ANGELS

THE FIRST JUDGEMENT

JOSE E VAZQUEZ

b

Angels

Angels/Angels Third Edition

Library of Congress Control Number:
00-191979

ISBN: 979-8-88757-239-0 (Paperback)
ISBN: 979-8-88757-241-3   (eBook)

Cover design by: 99designs/SusansArt.

Edited by: Leticia Cormier

Self-publishing Company: IngramSpark.

Printed in the USA: Lightning Source

Publisher: ANGpublishing

Version: A1

c

ANGELS

CONTENTS

d

This book is dedicated to humanity,
as a member, I was compelled to write
this narrative as a reminder of what is
beyond our daily routine: A choice!
By doing such writing, I did benefit from
its contents. I hope the book's message,
even on a small scale, equally affects you.

I also dedicate this book to the Raquel
of my life: Terry, our parents, and
our two wonderful children, Leticia
and Adrian. Last, to our three princesses:
(If you are a grandparent, you know what I mean.)
Cayley, Caitlin, and Claudia.

INTRODUCTION

FACTS

ANGELS!
Who are they?
Where do they come from?
Are these entities real or imaginary?

We have so many questions; the answers are few and elusive, sometimes even contradictory. Since we do not know much about these spiritual beings, our perception of their existence is hindered by ignorance. Furthermore, such perception is biased by our religious beliefs, eagerness to accept the intangible, and optimistic view of life. Even our overlaying insecurities and hidden fears could play a role in what is and what is not believable to us.

Modern angels are frequently portrayed as dolls that adorn our shelves or Christmas trees. We see their images illustrated in our churches, books, and movies; however, such appearances are usually portrayed as humanized figures with a pair of wings and *angelic faces!*

Reading the Bible[1], we find out that the angel described by Daniel[2] was an Archangel named Gabriel, and the angels Isaiah saw[3] were Seraphim. We also uncover that both men were scared to death at the incredible sight of their angelic forms and faces. Even our present outlook on the *cute* baby angels whom we call Cherubim is not even remotely close to the description that Ezekiel[4] gave us about them, "Fire creatures with four wings and four faces." Upon facing a Cherub, I do not think that any of us would have the courage to call the identity *"cute!"* Accordingly, the angels were and are powerful creatures that leave everlasting impressions on whoever has the fate to meet them.

Nonetheless, why do they appear so elusive, so out of reach?

Considering this, is there any possibility of meeting an angel in our lifetime?

Such an encounter is possible; however, in case we do, we may not recognize such an entity as an angel.

Why? Because angels rarely emerge in their natural form, they prefer to assume our human form. In addition, it is common theological teaching, by at least the Catholic Church, that a guardian angel is appointed at our

---

[1] The New American Bible, Copyright 1970 by the Catholic Press.
[2] Daniel 10: 4-9
[3] Isaiah 6: 2-6
[4] Ezekiel 10: 1-22

births to guide and protect us. If you believe in such a statement, an angel is, in reality, close to you and me!

Sometimes, I even wonder about the voice inside our heads, which we call our "conscience." Could it be the voice of an angel?

Everything gets more complicated once we get inside our heads because our minds can identify the presence of more than one voice. Both voices are diametrically opposite. One is from our guardian angel trying to help us; the other is from a malevolent voice leading us into temptation to do mischief and evil.

One is for *good* and the other for *evil*, for *light* and for *darkness*, for *obedience* and for *disobedience*, for *love* and for *hate*!

The first voice arose from an angel, the second from a fallen angel; we also know the latter by a different name, as a demon or the devil!

Our guardian angels are constantly chiseling us, making our appearance more acceptable to God's standard: perfection! The devil is committed to doing the opposite!

Whom should we believe?

As long as we are alive, we have a choice!

Returning to our inquiry, we ask: Do we know the names of the angels?

Other religions than my own, Roman Catholicism, have a more extensive list of angels' known names. I checked my Bible for such names.

This book mentions the names of only three Archangels: Michael, Gabriel, and Raphael. Up to today, these are all the official sanctioned names of the good angels.

Many years ago, in the early Church, more names existed that were venerated; nevertheless, due to contradictions related to their loyalty to God, those angels were dropped from the list.

We also know the name of the fallen angels' leader: Lucifer, better known in this modern age as Satan!

The task became overwhelming when I tried to find more names of the good or evil angels. Many names have variations, and different names merge into the same individual. The worst is the realization that separating the good angels from the evil ones becomes almost impossible.

How did this confusion get started?

Where do we get this information if it is not in the Bible?

At the beginning of the human race, our knowledge of the angels was practically none; since then, this knowledge has become progressive. This means that as time has passed, we have a better image of these creatures.

Old Testament passages pointed out that the people experiencing the event cannot always tell if the angels they met were good or evil. Sometimes, it was as if they did not know a difference existed! (e.g., Job referring to "Satan, walking into Heaven.")[5]

---

[5] Job 1: 6-12

In the New Testament, Christ sharply defined such difference when He said, "I watched Satan fall from the sky like lightning."[6]

This was an unequivocal statement that the devil did not belong to Heaven after his fall from grace.

To further our search, we know that the Bible has what is called "The Hidden Books," texts that were banned from the orthodox scriptures because of their controversial or confusing material. These writings from the Old Testament compiled earlier were translated from Hebrew to Greek around 200 BC and included in what was called the "Septuagint." Later, around the fourth century AD, St. Jerome proclaimed these "Hidden Books" to be *apocryphal*, meaning that they were not acceptable for the church's teachings.

The most critical rejected material was the *Book of Enoch*[7], written by a man who lived a few generations after Adam and Eve. Enoch loved God so much that He took him to Heaven without dying at the early age of 365 years. Enoch became the father of Methuselah, still the man who lived the longest: 969 years!

Enoch, the reputed author of this *apocryphal* book, claimed that he visited Heaven and Hell, plus many other places. He had an extensive list of angels' names; in some instances, he even mentioned some as fallen angels.

Most of the angels' names we know today came from this book, but due to contradictions and naming inconsistencies caused by many translations, it is impossible to be sure who are the good guys and who are the evil ones. After all, I could not accept assigning a name to a good angel where such a name might be of a demon! To clear my uncertainty about choosing names, I searched for help in other books about angels.

Therefore, I asked my church pastor for a good book; he lent me "A Dictionary of Angels."[8] The author compiled a vast list of angels and demons in this book, including variations and contradictions. He admitted to spending fifteen years accumulating this information. He also mentioned that his frustration in trying to separate the good from the evil reached an unbelievable level, causing him to approach insanity. Consequently, he decided to state the data without passing any final judgment.

I only spent a few weeks researching the subject and felt hopeless, so you can imagine that I readily agreed with his point of view about the confusion. Unfortunately, I did not extract one single name to add to the ones I already knew.

---

[6] Luke 10: 18

[7] One current version is "The Book of Enoch." Translated by R. H. Charles. 24th impression by SPCK 1994.

[8] By Gustav Davidson, The Free Press.

Here is another touching subject.

Why are there so many differences among the angels?

Is there a Heavenly Hierarchy?

Appropriately, the Bible says that not all angels were created equal. Therefore, a serious effort was made to determine how they were ranked. The accepted hierarchy, as seen by Dionysius, a Greek converted to Christianity by Saint Paul, remains as follows:

There are nine Choirs cataloged into three Groups or Triads.

The Highest Group: (*The one closest to God.*)

    1- Seraphim

    2- Cherubim

    3- Thrones

The Middle Group:

    4- Dominations

    5- Virtues

    6- Powers

The Lowest Group:

    7- Principalities

    8- Archangels

    9- Angels

I agree with this list, except for the Archangels, since most were Seraphim or Cherubim. Furthermore, they were like Overlords in charge of whole Choirs; I will place them at the top of the ranking.

From the scriptures, in the book of Tobit, Archangel Raphael told us.

"I am Raphael, one of the seven angels who enter and serve the Glory of the Lord."[9]

Out of these seven, we only recognize three valid names: Michael, Raphael, and Gabriel.

Lucifer's name is also considered accurate; all other names in the book are fictitious.

From the little we know about the existence of the angels before the creation of man, we can only deduce that they were given the same choice between Good and Evil as we presently face. However, unlike our current scenario, we could sin against God but still have the opportunity to repent and ask for forgiveness. This act could allow us to enter Heaven; the angels faced a different predicament. They only had to make one choice; unfortunately, this was as permanent as eternity!

All the angels must have been created without sin, which is an act of disobedience from what our Creator expects from us. Sin is a choice that encompasses the denial of God's will; for the angels, this step could not have happened in an instant; you cannot be an innocent creature full of

---

[9] Tobit 12: 15

love at one moment and become full of hate the next second; it took time for this gradual change.

It is not different from the way we presently are. If you are a person full of love for everyone around you, even if somebody did wrong to you, your first thought would not be to murder that person. However, suppose you gradually lower your moral values, letting anger, hate, envy, lust, lies, greed, and pride take over your soul. In that case, even murder becomes an option to satisfy your passions.

I see the angels as an alien race facing the same dilemma as us: to recognize God's existence and accept His commands. This similarity is the driving force behind such parallelism between our races, and it implies the following: As a civilization reaches a technologically advanced status, it becomes highly materialized and intellectually dependent. The harder we try to explain God's existence under such terms, the more elusive that understanding becomes; only something that comes from the inner heart, something as intangible as love, can make such a connection; it can open our eyes to perceive what we cannot see.

If an angel civilization ever existed, the angels must have lived very long lives, long enough for some individuals to gradually believe that they were eternal and they were gods!

FICTION

OUR TIME: 2,450,000 BC

PLACE: ANDROMEDA GALAXY
2,500,000 light-years away.

A green planet, third in a solar system, continued orbiting an average yellow star somewhere in the arms of a spiral galaxy. The planet had a friendly atmosphere and plenty of water; it looked like planet Earth, but it was not the same world.

Its name, *Terra*, had the same meaning as our planet *Earth* conveys. Three attached major continents existed over the landscape of Terra; the upper and lower landmasses were larger than the central section, with a shape similar to the American continents. Unlike our Earth, this planet had two moons; furthermore, it was located so far away that the light emitted by its star 2.5 million years ago, when these events happened, had not reached us yet, but it is expected to arrive soon.

How did life evolve on this planet?

It was carbon-based like Earth; however, the final DNA prints remained different; even plants and animals appearing to be the same as ours were not.

How did intelligent life start?

Identical twins were born that looked like humans, perhaps like Adam and Eve, but they were not humans but angels!

Did they evolve from mammals and apes?

It is a probability. We could use our imagination to figure it out.

Incidentally, one significant difference between the angels' anatomy and ours was that they were bisexual; by this, I mean they could choose their sex. The process was not complicated; by activating a particular hormone, the angel could switch from female to male or vice versa. It is as a hermaphrodite who has both sexes, and a specific hormone will trigger the characteristics of one side of sexuality while at the same time repressing the other. For the angels, such a change could take years to complete.

The more aggressive angels with ample motivation for leadership chose to be males. On the other hand, the angels with a passive attitude opted to be females.

Therefore, sex was a voluntary choice that could be changed; however, most angels remained at their original sex.

The lifetime biological clocks of angels were like early humans, who had life spans close to a thousand years. Although there was no Paradise, the early angels had no problem spreading across the continents. As the millennia passed, they populated the three continents, and race diversification started to appear. The Upper Triad of Angels (Seraphim, Cherubim, and Thrones) took over the central continent and named it *The Core*. From here, they controlled the whole planet.

The other kinds of angels who lived in separate and autonomous countries before started to mix and spread into the larger upper and lower continents. They created two great nations: *The North Alliance (NA)*, a conglomerate including seven nations, and *The South Alliance (SA)*, an aggregate of five countries. A solid but friendly competition existed between these two mighty nations from the beginning.

As millennia accumulated, the planet became overpopulated; food shortages and scarcity of basic needs caused a global accord to regulate and stop angel reproduction. The agreement said: "Further reproduction will be allowed only when all nations on the planet have unanimously agreed for its implementation and for a fixed length of time."

All three nations on Terra agreed on a maximum population of five billion. Each Alliance was allowed to have two billion angels; The Core was limited to one billion.

Later, as the implementation of significant advances in hi-tech liberated the angels from any hard labor or any primary needs, they enjoyed more leisure time. Properly applied, this caused the sciences and the arts to advance in giant steps. Synthetic foods, tough construction plastics, space exploration, supercomputers, and many more have proliferated.

Then, the big day came when the angels' DNA coding for aging was discovered. After a decade of hard work, they found the proper chemicals to alter their existing code; the angels became practically *immortal!* Accidental death, an extremely rare event, became the norm for an angel to die.

One significant exception lingered. A few individuals had a rare degenerating brain cell syndrome at the molecular level that not even bio-chemical engineering could fix. They had a fixed life span and would eventually die.

What could we become if we became immortals?

For the angels, as knowledge and skills accumulated, new mental and physical powers developed that carried the angelic race to undreamed-new heights. At this peak of their existence, a new super-being emerged from the central continent: The Archangel!

This entity was capable of telepathy, telekinesis, levitation, and other abilities we humans can only imagine. The Archangels quickly took control of The Core's government and the other two continents. At the time of this tale, we count fifteen Archangels, also known as Overlords. To recognize an Archangel, the last two letters of his name were separated by a dash: a sign of nobility.

Three Overlords managed The Core. Lucif-er, the most powerful Archangel, was the Overlord of the top and most prominent echelon of angels: the Seraphim. Next in charge of commanding the Cherubim was Gabri-el, a master in governing skills. Overseeing the Thrones, the youngest of Archangels, Dani-el, was a mere three thousand years old!

Magog-el, a Seraph, was the strong and stern leader of the North Alliance. He had six other Overlords under his command.

Micha-el, also a Seraph, was the spoken and dynamic leader of the South Alliance. He shared control of the South Alliance with four other Overlords.

This is the moment our story begins: all is peace and glory for the angels living on Terra, the same place chosen by God, where the crossroads of time and dimension intersect.

At this place, a pebble dropping into the cosmic sea could carry the mass of a whole planet, and the induced powerful ripples could overrun far-away shorelines. This pebble could be so small it could be placed on our hands; nevertheless, if such a thing were possible, undoubtedly and without remorse, it would rip our hand, our whole body, and the entire planet where we stood... to pieces!

In defiance of such a possibility, the pebble was not from a neutron star; it was from something immensely more powerful!

It relentlessly approached the planet in an analogous manner as we are approaching it too...

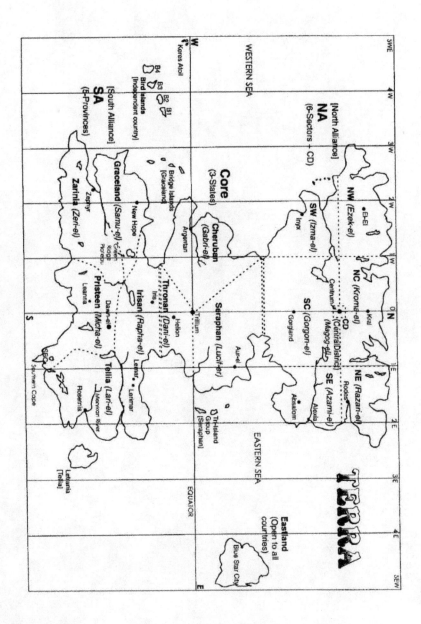

PROLOGUE

The immense emptiness of space is staring at us; we are floating millions of light-years away from our galaxy. Spread in front of us is the "Local Group," a small aggregate of galaxies in which our Milky Way, a large spiral galaxy with just one hundred billion stars sprinkled across its 100,000 light-years diameter, is the smaller of the two dominant galaxies of the group. The other four times more massive and called our sister galaxy is Andromeda.

2.5 million light-years separate these two galaxies, an enormous void compared to the mass of these large celestial bodies floating on the immense expanses of uncharted space.

The Milky Way and Andromeda come into sight as majestic but eerie disks, with their glow contrasting with the absolute blackness of the void surrounding them. They are a pair of jewels shining by the fire of billions of stars, where each star is a giant thermonuclear furnace piercing the darkness, a firestorm burning for a lifetime that seems to last forever!

However, at this distance, the stars glow so pale that they are hard to see. Accordingly, when we gaze at them, we can sense a mystical peacefulness; it appears as if the microscopic dots of light are incapable of affecting us in any way.

Both galaxies are not alone; each carries a complete set of satellite galaxies, which are companions in their cosmic travel across vast spans of the intergalactic void.

We can see the two large Milky Way satellites, the small and large Magellan Clouds, floating close to their parent galaxy. Several smaller ones are scattered around, shining like glowing cosmic firebugs on a summer night.

Andromeda has two large satellite galaxies, M32 and NGC205; a good-sized companion is not far away: M33.[1] Scattered nearby, another group of smaller satellite galaxies adds to the kaleidoscopic view.

Looking away into the depths of millions of light-years, we can distinguish other conglomerates much fainter and smaller as their distance increases beyond the grasp of reality. Only our imagination can transport us to such bizarre frontiers where time and space seem to merge into each other, in which the finite becomes infinite, where one single revolution of the arms of our galaxy takes 225 million years to complete, and where the light coming from the very faint and faraway galaxies has taken *billions* of years to reach us.

We mainly notice emptiness even with billions of galaxies scattered all over the cosmos. The staggering view could make us dizzy, a similar effect

---

[1] M= Messier's catalog. NGC= New General Catalog

as when we stand at the edge of a giant precipice and feel our muscles tightening, our perspiration increasing, and our attention becomes focused on the big hole attracting us like a magnet, pulling us into what resembles a huge predatory mouth ready to devour us.

If we had the sensation of falling from our floating location, this could be a very unusual feeling, since any direction we stare at, *up or down, front or back, left or right… we face a bottomless pit, darker than black, emptier than nothing.*

It must be a dreadful feeling to suffer the sensation of falling forever. Nevertheless, we are not plummeting; we are gracefully floating in space as we approach Andromeda and appreciate its inner beauty. Even though we could feel very lonesome at this isolated viewing location, time and space are frozen; nothing moves, nothing happens, and not even a whisper can be heard!

As we continue to approach the galaxy, the view becomes breathtaking. Andromeda expanded across our field of vision looks spectacular; its bright elliptical center is surrounded by a halo composed of older stars and globular clusters bursting with color, with yellow and orange dominating our visual perception. The spiral arms, which start at the nucleus's elliptical nodes, stretch outwards, coiling with overlapping layers that enhance their mystical display. Even when we cannot see the arms turn, we know that they do not rotate at the same speed, with the parts closer to the center moving faster than the outside component of each arm; in other words, they turn differentially.

The arms also shine with their own color, mainly white, with a blue tint adorning the better-defined edges where the galaxy-density waves create new stars.

Obscuring the entire stellar splendor are areas of dark material, mostly hydrogen gases, tightly intertwined with the galaxy's arms. These areas fuel the birth of new stars while dimming their splendor. By moving, the stars and clouds avoid collapsing into the gravitational whirlpool of Andromeda's nucleus, which is a supermassive black hole, a sinkhole of cosmic proportions!

Where is life?

We cannot even see the slightest indication that it exists!

Even when we can see the vast expanse of space, which equates to a vast expanse of elapsed time, we constantly witness *past events!*

Where is the present? Where is the future?

The present… only exists where you are floating!

The future is… the same as life, nowhere to be found!

Andromeda, you are so beautiful and majestic that you seem impervious to time; nevertheless, even for you, the clock is ticking… Apparently lifeless, the dominant galaxy off the Local Group ignores us, insensitive to feelings of any kind; it continues its journey to unknown locations and to an uncertain future that will eventually lead to its oblivion, with an eternal resting place in the universe. In cosmic terms, Andromeda is moving toward the Milky Way. After colliding with our galaxy, the massive black holes at their centers will merge in about 4.5 billion years and create a new, bigger galaxy!

We are still floating around admiring Andromeda as an unchanging three-dimensional holographic picture, an immutable image challenging our senses.

However, behold this image because something is happening... Overlapping the Andromeda spectacle, along a flat and almost transparent domain, bright dots start to appear randomly.[2] They are few and scattered alongside this translucent realm. Soon, they multiply, making the static image of Andromeda fade out as a background.

As their number grows exponentially, they start challenging the many billions of dots representing all the stars of the dominant galaxy. Our spectacle had changed; we could hardly see Andromeda anymore.

Then, suddenly, no more bright dots appeared; its number had become fixed. Their massive quantity relentlessly overpowers the cosmic plane above Andromeda; nonetheless, if the dots are observed individually, then it could be seen that they are independent. Each dot is free to move to any place on the celestial plane... *the dots are alive!*

Then, unnoticed by the dots, an eerie glow, far away from the infinite, self-initiates; it generates a cosmic disturbance beyond our imagination!

Time... space... dimension... There are no boundaries for the approaching shockwave! If only the dots could see it coming!

The disturbance arrives!

A bright, straight, thin white line suddenly appeared on the same plane where the dots hovered. It splits the semi-transparent domain into exactly two parts.

Now, there is a *left side* and a *right side!*[3]

The dots cannot see the white line but can detect its existence. The shockwave has affected the bright spots. Presently, they appear agitated and somehow erratic about which side to go on. Disarray is in command, but change is at hand; a subtle but drastic transformation occurs. Some of the dots are becoming whiter and brighter, with a glow similar to the disturbance's creator; from all locations on the plane, they start to drift and move energetically to the *plane's left side.*

---

[2] The bright dots represent the souls of the angels on Terra as being tallied and separated by a divine being after analyzing their affinity to Good or Evil.

[3] The white and good dots are on the left side because they face God, and it is His right flank.

The remaining dots are also changing; they have a new color, a sinister black with a red glow. They do not want to move, but regardless of their intentions, they are sliding to the *right side.*

The clock is still clicking. Not much time has elapsed since the shockwave arrived, but regardless, all the dots are now separated. All the white ones remained on the *left side*, and all the dark ones slid toward the *right side!*

Suddenly, an apocalyptic roar changes the universe's face!

The thin white line dividing *left* from *right* splits the cosmic plane, exposing an abysmal dark hole. It is similar to someone tearing apart a photograph of the cosmic plane and the galaxy behind, now revealing a black cavity that did not belong to the same dimension. Furthermore, the *left side* is not in our universal dimension anymore; it has shifted to a new realm of light and beauty: a place of joy and love without any bounds. The *right side* has also moved into a new but gloomy location: a nightmarish place where hate, despair, darkness, and confinement coexist.

We do have names for these two places: **Heaven** and **Hell.**

Two dimensions, which are separated by an abyss, a bottomless pit that is…

Immense!
Impassable!
ETERNAL!

The First Judgment

It was a different time and a distant place
where the angels faced their ultimate trial.
It was just a choice, but the aftermath became
astonishing and everlasting. Its shockwave,
even today, continues to affect our lives profoundly.

Then war broke out in heaven;
Michael and his angels battled
against the dragon. Although the
dragon and his angels fought back,
they were overpowered and lost
their place in heaven.

Revelation 12: 7-8

THE FIRST SIGNS

CHAPTER 1

A towering geyser of liquid fire burst into the clear sky. The bright yellow-orange molten lava, ejected with enormous force from the ground and searching for the heavens, looked like a giant tongue sticking out from the earth's guts, inquisitively probing its surroundings to assert a newly found freedom.

The scenic view, outlined by an extensive range of mountains, stretched for many kilometers. The heat from the thermal waves rising across the sky caused the landscape to undulate, like a reflection distorted by the ripples of an unstable water pond.

Heavy smoke dispersed by the wind at the top of the mountain marked the place where the new and tallest fire fountain seized its earthly possession. The pungent, searing smell of sulfur crept everywhere, spoiling the usually pristine forest scent. Fissures ran like loose ribbons of spilled molten lava at the lowest locations, which crawled downhill and obliterated the lush vegetation. Several rivers of liquified igneous rock moving deliberately toward the far outline of an ocean gave away their leading edges by the dark columns of smoke towering above the lush and green landscape, mimicking an advancing inferno.

Half of the higher ground still had vegetation; the other half was either black with hardened lava or amid gushing torrents of fire. As we approached the blazing edge of the igneous fountain, we began to see the shape of two angels; they stood very close to the fiery rim.

Another angel was located about twenty meters away on a lower slope. Even farther, at 100 meters below, one more stayed observing the blazing show. Several other individuals, taking measurements with diverse instruments, were scattered at the lower hills.

The angel at the top, closest to the molten lava, had his face away from the fire. He was athletic, with extremely well-defined muscles outlined through the synthetic soft and shiny jumpsuit loosely fitting him. His face, astonishingly handsome, had plenty of blond hair that graciously floated, mimicking the background's flames. His eyes were of the deepest blue imaginable, so deep that few could afford to stare at them without risking getting dizzy and losing their balance!

The scorching heat caused his high-temperature clothing to smoke with a faint whitish vapor. However, the same heat seemingly did not affect him. He looked at his companion a few meters away from the intense temperature and remarked.

"Magog-el! This is the largest eruption I have ever seen!"

The other angel received a clear and robust message even when no words were spoken. It was telepathic communication!

Magog-el turned around to face the telepathic speaker. This same person was intimidating and looked massive, and even when his facial attributes were similar to those of his companion, he did not look friendly, like a drill sergeant used to give orders. He was the Overlord of the Central District (CD for short) and the North Alliance (NA) leader. He replied, also telepathically.

"Yes, Lucif-er, I estimate the fountain's height to be almost two kilometers. That is a record!"[1]

Magog-el tried to move closer to Lucif-er and the molten wall of lava, but the baking heat of the nearby fire caused him to clench his teeth, and he moved backward.

His companion, seemingly impervious to the nearby furnace, barely smiled at the apparent discomfort that Magog-el endured; he proceeded with a statement.

I detect an increase in the tectonic friction; however, there is no apparent reason for this!"

The husky angel then asserted.

"I will assign a team to analyze the measurements taken at this site; we will eventually know."

"When the report is finished, send the information to my lab. I am very interested in finding the mechanism of this event."

Lucif-er looked at his associate with an analytic sweep from his piercing eyes; he momentarily watched the six faint blue rays symmetrically emanating from the angel before him, the trademark of a Seraph.[2] Lucif-er moved away from the fire and passed Magog-el, where he stood on his way down from the higher place on the mountain. At this moment, we can see that Lucif-er was also a Seraph, but unlike Gorgon-el, he displayed a double array of interlacing faint bluish emanations interpreted as wings. These wings were not static but a dynamic display continuously moving and undulating; he had twelve wings!

Lucif-er was the Overlord of The Core's state of Seraphan and the country's top leader. He stopped and looked down the hill, where the rest of the angels stayed busy doing specialized work. His attention was drawn to an angel intensely concentrating on taking ground measurements. This person stood 200 meters downhill but about a hundred meters in a lateral position.

---

[1] Obviously, the angels of Terra did not use the metric system or speak English. Their language and math were matched to ours to make it easier for us to follow their lifestyles.

[2]. I am capitalizing angels' choirs and the related title of Overlord because, in Terra, they were part of nations. For example: Mexican, from Mexico.

Lucif-er stared at another Archangel only twenty meters beneath, whose head remained turned away from him.

"Gabri-el!" The message traveling instantly to the nearby angel's mind specified.

Gabri-el's head swung incredibly fast. A pair of bright green eyes locked with Lucif-er's blues. This very handsome angel's face had a hint of femineity, and his blond hair looked slightly longer than the other angels. His sparkling green attire bordered the aquamarine. Four greenish wings radiated from his upper body; he was a <u>Cherub</u>.

A telepathic image without words or sound flashed at microsecond speed from Lucif-er's head to Gabri-el's. The image described a message of something not happening but a future event bound to occur, including the following visual event.

"The landscape where the angel stood taking the ground measurements: A fracture ripped the ground apart, isolating the angels from the rest of the land. In the next instant, the angel sank into the earth's bowels along with a large piece of land to meet a fiery death!"

Gabri-el rotated to now face the second angel standing lower on the hillside. Gabri-el's movement and the speed of the second angel had shifted to an incredibly fast overdrive.

For the next indented paragraph, the leading number inside the square brackets represents the speed at which we witness an event. Archangels can move and perform tasks much faster than other angels or humans.

To be able to follow speeded-up action, we accelerate our time reference to match the Archangel's faster speed. A 10 times faster event, slowed down ten times, should be our everyday perception. (Our eyes can only see one-tenth of a second frame intervals.)

[x]> = Start of faster time reference. <[x] = End of faster time reference.

[10x]>The angel standing at the lower location on the hillside.

He spun his near-ultraviolet blue eyes at great speed to meet Gabri-el's eyes focused on him; by the time this happened, the former was on his way toward the angel in imminent danger. The message from Lucif-er was not addressed to him, but he already knew its content because it was not delivered as a personal message. His youthful and superbly shaped face streamed toward the location where one angel faced death, similar to an arrow moving toward a target. As he continued accelerating, his blond hair became straightened backward, pushed back by the wind. Similarly, his clothes became tightly bound to his muscular body.

A Seraph and Archangel, we looked at him like using a high-speed camera showing an event in slow motion, allowing us to see an event happening ten times faster!

He reached the unsuspecting angel in no time, still holding a handheld instrument pointing to the ground and collecting data.

As the ground began to shake, escorted by a deep shearing sound emanating from below, fissures began to develop everywhere, causing many rocks to roll downhill. About fifty meters from the direction of the fast-moving Seraph, the ground started to split, and a red glow appeared from the new fissure.

Using only one hand, the Seraph lifted the angel from behind at the waistline as if he was weightless! The Seraph turned around and raced back to the place of origin. The incredible acceleration of the fast-moving individual took the air out of the transported angel's lungs; his eyes began puffing from their sockets as his mouth opened with disbelief. He looked like a blowfish out of the water.

The widening gap ahead, from its guts, spewed up large tongues of fire carrying chunks of molten lava like the fissure tried to prevent the two angels from returning to safe ground. As the Seraph sped across the gap, a new high wall of fire shot into the sky, engulfing the land where the rescue had just occurred.

After the Seraph safely returned to his former standing place, he stopped. <[10x]

Gently, using both hands, he placed the rescued angel on his feet. The angel was shaken, his glassy brown eyes staring at the wall of incandescent fire; he had barely escaped from its murderous grip. Due to the excitement, the angel's breath had changed to a faster rate.

At that moment, with a thunderous roar, the whole area where the angel stood before, taking measurements, collapsed into a fiery hole! The ground trembled under both angels' feet; the rescued moved back, ready to run in the opposite direction.

The Seraph placed a hand on his shoulder and spoke assertively.

"Do not be afraid; the place where we stand is safe!"

Similar to being given a sedative, the angel calmed down, and his breathing returned to normal. He looked at the Seraph and, displaying a big smile, exclaimed.

"Thank you, Great Overlord Micha-el! ... Thanks for saving my life!"

"My pleasure, Eugenius!" Micha-el identified him even when his name had not been mentioned before. This Seraph, also an Overlord, was the leader of the South Alliance (SA). Including him, the four most powerful Archangels of planet Terra were present on this blazing mountain.

Gabri-el, who was watching the event for a second time, turned toward Lucif-er; since the rescued angel was one of Gabri-el's assistants, with a look that included no words or messages, thanks were given. The rescued angel belonged to the second Triad; easily identified by his brown eyes and hair, he was a member of the choir named Virtues. It is noted that the second and third Triads were incapable of telepathic communication; this achievement was part of the upper Triad alone.

With a slow eye blink, Lucif-er accepted the message.

The angel named Eugenius walked toward two of his friends and engaged them in a lively conversation, which was hard to hear because of the nearby roaring inferno; however, the nature of the chat remained evident; it had to be related to the recent happening.

The four Archangels at the site, identified by the two separated letters from their names to be Overlords, started an intricate cross-telepathic discussion about the origin of the new lava fountain; they all agreed: It was an underground collapsed lava tube that caused the blazing display. Lucif-er added that it must have been a cavern underneath the lava tube hastening the collapse of the entire hill's side. At this time, he proceeded to the edge of the upper plateau and addressed everybody. His voice, thundering above the rumbling due to the lava eruptions, reached everyone.

The thermal updraft has changed, causing a reversal of the wind direction; consequently, the lava fountains will spill in our direction. We have fifteen minutes to clear this location!"

All the angels collected their belongings and moved to a nearby lower plateau, where they started boarding two silvery cylindrical machines. The Archangels embarked in one of the flying vehicles, and the other angels stepped inside the other.

Both aircraft lifted one hundred meters from the ground without noise or smoke and graciously sped away. They soon disappeared into the far, rugged horizon.

Fifteen minutes passed; the side of the mountain, previously untouched by the fire, became engulfed in smoke and flames as torrents of molten lava spilled downhill, burning everything in their path. The green and lush vegetation surviving on one of the flanks became obliterated.

Sixteen minutes had passed by.

Now, plenty of movement and action abounded on this small mountain... however, nothing remained alive!

****

The stars shone in the sky above Trillium, the capital city of The Core. The city's colorful and bright domes projected high into the sky like massive rockets ready to take off, easily outshining the celestial display. Below the domes, a symmetrical web of roads connected the large buildings; along those pathways, tiny but uncountable, many minuscule lights moved along predefined paths.

Dwarfed by the distance, the night sky was full of small cylinders following trajectories regulated by a three-dimensional matrix pattern. The flying craft generated no noise, but a white light glowing on its leading edge and a red one at its tail stayed clearly visible. In addition, the complete outside metallic frame emitted a faint bluish glow generated by advanced but unknown technical engines.

An antenna protruded from the center dome at the top of the tallest building. A circular terrace at the dome's base, enclosed in transparent plastic, was a high observation vantage point. The entire structure radiated a visible pale white light.

About fifty angels walked on the circular terrace, all following the same direction. Concurrently, the angels strolled in a mixture of small and larger groups. Most were males, making this observation the typical cross-section of The Core's gender. All of them communicated telepathically.

One of the groups casually following the curved corridor contained seven angels, including two females; everybody else seemed to maintain some distance from this elite assembly. Magog-el, one of the Archangels, addressed Lucif-er with a telepathic message everyone could hear.[3]

"The lab results of the eruption were inconclusive. We still have more tests to perform, but we cannot determine what caused such a large lava flow."

Gabri-el asked, *"What were the values of the 3-D Tectonic Analysis Program?"*

"If run in the internal mode, with all the local stresses accounted for, it is $TAP_I = 0$ ...However, the external method should also be: $TAP_E = 0$ It is not; the value is $TAP_E = 0.07$; origin unknown!"[4]

"All we could find was a minimal external force, not large enough to measure its direction. Indeed, since no internal forces caused this event, it is puzzling!" Lucif-er added while staring down at the 1,000 meters drop to ground level, a gaping hole between the building and the next tower. Many crisscrossing road connections flanked the empty space, but something else in the distance, a superbly illuminated geodesic sphere, called his attention.

"Most likely, the moons or the sun are responsible," Dani-el, the youngest looking of the group, ventured to mention. He had a single pale reddish halo around his head, with a similar glow around his feet; both became more noticeable when he separated them from the floor; they were his two wings. He was a Throne, the leader of his choir, and also an Archangel.

---

[3] Telepathic and verbal communication are very similar; the mental message is equally 'heard' as the spoken voice is processed in our brains.

[4] The Overlords, extremely intelligent individuals, engaged in complex dialogues without bothering to explain their conversations. If you find the chat hard to follow, treat it as science fiction jargon; ignore it and continue reading.

"The sun is the best choice due to its mass and nuclear activity; nevertheless, its gravitation, magnetic, and energy fields have remained normal," Lucif-er stated again as he changed his field of vision from the geodesic sphere to a Seraph standing behind Magog-el. This individual with a medium body frame, partially eclipsed by being behind Magog-el's massive body, displayed a foxy look that transcended his excellent appearance, an attribute attached to someone aspiring to go far; his name was Gorgon-el. He had been noticeably quiet during the conversation since the wife of Gabri-el, an angel of stunning beauty, had sexually disturbed him. On the third time, his casual and relaxed look scanned the heavenly curves of the lady. Lucif-er did notice and asked him.

"Gorgon-el, have you assembled a complete analysis of the event's location?"

"Yes! But I believe we are wasting our time; I cannot see how to resolve this problem!" He answered instantly. Archangels had the cunning ability to concentrate on several simultaneous tasks; thus, catching them out of balance remained practically impossible.

"You may be right!" Lucif-er hinted as the group continued to chat and walk around the sky-high terrace. He added, *"However, we expect another violent event in seven days. It will be in the form of a massive earthquake; this one is predicted to hit the city of Lemar. We should find out if there is a correlation between these two events. However, since that same day, I have an important meeting with the Overlords of the North, Gabri-el will be in charge of collecting the quake's data."*

Gabri-el asserted, *"Rapha-el and I have all the instrumentation already in place. Magog-el will have the results as soon as we collect them."*

They stopped walking; all seven stared at the dark sky at about noon high. Dani-el pointed toward a conglomerate of several bright points of light, seven altogether, and they neatly formed the letter A.

"Let me see," Dani-el said telepathically. *"The horizontal arm of the 'A' are the three stars named: The three sisters. At the top, we have a conjunction of two terrestrial planets. Also, two Jovian planets, one at each bottom leg of the letter, complete the character,"* after a brief pause, he asked, *"What does the intellectual nobility of this planet make out of this sign?"*

"You don't have to make it anything!" Quickly replied Lucif-er, *"It is just a particular arrangement of stars and planets as they move along their orbits."*

"To me, Gabri-el observed. *"It is a sign; I feel it means something!"*

After a swift mental analysis of the 'A' future orbital planetary structure, he further commented, *"There is more; in two weeks, the sign will become… a cross!"*

Lucif-er took two short steps to face the other six angels; then, he sharply stated with a very faint smile scarcely outlined by his lips.

"Furthermore, after another two weeks, the letter 'Z' will be displayed!"

"You knew and did not even mention it!" Dani-el jabbed while displaying a spark from his unusually reddish-colored eyes.

Without showing any concern, Lucif-er casually replied.

"I just mentioned... It is not important."

Raquel, Gabri-el's wife, a Cherub, moved closer to her husband. Her green eyes were not a piercing green as his, but a soft fluorescent aquamarine that any fortunate male angel glancing inside their glare would assert to be the most beautiful color in the universe. Her four-wing aura stayed smooth and tantalizing, reflecting her self-control and great personality. She placed her right hand on her husband's left shoulder as a velvet cloth would gently caress someone's skin. She advanced her opinion.

"It is conceivable that it is heralding the beginning of the end of our civilization!" Her telepathic message had the effect of a voice with a touch of melody.

Gabri-el's left arm partially embraced her while their eyes briefly met; in such a short time, only the spark outside their eyes gave away the intense exchange of several romantic thoughts and images that privately flashed between them. Gabri-el continued the conversation.

"Our earlier ancestors believed that our world shall one day end, and such an event will be preceded by great signs in the sky and massive disasters on the planet. You all know that they even prepared for such an end, thought to be imminent, and when it did not happen, they returned to their normal lives."

"You are correct!" Lucif-er snapped before anybody else had a chance to comment; he continued, *"But unfortunately, all are related to superstition... Why? Because I know that this celestial pattern will repeat in another million years; for the next time around, we should plan to have a celebration!"*

"Is it possible to predict what we will be doing in a million years? Raquel asked.

*"Certainly! As we live longer lives and our pool of knowledge continues to increase, we shall remove all the uncertainties currently embedded in our lives. A day will come on which we will **know it all!**"* Lucif-er emphatically stated.

"Do you mean we will be God-like?" Gorgon-el questioned.

"You said it!"

After a moment of silence, the other six angels tried to digest the theological implications of such a statement inside a strong, God-abiding society.

Lucif-er turned sideways and again stared at the crisscrossing roads in a breathtaking mesh that held the buildings together. His female companion, a Throne, had been noticeably quiet in the background. She also was an extremely beautiful angel whose stunning assets could only be eclipsed by Raquel's superb loveliness. She finally moved to approach Lucif-er from his back. Without looking back, he dropped his left hand behind and accurately grabbed one of her as she advanced forward. His piercing, deep blue eyes locked on her soft, beautiful purple ones; she held him as her strength drained away.

"You want to say..." he encouraged her.

"The A and the Z are self-explanatory, but the cross, I don't know what it means; I just know that I don't like it!" Liliel said, which was Lucif-er's female companion's name.

He added quickly.

"Do not worry; it has no meaning and is only a visual representation of a character... Anyway, Gabri-el is eagerly waiting to explain its theological implications!"

A glance between Lucif-er and Gabri-el became a swift acknowledgment from the latter. Gabri-el proceeded to talk to the group.

"I disagree," he said. *"I think that the cross is everything. The letters are just a projection of our existence, the link between the beginning and the end. The cross could be the crossroad between the divine and the angelic, as symbolized by the vertical trunk and the horizontal branch. The Lord has mysterious ways of conveying vital information to us, and for us to see it, we must open our hearts; then, our questions will become answers, driven by His will alone. However, if we try to impose our intellect to solve the riddle ourselves, the answer we get is one of emptiness or deception as true meaning will be sought but not reached."*

Simultaneously, Gabri-el thought.

"My good friend Lucif-er is becoming a skeptic; I don't know him anymore. We were close friends and agreed on everything. Now, it seems we are moving toward two diverging paths. I wish I knew where those pathways are taking us!"

"I entirely agree with my husband," Raquel soft voice asserted.

"I equally approve of Gabri-el's declaration," Dani-el followed.

Both Magog-el and Gorgon-el shook their heads, and the former expressed the opinion of both individuals, *"Lucif-er is correct; you are formulating too much out of a casual celestial display!"*

Lucif-er scrutinized the other six angels with his eyes; a faint smile appeared on his well-defined lips before he spoke without using his mouth.

"It is interesting to realize that I, Liliel, and the two Overlords of the North Alliance agreed on this, but the rest of you, including Micha-el, if he could be here... disagree!"

Next, after a glance at Raquel and then at Gabri-el, he asked.

"Tell me, Gabri-el, how did you manage to marry the most beautiful angel on the whole planet? Is it because you were a female long ago and concurrently knew the best approach to capture a female angel's heart?"

Liliel, looking sideways, glanced up to see Lucif-er's profile while she held his left hand. Concerned about his unexpected question, she stared for a second, then abruptly, regretting her reaction, lowered her sight to the floor.

Gabri-el, equally intrigued by the change of conversation, thought before answering, "Why is Lucif-er changing such an important topic of conversation for a menial one?" Aptly, he responded.

"Yes, a viable possibility. All male angels should try it at least once; we normally choose the male side because it is physically stronger and logical, but the female side has its subtleties and attributes that are unique to grasp a final wholesomeness normally outside the reach of the male counterparts. In addition, most of the drive for the fine arts and the roots of our social behavior are female in disposition. In conclusion, the role of a female as a mother, her primary goal for procreation, has exclusive feelings and emotions never matched by any male counterpart."

A moment of silence followed by only a few seconds remaining before midnight and the beginning of a new day. Trillium, the capital of The Core, controlled the only official time for the whole planet, although only The Core celebrated the new day at 0:00 hours. The rest of Terra's inhabitants acknowledged the event simultaneously but at different locations on the planet. There were ten time zones, only used as a reference for when going to work, sleep, etc. Terra had 10 hours/day, 100 minutes/hour, and 100 seconds/minute. A second in Terra was very close to a second on Earth.

A flash of light propagated from the tops of the city's buildings, bringing everything to a standstill, including the moving vehicles floating or rolling around the structures on their predetermined trajectories.

It was midnight... 0:00 hours!

Five million angels started to sing to the Lord, to praise and worship Him. No other place on Terra displayed this unique love. In unison, they expressed many songs vibrantly vocalized at the start of every day in their lives; The Core was all music and harmony to the Lord.

Everybody sang except four angels: Lucif-er, Liliel, and the two Overlords of the North; they stood still during the new day's song.

While singing his praises to the almighty God, Gabri-el thought, "My dear friends, what is inside your hearts and minds that you no longer express with melody the glory of our beloved God, to Whom we owe everything we own?"

♫ **"The heavens declare His glory**
and the firmament proclaims His work
the new day pours out His word
and the night imparts His knowledge."[5] ♫

The voices of the singing angels strongly reverberated because their vocal cords were made of three independent sections. Two of those

[5]Modified Psalm 19: 2-3

sections could follow the main tune while simultaneously changing the pitch or tone of the music's center frequency.

As we moved away from the city's central tower, their song combined with the rest of Trillium's angels became not noise but a pleasant undulating melody, where the words could not be understood, but the tune remained!

0:10 hours. The singing stopped, everything resumed regular activity, and the angels at the top of the central tower resumed their chat.

The night sky above the city remained undisturbed; above Trillium, clearly written by a cosmic hand, remained the letter **A**.

****

The sun, a red undulating disk, weakly emerged on the far horizon. Against the Trillium's silhouette, even its feeble performance was a blazing event; a light haze hanging close to the ground continued to diffuse its outline. In addition to the emerging light, a very delicate and pleasant breeze barely moved the leaves of the ornamental trees inhabiting the buildings' terraces or balconies.

In the far distance, we could hardly discern three individuals walking toward a transporting cylinder, a shiny vehicle resting near the top of a large structure's terrace.

While approaching them, the new daylight became brighter as the now fully emerged sun's disk, a pale orange, started turning yellow. Finally, the shape of the three angels became clearly visible. The one at the front was Gabri-el, dressed in silvery attire; his two companions, also Cherubim, wore similar outfits but in light reflective gray; they closely followed the Archangel.

They approached the parked vehicle, which was pointed at the front and somehow flat at the top and bottom. It rested on two sets of pads extending out from the main structure.

One of Gabri-el's companions pointed a finger at the craft; two doors on the side facing the angels rolled up to the cylinder's top section.

The assistants stood at the frontal door as Gabri-el walked into the rear section, where eight plush chairs with armrests were spaced in an oval pattern. The curved outside panels, which appeared as solid steel when seen from the craft's exterior, inside the vehicle remained transparent. The interior wall had see-through windows, with its unobstructed view only interrupted by structural stripes resembling the vessel's ribs, a minor occlusion of an otherwise spectacular panoramic view. Of course, if the passengers did not care about admiring the scenery, the windows could resemble opaque solid steel at the touch of a button.

Gabri-el sat in the frontal chair facing the forward section of the cylinder. He ignored the restraining accessories for safe flying; for an Overlord, they were unnecessary.

The other two angels boarded the craft and sat on the only two forward chairs reserved for the pilot and copilot. In front of them laid a vast array of lighted instrumentation. The angel seated at the left chair pointed a finger towards the open doors, and both became closed.

A pair of fins protruded from the vehicle's sides; after fully extending, their tips bent 30 degrees up.

"Great Overlord Gabri-el, we will arrive at Lemar in one hour... at 4:05!" The Cherub piloting the craft on the left seat spoke mentally.[6]

"Please, Reuben, take me there!" Gabri-el said in a soft telepathic message to his pilot, who was also a close friend.

A light whizzing sound with an almost unnoticeable vibration filled the craft's interior as it slowly lifted above the terrace's surface. After the pads retracted, the vehicle quickly accelerated and took a flight pattern not used by any other moving cylinder around the city; it soon became an undistinguishable dot in the sky.

As the new day's sunshine broke away the remaining shadows and the faint haze near the ground, any memory of the night's darkness disappeared.

The sun shone straight down at its zenith, minimizing any shadows below. At this location, the city of Lemar, Terra's time was 4:00 hours.

This large open area, like a plaza, was at the city's center, surrounded by rows of tall buildings. It would be empty if not for a large round and flat platform spread on its central location. Equally spaced semi-rigid pads projected from its bottom. The platform had dual hydraulic shock absorbers connected to the pads, making firm but flexible contact with the ground.

Except for an empty area located at the center of this raised part, the upper part of the structure showed many angels operating all kinds of instrumentation.

Only one lonely person out of two dozen above the platform was not busy working. He stood at the edge of this active stage, staring at the buildings marking the plaza's edges. These structures were smaller than Trillium's; the tallest building only reached 300 meters high. The architectural design looked different from The Core, with less pointed skyscrapers. No vehicle or individual roamed the city; its streets and pathways remained silent and empty. The ornamental trees gently gave way to a light breeze generated by midday's thermal updrafts; it produced the only noticeable movement.

---

[6] One hour in Terra = 2.78 hours in Earth.

Six faint rays, hardly visible due to the bright solar light at noon, emanated from him, symbolizing a Seraph. He wore a light purple outfit, his favorite color. He was Rapha-el, the Overlord of the South Alliance province named Irisan, in which Lemar, with a population close to a million, remained part of this region.

As his blue eyes focused on the city, dissecting every detail, a tint of sadness could be perceived in the piercing depth of his vision. He had a soft facial expression, and his hair was short and neatly styled to follow the natural contours of his head. While staring at the buildings directly in front, he thought.

"Lemar, oh pretty city! Soon, you will be gone; it is sad to see how much is destined to disappear. However, I thank You, my great Lord and loving God, for allowing us to predict this massive incoming earthquake. We are prepared, and with the measures we implemented, many lives will be spared when it strikes. All the inhabitants have been transported to a safe place inside the twin city of Lerimar, 400 kilometers away. I am extremely pleased that no one there will be hurt!"

His sight drifted to the left, and he gazed at a new group of buildings. A warning but faint signal flashed inside his brain, and he continued reflecting.

"Is it possible that someone remains in the city? I perceive something, but it is too far to know for sure." At the same time, he noted, "The time is 4:06; Gabri-el should be arriving."

Rapha-el turned around and started walking toward the edge of the empty central part of the platform. He looked up in the northwest direction and focused his vision on a small bright dot climbing on the horizon and quickly approaching.

When the dot reached nine o'clock high, it seemed to stop climbing, like it had become stationary; however, it quickly got bigger and brighter when approaching the site on a straight 45° downward line as measured from the ground's plane to the incoming object.

In just ten seconds, it slowed to a standstill 100 meters above. From there, it slowly descended to the platform's top surface while rotating about ¼ of a turn to align with the landing site properly. Finally, the landing pads popped out, and the craft settled down without hesitation.

Both side doors slid open; the pilot and copilot quickly exited the cylinder and stood outside in an attentive but not rigid position. Gabri-el stepped off the craft and walked directly to Rapha-el.

Both Archangels greeted each other by touching their open hands about chest high, a sign of a close friendship, almost family!

"My friend, I am so glad to see you again!" Gabri-el spoke telepathically; he immediately added, *"Let me empathize with you about this painful feeling associated with the impending disaster in one of your cities; I know what this means to you!"*

"I accept your comforting thoughts," Rapha-el responded to his concerned friend as both moved to the instrumental section. He next gently placed his right hand over Gabri-el's left shoulder and added.

"Only material things are being lost; the Lord has been kind by allowing us enough time to evacuate the city completely."

"His love has no limit," Gabri-el asserted; when they reached the instrumentation, he requested, *Please, show me the new Seismic Acquisition System, or SAS."*

Rapha-el began describing.

"The standard array of instrumentation is the same: RD: rock dilation; geodimeter: laser beam horizontal displacement measurement; magnetometer: local variations on Terra's magnetic fields; gravimeter: local gravitational changes; SC: scintillation counter for radioactive Radon; seismometer: seismic wave activity.

First, we have increased the sensitivity by a factor of ten. Then, SAS uses a new algorithm that allows an accuracy of one-minute deviation taken ten days before the quake; this divergence goes down to the very second on the same day of the event. The program has been tested to be valid inside these tolerances."

"This is not a fault-related quake. Is there any evidence of this happening before?" Gabri-el asked.

"Yes, we found that millions of years ago, this same area was hit by a powerful earthquake caused by mid-plate tectonic activity."

"What is the final predicted time for this incoming quake? I have 4:20 hours," Gabri-el inquired.

"It should be 4:21:05 hours!"

Two angels stood on a terrace outside the tenth floor of a building; both had black, medium-long hair and similar eye color. They looked alike, almost like brothers. Both wore two-piece light green suits; they had attractive faces but looked much plainer than the Archangels. The two angels belonged to the lowest choir: Principalities.

The terrace had a waist-high semitransparent outside border. Its spacious interior area displayed several flowering and broad-leaved shrubs on each side. The contour of the outer border divided the total area into two parts, with each side converted into a seating place delineated by ornamental plants.

One of the angels, a heavier-built individual, talked to his companion.

"Marcus, do you think we are doing the right thing? It bothers me that we may be doing something God disapproves of!"

"What do you mean... like us taking our own life?" His companion replied.

"Yes, exactly that!"

"Look, Sergius, we are not taking our lives; if God wants us to die today, it is His choice, not ours!" Marcus, the slender of the duet, emphasized.

*"I see your point, but I have some guilty feelings I never had before. I shouldn't listen to you and let you convince me to do **this!**"* Sergius spoke.

"My friend, we have been united since we were children; we have always done things together; why are we disagreeing now?" Marcus inquired.

"We did, but it never was suicidal!" Sergius responded while grabbing his companion's arms and lightly shaking them.

*"Your nerves must be getting to you... I am afraid to die, too. It burns me every time I remember that everybody else is supposed to live forever, but not us! We have the **DNA syndrome!** ... Because of it, we just have ten years to live!"* The other angel bitterly responded.

Reflexively, Sergius added.

"I know, my friend; the medical department said so, but nobody knows exactly how many years we have left. At least ten years are better than none, which could be what we have now by staying here!"

"I understand, Sergius! But knowing that I will be dying soon makes my daily life miserable and impossible to bear. All I do is count how many days I have left. I am tired of everyone being nice to us only because of our illness; it is easy to do when they are not in any danger of threatening their existence. I would be really nice to other sick angels if I weren't sick myself!"

"Yes, I clearly understand your feelings; they are my own!" Sergius nervously agreed while grasping both arms, which felt cold. Looking downwards at the plaza, he changed the conversation by asking, *"Anything new happening down there?"*

Both principalities gazed at an opening between two buildings where the platform stood with a silvery flying craft parked on top. Marcus, with a squint, tried to improve his vision by focusing on the platform; he gave up after a few seconds, and after relaxing his sight, he spoke again.

"It is too far; I cannot distinguish what is going on top of that thing."

"Do you think anybody important came in the craft that just landed?"

"I am sure he was an Overlord! I recognize their unique aircraft, which is used only by them."

Sergius agreed, *"You are correct... Marcus, I heard that our Overlord Rapha-el would be present; he is probably at the platform right now!"*

"Oh, yes! Overlord Rapha-el... I do like him very much; he is kind and a great rul...er..." Marcus stuttered as a nervous shaking attacked his right leg; he used both hands to control the vibrations, and the tremor dissipated.

"Are you OK?" Sergius asked with a concerned voice.

"Yes... What time is it anyway?"

Both angels looked at a tall building with a digital display.

It read: **4:19:91**

Their eyes opened with disbelief; it was almost the scheduled time!

"I cannot believe we are blabbing along and have lost track of time!"
Sergius exclaimed, exhilarated.

The pair of angels swallowed, clinched their hands into fists, and stared at the clock. The device continued keeping time up to the seconds.

4:19:96
4:19:97
4:19:98
4:19:99
4:20:00

Their eyes detached from the clock and quickly focused on the ground ten stories below. Their scared eyes searched for the approaching monster poised to devour them!

Nothing moved. Nothing at all!

Two strong heartbeats could be heard outside their bodies.

Seconds went by slowly... making it to be so long!

They glanced at the clock again.

4:20:11

The Principalities stared at each other. Then, realizing they were holding their breath, both gasped for air. After two or three deep inhales and exhales, the angels calmed down.

Marcus scratched his head and sighed.

"Nothing happened! Did the Overlords make a mistake about the quake?"

"I have never heard that **they** *make mistakes! As predicted by the electronic system, the quake could be late,"* Sergius replied while shaking a bit. He could not find what to do with his hands when he asked.

"Hey Marcus, do you think this building will stand a large earthquake? I don't recall any modern city being destroyed by a quake."

*'Neither do I, but this is not a large quake my friend; it is the **big one!**"*
Sergius looked around and pointed out.

*"Have you noticed that the breeze just stopped? ... The sun is high, but this deep chill is invading my body. **Marcus... let's go inside the building; I don't want to fall ten stories to the ground from this balcony!**"*

*"I agree; **let's do it!**"*

Both ran to the glassy wide door; it opened as soon as they got near.

Once inside, the door closed behind them.

Gabri-el attentively listened to Rapha-el's technical details; he knew his friend intended to end his discourse since only sixty seconds remained before the quake's arrival; he glanced to his left at the building's outline. Like a sixth sense, something clicked inside him, and he thought immediately, "Is somebody still inside the city?"

Rapha-el practically interrupted his meditation by grabbing him on the shoulder and exclaiming telepathically.

"You also noticed it!" He immediately added, *"Let's separate from each other by ten meters and triangulate the location!"*

In three seconds, both Archangels simultaneously stared at the same distant spot; in a synchronized thought, they communicated.

"There are two of them! On the tenth floor, inside a building in the third row from the plaza's left edge!"

At the same instant, Gabri-el's pilot received a telepathic message.

*"**Reuben**, emergency take-off! Get the craft ready for **priority E-1!**"*

All four individuals, the co-pilot included, scrambled to the cylinder. The doors barely opened when all went inside; the two Overlords climbing on the back section stood by the outside door, which remained open.

Gabri-el projected the location image to the pilot's brain, along with the message, *"Take us into the opening between those two buildings, to the structure directly ahead on the third row, and its tenth floor!"*

Before the message delivery ended, the aircraft began detaching from the ground. The engine's high pitch stayed substantially higher than during a normal takeoff.

The aircraft barely left the ground when it became aligned with the requested coordinates and sharply accelerated upwards. The two aviators became compressed into their seats as the G's accumulated, causing their facial expressions to be noticeably distorted. The Overlords hardly shifted their weights, apparently impervious to the acceleration.

The plaza's floor sped by, and the cylinder reached the first row of buildings, maneuvering between two towers at a screaming speed; the tenth floor of the targeted structure approached at a hair-raising velocity.

Standing at the edge of the craft's opened door, Gabri-el had a superb view of a gaping hole where large buildings sped precariously close by; he pointed to the balcony of a skyscraper's tenth floor. The pilot knew exactly where to proceed.

Gabri-el instructed, *"Get as close as you can; after we jump to the terrace, move away from the building and only return when you see us back at the balcony!"*

"Understood!" The pilot promptly replied.

The cylinder decelerated as it approached the terrace of the 10th-floor balcony. Swiftly, the pilot positioned the craft one meter above and away from the outside border of the terrace.

Both Archangels immediately jumped to the terrace floor; it opened before they reached the balcony door.

At tremendous speed, Rapha-el raced through the door. Close behind him, Gabri-el glanced back before entering the building. His sharp vision quickly identified the quake-s P (primary) wave approaching fast from beyond the plaza's platform, an incredible expanding circle expanding at **12 km/sec!**

As Gabri-el entered the structure, he relayed a mental message to the Archangel before him.

"P wave in two seconds!"

A spacious corridor faced him. Its rounded ceiling stretched far and made the hallway look like a tunnel. Plants and artifacts lined both sides of the hallway, with their shapes faintly reflected from the shiny floor by indirect illumination.

With no sight of the other two angels, both Overlords sprinted to the first corridor's intersection. When both reached the place, they stopped and simultaneously stared at the smaller hallway to the left.

About twenty meters away, Marcus and Sergius sat in the middle of the pathway, directly on the floor facing each other; the Archangels' eyes pointed to their location.

The P wave arrived as the Overlords began accelerating toward the two Principalities!

A high-frequency vibration rattled the whole building for a few seconds, causing weird noises and dust to fall from the ceiling; this longitudinal wave inflicted only minor damage.

By now, the Archangels had reached the two angels. When Rapha-el stretched his hand to grab one of the angels, the floor bowed and cracked loudly. A rolling wave deformed the corridor; the slower **S** (secondary) wave traveling at **10 km/sec had arrived!**

Just as a powerful bomb exploded inside the building, the big jolt sent the two angels sitting on the floor, flying about half a meter high while remaining in their seated position. At the same time, a roar saturated the place! The tremendous compressing power of the quake's wave overloaded the maximum stress allowances of the building's materials; not even the plastic reinforced with the TiO-B complex could survive the enormous shock.

Cracks and falling pieces appeared everywhere!

Rapha-el and Gabri-el did not fall because of their superior ability to stabilize; after hard-hitting the floor with their butts, the other two angels were tossed like grass reeds battered by a strong wind. Sergius' nose was dripping blood, while Marcus' right arm became seriously bruised when a falling wall section scraped it.

Every second became an eternity as chaos took over.

Sergius screamed, *"God, please forgive us and help us!"*

The earthquake roar drowned his plea.

The primary power blinked once and gave up; the sparsely placed emergency lighting took over. The corridor became an eerie place faintly illuminated through the dust and falling objects as the noise worsened!

A whole section of the ceiling began to collapse upon the four angels in the hallway! Gabri-el stretched up and held the collapsing slab with both hands while his mind locked with Rapha-el's, who was estimating the situation. Gabri-el mentally yelled.

"I will hold; take them out of here!"

"OK, but you move out as soon as we are clear!" Rapha-el's immediate response followed. He quickly grabbed both angels, one with each arm, and quickly disappeared when he turned into the main corridor.

A thunderous noise and vibration shook the side hallway, Gabri-el's legs, for an instant, bent downwards; his face showing intense pain!

"My Lord, the upper floors are collapsing... the weight is unbearable! ... I cannot get away and hold the ceiling much longer; I am trapped! ... Please... give me the strength to survive!"

Gabri-el's teeth squeezed hard against each other, and his forehead became moist with perspiration. Then, another big jolt rocked the place, causing more pieces to fall from the ceiling along with large quantities of dust.

A sharp pain ran from his neck, ending down his spine; his muscles and mind stayed working beyond their limits! Emanating from his hands, a greenish glow at the place of contact with the ceiling's surface showed his incredible effort to support the falling structure. At this instant, he thought.

"My God! If this is the end, I thank You for the great life You have provided me... I surrender my will; only Yours shall remain!"

The seconds continued to pile up upon the past, and painfully, he continued, **"It feels like the quake is going on forever... the floor is moving too much... I cannot hold it..."**

Intense sweat, mixed with dust, ran down his entire face. His arms and legs began to shake as he started losing control... his four wings made of light became fainter!

Suddenly, the quake stopped!

The building continued to make squeaking noises, combined with the rumble of large pieces crashing into it. From the outside, as nearby buildings collapsed to the ground, ominous vibrations and thunderous noises were heard and felt!

With the floor steady, Gabri-el regained some control and mentally exclaimed, **"Thank You, my Lord! ... I can feel You are with me and gave me new strength and hope... however, a strong aftershock is approaching, and I know this building will not survive... how could I?"**

His internal clock counted the seconds left before the ominous aftershock racing to finish the doomed city of Lemar, **"5...4...3..."**

Rapha-el was back!

The arriving Archangel promptly picked a round pillar-like section from the debris, which he pushed against the ceiling. Like a miracle, the piece fit perfectly when Rapha-el leveled it upwards between the floor and the collapsing ceiling. In this manner, he released the pressure bearing down on Gabri-el.

"Thanks to God and to you, my brother!" He exclaimed with utter relief and joy; he added, *"The stress must have been too great because I never sensed you coming back!"*

The aftershock hit the damaged building with a vengeance.

Rapha-el did not respond; he was evaluating his friend's battered physique and realized that Gabri-el could hardly walk; outside, the Cherub's body was not visible due to the dust and sweat covering his skin, but inside, he sensed severe damage, which caused almost unbearable pain.

Like a man with an injured back who hardly could place one foot ahead of the other, so tried Gabri-el to move away from the collapsing structure's deadly trap.

Rapha-el did not waste any time. He placed his friend's left side over his left shoulder and used his right arm to lift Gabri-el off the ground while holding him around the waist. Rapha-el, a Seraph, quickly proceeded to access the main corridor while placing special attention on not bending Gabri-el's back.

Rapha-el suddenly looked up at a large chunk of the ceiling coming down upon them; with his free left arm and hand, he grasped the heavy falling piece and tossed it sideways!

As they turned into the main corridor, the place remained immersed in almost total darkness; only a diffused bright light suggested where the end was. The opening, which was not steady at all, wiggled right and left, with the upper part gradually collapsing.

The passage appeared filled with a thick fog and falling dark objects; it was not fog but vast amounts of raining dust.

The noise level stayed intolerable, with rumbles, squeaks, bangs, and an eerie wailing of the structure, like crying from a building's impending death.

Similar to a time warp, the few seconds it took to exit the building stretched as a rubber band, apparently expanding forever!

Finally, the two Archangels reached the narrowing exit; the door was gone. When the two angelic entities passed the collapsing opening, they found only a narrow edge remaining; the balcony had fallen into the gaping hole underneath. All the building's balconies lay at the structure's base as large piles of rubble.

The panoramic sight from the narrow ledge displayed a vision of massive destruction!

Most of the buildings were demolished, while others continued adding to the piles of debris. When one of the few still standing fell, the quake's rumble increased noticeably; the collapsing towers sent large columns of dust and smoke upwards like growing thunderclouds in a menacing sky, with these layers of particles occluding the sun or giving it an orange tint.

The debris piled up on the ground made the vision even more frightening; it reflected the sunlight with a reddish color, moving and twisted like a tormented sea of blood!

Rapha-el swiftly located the aircraft floating one hundred meters away from the building. The cylinder moved toward the Archangels' location in seconds. However, due to the structure's precarious oscillations, it could not get closer than five meters.

"Oh my God, it is twice as far as my previous jump!" Rapha-el thought with concern when estimating the distance.

Without any other consideration, he backed as much as he could against the moving wall of the tenth floor, and he jumped while still holding his companion, the Archangel Gabri-el.

Like a falcon, he projected his wings of light, aiming at the aircraft's door opening!

One instant later, he swiftly ended his flight by firmly planting both feet inside the craft's main body after flying through the entrance.

The pilot and copilot stared in disbelief at their Overlord, Gabri-el. He was covered with dust and sweat, barely moving, and supported by his friend Rapha-el. They almost did not recognize him!

"Take us back to the platform!" Rapha-el commanded, interrupting their stupor.

"Right away, great Overlord!" Both Cherubim replied.

Marcus and Sergius stayed quietly, sitting in the back of the craft.

As the cylinder began to ascend, a louder noise saturated their location as the building they had just evacuated collapsed to the ground! ... One more cloud of dust and smoke rose, barely missing the ascending aircraft; only a large heap of rubbish from the previously elegant structure remained.

The craft zigzagging around the smoky columns of dust returned to the platform's surface. As far as it could be seen, the destruction was complete: There were **no** more streets, rows of buildings, or the city of Lemar!

Far on the horizon, about ten kilometers away, a rectangular building suddenly became a bright ball of fire! Next, like a pyrotechnic display, sparks, balls of fire, and flaming rivers of plasma came into view from the exact location. Lightning spread everywhere, even from the sky above; massive lightning bolts hit the exploding area.

"Oh, Lord!" Rapha-el exclaimed, *"The electric power plant superconducting storage coils have broken, and thousands of gigawatts are being released instantly as an immense river of electrons!"*

A mushroom ball of unusually red fire, with lightning surrounding its growing size, projected into the upper atmosphere at high speed. A local shockwave distorted and blew away the columns of dust from the collapsed buildings. At a distance, many nearby structures became vaporized into a whitish-red glowing vapor; some buildings melted away while others remained untouched. At the same time, a growing ring of lightning spreading its surface tentacles in a crisscross mesh of destruction could be seen moving away from the site's explosion.

The red glow on the horizon gradually faded and almost disappeared after just twenty seconds of incredible existence.

As before, the aircraft aligned and landed on the platform's surface, and all the occupants got out. Next, Rapha-el's attention became entirely directed to Gabri-el.

"My dear friend, it was a narrow escape! We thank the Lord for allowing us to stay around! You must know that you have several compressed vertebrae. Fortunately, the nearby Medical Center of Lerimar has a molecular decompressing device, and you will be as new in a few days!"

While talking, he reached Gabri-el's back; a glowing blue flash indicated a power transfer.

"Thanks, my brother!" Gabri-el exclaimed as most of the pain went away, and he could partially erect himself from the bent position he had maintained since the ceiling collapsed; he added, *"I will be eternally grateful to you!"*

"Not to me, but you should to our Lord!" Rapha-el replied. Next, he turned toward the two Principalities' angels with a stern look and addressed them.

Both remained wide-eyed and slightly trembling, but Sergius asked for forgiveness. His nose, still mildly bleeding, continued to stain the frontal part of his attire; he took one step forward and pleaded.

"Great Overlord Rapha-el, we are very sorry for all the trouble we caused, and..." He stopped when he saw the Archangel approaching them.

"Do not be afraid!" Rapha-el said clearly and friendly, *"I know exactly what you feel and its effects on you. I want you to know that I am extremely pleased you are alive and not seriously hurt. Equally, we, the Overlords, care for you, and we shall continue striving for a cure for your malady since it is painful for us to see the extremes that the anxiety from such illness pushes you to do!"*

Rapha-el pinched Sergius' nose for two seconds, and the bleeding stopped! Next, he touched Marcus' right arm, which the angel held with his left hand; the angel smiled as the pain disappeared or became numb.

"Please, both of you, enter the aircraft. In a few seconds, I will join you!" Rapha-el indicated with a louder voice.

Gabri-el moved to climb on. He paused at the entrance, looking around while feeling great joy. He felt as if a new life had been granted, and he was reborn! His memory banks added this new, unique experience to his lengthy lifespan!

Rapha-el advanced to the platform's edge; he needed to watch the ruins of one of his cities for the last time. The plaza had turned into cracks, uplifts, and debris. The buildings' outline looked utterly gone, even though some large chunks of some buildings had separated and fallen intact. Dust moved around like a light fog hanging everywhere, causing a sharp, irritating odor to pierce everybody's nostrils. At this instant, the ground did not move, but a rumbling noise of a few collapsing structures continued to be heard.

He looked at his clothes and noticed the dirt on him; his outfit looked grayer than purple. His brain triggered an ultrasonic wave that separated the dust from his skin and clothing!

The dust, just liberated, floated down from his body and joined the layer already covering the platform's top.

His appearance did not indicate that he had been inside a collapsing building; he and his attire shined. Nevertheless, his heart ached, but a feeling of accomplishment prevailed for what he had recently done.

At some distance away, he spotted one chunk from a structure tilted above the ground; his sharp vision identified the piece as the digital clock at the top of one building. Its backup power continued operating, but its display, now surgically removed from the central computer, stayed showing just one fixed number; he read it.

4:21:05

A time that will not change!

A time that will never be forgotten!

Rapha-el decided it was time to take his friends to the Medical Center.

The Overlord turned around briskly walking toward the waiting cylinder; as he passed one of the instruments, he glanced at the display. It was a seismograph; in a bright red, next to a graph's most prominent peak, a digital number continued to be indifferently displayed.

9.8

****

The sound from the steps of a fast-walking person resonated across the highly decorated walls of a wide corridor. The beautiful, shiny emerald marble-looking floor reflected from his attire a purple shadow. As he quickly approached a large door, a modulated multichannel laser read his DNA pattern and opened the sliding entrance before he even got close to the door.

When he entered the next room, a large circular area faced him; its rounded, centered section was a massive, polished surface that gave no clue of anything behind it. A peripheral corridor ran outside the edge of the central structure decorated with the SA (South Alliance) colors, alternating white and green segments. In contrast with the center section, which had no visible openings, the outside walls of this outer hallway had plenty of elegant windows offering a glimpse of the incredible outdoor landscape, which, at this time, close to midnight, offered a spectacularly illuminated view of a towering city.

Two Seraphim approached him when the walking Archangel moved around the curved corridor. Both saluted with one open palm at chest level, but only the one with the higher rank spoke mentally.

"Welcome, Great Overlord Rapha-el; our noble Prince Micha-el awaits you!"

"Thank you!" Rapha-el replied while returning the hand greeting. He added, *"For this meeting, I prefer not to be escorted!"*

"As you wish, Sir! We will wait here!"

Rapha-el walked around the circle until he completed one-quarter of its circumference, or 90°. He faced a curved entrance displaying an emblem, a five-piece triangular mosaic of white and green colors with six equidistant blue rays radiating outwardly.

The door, swift but almost silent, slid open.

Inside, Micha-el was sitting on a plush chair behind a semicircular desk. The desk, internally illuminated, resembled moonlight, and the whole room remained well-lit by a bright glow emanating from the walls. Four more chairs faced him along the desk's width.

Farther outside, another larger semi-circular row of chairs filled the space closer to the concave wall. Behind Micha-el, multiple displays and instruments stood in a niche.

When Micha-el saw his incoming good friend, he quickly got up and moved around outside the desk to meet Rapha-el.

Both Archangels greeted with both hands at chest level. Micha-el exclaimed without speaking.

"Greetings, my brother! I have been anxiously awaiting your arrival; please inform me of everything that happened."

"I am glad to see you, my brother, but I have sad news from Lemar!" Rapha-el immediately responded while touching his friend and superior's shoulders. The Archangels' eyes locked into each other, Rapha-el added.

"These are the events in Lemar and the information Gabri-el passed to me concerning the midnight sign displayed in the Trillium's sky."

Coming from Rapha-el, a stream of swift transfer of images, text, and even emotions was recorded in Micha-el's brain. Only seconds later, the communication concluded, and the two sets of blue eyes disengaged.

The leader of the SA knew the events with the same certainty as if they had happened to him! He touched Rapha-el's left shoulder and declared.

*"My dear friend, I knew you and Gabri-el risked your lives in Lemar, but I had no idea it was **that close! ... I shall acclaim the Lord for His generosity!**"*

Rapha-el sat on one chair from the first row, and the other Overlord followed suit on the next; they swiveled the chairs to face each other.

"My heart still aches at the face of such destruction," Rapha-el continued the dialogue while looking with an empty stare at the chair's electronic displays on top of the armrest, *"In all the thousands of years that I have lived, I had never seen such devastation. Lemar... a city built to stand any natural disaster... exists no more!"*

"I agree; I've never seen anything alike! My concern is that these extraordinary events are occurring between the signs in the night sky. Between us... the Holy Writings' predictions from our ancient past are becoming a reality. This world we love so much may be approaching its end; needless to say, I have no idea what our God has prepared for the future. Anyway, I am not afraid... I want nothing less than to be kneeling in His presence, to worship Him, and to give Him all my love plus my gratitude for my existence!"

"I feel the same way, Micha-el! Just as you said it!" Rapha-el agreed, and then he continued talking without using sound waves.

"Seven days have passed since the earthquake and fourteen days since the first sign; it's midnight; let's take another look at the night sky!"

"Exactly what I wanted to do next," Micha-el replied while pointing toward one instrument behind his chair located past his large desk.

The room's ceiling material, visually opaque panels, split open in the middle and quickly slid away in both directions; it allowed the black sky sprinkled with so many stars to become visible at the enlarging opening. Subsequently, the whole floor started to move smoothly upwards. The sidewalls gradually disappeared as the room's floor approached the beginning of the previous ceiling's level; at this point, when the floor passed such a plane, it stopped.

Nothing blocked the 360° full view of the sky. A dome farther above, made of transparent plastic completely clear and free of distortion, stayed practically invisible. Anyone inside the transparent dome's wall could see the city of Dawnel[7], the capital of the Pristeen Province, where Micha-el presided as the Overlord and ruler of the South Alliance.

The building marked the city's center. Four significant avenues merged into a large circular road constructed around this central structure, which was quite large at its base. Only four elevated connections, high above the ground and between each pair of avenues, connected the main building to

---

[7] In Terra's map, Aur-el and Dawn-el are written with a dash; in the narrative, the dash is omitted to avoid confusion with the Overlords' titles: -el and -er.

the first row of adjacent towers rising past the circular road. With its eight million residents, the city spread far beyond the first cluster of buildings.

Both Overlords stood at the edge of the room facing North.

At 9:00 hours, the stars and the planets had arranged to form a **cross**. Higher in the sky, both moons of Terra shined unimpeached. Each stayed 45° from the top of the cross but at different heights from the sign. Additionally, the moons appeared to be the same size; this was not the case since one was smaller but closer to the planet, thus giving the impression of equality. Their names were Moon1 (Moony) and Moon2 (Moon).

Both Archangels gazed at the 'sign' for several seconds as if reading something out of the pattern was possible. Micha-el, slowly scratching the right side of his head through his thick and undulating blond hair, mentally projected a statement.

"The High Council of Trillium has requested all the Overlords to attend a meeting in fourteen days. By then, the last sign should be visible, and we should discuss all the implications. Furthermore, we need to address another grave concern!"

"I know," Rapha-el said and quickly followed up, *"Gabri-el stated his great apprehension about the erosion of our traditional values by Lucif-er and the Overlords of the North!"*

"I will not accept any change that opposes or diminishes God's glory," Micha-el exclaimed, *"But I will do anything else for the sake of peace!"*

"We shall pray to the Lord for guidance and to enable us to see His Truth," The Archangel in purple added, making it sound like a continuous sentence following Micha-el's statement.

The two leaders, also close friends, exchanged their concerns about a changing world. In front of their eyes, the current sign steered deep emotions, mixed feelings, and incredible expectations. The disturbing events challenged their powerful intellects, but only one sense surfaced unchallenged: the Overlords, facing scary changes, had <u>no fear!</u>

•

•   •   •

•

•

•

****

Seven days later, North Alliance, SE Sector, City of Alexia.

A massive building only forty stories high stood at the top of a shallow sloped mountain; the slope started at the very edge of a sanded beach around five kilometers away and squarely faced a wide avenue, the main street in the city of Alexia. Several thick rows of buildings, rectangular shaped and with symmetrical additions, part functional and part decorative, stretched to the edge of the sea; no balconies with trees could be seen on the shiny gray and light blue colored structures. Instead, parallel rows of green belts filled with exuberant trees flanked the towering skyscrapers in an alternating pattern; low-level transparent pathways periodically and perpendicularly connected the buildings' rows.

Medium-sized mountains bordered the city, gradually diverging into a widening bay around eight kilometers from the ocean's edge.

The top floor of the 40-story square building had a transparent and tilted 45° protruding edge facing the bay. On the inside section of this tilted edge, many angels stayed busy operating all kinds of electronic equipment.

From the large group, two individuals stood next to the glassy front surface facing the shoreline. One figure with a large muscular build was Magog-el; next to him, shorter and not as thick as his companion but still showing an enviable physical profile, remained motionless. He was the Overlord of the SE Sector, Azami-el, second in command in the NA nation; with an incisive tone, he telepathically stated.

"The city's evacuation is complete. We are ready for this giant hurricane, which is scheduled to strike soon; all the equipment is in place to record the event."

"Fine!" said Magog-el while addressing two nearby tall Seraphim, both dressed in a white uniform with an instrumental gray belt and two noticeable black letters engraved over their right chests: CD (Central District, the governing sector of the entire North Alliance). They stood still in an open stand when their boss ordered.

"Cabal, Moriel, report!"

Cabal, a bit heavier build of the two, approached Magog-el and replied without talking.

"Sir! Winds next to the eye are moving at 110 meters per second, sustained!"[8]

Cabal pointed to the large room's rear, where twenty angels worked intensely with various instruments, including three huge video screens laid sequentially to cover the entire back wall.

He selected the left one, currently displaying a satellite image of the NA, specifically, the East Coast, where a massive hurricane began moving inland. He pointed his finger to the screen and, in the blink of an eye, had it magnified many times. The image showed a colossal hurricane's eye surrounded by a large, tightly packed, counterclockwise swirling mass of clouds directly moving into Alexia's Bay. After a second, he added.

---

[8] 396 kilometers/hour. (Earth's velocity/time reference.)

"The eye will hit the bay directly. We expect a tidal wave between 50 and 100 meters high, but we should be safe since we are 300 meters above sea level!"

The other Seraph, named Moriel, spoke mentally.

"Sir! The anti-cyclone crystal cloud seeding did not affect this cyclone!" He was ready to include more relevant info, but Magog-el dismissed them with a quick flick of one finger. Both subordinates quickly returned to their previous stand.

Azami-el's sharp eyesight concentrated on the surf along the coast. Without looking back, he pointed a finger to the first screen on the right side. The device instantly changed its view from the row of buildings alongside the avenue to the shoreline; a larger magnification also improved the new observation.

The image showed huge waves battering the front rows of buildings at the bay's entrance, devouring the sandy beach that had previously separated the land from the sea. Ominous clouds, like the tentacles of a giant octopus searching for prey, stretched from the ocean to the valley and the mountains.

The strong breeze gradually changed to a gale and beyond; it came and went as if mimicking the angry ocean's waves.

The afternoon sun gave way to partial darkness as the mother of hurricanes set food on the same ground claimed by a city named Alexia!

As the minutes passed, the intensity of the cyclone increased. The wind's hissing became a deafening, ominous howling, equally intimidating!

Everything outside turned dark, void of any color other than a dark gray shade. Heavy rain started to come down, although it continued to hit the square building's top-floor frontal glass at a horizontal angle, making any observation harder to discern. However, since the outside surface had some form of water repellent, the water did not stick to the glass but bounced off.

Waves of high-powered gusts swept through the city, making the frontal buildings at the shoreline sway. Debris broken away from many structures flew at dangerous speeds, breaking windows or taking chunks from the edges of other structures. The green belts became devastated as the invisible bulldozers broke and uprooted trees in a quest to slaughter the ones that could not run!

The sea became a destructive monster, generating massive waves that impacted the buildings at a continuously increasing water level. As another floor got underwater, the buildings became smaller and the angry ocean bigger!

The enraged waves rushed to destroy anything standing before them, even when the speeding hurricane's gusts clipped the massive waves' crests by blowing its water tops forward.

The front edge of the ocean began moving inland, the beach had disappeared, and a wall of water moved several kilometers inland.

A fast-moving blast of air hit the observation tower causing it to vibrate and oscillate after absorbing the vast energy of the speeding wind; it caused the front glass to bow inwards under the massive pressure.

Cabal and Moriel, standing close to the room's front, took one step backward; Magog-el, without moving, casually stated.

"Do not worry; the window will not break; its tensile strength is above what we expect from the storm." Then, he added, *"However, make sure team B is properly monitoring for incoming projectiles!"*

At this instant, one of the smaller displays inside the room blinked a red light. The operator, a Throne, quickly displayed the message. He turned around to address and inform the Overlords, but they already knew the message's context.

An infrared sensor detected one individual inside building AL2973, location F32, area B.

The area assigned to Adolphus AL1374696-VM

Magog-el interrupted the Throne's train of thought with a telepathic command, *"Make video contact!"*

"Yes, Sir! I am rerouting to the main screen." The Throne operator responded and dialed the angel's code as a video call number by just manipulating a finger.

The large, centered visual screen changed its display to show a spacious room furnished with modernistic furniture and adorned with indoor plants at several corner locations. About five meters away, looking outside a large glass window, an angel stood leaning forward. He was a Virtue, an angel's choir from the Middle Group. He wore a light blue tunic with a waistline belt. At this second, his back stayed facing the two-way video communication device.

He heard the transmission starting and turned to investigate the device by practically running to approach the instrument.

His concerned face covered most of the visual display on the central large screen inside the squared building's top floor, but at his apartment, he saw Azami-el's stern face framing two piercing blue eyes. The Overlord yelled at the Virtue.

"We ordered you to evacuate! Why are you still inside your residence!"

"Great Overlord! ... I apologize for any inconvenience I caused you!" Quickly but nervously, the Virtue named Adolphus spoke to the monitor; next, he hastily added, *"I cannot understand why I am doing this. I beg you, Noble Prince of the SE Sector, to send someone to help me out of here!"*

The thunderous voice of Azami-el echoed across the room.

"There is no excuse for this behavior! You deserve whatever happens to you!"

"Ah..." As Adolphus tried to speak again, Azami-el interrupted him with an open hand that meant: Stop!

The monitor went blank as the communication ended. The angel continued to stare at the monitor and showed his insecurity and confusion by running one hand across half of his face.

Seconds later, he remained frozen, still staring at the blank monitor.

Wham! It sounded like a bomb explosion!

A fast-moving projectile had blown the window away, scattering and shattering debris across the large room. A swift and deafening wind gust tossed and broke everything in sight. The comfortable temperature in the room changed almost instantly to very damp and cold; adding to the horror, an awful howling invaded the angel's apartment!

Adolphus could not stand anymore; instead, he lay face down on the floor. His light blue tunic had a hole in his upper back. Around this spot, the blue rapidly changed to purple... it was the angel's blood pouring out!

Adolphus, with his face distorted by pain, dragged himself toward the monitor. When close enough, he pushed the 'recall' button and pleaded to the empty screen.

"Please... help me!"

"I am sure the brains of the DNA Syndrome victims degenerate before they die. How else do you account for their idiotic behavior?"

Azami-el telepathically indicated selectively to Magog-el's mind alone. The addressee instantly replied.

"I agree; the special communication between the brain's lobes must be partially shifting out of sync!"

The Throne's operator saw another blinking red light and was ready to make the connection with a finger flip; nevertheless, he met Azami-el's authoritarian, deep blue eyes. The Overlord just barely moved his head negatively, and Adolphus's request fell into oblivion.

Again, Cabal approached Magog-el.

"Sir, building AL2973 is only three kilometers down the main street. There is an underground connection to this building; if you allow me, I could send a vehicle to rescue the Virtue named Adolphus."

"No need!" replied Magog-el. *I do not want to risk anybody's life to rescue an individual who does not deserve it. I already know that two Overlords almost lost their lives rescuing two affected DNA Syndrome individuals in the SA; we don't operate in that mode over here!"*

"Sir, your wish is my command!"

Another blast of fast-moving air caused the building to sway like a boat in the middle of the ocean. Noises mimicking moans emanated from deep inside the foundations. Except for the two Overlords, everybody else inside the room showed deep concern.

A tech group at the left side of the room suddenly became excited; the group leader, a Seraph, stood up and rushed a telepathic message to the Overlords.

"Sir! A massive 51-meter-high surge tidal wave is quickly approaching the internal shoreline!"

Without looking back, Azami-el acknowledged the message with a quick flip of his index finger. Afterward, he contacted Magog-el.

"It will arrive in two minutes!"

"Yes, it is too bad the water spray will impair our vision!" Magog-el added with anticipated disappointment.

The seconds inexorably continued to add; in the background, the red blinking light from building AL2973 requesting urgently needed help went unanswered.

Both Archangels (Overlords) stared into the partial darkness and the chaos the hurricane continued inflicting upon the city. The wind's howling became so strong that the building's insulation could not suppress its entire commotion.

Two minutes passed.

A hardly visible dark wall quickly began rising over the gray horizon, causing most onlookers to feel uneasy, even when observed at a 'safe distance'.

As it approached the beach, this dark monster grew taller and stronger. It even pulled most of the water that had flooded the bay's inner beaches and coastal roads. As it peaked at the shoreline, the fierce wind blew away their crest, causing vast amounts of water to the horizontally falling rain. The water's wall rose to the twenties floor of the shoreline buildings, most elegant 40-stories tall edifices.

Then, it came down with the fury of an angry giant!

Most of the structures lined up at the shoreline broke or fell by the massive impact, which even generated a seismic-like anomaly felt by the remaining residents: one unwilling, the rest just observers recording the event. The demolition roar was hardly heard since the storm's high-speed wind howling stayed too loud!

The falling chunks carried by the rushing seawater acted like massive hammers, demolishing other buildings farther inland and causing unimaginable chaos.

Building AL2973 was directly impacted by a large fragment carried by the turbulent waters. The fragment disintegrated into many smaller pieces when it hit and demolished the building; however, it only produced a minor noise increase to the outside roar.

Furthermore, a faint cry from an angel never reached the outside of the fragmented structure.

The two NA Overlords observed the devastation with a hidden hunger for a visually destructive phenomenon that gave them great pleasure and excitement, a spectacular form of entertainment. Nevertheless, behind them, a red blinking light blinked **no** more!

A plea for help vanished into the unknown as a whisper that the wind carried away… Adolphus was dead!

The water and the wind ripped Alexia apart. Enraged waters poured along the streets, looking for prey. Some building pieces remained visible, floating alongside the fast-moving currents, while other smaller pieces, flying like cannonballs, caused serious damage. The water did not reach the square observation building erected higher on a large hill, but the water's spray, so significant and violent due to the high-speed winds, made everything hard to see.

Another red light, this one noisy, began flashing on Group B's electronic array. The same operator exclaimed with a firm but excited message to the Overlords.

"Three flying large pieces approaching! The center one will hit the observation window!"

Everyone turned their heads, staring at the frontal tilt window, sprayed with so much water that the outside resembled a solid white wall; not much could be seen through the transparent surface. Although the two Overlords, staring out, focused their deep blue eyes on an outside location whose coordinates were only known to them, their internal clocks sped ten times faster than our average visual and physical speed.

[10x]> To us, visually seen as a slow-motion movie.

> As fractions of a second sped by, a dark and pointed sliver approached the window at tremendous speed, and the two Archangels began to slow it down.

> Two sets of radiant deep blue eyes stared at the lower front section for the incoming projectile. About ten meters away, the sliver's bottom, now slightly glowing blue, began to be deflected upward. Like sliding up a slippery slope, the flying chunk torn from a damaged building gradually moved higher while traveling forward. It cleared the observation window by flying above.

> With the blue radiance disappearing from their eyes, the Overlords stared at each other with a mutual spark of satisfaction.
> <[10x]

On planet Terra, the Archangels or Overlords had developed incredible powers, like the telekinetic ability to deflect fast and massive moving objects like the one that approached the observation window; these are powers humans don't have but dream of having. Consequently, this is why we endow our fictitious superheroes in cartoon magazines or movies with such abilities.

Moriel and Cabal, Magog-el's main assistants, moved two steps forward and returned to their previous position, their faces showing some relief.

From above, a nearby noise rattled the large observation room; the large screen on the left went blank. After the operator rerouted the input to another satellite antenna, the visual display of the storm returned to the screen.

The storm's eye lurking on the horizon was almost reaching Alexia.

A loud bang shook the building with fury, causing dust to fall from the ceiling!

Azami-el read the message from the leader of Group B before he could send it out telepathically.

"Sir, the third piece hit the tenth floor; the left section of this floor is demolished! Computer integrity is still at 100%; the building's internal support was not seriously damaged!"

Magog-el turned around and addressed everyone.

"The worst is over; continue your assignments."

To echo his statement, a swift gust hit the structure hard enough to rattle and sway more than ever; the Overlords ignored it. However, the rest of the crew tried to follow their leader's behavior, but the sweat wetting their foreheads gave away their true feelings.

The extreme storm persisted, pounding the city. The wind and the sea battered this coastal town with no mercy. The continually moving and twisting dark clouds provided a sinister upper sight. The howling, at ear-piercing levels, seemed to stay forever. Will the storm ever end?

Suddenly, the wind, rain, and noise quickly wound down; in a short time, they stopped altogether. The cloud cover lingered for a while before the sun shined through!

The hurricane's eye had arrived!

Just a gentle breeze caressed the city as blue skies opened above, and a burst of pristine sunshine illuminated the drowning town of Alexia. The only remaining noise was the gigantic surf still rolling out of control through the city; the powerful pounding of the waves could be felt along the building's foundations.

The devastation could now be easily assessed. Very few buildings near the inland bay shoreline remained standing; most had small and large pieces missing, and many were utterly gone. The streets could not be identified due to debris piled everywhere.

When looking inland, the damage decreased, but the destruction remained extreme. Most structures had missing pieces, and even fragments of trees impaled through windows and through walls.

Looking into the sunny hole in the sky outlined by towering tornado-like swirling clouds, what first appeared to be a star came down at great speed, turning into a shimmering flying cylinder. After hovering for a few seconds, it landed atop the observation building.

A side door opened, and two unarmed but military-like uniformed Seraphim exited. However, they stayed standing one at each side of the door.

Magog-el and Azami-el used a ramp to access the roof through a sliding ceiling door. When both reached the aircraft, Magog-el stopped to take one last panoramic view of the surroundings from the building's top. Afterward, he sent a mental message directed to the other Overlord. The top NA leader exclaimed with utter satisfaction.

"It was amazing; I am very pleased to have attended this spectacle! Tomorrow, bring me the final report at Centrum!"

"I will be there at 8:00 hours!" Replied Azami-el.

Using only the blink of an eye, they agreed to see each other later.

As soon as Magog-el and the pair of Seraphim pilots boarded the slick vehicle, a more advanced model than the average aircraft, it took off and swiftly climbed inside the hurricane's eye.

In no time, the vehicle gained altitude; now, the 'eye' looked like the gaping mouth of a monstrous tornado. The hole in the ground became smaller while the upper hole appeared to expand and became more prominent. The clouds at the bottom stayed close to black, but they turned into a dazzling white at the top, as seen by the aircraft's passengers flying above the clouds.

From this vantage point, the whole magnitude of a monster storm could be seen: It was like a galaxy with giant arms rotating counterclockwise and stretching as far as the horizon could allow. At its center, it had a well-defined dark hole.

The pilot sent a message to the Overlord.

"Sir! The clouds' tops are reaching 15,000 meters, and we are cruising at 20,000 meters. We will arrive at Centrum in 31 minutes!"

Using a slightly north but westerly direction, the craft locked into his programmed trajectory; the speeding vehicle left behind the great storm while on its way to the CD Sector's capital city.

On top of the square observation building, Azami-el remained analyzing the devastation. A cloud crossing above between the Overlord and the sun brought partial darkness again. The obscurity quickly spread over the city, like a spilled bucket of dark grey paint spreading on the floor. Azami-el wasted no time entering the observation building again.

In a short time, the wind, the howling, the rain, and the savage pounding returned!

Alexia faced the second half of this beastly hurricane, adding many more hours of torture and destruction, accumulating groundbreaking data for the computers' records. The storm spectators, except for two, remained here. Of the two individuals who departed this site, one left voluntarily, and the other had no choice... he left **permanently**!

****

Seven days later, at Trillium. 7:00 hours.

The Temple, a spectacular building with a diameter of 777 meters, encompassed the most beautiful and amazing structure adorning the city; it was committed to God and the Divine Trinity!

The all-encompassing dome represented the FATHER.

The SON, symbolized by a biconcave structure placed at the very center of the dome, was like an apple's core that rose from its base and ended at the exact inner center of the sphere, reflecting The FATHER's Glory.

The HOLY SPIRIT, exemplified by an incredible array of transparent and semi-transparent rods connecting the centered structure to the rest of the dome, pointed out the extraordinary and divine interaction between the FATHER and the SON.

The spherically concave central structure was not pointed at the base but truncated. A circular amphitheater built around the center could seat 10,000 angels at this location. The Core's elite, the Overlords, and The Core's citizens had all seats taken.

At the amphitheater's center, a circular gap bordering the outside edges of the spherically concave center was not part of the spectators' seating section but was reserved for the governing upper class. These seats stood higher and faced the audience. There was a space between the audience and the elite, about a five-meter gap of a highly polished translucent floor that could be illuminated with dazzling colorful designs. The elite's sitting arrangement had four sections: one pointed East, another faced North, one more at the West, and the last aimed to the South.

The eastern-facing section held twelve empty seats reserved for The Core's Council Members. They were in three rows on an upgraded slope toward the dome's center. One additional single seat at the front remained assigned to The Core's Council Leader, who was the only member of the Council allowed to address the Overlords.

The southern section held five chairs. One at the front and the rest in a semi-circled position just behind the front chair. The northern section had a similar arrangement but with seven seats. The western and last section had only three seats in a triangular configuration; this was reserved for The Core's three Overlords, where Lucif-er was the leader and the most powerful Archangel on the planet named Terra.

The Temple's architectural marvel was evident in its unique design, devoid of opaque materials. Instead, it boasted transparent, semitransparent, and translucent walls or rods, which when combined, created mesmerizing and unique effects.

At noontime, the amphitheater felt like the center of a giant, one-million-facet diamond! The light display induced by the channeled sunlight became incredible, with rainbows forming at every rod intersection in a million locations and the changing spectral colors propagating like ribbons through the center structure.

This caused a waterfall of light to proliferate along the transparent walls and floors embedded inside the towering central concave construction representing the SON. As the sun moved, the patterns constantly changed, causing the interior to appear alive!

By the afternoon, the colors changed to yellows and oranges, and later, as the sun went away, to reds; finally, at twilight, purples came to life in a frenzy spectacular display!

Even at night, when the moons came out, they caused tenuous but eerie spectacles. For moonless nights, internal lighting could generate the most unusual effects. To make things even better, electronic sound reeds sensitive to spectral light provided music enhancing the visual experience.

The angels walking the internal spiral array of stairways climbing through the many floors of the concave centerpiece, which ended at the truncated top where a sparkling circular lookout exposed the grand view from above, proclaimed that this place must be the closest location where God could be found in the entire planet. Of course, a speedy central elevator remained available if an angel did not feel like making the long pilgrimage upwards.

This Temple was not just a structure but a spiritual experience. It was a place where devout individuals could feel the presence of an invisible God, almost as if they could reach out and touch it. Love permeated the air, and the spirits of the angels reflected it back. In this temple, God was truly **present!**

At the eastern section, an opening on the shiny floor in front of the thirteen seats slid open. The lower sections stayed visible through the transparent floor, like seeing the bottom of a lake when the water was motionless and transparent.

Thirteen angels climbed a narrow flight of stairs, only made visible because they had a special light-dispersing coating, which prevented the two lower choirs from unexpected mishaps by making the steps and walls visible. Each higher step of this stairway acted like a piano being played with light instead of sound, a melodic wave continually changing the color of adjacent steps from a deep yellow to a rich orange; at the top, the empty circular section of the amphitheater came into view.

The angels dressed in fancy tunics came up in a single line using the following order.

The leader, a Seraph named Nobiel, was the first to step into the seating area. His blue tunic had patterns of green and red. He was tall and slender and walked methodically, showing a stoic personality.

Four Seraphim, wearing blue attire, followed behind him. Next, a quartet of Cherubim, wearing green robes, appeared. Last, four Thrones, wearing red, completed the group. All of them walked to their corresponding chairs and sat.

Using a similar opening from the floor, five Archangels came out from the southern section of the central layout; they were the Overlords of the SA (South Alliance).

Micha-el, the SA commander, wore a green and white tunic with interlacing color layers. He led his group with a dynamic pace. Behind him, the rest assembled in two rows of individuals, each positioned in a way that together resembled an arrowhead.

In the first row, at Micha-el's right side, stood the Irisan Province Overlord, Rapha-el, who wore his favorite light purple tunic. At his left, wearing a pale green garment, Samu-el, a Seraph, remained standing. Tall with a medium-built frame, Samu-el had an amiable, rounded face topped with curly blond hair: the Overlord of the Graceland Province.

From the second row at the right side stood a Cherub named Lari-el, with a slender face, wavy hair, and a golden-colored outfit. He gave the impression of being quiet, a listener, and the Overlord of the Tellia Province.

The last Overlord was Zeri-el, a Cherub of medium height but muscular build. He had long hair styled to meet his facial contours, wore a dark red tunic, and represented the Zarinia Province as an Overlord.

The SA's five Overlords moved to the southern section and took their proper chairs according to rank.

Next, a group of seven Archangels marched up from another stairway opening at the northern section of the central circular area adjacent to the supporting core's structure. They assembled in an arrowhead-shaped arrangement. They represented the NA (North Alliance) Overlords; they advanced according to their ranks.

First, the intimidating leader of the group, Magog-el. He wore a tunic with interlacing white and blue colors. This Archangel walked toward the northern section with extra firm steps that slightly echoed inside the amphitheater; he ruled the Central District (CD) as the leading Overlord.

Azami-el, the next in line, had a piercing stare and a constant serious appearance. Like the Overlord ahead, his tunic had one thin, solid blue stripe across the middle; he was the SE sector, Overlord.

Another Seraph closely followed him, a foxy-looking individual and third in command named Gorgon-el. He also wore a tunic with blue and white interlaced but had more stripes than his superior; two solid blue vertical thin stripes ran across the center part of his tunic, covering the front and back. He was the Overlord of sector SC.

The sector's abbreviations represented the four cardinal points, with the addition of CD, which meant Central District, similar to DC (District of Columbia) in the USA. White and blue were the NA's official colors.

A medium-built Cherub, Razari-el, ascended, walking energetically. His garment was solid light blue with a slender vertical white line across the whole center part. The tunic's colors were not flat but dynamic, as seen on silk and velvet. He wore his hair loose, but it hung straight down. Razari-el remained as the NE sector's Overlord.

Next appeared a Cherub named Izma-el, also medium built but taller, an astute observer and organizer and equally dressed in a solid light blue garment with two white vertical lines, the symbol for the Overlord of the SW sector.

Number six was Kroma-el, a Cherub, and Overlord of the NC sector. He wore short hair that made him more noticeable. He looked slender and tall, and his robe was like the other Overlords' but with one solid vertical black line across the tunic.

Last stood a Throne, Ezek-el, a stocky angel with a rounded face. He had lots of hair but in a managed way. His attire was also light blue, although it had two vertical black lines. He was the Overlord of the last sector, named NW.

All seven Overlords took their seats at the northern corner.

Three more Archangels climbed the stairway. The first one to come up was Lucif-er, whose imposing presence and handsome appearance demanded more than a glance. The blazing white of his tunic sparkled and graciously reflected the light around him but by no means overshadowed his tantalizing twelve wings. His movement resembled more of a flight than a walk, with everybody in the place looking at him. He was the Overlord of the most powerful state of The Core: Seraphan. In addition, he commanded the entire Core nation.

Next, a Cherub wearing a solid but iridescent green tunic elegantly followed Lucif-er. His deep green eyes gently scanned the surroundings; he was Gabri-el, the Overlord of The Core's state of Cheruban.

In a hurry, a youthful-looking Overlord stepped out of the entrance and caught up with Gabri-el. He made a triangle with the other two Archangels. His angelic wings defined him as a Throne. He wore a pale red tunic. His name was Dani-el, the Thronan's state Overlord.

The three Core leaders sat in a triangular arrangement at the opposite location (western) as the council members.

After all the Overlords finished sitting, the lighting started to change into waves of deep oranges and reds; the beauty of their interactions distracted the attendance from the center characters.

Note that an advanced holographic 3D electronic system monitored the circular seating arrangement on a partial segment of the central column. This allowed any spectator inside this dome to see all the seated VIPs, even if their location on the opposite side remained blocked by the massive, centered supporting tower!

Nobiel, the council's leader, stood up. He looked up at the dome's top and extended both arms toward the same spot.

Everybody stood up.

Soon afterward, he exclaimed with a loud, telepathic expression.

"Oh Lord of light and love, for this meeting to reflect Your will, please lead us down the proper path so our knowledge and wisdom can grow under Your divine supervision!"

Everybody sat again except for the speaker; he continued.

"You all know about the Holy Writings from our ancestors; you also know that we believe God conveyed these writings! In them, His command was simple and precise: 'Love your God with all your strength and your neighbor as yourself!'"

After a short pause, he continued.

"The writings included the prediction of the end of our world, an event to be preceded by great signs and catastrophes... Today, we are amid sky symbols and great disasters.

Lucif-er and the NA will explain that the present events are not predictions from our ancestors but only coincidences. The SA, Gabri-el, and Dani-el will state the opposite.

Our first speaker is Overlord Magog-el, who has requested to start the debate!"

Nobiel proceeded to take his seat at the front of the council.

Magog-el got up from the leading seat of the NA's triangular seating arrangement. Using slow but powerful strides, he walked to the central, slightly elevated circular podium in front of every seated dignitary. Once on the podium, he started a slow counterclockwise (CCW). Any angel looking at him could electronically see him at a distance straight on, directly at his face, or both. He sent a powerful mental message.

"Core citizens, the predicament is as follows: You have seen and heard the videos from three major disasters afflicting Terra, events happening at two-week intervals."

He paused for three seconds, then continued.

"The explanation is simple and has nothing to do with the Holy Writings... Our sun started a period of internal activity, like flares and sunspots. As it went into a mild nuclear core rearrangement concerning hydrogen and helium atoms, it produced one out-of-face gravitational wave that, due to the resonant characteristics of the atomic quantum interface, was repeated two more times. Consequently, these waves passed

across our planet, generating two internal upheavals and one major atmospheric disturbance.

Unfortunately, our best instrumentation could not pinpoint or measure the interaction of the waves and our planet's core. Soon, we will upgrade our solar detectors for better measurements to understand the unpredicted behavior of our sun.

The NA accepts this explanation as the only logical alternative for the three catastrophic events unleashed on this planet. Concerning the night sky patterns, we believe they are nothing else than that! To confirm our statement, Lucif-er has predicted: 'The same sky patterns will repeat in a million years!' Therefore, the claim that this is a divine warning is grossly incorrect!

Furthermore, all these rumors being fed by some individuals to the masses are creating fears that the population had long ago removed from their subconscious, fears based on ignorance and superstition!"

Magog-el stood motionless and silent for three seconds, then returned to his seat with solid and militaristic steps and rested his case.

The colors dancing inside the dome as the sun faded away for the day mesmerized the audience for one minute while the display became overwhelming. The eyes and minds of the present danced alongside the Temple's best orchestral disclosure, light itself.

The internal lighting turned on early due to the present conference, causing a new wave of interacting displays across the entire dome's surface, the floors, the walls, and even perhaps inside the angels' minds.

All these light displays happened after Gabri-el got up to respond to the leader of the NA; his green tunic sparkled with many other color overtones, a reflection of the incredible surroundings. He started to walk on the raised podium in the opposite direction than Magog-el, clockwise (CW). His steps stayed firm, but they did not follow a straight line.

Gabri-el's deep green eyes met another pair from the audience… Raquel's beautiful eyesight.

She quickly blinked her long eyelashes over her astonishing sparkling irises, like the curly lashes could talk and play music. Gabri-el got a personal message sent by her. (Personal: Only the selected person or persons could receive the telepathic message.)

"You are so precious to me; you are the light that embraces my soul… **I love you!"**

He responded also using a private channel.

"My sweetheart and beloved wife, only God loves you more than I do! I am sending you a tender kiss!"

Like a gentle breeze playing with your hair, so did the mental command by causing Raquel's brain to caress her lips tenderly. While briefly closing her eyes, she gently bit her lower lip with deep pleasure.

"Can you concentrate on what you are doing?" A personalized mental communicating voice interrupted Gabri-el's thoughts in a joking matter. Gabri-el glanced at Lucif-er, who showed a faint smile; the former responded with an equal smirk. Then, somehow concerned, he thought.

"Did Lucif-er intellectually deduce what I was doing? Or can he access a private telepathic message?"

He looked at the audience and started his discourse that compared to his predecessor, it was delivered with a milder touch.

"Dear citizens, we try to explain what cannot be with technology because we use material tools to explain spiritual events. After all, it is easy to deceive ourselves into believing materialistic truths, even when the spiritual and absolute facts contradict them. Let us mention that when we talk about absolutes, we also talk about God.

Furthermore, God's way, as it is in many instances, is not the same as ours... even if we think it is! Our ancestors had few material things, so they turned to their spirituality, a behavior that moved them closer to God. Consequently, all the writings from that epoch still command our current existence.

In contrast, nowadays, we have many possessions that erode the time that should be allocated to faith. We tend to solve all our problems with our machines and computers with a know-all-science trying to explain everything, even if it is incapable of doing it!

Dear Core members, I ask you not to be frivolous toward the signs and events being witnessed; they symbolize a message from God, and we should listen!

In conclusion, we should abandon materialistic habits and strive for a better relationship with our loving Lord and Creator!"

While Gabri-el walked back to his assigned seat, Azami-el sprung out from his sitting locale; similar to Magog-el, he assumed a CCW walking pattern when he reached the circular and slightly protruding podium; he moved briskly and assertively.

"Core citizens," he started. *"What you just heard is only an appeal to your emotions. Gabri-el's statements are irrelevant!*

Look at the facts; they speak for themselves. We, the people of Terra, have evolved a long time since the old era. We can now support and take care of everything ourselves. Our knowledge is vast, diverse, and increasing at astronomical rates. Our powers and lifespans continue to grow daily!

*These statements acknowledge one crucial fact: **we oversee our destinies!"***

After his brief discourse, Azami-el quickly returned to his NA-assigned position.

Five seconds later, Micha-el's sharp blue eyes sparkled as he sprang forward in his usual dynamic style toward the podium. Once there, he strolled, following the CW circling.

He stared at the NA Overlords, ultimately ending with Lucif-er, who returned the stare without blinking. Then, using a milder glance, he pivoted on his left foot for a 180-degree turn using speed and elegance; his tunic twisted with ripples along his muscular body. Everybody in the audience focused on his alluring deep blue vision and noticed it; after this call for attention, Micha-el stated.

"I know you want me to talk about the recent events unfolding in and on the planet. Their interpretation seems a matter of choice, though it is a message we cannot ignore!

As you already heard, the representatives from the NA, and The Core's sympathizer, Lucif-er, are doing their best to promote their materialistic points of view. I am not concerned about the physical events bewildering us; what concerns me is the visible decline of our moral values, which are already eroding our primary goal: To serve God!"

Micha-el paused and again stared at Lucif-er; however, this time, The Core's leader stood up and exclaimed.

"Micha-el, you can save us some time and go directly to whatever bothers you!"

Before Lucif-er sat again, like responding to Micha-el's eye-catching call for attention trick that he used before speaking, he pointed his right hand's index finger up and made a small circle with it.

Everybody saw Lucif-er's amazing deep blue eyes without him looking at anybody other than Micha-el! The audience got startled and somehow intimidated; a mental murmur rose from The Core's citizens' general audience but quickly disappeared.

Micha-el, still looking at Lucif-er, responded.

"As you wish... Lucif-er! I want to know why an angel died in Alexia while your NA friends just watched it happening?"

Magog-el jumped up from his chair and burst out aloud.

"What are you implying with this question!"

Lucif-er quickly glanced at him, and Magog-el understood. Unwillingly and angrily, he retook his seat. Without delay, Lucif-er replied, *"He just wanted to die... and he did!"*

"Lucif-er, for many years, nobody else had died in an accident that could have been prevented!" Micha-el responded and immediately added.

"Why nobody assisted him when he asked for help?"

"You saw the video; not enough time and too dangerous!"

Micha-el turned 180 degrees and raised both hands toward the audience, he mentioned.

"Gabri-el and Rapha-el, they rescued two similar individuals in the city of Lemar; it was <u>more</u> dangerous and had <u>less</u> time!"

Lucif-er got up and walked to get closer to Micha-el, stopping about one meter away. Both Overlord's blue eyes met, turning to a more profound and shinier hue, but their intensified color returned to a normal level in two seconds. Lucif-er continued the mental dialogue at a slower pace than the SA leader.

*"I know... except that they almost lost their lives while doing it. How would you feel if by now... **they could be dead**?"*

Micha-el paused for a second, trying to understand the other person's thoughts; being Lucif-er's, this possibility remained too close to zero.

"I would be as thankful to God as I am for them to be alive! I will know their sacrifice was for what we stay on this planet for: To serve God and love our neighbor as ourselves! If dying is a requirement, let it be so!" We are here not to be masters, but to serve!

Correspondingly, let me ask you, Lucif-er. Do you believe an angel from a lower choir is less valuable than an Archangel?"

Lucif-er disengaged eye contact and glanced at the spectators, he said.

"We are all equal... spiritually talking; nevertheless, the knowledge accumulated in an Archangel is immense as compared to the common angel; it is like day and night! ... The loss of an angel will hardly affect the whole community, but the loss of an Archangel will be vast indeed!

Furthermore, as you are waiting for me to say... Yes, Micha-el, I recognize that for God, there are no material possessions; He only cares about the spirit!"

Micha-el communicated slowly, emphasizing his reply using a direct and piercing mode.

"Exactly! You know... Do you still believe it?"

Lucif-er stared again at the SA leader; he snapped.

"What we believe is very deep inside our brains; even you may not believe what you assert!"

Micha-el did not answer. He turned around, and with energetic steps, returned to the leading chair in the SA seating segment.

Lucif-er continued staring at Micha-el's back for a moment, then returned to his assigned and prominent seating location. While looking at the audience, his eyes locked with Liliel, his beautiful Throne companion, seated at a frontal auditorium spot.

She sent him a personalized message, her lips opening slightly and the tip of her tongue barely touching her front teeth.

"I want you, handsome!"

Lucif-er did not reply; he must have felt deep anger inside, even when nothing was shown outside him. A spark from his eyes caused a mild frontal shock while his unmistakable message was delivered.

"Be quiet!"

She was startled, and then she lowered her gorgeous purple eyes. Nobody else knew, but she felt humiliated, as if everyone inside the dome had heard.

Ten seconds of almost silence vanished before Rapha-el rose and moved to the forum to speak. His mental voice reached everyone.

"Dear brothers and sisters!

I need to mention that the angels with the DNA Syndrome, the same individuals who got in trouble, need not blame, but our compassion!

This unfortunate group of angels, unlike the rest of us planning our lives for millenniums to come, has the hopeless affliction of dying in the near future. We must understand that we are not doing enough for them. Additionally, we should take a more active role in preventing similar occurrences as the two recent events.

It has been officially proven that the Syndrome's victims, in advanced cases, have serious psychological issues due to complex brain decay. As seen in Alexia and Lemar, these angels are not responsible for their actions when subject to stressful situations.

If you are already giving them love and understanding... please, give them more!"

Rapha-el returned to his location.

The debate continued for one more hour to no avail; the NA and the SA remained diverging. Micha-el tried one last time toward more unity between the North and the South by renewing the spiritual to avoid drifting apart. His last words transpired like a prayer.

"I plead with you, my brothers. Let's grow together, respecting God's will! It is not too late!"

While Micha-el finished imploring for unity, Magog-el privately complained to Lucif-er, *"You were not aggressive enough; I expected you to intimidate them! To show that we are in control!"*

The Core's leader replied, *"This is not the time or the place. Remember that you are at The Core, and its citizens remain a very pacifistic nation that dislikes aggressive or violent behavior. You must be a politician like Gabri-el; watch him when he talks!"*

Nobiel, The Core's council leader, stood up and stated.

"I regret to admit that after debating for so long, this is the first time the NA and the SA failed to reach any agreement. Let's note that the council abstains from any resolution and allows the debating Alliances to resolve their differences!"

After this last statement, he raised his hands toward the dome's ceiling; everybody stood. Solemnly he proceeded to express a closing prayer.

"We thank You, Lord, for your love and understanding. Help us move closer to You so we can benefit from Your wisdom. Praise to God; praise to You, forever!"

When he lowered his hands, the meeting ended. A high level of mental telepathic noise immediately inundated the entire amphitheater.

High above the circular raised podium, a massive holographic display replicating the outside night sky came into view. The intensity of the angels' mental talk got much louder!

Rising above the virtual horizon, crispy visibly, the last letter of the alphabet was now present... **Z**.

What did it mean?

Was it heralding the end of Terra?

Was it just a coincidental arrangement of planets and stars?

If this unusual night display appeared on Earth, should we prepare for an Apocalyptic event or ignore it?

Should we, also need to make **a choice**?

THE SHIFT

CHAPTER 2

After the conclusion of its journey across the sky, the vanishing sun faded away, triggering the twilight between the day and night. A chain of undulating mountains came into view as a gray silhouette, sharply contrasted with the crimson and purple glimmering above the western horizon. Against this brighter background, the darkened shapes of two Seraphim, identified by their six rays or wings as being Overlords, stood motionless.

As we got closer, we could see one of their faces; it belonged to a handsome Archangel with lots of undulating blond hair, which appeared to be pale bronze rather than gold in the minimal light remaining. This Archangel's muscular shape, faintly delineated against a distant dark hillside, was Micha-el. He turned to his companion, not visible, and spoke, an unusual method of communication between Overlords.

"Rapha-el, the sign we saw in the night sky seven years ago, deeply disturbed me. I did understand most of the message; however, something important is missing... What is the whole meaning? Were the signs commanding us to do something?"

His companion did not answer; he just stared at the darkening horizon, now allowing a few stars to become visible in the blackened sky.

Micha-el slowly turned and looked in the same direction. Behind the hills, massive columns of clouds rose like erupting from outraged volcanoes. The clouds had a unique glow, a deep purple with silvery gray outlines illuminating the hills' tops. Quickly, they merged into one ominous thundercloud that, in no time, obliterated the twinkling of the emerging stars. The surroundings turned into night in only seconds, and the clouds above became menacing!

Lightning struck far away, and it did again... nearby! Micha-el, noticeably alarmed, took one step backward.

"What is going on?" He asked his friend,

His companion did not answer; Micha-el spoke again.

"The approaching storm looks horrible! Rapha-el, we should look for a cover!"

The addressed Overlord replied with a tone of voice, seemingly unconcerned about what was happening.

"No need to worry; everything will be fine."

Micha-el looked at his friend and thought, "Rapha-el is behaving oddly like I am talking to a hologram; furthermore, I had never seen any clouds as strange as these ... **I must be dreaming!**"

He noticed how odd it was. Why the circular black pupils in Rapha-el's deep blue eyes? When I look inside, I see glowing white crosses.

Before he could make a related remark, his companion exclaimed.

"I know your need to understand the meaning of the cross; it will be revealed to you soon!"

As Rapha-el started to walk away, he glanced in the opposite direction from Micha-el. The latter Archangel, still confused, watched the other entity, adding distance between them.

A dazzling, bright, and thunderous beam of lightning struck where Rapha-el stood!

Micha-el was still there when the dust cleared away, but Rapha-el was **gone**!

He looked around but found no trace of his friend. He noticed that the ground where he stood had no vegetation, the same as a desert.

"Rapha-el!" He screamed while running around the place; only a distant thunder answered. The surroundings, to his astonishment, began to look familiar.

"Yes!" When he was very young, he visited this desert: The Gray Desert, about 300 kilometers west of the capital of the province of Pristeen, Dawnel. He suddenly remembered all the good times he had enjoyed with his parents long ago, right at this place!

For a fleeting moment, a warm feeling filled his mind and body; events long gone became briefly experienced again.

The clouds above never looked so menacing and intimidating as they did now. As a sense of doom gradually invaded his being, Micha-el felt so cold and alone that it hurt. While standing still, he closed his eyes...

A DIFFERENT BUT CONTIGUOUS DREAM SEGMENT[1]

A chill ran down his spine when the scream from millions of mouths forced him to open his eyes!

He stood in the middle of this wide street with poor lighting but not pitch black, like a night's brightness provided by a partial moon. The sky remained covered by threatening black clouds that made the large buildings erected on both sides of the street look like gray, featureless boxes. In addition, he stared at countless angels with their hands raised at him, almost faceless and colorless but not calm or silent!

In unison, they yelled at Micha-el.

"Great Overlord, Micha-el!
Please, save us!
Please do not abandon us; don't let us die!"

---

[1] With a dream segment, I mean: When we dream, it usually happens with short bursts of visual experiences. These could be followed by related additional segments that are considered contiguous to the original dream. Or it could be something unrelated to the initial segment, then becoming a different dream.

The crowd, screaming at him, begged as loud as their lungs would allow them. They screamed in Micha-el's face while pushing him backward and simultaneously trampling over each other.

The Overlord felt powerless; he had no words or strength to help anybody. With so many people around him, why did he feel so **alone**?

The out-of-control multitude seemed to have all the strings to take the Archangel to whatever place they desired. They pushed him along a narrow alley that opened into a large plaza; here, they did not push anymore.

Micha-el walked to the plaza's center, where five avenues originated, and all were packed with screaming angels; however, this time, he remained alone at the center of this large circle, which was one step higher than the avenues' pavement and had a diameter of ten meters; all the noisy angels stood outside this circle. The wailing became stifled and incoherent, more like a noisy background when talking to another person in the middle of a bustling and crowded street.

The Overlord slowly raised his head and looked up. Three massive round and black pillars projected way up into the sky. As if the clouds were waiting for the Archangel to glance upwards, they began to dissolve. In no time, the stars shined brilliantly in the sky.

Then, for three seconds, the crowd remained silent!

Unexpectedly, the stars began to fall from the sky!

The crowd went crazy! They yelled, moved their hands in panic, and ran in all directions, like the sea in the middle of a storm, chaos at its best!

Micha-el's heart ached at the sight of his people panicking over his lack of understanding and inability to help anybody. In despair, he raised both hands to the sky and pleaded.

"My Lord and God, please, I beg You! ... Help us!"

Over the whole place, an ominous feeling of increasing doom could be felt. It was like a mountain collapsing on top of them, and they could not get out of the way!

Micha-el felt as if the air itself was being sucked out of his lungs like his brain wanted to explode, and he started to dissolve into thin air and **nothingness**!

Suddenly,

A dazzling white cross appeared at the center of the night sky!

A cross that was... that was...

                    END OF DREAM SEGMENTS

"Sir! Please, wake up!"

Micha-el's eyes opened. His heart was pounding, his breath remained short and fast, and his body, including the loose white tunic he wore, was completely soaked in sweat.

Looking down at him at close range, his assistant, a Seraph named Arkyn, exclaimed with disbelief.

"Sir, you had a nightmare!"

****

A small but bright red light blinked on and off, with a noticeable "ding" sound after each pulse. Above the light, a large, darkened screen displayed a code number at its lowest section.

M-PD-001

Inside the obscured habitational area, a motionless person lying on a bed, only visible with each flicker of the vermillion glowing light, mentally identified the code.

"Micha-el, Dawnel in Pristeen, his private quarters."

The angel in the room flicked his index finger, and the room's illumination came on at about 50% of average intensity. Concurrently, the large, embedded display in the wall displayed Micha-el's face plus half of his upper body in a quasi-3D format, with the body's contours remaining partially projected above the display's surface.

The individual in the bed chamber moved to a sitting position at the center of his cushioned bed, like a yoga meditating action. He wore a light purple tunic, which identified him as Rapha-el. Without moving a muscle, analogous to floating above a surface, the seated Archangel rotated ¼ turn to face the display!

"Micha-el!" He telepathically acknowledged through the electronic machine. Next, after noticing the sweat on his friend's face, he asked with sudden concern.

"What is going on?"

"Please excuse me for interrupting your sleep. I am fine; I just had a nightmare!" Micha-el's image spoke after the incoming electronic response was translated to sound waves.

"But Archangels do not have any!" Rapha-el noted.

"I know; I was a young boy the last time I had one, so many years ago. Regardless, it was beyond a dream... it was a premonition!"

"You got my attention; send me a digital record of your dream!" Rapha-el suggested, his eyes sparkling as he chatted with his boss and equally close friend.

As seen from Rapha-el's side, Micha-el's image touched the screen with his index finger. Rapha-el did the same on his monitor, matching the exact location as his boss's fingertip.

Two seconds later, Rapha-el's finger jerked away from the screen like he had an electric shock! He exclaimed.

*"My friend, it was indeed a confusing and depressing dream! I was in it, but **he** was not **me**!"*

"*Exactly,*" Micha-el responded, quickly adding, "*I regret that Arkyn woke me up! I needed to know what the full meaning of the cross is. I am sure it represents something from God, but I don't comprehend the complete extent of His message.*"

"*My assessment of your dream is equal to yours.*"

The SA leader concluded, "*My friend, I am glad to share the vision with you. I will see you here at Pristeen in five hours. The SA monthly meeting will start twenty minutes later, at 6:20 hours.*"

"*Is Samu-el still vacationing in Eastland?*" Asked Rapha-el.

"*Yes! We all wish to be on such a beautiful island; see you soon!*"

Micha-el's image blinked out.

****

Early in the morning, the sun, near the ground in the eastern direction, spread its caressing warm radiation over the visible landscape. A cool and gentle breeze tenderly moved the trees and bushes, barely rocking the vegetation back and forth as if it wanted the plants to go to sleep.

A Seraph stood alone at the edge of a tall hill overlooking a bay with a breathtaking view. This bay was decorated with fabulous, sandy beaches displaying hues between light green and deep blue related to the water's depth or the distance from the shore.

A group of single-file white birds flew effortlessly nearby, with its leader aiming at a distant shoreline; furthermore, all the birds seemed to be connected by invisible strings that made them keep their distances from each other and turn at the exact same spatial locations.

The vegetation was a lush tropical forest, with rows of palm trees marking the inland edges of the sandy beaches. The thick green forest took over where the palms ended, displaying uncountable flowering trees that dotted the green sea of chlorophyll with all kinds of colors.

Far away, a cone-shaped peak rose high against the far horizon, an inactive volcano now covered by abundant foliage, the green color of life; the entire panoramic view was a Hawaiian landscape. This place was Eastland, an independent country not aligned with the NA or SA alliances but friendly to all.

The Seraph, a tall individual with a medium build, let the breeze play with his golden-colored hair. He wore a light green loose-fitted jumpsuit, which had the addition of a waist-high belt, carrying a medium-sized golden buckle.

Far away, a beautiful city could be seen on the shoreline on the right side of the bay. Its buildings looked like shiny emeralds and commanded attention. The town had a few tall buildings, with most of them just inching upwards from the long rows of flowering trees that, at this distance, appeared as multicolored ribbons adorning the sparkling structures.

At a much closer distance, walking on the shoreline and coming from the distant city, ten angels approached the hillside where the Throne stood. At this relatively shorter distance, they still appeared to be the same size as ants. From this group, one individual stayed at the front while the other nine formed a square of three rows of three individuals each.

A faint 'ding' came out seconds later from the Throne's buckle. He removed the buckle from the belt and rotated it so the front would face him. Four fingers from his right hand were positioned on the left side of the rectangular device, and with his right thumb pressing against the right side of the item, it rested on his palm with a complete view of its top surface.

The image of Micha-el's face appeared at the top surface of this gadget.

Micha-el calmly requested, *"Samu-el, it is midnight, and we just finished the official meeting; now, we want to know if you are having fun!"*

"That is easy to show," the Throne replied while he slowly scanned the countryside; he added, *"You can see it for yourselves!"*

As he moved the device around, he pointed toward the beach section where the ten ant-sized angels continued marching. At that instant, they stopped; their leader moved to the rear side of the square, and with an "about face," guided them away.

While Micha-el praised the place's magnificence, which he remembered well from his experience, Samu-el thought.

"How odd; it is like they spotted me and are going away just to avoid me! What possible rationale could they have for such behavior?"

At the same time, he spoke to his friends, listening at the other end of the communication device.

"I will be hiking back to Blue Star City and should be at the main plaza tonight. My brothers, I miss you; I wish you could be here at this fabulous place. I will be back in Dawnel in two days, so long!"

The small screen became deactivated and returned as a shiny gold buckle. Samu-el placed it back on the front of his belt and proceeded to signal two Seraphim sitting under a neighboring tree to join him, which they did.

All three angels quickly vanished into a sinuous dirt path leading to the city but through the forest's depths.

Pristeen Province, Dawnel.

Micha-el and three additional Overlords stood inside his main office together on the side where the SA leader usually sat; all were looking at a large screen displaying a frozen image of the ten angels marching on the beach, the same place where Samu-el's electronic scanner took a video image. A muscular Cherub, Zeri-el, telepathically exclaimed.

"We all agreed on the ten angels' suspicious behavior on the beach; 100-magnification should tell us who they are!"

Pointing to the spot on the screen where the ten stood motionless, the magnified image immediately showed one individual followed by a block of nine additional angels. They had distinctive blue and white uniforms with gray belts.

All four Archangels noted immediately, *"NA, CD personnel, basic platoon group!"*

Nevertheless, it remained hard to identify what they carried in their hands.

"Since we cannot get more information by using a larger magnification, let us use a 3D differentiating algorithm to reconstruct a better image," Micha-el suggested, and the program was swiftly implemented.

The image, after some jittering, settled down into a crisp sharpness.

"The leader is carrying a long-range scanner and telemetric locating device," noted Rapha-el, the Archangel in a light purple tunic. *"And the other nine…"*

Micha-el felt a cold chill running down his spine as the darkness and fear of his recent nightmare invaded his soul again. In disbelief, he had an intense thought.

"My Lord, am I dreaming again? I cannot believe my own eyes!"

For a few seconds, the four Overlords of the South Alliance said nothing, even when their brains stayed overactive. One of the Archangels, a normally quiet and listening individual, rotated 90 degrees to face the other three. Lari-el's golden tunic made a high-pitched whistling sound due to the speedy turn; simultaneously, he mentally exclaimed to his companions.

*"Are they carrying… **weapons?**"*

In the early evening, Samu-el comfortably sat with his two Seraphim companions inside a spacious and lustrous balcony resembling a squashed sphere. The balcony hung from the twentieth floor of a structure overlooking a vast plaza that resembled a giant five-pointed blue star. Each arm was 100 meters long; the centered main body stayed higher than the rest but below the balcony's height. Using multiple steps downward, a fantastic display of thousands of waterfalls originated at the star's center and cascaded water to the lowest surface. Situated at the tips of the arms, the vast liquid became collected and recycled back to the higher center.

From many locations, a fine mist was projected up, causing the solid blue illumination to have a foggy effect, neatly superimposed on the overall display. It was an enormous three-dimensional star that appeared to have its own life, like the center was always moving toward the tips of its arms.

From the balcony, the sight was spectacular; the blue star at the city's center gave the town its name: Blue Star City. While observing the vast array of waterfalls, Samu-el mentally spoke to his assistants with two messages sent simultaneously.

"Yasar, I do not get tired of looking at this beauty!"

"Ravyn, I do not get tired of looking at this beauty!"

Yasar, the younger-looking, with a quick smile frequently adorning his face, answered first.

"Sir, I don't either! I still remember walking the underground maze under and around the waterfalls yesterday. And the best view at the star's highest point, which we reached through a tunnel, was just incredible!"

Ravyn, more profound and formal, including his hairstyle, also replied.

"Sir, I have been to Eastland several times. What I like best are the star's daytime rainbows."

A gentle breeze moved across the balcony, briefly stirring the Seraphim's blond hair, he added.

"Sir, I love this night's temperature. I think it is about 22 degrees centigrade."

"It is 21," Samu-el calmly asserted.

Ravyn mentally commanded a side-view monitor to turn on. The viewing screen was connected to a hi-power binocular, which gave a crisp magnification of any place in sight from the building's terrace.

He commented as he focused on a handful of waterfalls and a crowd of individuals walking alongside the edges of the blue star.

"Sir, the NA citizens must like this place; they are all over!"

"Yes, Ravyn," replied Samu-el. *"I did notice that 90% of the visitors are from the NA; they must appreciate the wonders of this island."*

A faint ding came from the room; Samu-el knew it was for him by its frequency. Yasar immediately pointed a finger at the door leading inside the building from the balcony, opening it.

Samu-el, closely followed by his assistants, walked into a huge tri-level apartment lavishly adorned with artifacts and beautiful plants. All three Seraphim stood in front of a life-size screen; then, when glancing at the bottom of the screen, they saw.

M-PD-001 ***

It meant: Micha-el, Pristeen, Dawnel, Main Office.

*** = DNA acknowledgment required. Message encoded.

All the angels' smiles disappeared when an invisible eraser had **them** removed because… **this code had never been used before.**

Samu-el placed his right-opened hand over the center of the screen. One second later, the full image of Micha-el appeared on the display; with no smile, he briefly said.

"Samu-el, please report to my office ASAP!"

The addressee replied, *"Micha-el, I am leaving right now!"*

The screen blinked out. Immediately, Ravyn questioned.

"Sir! What could be so important to require code ***?"

Again, at Micha-el's main office in Dawnel, all five Overlords of the SA were present this time. Micha-el faced the other four Archangels sitting on their plush chairs according to their ranking order, from the right was the most important to the left the least; Rapha-el held the highest rank, next were Samu-el, Lari-el, and Zeri-el.

The ceiling stayed open, showing a clear view of the night sky, with the stars shining brighter than ever. No moons were in sight, and no 'signs' were in the black sky. Next, Samu-el exclaimed telepathically.

"I never had any difficulty understanding anything! Nevertheless, what all of you expressed to me makes no sense! Our Lord created us to live on this planet to serve Him and to love each other. How do weapons, tools of destruction, have any need to exist among our NA brothers?"

"My dear friend, we have the same problem assimilating information from Eastland. Our eyes reveal the facts, but our minds refuse to accept them!" Micha-el declared and immediately added, *"As you know, weapons were utilized many thousands of years ago for hunting purposes; presently, we do not use any animal for food. Our entire food supply is processed from prime ingredients that we can manipulate to have the nutritional value, shape, taste, and flavor we please. Consequently, in our present time, when an angel carries a weapon, it can only be with the sole purpose of attaining dominance over other individuals of his species.*

Would they reach the extreme scenario, where they use their weapons against their neighbors to hurt and even kill them?"

"Will God allow such a horrible scenario?" Rapha-el questioned while restlessly rotating his chair from one side to the other.

The NA's leading Overlord locked his deep blue eyes with Rapha-el's similar eyesight and spoke using his mind to his close friend.

*"Rapha-el, you know as I do that the Lord gave us the freedom of choice. This is an incredible power that has not even been considered until now. Just ponder that not one atom in the universe will do anything other than **His** will! ... But we, the angels of Terra, can say to the almighty God... NO! ... Just the thought of this possibility makes my entire body ache!"*

Micha-el's eyes sparkled almost to the color of fire.

Rapha-el promptly commented while moving closer to his friend.

"If **'choice'** *is a coin with two faces, mine has only one image, and it is the face of **God**! ... It is the only option that I have!"*

"You and I are alike!"

"And we choose to be like you!" The other three Overlords announced in unison as they stood up from their chairs. After everyone returned to their sitting positions, Micha-el continued talking.

"Before we notify the citizens of the South Alliance about this incident, it is essential that we uncover the extent and intentions of the NA.

Rapha-el and I will conduct an in-depth satellite study of the whole NA territory to analyze the activity level.

Samu-el, you will send a team of fifty angels to investigate what is happening in Eastland.

Lari-el and Zeri-el, each of you will organize a team of 100 angels to be sent to the NA Sectors to gather whatever information is available. The two teams should work independently.

I will give you 30 days to complete your tasks!"

Zeri-el, showing concern, asked Micha-el.

"Micha-el, what are we doing if we find out the NA is arming their population? For our protection, we must arm the SA with no delay!"

"I would rather not debate such a possibility. I am still hoping to find out that our concerns are unfounded and not to be taken seriously."

"If you authorize it, I could at least start some weapons research during this waiting period," Zeri-el insisted.

"No, my friend; just concentrate on your task and bring me an accurate report."

Addressing everyone, Micha-el added, using a louder mental output.

"In 30 days… report to me!"

****

The Core, Seraphan, Aurel: the golden capital, in the downtown area.

Lucif-er and Magog-el entered an elevator inside the city's most prominent building. The elegant device swiftly took them twenty stories below and silently opened its wide doors to expose a massive underground structure; indirect lighting brightly illuminated the whole place.

Very spacious and polished corridors merged into a central area housing an aerodynamic train. Its front edge was like a jet engine intake, and the remaining body was made of highly polished material. The frontal engine had many long sectional cylinders attached.

The high ceiling concentrically reduced as it approached the back end of this boarding train station and ended up in a narrow tunnel where the subway train had no other choice than to be channeled into an underground conduit, a guiding tunnel with a preset destination.

The train terminal was almost empty; a few angels stayed busy doing the perfecting touches of a brand-new station. The frontal train engine acquired most of the attention; there, ten Seraphim dressed in white and blue uniforms stood in formation, the basic NA platoon.

Close by, two more Seraphim wearing glossy gray jumpsuits were having a mental chat; the color of their attire identified them as technical personnel. When they saw the two Overlords approaching, they stopped their conversation and stood erect formally. One of the pair, a rounded-

faced Seraph, first glanced at Lucif-er's eyes but quickly lowered his sight
and delivered his welcoming statement.

*"Great Overlord, I am the chief engineer of this project. We immensely
appreciate your Eminence for taking the time to solve our nagging
vibration problem. Let me…"*

*"Morrie, there is no need to explain anything; we have been briefed
and know the issue,"* Lucif-er interrupted and then ordered, *"Start the test
run!"*

Magog-el flicked a finger, and the NA platoon orderly climbed into the
frontal engine's section through a sliding door. They moved to the rear
section and took the available seats.

The two engineers boarded next and took the two front seats reserved
for the railroad engineers, the only two swivel chairs in the engine's
interior. In front of them was a completely unobstructed view of the tracks
ahead because it was a virtual display generated by many video cameras
on the main engine's frontal surface.

The two engineers ordered the frontal display using their fingers and
mental commands. At the bottom left side of the display, a square orange
indicator came on. It read.

Manual Override > ON

Four seats, split into two groups, were behind the two frontal seats
separated by a gap. Lucif-er took the left two, and Magog-el sat on the
right sectioned pair.

The chief engineer turned to ask Lucif-er for speed and acceleration,
but the Overlord got ahead of his question and commanded.

*"Trillium is 5,000 kilometers away; trip duration should be one hour;
maximum acceleration at 10 Gs, sustained… **Start the test.**"*[2]

Morrie and his assistant glanced at each other since the unusual format
requested for the acceleration was the Seraphim borderline of sustained Gs
endurance, about when they began to lose control of their actions.

"Yes! … Sir!" A concerned chief engineer accepted the order. He
quickly moved a few fingers, and a screen section from the whole frontal
screen emerged with the requested parameters and a graph with elapsed
time as the x-axis. One last electronic click and the doors shut closed.

The train began moving toward the exiting narrow tunnel. It floated on
an air cushion about 30 centimeters above three guiding metallic and flat
strips alongside the ground; they provided magnetic levitation and
propulsion using superconductors.

After the train entered the underground passage leading to Trillium, the
guiding metallic rails stayed in a straight line, which allowed much higher
speeds; the acceleration climbed sharply, causing all passengers, except

---

[2] Note that Terra's hour is 2.4 times longer than one Earth's hour since the alien
planet has ten time zones while we have twenty-four.

the Overlords, to feel squashed against the back of their seats. A humming noise was gradually increasing its pitch.

Unperturbed, Magog-el started a private mental chat with Lucif-er.

"Today, Gorgon-el notified me that several teams from the SA are looking through all the sectors for information related to weapon manufacturing. In addition, the SA is satellite-mapping the NA! Should I stop the intruders?"

"No! It would not make a difference. The data gathered by the satellites is enough to prove that we are manufacturing weapons. Detaining the spies will publicly show that we are hiding something and that we are the aggressors."

Magog-el, the Overlord of the CD, Central District, which oversaw the whole nation of the North Alliance, replied.

"The SA will start arming as soon as they verify that we are doing it!"

On the frontal display, the graph tracing spot showed a speed of 24 km per minute at 5 Gs. A noticeable vibration started to roll along the train's length. Morrie wondered if he should ask to slow down the increasing acceleration.

"No!" Lucif-er's telepathic message anticipated the question. Concurrently, he continued his conversation with Magog-el.

"I am sure they will do it. Nevertheless, I plan to make them look bad, but we need to wait until after they start manufacturing weapons; then, we can make our move!"

The tunnel's lighting had 100-meter green markers and 1 km red markers. The green markers zipped by, while the red markers passed by every four seconds!

The Archangels continued talking while the anatomy of the rest was under severe stress, including serious facial distortion; inside their minds, they tried to stay focused.

"Stay awake!" Or "Focus, concentrate!"

The train's mild shaking peaked and then went away.

Seconds later, the bright spot on the chart reached 10 Gs at a speed of 48 Km/minute! The tunnel's red markers were now speeding by every other second!

Morrie's body shook violently, the whites of his eyes rolled back and forth, and he passed out. His assistant was barely hanging on, but body fluids dripped from his eyes, nose, and mouth. Both engineers had their bodies squashed against their seats, making breathing difficult and their faces severely distorted.

The NA platoon remained sitting straight, even under extreme stress.

The vibration came back twice as strong! Soon, it reached an apex, then it subsided and disappeared.

Lucif-er communicated with Magog-el.

"At this moment, my priority is to find a way to convince Gabri-el to join us. Dani-el will do the same if he does, and we will take over The Core; subsequently, the SA will not have a chance against us."

"My opinion is that Gabri-el is too close to Micha-el and Rapha-el to go against them," the NA's leader retorted while looking straight at his boss.

Lucif-er's stare stayed focused on the monitor's central and remote dot, which, at a far distance, was the only visible part of the retreating diameter of the tunnel that continued swiftly passing by and always approaching. He responded.

"I agree! But then, since he is also a good friend of mine and a good politician, there exists a small possibility of convincing him. I will try just one more time!"

The bright green light tracer on the graph remained at 10 Gs, but the speed was now 98 KM/minute. The tunnel's green markers were now just a blur, the red ones flashing by every second.

The shivering came back four times as strong as compared to the first time!

The assistant engineer and the platoon personnel looked concerned enough to be noticed beyond the mask of their warped faces; heavy perspiration continued to extrude from their bodies. Suddenly, one of the platoon's soldiers lost his straight sitting position, and his head went back sharply; he tried to regain his posture but failed!

Magog-el glanced at the platoon leader, and while pointing to the soldier in distress, he ordered with a tone full of disgust.

*"As soon as you return to Centrum, replace this individual with somebody **better**!"*

"Yesss... Sirr!" The platoon leader telepathically mumbled through his tightly squeezed teeth and brain.

One more time, the vibration faded and vanished.

Lucif-er commanded the assistant engineer, ***"End the test!"***

The only engineer still conscious smiled with satisfaction. He immediately set the train's speed to its average cruising velocity. The superconducting engine, running with a high pitch, settled down to an imperceptible hum. All the Seraphim under stress, except Morrie, the chief engineer, and one soldier, juggled on their seats to regain a comfortable position. The assistant engineer wiped the sweat from his face using a sleeve from his clothing; the soldiers did not move.

"It looks like a damping problem!" Magog-el spoke in a private message to Lucif-er.

The latter entity stated, *"You are correct! The tunnel has automatically activated fans, which pump air out of a frontal sector to reduce the train's friction; the same air is pumped back into the train's rear to increase the impulse power. However, the air is also being channeled from the engine's frontal intake to be equally discharged at the rear. The turbulence generated by the train's high speed interacts with the tunnel's airflow; this is coupled back to the train's total length every time a resonant frequency and its primary harmonics are encountered.*

The solution is to automatically increase the distance of the fans' air discharge to the rear in a ratio-metric proportion correlated with the train's speed at the measured concurrent times. This shall effectively dampen the vibration to non-existence!"

Lucif-er proceeded to implant the solution inside the engineers' brains; one was awake, the other still unconscious.

"Thank you, Great Overlord; we are most grateful!" Quickly replied to the assistant engineer.

Lucif-er minimally nodded down. At that instant, Magog-el privately requested.

*"Now, tell me about your plan... How can we compel the SA to **look bad**?"*

****

Thirty days had elapsed since the last meeting of the SA Overlords. Micha-el stood behind his chair, and all four subordinates stayed in their allocated positions. He had both hands on the back of the piece of furniture, which could loosely be called his throne. He glanced at Samu-el and mentally requested.

"Samu-el, tell us what you found in Eastland!"

The addressed Overlord paused for a moment, then he stated.

"Eastland, as agreed by the NA, the SA, and The Core, is supposed to be an independent country with no interference in their government by any of the mentioned coalitions.

The NA is changing this by infiltrating all the needs of their citizens with the obvious intention of taking over the nation!

They currently control one-third of the nation's assets; at this rate, they will completely take over Eastland in five years!"

Samu-el proceeded to display images of documents from NA's activity in Eastland as military personnel, land acquisition, and political influence. When he concluded, Micha-el, with great concern, mentioned.

"It is hard to believe, but the NA is in an unlawful expansionist drive!" Turning to face the two Overlords in the left seating section, he requested.

"Please, go ahead with your reports inside the North Alliance!"

Zeri-el was eager to start, so he took the first turn for the disclosure of his findings.

"My team found three major centers doing weapons research; one thousand kilometers west of the SC capital's sector, we found a plasma center called G-57; Gorgon-el runs the place. Two hundred kilometers

*north of Absalom, in the SE sector under Azami-el, there is a site building conventional weapons: A-23. One hundred kilometers west of Centrum, Magog-el oversees site C-14; the objective of this place is to develop... **nuclear weapons!**"*

Zeri-el went ahead and transferred the information to the other Overlords.

Lari-el took over the mental discourse and explained.

"We found the same three sites with similar objectives, although we also found that the universities in all major cities are actively recruiting technically oriented individuals for the weapons research programs.

*I want to add that this gathered data has greatly disturbed everyone on our team. It is hard to believe because there is **no** precedent in our planet's history!"*

Lari-el touched both temples using two hands while lowering his eyesight, like being mentally in pain.

Micha-el stretched his right hand across the lustrous desk's counter and firmly touched his friend's left shoulder. When their eyes met straight on, he exclaimed with overwhelming zest.

"My brother, my heart aches with similar distress as yours! Recently, I had a nightmare that caused me pain and anxiety I had never felt before. Today, the same pain and anxiety are here, but this time, I cannot just wake up and see all my worries disappear!"

He retracted his hand and addressed the entire group.

"Rapha-el and I did a satellite survey of the NA. The scanning probe clearly shows and confirms that our brothers of the North are up to no good; therefore, we are not surprised by your conclusions.

However, at this point, most of the NA do not know what is happening inside their country; this information appears to be restricted to higher-ranking officials!"

A large display behind him showed satellite images and close-ups of the previously mentioned sites. The three Archangels, not previously exposed to the data, quickly added the information to their mental memory banks.

Micha-el, without turning, pointed to site C-14, distinctly highlighted on the display, *"This place is our biggest concern. It was undeniably confirmed as a nuclear weapons research center with lots of uranium, lead, plutonium, and other heavy metals; obviously, it is not a nuclear reactor to generate electricity. Two other similar sites are now in construction in sectors NC and NE!"*

The display split to show all sites and a close view of them by using a powerful zoom.

"East of Centrum, we found an isolated site inside a valley surrounded by mountains. A military base training an army; obviously, they did not want anybody to find out!"

The displayed image changed again. When the zoom reached its maximum, they could see small squares of angels marching and interacting to form larger groups, companies, and even battalions!

Zari-el stood up, motivated by a strong determination for action; he requested, *"Micha-el, the evidence is beyond contradiction; the NA is geared for a plan of aggression and perhaps world domination!"* Give the order to arm the SA; we must protect ourselves!"

Micha-el turned to face him and replied.

"I agree with you, but to give such an order rips my heart! How can I develop instruments of death and destruction against whom I call: My brothers of the North, people that I love, and my God know that I don't seek any harm for them!"

Rapha-el stood up and cut into the distressful conversation.

"Micha-el, you know that I am against aggression and violence more than anybody else, but the results of the inspection demand a response. At this moment, I am concerned about the safety and future of our citizens. If we must arm, let's do it with the proper perspective and the values that God expects us to follow.

We should build weapons only for our protection, never to be used for the sake of revenge, hate, or even self-righteousness! **Always, as the very last resource!**"

A pause followed while the three standing Archangels sat.

The SA leader spoke again. In his mind, a maelstrom of ideas, images, and commitments merged across multiple paths so he could visualize the alternatives to peace and war, life and death, and the ominous threat of vast destruction by nuclear warfare. He managed to channel the turbulence and returned to his dynamic self; then, he spoke vigorously and with conviction.

"I am asking all present to stay with me through the night; needless to say, I appreciate your commitment and support. Together, we should find the best solution to this emerging severe threat.

Lucif-er and Magog-el are behind this dreadful scenario. They and I seem to be moving in opposite directions, impeding meaningful dialogue. I will ask Gabri-el, a friend of Lucif-er, to help us find a peaceful solution. We will pray to the Lord that such a solution will include the reversal of the NA's increasing weapon manufacturing.

At the central plaza at 7:00 hours, broadcasted to all places inside the South Alliance, I am scheduling a public meeting. Notify all ten council members of each province to be present.

At this time, I will inform the SA of the impending danger and what our response must be!"

Above the western horizon, the sun approached the end of one more day across Terra's almost cloudless sky. Much before 7:00 hours, an enormous multitude had Dawnel's central plaza packed solid.

On a higher podium, five Overlords stood separated from the crowd. They faced the huge gathering assembled among the strips of vegetation, starting close to the podium and projecting radially so the empty spaces left were triangular. There were five of these strips, all ending in a circular road about 100 meters away in all directions. The wide avenue also defined the location of the skyscrapers around the city's main plaza.

Most of the eight million inhabitants appeared to be present.

Next to the podium, underneath and facing it from each of the five strips, ten angels stood at each one representing the five provinces; a gap separated them from the large congregation, with their dressing colors correlating them to the province being represented.

The crowd radiated a mix of mental and voice rumble. With only one minute left for his announcement, Micha-el separated from the other Overlords and moved to a centered position. He looked at the vast gathering of Dawnel's citizens facing him. He asked himself a hard and painful question.

"Lord! Do I have the right to ask my loyal citizens about the hardships and sacrifices expected from them? Do You, my loving God, approve of this drastic decision that we could be incapable of reversing? I just want to say and do what is right, for Your sake, not mine!"

A mechanical, hydraulic noise could be heard, coinciding with a slight vibration from the podium's floor. Adjacent and surrounding the elevated platform, five massive virtual screens became electronically projected upwards, floating higher than the podium; they looked massive, 20 meters high by 30 meters wide! The visual display could give a much better view of the Overlords when addressing the enormous number of angels gathered around for many kilometers, as far as it could be seen.

Micha-el looked at the distant tall building at the outside plaza's edge. He stared at its three massive towers, connected by intertwining pathways from the bottom to about two-thirds of the way up. After that, the three towers projected unimpeached, piercing the blue sky as shiny golden obelisks bathed by the late afternoon sunshine.

The wind remained relatively strong. A gust partially blew Micha-el's curly hair over his face. He did not try to fix it because his mind was far away. At this instant, his internal clock highlighted: **7:00 hours.**

The Overlord raised both hands, open palms, high above his head. The hair on his face cleared away even against the wind's determination to do otherwise. In a few seconds, the crowd's murmur disappeared.

Micha-el took a few steps closer to the podium's edge, where a stairway went down two meters to the next flat area, where his ten council members stood in two rows of five angels. Further down, another two meters of stairs ended on the central flat plaza's floor.

He spoke with a powerful voice that everyone nearby could hear; nevertheless, the electronics magnifying his voice made sure that everyone present and even beyond the farthest reaches of the South Alliance could still be listened to. His electronic voice started the message.

"Dear citizens of the South Alliance!

As on many other occasions, we assemble to announce a very important event. I am sorry to mention that, unlike on previous occasions, I have terrible news this time!

We discovered by accident that the NA is moving people and resources into Eastland; now, their presence and influence are significant.

You must know that there is an agreement among all three coalitions to respect such land as a sovereign state. Nonetheless, this in itself was not as shocking as the following finding.

A basic NA platoon doing some kind of operation on Eastland's beaches... was carrying weapons!

This finding led us to extensively search inside the NA sectors for proof of arms development or manufacturing. We backed this search up with a complete satellite scan of the whole country... The results were just unbelievable!

The NA is, at this instant, engaged in the research and manufacturing of conventional, plasma, and nuclear weapons!"

Because of this message, even the wind stopped. For a few seconds, not a single voice or noise came back from the massive crowd; just like a sea with no wind, it became dead calm.

Next, like the increasing roar from an incoming quake, the multitude expanding beyond sight burst into a deafening roar!

Micha-el raised his right hand with a sign intended to calm the crowd and be silent. The noise declined to almost being unnoticeable.

Now, the large screens showed the data found by the Overlords, like a slide show using the whole screen or segments of it. With no data being shown, the screens focused on the speaker's face. An angel's voice would be magnified many times for the plaza's congregation to hear him; however, since the speaker was an Overlord, he did not need the electronic support inside the plaza; he only needed it past this boundary.

"My brothers, I find these findings extremely hard to comprehend. I understand your concerns and worries are overwhelming; nevertheless, we must focus on the future and evaluate our alternatives.

What could possibly happen to the SA if we do nothing? Otherwise, what would be the consequences if the SA needs to arm to preserve the status quo of the two alliances?

The first choice, doing nothing, is easy to implement; the outcome, on the other hand, could be catastrophic for our nation!

The second and opposite choice, matching the NA in an arms race, requires enormous work and commitment; unfortunately, our results will be against our lifetime moral values because we will be building war artifacts! ... After a painful debate, the SA's overlords agreed that there was only one choice: arm the SA!"

A noise from the attendance came back, but this time, it was not so loud and somehow more coherent. Micha-el raised his hand again, and the clamor went away; he added.

"I want to emphasize that we are in no way thinking of promoting any kind of aggression or bad feelings toward the NA or any of its citizens. We shall actively scrutinize all possibilities for a solution to this crisis and reverse this decision. We also pray to our Lord that the love and peace we had enjoyed on Terra for so many years remain with us!"

Following a short pause, he asked the council members.

"As representatives of our five provinces, do you have any suggestions or objections to arming the SA?"

One angel in a center group raised his hand. After Micha-el accepted with a hand gesture, he spoke in a moderate voice, but his words became magnified for the whole city's audience to listen to.

"Great Micha-el, we, the people of Pristeen, have complete faith that you will always do what is best for the SA; we accept your decision as our own!"

The crowd suddenly had a loud, short burst of approval; this rumbling coming from millions of mouths sounded different, perhaps like a distant volcanic eruption.

The SA's leader nodded with a brief thankful mannerism; next, he continued.

"Thank you, my people. I want to remind you that on this beautiful land named the South Alliance, we are all equal; there is no angel whom I consider less valuable than I am.

I am here to serve you! ... Make sure you never let me forget it."

The multitude roared, exposing their empathetic support.

As Micha-el raised both hands to his shoulders with his open palms facing the congregation, as seen through the large screens displaying his image, showing a grateful acceptance from the outburst of support from the citizens of his own province, Pristeen, the sun on its way down hid behind a tall mountain range in the far horizon. The plaza's lower section quickly turned darker as the sunshine that warmly bathed the spectators and the adjacent trees vanished. The three towering buildings, still illuminated, now changed their reflections from golden and shiny surfaces to dark greys.

Micha-el turned around to move back as Rapha-el, the next speaker, approached the podium's frontal section. Analogous to a lightning strike, Micha-el saw inside his mind the three towers in the instant he walked away from them... but in **black!**

The warm feeling that the ovation left in his heart instantly vanished; despair and anxiety replaced it. A chill invaded his entire body; he practically screamed inside his own mind.

"My God, this is the same place as my dream. I did not recognize it, but it happened in my own city! ... Am I the one to blame for the terror and misery that I saw my people suffer?"

Before Rapha-el passed by, his eyes locked on his friend's. The former, in a personal question, immediately inquired.

"Anything wrong, my brother?"

Micha-el took a full second to respond.

"I hope not... Let's discuss it later!"

****

The Core, Cheruban, Argentan's downtown area.

Argentan was so named because many buildings had a distinctive, silvery color, like gleaming pearls facing the Western Sea. The capital of the Cheruban State inside The Core was a bit smaller than Trillium and did not have as many spectacular structures, but it held its unique beauty.

Zeroing down into the downtown maze of skyscrapers' connecting pathways, specifically between the most significant central part of two massive buildings, hung a transparent tubular semicircle dome.

Inside this tubelike covered area, the bottom flat surface remained spacious, about ten meters wide. At the center of the span, which was also the mid-distance between the massive, towering structures, the tunnel inside the dome appeared to be never-ending; however, looking outside, the panorama was quite different and much more impressive.

The spectacular view of the downtown web of buildings was blessed with a nearby bay that exposed a sandy beach and a pleasant oceanic sight. Along the bay's coastal outline, a wide road lined with trees on both sides hugged the shoreline as far as it could be seen, creating an enchanting vision. All around, cylinders used for transportation crowded the roads and the skies, producing no smoke or noise; all vehicles followed preset trajectories. At the ground level and the connecting pathways above, many of these were only for pedestrians. These paths resembled our walking avenues where cars are not allowed, but in Terra, the length, landscaping, and decorating remained outstanding by making the walking avenues incredible gardens dedicated to the true beauty of nature, with an architectural design focus to enhance the splendorous flora.

The cavity inside the sky walkways occasionally bulged another two meters on each side to accommodate resting areas, which provided seating, food, and enhanced visual equipment to scan and magnify the city's splendorous sight for walking or running angels moving alongside the sky-high connecting domes.

Few angels moved along this pathway; therefore, most bulging rest areas remained unoccupied. Two runners, a fast-jogging couple, quickly approached the mid-section. When they reached an empty rest area, they slowed down and stopped. Both wore silvery, tightly fit jumpsuits.

The couple was Gabri-el and his wife Raquel. He wore a waistline buckle similar to Samu-el's in Eastland. She was breathing heavily with her head bent down and both hands holding her legs. Gabri-el, standing directly in front of her, showed no sign of any exertion and mentally told her.

"Your performance today was outstanding; best 10 km you ever ran!"

Raquel bounced her moist, partially tangled, and about shoulder-length fabulously golden hair to her back as she looked up at her consort. Perspiration showed, trickling down her face like tiny shiny marbles enhancing her flawless skin before dripping away.

"It is not fair... You never get tired when running with me!" Raquel exclaimed while taking a deeper gasp of air; she added, *"You don't even break a sweat!"*

Then, she softly touched him on the chin and spoke again.

"Could you, my sweet, at least fake, be a little bit tired?"

"No," Gabri-el softly replied, using his right hand to untangle some of her hair strands. He continued, *"It is equally not fair that no matter what, you always look like the most exciting and lovely being on the planet; my love, this is truly disturbing!"*

She slowly grasped his hand, and with tenderness, her lips briefly touched his index finger. Next, their eyes met, and their greens liquified into a sea of love.

Both sat on two adjacent swivel chairs anchored to the floor. The two Cherubim, facing the transparent outside wall, looked at the nearby and peaceful sea, which at this distance appeared as a gray-silvery vast surface only disturbed by rough streaks caused by downward winds.

Moments later, Gabri-el's deep green eyes looked empty at the crisscrossing connecting paths among the buildings and the 300-meter drop to the base of such structures.

His alert and intelligent wife immediately noticed it; she placed one hand on his shoulder and asked.

"My dear husband, is there anything troubling you?"

Turning around to face her squarely, he gently held both hands and answered with a somber tone.

"Raquel, last night while attending an important meeting, I got an encoded message from Micha-el stating that he had ordered the SA to begin a plan to arm the country due to the NA's overt development and manufacturing of many kinds of weapons!"

She stared at him in disbelief, tightly squeezing her companion; her telepathic exclamation proclaimed her great concern.

"My dear husband, I heard you, but I cannot comprehend what you are saying! Does this mean that the peace we have enjoyed since the beginning of the angelic race will end? ... Are we reaching the end of time, as predicted in the Holy Writings?"

Gabri-el paused momentarily while looking outward at the far and serene ocean. At the same time, he was tenderly caressing his wife's hands. He responded slowly, stretching the words.

"My precious wife, as I look outside, I see the same beauty and peace we had always enjoyed. If I could look into tomorrow, would it all be gone and become part of the cosmic dust floating in our universe?

My brain, as yours, will not accept it, but my heart feels that your fears are sadly true!"

Both Cherubim stood up and firmly embraced each other; Raquel buried her pretty face in his chest. He responded by placing both hands on her back and gently rubbing up and down. Gabri-el felt pain for conveying distress to his wife; this grim news couldn't be worse.

In addition, he proceeded to make the back rubbing part of a soothing experience. For an instant, his four wings increased to a deeper green and returned to their typical radiance.

Her tension, fast-beating heart, and deep breathing returned to normal; consequently, Raquel's tight embrace loosened to a gentler one. Still using a low tone of voice, the Archangel continued the dialogue.

"We always knew that this life would not last forever. We also understood that if we place our trust in the Lord, He will take care of us by providing all we need until we will joyfully stand in His presence. Sharing His love with us is all that matters."

Raquel glanced up at Gabri-el to give thanks and continue the chat.

"Thanks for the soothing massage; I appreciated your kindness... I have a question about something I need to know: The day we meet our Creator, do we stay married?"

He looked at her with affection while a slight smile shined on his face; he responded, *"No, I do not think so! But I know that I will love you even more than I do now!"*

"Aha! ... But will you make love to me, even then?"

The Overlord slowly ran a finger on her slender neck while awarding her a wider smile.

"Sweetheart, I wish we could; however, I believe that being in God's presence and being able to see Him as He exists shall deliver to all our senses such incredible joy and pleasure that <u>nothing else</u> should matter!

Another possible reason: To Love because it is spiritual... yes! To Sex because it is materialistic... no!"

She rose upward and gave him a warm kiss, *"Fine! You make sense!"*

Three Cherubim briskly walking by got very close and made eye contact with Gabri-el. As soon as they recognized the state's Overlord, they apologized, nodding with respect.

Gabri-el responded with a brief nod while sending a mental message to all of them, *"No need to apologize, my friends! Please continue your walk and have a great day!"*

The passerby trio renewed their brisk hike, quickly distancing from the couple.

The communication buckle on Gabri-el's belt emitted a soft 'ding.' He picked up the central piece for viewing; the image of Dani-el appeared on the device. The youthful-looking Overlord spoke immediately.

"Greetings to both of you! ... Gabri-el, I am departing for Trillium. Pick me up there. We should visit Lucif-er at his residence at 8:00 hours... Raquel, it is always a pleasure to see you again!"

"Same to you, my friend," Raquel replied with her melodic voice.

"I will be there!" Gabri-el responded.

"See you soon," said Dani-el as the display blinked out and reversed to its normal golden appearance.

Gabri-el returned the device to his belt and, along with his wife, remained seated for a few seconds, just admiring the beauty of their surroundings.

Another 'ding' interrupted their state of meditation.

Again, in a flash, the buckle returned to full display on the Archangel's hand. This time, the face of Ruben, his assistant and pilot, filled the small screen; he hastily requested.

"Sir! Please, locate a terminal! The NA will broadcast an extremely important announcement through the international channel in only 30 seconds!"

After acknowledging with his right index finger, he said before ending the transmission, *"Thanks, Reuben!"*

Gabri-el and Raquel got up and walked to face one of the side walls defining the rest area. At his mental command, the transparent wall delineated a rectangular area one meter high by two meters long.

The newly opened viewing screen was blank. After swiveling two chairs to face the display, both angels took a frontal seat.

A few seconds crawled by. Next, the entire face of Magog-el came sharply into view. After a brief pause, he started to talk angrily, which carried a clear and powerful, almost intimidating message.

"Citizen of Terra!

This broadcast is necessary for you to understand an ongoing travesty. We, the people of the NA, people who love peace and justice, who intrinsically believe these norms as you equally do, have our lives threatened by overt aggression from the SA!

Yes... I know that you cannot believe what I am telling you. Our hearts became distorted with pain and disbelief when we heard this ugly statement.

Yesterday, an Overlord whom I considered to be <u>my brother</u>... Micha-el... he ordered the SA to arm with weapons of mass destruction, with the sole intention of destroying our loving country: The North Alliance!"

Passersby angels started to stop and piled up behind Gabri-el and his wife, who by this instant were holding hands again. The newcomers were attracted to the disturbing news, as bees are to nectar, avidly listening to the NA's broadcast.

"I understand if you cannot believe what I am saying. If you have not heard it yet, yesterday at Dawnel, 7:00 hours, Micha-el gave a threatening speech of intimidation and aggression against the NA.

The excuse Micha-el and the SA's Overlords gave for this barbaric action was that we, the peace-loving people of the NA... were planning for war!

People of Terra, this allegation is entirely false!

No grounds exist for anyone to make such outrageous accusations; we feel deeply hurt by this lie!"

Magog-el lowered his head briefly, then raising it even higher, he shouted, "Consequently, since we cannot stand idle under this threat, the NA will also be armed, but only for self-defense!

I warn the SA about further intimidation attempts; we will not tolerate such aggressive behavior.

Nevertheless, we do not intend to start an arm's race; after all, we don't have any bad feelings against the SA. I encourage the South Alliance to show its goodwill by reversing the unprovoked order to arm its nation and eliminate all weapons of destruction!"

Magog-el relaxed, using a softer tone, he requested.

"People of Terra, let us work together to stop this madness and to stop Micha-el from his wicked dreams of world domination.

In addition, let us pray to the Lord for peace and the repentance of the SA!"

The Overlord in charge of the North Alliance paused for three seconds, then concluded his speech with an almost hypnotic stare from his deep blue eyes.

"The NA wishes you to continue enjoying peace... the same peace you always enjoyed."

The screen went blank as the speaker's image vanished. The image of Magog-el was gone, but the aftermath of his message lingered as a thick fog; even Gabri-el remained motionless with incredulity after hearing such an unprecedented broadcast. His consort, still holding his hands, looked confused while staring into the depths of his green eyes; she needed an explanation. He sent her a consoling personal message.

"My love, this conflict is much worse than I thought. Do not believe anything that you just heard!"

Around twenty Cherubim gathered around the couple; they were extremely disturbed, and they asked the Overlord in unison.

*"How could the SA engage in such a horrible action? **Why?**"*

Gabri-el raised both hands to calm the angelic group.

"Why?" He mirrored the question, then quickly delivered a statement that was emphasized by his authority.

"We used to live in a world where peace and truth ruled! ... Now, we have begun a new journey, where along its path, there is no peace; furthermore, instead of the truth, you will hear lies. It is a new world of fear and deception!

Make sure you make the correct choices when selecting what is right and what is wrong! ... What is true and what is not!"

The Core, Seraphan, Aurel, Lucif-er's residence.

It was 7:00 hours, close to the end of a nice warm day. Lucif-er's mansion, a massive modern residence on a hillside facing the city of Aurel, had the aerodynamic shape of a three-story building, with all levels ending on a large terrace overlooking the superbly landscaped downhill side. The terrace was not flat but staggered, similar to cruise ships, where the outside borders have rails. A six-pointed star landscaped with trees and flowers adorned the middle of the lower patio; a large circular swimming pool was included at the star's center; the pool's circumference touched the edge of the six-pointed inside edges. Last, starting at the star's top surface, six widely separated and curved steps led to the center pool.

The pool's diameter was 33 meters across, although it was a bit harder to see because of the water's depth; the pool also had six terrace levels, each two meters deeper than the upper and adjacent levels. The deepest part was located away from the building, and each terrace inside the pool was shaped like a crescent moon.

At the top of the large star, three numbers pointing toward the building were engraved on the marble-like floor; in a deep blue, equal to the color of sapphire, they read **666**.

At the opposite side of the building, another rectangular flat surface was visible, a landing pad capable of holding a dozen flying vehicles. Two large cylinders were parked closer to the building, plus four smaller ones farther back.

A large cylinder approached the landing pad from the southwest. As it came down, the late afternoon sun made it shine with golden overtones. The craft positioned and landed next to the other two large, parked vehicles. Promptly, the two assistants and pilots of Gabri-el, Reuben, and Norvel exited the craft and took standing positions next to the side door.

The middle side door slid open; two Overlords, Gabri-el and Dani-el, stepped down.

Immediately, a platoon of unarmed Seraphim encircled the aircraft. The leader addressed the Overlords with a respectful, low-tone communique.

"Welcome, great Overlords; we will escort you to the meeting site!"

"It is not necessary; we know the way!" Gabri-el replied but quickly added, *"However, I sense this is a new order you must follow. Please, show us the way!"*

"My pleasure, Sir!"

The platoon leader walked ahead with the Archangels closely following him. A column of three soldiers marched on the right side, and a similar column on the left, with a row of three staying behind.

After entering the building, the group moved through spacious and fancy-decorated corridors and arrived at the top balcony, where Lucif-er sat on a plush chair. This piece of furniture was part of a group of four chairs and an impressive glass table next to a rail marking the outside edge of the balcony, where the exterior view was superbly designed for the best view possible.

Lucif-er stood up; next, using a finger, he promptly dismissed the escorting platoon.

"My brothers!" He exclaimed as he greeted the arriving Overlords by touching them at chest level, both of their open palms. He announced.

"Welcome to my home; I am pleased you both agreed to this meeting!"

After reciprocating the welcome, all sat down facing each other.

Gabri-el mentally said, *"Dani-el and I need to discuss with you the recent announcements given by the SA and the NA; we hope you are willing to help defuse the ongoing confrontation."* He swiftly added, *"We know that you are a close friend of Magog-el; we are sure he will listen to whatever you say!"*

"Yes, he will usually do what I request; however, I heard the terrible news about Micha-el; I never thought of him taking the warpath!" Showing noticeable concern, Lucif-er replied.

"It is not Micha-el who is doing wrong; the NA and Magog-el started this crisis!" Retorted Dani-el, the younger Archangel.

"Dani-el, my friend, don't jump to conclusions; I saw Micha-el's speech. The facts presented by him as proof that the NA is arming, all are digital images; we all acknowledge that with a computer, it does not take much effort to change anything good to look bad!"

"I am confident that Micha-el speaks nothing else than the truth!" Dani-el insisted.

"That is your personal belief; not everyone would agree with you," responded Lucif-er, lowering the intensity of the mental exchange.

Nonetheless, Dani-el remained internally warmed up. His upper wing, showing luminosity above his head, and his lower wing radiance around his feet, both emitted an increasing reddish glow, making the radiance more noticeable. He sharply asked.

"Lucif-er, please tell me; did you know anything about the weapons research and manufacturing inside the NA?"

Gabri-el's eyes stared at Lucif-er; Dani-el's stare was already a fiery arrow!

Lucif-er just looked between both stares, observing a faraway place on the hills. With evident calm displayed, he assured his Core associates.

"Trust me, my brothers; if I had known of such deeds, I would have asked Magog-el to stop doing it!"

Dani-el got up, and with his back leaning against the rail, he keenly stated, *"Even so, my friend, many believe that you are the one running the NA!"*

After giving Dani-el a visual sign to sit and be calm, Gabri-el interrupted.

"We are not here to accuse anyone! We, The Core Overlords, must take an active stand to stop the senseless arming of both Alliances."

"Gabri-el, I totally agree with you; it is the most demanding task facing us," Lucif-er stated while Dani-el took a seat to calm down, at least what he showed externally. Lucif-er continued.

"Look, Dani-el; many people believe that your statement is accurate. I do admit that I have a considerable influence in the NA's affairs, but I don't rule the Alliance, Magog-el does.

As you know, no Overlord from The Core can rule another country without him losing his Core's position, which demands a unilateral commitment to The Core and neutrality."

"Will you discuss this escalating issue with Magog-el? It is important to find a solution to reverse his order to arm the NA!" Gabri-el suggested.

"Of course, I shall do it! However, I am certain that he will refuse unless the SA demonstrates its good intentions by canceling the development of its weapons. Can you convince Micha-el to do such a thing?"

"I am not sure... It has become obvious that unless both Alliances accept a bilateral agreement, no one will volunteer to disarm first!" The Overlord named Gabri-el stated.

Lucif-er looked deep inside Gabri-el's green eyes and replied.

"Your observation makes sense! You and Dani-el should work with the SA; I will do the same with the NA!"

"Do you have any plans to talk to the SA's Overlords?" Gabri-el inquired.

"I am eager to do so, but Micha-el does not want to talk to me... Did he mention to you that he wants to do it?"

"Not really; he asked me to help solve this crisis!"

Lucif-er, communicating with a serious mode's shift, exclaimed.

"If he is serious about solving this crisis, he should have come personally!

I am sure of one thing about Micha-el: As the years have passed, we have become further distant from each other. Part of the problem is that he lives in his own metaphysical world, cramped with strict moral principles. He thinks of God as his private friend, and nobody else knows what they talk about. I even theorize that Micha-el may have lost his mind, but we must prove it!"

"I did notice... that you don't like him either!" Gabri-el retorted while Dani-el looked away from the Seraphan's Overlord.

Changing his tone, Lucif-er displayed a faint smile when asking his Core associates.

"I hope you are staying for dinner; I took the liberty of ordering some special food for this meeting. It could be an opportunity to discuss this problematic issue further."

"Yes! We gladly accept!" It was the joint response from the other two Archangels.

Gabri-el got up, placed both hands on the balcony's rail, and stared down to the lower terraces, which were part of the vast star complex facing the backside of the main building.

Each terrace had around ten to twenty angels, with some walking, others sitting, and even just standing against the railings border defining the star's perimeter.

Looking sideways at an adjacent balcony, the Overlord of the state of Cheruban saw a beautiful angel with long, wavy, and reddish-blond hair; she wore a white tunic that accentuated her exquisite shape as she stood against the bordering handrail. When she spotted Gabri-el, she slowly leaned backward, allowing her hair to fall behind her into the open space. At the same instant, she thrust her shapely breasts upward in a sensual and provocative tactic; only then did her bright and seductive purple eyes meet with Gabri-el's.

"Hi... Gabri-el! It is a pleasure to see you again," she mentally spoke with her best melodic tone.

He paused for two seconds and responded while admiring her beauty and wings, which were faint but had highly pleasant halos adorning her head and feet; yet, their color was not the usual Throne's red but pink!

"The pleasure is mine! You remain, as always, outshining the flower's beauty from this fabulous garden!" He replied and mentally continued with a thought.

"Liliel, you are the only female I know who can change the color of her wings to pink. A strange color capable of draining the strength and mental stamina of any male. Is it possible that the spectral frequency of this color interferes with some brain activity that only males possess, and females instinctively know about it?"

A minute later, Liliel walked into the conference room, where the three Overlords remained on the balcony. Lucif-er looked at her with a broad smile; she responded by slowly opening her lips as if giving a gentle kiss. Then, Lucif-er stipulated.

"She will join us for dinner, which will be served in exactly ten minutes!"

Dani-el, after returning his eyesight from the backyard, asked.

"Why did you add a triple 6 display by the pond?"

"They are Lucif-er's favorite numbers!" Gabri-el responded ahead of the addressee.

Lucif-er glanced at the location of the triple-digit and replied.

"Gabri-el knows why! It is a simple statement based on the fact that I possess twelve wings instead of the standard six for a Seraphim.

6 are my primary wings.

6 are my secondary wings.

6 are the interactions between my primary and secondary wings!"

"I see," acknowledged Dani-el, who gazed at the twelve pale ultraviolet glowing wings for an instant, *"In other words... it is you!"*

Just slightly, Lucif-er nodded affirmatively.

Gabri-el, touching the only twelve-winged Archangel on his left shoulder, took the word.

"By the way, congratulations on successfully completing the underground high-speed train linking Aurel and Trillium!"

Lucif-er reciprocated the left shoulder amiable gesture and articulated.

"Thanks, my brother! I know you two are interested in starting a similar project linking your capital cities to Trillium. I will send you the plan's details so you can start building immediately."

"Very generous of you," both Overlords facing Lucif-er replied, *"We need this project to relieve the increasing air traffic congestion!"*

Terra's sun, as it had done for billions of years, faded one more time behind the gracious hills surrounding the leader of Seraphan's huge property. The bright yellow glow in the west began to turn orange when another pristine and peaceful day concluded.

How many more remained in the angels' paradise?

A large silvery craft, only discernible at nighttime because of the intense local lighting on the parking lot of Lucif-er's home, quickly lifted vertically with only a mild hum.

The two passengers sitting on two oversized swivel chairs had a last look at the mansion when the craft made a half circle while climbing toward the southwest. The place looked spectacular at night, with the main building, the landing pad, and the star-shaped pool complex superbly illuminated.

Gabri-el remarked, *"The synthetic meat dish was remarkable; I cannot imagine a real beef steak tasting better!"*

Dani-el, returning his sight from the outside scenery, looked at his friend and responded.

"I absolutely agree with you; my only complaint about the dinner was the tension prevailing between Lucif-er and us; I would have enjoyed it much better if such hostility could have been removed!"

As the young Overlord shifted his eyesight toward his friend's elegant tunic, Gabri-el sensed a need for Dani-el to expand his response; therefore, he enticed him, *"Please, continue!"*

"My friend, I cannot be as cool as you are when talking to Lucif-er about the SA and Micha-el when I know he is wrong! I feel like a hypocrite sitting next to him and unable to tell him exactly what I believe!"

"Dani-el, you know that Lucif-er and I were close friends for many years. It breaks my heart to see him moving away from God; if there is a way to reverse this, I will search for such a solution with all my power. In addition, Lucif-er is one of the few open doors to stop the SA from arming!

We cannot foster a dislike for anyone just because we believe they are bad; we must give them the opportunity for friendship and love; we must reject their lies and wicked deeds as a demanding duty, but we shouldn't be judges condemning an angel to a place where there is no return... and that includes Lucif-er!

To do this, my dear brother, we must walk in the right direction. Yet, in our search for God, we encounter many side roads going nowhere: these are the roads of materialistic illusions.

Only one road leads us to the right place, the one dwelling within our spirituality, the route to light, truth, and love. All of these originate from our God and Creator!

However, this same path could take us away from Him because, in the opposite direction, you will find lies, hate, and darkness. Therefore, we must choose carefully what direction we take... Unfortunately, this makes it more challenging: the way to God... is uphill!"

****

SA, Irisan, Iris' downtown.

Two angels stood facing each other; they were the two Principalities with the DNA Syndrome, Sergius and Marcus. Close by, along the pathways lined with trees crisscrossing the areas not occupied by the towering skyscrapers, many angels moved around them, some walking rapidly, others casually strolling. In the sky, lines of smaller cylinders followed preset pathways, the skyways of Terra. Even higher, the larger crafts, in smaller numbers, also adhered to their routes. A master computer controlled all the crafts since all kept the exact assigned altitudes, separation, and pathways. Marcus complained to his companion using voice communication.

"We have been waiting for Rapha-el to show up for too many hours. I am tired!"

"Just hold on; we know he is in the building, and he will come out sooner or later!"

"You can forget about sooner!" Marcus complained while displaying a sarcastic half-smile.

Sergius glanced for the hundredth time toward the main entrance of a nearby structure. The angelic traffic stayed congested at the building's frontal entry. Sergius, visibly affected by the frustration of waiting, commented.

"You are right about that; I hope Rapha-el doesn't leave by aircraft using the roof!"

Marcus quickly replied, *"It is a possibility; I will check again in 15 minutes to make sure he is still in the building."*

Sergius, squarely looking at his friend, asked a direct question.

"Do you still believe what Magog-el broadcasted the other day was true?"

Marcus stared back; then, looking at the flying traffic above, he responded in a lower tone of voice.

"I do... What he said it makes sense!"

"But Marcus, they were mostly lies! I cannot believe that you actually said: 'It makes sense!'"

"No, my friend!" He exclaimed while pointing his index finger toward Sergius' face. *"He was right when he said that anybody could modify a digital image to fit their needs!"*

"True, but Micha-el and the SA would never do such a thing!"

"That is what you say! How do we know who is lying to us? Our world used to be much simpler; it is becoming too confusing nowadays!"

"Your brain is the one confused; it must be corroding faster than mine," replied Sergius, simultaneously touching Marcus' index finger with his own. Next, he added.

"Aren't you grateful that Rapha-el saved our lives? Isn't he from the SA?"

"Of course, I am grateful to him for saving us, but the issue is beyond him. It is about the politics that the Alliances are imposing on us; I still believe the NA message was accurate!"

Sergius, slightly nodding his head, replied.

"You have a strange way of being grateful!"

From inside the building, on the third floor, a Seraph dressed in a light purple tunic glanced outside through a transparent window panel. Like hawks with super-sharp vision, his eyes scrutinized the distant people on the building's frontal section. Before long, he had spotted the two angels waiting for him. He thought with empathy.

"My friends, Sergius and Marcus, are here. They must be waiting for me, and since I will stay busy for the next four hours, I will spare them the waiting by meeting them now."

Rapha-el turned around and walked with cadence and speed through a corridor leading to the exit of the closest building.

Sergius and his friend continued observing the people exiting the building's main entrance; he coerced Marcus to do something by saying.

"Marcus, while I wait here, why don't you go inside the building to see if Rapha-el is still around!"

A voice, profound and concise but friendly, asserted.

"At this time, he is not there!"

Sergius, startled by the statement, began turning around to identify the speaker, with Marcus doing the same.

"Who said t..." Sergius stopped suddenly when his black eyes met the owner of a set of ultra-blue ones; the black ones could not stand the intensity of the blue; hence, they swiftly disengaged and looked down. Sergius exclaimed apologetically.

"Great Overlord, please excuse us for our manners!"

"My good friends, there is no need for that; I am delighted to see you again! I can sense you have been waiting for a long time; in the future, since I have become increasingly busy and new security measures will make me less available, please send a message to my electronic address. I should answer as promptly as I can!"

The Overlord, displaying a smile and pointing a finger at the two Principalities, continued talking.

"I have great news from the lab. A newly developed drug will add seven years to your lifespan after you take the pill. Just go inside the building; there is a test center on the tenth floor where you can ask for the medicine; only mention that I sent you, and they will give you the pills."

Rapha-el touched the two speechless angels on their shoulders to relax them; however, as a side effect, the Archangel also accessed their subconscious fears and anxieties; he continued talking using his vocal cords.

"Yes, Marcus, dealing with the new world of politics is confusing. We are not prepared to distinguish between conflicting reports since, up to the present, we have only heard the truth. Now, we need to learn how to select what is good and what is not. Just remember, the truth is permanent and uncompromising... lies are not!

Even when smothered, twisted, and denied, the truth will eventually resurface to testify again. Picture this inside your mind: the truth is equal to a brilliant diamond. If you cover it with mud, you cannot see its beauty or shine anymore; although after you wash it, the mud is gone, but the diamond and its brilliance are not; they remain unchanged!

Go now, my friends; I wish you a long and happy life!"

The two Principalities gratefully acknowledged Rapha-el's message and moved away. When Sergius thought they were safely far away from the Archangel, he moved closer to his companion and said, with a shallow voice.

"Listen, Marcus, talking to the Overlords is a one-way conversation; they know what you want, what you feel, and even what you are thinking! Rapha-el is very kind to us; even so, I find talking to him grossly unnerving!"

Marcus glanced at him and uttered one word.

"Likewise!"

Meanwhile, Rapha-el, standing in the same place, was spotted by a group of five angels. They had brown hair and eyes; all the individuals were Virtues. They rushed to meet the Overlord of the land and exclaimed in unison.

"Dear Overlord Rapha-el, please explain to us what is going on... We are utterly confused!"

Rapha-el smiled and almost joyfully exclaimed.

*"Do not feel bad; you are **not alone!**"*

****

Cheruban, Argentan.

Raquel sat alone in her plush apartment located on the top floor of the largest building in the city of Argentan. She was in the lower section of a multilevel design. The inside had an ample open space that met the requirements for large meetings or conferences. Two semicircular stairways connected the three levels. The entrance to the apartment was located at the middle level through a fancy lobby.

Behind the female Cherub, a large tri-sectional window stayed open, exposing quite a spectacular view of the city, the bay, and the ocean. The city sparkled like a Christmas tree, lighting the night sky in a manner comparable to a giant firebug; however, at this late time of the night, the air traffic dwindled to a few aircraft on sight. The bay illuminated like a diamond necklace, sparkling with white but also with some minuscule-colored lights moving along its contour. The ocean, dressed in faint silvery attire given by the full Moon, the larger of two satellites, appeared still because of the distance.

Instead of watching the beautiful sight, Raquel stayed focused in the opposite direction. From a semicircular array of instrumental displays, only one remained turned on; this monitor continuously showed the building's roof, a landing pad for aircraft. Some angels stood or walked around in this area, but no cylinder activity could be seen.

She looked nervous; this stunning angelic beauty who constantly displayed outstanding self-control appeared to have lost it. Staring at the display with both arms across her chest, she avidly followed any bright dot moving above the building until it passed the landing area.

She looked at the display's lower right corner, where a digital counter and a clock read **00:95:87.**

"Oh, my Lord," she thought, "It is almost the first hour of the new day, and Gabri-el is still not home. I am very concerned about his well-being; he has been working over ten hours daily for several days with no rest or sleep, and this horrible conflict getting out of control has taken all his energy and time."

She got up and walked to the transparent window panels; although glancing at the ocean side, she kept her attention on any moving bright dots in the night sky.

She squeezed both arms with her hands, feeling a deep cold. Her white, soft, and loosely fitting garments stayed temporarily wrinkled at the front, but she continued pondering.

"I feel exhausted from what is going on. I surely miss all the good times we had together, but most of all, I miss the smile now fading away from his face! ... A strange complaint because my own smile has been scarce in the last few days.

I will pray to You, my God, for the gift of understanding so I can have the wisdom I see in the eyes of my beloved husband, so I can better judge by myself what is true and what is not! ... Please, give me the strength to help Gabri-el instead of being another burden added to the many he already holds!"

She returned to her seat and continued staring at the same screen.

A faint star in the dark sky became brighter; Raquel's attention shifted to it, hoping for the best, the arrival of her cherished spouse. When the angels working on the landing pad cleared the center and aligned next to a perimeter marked by bright yellow lines, her heart began pounding joyfully; the large cylinder approaching the landing site was Gabri-el's craft!

With happiness flowing again through her body, she instantly forgot the long wait when she saw Gabri-el stepping down from the vehicle after his assistants stood outside.

On his way to enter the building, he walked briskly and waved one open hand in return for the greeting that all the angels on the landing pad utilized to welcome him back. Just before entering the building, he glanced at the camera's input for two seconds while Raquel observed him squarely facing her through the display. A complete smile unfolded on her while Gabri-el used his index finger to send her a kiss.

Only two seconds later, he was gone from the view. Even when she knew that Gabri-el could not listen, she exclaimed telepathically.

"I love you! I was just complaining that I didn't see enough of your smiles... Do you guess my inner desires, or do you actually know that I have them? ... I know, but I will ask you anyway."

She got up and walked with the grace of a swan toward the main entrance. For several seconds, she stood impatiently waiting next to the door... Finally, the door slid open.

The Cheruban's State Overlord walked in with his arms partially open, inviting her for closeness. She quickly embraced him and remained tightly intertwined. His body's warmth comforted her; his powerful muscular physique restored her confidence. His affectionate love, on the other hand, had the same effect as opium; it clouded her intellect. Nevertheless, to her satisfaction, she finally had peace of mind.

Raising her outstanding and gorgeous-looking face at him, she smoothly expressed her feelings.

"Now that you are away so often, I miss you so much that it hurts!"

"I understand how you feel, my love; the present conflict demands too much of my time!" Gabri-el responded without loosening his romantic embrace with her. To him, she was the most important concern in his extremely long life: the incredible joy of sharing your life with the most beautiful angelic female on the whole planet!

"I have two questions for you," she requested with melody.

Gabri-el gently kissed her between her naturally arched eyebrows and softly replied.

"Both! I do guess, but it is also my knowledge," anticipating two previously thought-provoking questions, he answered using one single sentence. Next, he quickly added, *"My dear wife, you already knew the answers...Don't worry; it is OK because it is like asking, 'Do you love me?'... You already know the answer, but it is comforting to hear it again!"*

The couple, now walking side by side, sat in the same chair, which was spacious enough to fit both snugly; Gabri-el pointed to the same terminal that Raquel had been watching.

The machine speedily showed eleven boxes, each containing messages sent to him and arranged in a hierarchical order of importance. The top one contained a code number and a private message from Micha-el.

At this instant, Raquel had a much better view of her husband's face; she felt great concern when she saw an exhausted individual staring at the screen. He pointed again, and the top box changed to a message.

>Linking in progress.

Still looking at Gabri-el's facial profile, Raquel softly rubbed his partially curly blond hair at the back of his neck using her right hand.

He glanced at her, anticipating her next move; for an instant, it appeared that Gabri-el would stop her by rationalizing her following action. However, what he saw inside that pair of slightly oversized aquamarine jewels that Raquel had for eyes convinced him of her unchangeable determination; he listened to her sensitive mental communique when she asserted.

"My sweet and loving husband, as much as I am your responsibility, you are also mine. Please, let me proceed; you know that mine is the proper action to take... and it is for your own good!"

Gabri-el, stretching his back, deeply yawned; he placed his hand over his wife's hand, still rubbing his neck. While he gazed at her with caring eyes, she extended her left arm and touched the screen with her index finger.

"ID check!" she spoke using her gorgeous voice.

A bright star-shaped icon blinked at the upper left corner of the screen. After being identified, she methodically stated.

"Computer, except for the link in progress, reschedule all other communications and meetings for Gabri-el... New starting time: 05:00:00 hours. End."

The center of the screen read.

Done

"After you talk to Micha-el, please come upstairs to our bedroom. I will be anxiously waiting for you," she telepathically indicated while standing up and walking gracefully toward the stairway.

"My precious Raquel, I shall be there in no time!" He assured.

Merely five minutes had elapsed when Gabri-el entered the bedroom. Sitting at the edge of a large round bed, Raquel had her right leg crossed over the other. Her silky white tunic gracefully outlined her superb contours even further; when she moved her head to see her incoming husband, her shoulder-long hair spread like a sparkling, beautiful fan made of pure gold, which gradually rebounded to stillness.

Raquel resembled a Greek sculpture of the most beautiful woman carved in marble, where the sculptor used the utmost care for every single detail; all the lines, straight or curved, were perfect! Needless to say, no sculpture could capture her radiance, graceful movements, vitality, and precisely, her sophisticated personality.

She extended her right hand, palm up, and Gabri-el grabbed it with both hands when sitting beside her. Their eyes met at close range; the shine of deep green and aquamarine fused into a new shade of green. Softly sent across his mind, she suggested.

"My love, you are very tense and tired; please, let me help you relax."

"Thanks, sweetheart; I know you want to give me your best massage ever, knowing what you can do with your tender but skillful hands... I am already grateful!" He communicated with her while releasing one hand and using it to caress her silky hair gently. She reciprocated by rubbing the top of his head and with a gracious smile, replied.

"My love, I will do better than that... I even have a new song for you!"

Gabri-el removed his clothing by unzipping invisible zippers, then laid face down on the bed. She, equally on the bed and next to him sideways, her soft hands touched his naked back; his well-defined muscles were as hard as rocks. To her, this did not matter; like a musician who knows all the notes on the keyboard, she knew all the places where the nerves, tendons, muscles, and bones met. Her skilled hands played an entire symphony over his tense body.

Due to the relaxing pleasure, Gabri-el's breathing became more spaced and profound. His four greenish rays or wings merged with hers.

Afterward, she started to sing, not loud, more like a breeze caressing our faces, and so did the melody of her song tickle his mind. Her voice, which carried two additional parallel channels, reverberated and complemented itself without the help of any musical instrument; indeed, it was an angelic voice!

Like seductive and alluring sirens who capture men with their songs, the angel's singing could seize the attention and heart of anyone listening! Her exquisite voice entered Gabri-el's ears with relaxation; very softly, she sang with all her heart.

> ♫ **"When the moons brighten your handsome face**
> **and the wind fondles your golden hair**
> **when your wings cover my face like an embrace**
> **then your tender touch is like a gentle breeze of air**
>
> **As your eyes, green as a forest**
> **meet mine that are like the ocean near the land**
> **as the soft pressure of your lips causes me unrest**
> **the sparkle from your eyes shines on the wet sand**
>
> **The murmur of the approaching wave**
> **the glimmer over the water that the moon graciously gave**
> **the stars above the sky that God had shown how to behave**
> **became our memories that we have learned how to save."** ♫

Very close to his ear, using her melodic voice, she whispered.

"Archangel Gabri-el... I love you."

He responded by touching the closest part of her with one of his hands, which she understood to be a sign of appreciation or gratitude; Raquel also saw a faint smile on his partially hidden face.

Next, his whole body relaxed; Gabri-el was asleep.

Raquel continued to cast her hands over his back, but her touch became almost imperceptible. She looked up at the modernistic décor above the bed and pointed a finger at it; the room's lighting gradually faded until a faint glow breaking the darkness remained.

Once more, she began speculating about the future.

Her eyes sparkled in the near darkness because they were wet; if angels could cry, she would have; after all, this was as close as she could ever get to the act of crying, and she felt as bad!

How would you feel watching 'paradise' crumbling under your feet? Would you also weep?

THE BAD SEED

CHAPTER 3

Seven more years have elapsed, fourteen since the First Signs.

A powerful lightning bolt blasted a nearby hill, ripping apart the darkness of the night; one second later, a deafening thunder shook the ground. Before the illuminated land could return to its previous darkness, two isolated individuals could be seen standing as shiny obelisks against the background. They were facing each other as the black veil of the night took over; a bluish glow emanating from them showed six robust rays per entity; they were Seraphim and Archangels.

Massive columns of strange-looking clouds quickly eradicated the brilliant stars populating the black sky, with their colors again the same bizarre purple and gray. The hills swiftly shifted to a luminous silvery hue, which induced an unrealistic feeling.

The menacing clouds covered the sky in no time, submerging the land beneath into an ominous, deep darkness. This lasted a short time because the blackness began to be pierced by almost non-stop lightning strikes.

Micha-el, one of the Archangels, sinking into despair, exclaimed.

"My God... the dream is back!"

Micha-el tried to touch his nearby companion on the shoulder, but to his surprise, he missed. After he stared into Rapha-el's face, the SA's leader noticed again that the circular black pupils inside the unusually blue eyes of his companion were not round but had the shape of a **cross**!"

Micha-el leaned toward his friend to get closer and gazed into his unique pupils. His mind was unraveled! He felt like staring into a boundless space!

The enormous stresses that instantly overtook his entire being shook his body. He did not know if he was standing, flying, or falling; perhaps he was doing it all simultaneously. Completely confused, he vocally begged the question.

*"I know that you are **not** Rapha-el! ... **Who are you?**"*

'Rapha-el' looked at him, smiling kindly, and softly replied.

"I am who I am!"

Still confused, the Overlord did not ask the same question again. Instead, he requested, *"Is this just a dream?"*

"No, Micha-el; it is much more than that."

The Archangel begged in a tone that even he identified as the same when he asked his father as a child.

"I remember now. You are the one who promised to me that I would reveal the meaning of the cross soon! ... I have been waiting for seven years!"

The face of 'Rapha-el', illuminated by the constant lighting, smiled even more before replying.

"Micha-el... for me, it was just an instant!"

With flowing steps that appeared not to touch the ground, 'Rapha-el' moved backward. Micha-el knew what was happening next; with his right hand, he covered his eyes.

The intense light penetrated even across his hand; the following deafening thunder shook Micha-el's entire body!

He slowly reopened his eyes; 'Rapha-el' could not be seen anywhere!

The Archangel's body gradually got colder and apprehensive, yet this time, he did not feel a sense of doom; instead, a strong desire to reveal the unknown dominated his mind.

He could not avoid the chill running down his spine; the unknown was approaching, and he knew it could not be stopped.

Just like his previous dream, he stood still while closing his eyes...

A DIFFERENT BUT CONTIGUOUS DREAM SEGMENT

Again, as a repeating mental shock, the scream of millions of mouths forced him to reopen his eyes!

Although deep inside, he hoped the vision could be different this time, it was not. The black clouds remained above; the almost complete darkness barely made the tall buildings visible, like dark silhouettes. The countless people crowding the broad street to its limits remained faceless, colorless, and <u>not</u> silent!

Raising their hands toward him, they screamed.

"Great Overlord, Micha-el!

Please, save us!

Please do not abandon us; don't let us die!"

The crowd moved closer to the Archangel, pushing him backward. This time, he desired to speak and comfort his subjects, but the multitude knocked the wind out of him!

For a second time, he saw himself being dragged along the narrow alley that opened into the large plaza; once there, the pushing stopped.

Micha-el walked the same path toward the plaza's center. He saw five avenues full of screaming angels, and as he climbed the ten-meter-diameter circle, the loud noise became damped and incoherent.

The Overlord looked up to the three massive black pillars piercing the clouds above. When the cloud began to dissolve, he exclaimed with renewed hope, *"This time, I know this place. It is Dawnel's main plaza!"*

With the clouds gone, the stars shined in the night sky again.

It was like somebody turning off a loud stereo system, so the pandemonium stopped for three seconds. Even before the stars began to fall, Micha-el had his hands lifted in a praying motion.

"Lord, please tell me that I am not responsible for my people's suffering; yet, if I am, take the life of this worthless servant. I beg You to spare them the suffering!"

The crowd's screams, arriving as suddenly as a sonic boom, heralded the vision of the stars falling from the sky. Chaos reigned again; the screaming, running, and impending doom had returned!

Despair tried to invade Micha-el's heart, but this time, with renewed energy, he refused it and exclaimed.

"Please, Lord, listen to Your faithful and humble servant's request. Show me how to attend Your will; it shall be my command!"

God must have been listening; instantly, out of nowhere, a bright white cross appeared at the center of the chaotic night sky. Micha-el, while staring in ecstasy, raised his arms even higher, outlining his magnificent physique with his powerful muscles moving upwards. His hands seemed to touch the cross's edges. He felt his mind and soul detaching from his body and projected above to a higher dimension.

An incredible flash of light obliterated all the night shadows!

Brighter than daytime, everything became overpowered by a blinding flash, **except the cross!** Its dazzling, pure white glow stayed impervious!

Now, the cross came alive. A beam emanating from its shape focused on the Archangel's forehead. His internal cranial structure appeared transparent as a small cross glowed inside his brain for a second... then, it disappeared! Micha-el's body and clothes turned to the same glowing white as the cross; together, they defied the other blazing light, and even his blue eyes became visible above the background glare.

The multitude, which became speechless, shared the new dominant white shine. They were not faceless anymore, with the color of their eyes sparkling like beacons with a fresh glow. There was no fear, only joy!

The SA's Overlord felt what he had never experienced before: It was beyond pleasure... beyond happiness... he had reached the realm where Love, the ultimate power in the universe, was part of him. In addition, at this instant, a message materialized in his brain's convolutions.

My dear son, Micha-el
My love is with you.
I am your God, the only Son of my beloved Father,
the creator of everything that exists in the universe.
A sign of the future,
the cross is tribulation.
The cross is sacrifice.
The cross is redemption.
It is the way to my kingdom,
it will guide seven like you
to share the Glory with Me.

Micha-el's ecstasy attained a sublime high; nothing else mattered anymore, only to continue communicating with his Creator!

It was like a wildfire out of control; his mind, body, and everything he owned were being burnt by a holy fire that did not consume but enhanced the quality of what he already had.

The feeling was so intense that…

END OF DREAM SEGMENTS

Micha-el's eyes opened quite wide; he was awake!

Everything in the dream remained so vivid that the extraordinary feelings it fostered did not fade away; he did not remember ever having such exhilaration in his whole life. He jumped out of the bed, and trusting both arms to the ceiling, exclaimed joyfully.

"I thank You, my Lord, for sharing Your love with me; I apologize for reflecting such a tiny portion to You! I am impatiently waiting for the day I will be called to Your presence so I can sing to Your Glory and adore You as You rightfully deserve!"

After the vocal outburst, he sat at the bed's edge; his eyes sparkled because they were full of moisture, while his breathing remained extremely deep but calm. All his muscles were tense and sweaty, as when a person had finished a workout; his mind, on the other hand, resembled a turbulent and swollen river created by the aftereffects of a big thunderstorm.

The Archangel's room entrance slid open, and his assistant, Arkyn, rushed into the slightly lighted room.

"Sir, are you OK?" He asked inquisitively.

Micha-el smiled as he stood up, approached Arkyn, placed his right hand over his shoulder, and replied.

"My dear friend, Arkyn, I am far beyond being OK!"

"I do not quite understand what you mean, Sir!"

"This is what I meant: I did not have another nightmare… instead, through a dream, I had the most inspiring revelation!" Micha-el joyfully exclaimed. He continued, *"Thanks for checking on me; if I am not too busy during the day, I will explain the theological implications of my dream… Good night, Arkyn!"*

Alone again, the Overlord did not want or could not get the latest events off his mind. His spiraling thoughts persisted in returning him to the same place where the dream ended, like a craving to resume the vision.

Even when Heaven had yet to be created, Micha-el had a brief taste of it…**and he will never forget it!**

The first rays of light from the emerging morning sun twinkled through Micha-el's bedroom window on the highest floor of the tallest building in

Dawnel. He was awake but still digesting the extraordinary dream of the ending night. The exhilaration finally returned to normal angelic levels, but he still felt fantastic.

He stood in front of the transparent window, looking at the warmth that the color of the emerging sun brought over to the eastern horizon. The view furthermore filled his being with renewed peace and love.

He thanked the Lord for the beautiful morning, which reminded him of the warmth of God's love. He thought about Rapha-el and Gabri-el, his two closest friends; consequently, he urgently needed to share his experience with them.

As he walked to the display, he sensed something on his forehead that was not normal. He stopped at a nearby mirror to scrutinize himself. To his surprise, but with enormous joy, he saw a small cross etched on the middle of his forehead! It looked like a sunburned mark, a bit reddish yet highly defined.

"Thank You again for last night's message and this reassurance, which proves the event was much more than a dream!" Micha-el thought emphatically while touching his heart and the cross on his forehead; this was his way of signaling to God how much he loved Him.

When he finally reached his private terminal and sat facing the viewing screen, his short command was displayed in the terminal's center.

Search> Dual/split link/Rapha-el, Gabri-el.

Five seconds passed before anything moved on the display, which split into two sections. Micha-el could give telepathic commands to the terminal, but for conversation, it was easier to talk to the machine; he addressed both sides of the screen.

"Good morning, my brothers!" Micha-el greeted the other two Overlords displayed on the screen. After their corresponding reply, he said.

"I have the most important good news for you: I had the same dream that I mentioned to you seven years ago!"

"And this time, it was not a nightmare!" Rapha-el remarked after seeing his friend's happy face.

"That is absolutely correct! It was the opposite: the best experience of my whole life! It was a revelation, a message from God!"

"Please, Micha-el, you have our attention!" interrupted Gabri-el, who then asked, *"And by the way, why did you sunburn a cross on your forehead?"*

Micha-el paused for an instant; next, with a calm and pleasant smile across his face, he spoke.

"Dear friends, listen for a few minutes; I will tell you about the dream. I will only use normal speed because I want your thoughts to analyze the message conveyed to me carefully!"

The commanding Overlord of the South Alliance proceeded to narrate the vision; he did not skip any detail. The captive audience stared into the speaker's eyes as if they wanted to extract additional information. At the end of the dream's description, Gabri-el quickly took the first response.

"Micha-el! I envy you for having the greatest honor of communicating with our Lord! I cannot wait to meet you in person so we can mentally share your experience!"

"I will be leaving for Dawnel in two hours!" Rapha-el added, visibly affected by the news, *"This is too important; I am dropping all my morning appointments!"*

Micha-el serenely responded, *"It will be my privilege to share this ultimate experience with both of you. I only regret that my memories will not be even close to the real ecstasy that only the Lord can provide!"*

"God has revealed to us the meaning of the cross!" Rapha-el spoke enthusiastically, *"I suggest that His symbol becomes part of our formal dressing; in this manner, we will acknowledge that we in the SA are willing to make any sacrifice that could guide us toward perfection, the same road taking us to our God and Creator!"*

Micha-el responded quickly, *"I think it is an excellent idea; the cross should be our emblem. It will bring new meaning to our dress code!"*

"Dani-el and I will include it on our uniform tomorrow!" Gabri-el quickly followed up.

Rapha-el's image, for an instant, appeared to be introspective; thus, Micha-el asked in the next fraction of a second.

"What is it, my brother?"

"I was pondering on God's message... It caused me a sudden pain in my heart. There are fifteen Overlords on Terra; however, He said: **'Seven like you!'** *"*

****

NA, CD, Centrum.

"I told you; I am sure there is no chance to get Gabri-el to our side. I am acknowledging that he and Dani-el have decided to be part of the SA, and the only way to stop them is to kill them!" Magog-el growled.

"I know you are accurate, but I want to try... one last time! Tomorrow night, we are celebrating Eastland's successful takeover; the party will be at my home. I am inviting Gabri-el, Raquel, Dani-el, and his new girlfriend, Maryen... Of course, I am not telling them the reason for the festivity. Instead, I will mention that it is for increasing the goodwill between our Alliances!" Lucif-er remarked while casually looking outside his personal aircraft's window, where the neatly arranged skyscrapers of Centrum became rapidly dwarfed as the advanced flying cylinder sped toward the sky and away from the city.

The two Overlords sat on the passengers' front seats, and behind them, on the next row of seats, two more Overlords, Gorgon-el and Azami-el, were equally sitting. Farther back, a whole platoon of Seraphim remained sitting; Lucif-er's personal guards sat straight, and they were fully armed!

Azami-el, addressing the two Overlords in front of him, indicated.

"I need to mention that I just sent 5,000 troops in civilian clothes to all the islands comprising the country of Bird Islands. This will be the initial phase for our plan to control the area; I am certain that the SA will deliver a stronger response this time; therefore, I am assembling a 50,000 army to back up the operation!"

Magog-el turned around and responded.

"Good! Do whatever is necessary to achieve the goal!"

The flying vehicle, moving at incredible velocity, pointed southeast.

The Core, Cheruban, Argentan.

As Gabri-el walked into his home, Raquel greeted him at the door with a hug and a warm kiss. With her usual sweet telepathic message, she mentioned.

"We have been invited to a party at Lucif-er's residence tomorrow at 9:00 hours. Dani-el and his girlfriend, Maryen, will attend and have requested that we pick them up at Trillium."

"I am glad they accepted the invitation. I will notify Reuben to arrange the trip," Gabri-el responded with a smile while caressing her silky hair at the back of her head. He added, *"I can see by your wings that you are feeling much better today! It is stressful when you worry too much, but the current world's events are frightening... even we, the Overlords, are not immune! ... Related to your wings, if you want it, could you change their color to pink?"*

Raquel stared into his eyes inquisitively, thinking, "Is he joking?" Next, she mentally asked, *"Why do you ask, my love? ... Oh, I know; you saw Liliel again! Well, you know that my natural color is green; although, if I try hard enough, I am sure I could do it!"*

Rubbing with her hands both of his temples in a smooth and circular manner, she stared into his deep green eyes and playfully continued.

"However, as it is now, I am having a hard time convincing my male friends that when I look or talk to them, I only offer my friendship, and I do not have any romantic feelings toward them... If I use pink, they will probably lose control of themselves, and they may even attack me!"

Turning her pretty face slightly sideways, teasingly, she asked.

"Is this what you want?"

The Core, Seraphan, Aurel.
Lucif-er's Personal Residence, the next day at 8:50 hours.

A blinking spot in the night sky populated by many stars swiftly approached the landing area. The only open space left in the mansion's aircraft parking zone turned bright yellow.

After the final approach, the flying vehicle positioned and landed on the designated slot. As usual, the two pilots quickly exited and stood one at each side of the vessel's main exit. By this time, the platoon guarding the parking lot moved to inspect the newly arrived cylinder.

All four passengers stepped out. The two Overlords moved to the front, facing the platoon leader, with the ladies following closely behind.

Raquel, in a white sleeveless evening gown encrusted with tiny, sparkling emerald-looking stones, was narrow at the top and spread out at her feet. The closely packed 'emeralds' flowed to the floor in down-spiraling lines like a water fountain splashing at her feet. Needless to say, she looked outstanding!

The other female, a Throne, had a pleasant salmon-colored dress. It was adorned with ruby-like stones that started at the shoulders, and in two single lines, merged to the center of her chest and equally on her middle back; then, the front and back became connected by a double stone line defining her slender waistline. She was a very attractive angel, but even if you are the moon, when you are standing next to the sun, your chances of being noticed are slim!

The platoon leader addressed the Overlords.

"Welcome, Great Overlords and distinguished companions; we will escort you to the main entrance!"

When Dani-el saw the handgun on the platoon leader's waist-high belt, and the high-power rifle slung straight up on his right shoulder, like the rest of the troops, he took a step forward and spoke with a stern telepathic message, *"No, you will not!"*

"Sir! My orders are to escort all visitors!" The platoon leader replied, a bit uneasy; he added, *"We have escorted you before; what is the problem?"*

"Kragen!" Dani-el called him by his name, *"Last time, seven years ago, you had NO weapons!"*

As Dani-el's sharp stare got closer, Kragen moved one step backward.

"I agreed with Dani-el's decision," Gabri-el intervened, *"We cannot be escorted by armed militia. If you are not allowed to drop your weapons, ask Lucif-er for instructions!"*

Kragen straightened up and replied.

"Sir, I shall do that!"

He touched his buckle. Two seconds later, the voice of Lucif-er said.
"Yes?"

Kragen spoke to the device.

"Sir! Sorry to interrupt you; the arriving guests refuse to be esc...!"

"Allow them to come unescorted!" The supreme boss, using a concise and snappy order, interrupted him.

At the instant the message ended, Kragen addressed the Archangels.

"Distinguished guests, I apologize for the delay! The platoon will stay here; please, you are welcome to walk to the mansion!"

Many angels were across the premises, alongside the spectacular hallways, or inside the massive ultra-modern chambers; nonetheless, there was a hierarchic arrangement where the least important stayed at the center while the VIPs enjoyed the best-decorated areas plus the balconies for outside entertainment. Either way, the whole place had a cheerful, celebratory atmosphere.

After moving through a few hallways, the four incoming angels strolled onto the structure's top floor. Lucif-er rushed to greet them, with three Archangels, Magog-el, Gorgon-el, and Azami-el, closely following him.

After the usual multiple cross-greetings, the whole group sat on single plush chairs aligned in a semi-circular fashion facing the balcony and the huge patio.

Three circular tables covered with food stayed behind them; the tables were set up buffet style. On top of them, synthetic meats, vegetables, fruits, and even sweet desserts abounded.

The elegant food display could be the sort of thing that a French chef would delight in. Drinks were separated and delivered in elegant plastic containers, with their kind and flavor color-coded.

Lucif-er, sitting on a central and prominent chair, directed everyone's attention to the illuminated star-shaped patio and the location of the swimming pool and telepathically spoke to Gabri-el and everyone else in the room.

"Soon, the diving team from Centrum will provide some of the entertainment!"

The Seraphan State's leader pointed to a place next to the pool, where ten Seraphim stood in a close triangular group, all wearing skintight wet suits.

Lucif-er raised his right hand above his head for two seconds as a signal and then put it down. A slight rumble from the pool area became noticeable when a sizeable U-shaped section separated from the adjacent pool's floor and raised to ten meters high, about the same height as the third floor's standing ground where it remained still.

The diving team stood on top of the platform, which had just been moved upward. Afterward, the flat top section of the U-shaped platform separated from its base and moved forward above the water. The team standing on the extended section repositioned to become a circle and bent their knees.

With a brief jerk, the extended base catapulted the angels up, as a springboard could do; next, moving at extreme speed, the base retracted backward and out of the way.

The ten Seraphim's feet went up, and their arms spread apart until they touched each other's hands; they followed by diving headfirst into the waiting waters. It was sort of a "swan dive" with ten people doing it together. The three characteristics of this dive are a bent head, a slightly hollowed back, and a straight line from the toes to the hip.

Just before hitting the water, their arms moved forward in unison to break the impact; all ten went inside the water with minimal splashing. As ten heads emerged from the rippling water surface, the spectators raised one opened hand upwards!

This act meant 'Good performance!' Two hands up would have meant: 'Superb performance!' Sort of a standing ovation.

Raquel was impressed, she exclaimed telepathically.

"They are good!"

"Better than good; they are superb," Dani-el calmly stated, *"They only had an individual variant spread of 0.1 seconds! But judging by the audience's response, I am sure they are capable of even more spectacular performances!"*

By this time, the U-shaped platform, or diving board, had descended to the pool's floor; the ten divers climbed above it and went up for another diving performance.

While the diving continued, Magog-el asked the two visiting Overlords.

"When you came in, I noticed that both of you were wearing a white cross symbol over your garments. What is the meaning of this gesture?

Furthermore, since we already know that the SA's Overlords started to do the same today, does it mean that you two have joined the SA?"

Before Dani-el could say anything, Gabri-el quickly responded.

No! We are not politically associated with the SA; it is a moral issue to which we agree, an act of faith."

"I have been informed that this is a response to a dream Micha-el had," Lucif-er indicated while turning to squarely face Gabri-el; the latter replied.

"Yes, it was! However, it was much more than a dream; it was a revelation!"

"My brothers," Lucif-er exclaimed, *"Why do you place so much trust and give so much importance to somebody else's dream?"*

Lucif-er looked at the other two Core's Overlords with a complacent and almost sinister grin; then, he continued, *"A dream is an immaterial stage of our minds where we have slight control over its content, but in the long run, it is only a fantasy. Our brains use this medium to relax our* *tensions, anxieties, and fears. I could provide myself with any dream that I want! And I could also provide to <u>anyone</u> the dream of their choice!"*

"Is there any possibility that Micha-el could be deceiving you?" Magog-el suggested while simultaneously raising another open hand for an additional cheer for the drivers.

"None!" Almost immediately, Dani-el responded.

"Personally, I would not accept anybody's dream to coerce me into doing anything!" Azami-el, restless in his chair, retorted.

Lucif-er retook the lead.

"My dear friends, the NA Overlords and I are no longer concerned about immaterial things. We want to shape what we hold in our hands and build what we can conceive in our brains. We have decided to oversee our destiny; we want to be the force that shapes the planet where we are living.

My brothers... join the NA and my new commitment; we can control The Core together, and the council will not be needed anymore!"

Moreover, with The Core on our side, Micha-el and the SA will have no choice but to give up the futile resistance they are building up. Then, there will be no need for arms or conflicts; we will be as a family again!"

Gabri-el, calm under pressure, took a quick look at Dani-el, who seemed restless in his chair. The youngest Overlord was also showing faint signs, only picked up by the other Archangels, that he was turning introverted. He was trying not to give away the turmoil brewing in his uncompromising mind.

Lucif-er continued, *"Our present technology has a long way to go. The future promises to be great; indeed, united, we could conquer the universe!"*

"You surely have big plans!" Gabri-el responded.

The divers' platform moved up again, this time to a higher level situated about the same height as the ceiling of the third floor; the angels on this floor could see the diving team almost by looking straight out.

"It is very high!" Maryen exclaimed. Turning her face toward Raquel, she asked, *"Is the platform elevation about twenty meters above the water?"*

"Yes, my dear; it is exactly twenty meters high," Lucif-er answered instead, *"The maximum elevation that this diving structure can be raised is thirty meters; only the Overlords use this elevation!"*

After digesting the information, Raquel inquired, *"I am not a physicist, but is the depth of the pool too shallow for this height?"*

Lucif-er smiled at her inquisitive but gorgeous eyes and the shiny emerald-looking stones of her dress, trying futilely to compete for the same attention. He mentioned next.

"Not at all; the pool's depth is twenty meters! After the diving event finishes, I will be pleased to show you ladies the lower patio and pool area!"

"Our favorite diving exercise is to jump from the thirty-meter position and fall flat on our faces, accelerating to 10 meters/second^2. Then, in the last tenth of a second, we activate our skin to cancel the shock!"

One individual who otherwise had been mostly quiet, Gorgon-el, exclaimed.

"It is a superb tool to tune our Archangels' skills to their utmost limits," added Lucif-er, who used his peripheral vision to see Liliel approaching the balcony's terrace and aiming for his direction. A quick mental command, only directed at her, made her stop before reaching the open terrace; subsequently, Lucif-er communicated with everyone.

"Please excuse me for a few minutes; I must handle some personal affairs."

Liliel watched Lucif-er as he briskly walked toward her. As he got closer, she tried to ask him about the need to stop outside the balcony. Yet, before she could send the message, his overwhelming mental voice overpowered her.

"I need to talk to you before you contact the guests! ... I have a job that fits your qualifications. When the diving team finishes its performance, I will take Raquel and Maryen for a tour of the lower patio; afterward, I will take them to the basement, to the room with 'the stone.'

I want you to take Gabri-el and Dani-el to tour the mansion; just stay away from me! In addition, look for any opportunity to be alone with Gabri-el... and if you do, try your best to seduce him!"

Liliel's eyes opened widely, showing her pretty, purple-pigmented irises. Even her sensually fuller lips opened slightly like a questioning sound was ready to come out of them. Again, a dominant voice overcame her mind.

"You heard me correctly... seduce him!"

Her right hand barely touched her muscular chest; she asked.

"You don't care if I have sex with somebody else?"

"If it is done for the sake of achieving our goals, I have no objections! Besides, knowing that your chances to attain this request are small... think of it as a challenge; if you win, you must be prettier than Raquel, and you could earn the title of the most beautiful angel on the planet!"

Liliel stared into his deep blue eyes and instantly lost her willpower. Softly, as a telepathic thought could be, she did the equivalent of whispering into his ear.

"I will do anything you want... my dear lover and master!"

Lucif-er took a second look at her, then at her dress, a beautiful light blue with a pearl-like tone adorned with two interlacing ribbons made of diamonds. At the bottom, the dress split at the sides to allow the display of two fantastic pairs of legs, if the wearer so intended. The top, with a low-cut neckline, partially exposed her full and perfectly shaped breasts. Her companion smiled with approval as his message equally suggested.

"You look outstanding tonight!"

After a brief pause, while a spark sparkled from his eyes and his wings strangely interacted with each other, he abruptly suggested.

"Liliel... let's go hunting?"

All the seats were taken at the VIP's top balcony. Everyone kept staring at the diving platform, where ten divers stood separated by one arm's length in a tight circle, forcing their faces to be oriented toward its center.

The protruding centerpiece at the top sprung the divers upwards and quickly retracted from the falling angels.

Simultaneously, all ten did a back summersault. As their legs projected upward, their hands touched, forming a circle that, for a second, was horizontally flat. Next, the Seraphim divers held the back of their necks with both hands while simultaneously bending their legs toward the back to induce rotation.

Three complete rotations and a final stretch to smoothly part the waters culminated in the tall plunge. Seconds later, as ten heads emerged to the surface, everybody attending the show cheered them on, awarding them two open hands high in the sky: A fantastic job done!

"Magog-el! Congratulations, you have a fabulous diving team!" Gabri-el exclaimed.

"Thank you! Although, let us continue talking about more important issues!" The leader of the NA quickly responded," *"It is essential for us to know if you accept our proposition!"*

Gabri-el leaned back in his seat; he knew that Dani-el stayed intensely waiting for his answer, so he took his time to proceed cautiously.

"I have no problem with your political organization; what Dani-el and I find irreconcilable is the moral issue. The NA's present trend of moving away from God is impossible *for us to accept!"*

"We don't ask you to give up your faith in God; you can believe anything you want!

I find the NA to be a tolerant Alliance where everyone can find a place to succeed; the only thing that is asked of you is that you take care of your own destiny. It is like dropping your own stone in a pond of water; you generate your own ripples, and these ripples interact with other people's ripples, and together we make our destiny!"

Gabri-el responded, *"No, Lucif-er, destiny is more like the ocean; we are the little fish causing our small ripples; however, the big waves come and go by undisturbed, relentlessly moving to the shore and their completion! We can modify certain events we generate; there are others we cannot because God made them that way!"*

Magog-el slightly shook his head with disapproval; next, he insisted, but his face looked more severe than ever.

"This new way we look today at our world has opened our eyes by removing all the restraints inhibiting our vision so we can see more clearly and farther away! If you are willing to try, you could find it out yourself!"

"I do not agree with your view either," rebutted Gabri-el. *"Sight without the guidance of God is not sight at all. It is like walking with your eyes closed while standing at the edge of a cliff. The ground below feels very secure, but disaster is only one step away, and it could be your blind choice to take such a step!"*

"Gabri-el, you are very hard to convince!" Lucif-er stated. *"My dear friends, the night is still young; just take your time before you give us an answer. We still hope you can acknowledge our request and become part of our great undertaking to improve the angels' race!*

Now, as I promised, I will take the ladies for a tour of the central patio and pool area. Liliel has volunteered to take Gabri-el and Dani-el on a mansion sightseeing tour!"

Gorgon-el got up, ready to offer his companionship for the ladies' tour, when he met Lucif-er's piercing eyes; he knew 'Just forget it.' was the only choice. Slowly, with his right hand, the disappointed Overlord dressed in his blond and curly hair; deep inside, he became unhappy for losing an opportunity to be close to Raquel. He watched the two groups moving toward the balcony's entrance, specifically Liliel's sensual behind as she grabbed the two visiting Overlords using one hand on each arm while staying in the middle. He followed her sensuous walk as the trio left the terrace, moving inside the third floor.

With a growing warming of his blood, he thought.

"I would not mind having her either! ... She has outstanding curves with amazing movements! These two females are incredible; Raquel, still your heart, Liliel set you afire! I am sure... Magog-el is going to touch my left shoulder!"

Gorgon-el started to turn around just as the NA's boss lightly touched him on the shoulder. He looked at the muscular Archangel, who, displaying a stern face, gave him a message.

"If you are thinking of taking Liliel from Lucif-er, you are insane!"

While glancing at Azami-el, who approached and stood beside him with a cynical grin, Gorgon-el replied.

"I would not even consider the possibility; I was just admiring how beautiful she looks in that new dress!"

With Azami-el's piercing eyes focused on him, Gorgon-el noticed that Azami-el's smile became wider. At this instant, Magog-el sort of commanded.

"OK, let's have some food!"

This spacious room had all the walls covered with fancy decorations. Some were relics of some kind, trophies, and artifacts of great beauty, like a museum's showplace where all the outstanding objects had been illuminated with soft and pleasant indirect lighting for easier viewing.

Accessed through a wide pathway in the center of this room, a very dazzling stone sat on a pedestal about waistline height. The stone with a similar cut to a diamond had the same qualities. Six flood lamps from a hexagonal overhead cluster caused the stone to shine intensely; this light turned strangely since it appeared not steady.

The only door in the place slid open. Lucif-er and the two ladies casually walked inside his room. He advanced to a location directly before this mesmerizing gemstone and mentally spoke to his companions.

"This is my personal collection; to start, let me introduce you to what we call the 'stone'!"

Moving out of the way, he exposed the spectacular jewel to the visitors. He continued, *"This is a synthetic crystal that I manufactured; it has 666 cm³ after my favorite number; its reflective index is incredible, much larger than a diamond. The overhead lights generate high-frequency scans mixed and synchronized to produce special dispersion patterns through the stone; this could be considered a symphony of light!*

For you to admire its beauty, you must see the performance... Raquel, please move a bit closer!"

After Raquel walked to the pointed location, he exclaimed.

"Perfect! From this place, you will have a much better viewing of the show, which I am starting now."

He pointed a finger upwards, and the lights above started an almost imperceptible dance. Following this introductory display, the stone began an extraordinary spectacle of the light's spectrum; solid dots of monochromatic colors spontaneously appeared. Flashes caused by the dispersion of rainbows created multi-patterned arrays that materialized inside and outside the gemstone.

The two female angels gave their complete attention to the luminescent spectacle. It was like being hypnotized by the incredible display on their faces, Raquel thought while admiring the show.

"This light display is fantastic! I had never seen anything so pretty, with the only exception being The Temple in Trillium! I can feel the energy emanating from the stone... It seems to be alive! Yes, the rainbows are unbelievable... However, how strange... is the stone getting bigger? Oh, my Lord! I feel like being drawn into this thing! ... Another weird feeling? ... Now, I feel like floating in the air... I am getting dizzy..."

She looked away from the stone and found Lucif-er's squarely staring at her; she felt like his eyes and the stone were the same!

She thought again.

"Lucif-er, the color of your eyes is a beautiful deep blue; they are changing to a deeper blue, just like the stone! ... A darker blue... darker... Oh my God, my head hurts! I cannot keep my eyes open... I feel so cold... and d..."

Dark was **black...**

"Raquel, are you OK?"

She opened her eyes; she did not answer.

Once more, she found herself staring into the blue eyes of Lucif-er. The ringing inside her head bothered her; at least, it was quickly disappearing. Lucif-er, who was holding her, cited.

"I should have warned you about the possibility of getting dizzy while watching the light show!"

The extremely beautiful female Cherub felt comfortable and enjoyed his arm supporting her; it was the same feeling as when her husband held her... but **he** was not Gabri-el!

Like waking up, she stood firmly separating from Lucif-er's arm and took a deep breath; she calmly said, *"Thanks; I am feeling fine now!"*

A hand touched her own; she turned her head and saw Maryen. She was being supportive.

"Thank you, Maryen!" She exclaimed while adding a tender smile.

"OK, ladies, let me show you the rest of this room!" Lucif-er said, turning sideways and pointing to another magnificent object. His fancy white tunic gracefully outlined his perfect profile and superb muscular body.

Raquel noticed how incredibly handsome and well-shaped he was. She felt a sexual itch that only Gabri-el had kindled in her before; inside her mind, his attractive blue eyes returned to be seen again. She reflected immediately.

"How strange; I always thought Lucif-er was extremely handsome, but this is the first time I think about him... in a romantic way!"

Liliel, sitting against the second-floor terrace's rail, faced Dani-el and Gabri-el, both also seated, the latter said.

"Liliel, we are thankful for the thorough and delightful tour you offered us; you definitely know this mansion from the top to the bottom. It was very graceful of you to volunteer for the occasion!"

"I equally enjoyed it very much," indicated Dani-el, *"However, it has been a while since the last time I saw Maryen. I am concerned about her since she has no previous experience with this kind of event. I should look for her!"*

Liliel glanced at him, not straight but at an angle. She displayed a friendly smile before replying.

"No need to be concerned; she is in Lucif-er's good hands!"

"Exactly why I am worried!" He immediately reflected on her statement.

"However, I can see your point of view," continued the beauty of an angel, *"You shouldn't leave her alone for such a long time!"*

Dani-el thought again, "She wants me to leave so she could be alone with Gabri-el. I do not think he will need my help; therefore, I will search for Maryen!"

The Throne's Overlord, while mentally analyzing the situation, telepathically communicated with his two companions.

"Please excuse me; I am leaving to find Maryen. After I do, we will return to the main third-floor terrace and wait for you!"

He got up and walked inside the building with a fast-paced stroll. Liliel, who had her attractive sight lowered, slowly raised it to match Gabri-el's gaze.

Liliel moved her left index finger across her lower lip, then slowly licked her upper lip while partially opening them with a sensual overtone. With melody in her voice, she spoke telepathically.

"I was thrilled when I found out you were coming to the party," she suggested, *"I was hoping you would come alone!"*

"It is my pleasure to be here, but you know I was not supposed to attend the party alone!" Replied Gabri-el, while simultaneously thinking, "Liliel, what are you up to? Are you trying to seduce me when you know very well that I am married? I must be polite while rejecting you, so I don't hurt your feelings!"

He also said, *"You are Lucif-er's girlfriend; I assume you have some kind of commitment?"*

"Not really; we are free to pursue our own interests and choices."

"If this is the new trend, I must be old-fashioned because I believe in moral values and obligations concerning relationships!"

Liliel took her time to answer back; before she did, she wetted the center of her upper lip with the tip of her tongue again; perhaps, she felt an erotic pleasure when doing it.

"Lucif-er and I are free from those binding rules; we have the liberty to do as we choose!"

Gabri-el leaned a bit closer and kindly responded.

"Liliel, you can ignore the old rules, but you could end up being bound by other decrees that may not be as kind to your existence!"

She looked perplexed for an instant, but she was not the kind who gave up easily; she crossed one leg above the other and purposely left it high so her pearl-toned light blue dress adorned with diamonds split in the middle, could allow the Overlord to have a clear view of her provocative posture which deeply exposed her fantastically shaped tights.

He had no other choice than to admire the alluring view!

She noticed, and she was gratified. She insinuated to her companion.

"Perhaps... you don't find me attractive?"

"Are you trying to be mischievous?" the Archangel replied. *You know exactly how attractive you are!"*

She got even closer and leaned slightly forward so the cleavage of her dress uncovered a larger part of her exquisitely molded breasts. The aura of her wings turned to a deeper pink, a tone more pleasant to the senses; in a very seductive tone, she murmured.

"I know, but since I am allured by your presence, I would be delighted to hear it from you!"

This time, the Overlord kept his sight in her eyes. His response remained biased by a reproachful disposition.

"Liliel... do not insist anymore! You know how much I love Raquel; I cannot do anything wrong to her.

If I offend my wife, I will be offending my God! My dear friend, for me and anybody who loves Him, that is not an option!"

After a brief pause, he continued, *"Listen! To have consensual sex, to love your partner, has been a requirement! This also implied some kind of commitment and mutual understanding, which in most cases ends in marriage. This ceremony has been just a public promise to honor and care for your consort, addressed to all angels on the planet and God!*

Since being married without the procreation of children, which cements an everlasting relationship, is the standard norm today, sometimes, couples married for many years find themselves drifting away from the love they initially had for each other. In these cases, in another public ceremony, the married couple agrees to dissolve their union. Only then are the angels involved allowed to start a new relationship with somebody else.

Now, what you are proposing is sex without love, a promiscuous encounter that is destructive in nature. An act with the only goal of self-gratification, without any concern for your mate or God's commands!

If we do such a thing, we will be no different than the wild beasts hunting for prey!"

Liliel did not like what she heard. First, she adorned her gorgeous face with a puppy eye look; then, she placed her right hand on his left knee; and last, she sent her best melodic telepathic transmission.

"This is not what I wanted to hear!"

Gabri-el grabbed her hand with his own left and got up; he commanded his female tour's escort.

"Let's return to the upper terrace; my wife is waiting for me!"

Later in the evening, Lucif-er stood beside Liliel, who was hugging his left arm; next to them, the other three Overlords from the NA remained in a tight group looking up from the top terrace at the night sky, specifically at an aircraft zooming away toward the southwest. The supreme leader of the group solemnly stated.

"Farewell, Gabri-el... someone I used to call my brother; you are not under my protection anymore. From now on, you and your friends are fair game!"

Liliel did not show any emotion; the other three Overlords smiled sarcastically.

Raquel gazed at the terrace's third floor from a flying aircraft as the cylinder flew away. She could see Lucif-er's blue eyes even when she did not want to see them anymore; therefore, she closed her eyes. Next, she turned her sight eastward, where a bright glow from the now emerging morning sun could be seen. Raquel found this light more relaxing, as the dissipation of the darkness made her feel more secure.

While touching her, Gabri-el gently contacted her with a personal message, *"My love, it seems not all was fun for you!"*

She responded with a pretty and kind smile.

"I was doing fine until Lucif-er showed me the 'stone.' After I got dizzy looking at that jewel's display, I felt strange, including chills and fear, like someone was chasing me!"

"You will be fine!" He affirmed, *"I also sense that you don't want to return to this place; I promise, I shall not bring you back! ... By the way, I must tell you that Liliel tried to seduce me."*

Raquel eyes opened in disbelief about something she never heard before in her long life on Terra. She questioned her husband.

"Why did she do such a thing? It is immoral; she knows that you are my husband, and she is Lucif-er's girlfriend!"

He looked deep into her aquamarine eyes, which had a mystic effect on his mind; he disengaged and tenderly advanced his thoughts.

"I asked myself the same question... I am sure she did it for Lucif-er; however, it does not make sense. If you apply logic to his motives, what comes out is so bizarre and evil that it defies understanding!"

Gabri-el turned to glance out of the craft's window. He stared at the now faint lights from the mansion, which quickly faded out because of the increasing distance and the dominant glare from the rising sun.

He remarked with a touch of sadness.

"Between my friend Lucif-er and I, a deepening abyss is expanding as time passes. Soon, it may become impossible to cross! I will pray to our Lord for his soul!"

Dani-el interrupted Gabri-el's conversation with his spouse by exclaiming, *"Gabri-el, there is something of the utmost importance that I need to share! I had a chat with two other NA guests, and what I extracted from their unsuspecting brains was a shocker. The party had not much to do with us; Lucif-er and the North Alliance's Overlords were celebrating... **the final takeover of Eastland!**"*

Pristeen, Dawnel, Same day: 5:00 hours.

Looking down from the top of the leading skyscraper, one of the three towers bordering Dawnel's central plaza stood a truncated upper terrace. This place resembled a triangle, with an aircraft landing pad occupying one-third of its center. The other three outside sections were like miniature parks with small flowering trees and sitting places to admire the high-ground view.

At this height, the wind was blowing very hard; only because the building had wind deflectors did a moderate breeze affect the ornamental trees planted at this considerable distance from the ground.

Even at noontime, the gray clouds overhead made this day dark and chilly, forecasting an approaching winter storm.

Inside one of the three garden-like sections, all five SA Overlords continued their outdoor meeting. Three modern benches bolted to the ground stayed in a semicircular array, with the terrace outside rail as one of its borders.

Micha-el stood leaning against the outside rail. He faced two Overlords to his right and the same number to the left, all four sitting on two benches.

The Archangels, dressed in light tunics, seemed impervious to the low temperatures prevailing at this altitude. The South Alliance's leader, glancing at the first Archangel seated at his left side, inquired.

"Samu-el... explain why we lost Eastland?"

This individual got up and walked to the outside rail, where he spoke telepathically to the others.

"We did not have a chance! ... The NA was ruthless. As they carried their insidious plan to a conclusion, they intimidated the population while lying outrageously. They disregarded God's laws, behaving in a selfish and materialistic way, which I have never seen before!

We were afraid that we would have to behave similarly to stop them, but if we did, we would have no better moral values than theirs! ... This was the reason for not stopping them!"

Micha-el paused for three seconds while the mild breeze played with his curly hair, he said calmly.

"I understand the situation; this was an event for which we were physically and mentally unprepared!"

Rapha-el mentally spoke from the opposite side.

"My brother, what are we doing with the new problem of Bird Islands?"

Micha-el grabbed the metallic rail and squeezed the top portion hard enough for the structure to complain with a high-pitched moan.

"My dear friend, I am not ignoring the NA's callous influx of thousands of military-trained individuals into the islands!"

He pointed to Lari-el, Tellia's Province Overlord.

"I am assigning you to counter the invasion. Send as many military people to the place as possible to equally match the NA's deployment. I want this force to be aggressive in canceling their wrongdoings; nevertheless, only as far as our moral boundaries would allow it.

Make sure our troops don't become part of the hatefulness being spread by the NA. We are fighting against their distorted beliefs, but we should be open to mercy and understanding toward our opponents. However, if the NA personnel threatens in any way the Islands' population, ensure them that we will fight to protect them!"

Samu-el nodded and acknowledged, *"I will start assembling the task force immediately!"*

Micha-el turned around to observe the menacing black clouds approaching the city's plaza and pointed out.

"Tomorrow, I will send a message condemning the NA's actions; it will be broadcast at 6:00 a.m.! I can see the rain coming. We should move inside; the storm has arrived!"

The Core, Cheruban, Argentan's University Building, 5:30 hours.

A large classroom, almost like an auditorium, was full of students; most were Cherubin, with fewer Seraphim and Thrones and a third of whom were females. They were all seated on spacious rows of chairs with a tilted frontal display facing the occupant. A podium raised about one meter at the auditorium center showed many electronic gadgets attached to its frame. The large room remained partially lit except for the podium area, which stayed brightly illuminated.

The angel standing next to the podium had all the students' full attention as he was a prominent scholar teaching astronomy. His magnified voice addressed the audience while resting his left hand on the podium.

"After inspecting our galaxy, we can move to the Local Group: The immediate conglomerate of galaxies which includes our own."

He pushed a button from the podium's controls. A three-dimensional holographic appeared above the entire auditorium. Andromeda and the Milky Way were separated at the center, with their satellite galaxies following each dominant member. Grabbing a small rod, he pointed to Andromeda, making it brighter, and spoke.

"This is our galaxy, Galaxia1, or just G1; its diameter is about 130,000 light-years, and its mass is 0.8×10^{12} solar masses, just about a trillion solar masses.

Galaxia2, equally known as our sister galaxy," the floating display representing the second stellar mass got brighter, *"is 80,000 light-years across, but its mass is very close to ours."*

The teacher pointed the thin rod up, and a red line connected the two dominant galaxies with a written label above it: **2.5 million light-years**.

The professor proceeded, *"This is the distance between G1 and G2; however, these galaxies are merging at a speed of 110 kilometers/second; in 4.5 billion years, they will collide and transform into a bigger galaxy.[1]*

Now, if we start a dynamic time representation of how the Local Group's galaxies behave... let's try 1 billion years = 10 seconds."

When he pointed the device toward the cosmic display of the Local Group's celestial display, it went into motion. The spiral arms of the galaxies could be seen rotating, the satellite galaxies moving around their gravitational mothers, and the whole Local Group spinning around a central point of gravity. He continued the lecture.

"Notice the rotation of the two central galaxies. A full rotation is considered a Cosmic Year; for G2, this amounts to 225 million years.

Also, notice the complimentary rotation of both dominant members. It is too bad we are at a tilt of less than 12° concerning G2. Otherwise, the view of our sister galaxy could be a grandiose one!"

As the 3D cosmic display moved to the colossal collision of two large galaxies where the merging of the two central massive black holes released an unimaginable amount of radiation and the scattering of billions of stars became mind-boggling, a red light appeared in the podium's instrumentation.

The lecturing angel inquired, *"Yes?"*

"Our illustrious Overlord Gabri-el has arrived; he is ready to talk to your class!" A deep tone of voice projected from the podium. After that, the professor replied.

"Don't make him wait! We are ready!"

Since the cosmic 3D show above had reached its conclusion, the professor turned it off. All the lights in the auditorium returned to a standard visual intensity.

A few seconds later, a side door slid open. Gabri-el and his two assistants, who were also the pilots, walked in.

Reuben and Norvel stood at both sides of the door, which silently closed again. All the students rose until Gabri-el reached the podium; then, they sat again. The professor mentally greeted the Overlord, showing great joy.

"Sir, it is my greatest pleasure to have you in my class! Please, take my place!"

"Thanks, Eryk," the Overlord responded telepathically while displaying a broad smile and an open-hand salute at chest level. Next, he faced the students and spoke through the voice magnifiers.

"Dear Core citizens, it is my delight to lecture you on my favorite subject... Astronomy!

---

[1] Most of the Andromeda and Milky Way information was gathered from Wikipedia or Google.

When you look at our planet and then move to the stars, galaxies, and the Cosmos, you must gasp in awe at the grandeur and immensity of the Universe. You have no choice but to believe in our Creator since the entire object is just a shadow of His image!

Here in space, where millions of light years and billions of years are as common as centimeters and seconds in our daily lives, we find that the only thing that will allow us to transverse the vast dominion of the Cosmos... is our imagination!

Use it and use it well. It can take you to places where it is impossible to go physically! Out there, you will find a place where the reality of our Creator becomes apparent; consequentially, you will also see what you are... stardust! ... Yes! Most of your body is made of atoms created by supernovas; therefore, you are an intrinsic part of the Universe.

There is even more; if you have a soul, you are beyond the Universe and material things since you have inherited one of God's attributes... ***eternity!*** *"*

The Archangel paused momentarily while making eye contact with all the students; next, he spoke.

"I will be glad to answer any questions related to this curriculum; feel free to ask."

A male Cherub in the last row stood up and inquired.

"Sir, please tell us if G1 rotates clockwise or counterclockwise?"

Gabri-el revealed a faint smile, and he commented.

"My dear Zorian, I can sense a motivation for a trick question; since you already know the answer, would you please explain it to us?"

Because of the student's question, the professor slightly rubbed the right side of his head while nodding in disapproval.

Zorian, a slender young Cherub with partially curly hair, eagerly to show his skills, proceeded with the explanation.

"Sir, it depends on the point of observation, if it is above or below the galactic plane!"

"Very good! Now, there is an absolute rotational direction for every galaxy in the Universe, and it is related to the Big Bang theory. As a project assignment, I suggest the whole class find our galaxy's actual rotation.

It will require lots of work. The absolute reference is the matter/antimatter interface generated by the creation of the Universe by the collision and annihilation of the most basic and primary atomic particles, what we call P-particles. As you all know, these particles can be +charged with a clockwise rotation, making normal matter, or -charged with a counter-clockwise rotation, making antimatter!

This interface is your zero reference. Your job is to find the inclination angle of the galactic plane, so you know your absolute rotational direction!"

As Zorian sat again, one Seraph in the second row stood and spoke.

"Sir! What happens if, by any chance, our galactic plane or any other galactic plane is exactly at a 90° angle?"

*"Muriel! ... You can define exactly 90° in mathematical terms, but in real life, you have infinite decimal points at your disposal; therefore, it will **never** be <u>exactly</u> 90°!"*

A Cherub, an attractive female showing a pleasant smile, stood up and inquired further.

"Sir! ... Would this inability to define an exact angle also apply to the matter/antimatter interface?"

Gabri-el returned the smile and responded.

*"No, Adeline; the interface is an absolute value, and by definition, is **zero**!"*

She did not sit, but she proceeded to ask another question.

"Sir, this is not related... Since you and all the other Overlords can read our thoughts, do you listen to our most private mental reasoning as we approach you?"

The Archangel gave her a sympathetic glance before explaining.

"Only when it is related to an important task that may require it. Otherwise, it would be an improper action on our part to invade your privacy! ... Next question!"

In the middle of the amphitheater, another Cherub stood up. He was the densely built type, but his eyesight revealed a keen hunger for learning. He calmly said.

"Sir, at the beginning of the course, we learned that the sun does not have enough mass ever to become a supernova. Is there any possibility of such an event happening?"

"Galvyn, you know there are Type I and Type II supernovas. In addition, they require bigger than 1.4 solar masses for such thermonuclear reactions to occur. We have never seen such an event for the size of the sun! If it does take place, we will name it... a Type III supernova!"

Galvyn replied with a laughing giggle, *"Nobody will be left to record it, Sir!*

Several muffled chuckles reverberated across the auditorium. Gabri-el openly celebrated what the rest of the class thought was funny. Finally, he closed the topic with a remark.

"Have no fear; the laws of Physics tell us that such a phenomenon is not possible!"

After the last student sat, Gabri-el pointed to another female Cherub in the front row, and as he made eye contact, he indicated.

"You have been anxiously waiting... Go ahead, ask!"

Sitting in front of an electronic display, Raquel continued using the terminal. Inside her residence, all was comfortably warm and quiet. Her eyelids began to feel heavy, so she rubbed her pretty eyes with both hands. It felt good when the cool fingers soothed the warm skin of her eyelids.

"I went to bed too late last night; if I take a short nap, I should feel much better…" She thought while remembering events from the last night. As she leaned backward into the plush chair, her eyes closed briefly.

Almost right away, she fell asleep!

Sitting on her bed's edge, Raquel's loose and glossy hair gently flowed from one side of her head to the other, following her rocking movements. Lightly dressed in a smooth nightgown that ended just above the knee, it outlined her outstanding physical shape by displaying a detailed contour of her heavenly curves.

She felt abnormally warm; she ran both hands to the side of her head, intertwining her fingers and lustrous hair as she pulled it backward. Next, her fingers slid down her neck and around her slender throat, but when they touched the hard nipples of both breasts, she shivered like somebody else had felt her!

She was waiting for her beloved husband to arrive; it was hard for her to figure out the burning feeling between her legs, a desire bordering on lust! A sensation still unknown to her!

A piece of soft and sensual music could be heard as Raquel looked around her bedroom. How strange, it seemed so different, even with a gentle fog hanging around… and what was all the stuff placed on the counters or corners that she did not remember to own?

Notably, the spectacular stone on the back of the room shined as if it had its own spotlights even when the lights stayed at less than 20% of normal lighting! Sparkles of all colors, sparse but powerful, were being lasered across the bedroom, although the dominant color remained…blue!

"Where had she seen a similar stone like that?" Raquel questioned herself.

Steps could be heard from the aisle leading to the door; she got up, impatiently staring at the door. When it finally opened, there he stood… the most handsome and desirable male on the entire planet.

She threw herself into his open hands; their lips touched, fanning the flames inside her exquisite body. She felt ardent but comfortable inside his muscular grip; when she finally opened her unique aquamarine eyes, she stared with passion into his deep… **blue eyes!**

Her eyes instantly became wide open! A nervous shake rattled her whole body while fighting to free herself from the vice-grip of his arms… then, she screamed… **"No!"**

Raquel woke up.

Her intensely disturbing emotions triggered sweat on her forehead, causing her heart to beat quickly; however, how incredible this was! The feeling of being in his arms did not go away, nor did the insane burning desire!

In disgust, she bit her index finger hard… and harder, until it almost bled! Under the severe pain, the dream's aftermath started to fade away.

A blinking red light and a deep beep caught her attention. At the upper left corner, the display revealed a short note.

International Network Message

Reuben heard three quick but low-tone beeps from his belt. He quickly detached the centered device and saw the message; he immediately sent a message to Gabri-el.

"Sir, the NA has an important announcement in the I-N. in nine seconds!"

The Overlord acknowledged the message; addressing the whole class, he exclaimed.

"The NA has an International Message that may be important for us to listen to. I am switching to the frontal main screen!"

Without looking, Gabri-el touched the podium's control screen. The cosmic display vanished, and the entire front wall came alive with a visual display.

The professor and the Archangel quickly moved away from the center to give the class a clear view.

In a few seconds, Magog-el's smiling face filled the screen, with both arms and hands opened in a welcoming sign.

"Citizens of Terra!

I am bringing you great news! … The nation of Eastland has joined the NA!

We are overjoyed at our brothers' desire to share the wealth of our great Alliance…"

As Magog-el emphatically praised the new partnership, Gabri-el looked at the concerned students' faces. He felt stressed by the news of an event that was the result of oppression, deception, and intimidation. His face showed little emotion, but his spirit remained in turmoil. He knew that Micha-el's speech was scheduled for 5:00 hours!

The NA tactical speech had preempted his SA friend's speech, so he was unhappy!

Magog-el continued to talk for 29 minutes. After that, he concluded by saying.

"… finally, my brothers, I wish you enjoy the peace you rightfully deserve!"

The screen blinked out. At the center, a new message appeared.

I-N will broadcast the SA message in 1 minute.

Gabri-el walked to the podium and addressed the class again. He made a short announcement.

"The NA purposely overlapped a speech scheduled at 5:00 hours from the SA related to the same subject. For a minute, think about what you have just heard. We will be discussing it after the next speech is over."

Ninety seconds of silence stretched for a while but eventually ended. Only five seconds before 5:30 hours, the lights at the console blinked again; this time, the teacher, also a professor, knew the reason for the signal.

You almost heard the students' minds counting down the seconds to zero. The wall screen lit up again; this time, it was Micha-el. He looked more serious than usual, as he probably remained upset about the previous NA's sneaky move; he started his discourse with a forced calm voice.

"Terra citizens! Greetings from the SA!

Just moments ago, you heard the SA's announcement celebrating the joining with Eastland; the NA knew my plan to condemn the same event they have maliciously twisted into something glorious to celebrate.

People of Terra, listen!

Eastland was not attached to the NA by any friendly means. It was forced to join an Alliance that had plotted to steal their independence!

We did try to stop them, but we started that process too late. Besides, we were not prepared for the deception, coercion, and even brutal force that the NA leaders and their military personnel displayed on that beautiful land.

After this unworthy action has been accomplished, the NA is on the move again! This time, they have set their predatory eyes on another defenseless victim... The Bird Islands!

I warn the NA that the SA will not allow another country to fall into the crazy expansionist desire of the northern Overlords. As God is my witness, I promise to use all the resources available to prevent the Bird Islands from being enslaved by the North!"

After a brief pause, Micha-el stared at his electronic audience, and in a sort of personal appeal, tried talking on a one-on-one basis with the viewers and listeners.

"My brothers, I strongly encourage you to pray to the Lord for a peaceful solution to the current confrontations. I will always be available to reverse the dangerous course we have unwillingly taken.

Pray for the NA! ... Pray for all of us!"

Micha-el's message stayed short; he probably discarded the original prepared speech and improvised this one. The auditorium screen went blank; it returned to its normal-looking format.

Gabri-el quickly returned to the podium. He sensed the apprehension and inordinate confusion that both announcements stirred into the minds of all present. Softly because of this understanding, he told the class.

"Today, you are witnessing the conflict affecting the lives of all the planet's inhabitants. Even if you decide not to fight against your aggressive brothers from the North by choosing a pacifist approach, which is The Core's way of life, you still have to make a choice!

I understand that the current events appear very complex, but I assure you," his green eyes sparkled towards the class's stare, like a laser beam impacting their eyes' corneas. *"It is the opposite because of a basic truth:* **You are either with God... or against Him!"**

Shortly after Micha-el's speech ended, Gabri-el also finished his involvement with the class at the auditorium and exited the classroom; his two assistants closely followed him.

A Cherub came running from the spacious hallway. His formal attire identified him as a member of the University's staff: dark green pants with a brown-gold jacket fitted to the contours of the waistline by a golden belt. He became slightly agitated by the running; raising his open right hand to salute the Overlord, he mentally and enthusiastically said.

"Greetings, Great Overlord Gabri-el!"

Gabri-el looked at the angel, displaying a broad smile; he used both hands to greet the approaching Cherub.

"Greetings to you, Mervyn! I am glad to see you again!"

The addressee gave Gabri-el a joyful smile for his greater appreciation, as shown by a two-hand salute; next, he expressed his concerns.

"Gabri-el, dear friend, I was worried about missing this chance to talk to you!"

The Overlord, anticipating an additional remark, stipulated.

"You had no need for concern; I had specifically reserved some time to meet you. Micha-el and I are aware of your special skills in computer science. It is important to us talking to you, the leading scientist in the field!"

"Thank you! I must mention that the NA offered me the most lucrative offer ever. Nevertheless, material possessions are not important to me; morality, on the other hand, is everything! Therefore, after listening to Magog-el and Micha-el's speeches, my conscience demands that I do something about it... Please tell Micha-el that I am at his service for anything he may need!"

Gabri-el touched his companion's right shoulder as his face approached Mervyn's. In a mental low tone communicate, Gabri-el told him.

"Mervyn, you have always been a leader on moral issues as you are in your expertise. Micha-el and I are most grateful for your decision! ... As

soon as I return to my office, I will send him the details of your valuable decision!"

Mervyn excused himself and walked away. Gabri-el watched his accelerated short steps, which caused his curly blond hair to float behind him. Gabri-el felt better; the news that this individual wanted to help the SA was great, indeed. He proceeded to relegate Magog-el's negative statements to a background location inside his mind; in this manner, he focused on the more positive endeavors now challenging his intellect.

He had thought about Raquel since he had left his residence in the early morning; now, his heart ached for her affection and company. He had one more thing to do, and then he would rush to her warm and loving arms, always ready to welcome him.

As if she could hear him from this far away, he sent a private message that only he could listen to.

"My love... I will be home, soon!"

SA, Irisan, Iris, Central Transportation Building.

Two Principalities were talking to each other. One of them, the heavier build, grabbed his companion by his shoulders and shook him firmly while articulating a demanding request.

"You cannot do this! You have to stay here!"

"Sergius! ... Let me go!" Protested the angel being shaken.

Sergius released his grip but continued staring at him sternly; then, he complained.

"Marcus, why do you always choose to do the extreme?"

The individual questioned, raising both hands like trying to explain something difficult, exclaimed.

"We are running out of time!"

He practically yelled to his friend, then he added.

"This is the last year of our lives! Do you want to sit and wait for the end without attempting anything at all?"

His companion replied, *"Since science cannot help us anymore, Rapha-el asked us to place our faith in God and pray for a miracle; you won't change anything by asking Lucif-er for help!"*

Marcus replied, *"You do that; I have to try something different; after all, Lucif-er is the most powerful of the Overlords... if anybody can help me, it must be him!"*

Sergius glanced at the concave row of windows, allowing him to gaze at the area outside the building. A large and well-illuminated section was only four meters high where the concave windows were located; however, in the opposite direction, the terminal opened in a massive arrangement of connecting floors, seating areas, and beautiful planters filled with flowering vegetation arranged in neat clusters. Overall, ultramodern decorations of glassy and transparent plastics illuminated from the inside stayed strategically located.

On the outside, a massive and shiny cylinder was mating with the concave section of the building, a curvature encompassing three floors; this craft could take up to a thousand passengers in a single trip.

Inside the airport on the second floor, Sergius sadly watched many angels gathering at the main wide sliding door to enter the vehicle. He returned his sight to Marcus' black eyes; the departing angel looked back with unchanged determination.

A wet glaze covered Sergius' eyes since his friend had been his inseparable companion. In fact, he considered Marcus to be closer to him than his brother did. He muttered.

"Any last thing I could say to change your mind?"

Marcus sadly looked at his friend while crossing his arms, stomach high, like masking an internal pain; he nodded.

Sergius, composing himself, asserted, *"OK, Marcus, have a nice trip, and let me know what happens!"*

Marcus smiled; he started to move toward the sliding door, which was now open and allowing boarding passengers through. He placed both index fingers at 45° in a symbolic sign.

Sergius' smile got wider; he recognized the symbol they used as teenagers when playing together. It meant, 'I will see you later... for sure!' He responded identically.

After Marcus boarded, the place became almost empty. A high-pitched humming sound could be heard as the craft separated from the building. It was followed by a high-frequency vibration, which mildly rattled the building. As the aircraft powered by a massive engine lifted vertically from the ground, it quickly disappeared from the windows.

Sergius felt a chill propagating from his spine. His inseparable friend of so many years was gone, and then he felt this strong, bizarre, and unnerving premonition declaring.

*"You will **never** see him again!"*

The next day, working at the computer, Raquel was restless because of the previous day's nightmare aftermath. Last night, she had a tough time sleeping; however, to her surprise, when Gabri-el lay in bed by her side, the sensual desire driven by her bad dreams faded away. Now, alone again and with the screen's glare making her tired eyes worse, the insane lustful feeling had returned. She thought.

"My God, I don't want this to happen again! ... After all, it was just a bad dream... still, I remained so ashamed of its contents that I did not even tell my loving husband. I am not sure that was the right thing to do since this disturbing nightmare was so real! I am so tired... so sleepy..."

Raquel tried to fight back, but the terminal seemed to conspire against her, the blinking lights triggering a hypnotic effect on her. Her long and lustrous eyelashes started sticking to her lower eyelids, effectively reducing the incoming light and encouraging sleep. Raquel gradually lost her ability to resist, and eventually, her head bowed down as she fell asleep…

Again, inside her bedroom, she caressed her silky hair and felt a tingling sensation all over her skin in anticipation of her incoming mate. All the erotic zones outside and inside her body climbed to above-normal temperatures. She recalled being in the same location as in the previous dream, but she felt much more excited this time than in the last dream!

The fog, the music, and the stone at the room's back all were the same; the stone sparkling into the partially illuminated room appeared brighter and bluer.

As the steps in the hallway got closer, her heart began pounding faster. When the door slid open, she ran into his powerful arms again; she practically melted during the tight embrace, with exhilaration emanating from every pore of her gracious body. Nevertheless, as his lips touched hers, setting her body on fire, she remembered… his eyes were not green but **blue!**

She pushed herself away from his grip, searching for the color of his eyes; in terror, she saw the hypnotic, deep blue eyes staring at her so close!

Raquel screamed again, *"No!"*

She was expecting to wake up. It did not happen!

He displayed a sneer as if he had planned this; then, his powerful hands grabbed her gracious and slender waist, lifting her off the ground. To her horror, her whole body trembled with pleasure and desire at the touch of his robust masculine hands. It felt like her mind and body had become two independent entities, one fighting the other!

Slowly, he placed her on top of the bed with his body pinning her down; she wanted to resist, but it seemed so futile. Under the pressure of his weight, her desire increased to levels of derangement; she began shivering!

In a masculine and sexy voice, he declared.

"Raquel! … Do not resist; I know you want me… just be mine!"

He touched her everywhere; his ardent lips ran around hers and alongside her stylish neck. Her groin and nipples started to hurt by the pressure of the sexual craving; she could hear her heart pounding hard as a hot sweat began to cover her whole body's skin.

With both hands, he grabbed her knees, separating her legs.

Anticipating with terror the imminent consummation of her insane craving, a chill running from her legs to the whole length of her spine appeared to allow her to gather all the strength needed to push away her ardent companion. She yelled at him.

"I cannot do this to my beloved husband… stop!"

When the dream commenced fading away, she heard one last message.

*"Twice, you have rejected me… there is **no** third time; you will be mine… **soon!**"*

Raquel's eyes opened slowly; she lay flat on her back on the plush chair next to the electronic terminal, with her legs spread apart. Slowly, she sat properly, and with both hands wiped the sweat dripping from her face; her heart continued beating hard, almost painfully. Her heavy breath forced her to partially open her mouth to facilitate the air's passage. She felt horrible; her nipples and groin burned with pain as if for one hundred years she lingered having sex, and finally, when the time came to do it… she said… NO!

If she was ashamed of the previous dream, she felt much worse this time because she loved her husband beyond any doubt or hesitation. How was it possible to feel such adulterous desires when your mind cannot even allow it?

She got up and started walking around the spacious room. Even when it did not happen, she felt violated as she showed it by pressing her hands against her breasts and lower abdomen.

Raquel finally stopped next to a food-dispensing machine. With her head bowing down, she mildly bounced her forehead against its wall several times.

Afterward, she dialed the machine for: **Water at 4° C.**

Picking up the dispensed cup almost full, she drank it slowly…

Compare this to a squelching rain obliterating a forest fire!

SA, Irisan.

Rapha-el's private aircraft was zigzagging alongside the picturesque canyons of Irisan's northern borders. The tall green coniferous trees gave the mountains a lush appearance from above, mimicking a thick green carpet on top of the mountain range's surface.

Ahead, quickly coming onto view, a small town appeared. It comprised a few taller buildings at its center, not higher than five stories; they neatly followed a hill's side, so the structures blended with the pine trees growing on the slope.

A small triangular central area was selected for landing, which the vehicle did after a brief hovering.

When the pilots and all passengers exited the craft, they faced a group of about fifty angels, who approached the arriving Overlord's team after waiting outside the landing area.

The two pilots dressed in their province's colors, a light purple uniform with a white belt, stood at the vehicle's exit door; they were armed with power rifles and handguns in a similar way as the NA military troops did.

Staying close to his craft in his usual light purple tunic, now displaying a white cross over his heart, Rapha-el walked with firm steps toward the local group, specifically at a set of five angels bunching together around one female.

Rapha-el strode directly at her; after getting close, he extended both hands, grabbing hers.

She was an average-looking female from the Angel's Choir of Dominions with long brown hair and a similar eye color. She wore a maroon tunic with a black belt.

All her companions were in the same choir. The Archangel swiftly noticed that two were her sons and two were family friends.

The female angel felt great emotional pain, causing her eyes to redden and her whole body to tremble. A thin layer of perspiration on her face made it appear waxy.

The Overlord did not waste any time to speak first.

"Dear Gylda, my heart feels your pain! The news of your son's death hurts deeply; I hope my presence can in any way diminish the anguish afflicting you, your family, and your friends!"

Her glossy eyes looked up to the Overlord for just a second, and then she asked with a trembling voice that reflected her deep suffering.

"Great Overlord... Why my son? ... Why is he dead?"

Rapha-el released her hands and placed one on her left shoulder. His compassionate touch felt like a healing elixir. Gylda's pulse and respiration stabilized almost instantly; even her distressed face relaxed from its torture. Next, his face got closer to hers, and Rapha-el stated.

"Your son was an unfortunate victim of a terrorist group that ambushed and killed two and left three more seriously injured. We are sure they came from the NA; since your son acted as the Town's Supervisor, he was targeted because of his position!"[2]

She responded with distress, *"My son, he never hurt anyone! Why does anybody want him dead? ... We have lived for many thousands of years without violence and murders; why now? ...* **What have I done that God punished me so painfully?"**

Rapha-el looked at her with deep empathy. He felt the searing pain of a mother who had just lost a son, the emptiness left by someone deeply loved and now departed. A suffering far beyond any that could be felt on her own body; not even her death could have been so painful! In addition... anger was present!

"Gylda! Gylda! God is not punishing you; you must see it from His perspective! Your son Antonius was a good angel; right now, he is with God, enjoying his reward!

---

[2] A position like our city's mayor.

For us, he is dead, and we ache because of his absence; nevertheless, we should rejoice! ... His spirit has found what we are striving for, eternal love and happiness... he found God!

Gylda, believe me, none of us is going to live forever. If we obey our Lord's commands, someday we shall be privileged to join your son where he resides now; my dear lady, he just went ahead of us!"

Somehow puzzled by Rapha-el's words, which were sinking in like sunshine through stormy clouds, warm and invigorating, she accepted what he had spoken. She kissed him on the cheek and uttered.

"Thank you, Rapha-el... we love you, Illustrious Overlord!"

The rest of the group equally thanked the Archangel for his dedication to his people, his ability to heal, and the wisdom of his thoughts.

After comforting the quintet, the Overlord and his assistants took off to a new destination. The mother, along with the people of the small town, stood still as the flying vehicle disappeared behind the walls of the sinuous canyon. She felt much better now; the unbearable sorrow had subsided to some acceptable grieving level. She looked at her two sons, sharing with her the loss of Antonius; she could almost see the image of her third son standing next to his brothers as he did for so many years. Even when she understood Rapha-el's consoling words, Gylda still wished that the Lord had taken her instead of her son!

For Raquel, one more day had elapsed; she continued pacing the big room in her residence, avoiding the seat in front of the terminal. The amazing Cherub showed great stress, with her four back wings glowing in disarray, opposite from her usual self. She was scared to get even close to the sofa-like chair next to the computer's display. By now, Raquel doubted her ability to resist another sensual nightmare, perhaps her last! Why didn't she confide in her loving husband for help?

Indeed, her husband must have noticed her unrest, but he did not ask, perhaps, to respect her privacy. And of course, when she went to sleep with Gabri-el, there were **no** nightmares! She should have ignored the shame and asked him for help; instead, she was now sweating it again... alone!

The craving began returning to her breasts and groin; while squeezing her thighs together, she bit her bent index finger hard. A quiet moan came out of her partially blocked mouth... Even the pain felt pleasurable!

What was this? An internal clock triggering these insane thoughts at the same time... every day?

Her body temperature rose again, and tiny droplets of sweat started flowing from every pore on her lustrous skin. In addition, this large organ started to become sensitized to the minutest touch, becoming an erotic event. She felt her eyes closing; Raquel knew that she may not have the strength to resist this time. She would not give up on the evil lust; she intended to die first!

The thought of losing her husband stirred sad and painful feelings. Raquel reflected that she must be confused; she was not losing him... He was losing her!

It turned into a fight to stay awake, but her eyelids got heavier as the night moved in, inexorably undermining her most precious defenses.

She decided: I cannot fight this alone; I will go jogging outside until I drop!

She started moving toward the exit when she heard this 'ding' noise behind her. The extraordinary, beautiful female looked back... and found herself staring at the electronic display.

She saw blinking lights; then, her vision started to spin. Before Raquel's collapsing body hit the floor, she managed to articulate one last pleading telepathic message.

"My love... please... help me..."

Gabri-el stayed very concerned about his wife during this important meeting on the outskirts of Argentan, as she had remained in an alternate channel inside his mind. He knew she had an erotic nightmare turning so disturbing that she was ashamed even to mention it. He thought next.

"I avoided intruding into her privacy because I did expect her to overcome the dream! ... One thing does not make sense; a dream, regardless of how disturbing it can be by bringing up deeply repressed fears or inhibitions afloat, remains just a dream! Nonetheless, Raquel is behaving like the dream is real!

In addition, it is strange that she only had those bad dreams when I was not around. What mental pattern could trigger such a nightmare?"

"Sir! Please tell us that you agree with engineering on how to use liquid Li-221!"

The message from the Cherub sat at his left side from a triangular-shaped conference table where the Overlord was presiding; it came into his mind from another mental input. The two Cherubim facing him stayed busy accessing or entering information into integrated controls embedded in the table. The Archangel also kept track of the other ten technicians attending the meeting and standing next to the triangular table. While still analyzing his wife's problem, he looked at the small transparent container made of a rare glass alloy; it held inside a pure black liquid. Its black color became more evident since the vial sat on top of a white piece of paper-like square of 50 x 50 centimeters.

Simultaneously, he thought, "This Lithium-based molecular-activated glue is stronger than anything manufactured before. I do have some concerns about inhaling its fumes or dust when it is created from chemical reactions or mechanically ground."

As Gabri-el picked up and opened the container to show its bonding characteristics, the vial slipped off his fingers and began dropping on top of the white sheet of paper.

An Archangel is fast enough to intercept a falling object, but to his surprise, he just stared as it felt and spilled the black liquid, which instantly stained the center of the white sheet of paper.

For a second, the twelve angels facing him watched with disbelief. This could be something they may have done, but for the Overlord, it was not an option!

The Archangel watched the small spill grow sharply pointed tentacles spreading in all directions. It quickly devoured the sheet's pure white color, converting it into a sinister obsidian color. The glue-active molecules invaded every microscopy crack of the weaker molecular bonds of the white material. It became like a malevolent virus taking over its host... in a merciless manner!

In a few seconds, the whole sheet turned black. The dark tentacles proceeded to attack the table's surface; however, around 10 centimeters beyond the sheet, the black and pointed tentacles stopped propagating; next, they coalesced to form a rough circle of approximately 70 centimeters in diameter.

The Cherub left of Gabri-el exclaimed.

"Oh Lord! Removing this spot from the table will require a laser blaster!"

The Overlord, undisturbed by the nearby onlookers, glanced at him and said, *"You are right, Zantiel; please, contact the chemical engineer to blast the spot away and then plasticize the hole in the table. Make sure he uses a 0.02 sub-micron filter mask and eye goggles when he removes the glue!"*

Gabri-el engaged in his own meditation.

"What is going on? Am I losing my powers? ... I dropped the container, but I also failed to stop it from hitting the table!"

The image of the devouring black liquid above the white paper continued to be played back, refusing to go away. One more time, he saw the white paper sheet being stained by the dark advancing liquid.

He thought, "It is like the paper lost its purity!"

But when he glanced at the black circle on the table, he saw a faint image appearing inside the darkness... It was Raquel's face!

The image, motionless for two seconds, suddenly voiced a faint murmur.

"... help... me..."

With a chill drilling through his spine, Gabri-el suddenly realized the grave danger his wife was currently facing. In a message sent to her, even when she could not hear it, he mentally screamed.

"Raquel! Do not surrender to evil! My love, hang on... I am on my way!"

With a speed that may look supersonic to the angels attending the meeting, he ran out of the room, almost ripping apart the sliding exit door when it did not open fast enough!

A lingering message floated in the air.

"I have an emergency; Zantiel will take over the meeting!"

[10x]> Gabri-el, raced through the corridor at top speed.

He sent a message to Reuben. Due to his fast speed, the Archangel did slow the electronic message to his pilot.

*"**Reuben**, emergency take-off, priority **E-1**!"*

Gabri-el was outside the building in no time, racing toward his personal flying cylinder parking location. A verbal signal activated his communication device, and the incoming message was delivered so slowly!

"Sir, activating the aircraft! ... Norvel won't be available!"

As he approached the craft, Gabri-el sent a command.

"I will pilot! You will be the copilot!" <[10x]

Raquel, already sleeping against her will, was waiting for her beloved husband with an uncontrollable desire for him. Her heart was pounding while sweat ran from her face down to her neck and into the cleavage between her full breasts. She ached for sex so hard that she did not recognize herself; it was not the way she usually behaved, like this new Raquel was resembling somebody else.

This time was different; even when she felt her bodily cravings, her mind stayed detached. It became a spectator, looking at what went on with her body.

Did her brain make this up?

The blinking of the stone at the back of the room made her dizzy. This time, its light emissions became twice as prolific.

The door opened, and a gorgeous male walked inside the apartment. She saw herself jumping into his arms, and her lips became compressed by a searing kiss. Before her body could see his eyes, her detached mind noticed that they were **blue**!

Even more disturbing, while his eyes looked directly at her mind's eyes, he displayed a sinister smile adorning his irresistible face, pointing out her ineptitude to change or stop the horror of the approaching sexual outcome.

She screamed to her own body, still unaware of the horrific mistake…

*"**No… Don't do it!**"*

Gabri-el, piloting his craft, reached speeds far beyond the ones allowed inside the city limits. His companion, Reuben, had a hard time compensating for the vehicle's maneuvers as initiated by the Overlord; as

a result, large droplets of sweat began appearing on his forehead. A
chilling effect caused his body's hair to stick up, reflecting a serious
concern related to the zigzagging through the towering downtown
buildings, which were approaching too fast as the craft moved along the
urban canyons at supersonic speeds!

Reuben had to remind himself that this was OK... Only because his
boss did the steering!

The vehicle left behind a vapor trail as the skyscrapers became shaken
by the cylinder's speeding sonic boom.

Gabri-el, in control of the vehicle, made it swerve and behave like a
toy in the hands of its master. The Archangel had a goal: to get home
immediately!

The silvery central tower, Gabri-el, and Raquel's home came into
sight... approaching fast!

Reuben moved his hands and feet forward while clenching his teeth.
For the short distance left... he anticipated a horrendously hasty braking!

The light fog drifting alongside Raquel's spacious bedroom looked
bluer than before. The fantastically muscular-shaped Overlord had placed
Raquel on the bed; he lay on top of her body with her legs split open! He
was not looking at her body but at her mind's image overlooking the event,
requesting her approval.

She felt her entire body trembling with anticipation, crying for its
carnal consummation while begging her observing own mind for
permission!

Raquel painfully knew... only a second... an instant of weakness...
and she would have engaged in an adulterous and sinful affair that had...
no recourse!

She screamed again, *"No! I cannot do this to my beloved husband!"*

Raquel's beautiful body, even as it trembled while covered with
copious perspiration, pushed away her persistent assailing companion, he
replied using a sensual voice.

*"Raquel! ... Why do you resist? Gabri-el will never forgive you for
what you have already done! ... If you feel ashamed, how do you think he
will feel when he finds out about your cravings for me? ... On the other
hand, I am offering you pleasures that you have never experienced
before... it only takes a second... say YES! ... **And be mine!***

*I promise you that all the anxiety and pain you are now enduring will
become an <u>exhilarating enjoyment!</u>"*

He started to push forward, getting closer and much closer to her most
private parts!

Terror sank in as her pushing and resisting seemed incapable of
stopping his powerful advances. She prayed for help! ... She prayed for

death! ... She would have preferred this rather than stain her marriage, rather than to **sin!**

Her head began hurting, her breathing gasping for air, and her heart... she could now feel the loud thumping becoming painful! ... Cardiac arrest was not far away!

She begged, *"Please, my God... wake me up!"*

Her assailant, slowly overpowering her, was like a tiger waiting for a single instant of weakness to devour her. He laughed diabolically, and while licking her neck, exclaimed.

*"I told you... You **cannot** wake up! You must accept me... **or die!"***

Sounding like an overloaded electrical circuit ready to rupture, the mind's image of her shakily inquired.

*"**Who are you? Why do you torture me like this?"***

"My sweet and sexy lover... You know me! ... I am the most powerful and handsome male on the whole planet. You are the most beautiful and sensual female in the same place! We are made for each other; together, we will reign over Terra as supreme rulers, and everyone on the planet will bow down to us in obeisance!"

The detached image of her mind, under severe shock, merged back into her body. This time, using her body's own eyes, she saw the piercing blue eyes so close to her. She felt her heart skip a bit while looking at her handsome tormentor, who suddenly became so familiar!

The fog lingering inside the bedroom distorted her vision; once it cleared, the angel facing her had a name!

*"**Lucif-er!"*** Raquel mumbled with uncontrolled anger. Her desire continued burning her whole body, but with determination, she fought harder. However, her stressed heart was reaching its limit... it skipped a long beat! Her pulsating organ almost went into an arrhythmic pulsating frenzy or fibrillation!

The Overlord, looking cynically at her, insinuated.

*"My dear Raquel... be mine! ... **This is your last chance.**"*

She felt like falling into a dark well or plummeting inside an endless hole. Her head and chest hurt painfully; the music, the lights, and even Lucif-er began to change. The room became brighter, the fog mobilized and spun around, the sounds reverberated, and finally, Lucif-er started to dissolve!

Inside her mind, Raquel knew the end was near. When her body began trembling, her mind articulated a faint farewell to Gabri-el, and then she was ready to meet her Creator!

"Gabri-el...my darling husband...I will love you forever... Now... my God... please... accept my humble soul... I am..."

She stopped when interrupted by Lucif-er's image shaking her vigorously; he screamed!

*"**Raquel! ... Wait!"***

She barely looked back at the now fading Archangel, who insisted.
"Please, look at my eyes!"
Faintly, she responded, *"... Nooo..."*
He grabbed her by the head and forced her to glance at him. Almost at her last breath, she did look... his eyes were... **green!**
Lucif-er had vanished! Instead, she saw **Gabri-el!**
Her lungs suddenly sucked air, like bringing back her departing soul; life returned before being too late. An incredible rush of well-being and happiness came back to Raquel. Still inside her dream, mimicking reality, she embraced her husband so tight that her ribs made cracking noises. She would have drowned the whole room in tears if she could cry. She thought Lucif-er did not have the most handsome face and physique; Gabri-el did!
The sensual music and blinking lights caught her attention, and they caused her to shake nervously, with an added chilling effect, she stated.
"Lucif-er said: This time, you cannot wake up!"
Gabri-el's comforting presence kissed her on her sweaty forehead and softly murmured into her ear.
*"He... **lied!** There is an exit for this evil trap!"* When she lifted her head to listen better, he added, *"The blinking 'stone' is the key; destroy it, and you will be free!"*
"Please, do it for me! ... I feel so weak!" She graciously asked him; nevertheless, he replied.
*"I cannot! **You must do it yourself!"***
He helped her to the large bedroom's back location, where the diamond-like stone continued sending all kinds of blue sparks.
"I don't have anything to break it," Raquel suggested.
He caressed her silky hair and replied.
*"This is a dream... just think that your hand is made of the most powerful force in the Universe: **Love!** ... Then, hit it, **but hit it hard!"***
Raquel closed her right hand, making a fist; for a moment, she hesitated, but squeezing her teeth with determination, she swung with all her strength to the 'stone'!
The seemingly diamond-hard artifact blew into a million pieces scattering throughout the room. The blast silenced the music, evaporated the fog, and instead of the threatening blue, glowing spectacle inside her bedroom... a pleasant green glow eclipsed all... a green glow... green...

Raquel eyes opened slowly. She stayed lying on the floor, but her head was comfortably on top of his thighs; her husband, sitting on the floor, thrived with caring love. His head leaned forward to examine hers better. His hands caressed her gently, wiping off the copious sweat from her pale face.
The beautiful female felt her whole body aching, but fortunately, the lust had disappeared. However, the pain became nearly unnoticeable

because, with a rush of enormous joy, the sight of her loved one overpowered anything else!

The Overlord kissed her on the lips; she responded avidly. This time, she felt a renewed burning fire encompassing her entire being; it did not hurt or cause anxiety or lust; it was the most comforting, healing, and pleasurable feeling that went beyond her material senses... It was the gift of **Love!**

Greatly enhanced by her unselfishness and sacrifice, it abundantly flourished. Moreover, as it overflowed beyond herself, it interacted with her husband's love to produce a greater love that erased all pain or fear in its perfection.

Their wings intermeshed in a symphony orchestrated by the most noble of feelings. Their glow was angelical... but it was a gift from God!

Raquel moved around and sat on his lap; she crossed her arms behind his back and rubbed her terse and wet facial skin against his. While dropping her eyesight, using a very soft mental message, she said.

"My dear husband... please, forgive me!"

While kissing her on the cheek, he responded.

"I have nothing to forgive you for... It was Lucif-er!"

A rush of anger and a desire to pulverize something emanated from his body. He calmed himself down by asking the almighty God to keep him away from those feelings of hate and violence; instead, he felt immensely grateful to the Lord for allowing him to save his precious wife's life... at the very last instant! The Overlord added to the last sentence.

"He is the only one responsible for all the horror you suffered; you were an innocent victim of the evil he now represents...Nevertheless, how did he become what he is now, a malicious deliverer of evil?"

She returned his kiss by tenderly doing the same on his forehead. The salty taste on her lips made her realize that her husband was hot and sweaty, an extremely rare condition! Looking into his eyes with an affectionate ecstasy, she inquired.

"Were you jogging before coming to my rescue?"

"You could call it... jogging!" He responded with a broad smile.

The apartment's front door slid open!

Through it, Reuben came in running; the entrance room was at a split level with the large bedroom, which had its door open. About halfway from the entrance, he saw Gabri-el and Raquel in a tight embrace through the bedroom's opened door. He immediately made a quick stop and apologized.

"Sir! ... I apologize for intruding! ... I was just concerned for your safety!"

Gabri-el looked kindly at his assistant and pilot and responded.

"We both are thankful for your concern!

Everything is fine now. Please return to the city council and tell them I am taking the rest of the day off; they can proceed without me. I will talk to them tomorrow at 4:00 hours!"

"I am glad everything is OK, Sir! I will notify the council!"

After the entrance door closed behind Reuben, the Archangel glanced into his consort's beautiful eyes while cuddling her with powerful but gentle arms; he proceeded to explain.

*"Lucif-er, the last time we visited his mansion, planted a hypnotic spell in your brain. I still cannot believe the evil that it contained... Indeed... **he planted a vicious evil seed!**"*

****

A few months have passed by. In the Northern Hemisphere, the cold winds of winter started to stream down from the North Pole. The first significant winter storm battered the North Alliance, descending from the Northwest, it slammed head-on over the whole west coastal outline of this Alliance. It brought lots of rain and wind to the shoreline, but blizzard conditions were present for the higher elevations. The existing balmy temperatures in the region quickly plummeted to chilly or freezing conditions.

On the other hand, the South Alliance enjoyed a sunny and warmer-than-usual climate as their summer just started. After a nice rainy spring season, the entire continent displayed a bright green and lush vegetation.

At the capital of Seraphan, Aurel, it was late at night, also cool and windy. Lucif-er's residence remained very quiet; only the armed platoon at the aircraft parking area had half of the troops patrolling the mansion's perimeter. Apparently, everybody else was asleep.

Regardless, on the upper terrace at the edge of the structure, where light and darkness became sharply separated, two dark silhouettes could be seen moving but staying away from the lighted sections.

There were two Overlords; one stepped out of the darkness and became visible... he was Lucif-er.

He pointed a finger at his companion, and the blue glow from his eyes almost revealed the identity of the Overlord staying inside the darkness. With a soft but dominant telepathic message, he pointed out.

"Listen! Let me explain it to you again!

You, moving inside the NA, does not help our cause. On the other hand, inside the SA, your contribution is invaluable!"

The Archangel in the shadow replied.

"It is my desire to actively participate in the NA's front lines and share the glories of its accomplishments!"

Stretching his right hand to the obscured profile inside the darkness, Lucif-er touched his left shoulder; then stated.

*"I promise! You will get... **the glory and the spoils!***

*You must keep a low profile and wait for my signal. When you receive it, you will proceed to sabotage their primary defense system, most likely a dedicated computer system, which Micha-el should know the location. Of course, you want to know what this signal will be... **Operation Code: Sapphire.***"

The shadow moved uneasily after the strong personal message drilled into his mind; he asked with a concerned mental tone.

"There exists the danger that Micha-el or any other SA's Overlord could detect my affiliation with you and blow my cover!"

Lucif-er grinned sarcastically about his associate's concerns. Next, he moved his face closer to the other Archangel so that his head disappeared into the dark shadow. His telepathic voice reverberated deep inside his companion's brain.

"I would not ask you to do this unless I was prepared to conceal your feelings!"

"And how would you do it?"

A gust of cool air moved the surrounding trees; when the wind flapped the dark Overlords' tunics, the clothes mimicked the oscillating arms of giant ghosts or the wings of enormous bats.

The hissing of the fast-moving wind caused the illusion of being much colder.

The stars above shined brighter; the ground below, even with the artificial lighting, resembled a dark, sinister site that the illumination could not dissipate. From the darkness, a mental message could be heard; it was from its new master.

"I have a 'stone' that will help me implant a mental block in your brain that nobody else can penetrate. It is dynamic; as long as it lingers in you, it will grow and become stronger, like artificial intelligence!

It will behave and grow like a seed!"

****

Two days later, the planet woke up early in the morning to a new global broadcast. This time, it came from The Core. The message content stated.

"I, Nobiel, representing The Core's Council, request that all the Overlords of Terra attend a conference.

Your presence is of the utmost importance five days from today; the fate of all the planet's inhabitants is at stake!

We must get together and seriously try our best to solve a conflict that is already out of control: NA><SA.

This confrontation has permeated inside The Core; therefore, drastic measures will be implemented to preserve its neutrality!"

Location : Trillium
Building : The Temple
Time   : 5:00 hours

Note: No weapons will be allowed in the city.

EXODUS: CONFRONTATION

CHAPTER 4

The most spectacular structure on the planet, known as The Temple, was teeming with angels. Not only did the amphitheater become packed beyond capacity, but also the spiraling steps leading to the top of the centrally truncated cone stayed crowded with spectators. Even the streets adjacent to this building became clogged by so many trying to get inside The Temple and not finding any empty spot, even to stand on.

The angels did not know that this could be the most crucial day of their existence. The ultimate war, the one fought inside our spirits, was ready to be unleashed!

Today, all angels had to decide if they stood for Good or for Evil! ... Only a choice, but with repercussions destined to go beyond their lives, the frame of time, and even the entire Universe! ... How frightening and amazing two options become when the consequences of such selection turn out to be **eternal!**

At noontime, the interior of the geodesic dome blazed with sparkling ribbons of white light, which were diffracted a million times, producing rainbows that seemed to be in control of their existence and numbers.

At the theater's center, The Core's Council and all the Overlords had already taken their seats.

The audience fell silent immediately as Nobiel stood up and pointed his hands toward the dome's top. Everyone else stood up. He spoke in a formal but emotional manner.

"Oh, loving God, we ask You to show us how to solve the conflicts affecting our planet. We need You more than ever!

Please... help us!"

As everybody, except the speaker, sat again, he continued.

"My dear friends, we have two critical issues to resolve in this meeting!

First, the conflict between the SA and the NA is getting worse as the years go by. I will request that Micha-el and Magog-el state why a peaceful solution cannot be found.

Second, we will deal with the increasing roles of The Core's Overlords, who appear to have taken sides in this conflict, therefore breaking what should be their commitment to neutrality!"

While pointing his right hand toward the SA's Overlords, he suggested.

"Please, Micha-el, start your opening statement!"

After Nobiel sat, Micha-el sprung out of his seat. He walked toward the center circle, where the three Core's Overlords remained sitting. His solid and firm steps strangely echoed across the amphitheater. When he began his forceful message, he stared at Lucif-er.

"Before I start this debate, I would like to make a correction! ... Since Magog-el is just a puppet, Lucif-er should answer my questions!"

When Magog-el stepped out of his leading NA's chair, the sentence was unfinished. Pointing his index finger at Micha-el, he retorted with powerful overtones.

"Micha-el, watch your tongue!"

The leader of the SA, still looking at Lucif-er, firmly spoke.

"We all know that you are the true leader of the NA; I think it is time for you to come out from hiding and speak for yourself!"

Lucif-er's eyes locked into Micha-el's, and a brief spark could be seen projected forward. His initial deadly serious look quickly changed into a complacent smile. He got up and approached Micha-el, walking across the area. At the same time, Magog-el got a private mental message, *"Just sit; I will take care of Micha-el!"*

Reluctantly, Magog-el turned around and fell hard on his seat; under severe stress, the chair made a mechanical noise resembling a high-frequency moan.

Slowly, almost silently, as a predator would move toward its prey, Lucif-er got closer to the opposing Overlord. When he was only two meters away, he stopped and said, in a deep tone, *"You first!"*

Micha-el started to walk in a large circle around Lucif-er with slow but dynamic steps simulating a needle threading a pattern in a cloth. A few seconds later, looking at the audience, he noticed The Temple's sound reeds giving away strange but impressive soft background music. For a moment, it seemed that the reeds began orchestrating his incoming message. He started his discourse.

"Let me start with this important observation! He spoke. After finishing the sentence, he briefly glanced at Lucif-er. Then, he looked back into the attentively listening large audience and continued, *"The main reason the NA and my Alliance cannot reach any agreement is that the situation is worse than it looks; Lucif-er and the NA have turned away from God!*

They no longer believe in our beloved Lord because their moral and spiritual standards have changed! ... How do you deal with someone who does not respect angelic or divine values!"

Turning sideways, with his loose head hair snapping in the same direction where his face pointed, he again faced Lucif-er. Micha-el asked forcefully.

"Lucif-er... tell us! Why don't you believe in God anymore?"

Lucif-er, after returning a piercing glance to Micha-el, turned his deeper-than-blue eyesight to the audience, who saw a much-mellowed version than Micha-el did. His voice, not loud, had the power to reach everyone present without needing electronic magnification. He equally provided his best smile since he knew that this meeting continued to be televised worldwide.

"Before I make a statement..." his eyes shined brighter than ever and bluer than anyone else could; in addition, against his sparkling white attire, they seemed to have strong hypnotic attributes.

"I am asking all the present, just one question...

Has anyone present... ever seen... or talked to God?"

His loud, challenging request rebounded even in the spiraling stairways. As the seconds passed, Micha-el exclaimed in a deep and absolute silence, **"I have seen the Lord!"**

Lucif-er, still posing for the cameras, partially raised both hands and spoke again, *"Is that the truth? Did you see God... **in a dream? Since when are dreams equal to reality?"***

Micha-el, fighting to control his disgust, explained.

"Our Lord is all perfection; we are not! Therefore, He does not appear to us casually or routinely!

He decides when or where we should see Him. All these appearances have a divine purpose, and He is the only one who knows the complete scheme; we only have minute picks about the outcome.

The Holy Books <u>do</u> mention several instances of personal appearances, plus many more revelations or visions through dreams. I claim I had a similar prophetic dream!"

Lucif-er moved closer to the attending crowd; with a cynical smile, he continued the argument.

*"If that is the case, let us argue about the possibility of a dream I could have... In my sleep, I saw myself as being a god! ... Will you accept this as a reality and worship me? ... **No!***

*The same reasoning applies to Micha-el... Why should we believe him, even if he deceives himself into accepting a dream as a reality? When we know... **it is not possible!"***

His argument ricocheted along the streets surrounding The Temple. The crowd gathered outside had huge holographic screens broadcasting the eventful meeting. Completely immersed in the dialogue, their attention had no viable mental space for any other thought or activity.

Lost in the middle of the vast outside congregation stood an angel from the choir of Principalities, with his black eyes avidly watching and listening to anything that Lucif-er did or said. The day under the blazing noon sun felt hot, but he did not notice; Marcus had the most crucial goal in mind... his life!

Lucif-er continued his extrapolation.

*"Since nobody on the planet has ever seen God... I, Lucif-er, declare that there is... **no God!"***

The declaration shook the entire place. Angels responded with mixed emotions as they inquired about the possibility. Some raised both hands with total approval, while most displayed either shock or anger.

A rising telepathic and vocal rumble filled the building and adjacent areas. Even The Temple seemed astonished by the previously unheard proposition since no sparks or rainbows could be seen inside the building for seven seconds!

Micha-el and all the Archangels from the SA stood up and proclaimed.

"Oh Lord! In the face of such unthinkable heresy, our angelic race implores Your forgiveness!"

Even Lucif-er and the NA's Overlords, who agreed with him, had a mutual consensus when staring at the vast and complex ceiling above and questioning the extremely unusual event of the missing rainbows. They came to the same mental conclusion.

"Incredible! Only a completely destructive interference pattern in a unified time matrix could have possibly caused this to happen!"

The noise inside and outside the structure began to reach a roaring status. Almost everyone stood up. Nobiel, raising both hands, requested silence.

The clamor became a rumor... then quietness. However, tranquility was gone! Everyone, except for Micha-el, Lucif-er, and Nobiel, returned to their seats.

The council leader, showing disbelief all over his face, sought an explanation.

"Lucif-er! ... You are The Core's leading Overlord; please, tell me that what I just heard is not true!"

Lucif-er turned his head to address him. He uttered a harsh and intense response, with an added cynical overtone, that hurt the nearby council leader.

"You heard me... accurately!"

Nobiel slowly took his seat back. Inside, his mind was spiraling out of control, trying to make sense of the unthinkable. His head sluggishly nodded while he placed his left hand over his head and squeezed it in disbelief.

Lucif-er pestered Micha-el with a demanding question.

"Micha-el! ... You believe in God; can you prove to us that He really exists?"

The leader of the NA, internally upset, responded immediately.

"Yes! ... But let me first mention that I am glad we can see you as you are: A conniving individual nobody should trust! ... Why did you take so long to tell us about your radical disbelief of God's existence?"

Unperturbed, Lucif-er lashed back.

"Be nice, my friend! ... Remember that we are 'live' in the International Network! Related to your question... I did not express it earlier because I

was sensitive to the feelings of all people who still think God exists. I did not want to offend their deep-rooted beliefs; however, since you are avoiding my question, how do you expect to prove anything?"

Micha-el paused briefly; then, raising both hands to the still awesome display of light and sound above, he rotated and pointed higher toward the incredible representation of God's Divine Trinity. Then he responded with a smile.

"Lucif-er, are you questioning me about God right here in His Temple?" Is it not enough just to look up to sense His presence?"

Lucif-er, not impressed by the remark, flipped his sparkling white tunic around and mentioned.

"Not to be forgotten; I was the chief architect for its construction! It is just an electronically controlled prismatic display. It is beautiful, but inside, there is no God!"

The Overlord of Seraphan, Lucif-er, raising both hands to the above structure, screamed loud enough to rattle most attendees' minds.

"God! ... If You are here? ... Talk to me!"

The loud voice rattled the building, resonating on many rods and crevices. A strong echo reverberated for three seconds; after that, only the soft and harmonic music from the building could be heard!

With a cynical, wide smile, Lucif-er stated.

"Guess what? I called God... but the only response I got back... was my own voice!"

Micha-el decided to proceed with the proof rather than continue to argue against his opponent's venality. As he walked away from the other Overlord, his adversary focused his sight on Raquel. In a private telepathic message, she not only heard his voice but also saw his piercing blue eyes facing her again!

"You are as beautiful as ever? Why did you sit so far back?"

She turned her pretty face away as fast as she could; regardless, a deep chill began running down her spine. She had dreaded this very thing happening, and sitting in the back section did not help!

Sensing his wife's discomfort, Gabri-el noticed the event; his internal temperature rose by 10° above normal.

Lucif-er must have felt the projected emotion toward his person; he turned quickly and glanced at Gabri-el with an inquiring face while both hands rotated partially away from each other. He questioned without saying anything: What is it?

For a second, Gabri-el showed no response; then, swallowing his anger, he nodded negatively.

Micha-el started his discourse to prove God's existence.[1]

"Certain truths, which exceed the reasoning of our minds, but are necessary for our souls to someday merit to be in the presence of God, can only be made to us by Divine Revelation!"

After a brief pause, Micha-el glanced kindly at the congregation. His words were clear and powerful; he wanted the entire world of Terra to hear and believe. However, this was not a need for him because the truths came up from deep, very deep inside his heart!

"God has proper knowledge of all things, by His own essence. For us, this is not the case since we have only common knowledge.

In our limitations, since Philosophical Science is discovered by reason and Sacred Science is obtained through Revelation, we can discern five proofs of God's existence.

First, we have the argument of motion. Anything that moves needs a mover. The first mover is God, the only One that is not moved by another!

Second, the notion of efficient cause. There is no known case in which a thing is found to be the efficient cause of itself. Because, if that is the case, it would be prior to itself, which is impossible!

Third, we can analyze possibility and necessity. In nature, things are possible to be, or not to be. However, it is impossible for all always to exist. If everything were possible not to be, then at one time, there would be nothing in existence. Therefore, things would have been impossible to begin to exist, and even now, nothing would exist. This is clearly false! ... We must admit the existence of some Being having of itself his own necessity, and not receiving it from another, but rather causing in others their necessity!"

The speaker paused briefly. He knew that most of the people listening in and outside The Temple and in the whole world had already heard these proofs of God's existence in one way or another. This time was unique since the very existence of the Creator was questioned. Therefore, the arguments were heard from a new perspective, like taking a refreshing crash course in theology.

None of the angels present missed a word. Not everyone listening understood everything, and not everyone attending wanted to understand.

"Fourth, graduation is to be found in things. Among objects, there are some more and some less good, the same as among beings... Now, the maximum in any genus is the cause of all in the genus!

Fifth, we observe the governance of things. Objects that lack knowledge, such as natural bodies, aim for an end. And they can achieve this not by chance but by design. Since material things have no knowledge

---

[1] The reasoning used to prove the existence of God, plus the inner essence of an angel, were taken from: Thomas Aquinas: I Encyclopedia Britannica, Great Books of the Western World – 19 Robert M. Hutchins, editor in chief.

or intelligence to move to such an end, an intelligence exists that by whom, all natural things are ordered to their end!"

As soon as the speaker stopped, Lucif-er exclaimed.

"Nice reasoning, but it does not change anything. The basis of all your arguments is what people who believe in God call… faith!

I do not have any; I see no God! … At the beginning of the angels' race, since they did not know anything better, it was natural to accept an omnipotent being as responsible for the creation of everything. It is logical that when our intellect and knowledge develop enough for us to stand on our own, then we reach a point where we do not need any Gods!"

Gabri-el stood up to speak, and the other two arguing Overlords allowed him to do so. Addressing the public, he expressed his opinion in a powerful message.

"Dear citizens, that God exists is not self-evident. For an angel, happiness is inherently desired, and he must instinctively know this. However, this is not the way to know absolutely that God exists!

The existence of truth, in general, is self-evident. The existence of the very First Truth, God, is not self-evident to us. It is impossible for the spirit of an angel in this life to see the essence of God, since the knowledge of God by means of any created likeness, is not the vision of His essence!"

As Gabri-el returned to his seat, Lucif-er spoke again. He chose to ignore Gabri-el's statement, and when he articulated his arguments, they progressively gained pace and intensity.

"People of Terra, I give you one crucial reason why you must believe that there is NO God! … This reason, which I am offering to you, is named **freedom!**

Yes! Freedom from any divine laws to follow, rules that infringe and limit your potential development. These laws were essential for our ancestors to cement and build our society; they served their purpose. Nevertheless, now we have no need for such laws, which are equivalent to superstition… anymore!

*You have the freedom to choose **your own destiny!***

*You have the freedom to be… **your own god!"***

After a brief pause, the audience, not only present but also from across the planet, was challenged to choose; his piercing eyes appeared to find everybody. He concluded.

"Join me! I promise you nothing less than the entire planet and beyond… forever!"

Micha-el, extruding fierce energy, could not wait to speak back.

"Citizens of Terra!

What Lucif-er is offering you… it is an illusion!

Without God… you have nothing!"

All the Overlords and the audience stood up, ready to speak their own. Micha-el and Gabri-el allowed the young-looking Archangel representing

Thronan to take the initiative and talk while Lucif-er gazed with satisfaction at the pandemonium he had created. Dani-el requested that all standing and not being part of the ongoing debate sit and be quiet. When the building returned to normality, he declared vigorously.

"If you choose to follow Lucif-er, you have chosen evil!"

Magog-el jumped forward and belligerently requested.

"What do you mean… evil?"

Dani-el turned around and answered him; his two red wings glowed equally brightly at his head and feet, a sign that the Throne was at his maximum focus on the subject's matter.

*"I said… **evil!** Because if anybody rejects God or any of his laws, he is committing an act of disobedience, a sin! Since sin is equated to evil, in the same manner that good is equated to God, by definition, the opposite of good is evil!"*

The group of God-abiding Overlords mentally agreed with Dani-el. Nevertheless, Magog-el took the stand to address everyone. His blue eyes appeared to have red inside them; it was from an internal fire to dominate anybody antagonizing him. He also addressed the international audience as well as the local. Even as he used a lot of restraint, his voice still sounded like a muffled roar.

"The South Alliance and their sympathizers are always trying to discredit the North Alliance representatives in any feasible way!

*We are… **not evil!***

The NA and I believe in the inner values of the individual. We encourage and nurture the best in each person to achieve their maximum life goals!

As a great nation, we want nothing but to attain the rightful destiny that our great angelic race deserves: First, optimizing the resources of Terra, then colonizing our solar system and beyond!

We have the technology and motivation to accomplish this tremendous task, but first, we need to be free from old taboos and superstitions!"

A family of six avidly watched the large screen mounted on the room's back wall; they were Virtues, all having brown hair and eyes of a similar color. A couple, the parents, hardly different from their four grown-up children, three males, and one female, sat together on a wide chair while their offspring sat individually on more compact fixtures.

One of the sons looked familiar. He was Eugenius, the angel Micha-el saved from the collapsing hill caused by a volcano's lava tunneling. He worked as an assistant for Gabri-el in the central science lab inside the city of Argentan.

He took a vacation to visit his family, who lived in a mid-sized town named Green Valley, so-called after the large plane of grassy rolling hills extending for a hundred square kilometers in the center of the province of Graceland, inside the South Alliance.

Since the international broadcast continued to be delivered, heated arguments ensued between him and the rest of his family. After Magog-el made his last statement, Eugenius insisted on defending his opposite point of view.

"I keep repeating to all of you! What you just heard from Magog-el is a deception! The NA has no intention of telling the truth; they only have one motivation, which is to conquer the whole planet!

Please, you need to believe me when I tell you that Micha-el and the SA have the only correct approach to God and ourselves!"

His father stretched from the sofa, grabbed Eugenius' right knee, and spoke firmly.

"Eugenius! ... Listen to Lucif-er and the NA Overlords; they make sense! How long have we lived? Close to two thousand years? Have you ever talked to or ever seen God?"

Eugenius returned his father's affection by holding his hand and touching his knee using both hands. With great concern, he tried to explain it to his father.

"No! ... But that is not the issue; we must believe in God even if we have never seen Him! And father, after so many years of believing, are you changing your mind so quickly?"

Looking straight at his son, he replied.

"I believed in the old ways because it appeared to be the only option... Now, I am hearing new propositions, which are opening my eyes to a new and different world with new rules and exciting goals!"

He spoke in a way that recollected the NA's arguments against God's reality. His son squeezed harder with both hands and implored.

*"My dear father... please, try harder to understand! We are talking about our future and about eternity! ... And it is **not** the eternity Lucif-er is offering you!"*

"How can you say anything against Lucif-er? After he saved your life!"

"Micha-el saved my life... not Lucif-er!"

Referring to Lucif-er, he glanced at Nobiel and the twelve Core council members, all standing in a tight circle next to their chairs, having a passionate exchange of arguments among them; he knew exactly what the discussion was all about.

After a few minutes of debating, Nobiel turned to face Lucif-er, ready to make a statement. Without allowing Nobiel any time to say anything, Lucif-er, directing his voice for the congregation to hear, exclaimed cynically.

"Our mutual friend, Nobiel, has a very important message for all of us. He wants my resignation as Overlord of Seraphan!

His conscience bothers him; he and all the council members agreed that I have broken The Core's two main rules binding such title!"

He stared so menacingly at the council that they moved backward to reflect their immediate concern. Nobiel did not say a word, so Lucif-er continued.

"Of course, the two main rules are: To serve God, and always be politically neutral!

Listen to me, Core Council, and all inhabitants of Terra!

I am resigning my position and title as Overlord of Seraphan. I have new goals that are much more important to accomplish, and because I cannot be a static observer of my planet's needs due to some ludicrous Core rules, from now on, I am relocating to the NA to a place where I can best serve you all!"

Loud cheering overcame the locality inside and outside the structure; only 10% of the angels inside the auditorium stood up in support, while outside, the noise turned much louder since 30% backed up Lucif-er.

Nobiel pointed to Gabri-el and Dani-el; it was more like a plea than a request, hoping these two Overlords would choose to stay.

Gabri-el felt compassionate toward the leader of The Core's Council, who had been a special friend for a long time. Nevertheless, Gabri-el had **no** other choice.

Loud enough, Gabri-el vocalized his declaration.

"Considering that I cannot be politically neutral because of the present conflict, I, the Overlord of Cheruban, equally renounce my position!

I am joining the SA; to me, this is clearly the only way to serve God and the Truth!"

Almost instantaneously, Dani-el followed Gabri-el's statement nearly word by word!

A new wave of cheering arose from another 30% of the auditorium and half of the outside crowd; this time, the cheering was from Micha-el's supporters.

Far behind the amphitheater, after hearing her beloved husband abdicate his prominent position at The Core's tri-state country, Raquel shook nervously, her face showing extreme apprehension.

A male Cherub seated next to her exclaimed.

"What is happening? Is our world falling apart?"

Nobiel closed his eyes when he felt a strange pain he had never experienced before. He rubbed his forehead with both hands for a few seconds, like trying to erase a bad dream; however, this one was far from being over!

Meanwhile, Micha-el moved quickly to meet the two Overlords who just abdicated their illustrious positions to join the South Alliance. He touched each of them with both hands at chest level, a sign welcoming the Archangels to the SA.

Nobiel raised both hands to calm the chaos ruling the auditorium; it gradually vanished away. With a sad overtone, he made the following remark.

"To all Core's citizens!

No more Overlords rule this country; the council will take control of all governmental duties... starting immediately! Please keep in mind that The Core is a <u>neutral</u> country!"

All the council members took their seats. Micha-el returned to address the congregation; he spoke.

"I need to make two points... They are necessary to understand this situation, which many of you are plunging into without fully comprehending the vast implications attached to this act!"

Micha-el forced himself to appeal to all the listeners. He knew that this moment in the history of Terra was the culmination of the angels' existence! ... The ultimate test!

A choice between a materialist and palpable atheistic reality or an intangible spiritual alternative only accessible by faith!

In an alternate channel inside his mind, Micha-el questioned his own knowledge of such incredible awareness. With no other logical interpretation, since he knew the Lord dwelled in him, he thanked God for allowing him to have the foresight to understand His direction.

When he continued, the delay remained a fraction of a second; hence, nobody noticed anything.

"The motive of pride... is excellence!

For an angel, a desire to be godlike... is <u>not</u> sinful! ... Providing that he desires such likeness in the proper order; by this, I mean that he may obtain such grace from God!

However, he should sin... if he desires to be like God, as of his own!

Accordingly, regarding God, some of us have already chosen to honor or ignore Him!

For the vast majority who are being confronted with making one today, let me tell you that this decision is not related to being convinced by argumentation but solely by the immediate acceptance of the Truth!"

His powerful rhetoric resounded across the building but much deeper across the angels' minds. His loose blond hair seemed to vibrate alongside his words while his well-defined muscles bulged over his interlaced white and green colored tunic. He added one more piece of advice.

"My dear brothers and sisters, I pray to our Lord that you choose Him!

Do not forget, once you are committed, there is __no__ turning back!"[2]

Lucif-er jumped to the center of the barely raised podium and demanded everybody's attention. His mighty appearance and voice did it very quickly.

"Citizens of Terra, do not allow Micha-el to scare you with words; ask for tangible proof!

*I am not trying to confuse you with fancy words; just consider that what I am offering, you can see, touch... and **be!***

If you are not already part of the great North Alliance, this is your opportunity for freedom!

I will give you ten days to pack and move North to our eminent and prosperous country, where you will become much more than whatever you are now!

*Let us show Micha-el and the SA what we consider to be true. We do not want our future restricted by ancient beliefs acting like binding chains! Anybody who is or wants to be part of the NA... **stand and raise your hands!"***

The roar that followed was deafening. Inside The Temple, outside, and in many places over the entire planet, the angels who believed and trusted Lucif-er stood up. He smiled with sinister satisfaction.

Yet, right in the middle of his celebration, he stopped his malevolent smirk; anybody close enough could hear the creepy cracking noise generated by his teeth being ground against each other. Even when facing the opposite direction, he knew that for his ideological support, one of the NA's Overlords... **did not stand up!**

Slowly, he turned around; his piercing blue eyes glowed as two powerful lasers ready to vaporize whatever he could focus on.

Izma-el, the Overlord of the NA's SW sector... remained seated!

He faced the invisible fire emanating from his foremost boss. With a concerned but determined message, Izma-el expressed his dissent.

"I apologize for letting you down at this moment, but my belief in God has precedence over anything else!"

Raising his voice, he added.

"I made my choice! Since I cannot stay in the NA under the present conditions... I will resign as the SW Sector's Overlord and relocate to the SA!"

Lucif-er disguised his furor and promptly tried to salvage the situation. He made the following remarks with a friendly smile while facing the network broadcasting cameras and ignoring Izma-el's presence.

---

[2] Micha-el's last statement is valid because the angels in Terra will remain sinful once they embrace evil. The same would have applied to humans if Jesus had not paid the Father for our immoral debt.

"Izma-el, if you cannot get rid of a deeply rooted belief of a divine being that you need for your emotional and moral support, we from the NA do encourage you to leave!

Contrary to what you frequently hear from the SA about oppressing our people, we are just the opposite. To prove it... I will allow anyone from the NA who still believes in God to freely move out of the Alliance to any place of their choice!

Do we hear the SA making a similar pledge?"

While Izma-el received many personal congratulations from the SA's Overlords, he also received some fierce private messages from the NA's Overlords, labeling him as a repugnant traitor.

Micha-el's candid walk quickly placed him next to Lucif-er, but he spoke to the whole planet instead of addressing him.

"I promise that I will let anyone who chooses to join The Core or the NA have the freedom to leave the SA.

In addition, they are welcome to take all their possessions with them!"

Nobiel, who remained standing but leaning against his chair as in need of support, took the word.

"As I currently represent The Core, I also make a similar pledge! ... Any citizen of this country who cannot remain neutral as the law of the land requires can move to the Alliance of their choice!"

This was the last link of the chain; it completed the highway for a global event named... **Exodus!**

The stage was set for the angels to choose and for the ones living in the wrong place to have the opportunity to move to the country of their choice.

Two hours later, Nobiel stood at the podium's center; he looked so tired that he even appeared to have aged, raising his hands to the distant ceiling for the session's closing, usually done with everybody standing. This time, a substantial number of angels remained seated!

He loudly proclaimed.

"We beg our Lord for forgiveness!

We called this meeting to erase our differences. Instead... we had plunged into a darkness never seen before!

What has been my worst nightmare... today... after what I saw and heard, it became a reality!

Go, my brothers and sisters... do whatever you have to do. We, The Core... will continue serving God, not with violence, only with the peacefulness of neutrality!"

Gabri-el was on his way out of the podium, moving into the central stairway, when Nobiel came almost running to intercept him. The

Archangel sensed his approach and stopped, allowing him to catch up. The council leader requested.

"Gabri-el, I need to talk to you!"

One of the Overlords, who had just relinquished his title and was in a hurry to intercept Lucif-er before he exited the auditorium, knew what Nobiel wanted to discuss. So, for an instant, he felt like postponing the talk to another time; however, he also sensed the painful urgency that Nobiel had placed with his request to communicate with him; thus, he yielded in his favor.

"I was in a hurry, but I will gladly discuss those issues that are seriously disturbing you!"

Nobiel, still uneasy after the meeting, touched Gabri-el's left shoulder and expressed the following.

"Thank you, Gabri-el... I wanted to go with you and Dani-el to the SA, but The Core desperately needs leadership. If I also left, I am afraid my country would sink into despair, and the consequent confusion could harm our citizens!

I need your help! Since the Council is now controlling its government, I need your advice on what is best for The Core. You know better than I that our commitment is for neutrality, and since the conflict between the NA and the SA may spill over the borders, I am concerned; rather... I am scared!"

Gabri-el grabbed both of his friend's shoulders and explained.

"My dear friend! ... Do not let fear distort the difficulties we are presently enduring. Otherwise, fear will lead you into panic and into a situation where there is no hope!

Instead, fill your heart with hope; it is the antidote to fear! You know that God is on your side and that He loves you! He will not let you down!

Let me add that there are many ways to serve the Lord; staying at The Core may be just what He wants you to do!"

Gabri-el walked his companion to the nearby exit, he added.

"Since this will take a few hours, let's go to your office. Furthermore, I must transfer many of my operating files to your computer system. I did have several important issues to take care of... but they can wait!"

At Green Valley, the large viewing screen was now turned off. Inside the spacious living room, five angels stood facing one individual... Eugenius.

With her eyes wet from the stress, his mother pleaded with him.

"My dear son, you must come north with us! We are a family; you cannot stay here alone while the rest of us move to the NA!"

Eugenius' heartbeat remained painful. He felt like a sharp object had been thrust inside this vital organ. Distorted by emotional pain, his face became wrinkled at several locations; he pleaded with his parents and siblings.

"You have no idea how much your decision is hurting me! It is not because we are separating, but because I know without any doubt that God, Micha-el, and the SA are the only realistic choices!

Please... for many years, I worked for Gabri-el and Micha-el... I trust them! ... Lucif-er used to be like them, but he has changed! ... Don't listen to him; he will instigate you to oppose our loving God!"

His father grabbed his hand and exclaimed.

"Come with us, son! We understand you have some attachments to the Overlords with whom you worked so long, yet we just heard Lucif-er, and what he said does make sense! ... Do not break your mother's heart by staying behind... get ready, and we will all depart together!"

As his father talked, he pulled Eugenius' hand toward him. Eugenius resisted, then, in an action that ripped his inside apart, he separated by backing up. From his trembling lips, he said something that sounded like a voice coming from somebody else's mouth, and these words became instantly written in blood across the gray matter of his brain.

"You go... I stay!"

Inside his mind, Eugenius cried to himself.

"Dear God... are You asking too much out of me?"

On the same day at nighttime, in the same city inside The Core.

Sitting on a comfortable chair, Lucif-er had Magog-el seated at his right side and Gorgon-el to his left. Facing them were five additional chairs: four occupied, one empty!

The spacious and modernistically decorated room where the meeting occurred had a huge window with a breathtaking view of Trillium. The downtown area occupied the center view, but The Temple, with its radiant light display, could not be ignored. Since it remained a clear night, all the buildings could be seen in their entire splendor; however, the movement of numerous flying cylinders did interfere with the bright emerald background shine of the towering structures.

The leader of the NA had his sight on the empty chair. Suddenly, he walked less than a meter away from it and burst into fierce anger.

*"Everything was going precisely as planned! Until... **this idiot screwed it up!**"*

Faster than the eye can see, he kicked the chair! He did it so hard that the front became pulverized and sent a multitude of small fragments toward the back wall. Only a large section survived but broke apart after crashing against the sturdy wall.

A loud cracking noise briefly reverberated across the enclosed space. When all returned to rest, a light dusty cloud slowly and reluctantly settled down. Lucif-er continued the angry telepathic exchange.

"He chose the location for his treacherous deed very well indeed! If Izma-el would have said that in any other place... I would have killed him!"

Magog-el, still seated, snapped with anger.

"It is not too late; we still could rectify... that!"

Lucif-er, playing with his long, wild, and spectacular golden blond hair, remarked, *"At this time, with the whole world watching us... it is not a good idea!"*

Moving uneasily in his chair and avoiding looking directly into the eyes of Lucif-er, Azami-el questioned.

"My concern is about security! ... Izma-el, that piece of garbage leaving our Alliance, did he compromise any of our top projects or secret information?"

Magog-el answered back.

"Nothing important; he never got involved in any depth into the top projects, only in manufacturing conventional weapons, aircraft, and defense equipment!"

"At least he is not taking anything that could hurt us with him," added Lucif-er. Then, lightly squeezing his front teeth, he emphasized, *"And by the way... when Izma-el leaves... the only possessions that he will take out of the NA are the clothes he will be wearing! As of this moment, all his possessions belong to the SW sector! Furthermore, anybody moving to the SA will relinquish everything they own!"*

Following this rowdy statement, Gorgon-el immediately inquired.

"Did Micha-el promise that the SA citizens moving to the NA could take all their possessions with them?"

Lucif-er did not look at him; instead, he stared at the space previously occupied by a chair, retorting in a malevolent tone.

"You said it correctly... Micha-el promised, I did not!"

With a twisted smile, Magog-el nodded in agreement; he mentioned.

"It is an excellent idea! It will discourage many from leaving!"

A 'ding' sound implied that someone was requesting access to this huge room, but the Overlords ignored it. The doorbell-like device emitted its peculiar sound a second time.

Lucif-er, somehow annoyed, pointed to the entrance; the door slid open. Standing outside was Kragen, the platoon leader, this time unarmed; he apologetically exclaimed.

"Sir! ... I apologize for interrupting! This individual at the front door insists on seeing you personally. Should I send him away!"

"He did mention that his name was Marcus!" Lucif-er alluded.

After a brief pause, he also recalled, *"One of the angels rescued by Gabri-el and Rapha-el during the earthquake at Lemar... Send him in!"*

Only a minute later, a shy individual with his black hair messed up by the wind stood at the entrance. The piercing stare of so many Overlords intimidated him; for a moment, he wanted to do a U-turn with an 'I will see you later' retreat. However, when he saw Lucif-er's welcoming eyes, hypnotically pulling him inside, he quenched this feeling.

Lucif-er moved his open right-hand fingers in a slow inside bending motion. At the same time, he insinuated with a soft voice.

"Come! ... Here, next to me."

Marcus advanced with shaky steps. Slowly moving, he took his time facing the NA's leader; he did not dare look up at him. Lucif-er calmly said in a soft voice, *"Take a seat."*

The angel of the Principality choir looked around, and when he could not find a place to sit, he decided to do it... on the floor!

Lucif-er smiled; he showed him his chair and commanded him.

"Take mine!"

Marcus felt very uncomfortable, and his voice could barely be heard when he talked.

"Great Overlord Lucif-er... I cannot do such a thing!"

The most powerful Archangel on Terra guided him to his chair and remarked.

"Nonsense! Just do it!"

The top three Overlords, all Seraphim, Magog-el, Gorgon-el, and Azami-el, jointly glanced at Lucif-er and mentally exclaimed.

"You wouldn't do it... here, at The Core!"

The other three lesser Overlords, picking at his boss' direction, tried to guess, "What is Lucif-er up to?"

Marcus sat nervously on Lucif-er's chair, erratically moving his head. The Archangel, who wore a shiny white tunic, moved behind Marcus and began explaining.

"Marcus came from the SA with one specific reason: to find somebody to cure the DNA Syndrome sickness that afflicts him. Nobody in the SA can help him anymore. Furthermore, he has embraced our beliefs after hearing me talking at the Temple."

The angel being referred to quickly nodded in approval. With a devilish grin occulted from Marcus, with a deeper tone of voice, he noted.

"He thinks I am the last Overlord capable of helping him. How lucky can he be? ... Today, I am in the mood for healing!"

Lucif-er bent over sideways, so Marcus could see his well-formed face; then, he spoke.

"For your anxieties and suffering...I promise, today is the last day!"

Marcus' face came alive with joy; he had been accurate on Lucif-er's powers. When seeing Sergius again, he became excited about the prospect of telling him about his incoming miraculous cure, which brings back hope and life again. Now, freed from the claws of death, he could live forever as any other average angel did. His last words were.

"Great Overlord; please, I cannot wait!"

Maybe it was better that he couldn't see the sinister smile on Lucif-er's face, who currently stood behind him and placed four fingers on Marcus' left cranial side with his thumb on his neck; he equally pressed with his right hand's fingers on the opposite side.

A blue glow grew from Lucif-er's fingers.

Marcus envisioned being in paradise, devoid of pain, anxieties, and problems. Only joy, pleasures, a... n... d...

The sinister vision of something crawling inside his head scared him.

He tried to run, but by immobilizing him, the black tentacles taking over his mind prevented it; they were also squeezing his life away. Marcus screamed, but it could only be heard inside his mind.

"Please, let me go! ... Nooo... help..."

The invading mental monster destroyed all activities in his brain. A sudden pain shook his entire body, and no more thoughts could be created.

Everything faded into numbness... then darkness... and finally, **emptiness!**

Marcus took a shallow breath, shook once, and lay utterly motionless...
He was dead!

Magog-el looked at the event undisturbed, with no feeling displayed.

Gorgon-el looked the other way: 'I didn't see anything attitude.'

Azami-el smiled; his eyes sparkled with hidden pleasure as he had killed Marcus!

The other three Overlords stared for an instant; they remained incredulous at what happened before them.

Lucif-er released the lifeless head of an angel previously named Marcus.

Like coming out of a trance, Lucif-er concentrated his sight upon his ten fingers. He placed all five fingers from his left hand apart; by just barely touching the tips of the opposite hand's similar fingers, he made a triangular tent at about 45° from the horizontal plane. Next, in a slow rotating motion, he touched his lips with his index fingers. He disclosed his rarely heard inner thoughts with a profound but chilling telepathic statement.

*"When we have at the tips of our fingers... **life or death**; it is when we truly realize... **that we are called to be gods.**"*

After a few seconds of undivided attention from his companions, he went on, *"I provided him with a quick exit from his suffering. I am glad that in a few years, our angelic race should end the generic cleansing of the only chromosomal defect still affecting us... When the last abnormal DNA individual dies, we will bear testimony... **of evolution at its best!**"*

His keen sixth sense and hearing notified him of something unexpected. With a sign of alertness, he raised his right hand and communicated with the rest.

"We have a visitor," he quickly mentioned.

The first imperceptible steps soon approached the sliding entrance as a fast-moving individual arrived at the door.

The sliding door entrance made a weird mechanical noise as its internal security locking mechanism became overridden and forced to open.

Lucif-er welcomed the intruder.

"Gabri-el! It is nice of you to come around! Have you changed your mind and decided to join us? By the way, what happened to your refined good manners?"

The incoming Overlord looked at the inert body sitting on Lucif-er's chair. His heart cried with pain at the sight of the departed angel whom he had saved his life. His stare changed to the standing Archangel; he felt anger invading his whole body; with almost fire extruding from his mental words, he uttered.

"I was coming to complain about the evil you imposed upon my wife! However, I can see that you are much worse than I thought! ... You killed Marcus!"

"Lucif-er, undisturbed, responded.

"Calm down, my friend; I just granted him... a wish!"

"Don't lie to me, Lucif-er! I heard his scream as it dispersed along the building's walls on their way to the ground... I heard him begging for help! ... I know that a defenseless Marcus asked you for life... and you gave him... death!"

The leader of the NA lost his smile, and his eyes started to intensify the deep blue in them. Once more, he denied any wrongdoing.

"Since he was dying anyway, and Marcus was in agony, I just removed his pain! I saved him from years of suffering, I just..."

Gabri-el interrupted; he toned down his outrage when he said.

"I loved this unfortunate angel; his pain was mine! ... You destroyed him! You... who were a close friend... even more... a brother! Now I see you, but I don't recognize the person I have known before! ... You have become some alien being! Alien and evil; I..."

This time Lucif-er interrupted.

"Stop! I am not in the mood to listen to this nonsense!"

As he sent this telepathic message, his eyes focused on Gabri-el's garments, specifically, the cross displayed over his heart. Gabri-el felt the temperature of the cross-image rising fast to hundreds of degrees! ... He quickly moved sideways to dissipate the heat; otherwise, his garments would have burst into flames. As it happened, only a faint smoke came out of his clothing.

All the seated Overlords got up, intending to encircle Gabri-el!

Lucif-er threatened him.

"I advise you to leave... while you still can!"

Suddenly, Gabri-el realized the precarious situation he was immersed in but still managed to glance at Marcus' limp body. Lucif-er noted his concern, and picking up the dead angel by the neck, he threw the body at Gabri-el as if Marcus were weightless! Then, he shouted.

"You want him; he is all yours!"

Gabri-el grabbed Marcus, who was still warm, and held him tightly against his body; if he had been here just a few minutes earlier, Marcus could have been alive.

Carrying Marcus' body, Gabri-el quickly walked out of the room and out of the building.

Lucif-er sat on his chair again, and the other Overlords did likewise. He stared at Azami-el and commanded, using a softer tone.

"I want you to set up three platoons and name them A, B, and C. Use your best-qualified Seraphim for this job. They will infiltrate the SA using the Exodus.

One of the teams, platoon A, must be trained explicitly so we can get rid of Micha-el... The second should eliminate Gabri-el... the third, just on standby; their overt mission is concealed until we assign them a target, perhaps Izma-el!"

"Consider it done!" Azami-el responded.

There are many shades of gray between white and black. God is light, and we see Him as being whiter than white, the color that encompasses all the colors of the light spectrum.

Evil, being the antagonistic opposite, is darkness. While black is the absence of all colors in the same light spectrum, Evil is darker than black because it claims even the exclusion of God.

Is it possible to be in a shade of gray and still be with God? Or vice versa, being with Evil?

Very few humans are genuinely holy or saints, and very few are truly evil or satanic! Because most humans live in a twilight zone where multiple shades of grey exist, we sit at some specific shade and rationalize our actions into believing we are pure white or black.

Regardless of what we deceive ourselves to believe and accept, there are **no** shades of gray in the end!

This was the case for all the angels living on Terra.

You chose God, or you chose against Him!

Are we going to be judged by the same standards?

****

Exodus! Two-way Exodus! NA><SA Also: NA<The Core>SA.

The giant ripple caused by one Choice uprooted millions of angels as they migrated from their native places to new locations. Many split their families by doing so, equally abandoning thousand-year-old friends and experiencing the pain of saying goodbye to places called 'home,' the same place they had claimed... never to leave!

Convoys of flying cylinders going one way dotted the sky; at other places, many could be seen going in the opposite direction. Great concerns and anxieties became stirred; the souls of many had been awakened, for good or evil.

In Inyx, the capital of the SW Sector of the NA, Izma-el was giving his farewell speech to the inhabitants of his sector. Millions had decided to depart with him; nonetheless, millions who agreed with him decided to stay since they could not stand the threat of losing all their belongings.

Perhaps their will was borderline, a shade of gray that shifted to black only because they could not commit and were unwilling to accept sacrifice. Now, what they could see and touch became more important than God and His commandments. It was like a short-term investment: narrow-minded and without concern for the future.

You could almost hear Lucif-er proclaiming.

"Collect now; you are already a winner! Choose God who probably doesn't exist, and after all your sacrifices, you will get zero, nothing!"

We know what happens to businesses and companies with only short-term profit marketing. For a short time, they enjoy significant profits, but in the long term, they crash and vanish!

At the city airport, the angels present had never seen anything alike; the crowd was immense, the number of cylinders on the departing strips enormous.

There were mixed feelings about the departure of the Sector's Overlord; many came to watch, others were departing, and some stayed angrily yelling at Izma-el.

"Traitor! ... You sold out to the enemy! ... What are you waiting for? ... Go away!"

A raised section commonly used for boarding was presently improvised as a podium. Magog-el climbed the ramp to its top surface, immediately raising both hands and requesting silence. The crow calmed down and became silent.

Many angels stood at this higher section or podium, but only one stood alone, Izma-el. He did not wear his NA uniform anymore because his fancy blue and white striped official attire was gone; instead, he only had a plain gray tunic with skin-tight pants underneath.

Magog-el wore his shiny blue and white interlaced uniform. He had now assumed control of the SW Sector. At his command, two whole platoons of his military escort fanned outwards behind Izma-el. The soldiers told the multitude at the location.

"Move back ten meters! Clear the front!"

As the area was cleared of angels, except Izma-el, they lined up behind the Overlord and stood in attention. Magog-el stared at the Archangel facing him; then, he publicly communicated with him with a cynical smile.

"You are stupid!

Here, you had the power and all that goes along with it! ... Now, look at you! All that you owned is gone! Do you think the SA is giving you back all your losses? Or perhaps... your chosen God will do some magic and restore your possessions?"

Magog-el chuckled several times, then, wiping out any smile from his face, he sharply ordered.

"Get out of my face! If Lucif-er had not allowed your departure, I would have killed you! ... Right here! In front of everybody!"

Inside Magog-el mind, he simultaneously replayed <u>why</u> he could not kill Izma-el at this time, as Lucif-er had explained to him.

"Listen, Magog-el, I agree with killing him! But if we do it now, as he departs from the NA, it will seriously damage our publicity. We could lose millions of new members when they ask themselves: If a powerful Overlord is killed when he rejects the NA and tries to depart, what can <u>we</u> expect from this Alliance if we move there? The average angel does not appear to us as being very smart, but they can figure out what happened if we do it!"

Coinciding with his following command to start the departing exodus, he lowered his anger and ordered while pointing to a nearby aircraft.

"Get out of my sight, leave!"

For two seconds, Izma-el stared back at his previous boss. Next, as he glanced at the enormous congregation of angels, he started walking slowly but forcefully. When he approached the downward ramp, his sight returned to Magog-el, who stood by himself before the podium. Izma-el sent him a departing message.

"I feel pity for all the North Alliance and their Overlords! ... You have given up <u>so much</u> in return for <u>so little</u>! ... I am leaving with only the clothes I am wearing, but what I am taking with me, in my heart, is immensely more valuable than anything you could ever own!"

When Magog-el showed his clenched teeth and became angry enough to kill Izma-el, only the mental image of his boss reminded him to let the renegade Overlord go. Not ready to listen to what he considered insults, the former leader of the NA turned his anger away by focusing his sight and hearing somewhere else.

Izma-el moved down and away from the podium. As the Archangel continued walking, the ocean of departing angels parted, allowing him to reach the first massive aircraft. This enormous vehicle led a column of ten transport vehicles capable of flying one thousand passengers in one trip.

Only one hundred meters apart and at both sides, other columns of ten cylinders continued boarding departing angels. Then, beyond that, more columns... extending as far as it could be seen!

When Izma-el reached the entrance of his assigned transport cylinder, which displayed the NA colors with the hull painted with a light blue color and a horizontally centered narrow white stripe, he waved goodbye to his previous sector's citizens and went inside the craft.

Soon, the sliding door of the leading craft closed; the nine flying machines behind followed suit, all waiting for the Ex-Overlord to board as a sign of departure.

One minute later, Magog-el raised one hand, the assigned command for the pilots to take off.

The leading column of ten aircraft lifted from the ground. As they ascended into the sky, they positioned so the cluster looked like a migratory wing of flying birds, except the leading was done with two crafts instead of only one bird as usually seen in their 'V' flying formation.

When the first wing reached three hundred meters high facing south, it sped away. The second wing or column did the same, and the remaining columns of cylinders took their turns.

The initial humming and ground vibration increased as two hundred large transport cylinders moved to the skies. Wing after wing kept adding to the noon blue skies, and their large shadows could be seen moving over the ground. Meanwhile, the sky became crowded with 'V' formations that diminished in size as they moved farther away.

The powerful superconducting engines caused an electromagnetic storm on the ground, with shockwaves rippling the iron reach dust of the region; even larger rocks became affected. The noise was not overbearing but certainly annoying.

It did not take too long… soon, all that remained of the flying cylinders was a bluish cloud vanishing at the far horizon.

Inyx, the SW Sector capital, had just lost 200,000 inhabitants. Many more continued anxiously waiting their turn while sweat ran down their heads. They stayed packed as sardines in long and multiple lines, as they had to wait one long Terra's hour; only then would the next scheduled departure fill the empty spaces vacated by the aircraft now gone. None of the waiting had any luggage.

The blazing sun continued baking the land, making it a scorching day, unusual since it was the beginning of winter. However, with the parting of its best citizens, the bright light emanating from the sky could not dissipate the increasing moral darkness slithering inside the city.

NA, CD, Centrum.
The next day, at some secluded area not far from the city.

Lucif-er and Azami-el walked together, closely inspecting three NA platoons; all members of each unit were Seraphim. Azami-el pointed out the following statement.

"These are the A, B, and C teams you requested; they are our best. The C-1 platoon leader is our number one soldier with superior weapons and explosives expertise!"

Lucif-er approached the A-1 soldier, a platoon leader, then stood squarely in front of him and stared him down. The military Seraph, avoiding Lucif-er's piercing eyes, only gave away a minute sign of uneasiness; nevertheless, he felt his brain's contents being emptied. He again breathed normally when Lucif-er moved to face B-1, the next platoon leader.

After two seconds, this soldier blinked and lowered his eyesight; he became noticeably disturbed.

Finally, the Overlord faced the last platoon leader, C-1. Compared to this individual's strongly defined gaze, Lucif-er's eyes appeared as bright as lanterns.

The Seraph did sustain the Overlord's stare for three seconds, even when such achievement required most of his bodily resources.

When Lucif-er released his scrutiny, C-1 felt drained but relieved. The Overlord placed his right hand on his shoulder and spoke mentally.

"Dagon... I am very pleased with your abilities and your competent knowledge of weapons! I also know you are an extremely accurate shooter, up to five kilometers. That is great, but it is only marginal for what we need; you must do better to avoid an Overlord's danger-detecting range.

*Therefore, you need to double this distance, and for this assignment, missing the target is **not** an option! ... However, we need to finish the development of a new 10K sniper rifle with a high-power laser/plasma envelope. This weapon will have to be specially stabilized for accuracy and rapid fire; it shall also be uniquely designed to avoid satellite detection using advanced AI detection...Unfortunately, the weapon is not ready yet! But when completed, we will find a way to deliver it to you."*

The Archangel moved away from C-1 and faced all thirty soldiers, he added in a louder telepathic communication.

"I will be asking a lot from all of you! But if you perform the assigned tasks, the rewards will exceed your expectations!

No more names will be used; you will be addressed using your platoon's codes. Since you know this is a high-risk operation, do you have any concerns or questions about this mission?"

Lucif-er knew who was to answer first; the soldier did not disappoint him.

"No, Sir! I will do my best to serve you and the NA!" Dagon speedily replied. The other two platoon leaders sounded off shortly afterward.

"Sir! We will do likewise!"

Lucif-er looked one more time over the whole group and remained satisfied, so he ordered.

"Report to headquarters!"

As the soldiers marched away, Azami-el approached Lucif-er and commented.

"Since you did not tell Dagon that a prototype of the super-gun is already operational, I assume you want to surprise him!"

The leading Overlord barely moved his head affirmatively and added to his subordinate's statement.

"Unfortunately, only the prototype is operational. You know that there is no time to manufacture similar weapons. For this reason, I will give it to Dagon; however, it will be especially packed and with a label demanding: 'Do not open until you are ordered to do it!'... You can imagine how pleased he will be when he finds out about this weapon!"

Azami-el, with an evil intent, smiled before he proceeded to inform his boss about the operation.

"I wanted this gun to be mine... the long-range hunting could be spectacular!" After expressing his feelings, he continued his dialogue.

"Returning to the operation details, the troops will wear unique clothing with internal air conditioning to prevent IR detection and nu-metal shielding to block electromagnetic detection. All the uniforms required are ready to use.

In addition, the Exodus transport, modified to hide the three platoons infiltrating the SA, will be fully refurbished tonight.

I arranged for one group of transport crafts to fly low into Dawnel while another group departs from the city but is flying above. The interference will prevent the detection of the parachuting teams... I will set up this scenario for tomorrow at midnight!"

Lucif-er glanced to the nearby hills that partially hid the military complex, then he noted.

"No! Do it the next day... at noon!"

Azami-el understood immediately. The satellite IR detection did not work when the sun was at its zenith. With a self-satisfying smile, he thought, "Also, at noon, it will be less expected!"

Micha-el was supervising the arrival of 100 aircraft from the NA. The airport of Dawnel remained crowded and in turmoil as many thousands were arriving and many thousands equally departing. The logistics of the redistribution of so many angels moving from one country to another turned into a nightmare!

Most immigrants came to the big cities, some to the small towns across the provinces, and all had to be briefed for security reasons; at least, the lack of personal possessions positively impacted the initial inspection.

The hot air produced by the summer afternoon produced thermal updraft breezes, which stirred the Overlord's curly hair from his face, thus revealing his deep concern for his province's departing citizens.

What could he have done to prevent so many from choosing Darkness over the Light?

Every single one moving to the departure line broke his heart. He knew that his Lord was painfully looking at the angels He loved but now had chosen to reject Him!

Micha-el stood at the top of the airport's building where some sections were used as landing sites; however, the place remained as a military-restricted section. He stayed beside a rail overlooking the vast space reserved for the airport's activity.

An aerodynamic craft, a new military version more streamlined than the average cylinders, flew to a landing site only thirty meters from the Overlord's location. The military vehicle displayed the SA colors, a silvery body with its pointed nose as a green cone and with the stabilizing wings and tails equally painted green.

As soon as the craft landed, even before their escorts could stand at the exiting doors, two Overlords got out, Lari-el and Zeri-el; both briskly walked to meet Micha-el.

He greeted using one open hand for the other two Archangels' right hands. He welcomed them telepathically.

"Greetings, my brothers! I requested your presence because I need to inform you about a resolution I took related to the Bird Island country.

The NA suggested splitting the islands into two parts to avoid unnecessary bloodshed. The two northern islands will join the NA, and the two southern the SA. By this action, we should also implement the Exodus in the country. Their troops and the citizens of the islands that agree with them will migrate to the northern section. We are expected to do a similar move to the southern islands!"

Zeri-el became disturbed by the news, and he quickly replied.

"Micha-el! We cannot do this; we will give half of the country to the NA! ... Furthermore, we have promised the citizens of Bird Islands that we would never abandon them!"

Zeri-el, while speaking, articulately moved his left hand.

Micha-el grabbed his hand in a friendly way and exclaimed.

"My brother! ... I know!

Analyze the situation; the island will be devastated if we engage in a bloody war! The ones who will suffer the most will be their citizens. In addition, with the Exodus now in progress, everything has changed. It is no longer NA versus SA but something much bigger: Evil versus Good!"

"Did Samu-el and Rapha-el agree with this radical decision? What about you, Lari-el?" Zeri-el questioned.

Micha-el waited for Lari-el to express his concerned opinion; this Overlord looked down when giving his opinion.

"I oversee the island's operation, and I feel as if I will be abandoning half of the country to the NA, but as much it hurts to accept, Micha-el is

correct! ... We have enough soldiers and weapons on the islands between the NA and us to make them a wasteland! ... I care for the unfortunate residents... I don't want them dead!"

Micha-el replied immediately.

"Rapha-el and Samu-el did agree with my decision!

Lari-el, I know this is a challenging and busy time, but in addition to the Tellia Province, you must supervise the Bird Island Exodus."

Lari-el nodded with approval. Zeri-el, still looking disappointed, relinquished and added.

"OK, Micha-el! Make it unanimous! ... Would you please excuse me now? I am losing a substantial percentage of my population, and I am returning to Zarinia to find out why."

This time, the two recently arriving Overlords each boarded their own aircraft and soon soared into the crowded skies above Dawnel; however, one went east, the other west.

Alone again, Micha-el returned to watch the multitude climbing into the large transports; the induced sadness returned to hunt him.

He stared at a vast line moving inside a nearby craft. In the massive conglomerate of angels, someone appeared to be familiar... He froze! The one just being recognized was his personal assistant and friend... Arkyn!

The Throne supervising the boarding at location C-16 heard a powerful electronic command coming from the airport's roof.

"C-16! Stop the boarding! This is Micha-el; I will be there in one minute!"

Startled, the angel gazed around, looking for Micha-el; he could not see him, but he stopped the line boarding the large cylinder. Two of his nearby assistants, also Thrones, mentally inquired.

"Sir! Why is the boarding stopped?"

He made a manual sign to calm them down and sent a quick explanation.

"Micha-el, the Overlord, he is coming!"

The assistants glanced around, looking for the Overlord. A moment later, one of them pointed to a fast-moving individual approaching from the massive airport building.

Arkyn, a Seraph with a neat hairstyle, was part of this stagnant, long single line when a mighty and friendly hand touched him on his back. Before turning back to identify the person, he instinctively knew from whom the touch came, which caused a deep chill to run down his spine.

An individual dressed in a shiny green jumpsuit with an interlaced green-white belt, the standard golden buckle, and a pure white or silvery cross imprinted on the cloth over his heart was facing Arkin. In front of him stood the dynamic Overlord in charge of the SA.

The departing Seraph's heart almost stopped when he faced his boss; he felt guilty abandoning his job, so he tried to leave inconspicuously and silently by taking advantage of Micha-el's extremely busy and mostly being away from Dawnel.

Even when he could anticipate the answer, the Archangel mentally talked first.

"My dear friend, why are you leaving?"

The Seraph lowered his eyes to avoid direct contact with Micha-el's. In a somber tone, he replied.

"Sir! ... Forgive me for leaving! ... It is not because you haven't been good to me; on the contrary, you are a great Overlord who has always been concerned about my well-being! ... Nevertheless, after I listened to the NA's appeal... I decided it is the way I want to live!"

"What you heard is not true, only an illusion! ... Arkyn, please... stay! Do you know what is at stake? I am referring to your spirit and eternity! You must avoid being on the wrong side!"

The Seraph swallowed once; he briefly glanced at Micha-el and spoke.

"Sir! ... I know what you are saying; however, when we can live forever, we have little need to worry about our spirits. I like the idea of choosing our own destinies!"

Micha-el shook his head; how insidious were the tentacle of evil, who so easily stole the souls of so many angels! **And how willingly their victims relinquish such a vast divine gift!**

Sadly, the Overlord made his last testimonial message.

"I can assure you one fact... <u>nobody</u> on this planet will live forever!"

The Core, Cheruban, Argentan.

The next day, around mid-morning.

Next to his personal craft, Dani-el stood with Raquel close to his left side; his two pilots stayed guarding both sides of the machine's fully opened sliding door. The council's leader faced the married couple, who stood only two steps before him.

They were not at the airport or some landing site on top of a skyscraper but at the avenue that followed the contours of the shoreline. Raquel had chosen this place for the last goodbye to a city that had given her so many good memories, especially the romantic moments with her beloved husband. This incredible ocean breeze felt so good after a hot day, the beautiful sunsets that both enjoyed together and the long walks along the picturesque road they took for exercise and pleasure.

Above all, she remembered the nights both enjoyed at its sandy beach while the ocean played music orchestrated by gentle waves breaking along its shallow shores. One or two moons did illuminate the beach and made the sea appear like a silvery blanket that had the power to stir a deep warmth inside her, a feeling that only her husband could quench with his lips.

A large crowd had gathered around them, comprised of many friends who wanted to participate in this final farewell. When you live for so many years, you have the time to develop numerous close friendships.

"Before you depart, I have one last question!" Nobiel declared using a public mental discourse.

Gabri-el answered without delay, *"My dear friend, you want to know why Evil is so complicated? ... It is not! It is as basic as a feeling... only the opposite of what God stands for!*

Its complexity arrives due to its inner simplicity, which allows it to interact with everything considered part of our lives; conversely, Evil is very simple-minded... Its primary motivation is the destruction of anything that is Good!

*Finally, remember this: **Evil's primary weapon is not complexity… it is deception!***"

Nobiel kindly smiled at Gabri-el while touching his opened right hand against the Overlord. Next, he did the same with Raquel and followed with his final statement.

"Gabri-el, The Core is painfully going to miss you even more because you are taking with you the most beautiful flower this land has ever seen!"

The couple gave the Seraph a wide and happy smile.

Gabri-el raised both hands, and his powerful telepathic message propagated to the whole congregation. His farewell said.

"Goodbye, my dear friends… As I leave now, my last wish is that God stays in your hearts… forever!"

The audience loudly responded, sounding more like a roar than a coordinated response; everybody thrust both hands up and mentally yelled.

"Dear Overlord, we equally wish that God be with you, always!"

After all the departing angels boarded the aircraft, it slowly lifted and moved toward the sea; in this manner, the passengers took a last spectacular but melancholic view of their now ex-citizens and their native city.

As the distance increased and the city became smaller, the void it left in their hearts grew bigger; the speeding vehicle taking them away sharply turned, traveling south.

One more day has transpired.

At noon, a large concentration of NA transports hummed to their destination, Dawnel, the city only one hundred kilometers away. The transporters stayed flying relatively close to the ground.

Higher in the sky, a comparable large concentration of cylinders approached the previous group, moving in the opposite direction and dotting the sky above.

Inside the centered flying wing going to Dawnel, a hidden cabin at the bottom of a large transport harbored teams A, B, and C. Dagon addressed the A-1 and B-1 team leaders, who stood while the rest of the troops sat facing each other.

All had camouflaged clothing with folded parachutes attached to their backs. They also wore transparent helmets with sophisticated internal displays showing the local parameters: wind, velocity, temperature, etc.

The leaders stood on a flat rectangular section in the middle of the compartment; Dagon spoke mentally to all soldiers.

"Do not forget, once on the ground, each team is independent and on its own! ... If you need to communicate with the NA, use a u-channel with a data burst aimed at the assigned communication satellite. Each team for receiving messages has its decoding machine... this code is changed daily!

Our leaders expect only success... Do not fail!"

As A-1 and B-1 nodded in approval, a green light started blinking inside the compartment; without any other comment, all three platoon leaders took their assigned seats. They knew they had only ten seconds to prepare for parachuting, an ideal infiltration method.

C-1 pushed another button, and the light changed to red. Three seconds later, the centered flat section on the floor slid out, showing an empty gap. Not far down, a rugged inhabited terrain was continuously moving forward. Deep canyons and mountains with thick forests are inaccessible places to parachute, but the three teams practiced hard and were undaunted by the impressive view.

Three large boxes, one in front of each platoon, moved to the edge of the gap; these were their supplies and weapons.

Team A's box detached and fell into the opened space; in seconds, all A's team members had jumped into the emptiness. Team B's box also detached and fell through the opening, closely followed by its members. Likewise, team C jumped.

Looking outside the flying transport, the underbelly door closed shut. All three teams kept falling until they looked like little dots approaching the ground. Their parachutes opened when it appeared they could crash into the trees on the mountain's slopes.

Only seconds later, all had disappeared into the forest; it was remarkable that no one became entangled on top of a tree. Their fall-breaking equipment and personal abilities allowed them to achieve excellent maneuverability. When the last transport's aircraft wing moved away from the low and high sky... nothing remained visible on the ground!

****

The great Exodus of Terra had ended. Millions of angels had changed their country of residence. Both Alliances' resources became stressed to their limits to keep track of the incoming and departing, plus the relocation of the newcomers.

At the top of Dawnel's central building, Micha-el used his command chair facing the semicircular desk. His four subordinated Overlords remained seated and faced him. Micha-el pointed out to the new group of three empty chairs adjacent to the occupied and announced.

"I am sure that you already know... These chairs are the new positions that will be occupied by the three new Overlords who have joined the SA.

Since they lost their titles when they resigned from their positions, we have previously agreed to give them an honorary administrative title.

Gabri-el and Dani-el want to work together, so I will assign them the command of the critical defensive complex at Southern Bay City, or SBC."

Zeri-el, Lari-el, and Samu-el all appeared concerned with the announcement. Zeri-el leaned forward to get closer to Micha-el, with his green eyes sparkling due to mental activity. He telepathically spoke first.

"Micha-el, I do not understand the wisdom in this decision! Izma-el just came from the NA, and if you give him a critical position in the Alliance's defense, would such an act cause a potentially dangerous breach of our internal security?"

Lari-el and Samu-el nodded in support, the latter noted.

"We heard a report that Lucif-er is capable of installing a mental block that prevents even an Archangel from identifying an enemy pretending to be a friend!"

Micha-el stared at the three empty chairs; then, he softly replied.

"I understand your concerns; however, since Izma-el is an Archangel, we cannot give him a managerial job. He has to be involved with something meaningful!

Furthermore, with his knowledge, Rapha-el and I probed his mind. The result unequivocally told us that Izma-el is with God... and consequently, he is one of us!"

Rapha-el glanced at his three associates and quickly added.

"The test that Micha-el and I did would have exposed any mental blocking. On a one-on-one basis, it is possible to hide evil from your companion; nevertheless, when two Overlords scan your brain simultaneously, not even Lucif-er can devise any scheme for such deception!

Dear brothers, it is of the utmost importance that you support Izma-el; he has given up so much to be here. If he can sense our distrust or even a cold acceptance of his presence, he will be hurt! ... Our knowledge and instincts tell us he is sincere... accordingly, try your best to welcome him!"

When the three Overlords admitted the explanation, Micha-el felt relieved and pressed an invisible button on a large electronic display adjacent to him with one finger. In less than a second, the face of a Seraph in a white and green uniform appeared; before he could say anything, Micha-el ordered, *"Send them in!"*

"Yes, Sir!" The military individual replied.

Shortly afterward, the main door opened, and three Archangels entered.

All five SA Overlords stood to welcome them. Wearing his official green attire, Gabri-el was the first to reach the chair next to Rapha-el. With one open hand, this Archangel saluted him. Leaning forward, he did the same with Micha-el and then enthusiastically exclaimed.

"I assume my chair is the one next to Rapha-el!"

"Of course, my brother!" Rapha-el responded.

Wearing his Core outfit, Dani-el promptly took the adjacent piece of furniture.

Izma-el became acquainted with the other three Overlords standing further away from him. They exchanged the usual open-handed greeting; nothing was said, but a lot of information was traded. Last, he did the same with Rapha-el and Micha-el.

After all sat, Micha-el glanced with satisfaction at Izma-el's new uniform; it was grey with a belt of alternating white and green sections. However, the most important feature was a silver cross over his heart! Elated by this sight, The SA leader addressed him.

"Izma-el, you are most welcome, but we also need to extend our gratitude for bringing so many former citizens of the SW Sector with you!"

"I am glad they chose to serve God as well as I did!"

As all the Overlords happily agreed with Izma-el's response, Micha-el announced the following.

"Samu-el will inform us about the most important item in today's agenda: The Exodus final demographic breakdown!"

Samu-el's inquisitive but friendly face had a hint of sadness, he stated.

"I still cannot believe that the NA absorbed 10% of the SA population. Computer calculations showed that the SA should have gotten an equal percentage from the NA; yet, since Lucif-er did not allow the departing citizens to take any possessions with them, this drastically affected the final count; we only received 5% of the NA population!"

Rapha-el shook his head and mentally spoke.

"Why does Evil appeal to so many? Perhaps because it offers immediate rewards compared to the uncertainty of the faithful's long-term commitment! The narrow-mindedness is appalling! Why were so many deceived into taking so little when they could have much more of what is valuable by waiting a bit longer?"

"My brother, our hearts bleed as yours for those unfortunate souls!"

Micha-el responded with noticeable distress caused by the wrong choice of too many angelic beings. After a brief pause, Samu-el continued.

"I see Evil as a mold that grows on us, numbing our senses. It is the same as the darkness at night, which, by impairing our vision, prevents us from seeing the proper direction where we are going!

It is mentioned that many search for God everywhere but forget to look inside their hearts. When we believe in Him and obey His commands… it is the easier place to find Him!

After these thoughts, I am displaying the final Exodus tally!"

He pointed to the screen next to Micha-el. A data table became visible.

EXODUS FINAL REPORT

	SECTOR	NA%	DEPARTED
	NW	0.5	10 million
	NC	0.5	10 million
NA	NE	0.5	10 million
(2 billion)	SW	3.0	60 million
	SC	0.3	6 million
	SE	0.2	4 million
	CD	0.0	0

100 million moved to the SA.

	STATE	CORE%	DEPARTED
CORE	SERAPHAN	0.1	1 million
(1 billion)	CHERUBAN	0.5	5 million
	THRONAN	0.4	4 million

10 million moved out. > NA: 2 million, > SA: 8 million.

	PROVINCE	SA%	DEPARTED
SA	GRACELAND	2.0	40 million
(2 billion)	IRISAN	1.0	20 million
	ZARINIA	4.0	80 million
	PRISTEEN	1.0	20 million
	TELLIA	2.0	40 million

200 million moved to the NA.

"Look at these statistics; now you can see why my heart was so burdened today!" Micha-el exclaimed; after that, he added.

"Furthermore, I will mention that the ten million inhabitants of Bird Islands were split in half. Five million settled in the northern islands, the other five in the southern islands.

Of Eastland's twenty million residents, only five moved to the SA… It was a similar situation as in the NA… many stayed only because they did not want to lose their possessions!"

Micha-el and the NA Overlords did not celebrate; the numbers showed that the forces of Evil continued their relentless takeover of the planet. Nevertheless, despair was not inside their minds because they did not have a place for it; instead, the Grace of the Lord dwelled inside them!

Lucif-er was in a good mood. He smiled at Gorgon-el's report for the Exodus, which clearly showed the NA, on a planetary scale, to achieve a much larger take of the angels' population. Even Magog-el unveiled a broad smile, sharing his boss' enthusiasm, a rare event for NA's now second in command; actually, he always was second because Lucif-er stayed undercover for quite a while.

Standing on an empty landing pad, the three Overlords enjoyed the view from the 1,300-meter-tall, tallest building in downtown Centrum and the planet Terra.

Also, this location's large central dome functioned as Lucif-er's and Magog-el's business office and reception area. Six similar but shorter buildings surrounded the main structure in a hexagonal pattern, with blue as the predominant color of their walls. A substantial number of military flying vehicles stayed on the sky-high landing pads of the seven structures.

Dressed in his favorite silvery jumpsuit, which gave it an aural appearance with his reflective powers, Lucif-er also wore an interlaced white and blue belt with the standard golden buckle. He addressed his companions.

"I am still furious from the trick Isma-el played on us during the international broadcast! I am sure he is to blame for the millions of Southwest Sector citizens defecting to the SA! Regardless, we did an excellent job extracting angels from the SA."

"All the propaganda we launched to discredit the SA... paid off!" Magog-el asserted with enthusiasm.

A faint 'ding' generated by Lucif-er's buckle interrupted. Without touching any controls, he requested, *"Yes!"*

"Sir! The Seraph named Arkyn has arrived!"

"Tell Kragen to escort him to the upper landing site!"

Lucif-er cut the communication before the soldier at the other end could acknowledge.

Deviously, Magog-el inquired.

"I assume we are referring to Micha-el's personal assistant?"

"Of course, I requested his presence to inquire about a weakness or a pattern of behavior that could assist us in getting rid of Micha-el!"

"Excellent!"

Shortly, a sliding door located at the centered dome opened. Walking to the landing site, two Seraphim approached the Archangels. One was a muscular individual dressed in the NA's military uniform and fully armed; the other, a civilian, moved uneasily as if being afraid of intruding.

When two steps from the Overlords, they stopped. The military angel immediately backed up ten paces and stood still.

Lucif-er stared at Arkyn, who quickly looked down and gulped some saliva. The Overlord, with a friendly smile, exclaimed.

"Arkyn! ... Welcome to Centrum, the NA's most renowned city!"

The Seraph, being welcome, managed to glance up and respond.

"Thank you, Most Eminent Overlord! ... I am glad to be here... and if I can be of any assistance, please let me know!"

The face of Lucif-er got closer to Arkyn's, but the Overlord made sure it was at an angle to avoid intimidating his companion; in addition, his smile got wider while mentally speaking.

"I am pleased that you want to be helpful. Since you were Micha-el's personal assistant," Arkyn tensed up when he heard the name of his previous boss, *"I would like to know more about him so we can improve our communication; perhaps we could even end this conflict!"*

As the Overlord noticed that Arkyn had become disturbed, he proceeded to calm him down.

"Relax!" Lucif-er suggested as he gently touched his left arm, *"I have no intention of asking you to give me the SA's computer codes or any secret plans that Micha-el plans to use against the NA, and you could have overheard... I know you are worried about betraying Micha-el, who treated you so well!"*

Looking up to Lucif-er with an incredulous glance, Arkyn felt uneasy. Lucif-er, scrutinizing every corner of the Seraph's mind, continued.

"No! ... I do not need any military secrets; I only want to understand Micha-el as a person. Just tell me what he likes or dislikes, his hobbies, his friends, and so on."

As Lucif-er's touch removed his inhibitions, Arkyn talked freely.

"Sir! ... Micha-el is an Archangel very dedicated to God. He follows Trillium's midnight prayer every day, but he does not have much of a social life... I think the most he does for entertainment is take a thirty-kilometer hike along the Blue Canyon!"

"One hundred and fifty kilometers northeast of Dawnel," interrupted the NA leader in a soft, telepathic tone.

"That is the location, Sir!"

"My friend, I have been there. It is an excellent choice for hiking, a wonderful location for enjoying nature, and a place where you can even forget the stresses of our methodical daily working routines!"

Arkyn, feeling better, talked a lot. Five minutes later, Kragen escorted him back to the building's interior. Gorgon-el cynically inquired.

"We don't need any military secrets from Arkyn?"

Lucif-er glanced at him and replied.

"You will find him a job, where, to accomplish his assignment, he will have no choice but to spill everything he knows!"

"I have the perfect job for him!"

Lucif-er, showing some facial satisfaction, malevolently insinuated to Magog-el, *"When the time comes, make sure team C has this information about Blue Canyon!"*

Same place, one hour later.

The discussions related to relocations had been long and tedious. As a closing statement, Lucif-er returned to mention the undercover teams.

"In three months, all this commotion should be over, and we will return to normality. At the conclusion of this period, I will order teams A and B to carry out their plans... In case they fail, Team C will be on standby waiting for orders!"

Gorgon-el replied eagerly.

"I extensively analyzed several scenarios for ambushing Micha-el or Gabri-el; the best result any team could achieve was less than 50%. We are working on improving the odds!"

"I already know!" Replied the NA's leader with a cold-blooded response since they were discussing the assassinations of Archangels; he continued, *"We will continue this later; now, I want to test the new anti-aircraft cannons just installed on the dome's exterior!"*

After the last remark, with a small side flicker from his eyes, he requested his colleagues to start moving. The three Archangels walked briskly toward the central dome, where the entrance door opened as they got close. Inside, they boarded the closest elevator, which took them to the very top of the dome, where the city's spectacular view improved.

The Overlords stepped out of the elevator into this small circular room where the back end of four massive guns could be seen above their heads. Bundles of cables and pipes extended from the guns to the floor, where all these connections disappeared into the level below.

Attached to each gun at the floor level, four large screens displayed the outside's four visual quadrants. One militarily dressed Seraph sat in front of each display, showing many complex controls, many operated even telepathically.

One armed soldier stood at each side of the elevator's door; they were aware of the Overlords' arrival by the visual information gathered by clusters of monitors located everywhere, inside and outside this massive building. The operators did not stand up but continued working at their terminals.

Leading the other two Overlords, Lucif-er advanced to the farther screen, where the north-sector operator stayed seated. When he noticed he was being approached, the Seraph at the station stood up straight and immediately exclaimed.

"Welcome, Great Overlord! I am at your service!"

Lucif-er, leaning to get closer to the screen, responded with a mild tone.

"I have a task for you... I want to test this cannon's total deployment and firing time!"

The Overlord pointed to the visual image of the northern sector, pointing to a white rock on the pinnacle of a small mountain, the last of a chain extending beyond Centrum's city limits. This metropolis' lined-up skyscrapers followed a height-decreasing pattern, tallest at the center and lowest at the edges, a similar view to a giant umbrella deployed on a valley covering one thousand square kilometers.

The selected location was about fifty kilometers away. On the electronic display, it was located at the bottom left corner, and since the cannon was positioned dead center, this meant maximum gun displacement.

"I am certain that nobody is at that location; nevertheless, take a satellite scan to ensure the area is clear!" Lucif-er pointed out.

"Yes, Sir! ... Starting the scan!"

The operator activated a device by pointing to the screen. The results were displayed in a section comprising 50% of the monitor's total area.

Satellite > CD   Scan > Centrum
NW > D= 50 Km   Area > 10 Km².
Search > Angels

Two seconds later, a new string of information appeared.

Scan completed.

There are no Angels inside the area, only wild animals.

"This is what I want: Three consecutive blasts at the white rock. Do your best!" The leading Archangel ordered.

"Yes, Sir! Command understood... starting... now!"

The screen showed a concentric series of circles, with the inner circle having a targeting cross. As the circles pointed at the white rock, the area became magnified many times, so the bull's eye stayed at the center of the white rock, seated on the mountain's top.

Next, a gun aiming sequence was displayed.

FREQUENCY	LOADED	ARMED	POWER	TARGET
3	YES	YES	80%	LOCKED

FIRE

At the same instant, the **FIRE** button turned green; the operator pointed to the triggering control, and the button turned **red**!

The part of the gun outside the dome was already pointing toward the target. A high-pitched sound and rumble flooded the control chamber since the rapid fire of three consecutive blasts coalesced into one single thunder.

The viewing screen showed a red laser bullseye, the target. Almost simultaneously, three hot plasma balls with a diameter of a meter and spaced only ten meters apart were projected outwardly from the cannon's tip. With incredible speed, they followed the path set by the laser and raced toward the white rock, practically disappearing in the distance in just an instant!

When the plasma bullets hit the target, the rock exploded in three huge balls of fire! However, they were so closely spaced that they merged into one fireball, mushrooming into the upper atmosphere. Debris began to fall all around the mountain's sides, and loud thunder spread at the speed of sound.

The fireball changed to a dusty and smoky cloud; the white rock on top of a mountaintop was gone!

An attention sound came out of the monitor!

The image of a soldier dressed similarly to the standing guards, except he had a small black circle with the NA letters in blue inside it, probably an officer, overrode the exploding image; he barked at the operator who had just fired a plasma cannon.

"What are you doing?"

Lucif-er, with a finger motion, displaced the magnetic convergence of the incoming signal plus the return image through the monitor. The angry officer's image now faced Lucif-er's location. The Overlord did not say anything, only pointed a finger at himself.

When facing the Overlord, the officer's face became visibly shocked; his anger quickly reversed to extreme caution. After a quick grinding of his teeth, he promptly exclaimed.

"Sir! ... My apologies for intruding!"

The Overlord, somehow amused by the response, noted.

"No need to apologize, commander! It is your job to supervise this operation!" Then, with his thumb, he made a quick signal indicating... Go away!

The officer understood and with a final, *"Yes, Sir!"* His image vanished from the monitor.

Now addressing his two colleagues, Lucif-er commented.

"It is acceptable... 3.2 seconds!"

Simultaneously, the operator also received a telepathic message.

"I prefer the time to be smaller than 3.0 seconds!"

The Seraph operating the cannon hesitated for an instant when the building moved, shaken by a slight vibration, but quickly followed up by responding.

"Sir! I shall do whatever is necessary to achieve such a goal!"

At the instant the three Overlords moved to the elevator's door to exit the premises, something analogous to what follows a lightning strike began rolling across the city's downtown area: a distant but loud thunder!

Standing under one of many ornamental trees adorning a main avenue of Iris, the capital of Irisan Province, Rapha-el relaxed under its canopy.

This boulevard was only for pedestrians, to be used for leisure, exercise, and even meditation when accessing the many botanical gardens dotting its long pathways, some straight, others meandering around trees, flower beds, or patches of grass.

Above the skies, the air traffic stayed heavy as many vehicles followed fixed patterns connecting everything, including the tall skyscrapers towering above the trees.

The Overlord knew that his friend Sergius was approaching his location. He felt sad since he had terrible news for him.

Consequently, he was not in any hurry to convey the message, which felt painful even as an Archangel. The Overlord, who stood for the underprivileged lower choir of angels, sharing their dreams and pains, equally felt the sharp edge of suffering caused by a missing friend. In addition, he experienced a deeper grievance: the strong possibility that Marcus could have lost something of immensely more value than his life... his soul! He begged the Lord that this may not be the case.

He spotted Sergius walking toward the spot where he stood, a lovely, shaded area still 100 meters away. The incoming angel stopped for a few seconds to admire a beautiful flower bed, whose beauty and aroma brought a mild, pleasurable smile to his face.

The Overlord would have preferred somebody else to notify the Principality angel, a statement that would erase many smiles from that face... for a long time!

When Sergius arrived at the tree, he finally noticed the Overlord's presence. His face lit up with joy because Rapha-el was more than an Overlord; he was a trusted friend.

"Greetings, my dear friend!" Rapha-el's soft voice welcomed the angel, who quickly responded with an exclamation.

"Great Overlord Rapha-el! ... I am so glad to see you! Do you have any news for me?"

Not wanting to postpone the sad news, the Archangel quickly replied.

"Yes! ... But it is bad news!"

Sergius felt a chill running through his spine in anticipation of something dreadful; he felt the right hand of the Overlord grabbing his. At such an instant, the chill was replaced by a surging warmth that relaxed him. He looked inquisitively into the deep blue eyes of the Archangel, who proceeded to vocalize his statement.

"Your friend Marcus... He is dead!"

The angel just gazed at Rapha-el. He did not feel pain, only a deep sadness; from the inside, he sensed a growing emptiness similar to a black hole sucking a large portion of his existence. When Sergius opened his mouth to speak, Rapha-el knew the question but allowed him to ask it.

"Did he die from the Syndrome sickness?"

"No... Lucif-er killed him!"

Sergius released his hand and backed up with wide-open eyes; he asked again, this time louder.

"Why? Marcus never hurt anybody!"

*"No, he didn't! But in his quest to extend his life, he asked the **wrong person**! ... When Marcus asked Lucif-er for help, he terminated Marcus' life in an evil action so he would not suffer anymore!"*

Sergius wanted to feel pain; however, the Overlord's soothing did not allow it. The angel stared at the busy skies while the emptiness inside him expanded; he felt incredibly alone; next, he thought.

"What is the use? I may not live much longer... It is so depressing that **nothing** can be done for us!"

Rapha-el interrupted his deep thinking with a comment.

"Do not allow despair to take you hostage! ... Have faith in God; He loves you as much as He loves me... don't give up!"

Sergius grabbed and squeezed his forehead with his left hand. The image of Marcus departing at the airport came into his mind. He could see him saying goodbye with two fingers at 45°, and the joy that this action brought him, plus the consequent feeling or premonition that he would never see him again!

He requested with a tone of sadness.

"Sir... Wouldn't it be better for everybody if God would take me out of this world?"

Displaying a kind smile, Rapha-el spoke to the Principality Choir's angel.

"Nonsense! Do not call it quits until the last straw is drawn out! ... If I am not giving up on you, why should you give up on yourself? Enjoy what you have; nobody knows what the Lord has prepared for our lives!

*You believe that I am living forever while you are departing soon; however, you could be destined to live longer than me... **only God knows!**"*

****

Three months[3] have swiftly elapsed, and the enormous hassle of the Exodus began fading away as the angels got new jobs, new homes, and everyday routines continued turning back for normality. Most relocated angels still missed their previous homes, but even that would eventually become a thing of the past.

One angel who stayed too involved in his new job to miss anything was Mervyn. Working at the Dawnel Research Center, or DRC for short, he was promoted to oversee the center only one month after his arrival. His

---

[3] Only ten months in one Terra's year.

vast knowledge of computers and Physics excluded him from doing anything else.

The section he could call his personal site at the lab was indeed complex. The quantum computer's large displays stayed arranged in 3-D matrix arrays, massive cryogenic piping for the superconducting experiments, high-power lasers, plasma generators, intricate electronic manufacturing devices, etc. All the equipment focused on a communal goal. The Argentan University professor had a whole team of engineers and scientists under his command running the best-organized lab on the planet.

Micha-el and Gabri-el, just arriving, stood behind him and his favorite working chair. He was slow to notice the two Overlords approaching him. Only when both started picking over his shoulder did he look around and exclaim.

"Greetings, Great Overlords! I am glad to see you again!"

Placing one hand on his shoulder, Micha-el replied.

"My illustrious good friend Mervyn, you are an important member of the Alliance; forget the titles, just call us by our names."

"Micha-el, I like it; it would be great!"

The two Archangels smiled at the Cherub, who had exceptional mental powers. His long, curly, and less well-kept hair matched the angel's opinion that professors were eccentric.

"We need to know if you are feeling at home. And of course, we would like to find out what kind of projects you are working on!" Micha-el conveyed telepathically.

Marvyn's smaller-than-normal eyes sparkled as he looked past them, visualizing the future. The Archangels saw his visioning, too, but they did not interrupt him, Mervyn explained.

"I have seen that the Alliance's security is questionable. We cannot do anything to stop electronic messages from entering our space; however, I will reprogram the existing satellite network to prevent messages from leaving the SA without detecting their origin. This will even include the u-channel satellite communications!

I will also include IR detection for the whole SA to track terrorist activities. I estimate that the new system will be operational in thirty days! ... Next, it may take years to implement, but nobody else must know about this project until it is completed! ... If ever! ... I have this idea about a 4-D satellite matrix that could provide an effective nuclear shield for the Alliance and give us an invaluable tactical advantage!"

Impressed by the project's complex implementation, Micha-el and Gabri-el understood the intricate mental images generated by Mervyn's intellect. They also comprehended the vast ramifications of a game changer. Micha-el spoke telepathically.

"You have my word about the secrecy of this extremely important project. Nothing will be mentioned about the matrix until it is deployed... if ever!"

Until now, just listening, Gabri-el added.

"I suggest that you allocate pieces of the project to different and isolated tech groups. With this arrangement, nobody will know what the final product is or what it can perform! ... If anybody wants to know what it is for, respond that you don't have any idea, but you can ask Micha-el!"

Micha-el mentally agreed with his companion Overlord.

Mervyn replied, *"Gabri-el, I think it is an excellent idea. With that arrangement, we can control internal security; I will take care of the details!"*

After a few more minutes of technical chat, the two Archangels said farewell. Gabri-el, who considered Mervyn to be a long-term, unique friend, touched open hands. The Overlord said.

"My friend, it was a great pleasure seeing you again! I will be dropping by anytime I have a chance!"

On their way out of the lab, Gabri-el mentioned.

"Micha-el, since you want me to be part of tomorrow's assignment, I will meet you at the departing pad at 3:15 hours. I am looking forward to visiting that pretty town named <u>Leanna</u>!"

Nighttime, later the same day.

Teams A, B, and C, already in their different assigned locations inside the SA, received the following message through their decoding machines.

A: Terminate Micha-el at Leanna's Central Building.
   Time: 6:10:00 hours.
B: Terminate Gabri-el at Leanna's Administration Building.
   Time: 6:10:00 hours.
C: A and B ordered into action. Your order: Standby.

C-1, also named Dagon, saw the message and burst into fury. Clenching his teeth, he mentally yelled.

"Why wasn't I assigned? I am ready to kill them myself!"

Leanna, 2,000 Km southwest of Dawnel.

A medium-sized city with half a million inhabitants, it was the most spectacular place in the Pristeen Province. Perhaps, the closest thing in Terra was like Earth's ancient Hanging Gardens of Babylon!

The buildings were not very tall, only around 20 stories high. However, every floor had a balcony, adding a new dimension to the conglomerate.

Just imagine being at the New Year's Rose Parade in Pasadena, California, with only one major difference. The parade would be not on the street but on both sides of every street in the city, with every spot competing for the first prize.

Therefore, the residents and many visitors strolling on the streets could admire the rows of buildings covered by flowers and ornamental trees. Still, the design would go beyond the individual structures to encompass the entire city. This was one of the few cities on the planet where arches among the buildings catered to plants as well as pedestrians. Even the parking lots looked different in this city; small terraces landscaped by artistic hands adorned the landing sites.

Micha-el and Gabri-el arrived almost at noontime. Raquel had anticipated her husband's trip by showing up in the city much earlier; she did enjoy the sightseeing of such a spectacular place escorted by two Cherubim soldiers. She planned to reunite with Gabri-el sometime after 6:00 hours when he should have finished all the business scheduled at the Administration Building.

Micha-el looked at a splendorous pathway leading to the circular top floor of the tallest and central building in the city; two armed SA Seraphim soldiers stayed close to him. Behind him was the building's edge, where the spectacular main avenue could be seen below. A room of about 20 meters in diameter comprised the entire top floor.

Before he reached the floor entrance, a small vehicle took Gabri-el and his two Cherubim personal assistants to the Administration Building, only five kilometers away.

5:30 hours.

In the middle of the city traffic, two small vehicles, each carrying three passengers, had arrived at Leanna. They were part of teams A and B!

Team A members inside a small flying cylinder, the equivalent of a flying car, continued programming the onboard computer to take an aerial scenic tour of the city. The prerequisite was approaching the central building from the direction of Main Avenue... at 6:10:00 hours!

Team B members quickly drove their craft to the Administration Building. They landed in the public parking lot and, after disguising a high-power handgun inside their outfits to make it unnoticeable, proceeded to enter the building.

Two armed Cherubim stood at the extra-wide main entrance doors; it appeared that Gabri-el had asked his personal assistants to wait outside the building. One of them, Reuben, pointed out to Norvel, the copilot, the incredible terrace across the avenue. It was a magnificent array of flowering plants with one large bush as a centerpiece; iridescent, mauve-colored flowers covered this plant.

Three Seraphim, walking casually, just passed them by as they entered the Administration Building.

6:08:00 hours.

On the flat section of a large emerald-green pentagonal table, Micha-el remained seated while presiding over a city council meeting. All five attendees on one of the pentagonal sides had an embedded computer display facing them. The Overlord announced, not using vocal sounds.

"I am pleased that we finished all the agenda in record time! Since I am anxious to go sightseeing with my friends, let us end this meeting!"

Everyone stood up; the Archangel quickly dismissed three city planners when he touched their right hands flat and open. They eagerly corresponded while showing big smiles.

Only one Seraph, the city's mayor, remained with Micha-el, who touched his back and remarked.

"Pavlen, you have done a great job implementing the city's defenses without deteriorating Leanna's beautiful looks. Next, you should..."

A bright flash reflected by the shiny circular floor, which was practically surrounded by windows, caught the Overlord's attention. His eyes, moving at high speed, tracked the direction of the incoming light as it became defined by the shadows it left on its way out.

Micha-el ran to the floor's corner facing Main Avenue. Two blocks away, he saw a ball of fire ascending into the sky; it took several seconds to dissipate and left behind a ball of faint smoke, which continued ascending to higher atmospheric places.

Since the Central Building was the tallest structure in Leanna, the Archangel could easily see that the explosion originated on a building's rooftop parking close to one kilometer away.

Pavlen arrived and stood next to the Overlord. While he also stared out of the window, somehow apprehensively, he asked.

"What happened?"

Simultaneously, the building vibrated, followed by a sonic boom rattling the transparent windows.

The closest defense deployment, part of a ring protecting the city, was five kilometers away. Its commander ran toward an angel staring into a large electronic monitor, which began displaying the downtown area.

The machine responded to the operator's request by pointing an arrow to a specific building and attaching a character string.

DC-256

The operator, a Throne, turned to the approaching base commander and exclaimed, *"Sir! It came from the downtown sector, building DC-256!"*

The commander ordered immediately.

"Deploy two aircraft, each with one platoon of soldiers. Investigate and report!"

In a room on the center of the first floor of the Administration Building, standing in a clearing next to a computer cluster, Gabri-el was listening to a group of angels facing him… Suddenly, he raised his hand to request silence!

After one second of acute listening, he announced.

"I felt an unusual vibration through the floor! … I am going outside to investigate, and I will let you know when I will return!"

Then, after turning around, he used vigorous strides to exit the room.

6:10:00 hours.

A Seraph, dressed in the typical SA's civilian attire, drove a small aircraft approaching the Central Building, with the vehicle staying alongside a standard preprogrammed flight path. The top of the tallest structure continued approaching the left side of the soaring cylinder; below, the multicolored balconies went down forty floors to a broad and spectacular boulevard named Main Avenue. The air traffic was moderate, with a line of small craft moving in the opposite direction twenty stories below.

A-1, the Seraph and platoon leader, had A-2 and A-3 fully concentrating on the aircraft's controls. A conniving A-2, showing noticeable pleasure, telepathically pointed out.

"The decoy explosion worked! I see Micha-el standing at the top floor's window, looking at building DC-256! I am ready for manual override!"

Two seconds later, A-1 ordered, *"Now!"*

The craft veered away from its allocated path, now heading toward the top floor of the Central Building. A-3, in charge of the concealed plasma gun hidden inside the vehicle's frontal section, saw the convergence of circles pointing at the exact place where Micha-el stood. The display read.

Target Locked

As A-1 and his two companions salivated with pleasure, A-3, the gunner, started to point one finger to a location on the screen where a square brightly read: **FIRE.**

A few seconds before, at the defense post, another Throne, sitting next to the one talking to the commander, saw a red light on his display. He screamed to the commander, *"Sir!"*

The Seraph in charge of the military post glanced at the terminal's urgent message.

The vehicle approaching the Central Building has a concealed plasma gun.

In a hurry, the Seraph commanding the post ordered the same operator.

"Code 3!"

The visual display, magnified many times, showed a flying vehicle moving above Main Avenue. The plasma gun integrated inside the frontal part of the craft could be seen on this display like the infrared light at nighttime identifies hot objects; the defense post operator was even capable of determining where the gun was aiming... now, at the Central Building's top floor!

The operator generated a new command string.

>CODE 3< Load: 1 Megawatt/microsecond; One 10-microsecond burst. Target: Locked

The operator and the commander barely had time to assimilate the information when a new message appeared.

Vehicle ID: PL357289   Path: Main NE↑30°

→Warning: Manual Overdrive.

The video showed the craft pointing to the Central Building's top floor. Without hesitation but feeling a deep chill invading his body, the commander immediately ordered.

"Fire!"

In the fraction of one second, when A-3 finally activated the firing button, and only an instant before the plasma gun hidden in the vehicle's front could fire its lethal charge... A bright orange/red ball of fire blasted across the avenue from a building only kilometers away, hitting the front of the flying cylinder!

A loud fireball vaporized the aircraft's frontal part, causing the entire vehicle to rattle!

Inside, the three Seraphim were tossed around; smoke spread quickly within the cabin!

A-2 got up and regained his position at the craft's controls. The frontal display flashed with many red indicators, showing that many controls or critical parts were damaged or reaching critical conditions. A-2, almost in a panic, calmed down and reported.

"A-1! The superconducting engine is failing soon! We only have enough time to land on the street..."

When his blue eyes stared at the large panel transparent window where Micha-el and his companion Pavlen stood looking outside, the building's top floor reached a bloodshot appearance, A-1 interrupted.

"Forget the street; crash the vehicle where Micha-el is standing!"

A-2 and A-3, in a speeded way, glanced at their platoon leader. A-2 struggled for an instant against his survival instinct; then, with a determination surfacing from deep inside his mind, he exclaimed.

"Yeah, let's get him!"

When A-3 nodded in acceptance, A-2, by pointing to a directional button, reprogrammed the craft to crash at the spot where Micha-el was standing!

The engine hummed unevenly but loudly as the cylinder sped toward the building's top floor, leaving a smoky trail behind.

Micha-el saw Team A's vehicle veering off its assigned path and pointing at his location. He was ready for a quick maneuver to get out of the way when the cylinder's front blew away from a plasma shot coming across the wide boulevard.

He did relax a bit, but suddenly, the craft aimed straight at where he and his companion stood. His deep blue eyes and six wings increased their glow, radiating beyond their usual boundaries.

The craft sped toward the Overlord like a bullet on its way to a target. He placed his right hand edgewise, just below the height of his nose; its edge glowed ultraviolet... The incoming vehicle started to turn right!

A-2 could now see Micha-el's radiant eyes; he fought with the craft's controls to go straight... he failed!

The vehicle steered to A-2's left at a sharp angle. All three craft passengers stared with sudden terror to the left side of the top floor as the cylinder plunged through the large window panels!

The Archangel's awesome telekinesis powers deflected the craft from a direct impact to a side collision!

Inside the top floor, a quadrant away from Micha-el and Pavlen, the aircraft hit the building's main frame and blew into a massive fireball!

Micha-el switched his movements to become ten times faster than our average speed, which caused his vision to see his surroundings moving ten times slower in motion.

[10x]> In slow motion.

The leading edge of a fiery, destructive explosion expanded across the top floor! When the pentagonal table was hit, it shattered into many flying pieces.

Sparks added to the chaotic destruction as electronic equipment ripped from their power sources shorted to the ground floor. Micha-el moved at his top speed as the fireball approached the two angels. He grabbed his companion, flung him on his shoulder, and then accelerated toward the closest transparent panel or window. Due to such sudden acceleration, Pavlen's lungs became squeezed out of the air, and his eyeballs almost were left behind!

The fire's leading edge almost touched them when Micha-el pulverized the window before him, causing thousands of minute pieces to fly almost gracefully outwards.

The two angels plunged into the vacuum, facing almost 40 stories to the ground floor! ... If they had the time, the view of the picturesque Main Avenue from there would be fabulous. Nevertheless, the crowd at the bottom of the building, standing on the street, was already expanding in anticipation of the falling debris.

As the Overlord and the carried companion fell to the 39th floor, the Archangel set both feet on a ledge from a colorful balcony populated with beautiful flowers and bushes. Almost to his landing, he placed his left arm above his head at a 45° angle. At this accelerated pace, the loud noise from the explosion was just a rumble passing by.

Fire and debris rained down on their way to the street's ground floor! Luckily, most angels on the street below had already moved out of the way because the previous plasma blast hitting the A team's craft had scattered small burning pieces over them.

Fortunately, none of the falling pieces hit any of the two angels on the 39th floor's terrace. Pavlen missed it all... he was unconscious! <[10x]

The post commander who ordered the cannon firing stared at the display with disbelief. He never anticipated a suicidal attack on the Alliance's Overlord! ... This kind of homicidal suicide was an incident that nobody had ever seen before!

When the fireball engulfed the top floor in flames, tearing apart the interior section of the Center Building's top floor, he squeezed his hands so hard that his fingernails dug into his palms. As fire and burning pieces of the vehicle and the structure rained down over the boulevard, he similarly squeezed his teeth intensely. Finally, as he closed his eyes, a faint murmur came out of his mind.

"Oh... my God!"

Raquel and both of her armed bodyguards, strolling along Main Avenue, two kilometers away, continued admiring the spectacular array of decorated bridges across the boulevard.

All three looked up and around when the decoy explosion rumbled by their location. Raquel inquired, *"What was that noise?"*

The closest soldier, a Cherub, answered.

"It sounded like an explosion! ... But I cannot see where it happened!"

Only seconds later, as seen from a distance, a supersonic small reddish plasma flash turned into a still small but larger ball of fire. This was the plasma shot hitting the vehicle as seen at a distant location; however, since it occurred over the boulevard, in a similar bearing as theirs, it was easy to tell that the flying craft moved away from its preprogrammed flying route.

Before they had time to comment about the incident, the vehicle plunged into the building!

The fireball that destroyed the Central Building's 40th floor looked impressive even at a distance. They watched fire rain down over the street below, the explosion happening in an eerie silence while they showed great concern. Everyone on the boulevard froze and focused their vision on the Central Building.

A few seconds after the large explosion, the blast's sound wave could be heard like nearby thunder. The pretty eyes of the beautiful female Cherub opened widely, and she exclaimed.

"My Lord! That vehicle crashed into the Central Building... intentionally!"

The same soldier, now much more excited, talked to her telepathically.

"Lady Raquel... I agree with you!"

He quickly removed his shiny buckle and sent a request to headquarters.

"We need transportation... Emergency: Code 2!"

Raquel, visibly concerned, pleaded.

"Please, my Lord... I beg You that nothing happened to my husband or Micha-el!"

One last sliding door, and he would arrive at the main entrance reception area of the Administration Building; as the door slid open, Gabri-el rushed through the door and into the room.

Five meters away, standing in front of the Overlord, a Seraph pointed a high-powered handgun at Gabri-el's head!

Gabri-el's peripheral vision instantly told him that two equally positioned Seraphim stayed, also pointing their guns to each side of his head. Regarding Gabri-el's location, the three Seraphim remained separated by equal distances at a similar angular spread of 120°.

[10x]> Gabri-el's green eyes glowed strangely.

He stared at the Seraph facing him. Then, with tremendous velocity, shown in slow motion to see his movements, he spun around! His eyes appeared to stop to face the second Seraph's eyes from team B personnel. Similarly, he stared at the eyes of the third Seraph and NA's soldier.

With the spinning, something strange was happening. It became like a prism splitting the image of the Overlord into its three primary colors: red, yellow, and blue... except for his eyes, which remained green in all three images! By now, their guns stayed pointing toward Gabri-el's three heads facing them.

The three NA soldiers fired their guns simultaneously!

The high-energy projectiles penetrated between the eyes of each head facing them!

These heads could have been made of holographic images because the power bullets just went through and blasted locations behind the Overlord's images.

The gun pointing to the first image of Gabri-el seriously damaged the sliding door that the Archangel used to enter this room; the other two bullets carved fiery holes in the lateral walls.

All these events were seen in slow motion; even the sound generated by the three blasts loudly rumbled across the room with an eerie reverberating low-frequency noise.

Gabri-el's three sets of eyes significantly increased their brightness. The Seraphim's trio, staring into the intensely bright green eyes, felt their eyeballs burned by an invisible fire!

All three screamed, dropped their guns, and utilizing both hands, covered their own eyes! <[10x]

Gabri-el's assistants and bodyguards came running into the reception room with their guns drawn and ready for action. Reuben and Norvel weaved through the angels that did not take cover, mainly unaware of what was occurring. In no time, they stopped next to Gabri-el while aiming their rifles at the attacking Seraphim.

These three made groaning sounds caused by the emanating pain extruding from their eyeballs; they continued to cover both of their eyes using their hands.

Reuben, glancing at his boss, inquired hesitantly.

"Sir, are you OK?"

The Overlord just nodded affirmatively; then, he took a few steps until his face got very close to the assailant directly facing him; even when he knew the condition of his eyes, he pulled both hands away from the Seraph's face and observed them, the outside surface was burned!

Knowing that the pain must have been excruciating, he felt compassionate; extending his right hand, he touched the Seraph soldier's head with the tip of two fingers.

The NA military angel let go of a sharp inhaling noise as the pain went away... he breezed deeply... The anger of failure overcame his mind, as shown by his teeth being squeezed... He did not want to be helped!

Regardless, the Archangel repeated the procedure to mask the pain of the other two would-be assassins. Afterward, he commanded his assistants.

"Take them to the Central Building!"

The two bodyguards guided the blinded assailants toward the exit door.

From the building's interior, an angel stormed into the room; he yelled.

"Terrorists! ... They just blew up the top of the Central Building!"

Pavlen, the city's mayor, slowly opened his eyes. As his vision cleared up, he shook his head in disbelief... From the 39th floor's balcony, he gazed down at a gaping hole extending forever before reaching the street's floor. He violently tried to move away from the ledge, but a steel hand across his chest did not allow it!

Micha-el had just stepped down from the terrace's outside edge to the lower inside floor. He used both hands to gently move Pavlen from the ledge to the safer balcony's interior, and then he let him stand alone.

The mayor's heart was pounding fast; he rubbed his sore neck and ribs... Shortly after, when he began to calm down, he exclaimed.

"Thank you! ... Great Micha-el!"

The Overlord smiled at him and replied.

"Thank the Lord, Who has been so kind to us!"

Subsequently, both angels visually peeked downward to see the smoke and fire scattered on the street's floor. Angels were rushing to the site to help and remove injured pedestrians. Air traffic over the city had slowed to a dead stop, but two military aircraft were approaching the building at a high speed.

Pavlen, while still looking down, commented.

"We were so lucky... to escape without a scratch!"

Micha-el placed his hand on the mayor's back and stated.

"My dear friend, just listen to this: God let us do His work and use His power through our hands... When we escape death or injury, and we don't understand how this happened, we call it... luck!

Nevertheless, under God's infinite vision, luck is not possible; everything is predetermined! When we witness an event with chaotic behavior, we have no idea where it will take us! Under our Lord's wisdom, the same event is as predictable as adding two plus two!"

After a brief pause, after seeing Pavlen looking at him with glazed eyes and still suffering a mild shock, Micha-el decided that the city's mayor was not ready to assimilate anything, so he concluded.

"OK, my dear friend; no more lectures. Let's walk to the parking lot on the opposite side of this floor!"

By the time they reached the place, which was like a crescent moon hugging the 40th floor from behind the side facing the boulevard, two military aircraft had landed, and military personnel began spreading out, taking defensive positions but also setting up a perimeter to fight the blaze remaining inside the top floor of the building.

When they saw Micha-el, they were delighted and openly showed their enthusiasm by cheering him on. The Overlord equally responded to the display of affection; then, he quickly moved to the location where several city planners were being assisted for injuries caused by flying debris and fire exposure. He examined them personally.

To his satisfaction, they were not seriously wounded. He ordered them to be removed from the place, loaded into a cylinder and sent to an emergency center.

At this instant, the flying craft belonging to the post's commander arrived. He was in a big rush to meet Micha-el; when he finally faced him, he almost mentally yelled at the Overlord.

"Sir! ... I thank God that you are alive and not injured! ... Please! Forgive me for endangering your life!"

Feeling empathy for his subordinate's concern, Micha-el calmly mentioned, *"There is no need to ask for forgiveness! ... You used Code 3 correctly and in the most efficient manner. By not blowing away the whole attacking vehicle, you prevented unnecessary debris from raining down over the people walking on the boulevard. Your choice was correct; the safety of the people was before mine.*

Furthermore, there has been no precedent for you to anticipate a suicidal attack as we have just witnessed. I thank you for a well-done job!"

The commander felt much better; he excused himself to take control of the military angels already on the site.

Another craft, this one more ultramodern, arrived. It was Gabri-el's personal vehicle. Both Overlords rushed to greet each other.

At the sight of the approaching Archangel, obviously in good health, Gabri-el felt relieved and spoke telepathically.

"My brother, I am so glad that you are well!"

When Micha-el got close and sensed the unspoken, he asked.

"They tried to kill you, too?"

"Yes! Our loving God was generous to both of us! ... The Seraphim from the NA who ambushed me, I could not detect their evil intentions. These soldiers were specially conditioned to prevent us from anticipating their attack. I only know one person who can achieve this kind of mental conditioning... Lucif-er!"

"Precisely! ... It will also explain why the Seraphim, inside the suicidal attacking craft, gave their lives in such an unprecedented manner!"

Feeling sadness invading his being, caused by the death and injury of so many, Gabri-el made a final comment.

"The Holy Writings briefly mentioned that at the End of Time, brother will fight against brother! ... When I thought about such fighting, I always considered it to be a verbal battle!

Are we literally going to fight each other... to the death?"

****

Thirty days later. NA, CD, CWC.

Lucif-er and Magog-el stood behind a seated Seraph operating a display from a powerful quantum super-computer. Many similar monitoring screens, all connected to the same CPU (Central Processing Unit), could be seen inside this huge location. Many types of complex electronic equipment were attached to this advanced AI center, where information from the entire planet Terra was continuously being gathered. This was the NA's Central Warfare Center or CWC.

The place located near Centrum, about 200 Km south of the city's center, was 2 Km underground.

Approaching noontime, a message from the SA was expected to arrive via u-channel, not from the platoon teams but from the undercover Overlord.

At 5:00:01 hours, the micro-code appeared on the screen; the computer decoded the message and displayed the finished process.

Starting at the top of a large monitor, the words began to pour quickly.

Code: 378-DKR-2

Greetings!

Teams A and B failed their assignments and have been decimated.

Samu-el was assigned to do the investigation. Molecular samples of soil and organic traces on their bodies gave away the Team A base location address and town's location.

After an Overlord mental scan, prisoners from Team B had no choice but to expose the rest of the team.

The remaining soldiers of both teams fought hard in a gun battle rather than surrender.

Two wounded members of Team A survived; only the three captured at the Administration Building from Team B are still alive.

All will be sent back to the NA, and a stern warning to stop this kind of terrorism will be included.

The SA knows about Team C but has no idea where it is located. Since the team members are registered as immigrants, they are safe if they keep from doing anything illegal.

Today, the SA is launching an additional set of satellites to complement the existing network. The new arrangement will provide maximum security for total ground coverage of the entire SA. It uses IR detection, DNA cross-reference, and an energy differential locator.

Inside and out-of-town raids are now out of the question; u-channel is not safe anymore. We must find another way for this communication or personal delivery is the only medium left. Consequently, this will be my last transmission using u-channel.

Mervyn engineered this security system...

Without taking his eyes off the screen, Magog-el requested a personal message from his superior using ultra-fast speed.

"Is this the same Mervyn from the Argentan University?"

Lucif-er, in a similar way, replied, *"Yes!"*

Without any visible delay, both Overlords continued reading the message that appeared to be flowing without interruption.

... which I suggest you duplicate for the NA. I am sending the programming code at the end of this transmission.

Mervyn is also working on a hot project, which I do not know yet. He works all the time without socializing. It will be hard to extract information from him. If his project becomes a reality and it is important, I will send a personal messenger with the programming code.

I miss not being in the NA... End of transmission.

>Satellite Programming Code: ▶ |╪⇔⇒⇟⊣ |≣⊚⊣🔲🄳⊣ .... ◀

Each symbol represented a programming macro, and because the hardware was built in a 3-D frame, the software was also a 3-D net wound-like a DNA chain that interacted with adjacent neighboring strings; the chains also extended for thousands of macro units.

Lucif-er ordered the operator.

"Tell him! ... We need you over there! Do not do anything that could expose your military secrecy!"

Thousands of kilometers south, another group of angels met in a similar underground facility. Micha-el, Gabri-el, Samu-el, and Mervyn stared at this large circular area with numerous large coils, cables, and rows of blinking lights. The coils were stacked straight, each on top of the other; a centered hole provided the space for the satellites to be projected upwards. This inner tunnel measured 1.5 Km to the outside surface.

Another horizontal and larger tunnel connected to the coil stack was the transportation section where the satellites were delivered for launch. A complex mechanical transport arrangement loaded a horizontal saucer-like device to the center hole of the horizontal coil stack, where it was flipped 90 degrees for launch. Many waited in a long line inside the large tunnel, with no end in sight.

The angels stood in a semicircular strip around the vertical coil stack, where many electronic panels and controls were located.

The vertical coil used to propel the satellites was 2 Km long, and since ¾ stayed underground, the last 500 meters were built above the ground.

This place, one of several satellite launching sites, had the advantage of being on a plateau of land around 4,000 meters high; the location had the name of Green Ridge and was 2,000 kilometers east of the capital city of Graceland. Only a few kilometers from the site, a mountain's cliff steeply dropped 2,000 meters. This location was ideal for implementing the satellite's side-loading tunnel, like loading a gun with a magazine full of bullets.

Mervyn, moving away some of his curly and a bit too long hair from his eyes, explained.

"I have twenty-four new satellites ready to take off! When they finish deployment, by 8:00, I will activate the Security Program. It should end most terrorist activities and any u-channel communication leaving the SA.

*From now on, we will be able to track the location of any transmission
originating from the SA!"*

Gabri-el was moved by the enthusiasm of the professor, a Cherub he
had known for so many years while still living in his native city, a town
extending along a stunning shoreline, now a metropolitan center named
Argentan. He missed this city and its beautiful surroundings, but most
importantly, his precious wife, Raquel, deeply carved the most recent
memories.

Laying aside the melancholy, with assertive energy, he stated.

*"I am impressed by your confidence; you work so hard on these
projects that they are guaranteed to go well!"*

"Thank you! ... Now, I will start the launching sequence!"

Mervyn turned around; he accessed the closest control/display panel.
Working at a speed only matched by an Overlord, he set the satellite
propelling software to a launch-ready condition. At the same instant, the
strings of lights along the climbing coils' stack turned blinking red.

An authoritative voice came out, saturating the whole area.

**The launch will be activated in 5 minutes. This area will be
pressurized to aid in ejecting the satellites. The launch will be aborted
if a sensor detects people inside this area.**

>Leave immediately!

A sliding door opened, showing the empty box shape of an elevator
compartment. All four angels got inside. One of the Overlords activated
the device; he requested the top floor.

The elevator started so fast that Samu-el had to support Mervyn by
holding one of his arms; because of the initial rapid ascension, his legs had
bent. The floor markers along the vertical path went by fast and continued
accelerating. This trend reversed about half the way up, making Mervyn
feel that he had become weightless alone.

After a complete stop, the doors slid open, and everyone strolled to the
sunny midday skies. The flat open area was like a lookout point where we
enjoyed the beauty of nature. In this case, this was the highest part of the
Green Ridge Plateau; from here, we could notice that this place had two
steps, almost flat areas, or plateaus, but with undulating areas: glossy green
grass and clusters of tall, colorful trees beautifully covered both sections.

The sudden change in lighting did not bother the Archangels; only
Mervyn squinted frequently to adjust his sight to the outdoor glare.

Behind them, a massive coil arrangement still went up another 500
meters into the blue sky; support beams arching downwards extended for
quite some distance.

The four angels climbed on a platform with supporting rails. The device
took them to a site two kilometers away.

This location was nicely designed as a lookout vantage point. It was a
semicircle pointing to the towering launching structure. A high-impact

transparent protective shield curved like a car's windshield over an area where a dozen equally spaced chairs faced the tall coil structure. At the front, but below the shield, several electronic displays could be seen.

All four angels took adjacent seats. They waited a full minute before seeing a bright ring of red lights moving up the coils' column at a faster accelerating pace.

At the very top, the saucer-like device, a satellite, was moving so fast that the front edge was glowing red beside the vapor-condensing trail. Seconds later, the angels heard a hushing sound followed by a loud, decreasing thunder; it was a sonic boom! At least this one was moving away from them!

As the satellite sent into orbit quickly disappeared in the upper atmosphere, another one came up through the stacked coils' column structure and became accelerated by the electromagnetic coils to supersonic speed before being released into the sky to become another satellite.

Micha-el padded Mervyn's back and exclaimed.

"Everything is on schedule! Our people in the South Alliance will sleep better tonight, including me! ... Thanks, Mervyn, for achieving this important security upgrade! Also, I thank God for you being on our side!"

Mervyn's little eyes wetted with satisfaction; he had never felt so needed and valuable as he did today. The broad smile he gave back to Micha-el was not only to thank him for his support but also as a promise! ... He was already working on designing and implementing something that had never been done before. It was so complex that 99.999% of the population could not understand, even if explained to them! Just imagine what kind of math will be required to predict anything resulting from the interaction between a 3D universe and a 4D domain at the quantum level. Quantum Mechanics is very hard to follow and understand in our dimension; now, in an upper dimension, all our knowledge could barely solve what would be the equivalent of us being inside our 3D realm trying to solve the entire universe when we only knew how a 2D flat piece of paper works!

Mervyn's idea could materialize as an umbrella that could protect his nation from any nuclear attack! ... In addition, yes! It could also have the incredible power to annihilate any aggressor! This unbelievable shield ought to be named: **The 4-D Matrix.**

A distant muffled thunder came from the opposite direction of the liftoff site, only an echo from a previous satellite sent into orbit.

A third saucer took off for the upper bounds of the sky. The previous two, already using their own power to reach their destinations, were swiftly moving along the very cold domain beyond the upper atmosphere.

Did the forces of Evil finally lose ground?

THE VISITANT

CHAPTER 5

Seven more years have elapsed.

The SA and the NA were almost equalized in the arms race, which discouraged the NA from attempting further aggression. The satellite security system first installed by Mervyn and later copied by the NA had further restricted any attempts at hostile activities.

Like the Cold War days, nuclear stockpiles grew, armies became bigger, and newer weapons were developed; all increased the price to be paid if a confrontation ever happened. An invisible nuclear dark shadow threatened everything they had, including their lives, but as we did, they just ignored it; however, the terror of an assassin sneaking when least expected was always hanging over their heads. In this manner, this shadow took away a precious gift that previously allowed the angels to enjoy life to its fullest. This gift used to be called... Peace.

Over the SA, it was late at night...

The darkness of this night reigned with absolute power; it was like being inside a cave where not even the starlight could illuminate the surroundings. The emptiness of perception, the absence of light, was appalling. When we look around and there is nothing or nobody to touch, communicate, admire, or love, we feel empty, and loneliness quickly sets in. The inner desire to be loved becomes painfully introspective; however, the seed for the ultimate love, God, which is deep inside our beings, is always striving to come out.

Like the Big Bang must have been, starting from an infinitely small point in space as its origin, suddenly...

A powerful burst of Light blasted away the darkness!

For the Divine eyes, no pixel in space was left unshaken!

Its intensity, emanating at an astonishing rate, minimally allowed the perception of several beings standing in its path; by comparison, these individuals appeared black and faceless.

Analogous to an echo's behavior, the amazing bright Light instantly rebounded from the end of the Universe. However, the effect was somehow slowed down for the benefit of our limited perception and understanding. A second bright Light had appeared!

This new Light was like the initial burst, but its peculiarities told us of its uniqueness. The two Lights were of the same essence, yet independent.

The standing dark images were no longer dark; they became illuminated by two sources clearly defining the individuals. One of these individuals stood in the front but was closely flanked by two other companions. Not too far behind, four similar creatures stood in a single line. Together, they were... **7.**

We still did not know their identities.

Next, the two Lights interacted; a new Light was begotten from their majestic exchange! This new radiant entity also had its own identity. Its glow revealed the faces of the three individuals in the front: Micha-el, Gabri-el, and Rapha-el. The faces of the four standing in the back remained beyond recognition.

An extremely clear voice manifesting attention arose from all three Lights. It came from everywhere and proclaimed.

*"**Micha-el, Gabri-el, Rapha-el... my three favorite sons.***
Your love for me has already earned a special place next to me... Soon, all seven like you, will see me as I am. You shall share my love and glory forever!"

One millisecond faster than his next two companions, Micha-el kneeled on both legs. He simultaneously extended his two hands diagonally upwards to signify adoration and prayer. Almost simultaneously, the two flanking Archangels kneeled next to him. Only an instant later, the four in the rear followed their leaders' example. Micha-el exclaimed ahead of his two closer companions.

"My God! I love You with all my heart and with my entire mind. Tell me what You want from me; I am Your unconditional servant.
If You want me in Your presence today, I am ready to leave this world, right now!"

The two Archangels flanking Micha-el using their own words equally pledged to the Creator.

The voice, with a deep, caring tone, responded.

*"**Not yet; I have more tasks for you.**"*

All seven Archangels pleaded, *"**Our loving Father, command, we shall do Your will!**"*

The voice, in a decreasing intensity, proclaimed one last time.

*"**When the time comes... you will know.**"*

The Archangels' eyes glowed with exceptional whiteness, including their faces. Even their tunics brilliantly reflected this new radiance from their natural wings, not visible before because the unique bright lights eclipsed them from perception.

Beyond visual and sound perception, dreams do not have much more as a sensory experience; this dream went beyond this point. As the euphoria of a sensation of well-being, pleasure, satisfaction, and love moved them above the upper boundaries of the senses, all three of the Archangels standing at the front woke up <u>all at once</u>: Rapha-el in Iris, Micha-el in Dawnel, Gabri-el in SBC!

For ten seconds, all three remained in a trance. Then, in unison, they rushed to their display terminals and frantically contacted each other. The three Overlords started the communication exchange by sending their messages directly using voice. Micha-el asked his two colleagues.

"Did you stand with me facing the Lord?"

Both responded at the same time, *"Yes, Micha-el, we were there!"*

Micha-el continued ecstatically, *"We thank You, Lord, for the beautiful experience that You so kindly shared with us!"*

The other two Overlords agreed. After a brief pause, Rapha-el expressed his sensitive mind, *"My soul remains sadly distressed because of one unnerving issue; we are eight Overlords in the SA, and this is the second time the Lord has mentioned, 'Seven like you!'*

Is it possible that Izma-el was exposed to Evil so much that he fell out of God's Grace? How can this be when I feel in my heart that his soul is with the Lord? In any case, what could one of the remaining five possibly do to be excluded from God's reign?"

Micha-el responded, *"My brother, I have no idea. However, I do not want to talk about sad things right now. On a deeper level, let us share this glorious experience!"*

Same day, same hour, only four time zones to the West.

It was the only DMZ[1] Existing between the NA and the SA, an arbitrary line drawn halfway between the second and third Bird Islands separated the warring armies. Only 100 km away from this line were the coastal areas of either island. Since The Core prevented any direct contact by the North and South Alliances, this was a unique place on the planet.

Approaching the DMZ from the south, flying at low altitude and moderate speed, a personal unarmed small cylinder on autopilot just crossed the line separating the Alliances!

Inside, one Throne scientist and his two assistants, both members of the Choir Denominations, were very busy working with an instrument at the center of the craft. All three of the craft's passengers wore casual civilian clothes or jumpsuits. After manipulating the device for quite a while, the Throne scientist complained to his companions.

"I cannot figure it out… What is wrong? The magnetic field is 90° out of phase, but everything seems to be working!"

One of the assistants, a stocky, short angel, scratched his brown hair fast and repetitively with the tips of his right-hand fingernails. He was sitting on the floor holding an analyzer in his left hand. He quickly replied.

"I agree with you, Tanner; I can't find anything wrong!"

Tanner, immersed in a more profound thought, spoke back.

"It looks as if we are flying one quadrant away from the west direction!" He directed his attention to the other assistant, a slender female, and asked.

---

[1] DMZ = Demilitarized zone.

"Carolyn, will you please check our flight heading again?"

She stared at the craft's front controls and replied.

"Heading: West, deviation: 0.00; altitude: 1 Km; speed: steady at 0.2 Km/sec. All settings are correct!"

She directed her sight at the pristine sky, full of bright stars without moons. Something called her attention... She concentrated on the ocean below; it seemed like a darker edge was approaching their location. Immediately, she thought.

"Is this real? Are we approaching the coastline of an island? With the craft heading west, this is **not** possible!"

She pushed some buttons on the front console. A location request appeared at the display showing the contour of the first island North of the DMZ; a moving bright dot began touching its southern tip.

Her heart started pumping faster, and a chilling effect invaded her whole body. She looked around frantically, suddenly stopping at an exposed blinking control panel close to the floor. She picked up a square metallic piece from the floor and plugged it into the blinking panel.

Her eyes avidly looked at the Main display indicator; it now read.

Heading: North; Deviation: 0.00

Her heart skipped a beat..., but she managed to mumble.

"Oh, my God... the magnetic shield fell to the ground!"

Tanner's head quickly snapped upwards; he questioned.

"What did you say?"

The base commander of the island north of the DMZ stood behind a seated military soldier who stayed busy operating a display with numerous controls; this soldier was part of a larger crew. The commander, a Throne, continued rubbing his eyes as he yawned for a second time; he had just been awakened to supervise something unusual. He asked the seated soldier, also a Throne.

"What is the current status?"

"Sir! There are no weapons aboard... I can only detect some large magnetic fields generated by the craft... IR detects three angels inside... Current location: Just moved inland, sector SW-17!"

"Ask them for an ID code."

"Yes, Sir!"

The operator pushed some invisible controls with the tip of his fingers. The device sent a message.

NA Command Post directive.

You have exactly twenty seconds to identify your craft, or you will be shot down. The count is starting, now!

Carolyn, with her eyes wide open, stared at Tanner and screamed.

"We are flying over B2 Island... the NA will shoot us down!"

The scientist scrambled to get to the front controls. As soon as he could touch them, he placed the cylinder in a U-turn; next, he started to type a message that read.

We are unarmed, and we are conducting gravitational experiments on the planet.

Then, Tanner anxiously looked at the angel sitting on the floor and nervously inquired, *"I need an NA ID code! ... Loren, some time ago, with the frequency analyzer scrambler, you intercepted a code from the NA... What was the format?"*

Loren stared at the machine before him, trying to remember. He talked slowly: "First, the 'NA' letters... next, the main sector... in this case: 'B2'... last, *a six-character alphanumeric! I have no idea what this code is supposed to be!"*

The scientist frantically made up the message and gambled with the characters.

We lost our course, but we are returning to our previous bearing. We have authorization to run this experiment on NA territories.

NA B2 34KT79

In another section of the front screen, the instrumentation displayed another message.

NA Plasma cannon's targeting telemetry.

Condition on this craft: LOCKED

The last word was in a bright red. The scientist's forehead, now wet with perspiration, leaned forward as he dived to send the message before it was too late!

Carolyn, visibly shaking, begged.

"Please, Tanner, use maximum speed to get away!"

While squinting in a disapproving mode, he responded.

"Are you out of your mind? The moment we try it, we will be vaporized!"

The soldier at the terminal, with a display of sector SW-17 on his screen, followed the bright dot moving into the open sea and in the direction of the DMZ. The dot had concentric circles that expanded and contracted. At the terminal, written next to the dot, the words indicated.

Target Locked

The soldier exclaimed, *"Sir! They are moving away... They are trying to get back to the other side of the DMZ! Do you want me to blast them away?"*

"No! Check the code first!"

Quickly, the soldier allocated the top left quarter of the display for the search. That section stayed separated from the craft positioning and the weaponry firing sequences. Some time passed; the searching display section finally reported.

All memory banks have been checked.
Code ID: NOT VALID

The base commander ordered the soldier.

"Request a new and valid code ID! Give them 20 seconds!"

The message went out. Nineteen seconds later, the display showed the response.

It is the only code we have. Is it possible that your memory banks have not been upgraded? If you shoot us down, somebody is going to be very unhappy!

"Sir! They are approaching the DMZ," the operator indicated. He quickly continued, *"Last chance to destroy them!"*

The commander squeezed his chin with his right hand. A decision had to be made, so he quickly asked one more question.

"On their way out, have they increased their speed?"

"No, Sir! Speed has been constant; it is the same since we first tracked them!"

The commander ground his teeth and unhappily retorted.

"Let them go!"

The next day, lunchtime at the main post on B2 Island.

The regional commander in a shiny white and blue NA outfit, with one single blue vertical line over the center of his white shirt, also displayed a black circle encompassing the letters NA in blue over his chest's right side. In gold, about half the height of the other two letters and below the circle, two more letters read BI. He was a Seraph; in front of him, a Throne, the commander of B2 Island sat at a glass table where some fancy food had been served on two large plates. Two different drinks in transparent glasses also stood next to each plate. He had a similar uniform, except that he had two vertical stripes over his chest, and instead of BI, in smaller letters, his read: B2.

The conversation was single-sided. In a stern tone, the regional commander continued, *"I got your report! I am trying to figure out if you are dumb or stupid!*

A flying craft from the SA just flew over your post... turned around, and went back across the DMZ... **and you let them get away?"**

The B2 island commander lowered his eyesight and apologized.

"Sorry, Zoltar! They were unarmed, we knew that they were doing scientific work off the coast of B3 Island, and they gave us a code ID that could be real!"

The Seraph's blue eyes stared at his companion angrily; after a brief pause, he replied.

"Denariel, I told you before! When we officially talk, even if you are my best friend, you should properly address me! ... Now! When you found out that the code was invalid... **Why didn't you blast them away?"**

Under fire, the commander just swallowed, meagerly trying to explain.

"Sir... I didn't think the craft was any threat to the NA!"

His boss, letting some steam escape between his teeth, commented.

"You didn't think! Does that mean that you actually have some brains?"

The top commander looked away from him while visualizing events happening elsewhere; his subordinate was his closest friend, but this situation went beyond friendship. He continued, *"I can see the whole SA laughing at us... The gullible and stupid NA soldiers from B2 Island!"*

Next, he stared into his subordinate reddish eyes and threatened him.

*"You are my best friend, but make one more stupid decision like this one, and I shall make sure that you will spend the rest of your life... **on the North Pole!**"*

****

A few days later, two Overlords, walking fast on a wide, white, and speckled corridor, advanced toward a hospital's ER location. Many angels were around; the ones not busy would take the time to salute Rapha-el as the Overlords passed them by.

Izma-el followed his colleague on his right side. Soon, both faced an opening sliding door that allowed them to walk into a spacious room.

A single bed surrounded by instruments was at the center of this room, where plenty of space had been cleared to permit easy walking. On the bed, one angel lay inside a solid plastic envelope covering his whole body.

He was awake, breathing shallowly, and its frequency spaced by longer intervals than usual. His face looked bony, reflecting that not many muscles remained inside his body. His empty stare showed his black eyes devoid of any spark. His heart struggled with every pump cycle; the machines were artificially compensating for his lack of vitality. This angel... **was dying!**

Rapha-el and his companion stopped at his right side; immediately, the leading Archangel ordered something to the control instrumentation that caused the top section of the plastic capsule to open, exposing only the patient's head. Simultaneously, two round chairs projected up from the floor. The room's illumination got a little brighter while remaining at a pleasant level. Both Overlords took a seat, which allowed their heads to be closer to the patient's.

This ailing individual slowly rotated his head to see his visitors; some spark returned to his weak eyes at their sight as a faint smile tried to split the skinny and dry lips. A word, like a subtle whisper, barely made his way out.

"Ra...pha...-el..."

The Archangel replied vocally, *"Hi, Sergius. I am glad that you are feeling a little better today."*

Then, as he anticipated a question from the angel, Rapha-el raised his hand in a sign indicating 'Don't talk' and added, *"This is Izma-el... I can see you cannot recognize him. Do you remember?... Seven years ago... during the Exodus. The Overlord from the NA, who joined our Alliance."*

A blink from Sergius' eyes told Rapha-el that he recollected now. Izma-el touched the angel's shoulder and talked very softly.

"Rapha-el told me all about you; I am very pleased to meet you... You should know that I also pray to the Lord for a cure for the Syndrome that afflicts you. I hope such a cure will be on time."

Sergius gave him another faint smile. He struggled to express himself.

"It is... too... late... God will... call me... very soon..."

"Not yet," retorted Rapha-el, *"We will fight to the end since I feel your time is not over!"*

"I want... to fight... this sickness... but, I feel... so... wea..k..."

Sergius' head leaned downward, and he dozed off. Rapha-el gently but briefly touched his forehead; like Sergius getting an insulin shot, his eyes popped open trying to follow the conversation; yet his mind skipped.

"Yes... What? ... What did... you say?"

"I said... you are exhausted, and the best thing is for you to rest. We are leaving now," Rapha-el replied with care.

Furthermore, as the Archangel saw Sergius' lips barely trying to talk, he added, *"Yes, we will be back; it is a promise!"*

Izma-el stood up and encouraged him again, *"Our Lord is very generous; focus on His love for strength and hope. So long, my friend; I shall be back when Rapha-el returns."*

As the two Overlords left the room, the body capsule closed again; the two chairs silently merged into the floor as before, and the lights dimmed. Moving into the corridor, Izma-el commented, now telepathically.

"It makes me sad to watch Sergius' life slowly disappearing."

Rapha-el extended his hands so both were facing his own face. He commented, *"With these hands... I can eliminate pain, heal a wound, and make a fever disappear!"*

Raising his hands higher, with an ardent zeal boiling through his veins, he exclaimed, *"My God, if You would allow these hands to be capable of curing the incurable, to make them capable of bringing back the lost vitality of the terminally sick; and to make me able of comforting their tormented minds by giving the suffering new perspectives on life! ... Merciful God, by curing them, they would become living examples of Your eternal love. I beg You, Lord... not for me, but for those suffering the most. Please! Help me terminate the nightmare called: The DNA Syndrome!"*

****

All eight Overlords, in a unique seating array in Mervyn's laboratory, faced the scientist standing in front of a huge display, ready to give the lecture of his lifetime. He looked nervously at the Archangels, who wore semi-formal attire, a jumpsuit version of their formal fancy tunics. The podium was only slightly raised from ground level, allowing a full view of the screen, but only when Mervyn would move out of the way. His hands became wet with perspiration in anticipation of an announcement that even he found hard to believe: The accomplishment of an almost impossible task!

If you could telepathically clear your mental throat, he would have done it since the starting time had arrived. He was nervous; he started a bit shaky.

"My dear friends... I have called this meeting, because I have the most important announcement affecting the future of the SA... I am jubilant to finally disclose that the '4-D Matrix Defense System' is operational and ready to be deployed. Once implemented, we will be free from the threat of any possible preemptive nuclear attack from the NA!"

Samu-el sat straight up from his chair and questioned.

"Why did I not hear anything about this System?"

"Neither I!" Zeri-el also commented.

Micha-el rotated in his chair and responded to the two Overlords.

"Only I, Rapha-el, and Gabri-el knew about it. We decided to keep it a secret for two reasons... First, the chances of this project ever being completed were very slim... Second, due to its awesome importance and the fact that the Satellite Security System programming code was leaked to the NA by somebody in a high position, I was forced to take this unusual and unprecedented decision."

When telepathic silence returned to the meeting, Mervyn continued.

"Let me explain how it works!" [2]

He pointed to the screen with a hand wired with a complex communication device. In response to his command, the center of the screen was illuminated with a 3-D visual display of the planet Terra. One satellite array became displayed over the SA and a similar one over the NA. After a brief pause, he continued.

"These are the current defensive arrangements for the Alliances. As you know, the satellites are armed with power lasers and plasma guns. Nobody has nuclear-carrying devices in space; they are too easy to shoot down!

---

[2] Reminder: Mervyn and the Overlords communicate with each other using complex intellectual dialogues; the reader does not need to understand everything they express. If Mervyn's cross-dimensional explanation is too hard to follow on the next four pages, please consider it sci-fi jargon, as you probably had before in Star Wars or Star Trek, and quickly move on to the next reading paragraph.

The fastest offensive or defensive weapon is the laser. Once fired, it travels at the speed of light but can also be deflected, absorbed, or reflected.

Next, at an intermediate speed, is the plasma gun. At short range, it is impossible to stop; however, once we are talking about planetary distances, it becomes susceptible to cancellation.

Last, the delivery vehicles used for nuclear weapons are extremely slow compared to the other two weapon systems. In the atmosphere, they are restricted by air friction, which at high speeds becomes a thermal barrier. Even if they were deployed in space, the time required to accelerate the delivery craft, even using hypersonic speed, is still <u>too long!</u>

*The present 3-D defense systems have many weak points that can be exploited. A war will initially start as a massive laser offensive, closely followed by a plasma gun barrage. Nuclear weapons can be used only after the two primary defense weapon systems are disabled! ... However, a 4-D matrix, which includes the relativistic effects of anything traveling at or near the speed of light, **is not vulnerable!**"*

Mervyn looked into the piercing eyes of the elite audience... he felt sorry that he did. The room oscillated momentarily, but everything returned to normal as he stared at the ceiling. He knew that he had the full attention of the SA's most powerful minds. After two seconds had passed, he pointed to the screen. The display over the SA changed to a new strangely skewed arrangement. He proudly exclaimed.

*"There it is... **The 4-D Matrix Defense System!**"*

All the Archangels scrutinized the complex satellite layout. The Overlord with a slender face, a Cherub named Lari-el, who preferred listening, asked.

"Why couldn't the NA use lasers to blast away the matrix?"

Mervyn felt more comfortable gazing at only one Archangel of the same gender as his, he quickly replied to Lari-el.

"The standard offensive and defensive laser systems operate at speeds of sub-nanoseconds. First, considering that it is physically impossible to shoot thousands of lasers in the span of a single microsecond, the spacing between the first and second shots becomes critical. The gap between a leading and a follow-up blast, separated by only one microsecond, is about 300 meters!"

After another brief pause, he moved away some of his curly hair, which was crowding his face, and smiled with some internal satisfaction commonly not expressed outwardly. He mentally spoke.

"At this point, all the rest of the satellite matrix will electronically deploy a plasma shield! Basically, this is the simulation of an optical mirror, which by deflecting the incoming laser beams, makes them <u>useless!</u>"

In the upper left corner, a 3-D simulation of a satellite unit was displayed; it showed the incoming lasers being deflected by the plasma shields. He continued.

"Since it is not practically possible to deflect a plasma blast, you must neutralize it. Network telemetry will identify the unit under attack, which will respond by shooting a smaller but opposite charge to the incoming plasma projectile. By hitting its center, the neutralizing anti-plasma will generate a blast of energy that will disrupt the coherence of the envelope by causing it to expand, and accordingly, destroy it!"

Another simulation showed the physical approach to neutralize a plasma cannon blast.

"Finally, after the enemy's satellite network is destroyed, the attack vehicles will rain down on the NA. They will carry multi-target nuclear warheads. They will be protected as long as they stay in the 4-dimensional vortex of the Matrix!

*Similarly, as an imaginary 2-dimensional being cannot see a 3-dimensional opening above, a 4-dimensional vortex hole is equally invisible to a 3-dimensional being. "The spatial arrangement does not allow a single hit, because, even when we can see the Matrix satellites from the planet's surface, they are at an elevated quantum state, and what you actually see is mostly a hologram... **the satellites are not there!** If a quantum computer tries to locate their actual location, at any chosen instant, it will find out that they are **everywhere**, and simultaneously, **nowhere!***

However, when the attack vehicles leave the Matrix, they will be susceptible to laser and plasma attacks, but only when they get closer to their targets, about the same time as they enter the atmosphere.

The first wave is designed to explode its multi-target payload high in the atmosphere just before the enemy plasma cannons destroy the vehicles. The 20-megaton nuclear devices are constructed in a way that will generate a massive magnetic blast, 99% directed toward the ground... In this case, the NA! The massive electronic disruption they will cause will pave the way for the second wave, which will be directed to programmed targets!"

A third visual emulation showed the nuclear technique used to open a window for the final devastating attack. Even when it was just a simulation, Rapha-el let some air out of his lungs in a way that sounded like a moan; then, he stared at the floor before him. Micha-el turned around, and touching his arm, said, *"I know how you feel my brother. I pray to the All Mighty that this Defense System is good enough to deter even the possibility of war... **and never to be used!**"*

Lari-el asked again.

"Mervyn, I know you plan to show us how Physics and Mathematics support your work function. Could you please do it now? I can hardly wait to see the Matrix layout!"

The Cherub with curly, not-too-well-kept hair rubbed the back of his head. After a quick affirmative smile, he said, *"My pleasure!"*

As the professor got ready to supplement his words with visual displays on the big screens, he paused for a short time. He decided to start with the basics, even when the Overlords knew all about it, just for the sake of continuity, *"You all know that for an object to move from a lower dimension to a higher one, it is not physically possible. If we could, we would be intruding into God's dwellings!*

However, we could simulate being inside such a dimension to experience its incredible advantages... Just note that any higher dimension is immensely larger than the lower one!

As you look down into lower dimensions, the first thing that draws our attention is the spatial restrictions. For example, 2-D is more restricted than 3-D, but 1-D is much more restricted.

Since it is impossible to explain a 4-D space as related to our 3-D world, let us assume the 4-D is the 3-D, which we can understand. In this manner, we can examine our perspective from a 2-D world.

How could the 2-D world we see simulate the 3-D space where we are? ... There are two ways. Both include relativistic approaches if we intrude into the 4-D, the dimension we are trying to simulate... To simplify, we further assume the 2-D world to be just a square piece of paper.

First, we could draw a three-dimensional image on the flat paper. It will still look limited to being a flat drawing to simulate the 3-D world we are in.

*Second, we could bend the edges or any part of the paper. Again, its flat surface will simulate a 3-D object, even though the beings living inside the 2-D piece of paper will only see a completely flat world, never a 3-D world; for them, the higher dimension world is beyond their sensing abilities. In other words... **it is invisible!**"*

The large screens visually reinforced the mentally spoken statements with lively demos. Mervyn paused for a short time while scratching his head; he briefly said.

"The next simplified drawing uses both techniques to simulate the fourth dimension. It is the basic unit, the foundation of my work!"

At the center of the huge screen, all other information was displaced outwardly, relinquishing the area to a new informative data set. Now, the letter **T**, plus additional information, appeared.

Pointing to the displayed image, Mervyn continued to deepen into his thesis, *"The 4-D spatial super-transform, which is time-dependent, has four handles!*

There is one for each of the three dimensions: X, Y, Z, and one for the T-Relativistic. As viewed in the Fourth Dimension, the handles are in a planar layout and equidistant. This is untrue *if we inspect the same drawing in our 3-D world!*

In a 3-dimensional drawing, the XYZ handles should be pointing in directions normal to each other, but the fourth handle, the vector T, is skewing everything. It is hard to sketch 4-D drawings in our 3-D world."

The professor paused for a moment. His soft green eyes managed to hide the great intellect behind his desire to make eye contact with the audience as a good speaker should; nevertheless, Mervyn stared at the ceiling instead. Pointing to the T transform drawing on the big screen, he exclaimed, *"It is the center of the 4-D Matrix! From here, as the equation above the display shows, the matrix propagates in all four directions. The interactions are complex within the matrix; the handles support the propagation of 3-D vector transformations, which are intrinsically connected ... Let me show you, the second step to integrate the Matrix!"*

He manipulated more controls connected to his hand, and the initial display with the **T** in the center started to grow in a similar way as a spider fabricates its web.

The more items added to the screen, the more complex the array became. Every new item would grow connections to the others to become part of the intricate network. The 4-D drawing was no longer flat but a superimposed mesh of 3-D images.

Next, he added three-dimensional X'Y'Z'T' to the equation; the web grew enormously. He went to double prime and finally to triple prime. The simulated 4-D array on a 3-D screen display was awesome. It covered the whole screen!

The 4-D Matrix defense system was obviously the work of a genius in his field of expertise. The Overlords, busily assimilating the concept, were amazed by its intricate design.

Enchanted by the display, Zeri-el asked, *"Mervyn! Are you ready to deploy this system?"*

The Physics/Math/Computer scientist smiled with satisfaction; he could not wait to announce the final glorious event. He took a three-second pause before exclaiming.

"I am building the final cylinders for its delivery... The SA will deploy the 4-D Matrix, fully operational... in only 20 days!"

The same night, in a small village 120 Km west of Dawnel.
Dagon, or C-1, was approaching the place where he lived. He just parked his personal craft next to a three-story building, where sections or flats were allocated to single individuals, similar to a condominium setup. The pathway to access the building stayed well illuminated; however, due to

the densely decorated trees planted along its curved and ascending footpath, large adjacent areas remained partially or entirely dark.

He was walking fast on the incline leading to his higher-located personal flat. It was late, and tomorrow would be a hectic day at work.

His sharp peripheral eyesight picked up a slight movement in the shadows! He looked in the direction, but nothing was visible. His muscles tensed up; he was getting ready for any action that could develop... he sharpened his hearing...

He listened with acute concentration. He could not hear anything else than a very soft murmur caused by a mild breeze caressing the leaves of the trees. There was something else... that repeating 'tick,' 'tick' sound from behind to his left side! What could it be?

After a brief analytical exercise, he thought, "I know. It is a night bird called Blue Crest.' It is probably digging for larvae in some tree's bark!"

Dagon rotated his head at tremendous speed to peek behind him. There was nothing... or did he see a shadow moving away into the darkness? He thought again. "I feel like I am being stalked. I hate to be in the open without any of my guns... just two more steps and the sliding door to the building's second floor will open!"

He could sense somebody standing behind him!

"Do not look back!" A strange but dominant mental voice commanded.

Dagon, now standing still, ignored it. As he tried to look behind quickly, his neck did not obey him; instead, a searing pain propagated to his neck and moved down his spine. He squeezed his teeth together to control the distressing ache; after a deep breath, he slowly let the air out of his lungs!

"Stupid luck!" He angrily reproached himself, **"An Overlord has picked me up!"**

The voice behind mentally talked to him again, *"I work for the NA, and I cannot risk that you could identify me in any way! ... We will continue talking in this manner. I have contacted you because I have two tasks that your team must accomplish for me!"*

C-1 was ready to think. "This is probably a trap to expose the rest of my team!" But he did not; he knew the Overlords could listen to his thoughts... Instead, cautiously, he asked mentally, *"What do you want?"*

The Overlord answered, *"An extreme crisis has developed. The NA is in danger, and only your team can prevent it!"*

Above his right shoulder, a hand appeared in his field of vision; it handed Dagon a small square and shiny cube. He picked it up; he knew it was a high-density 3-D memory module.

"You protect this module with your life!" The voice ordered. Then, he continued, *"Inside, there is a program on how to build a 4-D Matrix Defense System. Whoever launches it in the air first will control the whole*

planet! The NA <u>must</u> stop the SA from deploying the Matrix! Furthermore, we only have... **19 days left!**

I know you have found a job for C-2, where he commutes between Dawnel and B3 Bird Island... **He ought to deliver the module through B2 Island and to Lucif-er in Centrum... immediately!***"*

"How did you know about C-2? Do you have a master decoder?"

"Yes! Next, I have a personal job for you! ... Before the time for the 4-D Matrix deployment is up... **you must try to kill Micha-el!***"*

When hearing the name of his main target, Dagon squeezed his trigger finger against his same hand thumb, but rebelliously, he replied, *"I only take orders directly from Lucif-er!"*

The voice grew angry and impatient. It shouted.

"Do not play stupid with me!

This is a crisis! Since we cannot communicate with the NA without exposing ourselves, I am superseding Lucif-er's authority. I am risking my critical secret cover to bring you this vital information. If you refuse to do it... I will kill you!"

A moment of silence followed. Dagon started to believe the stranger; he did make sense. As he stared at the closed door before him, he reminisced about the last seven years of his life. What did he do? Nothing but holding that dumb job in the town's factory, a job that he hated. He could not wait any longer; every night, he would train for the moment he anxiously awaited. Would it be possible? That it was today?

Like a rising sun brings heat to the land, his blood gradually heated to what felt like its boiling point. Even when the Overlord knew his next move, he allowed it out of his feverish mind.

"Yes, Sir! I will do it!"

The Archangel gave some further instructions.

"You know where the Blue Canyon is located. It is Micha-el's favorite meditating place. Five days from now, he and Gabri-el will be taking a walk together. Fifteen kilometers north from the start of the trail, a large white rock protrudes into the canyon's riverbed. Before he turns back, <u>he stops there!</u>"

Dagon tried to interrupt with a sentence expressing that he had a minimal chance of success with the weapons at his disposal. Still, the Overlord continued, *"Your chances for success are much better than you think. That box marked 'Do not open until ordered,' which you have hidden in a closet... Open it! You will like what is inside!"*

C-1 visualized the box, which he had often been tempted to open; however, he knew Lucif-er.

Suddenly, he felt a new emptiness behind him. He thought about quickly flipping his head around, but his brain reminded him of a recent painful experience. Slowly, he turned around. The pathway was empty, with no Overlord in sight; the Archangel no longer stood around.

He rushed into the building and his apartment. He went straight to his computer terminal and sent a quick message to his teammates.

Report to me at once.

The business transaction that we have been waiting for has been approved. C-2, bring your gear tonight. We have a special delivery for B3 Island.

The screen cleared, and it went into standby mode. Dagon walked to a nearby closet with a burning desire. The door slid open; in the back was this gray rectangular box.

He stared at it for a second... On top, he could see five rectangular symbols; it was a unique code, and each symbol represented a word. He mentally deciphered the code, as he had done many times before.

DO NOT OPEN UNTIL ORDERED.

His eyes were fully opened, anticipating something good. What could it be? Just below the symbols, he placed both hands open and flat on a smooth surface. A green light blinked on.

Without removing his hands or even moving away a finger, he pressed a 10-digit code using additional pressure, only at his fingertips. The top of the box clicked and disengaged from the rest of the crate.

Dagon anxiously picked it up and threw it away! ... He stared into the opened cavity. With both hands, he raised a long metallic object. It had many instrumental devices attached to its main body. His heart raced with excitation... It could not be! ... **But it was!**

He raised the high-power 10-km plasma sniper rifle above his head. While shaking the hi-tech weapon with his powerful hands, he screamed with passionate satisfaction, which emanated from the dark depths of his unique and viciously oriented military training, **"Yessssss!"**

In the province of Graceland, an angel from the choir of Virtues stood alone outside his house. The place had a great outlook of the bright green, grassy rolling hills of Green Valley.

Many colorful birds flew in the sky with the intention of going west, a yearly migration to the Bird Islands, although most seemed not to be in a hurry to get there. From the east, a cluster of cumulus clouds was approaching; a gentle but steady breeze blowing from the same direction preceded the towering white clouds. The angel, Eugenius, sitting on a decoration encrusted on the front of his house, stared away from his home in the direction of the many homes around the countryside. The area around the houses was empty of angels; he figured out that most people must be at work or doing recreational activities. Well, almost everybody; this single angel was coming down from a street leading to the first nearby rolling hill and into a path connecting the structures, including his. The approaching individual remained far away.

Eugenius grabbed his stomach. A great emptiness existed inside, and it was not due to hunger. The angel missed his family, which he previously and currently loved so much. Seven years had passed since the Exodus, and he had no idea where his family now stayed since he had heard nothing from them.

His wet eyes showed the distress caused by a long separation. His love for God kept him going; he even dreamed of the future day when he would meet his Creator and end all this suffering. The price he paid for his faith had been high indeed.

He had taken for granted that he and his family would always be together as they had for so many years. However, the last few years without them appeared longer than a thousand years. How long before his soul could find peace again? ... An eternity?

He glanced at the clouds getting closer; it would rain soon. The wind gradually picked up; next, a distant thunder rumbled by.

He looked again at the individual coming his way. He started to discern his attire, a light green jumpsuit. He was walking fast, at a dynamic pace, probably exercising.

One more time, Eugenius submerged himself in the quicksand of loneliness, where an internal pain refused to go away. He realized that his desire to be loved was not properly focused, and if he could have his entire mind and soul dedicated to his God, there would be no place for loneliness to exist. So, why couldn't he deal with it?

He apologized to the Lord for this significant weakness in his character. He took a light bite of his thumbnail; self-pity does not solve anything; some real action was needed. With almost anger, he thought the following.

"I need to socialize, to do more physical activities. Maybe I need to move afar to a new house to start a new life, something that could heal the 'wound'!"

He looked up to see the dark clouds passing overhead. At the distance, the rain began coming down like undulating sheets of silk shaken by the invisible hand of a restless wind. The approaching lightning and thunder became brighter and louder.

The walking angel, now close to his house, looked directly at Eugenius. A reflection of the sunshine breaking through the clouds indirectly illuminated his face. The approaching angel's curly brown hair almost looked like gold as it became backlit by the sun's rays. His face was flawless, like a Greek… **goddess!**

"Oh, Lord!" He exclaimed mentally as he noticed the shapely form bulging beneath the jumpsuit. "It's not **he**, but **she!** … Furthermore, I have never seen such a beautiful angel in my whole life!"

As he recognized her as the next higher choir of Dominions, the clouds occluded the sun; now, she was in the shadow. Her previous image, already registered in his brain… did not change!

While walking by Eugenius's house, she suddenly stopped, changed direction, and moved directly toward him. He did not blink for several seconds. In a melodic and clear voice, she addressed him.

"Hi Eugenius, I am Claire!"

As he greeted her by touching her open right hands at chest level and admiring her long eyelashes, he just said, *"Hiii!"*

She continued, *"You don't know me; I am new in this town. I lived most of my life in the provincial capital city of New Hope. Somebody mentioned to me that your whole family left for the NA. You must be feeling very lonesome... My oldest brother also went to the NA... I do love him very much, and I know what the absence of a loved one does to our hearts... I have noticed that you have isolated yourself from everybody else. I could not justify walking by and ignoring you when I know you need some kindness and companionship to survive."*

The rain started to come down; some large droplets began smashing onto the ground. He woke up from the trance he was in and offered.

"Would you like to come inside my home to avoid the rain?"

She gave him a wide smile that showed her perfectly white and lined teeth but declined, *"No, thank you... I'd rather continue my walk."*

"In the rain?"

"Why not? I don't mind; it is a warm rain anyway! Would you like to share the walk with me?"

He hesitated for an instant but cheerfully accepted.

"I would love to!"

As both angels walked together into the heavy rain, her curly hair quickly straightened to flat bands running across her face. Minute streams of water were capriciously running down her face. He looked at her at close range, squinting his eyes to keep the rainwater away from them. He thought how beautiful she looked, even when soaking wet. When the rain hit him hard in the eyes, he glanced down. Then noticed he had forgotten to change and was still wearing his nice working clothes!

He quickly turned his sight toward her to see if she had noticed... She did catch him in the act and responded with a closed-lip smile. When he began to feel rather dumb, she touched him on the shoulder, and with a soft tone, she said, *"Don't worry... It doesn't matter!"*

He did not feel the rain anymore; he hardly noticed it. Lightning, thunder, heavy rain, and gusty winds accompanied the sudden storm. Outside, the storm raged; inside, the one that had lasted seven years had just vanished!

It is interesting to watch the crossroads in our lives. While some separate us from our loved ones, leading us into despair and never-ending suffering, other crossings merge two lonely souls into the same path, bringing love and companionship where none existed. Most surprising of all, sometimes this happens almost instantly.

Is the hand of God constantly molding our lives, much more than we can imagine?

****

Mervyn nervously waited outside the main lab complex, pacing back and forth on a large porch connected to a wide semi-circular entrance. He looked up above the towering structure, but no movement from whatever he was expecting appeared.

He scratched the back of his head, where his curly hair remained thicker. Even when the late afternoon radiated a pleasant coolness, he was perspiring. The stress emanating from inside wore him down, causing his four wings, visible as faint rays, to be in unusual disarray. He thought.

"Why is it taking so long for Micha-el to arrive? He said, 20 minutes!"

It must have been about 30 minutes since he communicated with the leader of the SA. He checked his watch and was shocked to see that it had been only 19 minutes! He stared at the busy sky where so many crafts passed by, but none was approaching his direction.

Only a few seconds later, a bright dot diverged from the scheduled flying paths. It bypassed the landing patterns and came straight to a small, restricted parking lot carved out from the building's decorating landscape, only 20 meters to the left of the porch.

The slick and powerful craft, the personal machine assigned to an Overlord, landed quickly. Micha-el, his dynamic self, was the first out of the vehicle and rapidly approached Mervyn. Two armed Seraphim soldiers ran in opposite directions, one to the main entrance, which he opened but did not go in; the other went to the front of the building, where the multiple paths from the adjacent avenue merged to give access to the main entrance. This soldier raised his hand to indicate 'Stop' to five individuals on their way to the building; obviously, they had special instructions for this meeting.

The Overlord stood next to the scientist, and his saluting hand, just by touching Mervyn's, knew about the severity of this meeting. A deep concern replaced the Archangel's smile!

"My dear friend!" He exclaimed, *"You asked for this meeting to tell me that somebody stole a copy of the 4-D Matrix Defense System?"*

Mervyn glanced down in an apologetic and emotional response. Micha-el fought to control his disappointment; losing such important information was no small deed! However, he quickly touched the professor's shoulder and gently commented.

"Please, Mervyn. Do not blame yourself for this incident! ... The building security is exceptionally high. Only somebody utterly familiar with its layout could have done it. In addition, to achieve this for a second time without leaving a trace tells me that the perpetrator is an Overlord!"

The Cherub looked into the depth of the Archangel's blue eyes and inquired, *"Do you think that Izma-el could have done it?"*

Without blinking or showing any other concern, Micha-el replied.

"No! I fully trust him!"

He could have extracted the answer from Mervyn's brain, but he needed to relax the scientist by letting him explain a significant detail. So, he asked.

"How did you discover that the program was copied?"

"The Matrix program has an additional but invisible supervisory program. The thief erased all data indicating that a copy had been made. Today, when I checked the transparent supervisory program, it told me about the clandestine copy!"

Micha-el, looking away from Mervyn, commented.

"It has been twelve hours since this happened. Data this important will be moved to the NA in record time. I will call a Yellow Alert on all our borders, just in case we are still in time!"

Micha-el, staring again into the green eyes of his companion, solemnly stated, *"Let me tell you what else I will do.*

Since the process of unmasking the traitor can be gruesome, I am very reluctant to accuse any Overlord of the SA, whom I consider to be my own brothers!

It is not easy to conduct this inquiry on the innocent, who always worked very hard for our Alliance; asking for proof of his loyalty could be quite a blow to his self-esteem. Nonetheless, if the NA has the information about the 4-D Matrix, they will threaten us with nuclear war before they allow us to deploy it. In this case, it will be impossible to implement the satellite network.

I will order all the Overlords to be present for the launch. If the NA does interfere with such launching... I will not stop until we have figured out who is responsible!

Only if I do not hear from the NA and we successfully deploy the Matrix... Then, I will not say a word. In either case, I promise nobody else will know about this innovative program tool you installed deep inside the 4-D Matrix program. The invisible supervisory program will continue to be so!"

****

A red light, part of a computer display, sounded an alarm in a South Alliance military base on B3 Island. The commander of the place ran to the main large screen, which showed a bright dot moving north and quickly approaching the DMZ.

Most commanders in critical locations were Seraphim; he was no exception. Addressing a soldier, a Cherub seated close to him, he mentally requested.

"Data!"

The subordinate quickly conveyed the information.

"Personal unarmed vessel from the SA! ... Refusing to be ID and moving quickly toward the NA-controlled space, the same sector as the incident involving a previously drifting research vehicle. There are two individuals aboard. It is too late for an aerial interception! ... Plasma cannon, locked!"

The SA commander remained silent for two seconds, reluctant to shoot down unarmed civilians. He remarked thoughtfully so his assistant could also mentally hear.

"It is possible that the passengers are NA agents returning to their country. If we had caught them, we would have to return them to the NA, anyway! ... Let them go!"

"Sir! May I remind you that we are in Yellow Alert, with orders to prevent anybody from leaving the SA!" the soldier said.

"I am aware, but we cannot prevent them from leaving unless we kill them! ... Order stands!"

C-2 and C-3 held the controls of the speeding cylinder. They were already inside the DMZ, and the red blinking message in the front display continued unemotionally stating.

SA Plasma Cannon, Targeting Telemetry
Condition on this craft: LOCKED

Their lightly perspiring foreheads with staring eyes focused on the control panel indicated the intensity of their concentration. Both Seraphim became elated when the last message turned to a solid green.

UNLOCKED

"Yes! ... It was easy!" Both mentally yelled together.

C-3, turning to C-2, exclaimed with noticeable joy.

"You were right! The SA soldiers are gutless... Incapable of shooting unarmed civilians!"

Their controls indicated that they had just entered NA-controlled air space.

Was it feasible that the kindness and respect for life from an SA commander would be the reason for the Alliance losing that needed edge, which the Matrix could have allowed them? All those benefits include peace of mind, a chance to end the world conflict, and most importantly, a device capable of pushing Evil to the lower places where it belongs... Apparently, all those benefits had now vanished!

An intruder's alarm rang with an annoying noise!

The North Alliance's B2 commander came running again to the same place where the big display was located. He stood behind the same Throne soldier that assisted him before. Anxiously, he requested.

"What is going on?"

The soldier carefully monitored the terminal and reported quickly.

"Sir, this is similar to the last incident! SW-17 Sector, SA vessel; unarmed, two individuals aboard! This vehicle is moving fast, about 1.2 Km/second!

Plasma cannon... locked!"

After being chewed out from the last incident, the Commander felt very uneasy about this new development. He had a limited time before the cylinder would overrun his post!

Nervously, he fought to give a sense of security and authority. He stared at the red dot approaching the island's coastline.

"Check ID!" He requested.

"Yes, Sir!... Done!"

Only two seconds later, the code appeared on the monitor.

NA CD 333333

A bit skeptical about the code ID, he squeezed his forehead skin as he stared at the code; he telepathically snapped.

"What kind of stupid ID code is that? The last group is supposed to have at least *one* letter!"

The operator manipulated some controls. The terminal responded.

THE CODE IS VALID.

"Sir! I have never seen this code format before, but the computer approved it! I am going... ***Commander! The vessel has changed direction! It is heading straight for this post... Time of arrival: 29 seconds!"***

Panicking inside his brain, the commander named Denariel assured himself that no such code ID existed, even if the computer said so. He felt time running out and choking him harder with each speeding second zipping by; furthermore, each second felt like a bullet on its way to his own heart!

He screamed, ***"Shoot it down!"***

C-2 saw the darkened outline of the island quickly passing underneath, but his mind was already on the NA mainland. This new course just plotted was taking him and his companion directly to the city of Centrum. There, by delivering an exceptionally important memory unit, they will be received as heroes!

Seven years away from his favorite city, how he missed it all! ... And especially that voluptuous girlfriend of his... Marcia! He could not wait! He squeezed his teeth together hard enough to cause saliva to come from his lips; while licking his upper lip, he complained.

"Why can't this piece of garbage or aircraft go any faster? Maximum speed...
is so slow!"

His side vision caught a red blinking message still going on. Without
turning his head to look at the display, he nodded about the slow response
of the inept personnel of this remote B2 Island base.

On the ground, a few kilometers directly in front of his pathway and
from a place entirely covered by darkness, a bright light blinked on!

Only a fraction of a second later, he saw a red ball of fire about to
impact the cylinder. There was no time to think, to react, or even to feel
pain.

C-2 and C-3 opened their eyes widely... and died.

A red ball of fire blew up the craft into tiny pieces. Like a lightning
bolt, a sudden flash closely followed by a thunderous blast illuminated the
night sky above the island.

Like a firework shot on Independence Day, the initial big ball of fire
disintegrated into tiny reddish pieces that rained to the ground below.
Seconds later, on the terrain where the pieces fell, only a few burning spots
remained visible.

What seemed hopeless to stop, the great secret of the SA carried in a
small electronic cube, was now reduced to tiny pieces of burned debris!

Evil, in its destructive ways, sometimes destroys itself.

****

As many times before, Micha-el stood alone, gazing over the beauty of
the Blue Canyon. A small river had carved this scenery out of a solid
mountain range; its brisk waters ran east, where it became a tributary of a
much larger river named Dekodda. The journey of the massive Dekodda
ended in a large delta on the eastern coast, separating the provinces of
Irisan and Tellia.

The canyon's color was due to one type of huge tree crowding the
valleys and slopes of the mountains; it flowered in the spring with a
spectacular show of blue flowers like the Jacaranda trees. At this time,
only a few trees started blooming to their total capacity.

The early morning began cool and clear, with the sun barely rising
above the surrounding mountains' rims. Many birds sang melodically but
avidly, using unique tones and sound sequences demanded by their
species, either looking for a mate or defining their territories.

Gabri-el appeared around a sharp bend in the trail and proceeded to
meet Micha-el at a post marking, which indicated the beginning of a trail
running parallel to the river's course.

The Overlords greeted each other with both hands at chest level.
Micha-el wore a white top with a solid green bottom jumpsuit; Gabri-el

had a completely solid light green outfit; both displayed a small golden cross over their hearts. With a welcoming smile, Micha-el mentally said.

"My brother, you got delayed by Mervyn more than expected!"

As both Overlords started a brisk walk along the compacted dirt trail, Gabri-el responded.

"Yes, Micha-el, this angel is in great distress. He cannot forgive himself for letting somebody break the lab's security system and steal the 4-D Matrix program. I keep telling him... It was not your fault, but he refuses to listen!"

Micha-el quickly followed.

"I can sense that you have figured out the procedure for finding the traitor. Your configuration is the same as the one I have drawn inside my mind... Each Archangel, being probed to find out who the traitor is, will stand at the center of a hexagon, with Overlords at each point where a circle intersects its corners. The radius, the value of π in meters, is the spacing of the questioning Overlords: equidistant over the circle's circumference, or $2\pi/6$." He finished with a statement, *"I will not participate in the questioning!"*

"I pray to the Lord that we will not have to do this," Gabri-el said.

"Exactly my own feelings!"

The two good friends quickly moved away into the picturesque canyon. As their figures got smaller in the distance, the murmur of the running waters soon overtook their emotionally charged conversation.

A scope-targeting device showed a magnified circle of a blue eye pressed against its rear objective. Red markings with a small cross at the center displayed a single tree standing at the top of this large white rock protruding into the river's canyon; the tree in sight was covered entirely with blue blossoms. The weapon's cross-reference remained precisely positioned in the middle of the tree's trunk. Inside the scope, away from the center, several messages merged into a single data table. It read the following:

Distance : 10,324.666 m		**Temperature/Outside: 25.1°C**
Stabilization: Active	<<<+>>>	**Wind SE/D** : 3.3 km/h
Power out : Maximum		**Security Parameters : Active**
Target : Not Locked		**Vital Signs** : Normal

C-1 smiled when he saw the least three significant digits of the 'Distance.' It was a good omen... the three numbers of his boss!

He was wearing a completely sealed suit, almost like a spacesuit, self-contained. A visor flipped up to expose a thin and transparent membrane, which allowed eye contact with the high-power sniper rifle's scope without compromising the secured internal environment. The air exiting the contraption was temperature and chemically compensated to match the outside ambiance.

Furthermore, the outside material comprised fiber optic bundles that transmitted the incoming light to the opposite exiting side. The effect was a perfect chameleon disguise, which optically matched the individual to its surroundings. Dagon was practically invisible, even to the IR monitoring security satellites.

The sniper gun did have a laser for telemetry; however, this device was not used against an Overlord to avoid detection; it would be a giveaway, rendering the gun useless. Instead, the auto-focus was computer-coupled to a complex high-quality optical triangulation that used an array of merging collimated beams at the point where the targeting-centered cross was located. This targeting point stayed through the whole zooming range, always in focus.

The rest of the C team waiting for action split into two locations. Four camped outdoors at a nearby place, 20 kilometers west. They were supposed to pick up C-1 if that was possible. The rest were busy in a small town nearby, which the team used as a base, and they worked together to organize a getaway.

C-1 arrived yesterday afternoon. He meticulously chose a site with an excellent overhead cover and a clear view of the protruding white rock with the flowering tree in its middle.

He was hungry… yet it was another kind of hunger: a sinister killing driving force that overrode everything else. The wait had been long, but its conclusion was in sight!

Thirty-five Terra minutes have elapsed; in that time, the two Overlords covered more than half of the distance to their destination: the white rock marker, a place for a break and then to return.

We could listen to their conversation as they approached this place during their brisk walk. Gabri-el made a comment.

"The smell of the flowering Hoshua trees is truly an intoxicating pleasure. It reminds me of the aroma from vanilla sticks!"

Micha-el did smile, but he immediately retorted.

"They do, my brother… although, do not change the subject.

Did we agree that the consciousness of self-being, as an identity, is a brain function brought about by our own spirits? Therefore, its manifestation becomes a driver for our mind, imprinting in this way our uniqueness… However, our perception of our identity is restricted by our perception of reality. It is like the electromagnetic spectrum, where visible light is only a window. Through it, we can see our surroundings; nevertheless, it is only a window that restricts the perception of all the events happening side by side around us. If we could see IR, UV, X-rays,

Gamma, and other mediums of perception, it would open new horizons, allowing us to see the reality next to us with a new and unique perception. Similarly, to find ourselves, our perception of reality must go beyond the perception of material things and the logic of our minds. As always, God always helps us to recognize this invisible and immaterial link!"

Gabri-el, listening with intensity, remarked.

"Yes, Micha-el, since the Lord gave us the gift of our souls, He should be the connection to understanding. As we ask Him... and take little sips from the ocean of His knowledge, we ascend one step higher in our wisdom! ... Conversely, what will be our perception of our identity if we do not have the following: language, knowledge of previous experiences, and contact with anyone else?"

Very briefly, Micha-el kindly looked at his companion; then, with a visionary perception going above his intellect, he continued.

"Even in those extreme conditions, our perception of self will be connected to our perception of the existence of our Creator because our Lord, in His generosity, allows the unintelligent, the inexperienced, and the uneducated to understand the most complex truths of our existence. Truths and realities that are beyond the grasp of the most intelligent and educated; we call this gift, a revelation!"

Gabri-el looked at the delightful scenic walk. The trail, making a sharp turn right, projected outwardly into the riverbed, allowing the angels to see what was coming ahead.

Still far away, a large white dot protruded over a distant cliff above the river. It was their midway destination... the large white rock!

Using the telescopic sight, the Seraph named Dagon began scanning ahead, trying to find anybody approaching from the south. He got impatient; the sun was rising but with no sign of the Overlords. His internal temperature increased a fraction of a degree; nevertheless, the suit air-conditioner quickly compensated for the difference. Because he laid flat on the ground, using an old log for cover and rifle support, he was stiffening up a bit; thus, he started some muscular tension exercises that opposed different muscle groups. He strongly tensed his muscular and well-toned body; a few minutes later, as his blood circulation improved, he felt much better.

Again, he gazed at the river turns in search of any movement. He hated the smell of these purple flowering trees, Hoshua, or whatever their name was... It made the task much more challenging to concentrate on... **Did he see something?**

He froze. Two small figures were moving along the outside of a protruding turn across the river. The Overlords were coming, and his moment of glory was coming soon!

The Archangels, approaching from the last stretch leading to the big rock, had Gabri-el talking at this time. He briefly looked at the approaching beautiful tree in the middle of the large stone as he expressed his perception of the eventualities being discussed.

"What about the reasoning we use to explain the events we have been discussing? Is it truly ours? Could we be repeating the same ideas and logic as many others did before us? ... Maybe we are just the product of our education; what we read, learn from others, and our computer memory banks tell us is our knowledge. Perhaps, also a consequence of our culture, one more piece on the aggregate that is our angelic race... Although, we both know that all knowledge and truth originates from God!"

The tree was only fifty meters away; while walking directly to its location, Gabri-el requested, *"Let's dialogue about God and His Divine Trinity?"*

Micha-el stared at the blue blossoms, now becoming more discernible; he softly replied, *"Just briefly... We know it is impossible for us to figure out our Lord's Holy Trinity! Only when we finally arrive at His presence will we see Him as He is; then, we shall understand. My soul, eager and impatiently, burns for the coming of this day!.... I will share a thought with you... Sometimes, I see God and the Holy Trinity as light itself.*
The Father is the higher energy Blue!
The Son is on the opposite side, the Red!
The Holy Spirit is the interaction between the Father and the Son.
It includes a range of infinite colors in between; all the hues together make White light, like what we call our Creator, <u>one</u> God!
All the Deities of the Holy Trinity are unique, just as the independent or 'primary' colors are. And <u>only</u> the combination of all colors is <u>White</u>!"

The Overlords now stood on the top and center of the large white rock, just at the same place where a beautiful Hoshua tree grew with such splendor.

Gabri-el looked up and touched a cluster of flowers shaped like small, inverted blue bells. While responding to his companion, he thought, "These flowers have an exquisite shape and a delightful aroma!"

"It is a great insightful thought, Micha-el! That must be why The Temple's light display makes us feel so close to the Lord!" After an instant of self-searching, Gabri-el continued, *"When I think that Lucif-er was the chief architect for the construction of such a building, I still find it hard to believe that now, he is determined to destroy it!"*

As Micha-el moved closer to the edge of the rock overlooking the riverbed, he took a deep breath from the pristine morning air. Somewhat sadly, he commented, *"It is a pity... God gave us a soul who strives to return to his Creator; however, it is our choice to decide if it will return to Him... or not!"*

Dagon was delighted. What else could he ask for? Micha-el was standing at the edge of the rock, squarely facing him. He could not have been supplied an easier target.

As seen through the scope, he placed the center targeting cross over the Overlord's heart. He chuckled and smiled when he saw the golden cross adorning his jumpsuit, just over his heart!

C-1 anxiously but in a malevolent way remarked, *"Thanks for the 'cross'... I will match my targeting cross over yours!"*

He set some controls; the scope's internal computer displayed the information. It read:

Distance : 10, 313.777 m	**Temperature/Outside: 25.7°C**
Stabilization: Active <<<+>>>	**Wind SE/D** : 2.1 km/h
Power Load : Maximum/0.1 Sec	**Security Parameters** : Active
Target : <<<Locked>>>	**Vital Signs** : Normal↑

Dagon could shoot Micha-el first; after that, he had the limit of 0.1 of a second to nail Gabri-el before he had a chance to take evasive action and move out of reach.

As he started to squeeze the trigger, his concentration reached a maximum, his whole body went on overdrive, and his sight became glued on two overlapping crosses. To conclude, he mentally remarked out loud.
"Say goodbye, Micha-el!"

Gabri-el joined his companion at the edge of the protruding rock. The scenery, the river, the forest, and the mountain ranges were fantastic. Everything was so gorgeous and so peaceful. He began speaking telepathically.

"Micha-el, I think..." he suddenly stopped and visually pondered about his surroundings, **"What is going on?"**

Suddenly, an eerie silence overcame the land! No birds were flying or singing. He could not even sense the movement of a single insect. The breeze was dead still, and even the river waters had lost their gurgling sound.

However, high in the sky, he saw something moving... it was hovering above them. It was a beautiful white eagle, and it looked so familiar. Gabri-el exclaimed to his colleague.

"Something strange is going on! However, look at that beautiful female royal eagle; she is so pretty and graceful... she reminds me of Raquel!"

Also concerned about the strange event, Micha-el stared up at the eagle. Her plush feathers gently broke the air; with minor adjustments from her large wings, she could majestically soar above. Her eyes were of a unique beauty, the same as Raquel's. Curious enough, she was looking at them.

"You are correct... She does remind me of your wife!" Micha-el agreed.

Both Archangels reflected on the mental communication they had. Even the telepathic messages sounded like they came from a reverberating electronic box.

Suddenly, they felt an extraordinary urge to look behind!

Both Overlords turned their heads backward at the same time. An unexpected presence caused a sudden chill to run along their bodies.

How could this angel get behind them without them feeling the slightest indication of his proximity?

He looked like somebody from the top triad dressed in a dark red tunic. However, the faint white halo emanating around his body did not match any group member. His face was pleasant and radiant. The two Overlords lost all concern about his presence by just looking at him.

He addressed their minds in a soft, most pleasant, telepathic message.

"Greetings, Micha-el and Gabri-el!"

The Overlords were surprised that the stranger knew them, while they could not read anything from his mind. For a moment, they felt the non-Archangels' frustration when conversing with an Overlord, as he knew all about them, but the angels could only guess what he was thinking about them.

"Who are you?" Both Archangels requested.

With a kind smile shining on his face, he responded.

"I am the One, whom you have been talking about!"

As the stranger communicated with the Archangels, they had many questions they wanted to ask; however, they were compelled to listen. After that, he talked about the mysteries of life they often tried to decipher together; they were impressed by the stranger's knowledge. He seemed so logical and truth-bearing. At the end, he indicated.

"I have three gifts for you."

Next, as he walked to the base of the Hoshua tree, where a bush had a single white flower, the unfamiliar angel picked it up effortlessly. It appeared as if the flower moved to his hands instead of his hands moving toward the flower, *"This is for you, Micha-el."*

He handed it to him. The incredibly beautiful flower was like a giant rose, but its petals stayed compacted in a large ball of incredible whiteness.

Micha-el took it in both hands, astounded that he had not seen such a flower before, even after stopping at this place so many times.

The stranger commanded the Archangel, *"Destroy it!"*

Even when Micha-el's mind remained confused by the unusual request, he followed the order. With a feeling of pity for the squashing of such an incredibly exquisite flower, he suddenly and powerfully compressed it with both hands.

To his incredulous eyes, a sharp pain made him reopen his hands! He had ripped deep cuts in both palms; blood began gushing from them. Even when the pain felt real, it was not overwhelming. He looked at his blood like it was not his... An Archangel does not get hurt at all!

The stranger spoke again.

"This flower, you cannot destroy by force alone.

Love, being just like a gentle breeze, <u>will do it</u>." After giving Micha-el a broader smile, he continued, *"Gently, blow air onto the flower, and its true nature will be revealed!"*

Micha-el, holding the stem of the white blossom with just two fingers, obeyed. As the breeze from the lips of the Archangel penetrated the flower, its silky petals quickly flew away... What remained horrified both Overlords!

All that stayed behind was a black core of twisted thorns and ugly vines. Like a giant black spider's tentacles looking for prey, the flower's core resembled it.

Micha-el threw it away! How could something of such incredible beauty be so horrendously ugly looking inside?

Micha-el stared into the eyes of the stranger; his heart pounded with excitement. This was not a stranger! He had seen these eyes before... **but where?**

The newcomer, with a soft smile, disengaged from the stare. He removed the largest bell-shaped blue flower hanging from the Hoshua tree. He offered it to Gabri-el.

"Give this flower to Rapha-el; his wish has been granted!"

Gabri-el did not understand the whole meaning of this statement; nevertheless, he quickly accepted the flower. Gently, he placed it in a pocket inside his jumpsuit.

The stranger made another serene comment.

"My dear friends, I will stay with you even as I depart. In a short time, you shall see me <u>again</u>!"

A sharp 'thud' sound behind the Archangels induced them to turn around to investigate. A small branch from the tree had broken off and fallen just behind them. When their heads returned to see the stranger, they found out that... **they were alone!**

Both glanced everywhere quickly. When they found nothing, they looked at each other with similar questions. Their confusion grew until Micha-el looked at the floor.

At the same place where the stranger last stood, on a thin whitish layer of dirt covering the massive stone underneath, they saw neatly drawn.

A cross!

Micha-el's eyes opened widely; inside the cross and his mind, he saw the eyes of the stranger... he remembered! **In his dream, they were the eyes of God!**

He raised both of his hands to the sky and screamed.

"Dear God... You were in front of me, and I did not recognize You! Please, forgive me for my blindness!"

As he lowered his hands, he looked at his palms; they were spotless, with not a single scratch left. He screamed again, *"Thank You; I love You **so much!**"*

He moved near the symbol on the ground and fell on his knees, facing the cross. He equally faced the riverside section of the rock.

Gabri-el was almost instantly on his knees by Micha-el's side; he touched the cross with two fingers from his right hand. He brought the dust sticking on his fingers to his lips and kissed it.

"Thank You, my Lord... You have made this day... the best day of my life!" He exclaimed loudly.

As he remembered the blue flower God had given him, he placed his hand in his pocket and touched it. What a strange but wonderful sensation! A flower petal always feels cool; this one felt warm!

Gabri-el raised his eyes to the sky above, reaching in ecstasy for his Creator. He saw the white eagle still hovering over them; however, just as quickly as he had noticed, the large, beautiful bird dived away toward the west at a soaring speed.

The Overlord had a place left in his mind to make a mental observation.

"You must have spotted prey... Good hunting!"

The pleasant touch of a gentle breeze caressed his face.

The distant melody of several singing birds pleasantly echoed deep inside the forest.

The rumbling sound of water splashing over the rocks vocalized the river coming out of its sleep!

C-1 could not believe what he had done in the past minutes. He just woke up from something analogous to a trance! At the instant, he was ready to wipe out the Overlords from the face of the planet, but involuntarily, he did not pull the trigger. Instead, he decided to watch their strange behavior. With anger in his mind, he began reminiscing about the last events... where he never saw the Divine Visitor!

*"These Overlords from the SA are a pair of idiots! ... First, they talked to the wind! Then, the 'great' Micha-el cut his hands with his own nails! Finally, the crazy maggots kneeled and kissed the dirt from the ground! **By killing them... I am doing the SA a favor!**"*

For an instant, Dagon glanced at the nearby trees fully covered with blue blossoms. As he squeezed together his teeth, he mentally commented with increasing fury.

*"Instead of watching, I should have done my job! ... These stupid and bad-smelling blue flowers... **are putting me to sleep!**"*

The Seraph proceeded to recalibrate the sniper gun. Again, the two crosses over Micha-el's chest overlapped! The two Overlords remained kneeling on the ground, facing the top-trained assassin from the NA!

His muscles tensed again. He had to be fast to kill two Overlords consecutively. As he gently squeezed the trigger, he remarked to the kneeling Overlords, *"No use begging for your lives… you are dead!"*

At the last instant, before he shot the powerful and accurate gun, he saw a shadow above his forehead. He was fast to investigate by glancing above the telescopic sight.

He saw the top part of his visor torn by two pointed objects!

For an instant, they faced both of his eyes. The next instant brought blackness and a searing pain!

He never saw the blood spraying away from his eyes. He tried to finish squeezing the trigger… his finger did not move! That specific part of his brain, which controls motor skills… **was already dead!**

Military Base: SA-P-175-Blue Canyon.

Several Seraphim soldiers jumped to action as a monitor showed a blinking red signal. This section was carefully monitored because the SA Overlords used it for unescorted walks along its trails. One of the soldiers, on edge since he knew that two Overlords, Micha-el and Gabri-el, were only 10 kilometers east of the disturbance, briskly asked his companions.

"What is it?"

As he magnified the sector for a better view, the Seraph beside him responded, *"Satellite IR picked up a signal! … Wait, I can see two signals now, 3 centimeters in diameter each!… Center to center spacing: 8 centimeters!"*

"Those are most angel eyes' normal dimensions and spacing!" Another sharp operator mentally mentioned.

"Yes… But I cannot find anything else! … Also, notice that their temperatures are going down… I think they are dead!" The Seraph added.

The first soldier said, *"There was no signal at that place before. Are those two small animals that came from below the ground… and they killed each other?"*

"Maybe!"

The sharp-minded operator asked.

"Can you detect any animal of prey nearby?"

The soldier pushing all the controls emphatically responded.

"None!"

The two Overlords were approaching Dawnel, flying inside Micha-el's personal craft, which had been summoned to the divine's vision site on Blue Canyon. With the downtown in sight, the craft approached the central building, aiming for the landing place on top of its towering structure. Micha-el, still in ecstasy, told Gabri-el.

"The guards I left on the white rock will prevent anybody from stepping on the cross! That place... I shall declare it a Holy Site! In addition, I shall immediately begin to build an altar for our Lord. It shall be a special place where the people and I will come to adore Him!"

Gabri-el smiled with deep understanding. It was not likely that an Overlord would do or say anything redundant... Micha-el already did it twice. However, he knew that it did not matter; the flame burning inside still reminded him of how close he had been to his Creator!

He could hardly wait to tell Raquel about this incredibly good news. Even at this distance, that small but graceful figure at the edge of the landing place was definitely her.

Micha-el interrupted his thoughts.

"Gabri-el, our Lord's first gift... I know that He was referring to Lucif-er, but what was the meaning of the white flower? A warning?"

"My brother, I know as much as you do. Perhaps in the future, we will know the real meaning."

After a short pause, with Gabri-el's eyes getting closer to Micha-el's, the first questioned, *"Also, what was the third gift?"*

Micha-el placed his right hand behind the neck of his companion. He gently pulled him closer. He exclaimed.

"My dear friend... To me, God's presence was the third and the greatest gift of all!"

The craft gently landed; Gabri-el saw Raquel, almost running to meet him. She stood before the cylinder's door before it would even open.

As the door slid open and the two Archangels stepped down, she jumped into his arms and kissed him. She was anxious to say something. Before her husband could announce the good news, she took the initiative and started, *"My dear husband and Micha-el, I have exceptional news for both of you! I..."*

Gabri-el could not wait, and in an unusual manner, he interrupted his wife, *"Sweetheart! We have much bigger news to tell you!"*

He was ready to start describing all the past events, but he stopped. He sensed a great sorrow from his wife provoked by denying her to talk first. It took an enormous effort, but he relinquished.

"Sorry for interrupting my love; tell us, what is so important?"

Raquel's face, the perfect image of beauty, lighted up like sunshine. She quickly proceeded, *"I had this incredibly realistic dream!... In this dream, I saved both of your lives! ... The dream started at..."* She froze.

Gabri-el had stopped smiling and was staring at her! Micha-el, one step backward, moved in and equally stared at her!

The Overlords, with anticipation, had read her mind. Gabri-el exclaimed, *"You!... You were the white eagle!"*

"Raquel, I saw you flying above us!" Micha-el exclaimed and quickly requested, *"Please! Continue!"*

Raquel, a little shaken since she became concerned about the behavior of her companions, after a second or two, softly but cautiously added.

"Yes... I was the white eagle! ... I was standing on the arm of this powerful but gentle angel. I do not know who he was, but I know I would trust him with my life!"

Her eyes looked away as she was reliving the dream.

"He told me... 'I am here to visit Micha-el and Gabri-el; however, they are in grave danger!

Deep in the forest, a beast is waiting to strike and kill them. I will meet Micha-el and Gabri-el on the large white rock; fly above us, look west. You have the power to stop the beast!

I flew up... the wind rubbing against my feathers felt so good! It gave me a mighty lift, so I soared high above the rock!" Raquel swayed like she was still flying above the forest, her face showing the joy of a pleasant experience.

"My eyesight was incredible; everything was so sharp! Even at great heights, I could recognize your faces. You were standing next to this gorgeous Hoshua tree when I saw the majestic angel who had sent me to protect you as he approached you.

At that moment, something strange happened! ... It was like time had frozen... and I was flying but going nowhere! The whole land was at a standstill!"

After a brief pause, she proceeded.

"Minutes later, everything went back to normal."

At this point, the joy in her face vanished as she became serious. Now, feeling the anxiety of some unpleasant event, she continued, *"Out of the west, I clearly saw it! ... An ugly large serpent with two bulky red eyes, a sinister monster ready to strike! It was far away, but I knew it possessed powerful poisonous darts that could hurt you! ... With no time to lose, I dived for its hiding place! ... Next, with my talons, I ripped its eyes apart and destroyed it! ... Afterward, I just flew home... and woke up!"*

Her smile used to end her story faded a bit as the two Archangels stared at her again!

Gabri-el calmed her down by saying.

"It is OK, my darling! Micha-el and I want to see the beast; the image still inside your mind!"

It was there crisp and clear. They saw the soaring eagle attacking the eyes of the serpent, but most of all, very clearly, they saw its poisonous dart shooter: An ultra-long range, high powered, with computer tracking...
a 10-km plasma sniper rifle.

This time, the Overlords became the ones being shocked! It was absolutely true; Raquel had saved their lives!

Micha-el, without picking up his communication buckle, spoke.
"Commander SA-P-175!"
Two seconds later, an image appeared on the tiny screen, he said.
"Sir! How can I be of help?"
"Has anything unusual happened in your sector in the last hour?"
"No! Sir! All activity has been related to our military personnel, including you!"
"What about 10 Km west from the site where my craft picked me up?"
The commander hesitated momentarily; then, he answered, *"It is strange that you asked about this particular place, Sir! ... There was a report about two small animals in such an area... that died in strange circumstances!"*
"What were their characteristics?"
"Sir! 3 cm diameter each, 8 cm spaced apart, c-c."
"Did you consider that those are the same dimensions for an angel's average eye size and in-between spacing?"
"One of my best operators did notice, Sir! ... However, there was no indication of any angels around... Thus, we discarded it!"
Micha-el, in a firm but clear message, ordered.
"I want these instructions to be carried out immediately!
First, send a platoon to the location we are talking about. Look for a body. It may be hard to see!
Second, send three platoons to check for activity around your sector. Exercise extreme caution if you encounter suspicious individuals; you will be dealing with highly trained enemy infiltrators!
Last, call Pristeen Central Command and request a search for departing individuals with no valid reason. The same caution applies!
Thank you, Commander. That will be all!"
"Yes, Sir! *It will be done as you requested!"*
While Micha-el alerted his Province command, Gabri-el has been talking to his wife. After giving her a tender kiss on the lips, he asserted.
"Raquel... you did not have a dream. What you saw, it happened. Call it... a transfiguring vision!"
As his nose touched hers, he asked.
"Now, my dear! Do you have any idea Who the Angel is?"
She reflected momentarily, then nodded negatively, *"No, my love!"*
Gabri-el's deep green eyes made ripples into her gorgeous aqua-colored eyes. Her arched, long eyelashes moved up and down fast as she blinked twice. In a deep and ceremonious tone, he gave her the good news.
*"He is... **God!**"*
Raquel backed up and refocused her sight on his face. Her forehead became wrinkled between her eyebrows in disbelief, not because of a lack of faith but due to the unexpected announcement!

She was shaken, startled, and confused. Also, she knew that her husband was incapable of lying.

She saw that face again in her mind. For the first time, she looked into those strange eyes. A mild shaking rattled her whole body; with incredible jubilation, she replied.

"My God... He was You!"

She jumped into her husband's arms and hugged him with all her strength. The excitement caused her to breathe heavily. However, inside her was the uncontrollable joy of being part of a divine event where the participants' angels gained so much.

Micha-el approached the couple. As Raquel turned to see him, the Archangel, while passing his hand over her silky hair, kissed her on the cheek. In a very emotional and sweet tone, he said, *"My dear and beautiful friend, Raquel... I am so delighted that you became the deliverer of our Lord's power... I thank you with all my heart!"*

The deep emotions running inside his mind lingered overwhelmingly. He felt full of life... like being born again. He was immensely grateful to God for His never-ending love and generosity.

When emotions become sublime and bring out the most noble of our thoughts and feelings, we get closer to our Creator. He is not idle; He continuously gives us opportunities to get even closer.

Micha-el's eyes were wet with intrinsic passion. Now, he knew what the third gift was: **His own life.**

****

Rapha-el, Izma-el, and Gabri-el were talking outside the main Hospital entrance in the city of Iris, the same place where Sergius was about to die. Gabri-el extended his hand; a purple flower was carefully carried inside it. He said to Rapha-el.

"Our Lord, in person, gave me this flower... He told me to bring it to you!"

Rapha-el dropped onto his knees; a deep emotion shook his whole being. He extended both arms and made a cup with both palms, ready to receive the divine gift.

Gabri-el dropped the still fresh-looking flower on his hands.

The kneeled Archangel gasped for air; its touch felt like fire! Its essence ran through his arms and to his brain; very gently, Rapha-el touched it with two fingers. The pretty bell-shaped flower felt cool on contact. Then, it quickly withered under the hot sun. In seconds, it was completely dried and disintegrated into dust!

A gentle breeze blew the dust away from his hand, leaving only a single grain. Izma-el quickly touched the speck with his index finger and brought it to his heart. There, he followed the path already marked on his uniform by making the sign of a cross.

Rapha-el raised his hands in a sign of prayer. In a soft, tender, and full-of-love exclamation, he said.

"Dear God! I thank You for listening to this servant of Yours. I will pass Your gift to the needy!"

He stood up and said to his companions, *"Let's give Sergius this great news!"*

"We should hurry up; he is about to die!" Izma-el commented.

Rapha-el kindly smiled at him. Without any sign of rushing, he calmly said, *"Not today! I know he will wait for us!"*

The sliding doors where Sergius was hospitalized moved to allow three Overlords to walk in. Two doctors, Thrones, quickly stepped aside. The capsule holding the sick angel had its top end opened. The Overlords allowed the lead doctor to state what they already knew.

"Welcome, distinguished Overlords! ... Sergius is dying; he only has a few minutes left... There is nothing else that we can do!"

Rapha-el took the initiative to answer since he was the province's Overlord, *"I understand your anxiety. However, there is no need for concern; our Lord has graciously given me the ability to eradicate the sickness killing him: the DNA Syndrome!"*

The statement baffled the doctors, but they did not question the Overlord.

Rapha-el moved very close to the opened capsule. Inside, Sergius's pale face showed his grave state. The angel had almost no muscle left; he was skinny, and his heart was struggling for the next beat, which could be the last. He stayed awake, barely breathing. He looked at the purple figure before him; he did not recognize the Archangel's face. However, the tunic's color was the giveaway.

In a voice so low that only the keen ear of Rapha-el could listen, he struggled to say, *"Ra-pha-el.... Than-ks... f-or com-ming to... say... g-good b-ye..."*

The Overlord smiled at him with innate pleasure; he gently said.

"I brought a gift!... By God's command, I give it to you!"

Rapha-el placed both hands on each side of Sergius' head. At the point of contact, a bluish glow briefly illuminated his head.

The angel took a deep breath... His soul, ready to depart his battered body, was strongly recalled! It was like fire burning inside his whole body... **his DNA code had been overwritten!**

The dying angel was not sick anymore. His eyes opened widely; a new life sparkled inside them. Now, he recognized the two other Overlords in the room.

"Gabri-el, Izma-el... Thank you for being here. Suddenly, I feel much better!"

He tried to push himself up, but his arms bent, and he collapsed back into his bed. Rapha-el, still very close to him, caressed his black hair, and with a caring tone, indicated.

"Be careful moving too fast. Even when you are cured of the Syndrome, you are still very weak!"

Sergius eyes lit up with a spark that had just recently arrived; he anxiously questioned, *"Rapha-el.... Did you say that I am cured of the DNA Syndrome?"*

"Yes! That is precisely what I just said!"

The two doctors, skeptical about their patient's sudden health upgrade and the even more incredible news from their Overlord, ran to the controls to monitor the patient. Many buttons were pushed, and when the awaited answer came out, both turned to Rapha-el and Sergius and, in unison, exclaimed.

"He has no Syndrome!... He is cured!... It is a miracle!"

Rapha-el responded in a manner that all understood.

"It is a miracle, a miracle of Love! Our Lord has kindly allowed this servant to be the recipient of His generosity!"

Sergius, holding Rapha-el's hand, remarked.

"Thank you, my dear friend. Your faith for my survival was greater than mine!" Next, raising his eyes directly above, Sergius gratefully acknowledged.

"Thank You, my God and loving Father, for this gift... A second life!"

Rapha-el later instructed the lead doctor to list all the surviving DNA Syndrome angels in the SA. Not long after, he quickly traveled to the provinces to heal them individually. In this manner, he eradicated the dreaded syndrome from all the SA provinces.

There was no greater reward than the sight of the cured, their joy, gratefulness, revitalization, and a renewed even greater love toward their Creator; it was the reward Rapha-el got from doing this great deed. His soul was increasingly lifted to new heights. He did not see God in person as his two companions did; it did not matter; he did not need to see the Lord. With Rapha-el's complete acceptance of the will of God, the Lord continued living inside his body and mind!

In a true sense of generosity, Rapha-el notified the upper command of the NA of his willingness to help the sick angels in the Northern Alliance. They acknowledged. No angel from the North showed up to be cured that day! ... **None ever did.**

In their selfish and evil approach to satisfy their narrow-minded goals, the NA command, by not notifying anyone of their dying citizens, had denied them their last chance for life.

With this method, they also eradicated the DNA Syndrome from their land by allowing all the sick NA citizens to … **die away!**

INCOMING STORM

CHAPTER 6

All the SA Overlords stood together in a remote part of the province of Graceland called the Green Ridge Plateau. Mervyn was included in the group, the only non-Archangel in this gathering, although, due to his unique qualifications, he appeared to be part of the elite.

All present watched the incredibly busy sky full of saucer-like devices being ejected into orbit to become deployed satellites. String after string of flying devices were powerfully shot upwards to fit their distinct place in the 4-D Matrix in space as the SA built the most crucial defensive and offensive system, ever!

The potentially dreaded response from the NA did not materialize; nothing was heard from the opposing Alliance. What happened to the copy of the Matrix program? Was it possible that the computer Matrix supervisory program misread the copying information?

Micha-el extruded happiness, and the program's duplication became meaningless. He did not have to search for an Overlord to be a traitor, which compelled his mind to be at peace.

As the leader of the Alliance looked at Mervyn, who stood nearby, the professor must have felt something because he turned his head to link his eyes with the Overlord's… they smiled at each other. Mervyn raised his shoulder and opened his hands, reflecting on a thought that said.

"Oh well! I guess it didn't matter!"

Next, Micha-el touched Gabri-el's shoulder and mentioned mentally.

"Today is a great day for our land. I hope this awesome deterrent will bring peace to the whole planet!"

His companion and a very close friend replied.

"Yes, Micha-el, let us hope for an everlasting peace!"

Central District (CD), NA

Chaos was the name of the ruling lord of this place. Red lights blinked everywhere, and operators hastily collecting data from their screens rerouted the information to the main computer for cross-analysis. Angels running around carried messages as they moved from one working station to another, all feverishly working.

Lucif-er, Magog-el, and Azami-el stayed close together. All three focused on the huge center display where all the data finally became assembled. Many dots continued rising from the SA territory, and after reaching a place high above the atmosphere, they were positioned in a specific but unusual pattern.

The base commander, a Seraph dressed in full uniform, quickly moved behind Lucif-er. There, he stood still, waiting for an order; without looking back, Lucif-er commanded.

*"I want a full alert... **immediately!"***

The officer responded in a snappy way, ***"Yes, sir!"***

Quickly, he ran to the closest available terminal to select an operator to whom he had passed the same command.

"Those satellites going into orbit are fully armed, including nuclear!" Azami-el retorted, *"However, we have not detected any ground activity signaling a full offensive plan from the SA!"*

Even when the last message was directed to Lucif-er, Magog-el did not wait for a response and inserted an opinion.

"I have placed the whole defense system, with orders to lock all laser and plasma cannons into this new satellite array. I am looking at their deployment, but I still cannot recognize any tactical pattern."

Azami-el quickly added his viewpoint.

"I have the same problem. I cannot match any 3-D pattern I know to the progression leading to the present orbital positioning."

Lucif-er remained silent; his piercing eyes intensely assimilated the progression displayed on the big screen. His breathing became longer and deeper; a growing concern bothered him. His teeth started to grind ominously; on that account, his companions decided not to interrupt him!

Swiftly, he approached a Seraph sitting close to his left side, one of the top operators in this underground military base; with a cracking intonation, he ordered, *"Run a computer analysis of the SA's new satellite network, use a 4-D Matrix algorithm!"*

The operator looked back in panic! He repetitively blinked nervously while responding in a meek tone, *"I don't know how to use a 4-D algorithm! Ssi-r-r..."*

Before he had time to finish saying 'Sir,' Lucif-er grabbed him by the front top of his uniform and lifted him out of his chair. He stared so hard at him that the Seraph thought his wide-open eyes caught fire. The Overlord, very close to his face, sharply announced.

"I will do it myself!"

With a flick of his wrist, he threw away the operator! He flew about six meters before he hit the hard ground. Since the floor was polished, and he remained in a sitting position, he slid another five meters before he ultimately stopped.

Noticeably in pain, by the squeezing of his teeth and the narrowing of his previously wide-open eyes, he could not get up; he remained in that position. Nobody dared to leave his post to assist him.

Lucif-er jammed the computer terminal with multiple requests using incredible speed. Shortly afterward, a smaller screen next to the main display showed the 4-D Matrix. Lucif-er saw it for a second, and it was enough for him to burst into a violent rage.

With a closed fist, he smashed down the terminal. Sparks and smoke came out of the unit, and small pieces dispersed around, making metallic noises as they bounced on the floor. Next, he picked up the damaged unit, ripping off all the cables and bolts from the ground beneath. More fire, sparks, and smoke ignited spontaneously. He angrily threw it in the same direction as the unit operator sitting on the floor!

The Seraph, seated on the floor, saw the large unit tumbling rapidly toward his body. He froze; his eyes remained fully opened, and his lips partially separated.

The unit barely missed him! Even when it went past him, his expression did not change. Except, now his hands showed a noticeable shaking.

Magog-el and Azami-el, looking concerned, carefully studied the matrix. With disbelief, both addressed their boss on a private channel.

"Is it possible, a 4-D Matrix defense system?"

In a sober tone, Lucif-er replied.

"It is… And it is impregnable!"

Reluctant to accept it, Azami-el said, *"I will have to see it to believe it!"*

"Go ahead!… Run a simulation!"

Azami-el's shorter but stocky body jumped into action. In no time, he accessed the next terminal, punching multiple commands to the computer. He ordered a simulated attack on the matrix with all the NA, nuclear, laser, and plasma cannon resources. As shown at high speed by the display, the computer sorted all logical possibilities. Finally, it showed the result.

→**Simulation: All-out attack on the SA Matrix.**

> **With all probabilities considered, the attack failed.**

> **The NA would have been destroyed.**

Magog-el raised his two fists in defiance; he angrily exclaimed.

"When Mervyn refused to join the NA… we should have killed him!"

Azami-el, disturbed by the results, commented.

"Micha-el has us by the balls; he could <u>wipe us out</u>!"

Lucif-er's assertiveness returned. With one hand, he moved his curly hair out of his face while staring at the panic-stricken Overlords; he cynically smiled at his colleagues. One second later, he stood up and slowly started to pace the room… he burst out laughing!

The other two Overlords questioned him.

"We are in deep excrement, and you are laughing?"

Lucif-er changed his grin to a satanic one. With coolness extruding from his skin, he expressed the following.

"Just calm down… Place yourselves in Micha-el's place; he is God's servant! The outspoken giver of Justice! All about Truth and <u>Love</u>! … ***He cannot allow himself, even to hate his enemies!***

How, then, could he order the slaughter of two billion angels? If we do **nothing stupid***, his conscience will not allow him to give such an order...* **he cannot do it!***"*

After looking at the interested faces, he continued.

"Consequently, we have the answer. We do... **nothing!***"*

After a fleeting delay, before anyone else could express his concerns, he added, *"Furthermore, do not forget! We have a wild card still waiting to be played!"*

Lucif-er got closer to the two other Overlords; in a different tone, he inquired.

"There is one pending question! Why did our 'wild card' in the SA not warn us about the Matrix? We could have declared war before allowing those idiots to take this kind of advantage!"

Lucif-er, intensely looking at Azami-el, stated.

"I must communicate with our accomplice in the SA. I know you have partially developed a new carrier to deliver the code... I need it now*!"*

Azami-el, reassured after listening to his boss, explained.

"To prevent detection, the new carrier will be attached to the noise spikes randomly occurring in the atmosphere. It is only operational for simple communications; we still cannot download complex programs during the transmission, or the location would be detected!"

Lucif-er interrupted him.

"No need to explain; just do it! And do it **soon!***"*

Same place, five days later.

The same three Overlords and Gorgon-el gathered at the Central War Center, waiting for a message to be displayed on the central screen. Azami-el had sent the instructions and coding patterns to the 'wild card' Archangel and the C-team to build the new device, which could send limited messages without being pinpointed. Then, they were expected to respond in three days, at a specified time late at night.

The requested time had arrived, but no communication was in sight. Magog-el, angry and impatient, mentioned.

"Fifteen minutes past 1:00 hour! **Nobody has responded!***"*

Somehow worried that his rushed communication prototype was incomplete for a reasonable exchange of coded messages, Azami-el replied.

"He could be... too busy!"

"At this time of the night?" Magog-el retorted using an unfriendly remark.

At this moment, in a dominant telepathic message, Lucif-er stated.

"A message is coming!"

They had to wait until the operators received and decoded the anticipated message from the SA. Soon, the screen displayed the response the Overlords of the North had previously summoned.

Code 378-DKR-2
Greetings.
C-Team is gone.
Two wounded survivors,
plus six bodies,
to be returned to the NA,
tomorrow.

"This mode of communication is incredibly slow!" Gorgon-el complained while looking at Azami-el. This Overlord just flicked his hands, insinuating: "That is the <u>only</u> available type of communication we have!"

C-1 tried to kill Micha-el,
he failed and died.
A stern message
will be sent to the NA.

A short pause followed the message string. Lucif-er just reflected on the 'stern message.' "I know Micha-el! 'Another incident like this one and the NA will be destroyed!' **Do not waste your breath!**"

I sent a copy
of the Matrix program,
18 days before deployment!
Why did you allow its deployment?

Lucif-er pointed one finger at an operator facing away from the displays. The Overlord briskly commanded.

"Interrupt message! Ask him, <u>where?</u>"

Somehow startled by the sudden and powerful order, the operator quickly recovered and did as requested. Ten seconds later, the answer came back.

I do not believe it...
You did not receive it?
It was delivered over B2 Island!

At this instant of the message, Lucif-er's eyes sparkled with fury! Magog-el clinched both hands up like he was strangling someone! Gorgon-el just nodded while clinching his teeth! Azami-el's blood, always ready to boil, did! As murderous hate showed up in his piercing blue eyes, he looked at Lucif-er.

Lucif-er, without turning to look at his subordinate, just pointed one finger at him. Angrily and speedily, Lucif-er pointed the same finger down to the floor!

Azami-el saw in his mind a graphical order: *"Bring Zoltar to Centrum... **immediately!**"*

Azami-el took off to the nearest terminal, which was currently occupied by a busy operator. When this individual saw the Archangel approaching at great speed, he dived for the floor! Before he could hit the ground, Azami-el was already sending a message through the terminal.

Code CD-C-666-ZMK-9
BI Commander, report immediately to Lucif-er.
Main Office at Centrum.
Bring all your sector activity records.

He ended the message and rejoined his upper elite companions. The displaced operator quickly got up and regained his seat. The message from the SA concluded at this time.

Let me know,
what is going on!
End.

Zoltar was leaving his main office at B1 Island for an early dinner. He was dressed in his fancy white and blue uniform and walked ceremoniously, a bit stiffly. Before he could exit through the door, his terminal beeped; a message overrode the strategic design he had been working on.

He quickly turned around and read the message. He felt a chill; Lucif-er wanted to see him… right away! He hoped that the big boss had not found out about the weak response of his friend Denariel, the B2 commander; he could be pissed off. He acknowledged the message.

Sir! The BI Commander is leaving for Centrum.

Next, at the terminal, he called his pilot. After his face appeared on the screen and he formally saluted, Zoltar gave his instructions.

"Top priority! Bring the fastest craft available to my office building; we are going to Centrum!"

"Sir! I will be there in five minutes!" The individual quickly responded.

After the last order, Zoltar instructed the computer to compile a copy of all sectors' activities. While the machine was compiling the data, he decided to review the previous two incidents on B2 Island.

The first string of data flashed quickly over the screen. The Seraph was a high-speed reader. Quickly, the second report flashed at great speed. Something caught his eye; he stopped the computer and stared at the line with the two words '**…wrong code…**'

The regional commander thought.

"Now that I am reviewing this report about the destroyed craft from the SA, I am noticing that Denariel never mentioned what the wrong code was?… It must be OK, but I should check it anyway."

Zoltar quickly requested the information. A memory module with the requested data, a shiny cube, emerged from an opening in the machine.

Concurrently, the requested code was displayed on a side portion of the screen.

NA CD 333333

The commander's heart skipped a beat. He knew the code... Lucif-er's special covert forces!

It was not a well-known code, but it was on the computer. He screamed at the terminal, even when he was thinking about his colleague.

"Did you check the code?"

The answer was displayed since he also had requested the information from the machine.

The request for Code ID was OK.

The commander lost whatever was left of his cool. He grabbed his forehead with both hands and after making a non-angelical sound, more like a beastly sound, *"Aaarrrr!"* He screamed again.

"You did not recognize the code... The computer told you it was OK!... And you shot the aircraft down!"

He lowered his head over the display. In deep despair, amid a mild shaking of his whole body, he just mumbled, *"You stupid jerk! This may not be the end of our careers; this may be... the end of our lives!"*

Standing alone in this huge conference room, Zoltar looked rigid and nervous, as tiny drops of sweat extruding outward from his facial skin indicated.

In front of him, a gleaming black counter, like obsidian, stretched around both of his sides. Its shape resembled a large concave U, with Lucif-er sitting at the other side of the counter at its center. Magog-el sat on his right while Azami-el was on his left. Four additional fancy chairs were at this location, but they stayed empty. A platoon of heavily armed soldiers, Lucif-er's personal guards, stood at the door, windows, and other strategic positions, but away from the Overlords.

An eerie silence hung inside this big conference room. Lucif-er remained looking at his hands and making snapping sounds caused by engaging his right-hand middle fingernail and left-hand thumbnail. A loud 'tick' sound could be heard as he pushed the two edges against each other, making the two fingernails snap away. In Zoltar's brain, the 'tick' noise reverberated ominously, causing a chill to run down his spine every time he listened to the noise... One more time, he swallowed.

Lucif-er, still looking at his nails, continued the activity without saying anything. The BI commander's legs shook slightly. He decided to look somewhere else. His eyes locked with the intense stare of Azami-el's fiery blue eyes. The heat on Zoltar's eyeballs increased instantaneously!

"Big mistake!" He said to himself as he decided to stare at Lucif-er; at least, he was not looking at him.

Lucif-er smiled in a sinister way. Without changing his stand, he expressed the following.

"To avoid Azami-el's eyes, you think it is safer to stare at me. You must not know that my <u>indifference</u> *is more lethal than the fire from Azami-el's eyes."*

As the commander swallowed in near panic, a sharp pain caused by an invisible line pressing all around his cranial perimeter forced him to hold his head with both hands. For a moment, he thought that this was the end; it felt like his skull could split into two separate parts!

Yet, all pain vanished as quickly as it came. While making audible sounds, his sweat started to drip on the shiny floor. Closing his now-opened mouth, Zoltar tried to compose himself; with his hands stretched down, he tried to stand erect.

Lucif-er, calmly looking at the commander, continued.

*"I know all that I wanted from you. Now, I have a task that you must accomplish... I want Denariel...**to be slaughtered**!"*

Lucif-er stopped as Azami-el got up and swiftly moved to leave the place; the latter exclaimed, ***"I am going to Bird Islands; I will kill him myself!"***

Lucif-er, with an eye movement, commanded him to sit. Then, he said.

"You are <u>too</u> *busy! I want Zoltar to do it."*

The commander blinked twice and swallowed simultaneously, meagerly complaining, *"Great Leader of our Alliance! Denariel is my best friend... Could someone else perform the deed?* ***Sir!***"

Lucif-er's hypnotic eyes approached his mind as a heavy dark blanket, ominous and lethal. The commander knew that it was an ultimatum. One wrong word came out of his mouth… **and he would be dead**.

He decided to live!

"Sir! It will be done… today!"

Lucif-er nodded affirmatively, almost unnoticeable. Next, he added, *"I am appointing a CD officer to take over the vacant position. Make sure that he is present when you kill your friend."*

"Your wish is my command, Sir!"

At a wide balcony overlooking a Hawaiian-like scenery, the afternoon sun just set behind some rugged mountains covered with exuberant green vegetation; most birds were returning to their nests or to their favorite tree to sleep the incoming night. Two Seraphim and a Throne stood on this spacious balcony or terrace adjacent to a medium-sized, ten-story building aerodynamically designed to blend with its surroundings. All three dressed in rugged outfits resembling army fatigues had handguns attached to their communication belts.

Zoltar addressed the angel facing him, Denariel.

"This is a short-notice military exercise related to the SA launching so many new satellites. The high command wants a new level of alertness to prepare for any new contingencies.
Also, meet my new assistant. He will have a position exactly like yours! His name is Akron."

Denariel glanced at his new colleague, a muscular Seraph with a narrow face; he saluted with an open hand at chest level. Akron responded similarly and quickly said.

"For a long-lasting and glorious service together!"

"Likewise!" Denariel briefly responded.

"It is dinner time. Let's go inside, and we'll discuss the details of this exercise," Zoltar said.

The sliding door opened to display the interior of a restaurant. There were no chefs, waiters, or servers. Everyone ordered their food at a flat display embedded in the eating tables. Individually molded and cushioned seats were hierarchically arranged on its extensive multilevel floors. The machines could dispense whatever was ordered at each station out of synthetic-grown basic proteins, sugars, fat, vitamins, and nutritional minerals; the machines prepared fancy drinks and cooked splendid, tasty meals. At the place of honor, the three commanders had a great dinner.

One hour later, all three stood on the terrace of the same building. The breeze had picked up, and the temperature was noticeably cooler. To the west, only a purplish glow remained where the sun had set. The three remained this time alone; all other dining soldiers or civilians had departed. By this time, the place was artificially illuminated.

"Thank you, Zoltar!" Denariel mentioned while leaning against the rail, *"Your recommended dish was exquisite. This has been one of my best dinners ever!"*

Akron, also leaning on the rail overlooking the panoramic view now in darkness, commented.

"Your local menu has exciting variations. I already like this new post; I am feeling at home!"

Zoltar, two meters away from the rail, while pointing west with his left-hand finger, said.

"Denariel... I am very pleased that you liked your dinner," he said. Continuing to point to the west, he asked his friend, *"Is that a satellite moving into orbit?"*

The B2 commander turned around and stared at the starry night sky. He asked, *"Where?"*

Akron intended to peek in the same direction, but Zoltar's right-hand index finger pointing up and calling for his attention prevented him from doing it. He watched the BI commander as he removed the gun from his belt holster and pointed it to the back of Denariel's head; he insisted.

"Look! Above the star triangle!"

He fired.

A reddish flash flowed almost from the gun to the head of the B2 commander! Since the gun was set at a minimum power level, the plasma blast behaved like a bullet, just penetrating the skull and frying the brain; it did not blow away the cranial cavity.

Denariel's eyeballs glowed red briefly, then became saturated with red blood. His faint two reddish wings separated from his body and dissipated... **He was dead!**

His limp body fell to the ground. However, his chin hit the rail hard on the way down with a loud 'thud.' Then, he slammed backward onto the floor at the feet of his best friend.

The two Seraphim's eyes lifted from the floor and into each other. Zoltar stated in a deep voice.

"This is a lesson for you to remember... Do not screw up!"

Akron, apparently undisturbed, maintained eye contact and remarked.

"Sir! I am sure this is related to the B2 island incident. This lesson is properly taken!

I will treat my subordinates in the same manner you have shown me, and for the greatness of the NA, I will expect no less from you. In addition, I commend you, Sir, for your tactful and considerate handling of this delicate matter! ... If you allow me, I will take care of the body!"

The new B2 commander impressed Zoltar. The latter thought.

"These last breed of officers from the CD are tough... I just killed my best friend... I don't feel too good; I think I am getting a headache! But I better not show weakness, or this Seraph will start considering taking over my job!" Then, displaying a fake firm stand, Zoltar replied with a militaristic mental message.

"Good! In one hour, I will brief you on your new job in my office!"

The value of life in the NA had been steadily decreasing. At present, a significant mistake could be the last. The day may come when just looking without permission into the eyes of the Lords of Evil could be enough to be submerged in boiling oil inside a frying pan!

Five days later, in Lucif-er's main conference room in Centrum, all the NA Overlords sat at their assigned locations except Lucif-er, who stood on the other side of the black counter. Lucif-er addressed the others.

"Before I explain the new incoming policy to be strictly implemented over the land, I will notify the present about the fate of the C-team!"

He paused for a few seconds, waiting for a large screen behind him to project upwards from the floor. When it was extended up, he continued.

"You all know that the C-team failed its mission. However, the circumstances of this failure, specifically about its leader's death, C-1, are bizarre!

Dagon was our best-trained covert fighter. He had an excellent chance to nail Micha-el, his primary target. We supplied him with the latest 10 Km-sniper gun and a complimentary suit that made him invisible to any known detection system. Even better, our Overlord in the SA provided him with information that positioned him in a perfect ambush location.

Why did he fail... because he was detected? ... No! Azami-el has a picture of his returned body."

He paused for a second while his colleague retrieved the requested image. Next, C-1's whole body was fully deployed on the screen. Lucif-er maneuvered the picture so that in a more significant mode, the head became displayed.

Dagon still had the special suit on. The scratched visor on his helmet stayed on his forehead. The only visible part of his face was the two conical holes where his eyes used to be. Not a sign of blood remained visible.

"You can see the problem... C-1 was killed by an animal!" Lucif-er continued. Then, his stare spanned across the audience, catching some eyes displaying incredulous glare.

"Azami-el's report stated: Killed by the talon of a Royal Eagle. By observing the size and angle of penetration, I will add, a female Royal Eagle!" He spoke telepathically.

Kroma-el, the Overlord of the NC Sector, a Cherub with a crew cut haircut, exclaimed, *"Is the SA training eagles to kill people?"*

Lucif-er looked at him condescendingly, then said, *"Not likely; nevertheless, you tell me... What is wrong with this picture?"*

The NC Sector Overlord sitting at the other side of the counter leaned forward and eagerly scanned the image into his brain. Kroma-el appeared to be concentrated on the task. Two seconds later, he stated, *"The angle of the scratches on the visor matches the final impact on C-1's eyes; however, that is impossible!"*

With a faint smile, Lucif-er remarked, *"Exactly! The visor was made with a special alloy of Ti(Si-Carbide)... The only material that can scratch it is a diamond!"*

Kroma-el leaned backward on his chair and jokingly retorted.

"Please, do not tell me! Are we going to fight Royal Eagles armed with diamond-tipped talons?"

The other Overlords chuckled with a smiling grin, except Azami-el.

Lucif-er continued, *"No need to worry! Very few Royal Eagles are alive, and finding many diamonds of that size is not feasible!*

I even think the SA intentionally made those scratches to confuse us into believing it was a supernatural event."

"I agree!" Magog-el barked out.

Lucif-er got closer to the counter, stopping just in front of Magog-el. The image on the screen now displayed a much-enlarged piece of a charred memory module. He mentioned, *"It was regrettable to have missed the arrival of this module to the NA. We would have gone to war before allowing the SA to deploy the 4-D Matrix! But since it did not get here, we are presently at a serious disadvantage!"*

Lucif-er's message got bitter and hateful. No smile appeared on his face, and none were on the faces of the listening Overlords; with a stern expression, he continued.

"From the debris of the destroyed vehicle, we have recovered all the pieces left of the memory module. We are reconstructing the Matrix program!
It seems to be an incredibly complex program. The only baffling factor is the vast number of extra handles for the program modules. We assumed that Mervyn wanted to add more blocks of peripheral supporting programs to enhance its operation, but the handles were unnecessary when the main program was finished."

Lucif-er mentally eyeballed every one of his subordinates, ensuring his following message was clear and concise.

"The following is going to be strictly implemented!
For the next 100 days, nobody will do anything that the SA could consider as an act of aggression, a threat to their security, or anything seen as a threat to the peace of their land!

After we lure the SA into a sense of secured superiority, as the Matrix protective umbrella currently provides, we will draw their SA leaders away from its protection! We could accomplish this by convincing Nobiel to call for a peace gathering at Trillium.

If we could get rid of Micha-el, we could overpower the rest! ... Once in our hands, we could use them as hostages to force the SA to drop the 4-D Matrix satellite system. The moment they do such a thing, we will be back in control!"

With an eerie glow from his deep blue eyes, he continued with self-convinced certitude. Evil did not intend to give up; even when they were the underdogs, they planned to cause ominous harm. Lucif-er uttered his last statement.

"There, at Trillium... after forcing Micha-el into a duel... **with my own hands, I will kill him!"**

****

The warm afternoon sun shined over this small but aesthetic garden. In this secluded place, The Core's council members enjoyed the relaxing atmosphere while unofficially discussing their nation's most critical issues. All thirteen were in a closed circle. The seats stayed comfortably spaced to give enough elbow room but sufficiently close for a face-to-face discussion. The council members, for some unwritten self-imposed law, whenever they appeared in a public place, always wore their official-colored tunics!

Even at this informal gathering, the council members kept their separation of states by preserving their assigned groupings: the leader Nobiel, four Seraphim, four Cherubim, and four Thrones.

Nobiel was seated straight, still a bit taller than his colleagues. His stoic appearance resembled a trademark that followed him everywhere.

He said, *"The SA Matrix defense system has done the trick. The NA cannot start a war and win! They have no choice; they must switch to a more peaceful approach to life. The last 100 days have been absent of violence, and the peace that the whole planet has enjoyed proves that point!"*

One of the Seraphim in a blue tunic, seated fourth to his right, pointed out, *"Even so, I cannot trust Lucif-er at all!"*

A Cherub to his left side also commented.

"After Lucif-er's last abomination at The Temple, I presently think that it will be impossible to have a meeting with him at the house of God, which he has betrayed in the most untrustworthy manner!"

Nobiel nodded in approval, and he quickly remarked.

"You are absolutely right! A meeting at The Temple is out of the question! However, what about the large plaza east of the city called <u>Atrium</u>*? ... We could build two raised connecting platforms at its center, the seating places for the Overlords; additionally, we could allow about 100 thousand participants per Alliance!"*

The Cherub eagerly responded, *"That would be an ideal place; I am for it! What about the rest of you?"*

The other eleven responded in unison, *"We agree!"*

Nobiel continued, *"Our security must be upgraded to a maximum. No weapons of any kind will be allowed! ... The Core will not participate in the peace debate unless requested; however, we will be in the front row, electronically speaking.*

We could announce the peace meeting tomorrow; it will take place in twenty days. Let's pray to the Lord for the end of hostilities and an everlasting reconciliation... Raise your hand if you agree with the conditions set for this peace meeting!"

At about face level, 12 hands showed up.

At 4:00 hours at Trillium, the long-anticipated day had finally arrived; it was a hot and muggy afternoon. There were 100,000 visitors from the SA facing 100,000 visitors from the NA; all stayed standing. Dividing them stood dual two-meter-high platforms. Both connected in a way that separated the people from each Alliance. The Core did not want any violence breaking out, especially from this large number of participants.

The two main platforms were square, ten by ten meters; in between, a diamond centerpiece, seven by seven meters, was placed. Two pathways, three meters wide and about six meters long, connected this centerpiece to the platforms.

Beyond the outside edge of the two main platforms, a thin wall two meters high extended to the buildings surrounding the plaza. This wall was not too tall, but its top was equipped with an electromagnetic array ready to give anyone a mild shock for even sticking a finger across the divider, but a more considerable shock, proportionally related to the speed and mass of the moving anatomical part to anyone trying to jump across to the adjacent area. The two large groups were effectively separated from each other.

The NA platform pointed north, while the NA supporters stood on the entire left side. The SA platform, in opposition, faced south, while the SA visitors stood on the entire right side. Clusters of trees towering above the angels circumvented the vast crowd area.

Four extra-large video screens, attached to the perimeter structures, where tall buildings approaching 100 stories high framed the gathering place, provided the visitors visual access to the activity on the centerpiece. The wall of skyscrapers was about 250 meters from the plaza's center. Of course, The Core's citizens packed every window, including the rooftops, as they anxiously waited for the reconciliation of the two Alliances.

Maybe this could be when peace, as we imagine, usually in the shape of a dove, would extend its benign wings to soothe the whole planet of the scars and pains brought by the increasing threat of war. Then, all should be back to normality.

We call this wishful thinking; without it, our existence could be in consequential danger of becoming a big bore!

The dynamics of our lives are not much different than the dynamics of matter. When an event disturbs the order of things, the affected matter moves from ordered to disordered. Ordering it again would take a lot of energy not used before. In other words, more related to Physics, we could say that we have increased the degree of entropy related to this isolated event.

The best way to picture this is by dropping a ceramic plate on a hard floor. The broken pieces are in a new, disordered state. Putting it back together requires a lot of work, which uses energy. The consumption of energy decreases the available resources of ordered energy, thus increasing the entropy of the event.[1]

The worst part is that the plate may never be the same regardless of what we do. It's not as strong or even as pretty. It could be much easier to obtain a new one, perhaps a better one! However, our sentimental

---

[1] Also known as the second law of thermodynamics.

attachments sidetrack us into preserving what is not there anymore. It is part of our human nature. Most likely, it was also part of the angelic nature…

A rumble caused by 200 thousand individuals talking to each other became interrupted by a sudden and reverberating 'ding' sound; it indicated that the Overlords were entering the plaza. In a few seconds, silence reigned in the entire place.

At the same time, as a wave affected the east-west ends of the centered and pointed diamond-shaped platform, the crowd on the NA side and equally on the SA side parted to allow their leaders easy access to the center platform. As soon as the centerpiece sides cleared, two ramps, one on each opposite side, moved up at an angle of 20°, connecting the floor to the top of the higher-centered platform.

When Lucif-er and his six Overlords entered the plaza, a deafening roar from his supporters filled the place; the noise even bounced back from the adjacent buildings. Lucif-er, leading the group dressed in his blazing white tunic, raised his hand in approval. His group walked up the ramp and through the narrower pathway to the NA platform north of the plaza.

Lucif-er took the lead seat. To his right and a half-meter behind him, Magog-el sat. Gorgon-el and Azami-el took the next row. The Overlords, Razari-el, Kroma-el, and Ezek-el took the third row. Lucif-er raised his right hand again, this time in a signal to appease the crowd.

The noise level died quickly.

From the east side, the crowd roared in recognition of their leaders. Micha-el, leading the eight Overlords from the SA, walked toward the center. Many hands from his subjects extended along the opened path to salute him. He corresponded quickly and accurately as he briskly advanced to the center platform; in this way, he touched as many hands as possible. When all the Archangels from the SA stood on the upper diamond-shaped section, the ramps quickly separated from the ground again.

When Micha-el started walking on the narrow path leading to the SA square platform, the crowd from the NA screamed at the Overlord with hate and fury in their eyes. Extending their arms over the top, they jumped, trying to grab Micha-el's feet; he knew he was out of their reach.

They yelled.

"Murderer! … Micha-el, we hate you! We want you dead!"

Nobiel and the whole Core's council, located in an eastside building, watched with surprise and concern about the behavior of the NA visitors. The council leader swallowed hard before thinking with sadness and concern, "Holy God! This meeting starts in the wrong manner. Have I made a crucial mistake by arranging it?"

ANGELS/ANGELS

In the middle of the screaming, Micha-el sat at the leading chair on the SA platform. In the second row, seated behind both sides of Micha-el, were Gabri-el and Dani-el. The following row was part of the typical SA triangle with Rapha-el and Samu-el. In the last row, Lari-el and Zari-el were at the ends, and Izma-el stayed in the middle. It was a tactical position to avoid conflicts and confrontations with the NA. However, he received his share of insults before he had a chance to reach his designated location.

"Traitor! You abandoned us to serve our enemies! You are a piece of garbage! Drop dead!"

The SA visitors started to yell to the other side to be quiet and to respect their leaders!

Micha-el raised his hand disapprovingly, reminding the SA visitors to be silent. Even when his citizens were unhappy about his command, the SA side became quiet in five seconds.

However, the NA crowd stayed out of control, and the deafening screaming continued. Lucif-er and Magog-el smiled cynically since they approved of their subjects' behavior.

Lucif-er got a private mental message from Micha-el.

"Lucif-er, ask your people to be quiet so we can start our business!"

The leader of the NA, looking away from his primary opponent, retorted.

"What is the problem, Micha-el? ... They are just expressing their feelings and beliefs. They have the right to do it. If you want them to 'stop,' you should command them to do it. Or perhaps you would prefer that I show you how it should be done!"

Anxious to start the essential element of the Alliances' gathering, Micha-el relinquished and exclaimed.

"We are never to accomplish anything in this manner! For the sake of this meeting... Please, show me!"

Lucif-er looked directly at Micha-el without looking away from him and stood up. With a sinister grin adorning his already too-handsome face, he commented, *"Since you said the magic word, I will be glad to help!"*

While still looking at him, he yelled mentally and vocally!

"STOP!" <> "STOP!"

The mental and sound blast propagated in all directions away from Lucif-er. In a fraction of a second, they reached the walls of the adjacent buildings. If the window panels had been made of glass, most would have been shattered by the wave; since they were not, they rattled violently, separating some dust from the walls.

Most people gathered on both sides covered their ears; some covered their heads! The sound wave bounced back, and the echo passed the Overlords in less than 1.5 seconds. Even a third and faint echo could finally be heard. Afterward, absolute silence dominated the place.

Micha-el, nodding with disapproval, touched his left ear.

Lucif-er, as he started to walk toward the center diamond piece, remarked, *"You are welcome!"*

Once he reached the center of the structure, Lucif-er opened his elevated hands and exclaimed.

"Welcome, citizens of Terra!" Everybody heard his voice, crisp and clear, *"We have gathered with the explicit determination of finding a way to end hostilities. The NA has the conviction and discipline to establish a lasting peace; therefore, we work hard to find ways to achieve such a goal... Today, our presence is proof that we want peace!"*

He continued in a tone that he knew would ring a sentimental nerve.

"We seek and want peace; with our open hands, we offer it! Nevertheless, our great effort is not matched because there is one major obstacle to prevent this from happening... The SA's determination to destroy our Alliance!"

Micha-el stood up and quickly marched to the center diamond platform. There, at close range, he faced Lucif-er only one meter away. Their eyes locked in defiance; Lucif-er's cold and menacing eyes clashed against Micha-el's energetic, self-confident eyes. A bluish glow emanated from the encounter as both Archangels' wings increased in intensity!

Disengaging, Micha-el looked and directed his reply at the NA visitors.

"Do not listen to your leaders; the SA wants peace! We will do anything possible to terminate this conflict!"

Lucif-er, still staring at his opponent, interrupted. He talked in an angry and bullying way.

"If the SA wants peace, what is the 4-D Matrix doing in space!"

He pointed at the sky in defiance and continued, *"It only has one intent: to kill us all! If you want peace, why is the Matrix not disabled?"*

Micha-el was slow to return to the staring match. With a sad grin, he commented, *"We are here, trying to find a way for a lasting peace, only due to the Matrix's deployment. Without it, the NA leadership would give us nothing!"*

Increasing the depth of his voice, he requested.

"If the NA disarms, we promise to remove the Matrix!"

With a cynical smile bordering on a gibe, Lucif-er retorted.

"We promise you the same. Remove the Matrix, lay down your weapons, and we will do alike. Then, we will enjoy an everlasting peace!"

Five individuals in the NA crowd near the platforms started yelling at Micha-el as part of a deliberate arrangement.

"Micha-el is a liar and murderer!"

They repeated the sentence over and over. Two similar groups joined in the offensive chanting.

The crowd became restless on both sides. The rest of the NA visitors were incited to join the shouting. Now, the SA visitors got angry about the offensive behavior of the other side.

Micha-el turned his attention to the closest group. He spread his five fingers from his right hand, pointing toward the five individuals screaming their heads off.

All five went mute instantly. Their mouths were opening, but no sound came out of them! They grabbed their throats in disbelief!

Micha-el extended his left hand while passing the other one underneath, with his fingers equally separated and pointing to the second group... he gave them the same treatment!

Five more individuals were now in complete silence.

As Micha-el pointed his right hand toward the third group, who had just watched what happened to their friends, they decided to shut up and close their mouths!

The NA crowd became unhappy. They resented how the leader of the SA treated their companions. They got angry and placed pressure on the platforms, making them vibrate. Only the space close to Micha-el stayed empty, as the nearby NA visitors had moved backward and away.

Lucif-er giggled almost unnoticeable; then, he remarked so everybody could hear, *"I can see that you did not wait for my permission this time. Do you think it is fair to mistreat my people this way, and I do nothing about it?"*

While still looking at Micha-el, Lucif-er snapped his right-hand sideways, pointing to the SA visitors. Ten SA individuals on the front row, next to the middle platform, dropped to the floor. There, they twisted as worms over a hot surface!

Micha-el looked sympathetic to his citizens' pain; after letting out some steam in a long breath, he commented to Lucif-er.

"You know very well that I did not hurt any of your people!"

"Yes! But the rest of the people did not know the difference!"

Some of the fallen angels' friends picked them up, and many nearby SA angels moved several meters from the center platform... Things were getting out of control!

At that moment, Lucif-er pointed a finger to Micha-el's chest, precisely to the location of the cross on his garments. He barely touched it, but it was much more than a touch; it was a highly charged pulse of energy, as seen by the stronger glow around Lucif-er's finger.

As soon as the pain became apparent, Micha-el blocked it away. A bluish field glowed between the two Archangels; it had a definite boundary between them. Lucif-er commented.

"Did you get the point?"

All the Overlords on the north and south platforms stood up in unison! The crowd, for the same instant, also stopped breathing!

Nobiel and the whole council were petrified. Their reaction to the developing contest distorted some of these angels' faces. They could not believe how fast the meeting deteriorated. Nobiel squeezed his teeth and pressed the tip of his chin with his thumb and index finger, realizing he had been deceived. Lucif-er had used him for the sole purpose of drawing the Overlords of the South from the protection of their Matrix! Only God knows for what dark intent. How could have been so gullible to Lucif-er's promises of finding a way for <u>everlasting peace</u>?

He was utterly depressed. To make it worse, he was powerless to stop the NA Overlords. The council and its leader were guessing what was next.

Overlord confrontations have happened before, but only as friendly exercises. Now, could it be something that has never been seen before?

The Overlords engaging physically and mentally in… **mortal combat?**

Lucif-er moved a hand behind him and asked all his Overlords to stay seated, *"This is just between Micha-el and me!"*

Lucif-er received a personal message from one of his Overlords.

"Let me fight Micha-el; I know I can kill him!"

Lucif-er did not look back, but he instantly responded secretly.

"Azami-el, sit down! That feat will be part of my own pleasure!"

Micha-el also requested his Overlords to sit. Slowly, both groups returned to their previously assigned sitting positions. Micha-el, squarely facing Lucif-er, speared a statement. His powerful voice filled the plaza and its adjacent buildings so all the visitors could understand.

"I did not come here to fight, just the opposite; I came for peace! Lucif-er, you could direct this meeting in the proper direction; give us something tangible that could be used for advancing peace!"

Lucif-er turned to the NA visitor's side with a sarcastic mannerism that included a smile and a pointed finger in the direction of his opponent, he commented.

"This Micha-el, who promises and offers peace, would not hesitate to push a button and bring death and desolation to our Alliance!"

After a brief pause, so the audience could digest the heavy innuendo meal, he continued, ***"Nevertheless, the same Micha-el, who is so brave behind a nuclear-armed attack Matrix, is apprehensive of fighting me! What does this tell you about the 'real' Micha-el, hidden behind a mask he calls his face?"***

Micha-el became frustrated with the upsetting insinuations. His tensed muscles were showing up beneath his fancy tunic, he retorted.

"Stop this nonsense. You can say anything that you want to me. But I have said: There will be… no fighting!"

Lucif-er glanced at him with only a half-head turn. Scornfully, he laughed, *"I could change your mind so easily that it is not even a challenge!"*

Micha-el, pointing a finger at his opponent, indicated.

"I meant what I said!"

Lucif-er, at lightning speed, also pointed the finger at Micha-el, crossing and touching the already pointed index finger. He also powerfully pushed Micha-el's finger to his right in a sort of finger wrestling. He exclaimed.

"So do I!"

Micha-el retrieved his finger before the sparks started flying; Lucif-er immediately commented.

"Are you afraid to find out how weak you really are?"

The SA leader, now breathing faster than usual, made a solid effort to calm himself. He spoke.

"Lucif-er, I promised God and the SA that I was coming here to talk peace. If you have NO intention of conducting this gathering for that purpose, we will exit this meeting."

Undaunted by the statement, the NA's #1 Archangel, with deep malice, indicated, *"Did you just mention… 'god'? … That useless being, seven years and 92 days ago, at a building called 'the temple,' we decided it had never existed!"* Lucif-er nodded his head with disapproval; while looking down at Micha-el, he added, *"Oh! I know… you still believe in him!"*

With a highly sarcastic grin, in which his face got closer to Micha-el's, Lucif-er continued.

"Perhaps, since you are a coward, you could ask your 'god' to fight for you!"

While rotating to address the whole congregation with his hands raised up and with a big smile, he loudly concluded.

"Unless… 'he' or 'it'… is also afraid to face me?"

He finished turning around with another half-stare to Micha-el's face.

Even before the last remark was completed, Micha-el's blood had reached its boiling point. He squeezed his teeth together until they made an unfriendly sound. Following the previous remark, the NA crowd roared with approval. In addition, a delayed but equally strong clamor rose with disapproval from the SA visitors. Micha-el's six wings were never so visible before; their glow bathed him in a blue haze. He just exploded with a remark that drowned the loud murmur from both crowds.

"If you cannot have any respect for God, leave Him out of this argument!"

His powerful voice rattled the audience, changing them from shouters to listeners. He lowered his voice to a less thunderous tone to point out the following to Lucif-er.

"God is everything to me, Lucif-er. Not even you, who denies His existence, could exist without Him allowing it."

Gabri-el's eyes met with Rapha-el's, both nodding in despair as they understood that a fight had become inevitable. Even if Micha-el could refuse to fight Lucif-er in God's defense, something that was impossible, they would have to take his place and fight Lucif-er; it would not matter if that meant to die! Unfortunately, they also knew that due to the circumstances, Micha-el should fight Lucif-er, and they were already confined as spectators.

The Overlords of the North smiled with delight; their sinister plan to get Micha-el out of the way was working to perfection. As soon as the leader of the SA died, they would overpower the remaining Overlords of the South. The task should not be too difficult. After all, they will have the surprising advantage of being eight against only six! Then, they could ransom them as a sure way to drop the 4-D Matrix defense system. After that, the rest would be... just a piece of cake!

Lucif-er was more than confident about himself. He was just playing with Micha-el before the kill, sort of a cat-and-mouse scenario, he exclaimed cynically.

"I sense anger; however, I am not talking to you; I am talking to your 'god'!"

Ignoring Micha-el, he took several steps away from him, raising his arms to the sky. He demanded with a thunderous electronic voice.

"YOU, WORTHLESS 'GOD' OF MICHA-EL... I, LUCIF-ER, CHALLENGE YOU TO A FIGHT! YOU CAN USE ANYTHING... METEORS... TORNADOES... LIGHTNING! I DO NOT CARE; YOU SHOOT FIRST!"

An eerie silence followed as the much longer-than-usual seconds crawled one after the other; it was like both sides expected something to happen. Except for the Archangels, just about everybody else stared at the bright and cloudless early afternoon sky; the sun did not even blink! The soft breeze, caused by the thermal updrafts, continued undisturbed!

Expectations stayed incredibly high. To their disillusionment... Nothing happened!

Lucif-er showed his favorite slimy smile. With open questioning hands, he stated, "Nobody answered! *OK, Micha-el... I guess you and your stupid 'god' deserve each other. Both of you are cowards!"*

Micha-el had it! He calmed down the volcano, ready to erupt from the inside to the outside. He reflected to himself.

"I apologize, my Lord; I came looking for peace, but since Lucif-er had something else on mind, I am ready for battle! ... I would not do it for myself but for Your sake and glory... I MUST!"

He did not address everyone; this time, he blasted a personal message to Lucif-er alone.

"You, the Evil one, defend yourself!"

Lucif-er faced his nearby opponent with an open smile, contradicting his darkening and hypnotic blue eyes. In utter satisfaction, he thought.

"Micha-el... you are mine!"

At the same time, he pointed his left-hand index finger up and exclaimed.

"Since all these visitors need to be entertained, I do not want you to die too soon! Let us start at level 1!"

When Lucif-er pointed one finger up, all the attendants knew he meant the first level of the Archangel vs. Archangel fight, an enclosed event!

Since not all of you know what I am talking about, I will gladly explain this unique event.

To begin, you must realize that before the angels had to choose between God and Evil, nobody fought intending to injure or kill someone in combat.

A confrontation was much like a boxing match; the two contestants fought to overpower their opponent inside the frame of a sporting event, a friendly competition with set rules and confinements as the boxing ring's fixed size remained the most important. A friendly fight between two Archangels could be hazardous to nearby bystanders if they were not Archangels themselves. All-out Archangel combat to the death, without the 'ring' limiting the area of confrontation, would be devastating to a multitude watching the event.

There were three levels of combat. Only the first and second levels of Archangel-friendly combat had been previously utilized as a training exercise or as a sporting event.

First Level- Imagine sitting in front of a 3-D video game, the best possible, with a virtual reality generated by computer graphics. Facing you, something is going to materialize. You must take countermeasures to cancel its effect if it is an offensive weapon or a dangerous object. Simultaneously, you could generate your own offensive game. Your opponent will see a mirror image of your field of view; accordingly, he will attack you and defend himself.

Next, consider the following event like a train moving toward you. Each wagon is an independent event or action; as one passes through you, it could display a distinct challenge you must undertake to complete. By then, the next wagon with a different challenge should be materializing.

Last, to increase the game's difficulty, the train passing over you could continuously increase its speed, as the acceleration could be fixed or increased in value.

The catch: as a sporting event, it is harmless; as deadly combat, it is not a game! You could indisputably die if you fail to defend yourself realistically and efficiently! However, since level 1 is frontal combat, if things get too hot, you could escape or disengage from the fight by just backing up and exiting.

Second Level- Same as the first level, but much more complex. The area of battle can be multiplied six times simultaneously. It is still frontal combat; however, each surface of your cube works independently as a Level 1 combat area. Exiting by backing up, even when much harder to do, can still save your butt!

Third Level- The ultimate battleground. Enclosed inside a very compact cube, individually, you and your opponent share the center of a much larger cube. Each of the six internal facets of the cube is a nodule for battle. You will be fighting six trains of dangerous events, approaching from all possible directions while continuously changing and increasing speed. If you do not think that is complex enough, you are confined at the center of two cubes, one frontal, and another backward; therefore, you have twelve battle zones! Last, the volume confining you at the center of two cubes is the 13th battle zone!

At this level, I do not wish you luck; none is left. Since you are attacked from all directions, there is no escape possible.

You must win... Or die!

Level 1 + 2

Archangels: visual frontal planes for battle. It includes an individual box: 4 x 4 x 4 meters. The winning Overlord can push the center plane forward, reducing his opponent's initial cube volume.

Level 1: Micha-el and Lucif-er, floating at the center of their own cube, will fight only through the center plane.

Level 2: Similar to Level 1, however, as you float at the center, the fight could escalate through all six planes of your own cube facing you. For both levels, the back wall is open for withdrawal.

Level 3

Three cubes overlapping, each 4 x 4 x 4 meters. Each Archangel is at the front of his cube, enclosed in his individual and skintight-centered rectangle. No one had ever considered this location at the center to be usable; this is the 13th battle zone; instead of the usual outward projection like the other twelve planes of battle, you fight inwardly for each inner facet of the larger cube for twelve cumulative times; six surfaces from the back cube, plus six surfaces from the frontal cube. I need to emphasize that Level 3 has never been used before. Even for the Overlords, this was uncharted territory.

Note that each Overlord's frontal battle area ends exactly at his opponent's location. Thus, even when separated, they share the center cube of the whole battlefield.

The spectators stayed silent; a bluish rectangle formed around the warring Overlords as the Level 1 battleground field unfolded. It was partially transparent, encompassing both Overlords in an 8 x 4 meters box. A distinct vertical interface remained visible at the center, dividing the two 4 x 4 cubes. Only this surface could be used as a battlefield for Level 1. The Overlords inside the so-delineated 4 x 4 cubes stood at the bottom surface or the platform's floor.

With their next move, the Archangels levitated above the surface of the platform to take a center position at their own cube. The preliminaries were over!

Inside the cube, the outside world disappeared into darkness.

Only Micha-el, facing Lucif-er, remained visible... A time shift started to slow down the fast-moving engagement!

[2x]> The action started gradually from a slower beginning.

Lucif-er's head grew quickly until Micha-el saw only a large frontal view of his opponent's face. His eyes turned from blue to a fiery red. At the same time, his enlarged irises were rotating hypnotically; from the black depths of his enlarging pupils, two extremely sharp conical darts shot at Micha-el with incredible speed; the direction, Micha-el's eyes!

The leader of the SA generated a large conical metallic object larger than his head, which was equally fast propelled and pointed towards Lucif-er's head. The two darts from the latter bounced off, deflected by the large cone's conical walls, and dissipated into the peripheral darkness. This happened not in silence; the projectiles carried deafening sonic booms!

[4x] Lucif-er blasted Micha-el's cone.

It blew up in a ball of fire, reducing the cone to smoldering pieces. For a moment, the leftovers, still in flames, appeared to have their own minds. They reassembled into multiple flat planes, with their edges as sharp as razors.

From the maximum field of vision and with different angles of approach, they tumbled down toward Micha-el. This Archangel introduced a sonic boom, which shattered the planes to dust.

Micha-el projected the sand-sized remains at his opponent at a speed resembling a micro-meteor shower on the moon's surface![2]

[6x] By now, things were moving six times faster than usual.

---

[2]. According to Google search, the moon has no atmosphere, and meteors hit its surface at speeds of 20 km/sec up to 72 km/second.

We still saw them at normal speed due to our time shift, which slowed things down.

An intense ball of fire came ferociously, expanding from Lucif-er's side. It vaporized all the dust particles and quickly approached Micha-el's face. The heat was intense!

Micha-el barely had time to produce a concave shield, which collected the expanding ball of roaring fire and converted it into a powerful laser of intense white heat. The laser emanated from the center of the shield was aimed at Lucif-er.

[10x] In front of Lucif-er, a prism materialized.

It broke the white light into a rainbow pattern. Each distinctive color, except indigo, merged into multiple laser shots at Micha-el.

Red, orange, yellow, green, blue, and violet, all six lasers smashed into Micha-el, now using a protective shield; a high-frequency sound also rattled his eardrums!

The six exploding blasts on the shield shattered it to pieces, causing Micha-el to move backward. He ended up closer to the back edge of his cube. The interface was no longer in the middle; he had lost substantial ground. He projected the broken pieces toward Lucif-er!

[15x] Like a shock wave, Lucif-er deflected the pieces upwards.

Simultaneously, he shot one-hundred blades; they were not only sharp but also had an internal high-explosive core. Unequally spaced, they moved around the shield fragments, so they were not visible until they were at short range. Micha-el had little room to maneuver; they were too close, coming too fast! He set himself as a repulsive barrier.

On impact, when the incoming blades hit the barrier before touching his skin, they violently exploded, pushing him backward! A scorning and reverberating voice filled the uneven rectangles before Micha-el had time to depart his compressed volumetric rectangle!

"Micha-el... are you leaving? We are just starting!"

Micha-el exited! <[15x]

To the other Archangels, the events unfolded as seen by their advanced faculties. However, to the rest of the audience, everything started with the cone fighting at a visible rate; then, the whole thing quickly became a blurry mixture of flashing lights and loud but high-pitched compressed noises!

As the bluish box encompassing the cubes disappeared, Micha-el came out, falling backward to the floor. He managed to place his feet on the ground first, but he still took two steps back due to the inertia caused by the last shock wave!

Lucif-er quickly lowered himself to the platform surface.

All the Overlords stood up; the ones from the North raised one hand, fist closed, a sign of power and victory. Their leader had won the first round!

The crowd from the West roared with approval. In addition, they all raised one fist to celebrate.

All the people from the East side, plus the Overlords of the South, remained in silence. A great apprehension started developing in their minds; they were concerned about Micha-el's future.

Still breathing hard because of the energy spent fighting, Micha-el looked at the large multitude of North visitors cheering his adversary. About 30 meters, diagonally SW from his location, he recognized someone.

For a second, their blue eyes locked on each other. Micha-el had identified his ex-personal assistant. He was enthusiastically cheering for Lucif-er's victory. Suddenly, he became noticeably disturbed when he realized that Micha-el had recognized him; he swallowed and at once looked away in the direction of the Overlords of the North. He did not stop cheering. Micha-el's heart became saddened; he, who used to be a friend, was no more. He thought of only one name... Arkyn! After that, his attention focused on Lucif-er publicly addressing him.

"Micha-el, aren't you scared knowing that you will lose?"

Micha-el looked at his opponent defiantly and replied.

"My strength is not mine; it comes from my Lord as He wishes to dispense it. I have no fear of Evil since I know God is at my side!"

Lucif-er hand-dressed his spectacularly blond and curly hair. He commented with a degrading look at Micha-el, the same way people with a steep nose look at whom they consider inferior.

"Have you ever realized that your 'god' does not answer because he does not exist? ... The only proof you have, dreams, cannot be considered as reality... I make you this offer, in which I am giving you a last chance to save your life: Join the NA, and I will make you second in command, equal to Magog-el. You still could rule over the SA. This is an easy way to have peace!"

Micha-el squeezed together his teeth again, and with ardent fervor in his voice, replied, *"Your evil heart has no room for understanding anymore!"*

The SA leader addressed the congregation seriously; by this time, all the other Overlords had returned to their seats.

"In the past, Evil meant an event that brought sorrow and pain. Now evil has a new meaning: 'Disobedience to the Lord.' It is a rebellious force bent on hate and destruction of anything Good and Holy!

It is something that is not light, but darkness... Not love but hate!
And not God, but yourself... That is you, Lucif-er! You want to be a god,
but you can only be: The Lord of deception!
All who follow you will only find what you intrinsically believe: hate
and destruction!"
Lucif-er's eyes sparkled with fury. He yelled to his opponent.
"Shut up! Your absurd babbling has exhausted any patience I had
left! Instead of pestering me, you should be worried about yourself since
your life will end ... soon!"
At that moment, he raised his right hand: Two fingers were up!

Once more, the cubes formed from the overall bluish rectangle of 8 x
4 meters. The two Overlords levitated to the center of their own cubes; the
second battleground was set and ready for action!
[2x]> This time, Lucif-er's head did not grow.

 Instead, his whole body got smaller and almost vanished into
a reduced single dot! Micha-el hesitated momentarily, trying to
figure out his opponent's intent. Then, it dawned on him. Lucif-er
had created a high vacuum! If Micha-el projected some form of
high energy, the projectile not only would not have any resistance
in its flight, but it would cause a forward drag on its originator,
causing him to lose his balance!

 Micha-el thought, "I could also bet that Lucif-er's location is not
where the reducing dot is!"

 Accordingly, he sent a capsule full of liquid gas with minimal
initial energy. It accelerated at a tremendous increasing speed but
was aimed high above the remaining dot from Lucif-er's reduced
figure. The expanding gas coming from behind this spot caused
no interactions. Micha-el's voice metallically echoed in the
rectangular tunnel used as a virtual reality battleground.

 "Nice try, Lucif-er!"

 Almost instantly, in a louder reverberating tone, the NA leader
replied, **"You almost ate it, Micha-el!"**

 Before the turbulent gas reached Lucif-er's actual location, he
rearranged the turbulence into a menacing tornado with powerful
spinning winds, increasing speed as it advanced to Micha-el's
side.

[3x] Micha-el materialized some rotating fan blades.

 They spun furiously in the opposite direction as the menacing
tornado. As both met, it was like another matter/antimatter social
event; they annihilated each other. The sound blast was violent!

 Screens 2 and 6, from Lucif-er's side, huge boulders were
aimed at Micha-el's head.

For screens 4 and 5, Micha-el sent sharp-edged small disks. In 5, they also multiplied by splitting in half, with irregular trajectories.

A high-energy plasma blast raced toward Micha-el at 1, out of Lucif-er's right-hand palm.

2 and 6- Micha-el focused on a high-energy laser to destroy the boulders. In 2, they were destroyed, but in 6, the boulders were hollow! The beams only made holes in the boulders dangerously approaching Micha-el's face from the bottom battleground! (as seen from the cube's surface 6)

At 4 and 5- Lucif-er used a powerful sonic boom to shatter the left side (screen 4) disks aiming at him! If the sonic boom reached Micha-el, he would be permanently deaf! Similarly, Lucif-er projected a high-power shock wave for the right side, which equally blasted away the multiplying disks.

[4x] The speed of the battle continued to increase.

The violence in the six screens mounted in ferocity, where the number of battlefield surfaces was the same for both warriors.

[6x] At six times faster than the average speed.

Lucif-er activated two more screens or surfaces using screens 1 and 3. Now, all six battlefields of the cubical surfaces have become active. Screens 1 and 3 turned into biochemical warfare areas, with cyanide-impregnated micro darts, chlorine gases, KCyanide vapors, botulism toxin, skin, eye-burning acids, etc.

How could they manufacture such chemical compounds? They probably used the available chemicals from the air, clothing, and bodies. Any means of destruction you could imagine were there, plus much more and much worse. The opponent had to correctly identify the toxin, cancel it, and counterattack.

[8x] Everything became faster and more complicated.

The worst nightmare of a lifetime was raging. Incidentally, the warriors were only one mistake away from becoming nonexistent!

[10x] At this incredibly fast pace, Micha-el struggled to keep up.

Given the complexity of all the battlefields and their extremely accelerated pace, this could be expected, mostly against Lucif-er, who was confident in his superior powers.

In the heat of the battle, just one moment of weakness could cause all the peripheral battlefields to collapse. That is what happened!

Micha-el had retreated against his cube's back wall for a second time! The rest was collapsing.

[15x] Lucif-er increased the speed even more.

He sent a blast of red-hot plasma to Micha-el's remaining space. As the heat rose, Micha-el knew that he had to get out and exit, or he would be burned alive. The drag of six battle zones made it extremely hard to detach. Milliseconds had passed, and he still could not do it!

A sarcastic voice overpowered the incoming roaring fire.

"Hurry up, Micha-el, or you won't have time to even say goodbye!"

The leader of the SA concentrated all the energy left in his body and broke loose. He moved out... Exited! <[15x]

Similarly to the first battle, the audience could see the initial skirmishes. After that, everything got complicated and too fast to follow, except for the Overlords. Flashes, noises, and moving objects seemed like a maelstrom, just impossible to trace!

Suddenly, Micha-el came flying from his cube's backside with his clothes partially smoking!

He fell to the ground and rolled twice. Next, kneeling on his right leg, he struggled to get up. His face was covered with sweat and lightly bruised; his glorious curly hair did not look so well-kept. Breathing heavily, he slowly rose from the platform's floor; a horrendous cheer from Lucif-er's supporters shook the whole place!

Something wet dripped from Micha-el's nostrils; he didn't look... He knew it was blood! He placed his left thumb and index finger on his nose... The bleeding stopped!

All the Overlords from the South Alliance stood up. Gabri-el and Rapha-el started to move to assist him, but Micha-el made a sign with his hand to stop. He mentally communicated with both Archangels, who showed great concern for their leader and close friend.

"Thanks... I am OK!"

Nobiel and the council members looked with horror at Micha-el, who had barely exited the second round of fighting in time. Using the cameras on the platforms, they closely focused on his face without missing any action.

The sight and imminent third-round implications caused Nobiel to shake lightly. The rest gave the impression of being shocked since, by The Core standards, Micha-el remained a highly respected individual.

How could the council members reconcile the thought of being deceived and bring Micha-el to Trillium for his destruction? Close to panic, they dreaded the incoming and deadly final battleground...

The Third Level!

In Dawnel, in front of another large screen, a small group of angels watched the meeting turn sour and become a combat zone. Raquel and Maryen, Dani-el's girlfriend, were seated in the front row watching

Micha-el's second defeat. They stood up like they were being ejected by a powerful spring. Maryen, using both hands, squeezed her friend's right hand. She looked squarely at Raquel and anxiously exclaimed.

"Raquel... I cannot believe my eyes; if he loses again, Micha-el will die! How can this be happening?"

Raquel looked at her companion, but her mind drifted away to Trillium. Disturbed by the current events, she felt the utmost concern for Micha-el, her husband Gabri-el, and the rest of the SA present at the meeting. She remained glad about her decision not to attend. However, her heart lingered in pain, sore for Micha-el's safety and the possibility of Gabri-el being next.

With a hesitant mental remark, she answered back.

"I know God resides in Micha-el; my dear friend should not lose... Why is God not helping him? I don't understand what is going on!"

After her troubled response, Raquel suggested her companion retake a seat. Her right hand remained trapped between Maryen and her; as she placed her left hand on the others, she continued using a milder tone.

*"There is **only** one thing we can do to help. Together, let's pray to our loving God for all the SA people attending the meeting in Trillium and for their safe return home!"*

Micha-el began a slow return to confront Lucif-er, who stayed celebrating with his whole crowd, both hands up and palms open when Gabri-el contacted Micha-el. Gabri-el's personal telepathic message reflected his deep concern and empathy, *"My brother, you are using the wrong approach! You cannot defeat Lucif-er on his own savage terms! Please... Remember the message from our Lord! You will endure, not by force, but with <u>Love</u>!"*

Micha-el listened with appreciation. He remembered the most crucial encounter of his life. He also recalled the beautiful white flower that he held in his hand. He opened his right hand and looked at his palm... A chill ran down his spine. His hand was partially stained with his own blood!

He smiled... Right now, the first gift ultimately made sense!

Lucif-er was the flower. Sumptuously dressed in that dazzling white tunic, he always looked much better than anyone else by the power of his mind and body.

It was now up to him, Micha-el, to blow that deceiving layer to expose that ugly monster hidden inside! He stood straight; a new vigor filled his body. He knew that God was inside his soul; therefore, how could he lose to Lucif-er or any other evil monster... **in Terra or the whole Universe?**

Lucif-er moved his hands, requesting silence. The crowd complied very fast. He remarked in his most sarcastic but powerful voice.

"People of the North!... I intercepted a message from Gabri-el to Micha-el... Just listen to this!"

For the following statement, he chuckled with anticipation.

"It is very amusing...
'Micha-el, if you want to win, fight Lucif-er with <u>love</u>!' Yes... l-o-v-e!
Who is he? A homosexual? Is he going to kiss me to death?"

As the Northern Overlords and the entire NA visitors burst out laughing, Micha-el stayed undaunted by the comment reflecting in the 'homosexuality innuendo.' Lucif-er, mentioning the subject, which had never been any sexual preference on Terra before, was like accepting that it had become part of the degradation rampant in the NA. His heart increased with sadness because he knew this to be one more offense to his loving God.

At the same time, Gabri-el reflected on Lucif-er's statement.

"My God! Even for such a narrow, mentally projected thought, since a personal telepathic message is equivalent to someone just whispering in your ear, Lucif-er can still listen to our private conversations. I suspected something like it, but it is tough to accept it!"

The leader of the NA looked beyond Micha-el and cynically stated.

"Yes, Gabri-el, I can do that and even more!"

Gabri-el's face got very serious; after calming himself down, he replied.

"You had an unfair advantage in all our meetings; however, it does not matter! What we think, what we personally communicate to each other, we could have told you in your own face. We have nothing to hide since we talk and live by the Truth!"

Lucif-er quickly responded.

"The only <u>truth</u> I see is the fact that all of you are a bunch of pathetic losers! As you will be painfully aware soon!"

He addressed Micha-el in a much louder voice.

"Are you ready to die? This time, there is <u>no</u> dreamscape."[3]

Micha-el, showing great confidence, just smiled before he retorted.

"You will be truly sorry about opening your mouth too much."

"You are dumber than I thought, Micha-el; this is not a virtual reality game. After this round of the fight, it is too bad that you will not be able to open your own mouth... <u>ever!</u>"

While looking at his right hand, Micha-el passed his left hand over it. The bloodstain vanished... This time, he raised his right hand... three fingers extended. He had called the third and final confrontation!

---

[3] With 'dreamscape,' I am referring to a movie where you wake up to escape death, similar to the First and Second Levels. Needless to say, if you cannot wake up, you are dead: This is Level Three.

Lucif-er burst out laughing, amused by what he believed were Micha-el's suicidal tendencies. Cynically, he stated.

"I sense a great confidence emanating from you... You are quite sure about winning!"

He chuckled a bit more. His Overlords and the NA crowd eagerly joined him in the celebration. Laughs, giggles, and scorning comments from his opponents came raining down on Micha-el. Lucif-er slowly caressed his chin; then, he deeply stared at Micha-el while loudly requesting.

"Do you know something? If you are so confident about winning as you believe, I would be eager to make some profitable bet... What about this? The winner... I mean, the survivor... takes it all!

You win: The NA is yours. I win: The SA is mine... It is an excellent civilized way to avoid nuclear war!"

Micha-el started to levitate; the rectangular bluish box began to materialize. He commented vocally.

"Stop the nonsense. In the same way that the SA is not mine to give, you cannot offer the NA as your own property."

The leader of the North responded with a personal mental message. At the same time, he levitated toward his place at the center of his cube faster than his opponent was moving to the center of his own cube.

"You do not own the SA?... That is too bad!
The NA... does belong to me!"

He continued with a loud voice statement.

"By the way, Micha-el... Good luck!"

Both Overlords stayed at the center of their cubes. Both remained absolutely sure to win the battle; however, there was a catch: only one could survive. It turned into the prize fight of a millennium!

The ultimate supremacy: The winner, the most powerful being on the planet. Micha-el did not care about the title; his opponent considered it a must!

Like the two previous encounters, a bluish rectangular box became visible for all to observe, but its materialized size was now 4 x 4 x 4 meters.

Each Overlord was not at the center of their cube; instead, they became encased inside a smaller rectangular volume at the center of their frontal cube's surface, previously named screen #1.

Back on the battlefield, there was a significant overlap. The center vertical face between the Overlords, the same area where the two previous battles took place, was no longer there. Four meters separated the two Overlords from each other; it placed Lucif-er's frontal surface right against Micha-el's skin and vice versa. Somehow, it looked strange how the two small and skintight rectangles encased the Overlords.

The third, and supposedly the <u>always</u> deadly confrontation, began!
[2x]> Lucif-er's eyes split into a deep blue and a fiery red.

Then, they rotated, generating two spiraling volumes that expanded to the side edges of the front battle zone.

In a fraction of a second, Micha-el faced rotating strands of high-temperature fire, alternating with strands of cryogenic super-cold temperatures. It was like a version of a small pin wheel-shaped toy with two colors alternating segments; when the wind makes it rotate, they have a hypnotic effect on the onlookers. The approaching threat of these fan-looking blades had the added feature of independently carbonizing some sections of your flesh while freezing solid the next adjacent slices.

Moving his right hand close to his body, Micha-el raised his palm outward. This happened at the front interface, where a dot, the tip of Micha-el's frontal pyramid, just ended in front of his body. This is the same place where Lucif-er's attacking fan occupied the entire plane of his frontal cube's face.

As the incoming hot/cold blast approached Micha-el, a whitish, semitransparent puff of light materialized out of his right palm and exploded, but not violently!

The blast mildly shook the interface facing Micha-el. However, the energy involved dissipated and returned to Lucif-er via the inside central tetrahedral perimeter of Micha-el's attack volume. This was unusual since the energy should have returned to Lucif-er from outside his tetrahedral volume. Before the last flashes of energy completely dissipated, it could easily be seen that Micha-el's frontal volume was lost to Lucif-er!

However, one whitish, almost ethereal puff of light remained at both Overlords' frontal starting point.
[4x] Lucif-er stepped up the pace.

He was delighted to have won so quickly in the first encounter. Sarcastically, he yelled at his opponent in a still reverberating tone.

"Did I catch you sleeping? Or perhaps you cannot handle hot and cold simultaneously?"

Concurrently with his statement, Lucif-er was puzzled by the light puffs. What were those tiny balls of light? He moved his hand across the puff in front of him like trying to hit a fly; his hand went through the puff, analogously to someone trying to touch a ghost. Next, he tried an electric zap, plasma, laser, magnetic shock, pure oxygen, pure acid, and a strong base.

Nothing... Nothing at all! It was like it did not exist, but it was there; it remained undisturbed in the same place.

Meanwhile, Micha-el seemed unperturbed after losing a sector. A faint smile adorned his attractive and confident face.

Lucif-er decided: if the puffs of light were in front of him and equally in front of Micha-el, it was logical that he did not have to worry about them; therefore, he attacked with fury.

Both the left and right sides of Micha-el underwent severe assault. His left side saw multiplying black needles that grew and shattered, then increased again in bigger numbers. His right side saw a solid wall of some strange kind of purple plasma ominously approaching with an increasingly loud noise!

Without even looking, Micha-el crossed his arms in front of him. He opened his right palm, touching the surface of his right side, centered in the 13th battle's zone. One oddity of this 13th battle volume was that it existed at two different places simultaneously, at each Overlord location. Was this a quantum effect?

His left palm stayed equally positioned against the left surface of the encased battle zone; two puffs of light confronted the two attacking sectors.

On impact, the black needles turned to dust. Its energy also returned to Lucif-er through the center walls of his opponent's facing surface. The high-pitched sound from the plasma just faded away like a moving vehicle; the noise and the purple glow returned to his originator, same as the other ones... However, Micha-el had just lost two more zones! Three zones now belonged to Lucif-er. The latter did not wait much to rub it in.

"Micha-el... This is too easy!

I was expecting to have more fun. It would be best if you tried harder, or you will have no place left to stand... And nowhere to hide!"

Micha-el still did not answer.

The leader of the NA stared again at the three light puffs, now in front and on both sides of his muscular body. They were the same as the three puffs in Micha-el's position... Lucif-er squeezed his teeth together with disgust; something told him that not everything was turning as he wanted!

Nevertheless, despite his great might, he remained powerless to change anything. Consequently, with increasing anger, he stepped up the fight.

[7x] Lucif-er decided that he was tired of playing this game.

He was going to attack in all remaining sectors, in this manner trapping Micha-el for the final kill, so he did.

Small balls filled with high explosives and cyanide gas rained over the back sector, speeding menacingly toward Micha-el!

A high-power laser blast, invisible because its frequency was in the ultraviolet region, emerged from above!

Spinning balls with sharp pointed ends and internally generated high voltages assailed Micha-el from below! The electrical cross-lightning turned awesome!

Micha-el deployed his left hand palm to stop the first attack from behind. Exploding bombs and nasty gases mixed briefly before they returned to Lucif-er.

Almost instantly, he crossed his hands again, his right palm facing up, the left facing down. The invisible laser became visible, a deep blue on impact; it quickly dissipated in a sharp hiss and returned to the same place as the others. The appearance of the white light puffs in this zone became more noticeable.

The electric storm made supersonic cracking noises as it hit the lower interface, but it shorted out, and by crisscrossing its way backward, it returned to the evil contender.

Lucif-er used all means of mass destruction against Micha-el, who repelled them all using the bright puffs.

As the barrage ended, Micha-el found himself trapped; all the sectors had been lost; there was no place to exit! In addition, twelve puffs of light closely surrounded him, the same amount next to Lucif-er.

The latter, drooling at the view, assumed his opponent had no chance to win this battle. His triumphant scream rattled the rectangles.

"You coward! If you had fought, you could have lived a few seconds longer. Now, it is over... Prepare to die!"

Before Lucif-er unleashed the final attack, Micha-el, still very calm, noted, **"You are wrong, Lucif-er... You are the loser!"**

The leader of the NA burst out laughing, looking at Micha-el with scorn and hate. The Archangel, the leader of God's abiding Alliance, was his for the slaughter!

In the middle of a chuckle, he remarked.

"Yes, I lost... It must be the reason that will allow me to see your flesh churning into greasy and charcoal-looking remains, a carcass that not even your mother will recognize!"

As all twelve interfaces showed the distorted face of Lucif-er with his deep blue eyes full of hate and intending murder, his muscles tensed because of the same vicious goal, and his curly hair moved like a sea of minute blond snakes; he thundered.

"Die!"

[10x] A powerful firewall raced through all twelve windows.

It moved to incinerate Micha-el; the Archangel disappeared in the wall of flames!

Hundredths of a second slowly passed by before the flames cleared out. Lucif-er peeked, looking for the Archangel's remains, but what he saw chilled his whole body.

Micha-el was still there, standing, untouched.

This time, Lucif-er saw twelve faces in front of him. Micha-el questioned in a sober tone, not displaying any smile.

"The puffs of light; do you know what they represent?"

Lucif-er's hateful and deepest stare became the only answer he got back. Micha-el continued vocally, **"The white light is a gift from God and represents Love. Even when we see it as a fuzzy dot, each dot represents a volumetric spot existing in a higher dimension; thus, it is almost invisible in our three-dimensional world."**

As the leader of the North ground his teeth and squinted his eyes with furor, his fingers on both hands malignantly twisted as if they could hold Micha-el's neck.

"I think you are getting the picture now," Micha-el noted; then, he continued.

"You must be aware that there were <u>thirteen</u> battle zones... The thirteen was a higher spatial dimension: It was made of dual cubes smaller than the others and located exactly where we stand; they tightly encompassed each of our bodies. Conversely, unlike the other twelve, you must fight inwardly to win!"

Micha-el paused briefly; his opponent was almost foaming at the mouth. He continued without any hesitation.

"You won all twelve of the 3-D battle zones. But, if you lost the thirteenth, the higher dimension battle's zone... You have lost <u>everything</u>... I know it looks like a paradox; unfortunately for you, it is a physical reality!"

Lucif-er burst with uncontrollable rage; fire and lightning shook the two 4 x 4 cubes encompassing Micha-el. The smaller third, the inner one, remained impervious to this violence. The evil Archangel emitted a vicious and deafening roar.

"NOOOOOO!"

Micha-el, like watching a video display, just ignored all the fireworks. Next, he pointed his right hand with his open palm facing Lucif-er. In the center, a bright puff of light materialized... He made a last statement.

"If your heart and mind were pure, this light would be the most precious gift ever presented to you. Nevertheless, you are an antagonistic representation of His essence; you became the Lord of Darkness.

For you, it will be like fire... It will not kill you because Love does not kill or destroy; however, it does purify!

Since you are beyond purification, I am sorry to mention...For you, it will burn so much that you will surely wish... to be... at some other place!"

The bright puff projected toward Lucif-er at one meter/millisecond.

[25x] Lucif-er's body felt a chill! For the first time in his long life.

He knew what fear was about. Like an ominous silver bullet aimed at his heart, the puff moved inexorably in a seemingly straight line toward him. However, whatever made the dot fuzzy, perhaps uncountable microscopic light spots, did not advance straight but followed curved planes.

Lucif-er knew: It was physically impossible to stop it. It looked so harmless... Would Micha-el be correct?... Something inside him said... **"Yes!"**

In slow motion, it got closer and closer until, all of a sudden, it went inside the NA leader's smallest cube. Then, as it touched Lucif-er, it ignited an eerie inferno!

Yet, not the slightest spark or hint of smoke showed outside the inner cube. Horrible noises that emanated from Lucif-er filled the total volume of the rectangle. The searing pain he felt was like a precursor of Hell! Since this fiery torture would not kill him, he concentrated all his might on a way out. Almost to the point of extinction, he managed to project himself out of this incineration chamber... He was out!

Lucif-er: EXITED! <[25x]

In real-time, after the battle started, the frontal attack by Lucif-er appeared clear and thunderous. The two-sided attack flashed and squealed very fast. The following last battle and non-intelligible, super loud noises came too quickly. To all non-Archangel visitors, the end of this battle appeared almost wholly attached to the grand final confrontation.

All the Overlords, who could follow the high-speed events, stood up before its dramatic conclusion.

As the entire complex battle arrangement dissolved into thin air, one Archangel, Lucif-er, came out smoldering as he fell over the center platform. He did not have enough energy to slow his fall; therefore, he hit the surface like a sack of potatoes!

Not the Overlords of the North, but the NA crowd at the west side, individuals anticipating a victory for their leader, started to scream in celebration!

Only when they realized that the Overlord who slowly levitated to the platform was the victorious **Micha-el** did they abruptly freeze in incredulous astonishment!

After two seconds of silence, a loud triumphant roar from all the SA visitors rattled the place!

The whole Core's council membership went wild. They jumped over the chairs, embracing each other in jubilation over Micha-el's victory over Evil, and raised both hands honoring the winner of a tough battle. Only one Seraph, Nobiel, looked up to the ceiling and did not jump joyfully; he probably was thanking God for the unexpected outcome. Furthermore, he was grateful for relieving him of the burden of guilt, which his conscience, had Micha-el died during the fight, would have been painfully placed on him.

As his noisy colleagues embraced him from all sides, he wiped off the sweat from his forehead. Then, he took a deep breath and smiled.

In Dawnel, the celebration turned as happy or perhaps even more. The crowd joyfully celebrated amid an incredible noisy euphoria triggered by their loved leader winning the last battle. The two female angels, now standing in the front, embraced each other with joyful affection. Micha-el, Gabri-el, Dani-el, and the rest will return home... **safe!**

Their wet eyes reflected the deep emotion shaking their beings while gratefulness manifested across their pretty faces. Raquel kissed the tips of her right-hand fingers and eagerly thrust them upward toward her Creator.

Lucif-er, lying flat on his back on top of the platform's floor, slowly got up. His visible skin, including his face, was red, like having a bad sunburn; even skin flakes could be seen peeling off from its normal smooth surface. His great hair looked damaged and in serious disarray. His white garment was gray, with burned black holes around. Yet, the most striking feature of all was Lucif-er's face, distorted beyond recognition by a murderous hate; it wanted to explode like a volcano!

He was seriously hurt, not by the flames, but by the painfully sharp edge of defeat! The humiliation caused his blood temperature to reach fuming levels. He defiantly stretched up; with his fingers twisted like claws in a beastly manner, he yelled.

"Micha-el cheated... He did not comply with the established codes of battle! He used unfair garbage, which he calls 'love'... Besides, this battle was supposed to be fought to the death! If Micha-el won, what am I doing standing here?... I should be dead!"

The rest of the NA Overlords, ready to attack the SA Overlords after Micha-el's death, became shocked and confused about what to do. They could not believe that their powerful boss could have possibly been defeated. Therefore, they decided to charge across the narrow walkway to assist Lucif-er and kill Micha-el, if possible!

An instant later, Micha-el yelled at the incoming NA Overlord mob.

"Stop!"

Since he would be ignored faster than the eye could see, he placed his right hand open, palm facing the NA Overlords. A bright puff of light emanated from the center of his palm, and with increasing speed, it raced toward the charging evil Archangels!

Lucif-er, who remained partially blocking the pathway connection to the northern platform, became the first to dive away from its path. All the other NA Overlords stopped dead in their tracks! Since they had followed the complete battle sequence, they were keenly aware of the incredible power of those innocent, puffy white lights!

It was not a pretty sight. The stronger pushed the weaker out of the way, and at the same time, everyone scrambled to move as far away as possible from the incoming 'Love' bullet.

Making a hyperbolic curve, the bright puff speeded past the NA platform and climbed almost straight up. For an instant, it resembled a shooting star rising backward.

With a stern expression, Micha-el mentally addressed all the scattered NA Overlords; he ordered.

"Sit down!"

This time, there was no argument. Even when furious, they obeyed and took back their seating positions.

Personal messages were pouring into Micha-el's mind, first from Gabri-el and Rapha-el and then from the rest of the SA Overlords.

"Well done, my brother!" "GOD was with you!" "Great fight!"

Micha-el glanced in the direction of the NA crowd, where his ex-assistant Arkyn was last seen. He was not there... Micha-el quickly identified an individual moving away into the crowd; since he was about 50 meters away, he must have taken off the moment Lucif-er fell onto the platform.

Micha-el looked back at the NA seating positions; all were seated and behaving. With one hand, he calmed down the still loud cheering from his SA sympathizers. He talked to everybody.

"Terra citizens!

As it was expressed today through the essence of Love, you witnessed the power of God!

Love, which transcends space and time, affects us in ways we can only dream of; the power of Love is beyond our reality.

Now you know... Love is not a passive and submissive force but the ultimate power!"

Micha-el started to make a clockwise circle as he slowly paced the center platform. After a brief pause, he continued.

"The SA wants peace, and we came to find ways to do it; however, Lucif-er and his Overlords had some evil plans to kill or subdue us. We prevailed, not because of our own power, but because of God's love!

We have no hard feelings towards anybody in the NA... No matter when, if you get serious about talking for peace, you could send a delegation to Dawnel. You will always find us eager to find a solution for resolving our differences!"... Micha-el stopped as all the NA Overlords got up and started jumping off the platform! They trampled some of their own citizens on their way down into the crowd. They decided not to listen to what Micha-el was saying, and since he stood on the center platform where the entrance/exit ramp was located, they took a short way out.

The NA visitors scrambled to move out of the way of Lucif-er's and his colleagues. Especially out of the way of Lucif-er since he had a scary and ferocious appearance!

All over the place, the NA visitors turned about-face, some walking, others running; they began to evacuate the westerly section. Micha-el, looking sadly as they left, thought.

"My God, I have no pleasure doing this... Is there any way to bring them back to You?" With great sadness, he admitted to himself.

"I know... it is too late!"

He felt two friendly hands touching his back. One was from Rapha-el, who must have seen his facial expression because he added.

"My brother. It breaks my heart to see so many souls... lost forever!"

Gabri-el, on his other side, also staring in the west direction, commented.

"They do not listen with their hearts because God has been excluded from them. They are like arid land... The good seed from your words will be wasted!"

Micha-el admitted such truth but could not help himself to preach one more time to the leaving NA visitors.

"Last chance, NA citizens!

God offers you light, love, and compassion; He represents eternal life!

Lucif-er; he is the Lord of darkness... He can only offer you eternal death!

He preys on your fear of war to deceive you into believing that the SA is your enemy. If you are worried about nuclear war... Don't!

Just ponder about one single fact. The suffering of <u>one</u> lost soul for eternity is infinitely more extensive than the lifetime suffering from the entire population of the whole planet!

This is one single example of the other war... The war between Good and Evil... It is the only important war. Any other war, by comparison, amounts to just NOTHING!"

The NA visitors continued their departure; they did not even look back. In their anger and hate, the humiliation of defeat became unbearable. They walked like robots, head down, same as their feelings. The west side of the place became empty very fast. Micha-el might as well have talked to the plaza building walls; at least, they would have returned an echo!

Even when the SA visitors continued loudly celebrating their victory, Gabri-el squeezed his friend's shoulder and in a sober tone suggested.

"There is nothing left to do here; let's go home!"

"Yes... I must go to the new shrine I am building in the Blue Canyon to thank Somebody Who loves me so much... personally!"

"We shall go... together!"

The next day at Centrum, the seven NA Overlords convened in the main conference room. Not a single smile could even be hinted at this meeting. Today, the actions of all seven appeared to be like Azami-el's normal daily behavior.

Two Archangels, Lucif-er and Magog-el, remained seated on the large concave conference table, which looked black and obsidian. The other five stood in front of the table in a single row that simulated a stairway. They stood hierarchically from left to right; each lower-ranked Overlord stayed one step behind their superior.

Lucif-er's bad mood was not completely gone. His face was almost completely restored to normal; only minute specks of skin could still be seen separating from the rest. His exposed skin barely showed a tint of sunburn, and his glorious hair looked as usual. His clothes, a short tunic with loose pants, were not his typical solid white. Its material, made from soft and pure silk, had two tones intermixed between white and blue, continuously changing as related to the angle of reflection. Silk being the best choice to soothe burned skin.

Magog-el sent a message to Lucif-er.

"The people are talking about the embarrassing affair in Trillium! Is there anything that you want to do about it?"

Lucif-er, staring at his five subordinates standing in formation, responded.

"No! If you want people to believe in our version of events, keep repeating it to them! Eventually, they will believe that it is the only truth. Only the ones that attended the meeting will know the difference, but even they will have to accept the official statement since it will be part of the population's consensus...

Also, they will understand that keeping their mouths shut will be much better for their health!"

Without any physical command, Gorgon-el knew to step into the center position of the concave space in front of the black table. He stood straight as his foxy blue eyes shifted aim from Magog-el to Lucif-er. The latter gave his new orders.

"I want you to specialize in the development of nuclear weapons!
I want enough warheads to destroy the SA but not so many as to cause a nuclear winter on the whole planet. Radiation from the explosions must be kept to a minimum for obvious reasons.
This goes for all of you; I want today's decisions to start being implemented immediately. The total waiting time for their completion is five to seven years, max!
Use all resources available, two or three working shifts, whatever is necessary!"

As Lucif-er dismissed him, the subordinate exclaimed.

"It will be done!"

Azami-el moved to the center. He felt at home today but only glanced at Lucif-er's eyes at an angle. He listened.

"Azami-el, all communications, security, and the logistics for the attack are yours! We need to upgrade the computer system; I want the plan to be flawless!"

"I will do my best!" Responded Azami-el, but before returning to his position, he added, *"I wish... I could push the firing button... today!"*

Both Overlords' deep hate emanating from their eyes coalesced by mutual consent.

Lucif-er added.

"So do I! ... Nevertheless, we must do it with absolute precision, there is no room for mistakes!"

Razari-el, a Cherub, energetically placed himself next to the center. His main boss ordered.

"You will oversee all conventional weapons, plus the training of all the Armies in the Alliance... I want to emphasize training them for a winter battleground. We will attack when it is summer here. Since our troops will move south into radioactive cold weather, I want everyone to be in top shape!"

"They shall be ready!"

Another slender, tall Cherub with short hair moved up. His leader's orders were precise.

"Kroma-el, your first and foremost concern will be building materials and devices to remove dust from the stratosphere and air; they will cause cooling and radiation problems!
We must mass-produce heavier particles that capture dust, either electrostatically or chemically.
We need barriers built along east and west shorelines to filter the incoming air currents!

Once the dust is removed from the air, the second job is decontaminating the ground, oceans, and our water supplies! It is a big job that needs to be done in the allowed time!"

The Cherub did not hesitate to answer.

"It will be done to your specifications!"

The last Overlord, a Throne, showed his rounded face and hairy head. He, too, listened.

"There will be hard times after the war. You Ezek-el, have to build two kinds of places that need to be connected. Massive food storage units should be built next to massive shelter units!
Start collecting non-perishable food primers for future storage areas. Also, secure deep-water wells for safe drinking water supplies!"

As the last Overlord acknowledged and returned to the formation, Lucif-er stood up. He still had a fiery look radiating from his eyes. He exclaimed.

"When all these requirements are fulfilled, our Overlord in the SA will disconnect the Matrix defense system...
Then, we will attack!"

His muscles tensed as if he could explode. Raising his hands intimidatingly, he angrily added.

"I do not want to play any more games!
I want Micha-el to pay for his offense to me and the NA!
I want every single citizen of the SA... dead!"

As his lips shouted the last word and his eyes almost emanated fire, he closed his right hand into a fist and, with tremendous fury, struck the obsidian-looking table!

The large and massive table split in half. Black dust and fragments of the smashed surface flew in all directions. Only his thunderous telepathic message overrode the loud explosion that violently resonated into the conference room.

Evil could not take defeat as a good sport. It reacted in the only way it knows best... with a vengeance!

Evil has an innate hate that will not rest until the destruction of all its enemies has been accomplished. The enemy is anybody who does not allow Evil to enter his heart!

In the South Alliance, the good angels continued celebrating their victory, unaware of the rising stormy black clouds that could foreshadow their extinction.

Had they underestimated the powers of Evil?

Or perhaps, even some of the most twisted plans that Evil so meticulously schemes could be part of a majestic divine plan, which has one purpose: glorifying the faithful!

Only <u>He</u>, our Creator, knows all the intricate details.

And <u>we</u> shall also know and understand His plan... in contrast, <u>only</u> after its completion!

CRITICAL MASS

CHAPTER 7

The most southern land on the planet: Southern Cape, Pristeen, SA.

Another seven years have elapsed. It has been 14 years since the Exodus and 28 years since the first signs appeared in the night sky.

Winter was already at its peak; Terra had a global temperature a few degrees centigrade warmer than Earth, so the South Pole had no permanent ice cap. The North Pole stayed colder; all three northern sectors had glaciers close to the pole, which advanced in the winter until coalesced into a small ice cap; in the summer, the heat would cause the ice cap to melt away.

A single towering structure pierced the sky as a beacon or lighthouse. Due to the cloudy skies, its glossy and smooth surfaces appeared gray. This building was a mixture of a station monitoring the weather and a military outpost. About one kilometer south of this structure, at the very tip of the cape, a rocky beach facing the ocean on three sides pointed to the turbulent waters coming from the South Pole's direction.

Standing as two airtight couples, four angels faced the cold and gale-force winds blowing from the south; together, they watched the vast and restless ocean facing them.

Due to a partial high cloud overcast, a lower and darker cluster of clouds began moving inland. These clouds emerged as a solid front coming from the same direction as the wind, which battered a land covered by thick layers of snow. Some dark rocks crested with snowcaps protruding above the snow, their color contrasting against the fluffy snow and the foam from the turbulent icy waters. The late afternoon's gloomy grayish tone made the shore rock formations appear almost black.

Against this background, the taller and more muscular individuals of each couple, dressed in light gray snowsuits with no head cover, stood facing the cold wind. In a more colorful and heavier snowsuit, their companions' heads were almost entirely covered by the hood attachments of their clothing.

A pair of gracious aquamarine eyes peeked at the ferocious waves battling against the shoreline. The waves howled like wild animals while the wind blew the foamy spray inland. She turned to her companion and exclaimed.

"My love... I think it was a mistake to come to the Cape. The ocean view is great, but a winter storm is approaching.... Besides, I am sure that I am going to freeze my butt!"

After a brief shiver that paused her mental dialogue, she briskly asked *"Sweetheart, how cold is it?"*

Gabri-el, whose blond hair was blown straight by the wind, smiled affectionately to his wife; then, he replied with a soft mental message.

"My darling, it is -10.4°C, with the wind chill factor. -27°C... To get warmer, get closer to me!"

Raquel quickly embraced her husband very tightly. Almost immediately, she felt a surge of heat running along her whole body; she expressed her joy with a melodic message.

"Oh, Gabri-el... this feels good! ... You must have an internal furnace or something similar that keeps you warm!"

The other female in the group also sweetly embraced her partner, she requested.

"Could you kindly endow me with some heat?... Please!"

Dani-el rubbed her head through her hood and replied.

"My precious, you can have all the heat you want from me!"

As she also enjoyed the warmth bathing her whole body, she exclaimed.

"Dani-el, in moments like this, I feel a closeness I have never felt for anyone else. I love you so much!"

Turning her pretty face toward Dani-el, Raquel inquired.

"If you love each other so much, why don't you get married?"

Maryen raised her eyes to meet Dani-el's. He looked at her with tenderness but delayed his answer long enough for Gabri-el to advance the following statement.

"Dani-el is worried about the future... Listen, my brother, the last seven years have been unusually peaceful and quiet for the SA. The NA still behaves like it is going to war at any time, but as long as the Matrix is deployed, there is no need to worry about them.

Except for our Lord, nobody else can promise you another seven years of peaceful coexistence... not even tomorrow! ... Take whatever you both have left and make the best of it!"

The Throne and Archangel paused for a second; the howling wind could be heard zipping among them, but nobody in the group cared about how cold it was anymore. He replied.

"My dear friend Gabri-el, I accept your logic. I will marry Maryen... in ten days!"

The female Throne felt her body filled with a different kind of warmth, a much deeper one. With apparent exhilaration, she exclaimed telepathically, like everybody else was doing.

"My love! In my heart and mind, your loving image is already equal to a husband's. However, in ten days, my anxious and affectionate body will accept this most welcome union!"

Feeling the outpouring of love from her companion, Dani-el responded with equal zest.

"My sweet Maryen, I am throwing all my worries away!

In addition, I will focus all my energy and knowledge to make our love flourish into the most beautiful flower, whose soft and aromatic petals will tenderly bind us into one loving couple!"

An intense emotion threaded their hearts together, inducing a passionate, airtight embrace that excluded the menacing storm. The touch of their lips in a warm, moist, and tender kiss said it all.

****

Gorgland, SC Sector, NA

Two kilometers underground, NDM Plant N-112, Nuclear Devices Manufacturing; three Seraphim, on a high platform in the middle of a vast multilevel manufacturing plant, were overlooking some complex machinery working at maximum load.

Shiny cylinders rushed along an automatic conveyor at the plant's ground floor. At about the middle of their run, a band flipped them vertically; then, many electronic components became attached to the cylinders' central bodies. Spot welding caused bright light and sparks to brighten the place sporadically. Laser beams cut patterns, made holes, and soldered joints. At the second level, massive overhead carriers moved parts to the lower section. At the third level, as high as the observing platform dwelled, spider-like machines moved their arms to above and below tiers. More moving devices could be seen at the fourth level. At the last but highest layer, a mixture of illumination, power distribution, and outside part acquisition crowned the large manufacturing site.

All three angels on the platform wore silvery and highly polished working suits. Attached to the center of their suits, a rectangular display device about 3 x 5 cm was divided into two sections, one read at its top 'Sum,' the other 'In.' Green messages, with digits at their right, added numbers very slowly. The 'In' counters had much smaller quantities than the 'Sum' counters; they were radiation counters. Also, as an integral part of their suits, fully transparent helmets covered their heads. Inside the front helmets' walls, small sectors processing data acquisition segments could be viewed in green characters.

Two angels faced their leader. The latter had a small golden circle encompassing the white/blue NA emblem on the left side of his chest. The other two had a similar logo but with a circle in silver. All three stared at an integral display mounted on a wide border edging the viewing platform. The increasing device number just read.

Multi-head nuclear devices completed: 10,000

The two angels with the silver emblems raised both hands, showing two fists up. In this place, it was a sign of power, praise, and recognition for outstanding technical achievements. Both exclaimed in unison.

"Hurray for Arkyn! Sir, you made the deadline!"

One of the cheering individuals, standing closer to Arkyn, remarked.

"Your suggestion to avoid thermonuclear reactor overheating by increasing the cooling liquid nitrogen pressure, which lowered the overall cooling temperature, was brilliant. It allowed us to work at full speed but with only 90% of the maximum reactor's power!"

Arkyn smiling with satisfaction caused his teeth to be visible. He solemnly spoke, *"I could not have done it without your support and hard work. Now, slow automatic production to 30% and reactor power to 50%; after that, notify Gorgon-el that the project he requested is completed! I'd like all personnel with no present critical jobs to join us in the above main recreation area for a celebration!"*

Twenty minutes later, after all tasks had been finished and the automatic machinery had started working at a reduced speed, the three Seraphim boarded the high-speed elevator that transported them to the surface, 2 km above.

The recreation area on the outskirts of the capital city of the SC sector took the space of the ten lower floors inside a large rectangular building; this vast volume spawned along increasingly higher indoor terraces, which started from the ground level. Also, the perimeter next to the inside walls, which included the main entrance, remained the lowest, with the center terrace the highest.

As Arkyn and his two assistants walked into the place, about a thousand subordinates stood up at the many multilevel locations. They cheered the plant manager and his two principal assistants. As the three walked almost in a militaristic way toward the place of the highest ranking, the uncoordinated cheer became a loud noise that bounced back from the unusually modernistic decorated ceiling. The clamor drowned the multi-beat entertaining music, which had previously saturated the place.

When Arkyn reached the center terrace, he raised his two fists high into the sky. The multitude roared so loud that it caused the stand where the three Seraphim stood to vibrate!

Arkyn breathed heavily with enormous self-satisfaction; he worked so hard to achieve this prize. While he bathed in the glory, the roaring brought back memories of seven years ago… at Trillium.

He, again! Micha-el's face appeared in front of him. His piercing blue eyes accuse him, making him feel guilty of non-existent guilt; the stare bothered him so much that he departed from the Overlords' big fight, even before it ended.

While squeezing his teeth together very hard, he simultaneously closed his eyes for two seconds. Angrily, Arkyn thought to himself. **"Leave me alone! Stop torturing me… I hate you!"**

The roar, which for a moment faded away, came back. The image was gone entirely. Arkyn took a deep breath in utter contentment and screamed with pleasure at his triumphal outcome.

"Yessss!"

Next, as the roar calmed down, he told the excited audience about all the great work they had done, the sacrifices they had endured, and their incoming rewards. Of course, he had to mention the NA's move to glory and the SA's defeat.

When the three Seraphim finally sat down in plush semicircular sofas, four females approached them. It became evident that somebody had anticipated the event and brought lots of companionship for the Nuclear Plant's working personnel.

A voluptuous Cherub female, leading the group in a tight mini dress that exposed her shapely legs, did emphasize her rounded buttocks and protruding breasts. At the same instant, she keyed for some fancy drinks at the center table; her attractive round face was seductively glancing at Arkyn.

He bit his upper lip lightly. He remembered the fantastic sex they had enjoyed together; while looking with lust at her shapely curves, he recollected her name: Deana!

An orange/green spiraling mixed beverage came from the computer-controlled dispensing machine. She picked it up, and after taking a few steps, she sat extremely close to him, poking his ribs with her firm breasts. When her green eyes finally met with Arkyn's, she softly mentioned.

"I am so glad to see you again! ... This time, I brought a friend!"

She called the next female in line to approach Arkyn using her right hand. This angel, a Throne, also wore a scanty dress but not a tight one; the soft material showed her sensual and attractive form. She moved to the opposite side of the Seraph and sat similarly close to him, Deana indicated.

"Her name is Gail. All three of us will have some fun tonight!"

After looking her over, Arkyn nodded with approval. Showing a mischievous smile, he retorted.

"You bet! Even now, I am anxiously waiting!"

He liked the NA females. They were quite unlike the ones in the SA, which had such puritanical beliefs that made it impossible to have a casual sexual encounter. You needed to be involved in lengthy and serious commitments to do anything.

The other two females, two Thrones, took seats next to each plant manager's assistants. First, they served drinks and food to these individuals; next, they helped themselves with the drinks and appetizers. One of the assistants noticed that the female angel keeping his company requested the table computer a strange mixture as a beverage. He questioned her.

"What did you ask?"

"This is a new drink; it has a mixture of drug extracts .10% H-30, 20% D-38, and 70% alcohol[1]... It makes you feel... fantastic!" She spoke telepathically.

"Let me try it!" Her companion requested.

Arkyn, who overheard the open conversation, interrupted.

"You people, be careful with those drug-enhanced drinks! I received a report which warns about the abuse of non-addictive chemically changed drugs. Even when they are physically non-addictive, you could psychologically become dependent on them. This, in turn, will affect your job performance, and you know exactly what that means. Use them, but only occasionally!"

"Thanks for the advice, boss!" the subordinate responded.

The other assistant leaned forward toward Arkyn and mentioned with a rather friendly and personal overtone.

"Sir, we have been so busy that we have only discussed our business and assignments. I hope you don't mind if I ask you something personal?"

As soon as Arkyn nodded in approval, the assistant continued.

"Somebody told me you were at the big fight between our great leader Lucif-er and Micha-el. Are the rumors true? Did our leader lose?"

Arkyn froze; he could not believe his subordinate asked him that question! Just a few minutes ago, he was thinking about Micha-el, and now this? He remained silent momentarily, with his jaws tightly drawn against each other.

"Sir, did I say anything wrong?" A worried Seraph inquired.

Arkyn rubbed his forehead with both opened palms. He regained his composure; after all, he was absolutely sure that his companions could not read his mind. He replied.

"Not at all... Yes, I did see the big fight. Our great leader did not lose. You all know that in the 'Third level of combat,' only one Overlord can survive... the winner!

Lucif-er is alive! Isn't that proof that he did not lose? ... Micha-el cheated... I don't know what he did; maybe he had a concealed plasma device with him! On the other hand, perhaps he used mass hypnosis! Who knows? The case was that the rotten SA Overlord just appeared... I repeat! ... appeared as if he had won!"

For the next ten minutes, everybody in the big celebration continued having a good time. Suddenly, the noisy party doers gradually came to a silent stop. The sound of hard steps on the shiny floor conveyed the message of soldiers marching inside the structure.

---

[1] H-30 = Hallucinatory $C_{15}H_{15}N_2CON(C_2H_5)_2$ = LSD

D-38 = Drug $C_{17}H_{21}NO_4$ = Cocaine

100% = Not by volume, maximum safe doses.

As Arkyn and everybody else stood up, he mentioned.

"The big boss is here!"

A platoon of heavily armed Seraphim soldiers marched into the place. They formed a pointed triangle that spread as the front ones moved to the central terrace. In the end, as they displaced the people previously crowding the place, they formed an empty rectangular corridor; two soldiers stayed at the entrance, one at each side of the door, and the rest stayed equally spaced along the opened corridor. The last pair stood next to the manager's table. The soldiers facing the adjacent column in pairs did not look at each other; they stared diagonally forward at a 45° angle.

A medium-built Seraph with wavy blond hair displaying a highly reflective light blue jumpsuit stood at the entrance. He had a round emblem over his chest, white and blue vertical stripes, with two golden superimposed letters: SC. He calmly walked in.

He was the Sector's Overlord, Gorgon-el; without any hurry, he strolled to the center terrace. Once there, the whole group standing next to the table saluted him. Arkyn addressed the Overlord.

*"It is a great honor for your visit!... **Most Eminent Overlord!**"*

Gorgon-el returned the chest-high, open-hand salute and stated.

"Arkyn, I am extremely pleased with the timely completion of a challenging task. If you are not afraid to pull the trigger against your former SA friends, I will recommend you for a commander's rank promotion!"

The Overlord knew what turmoil this news caused in Arkyn; he perceived the hidden desire burning deep inside the plant manager. After all, commanders will eventually be the first to be trained to become Archangels. A new NA directive commanded a new breed of Archangels to help dominate the planet. The Overlord watched Arkyn's eyes getting bigger with excitement. Gorgon-el was proud of what he had molded Arkyn to become.

The Overlord smiled... it was the same smile that an evil man has when he sees the child that he had perverted, shaking with desire.

"Sir! You can count on me for anything!" Arkyn exploded with joy.

"Excellent! Your true abilities were wasted in the SA. We have a new career for you; therefore, we will start your training immediately!"

Gorgon-el glanced away from Arkyn and checked the curves of his Cherub girlfriend. He took two steps to place himself in front of her. Deana, nervously, looked down.

Gorgon-el stretched his right-hand index finger until it barely touched her throat. Then, very slowly, he pulled his finger away toward her chin. The sensual sensation gave her a chill!

The Overlord knew precisely what buttons to push to get her; in fear, she shook lightly while nervously swallowing a big gulp of saliva.

At the same time, the Overlord gave her his trademark foxy look, he remarked to Arkyn.

"Your girlfriend is very pretty; she is a splendid choice," he said. Next, he ordered Arkyn. *"Tomorrow at my office, 6:00 hours!"*

Without any more words, the Overlord walked away. As he passed them, the soldiers followed him in pairs. Soon, they all strode out of the building.

Without delay, the big party resumed.

Deana, recovering from the shakes, kissed Arkyn on the edge of his lips. She just said, *"Congratulations... Commander!"*

Arkyn smiled widely, leaned backward against the couch, and wildly fantasized about the incredible news. As he stared at the lights above the ceiling, he forgot about his female companions and dreamed for a moment. He barely overheard Gail commenting to Deana.

"Lucky you!... The Overlord really liked you!"

Deana nodded negatively, she remarked.

"No thanks! A friend of mine told me that the Overlords' penises are as large as a horse's. I am not contemplating to die by an equestrian encounter!"

Arkyn, in the center of his talking female companions, just smiled about the remark. He thought, "When he becomes an Overlord, he will also have a BIG one!"

He felt his destiny now being fulfilled. After all, the most important reason he abandoned his job as Micha-el's personal assistant was envy.

The NA's flagship, Lucif-er's personal craft, began approaching Kral, the capital of the NC Sector. As it lowered its altitude, the large vessel slowed to 1 km/sec. The primary pilot keyed priority # 1 on a control in the center screen. Only two seconds later, a visual route layered over the city's normal air traffic map became discernible. The terminal displayed a message.

Priority # 1: Acknowledged.
Route: Kral-Sector 46 >>> is gridlocked. <<<
Destination: Defense Base K-225.
K-225 message: Kroma-el is awaiting your arrival at the building, AK3675 LA-1A

The pilot instantly keyed the building and landing area into the screen.
>AK3675 LA-1A
The machine responded to what appeared to be instantaneous.
AK3675 Locked.
Arrive at the destination in 4 minutes and 20 seconds.

A fancy NA uniformed Cherub displaying a round emblem on his chest anxiously awaited his boss's arrival. The uniform's emblem resembled a showy circle; inside the circle were white/blue vertical lines with the letters NC overlaid in gold.

His crew-cut hairstyle immediately identified him as Kroma-el. He was not alone; his heavily armed all-Seraphim platoon stayed deployed nearby.

Two massive towers stood 50 floors above the landing area on each side of the area. About one km long, the structures had a gap about ½ km wide between them. In this center channel, you could observe that about two kilometers away, at either building edge, another massive and dual structure was erected, not precisely aligned but slightly skewed to follow the city limits. The structures made a giant circle around the city of Kral.

A bright spot at 45° above the horizon started its approach from the south; as it slowed down, it aimed at the parking area. It was not long before the large, aerodynamic, and utterly armed cylinder rested on its assigned location. Kragen and the rest of his platoon became the first to get out and take strategic positions around the vessel. Next, Lucif-er and Magog-el simultaneously stepped out of the cylinder.

Kroma-el rushed to meet them. He used the chest-high, open-hand salute with both. As all three briskly walked to the building to the left, the two platoons stayed put. The leader of the NA spoke first.

"Everybody is ready, but you! ... Give me the details!"

Kroma-el made eye contact with Lucif-er and explained.

"This project is bigger than I thought! I could have finished it, but the NA resources have been shifted 80% toward offensive weapons, the rest for defense!"

"That is only an excuse!" Barked Magog-el.

After a brief pause, Lucif-er added.

"For this time, I am accepting your excuse for this project because you are correct about not having enough priority!" Then, as Lucif-er stared at Kroma-el, the first commented, *"You were going to tell me that Kral's dust removal system is operational, Centrum will be finished in two days, and all Sector's capitals in six days!"*

Kroma-el nodded affirmatively; he was used to Lucif-er anticipating questions and answers. He remarked.

"As we agreed in the meeting held two years ago, for the rest of the large cities, in the case of partial completion, we will build and protect only the side of prevailing winds. Of course, the nuclear bombing will affect the direction and intensity of all trade winds moving East/West or vice versa, but we assumed the computer's projections to be accurate enough!"

Lucif-er, almost interrupting, sharply stated.

"If we divert all resources to finish this project, it will take half a year! By then, it will be winter in the NA, which means that we will need to wait another half year to meet the conditions we have today... I cannot wait another year!

If we attack in eight days, the minimum extra casualties in the NA as related to radiation and contamination should be about 100,000! The worst scenario, 1 to 5 million!"

Magog-el smiled cynically and exclaimed.

*"That is nothing! We could absorb a 10% loss of all NA citizens without any serious detriment to our production schedules. **Let us do it!**"*

Lucif-er showed his teeth and shared an evil moment of pleasure with his Number One Archangel, while patting Magog-el on the back, mentally shouted.

"Let's nuke Micha-el and all the SA bastards that follow him!"

The impressive interior of building AK3675 was devoid of any decoration or facilities. Its primary function remained to suck air at three different levels: Ground, 25 floors high, and the 50th floor or the roof. The super powerful nuclear-powered turbo fans caused a tremendous sucking action around the cities surrounding air masses. All this enormous volume was then moved into a continuously rotating filter complex, which removed most of the solid particles in suspension. The filtered air mass was then ejected to the second sister building, which further purified the air by eliminating micron and sub-micron size dust particles.

Finally, the second building ejected the processed air at a 45° angle into the sky. The resulting effect was that the air inside the city became partially compressed, causing a pressurized volume that pushed outward to exclude other outside contaminated particles from raining over the city.

The only other addition to the dual set of structures was some strange ground-based multi-finned additions. The highly polished objects stood protruding at the intake and exhaust locations. They appeared to be decorations, but they were not. Their only purpose was to prevent ground dust from being generated at either end by the fast-moving air masses' turbulence.

The three Overlords walked briskly to the center of the building. The only narrow pathway to that place was a hollow grid with a square pattern of 5 x 5 centimeters, with the top surface of its walking width measuring only two meters wide. A round waist-high handrail could be used as a support at both edges. As the Archangels walked on the pathway's grid, the view below or above stayed impressive but intimidating, a straight drop to the floor at some places, 25 stories down! Or the opposite, 25 stories of clear view to the ceiling!

The trio of powerful walkers made a metallic noise that reverberated and echoed from all the crevices and large surfaces inside the building. As they walked, they looked at the hardware. The tubes conducting the air in the middle looked enormous. From the front, the turbo fans would suck air from the outside; then, like fingers merging into a hand, they integrated into larger tubes that had diameters as large as ten floors. Grids of supporting structures, power lines, electronic monitors; all of these, times three, completed the biggest vacuum cleaner you could ever imagine!

As the Overlords reached the center, they saw a merging point for eight similar paths. Each path was connected to each wall and each corner of the building at the 25th-floor level. At the center junction, a circular structure towered from the depths of the building to the very roof, an elevator. Two larger circular platforms protruded like two massive but squashed donuts just one floor above and one below where the Archangels walked.

The whole building's interior was not illuminated, only locally, like the pathways, the elevator, the two platforms, and other sections critical to the operation of this enormous piece of machinery. This made the view even more eerie and inhibiting, like standing in the middle of nowhere; the pathways looked so long that their destinations appeared beyond perception with intimidating and weird-looking surroundings. This could be a good setup for a horror movie!

The three Overlords stood in the center of the intersection, a five-meter diameter circle with a pedestal one meter higher at the center axis.

Kroma-el pointed a finger at the stand. The circular pedestal moved the three Archangels to the upper floor platform.

Kroma-el led the two other Overlords to a circular pattern bordering the circular edge. The instrumentation at this place stayed one meter from the floor in a slightly tilted array of displays and instruments.

The most prominent, 'MAIN CONTROL,' remained busy, with columns of information displayed and upgraded in real-time. These included Nuclear, Temperature, Wind velocities, and Power transfer in Gigawatts. Only a smaller square in its mostly empty center read.

Initialization > Completed.

Perimeter   > Secured.

>>>START<<<

This last control was green and blinking.

Kroma-el, pushing buttons without touching the screen, mentioned.

"With no wind, we filter 99.99% of all size particles. As the wind velocity increases, we lose the filtering process exponentially. At 0.01 Km/sec, it equals 95%; at 0.02 Km/sec: 85%; by 0.05 Km/sec, no significant filtering is left!"

Lucif-er, inspecting the layout while his colleague mentally explained the operation, looked at a video section showing that both platoons previously deployed at the landing place had moved inside the building.

"Just start the demo!" Lucif-er requested.

Kroma-el pointed to the blinking 'START' indicator in green. It changed to red. The last line, not blinking now, read.

START > ON

A massive electric power surge flowing along the superconducting bars transferred energy to the turbo fans. A humming sound, gradually increasing in intensity, filled the building's voids.

Moving slowly along the massive piping, the air soon made howling noises. With a mild vibration, the building started to shake. As its speed increased, the dry air started to generate large quantities of static electricity. Bright lightning bolts jumped at some specific places of the machinery to grounding rods. The whole area resembled a giant welding factory!

Even the Overloads became affected by the static electricity saturating the structure. Around them, minute electrical sparks jumped from one place to another. Their hair started to stand up. It seemed like invisible hands began pulling each hair away from their scalps.

Lucif-er flicked his right wrist, and all three Overlords' hair returned to normal.

Close to maximum throughput, the noise became unbearable for the average angel, passing 100 decibels! Finally, the vibration stabilized to acceptable levels.

The Overlords appeared impervious to the noise or vibration; Lucif-er addressed Kroma-el, *"I know you synchronized all turbo fans to reduce noise and vibration! Try one more thing... Run each pair of adjacent turbo fans, one CW and the other CCW. It will decrease the shaking by another factor of 10!"*

After an instant of reflective thought, Kroma-el enthusiastically commented.

"You are right, I can see it! It will increase thrust and reduce vibration by canceling most of the sonic waves' lateral interfering fringes!"

For a few minutes, Lucif-er looked over the performance of the machine. He showed his approval with a light affirmative nod and calmly stated.

"Kroma-el, I am satisfied with the performance parameters. Shut the machine off! Now, procure me a secured visual contact with the rest of the Overlords!"

The operating Overlord turned the power off. Everything wound down quickly. He moved to the next display and ordered the computer.

Search> 4 Links; Code Priority 1/Lucif-er
Gorgon-el, Azami-el, Razari-el, Ezek-el

The screen was split into four equal areas. Three seconds passed, and suddenly, all four sections were filled with the faces of four Overlords.

Lucif-er raised his hand to stop any questions. He sharply stated.

*"Meet me at Centrum tonight, 9:50 hours! I am initiating Operation Code: Sapphire! ... We start the countdown at midnight: Exactly for eight days... **80 hours for T = Zero!**"*

Razari-el and Ezek-el's eyes widened, but they smiled and quickly acknowledged. The first was inside a flying craft; after receiving the message, he mentally ordered his pilot to turn the vessel around and go to Centrum.

Gorgon-el stuck out his tongue with sadistic anticipation. He gave his boss a foxy but sinister acceptance of his command. Azami-el did not say anything; his eyes got reddish because of the evil thoughts in his mind. Only Lucif-er could infer what he thought and be correct.

Azami-el craved to be part of the army invading the SA and to hunt for the survivors of the nuclear attack on the Alliance. He had eagerly waited for this moment to fulfill his primeval desires: **To maim, rape, and kill.**

For Lucif-er, nothing was better than a <u>dedicated servant</u>!

$T_0 = -79:00$

In a secluded computer room inside the SA, an Overlord seated in front of a terminal remained obscure; we could not see his face. An encrypted message from the NA had arrived. After a few seconds, the computer converted the complex code to a readable message and displayed the following statements.

Code 378-DKR-1

Operation Code: Sapphire

The Overlord tensed at the sight of the last word; finally, the wait had ended! He had spent too many years living in disguise. He wanted to enjoy life in the same manner as the Overlords of the North. He hated the cage, the city where he was born, a place with good memories until he finally decided he needed no God to tell him how to live his own life!

After all, he could take care of himself with his superior power and intelligence. Compared to the NA, life in the SA remained a bore. He preferred the lifestyle of the northern Overlords, and except for a few bosses that he would have to contend with, he would enjoy unlimited power, multiple sex partners, and even the right to choose who would live and who would die! It was the closest thing to being a god himself! The message continued.

Greetings!

The operation is scheduled in real time.

$T_0 = -78:99$ **hours**

The Archangel immediately figured it out. At midnight, in seven days, plus 8 hours, and 99 minutes!

More information was shown on the screen.

We suggest, at $T_0 = -0:5$

You will be leaving SBC for a trip over the South Pole.

Please acknowledge.

END

The Overlord smiled for two reasons. First, the clock started running. Second, he always thought the NA was too cautious when sending coded messages. The probability of someone decoding this complex coded message stayed as close to zero as Micha-el surviving an overhead nuclear blast!

He, in a speedy manner, had the response sent.

>**Code 378-DKR-2**
Greetings
Message understood.
Monitor the matrix.
The moment it goes down,
at $T_0 = 0$
Attack!
Acknowledge
End

He knew he had to wait several minutes for the acknowledgment. His message was slow and hard to decipher. One part of his mind shifted to the 4-D Matrix program. He had left a hidden and dormant program on Micha-el's computer, the same place where the Matrix operation remained controlled by a computer network attached to the whole SA. It became an evil virus waiting for a command to attack and destroy the most essential defense ever deployed. To activate such a 'virus,' he would need minimal exposure; a simple coded command would do it.

As he reminisced about the procedures to follow in the coming days, he mentally set his schedule for his plan of deception to work smoothly.

He was ecstatic because, in a few days, he could abandon the facemask that Lucif-er had imposed on him for the so-called greatness of the NA. The mask worked since nobody could see through it and determine his true intentions. He could not wait to be just himself. A message appeared on the screen.

Code 378-DKR-1
OK
END

He immediately typed a new message to his computer.

>**Activate program. IZ797**
>**Encode message: Key RN-378**
>**Sunshine countdown: $T_0 = -78{:}93{:}39$**
>**Program access: None**
>**Lock: Activated**
>**End**

The destruction of the SA had a clock counting down; it remained invisible and inaccessible!

The Overlord, overconfident in his abilities, cynically thought.

"It is going to be so easy… Just like child's play!"

Dark clouds were menacing the good angels' nation. Would God warp such a carefully designed evil plan? A scheme like a spider web with a fearsome hidden black arachnid ready to jump for any prey caught into the net, ready to kill and devour!

How shall our Lord protect His loved ones?

****

$T_0 = -75{:}05$

On a cool winter day with a mild breeze and plenty of sunshine, Leanna, the most beautiful city in the province of Pristeen, sparkled under the noon sun. Even when the solar disk was not overhead but heavily shifted in the northern direction, its warm light provided enough energy to make the day pleasant. Winters remained much milder in Terra than on Earth because the obliquity of the planet's ecliptic, at its farthest point from its celestial equator, was only 19° 5'. Earth = 23° 26'

Looking down into one of the main avenues, a large crowd gathered around a circular garden at the boulevard's center. The terraces of the adjacent buildings looked prettier than ever. There were not too many flowers at this time of the year, but the towering structures surrounding the central circular park stayed adorned with the most colorful clusters of flowers. Spectators packed all the balconies overlooking the garden.

Many angels were anxious to witness a rare event: The wedding of an Overlord, Dani-el. The large attending crowd caused a rumble heard all over the place in both mediums, by sound and telepathy.

A large circular garden with shiny circular pathways and 90 degrees interconnecting walkways remained empty of angels but quite the opposite regarding its vegetation, where bushes appeared like necklaces around the most beautiful ornamental trees imaginable. The gorgeous landscape, endowed with the best available varieties of ground covers, some of them blooming in the middle of the winter, appeared to have no competition; however, to see flowers, it was imperative to look up to the adjacent towering terraces where the building walls gracefully complemented the center circular garden as an extension reaching for the skies.

Just at the edge of the empty circle, Micha-el and Gabri-el, dressed in their fancy tunics, began communicating in a personal telepathic manner that excluded everybody else. Gabri-el, showing great concern, stated.

"Dear brother, the military activity in the NA is increasing at an alarming rate; they are mobilizing everything. Their X-ray scanning of the SA worries me about an imminent attack!"

Micha-el placed his right hand over his friend's shoulder and retorted.

"The NA is probably having another massive military exercise. I have not ignored it; I placed our troops in alert status 9![2] In addition, I have ordered an X-ray map of the NA; this will soon reveal all their new underground facilities, and the results will be included in the Matrix program."

Gabri-el's green eyes locked with his friend's blues. The Cherub smiled at his companion at close range; his many years as a politician for The Core had given him a sixth sense for the incoming events. Furthermore, he used to be a close friend of Lucif-er, which gave him a more profound perception of the matter. He mentioned.

"Micha-el, the NA has never gone into an alert status 9; I know that Lucif-er is up to no good. I also know that he would never start a suicidal attack against the Matrix… Therefore, he must be counting on someone to turn it off!"

Micha-el placed the other hand over his friend's second shoulder. In a sober tone, he exclaimed.

"My cherished brother, I can sense that you are very serious about this matter. I know you want to ask me for permission to investigate the SA Overlords, even when you understand that I have always opposed anybody administering such a test. Nevertheless, I respect your tactical insight; I will allow you and Dani-el to start the investigation.

However, since today is his wedding, please do not do anything until tomorrow!"

Gabri-el, displaying a broad smile while placing both hands on his companion's shoulders, exclaimed with relief.

"I would not think of doing anything to spoil his day!"

Then, sensing that someone was approaching from behind, he added.

"Raquel is coming this way; the wedding must be starting!"

The prettiest angel on the planet, dressed in a long gown of the same color as the sky, approached both Overlords. Before getting close, she told them.

"You two look too serious! … Did somebody forget to mention that this is a moment of great rejoicing?"

When Micha-el finished speaking about the two angels being married, he returned to the same spot where he stood with Gabri-el. To his left, outside the circle, Maryen started walking toward the center.

She was dressed in white fleecy attire, which made her look her best. The dress tulle-like material was iridescent. From the center of her chest, in a triskele, three beautifully designed arms of clothing emanated to cover the top, middle body, and legs. The center of the triskele, adorned with a

---

[2] 10 is equal to war.

large diamond, held the materials in place by its compression against a rigid and similarly matched surface. Her dark purple eyes shined with happiness, while her fluffy blond hair stayed arranged in a short but pleasant multi-spiraling pattern. When she gracefully walked, the dress extending under her arms made her emerge as a lovely butterfly.

Dani-el, dressed in his best light red tunic at the opposite end of the circle, appeared younger than ever. Nobody could guess that he was three thousand years old!

Slender but dynamic, he approached his bride with tempo. Ardent but gentle steps moved him forward, resembling the smooth glide of a flying bird as it moved effortlessly in the sky. Dani-el's body motions remained powerfully elegant, subtly reflecting the best of his individuality. All his being, guided by one force that surged beyond the physical, was his connection to Eternity and the most precious gift from our Creator... Love!

His garment still had the silver cross over his heart. The only addition to his tunic was a belt, five centimeters wide, white, silky, and loosely bound around his waist. It was a wedding artifact.

Maryen and Dani-el faced each other at the center of the park's circle, their radiant faces looking intently at their consorts. Slowly, they greeted each other chest high, both open palms touching their companions. Without separation, they lifted their hands above slowly, like a joint praying position. They made a triangular-like tent with their arms extended at a 45° angle.

This gesture was required to open the ceremony. The couple spoke in unison.

"Dear God, as our witness, we ask You to bless this wedding!"

For a few seconds, they stayed motionless and in silence.

Gabri-el and Raquel approached from opposite ends of the open triangular tent made by the wedding couple's extended arms. She walked inside the angels' tunnel as her husband approached the marrying couple from the other end; Gabri-el's right hand faced Dani-el's standing position.

Still, under the triangular tunnel, Raquel and Gabri-el faced each other and gently kissed. Their open hands, extending down, touched together. Then, in an upward slow motion, while slightly backing out, they made a similar gesture as Dani-el and Maryen. However, as their hands reached their maximum height, they separated the palms of the wedding couple. The four angels rotated to make a square. Their contacting palms still pointed toward the sky.

At this moment, Gabri-el spoke with a powerful but pleasant voice.

"I am Gabri-el, a married angel eternally grateful to our Lord for having blessed my union to Raquel, my beloved wife.

I present Dani-el, who desires to be wed. Consequently, I wish him the best in this wedding ceremony, including subsequent happiness equal to or better than mine!"

Raquel spoke next. Her voice reached all the spectators because the whole place was wired for sound and video. Additionally, her voice sounded like a binding melody; it drew you to listen, like how the sirens' songs captivated passing sailors.

"I am Raquel, also eternally indebted to our God for the priceless gift of my husband, Gabri-el.

I present Maryen, who desires to be wed and to whom I wish a great happiness equal to mine!"

The four angels moved together until the eight hands projecting upwards appeared to be only one. At this moment, all spoke as a single person.

"Dear God, bless this union with Your most precious gift… Love!"

All four angels froze in their present position.

The first row of spectators moved toward the central two couples and made a circle. At each interconnecting 90-degree pathway, an Overlord walked in. They were Micha-el and Rapha-el on opposite ends, Izma-el to the left, and Samu-el to the right. Lari-el and Zeri-el were excused due to pressing emergencies.

They stopped five meters apart at equal distances from the center. In this way, they made a circle 10 meters in diameter in conjunction with the first layer of spectators.

Thirty angels, like the group in the center, touched their palms sideways and pointed to the sky. This new and larger circle was composed of the relatives of the bride and groom; the Overlords of the SA considered themselves as family or just brothers.

At Micha-el's mental command, with all in the circle trying to be one voice, the Archangels spoke together; their voices filled the surroundings.

"Dear loving God, bless Dani-el and Maryen with Your divine gift!"

Immediately after this statement, a much larger aggregate of angels moved toward the circle's center, stopping 10 meters away. They made a larger 20-meter diameter circle of triple-packed concentric rings, about 180 angels.

Usually, the second larger ring had only a single circle composed of the bride and groom's best friends. Important angels packed two external rings; only an Overlord's wedding could have three outer rings.

While the triple ring assembled, Dani-el, motionless with his hands interlocking with his three other companions still facing the open sky, at the sight of his beautiful bride, could not resist giving Maryen an invisible kiss, similarly as he had overseen Gabri-el giving them to Raquel, even in public meetings.

Maryen was startled by the warm and soft pressure on her moist lips. However, she responded quickly, giving Dani-el a sweet smile and responding with a faint kissing mannerism. She also sent a personal message to her consort, *"Not yet!"*

At about this time, the outside triple ring was completed. They similarly joined hands and projected them into the sky. Again, Micha-el gave the signal for this larger group to proclaim.

"Dear loving God, bless the union of Dani-el and Maryen, and bless all of us!"

The roar was much louder, the coordination less sharp, but the statement carried far away! The roar's echo rebounded from the many terraces that appeared as steps from giant ladders climbing into the clouds.

Dani-el and Maryen were not alone; their close relationships with everybody in the circles reminded them of the intrinsic interweaving in everyday life and the importance of our interdependence.

We humans are social beings; the angels were no different. The quality of our lives can be expressed in the same terms as the quality of our relationships with others.

The two couples at the center started rotating clockwise. The inner ring followed the motion but in the opposite direction, CCW. The outer rings rotated clockwise. The members of the inner ring took short side steps for their displacement. For the outer ones, larger steps became necessary to stay in synchronous rotation with the center angels and the inner ring rotating speed. After a full 360° rotation, everybody stopped moving.

This interaction between the wedding couple, their relatives, and their friends was a vivid example of the circles of life. We take many journeys in our lives, but in the end, as is true for many of us, we end up at the same place where we started!

The couples in the center separated and lowered their hands.

The first circle followed up accordingly.

The triple outside circle did last, likewise.

From outside the rings, two angels approached the triple circle from opposite directions. They carried two iridescent but transparent glasses of water, similar to champagne glasses. Two of the wedding angels' best friends from the outside circle moved the glasses to the inner circle. Micha-el got one, Rapha-el the other one.

Both Archangels walked to the center. They stood at each side facing Dani-el and Maryen, who moved to meet them similarly. Currently, Micha-el spoke.

"We are offering you water, the essence of life.
It represents what you are now and what you will become: two different glasses... but the same water.
Drink! Let your two bodies and your two minds become just one!"

The wedding couple received the glasses. Facing each other, they touched their forearms when they offered their cup to the lips of their consorts. They drank the pristine water.

The couple separated a short distance, swung from opposite directions, and then the glasses collided and shattered. This action indicated that no one else was allowed to drink from these identical cups; by breaking the glasses, you were, in a symbolic way, excluding any other mates.

By the way, standard Terra glasses were almost indestructible. These wedding glasses were specially made of a material that did not shatter into sharp edges and was biodegradable!

The marrying couple picked up all the glass pieces from the floor and walked together to the nearest flowerbed. Inside the planter, they found something like a coring gardening tool. It had two upper handles. Each angel grasped one side with their right hand. Together, they pushed the tool into the organically composed, sandy, and moist soil. As they pulled it out, they twisted and removed a cylindrical core off the ground; the remaining hole was about 10 cm wide.

They placed the glass fragments in the bottom as fertilizer. Both removed some flower seeds from an inside pocket in their attires, which were gently deposited inside the hole.

Last, they shook the coring tool to drop the inside dirt into the hole. Only a tiny bump remained at the location of the previous hole.

Since it was a fertility rite, the symbolism of this last motion had sadly lost its value because of the current ordinance that allowed no offspring from the angels. Especially for the females, this left a vacuum that any other pleasure could not fill. Many waited for a break in the law, which would bestow upon them the unreplaceable joy of motherhood.

Leaving the tool behind, the couple returned to their original center position.

At close range, their eyes focused beyond their irises as they reached deep into their minds, where a message of warmth and joy flooded their brains. They looked at each other with ecstasy since they knew that the last step in their marriage ceremony was upon them.

Slowly, Dani-el removed the first layer of the white belt around his waist. The material was stretchable and with some super Velcro at the tip. One end remained attached to the rest of his belt. He offered it to her and spoke.

"Maryen, will you accept that your body and mine become one?"

She tenderly glanced at the groom. She seized the belt and placed it around her waist, concealing it under her spiraling but elegant dress. She also attached the end to the front. A belt around their waists now connected both angels.

"Dani-el, I accept!" She responded.

The Archangel removed another layer from his belt and offered it to Maryen. He requested one more time.

"Maryen, do you accept that your mind and mine become one?"

Smiling to her consort, she placed the second belt around her waist and attached it to the front. With her sweetest voice, she responded.

"Dani-el, I accept!"

In his hands, he reached inside a pocket, and a shiny triangular object filled his palm; it was the wedding vows terminating device.

Since the marriages in Terra lasted for so many years, wives were allowed to terminate a marriage. The reason was apparent: a marriage enduring thousands of years may someday face situations where a significant burden was placed over one, or even conceivably, over both individuals inside the marriage bond. Moral law did allow for termination when this situation became stressful. After all, Terra marriages were not considered to be eternal, especially when you thought the next life in the presence of God to be the source of all Love. Terra marriages, even when including deeply shared angels' love, were only a feeble taste of the intensity our Creator can share with us, individually or together.

Our Earth's or Terra's marriages will not appear to have much importance once we meet God with all His glory, immensity, eternity, and the incredible power of love. It is too bad that we can only meagerly reflect a tiny amount of that love back to Him; however, it does not matter since He loves us the same because He has created each of us in His image.

The marriage termination could be done in the simplest public ceremony. Using this device, which had a slot to insert a wedding belt, the blade hidden inside would easily split the marrying belts. The wife publicly returning the belt's four pieces and the device to her husband was universally accepted as a final separation.

It is to be noted that this option was rarely recalled in The Core or the SA. However, in recent years, the NA had a marriage collapse that closely followed its people's increasing moral decadence. In that Alliance, a 'wedding' became synonymous with a sarcastic and sexual joke!

Dani-el presented the device to his consort and made a third request.

"Maryen, as the laws of the land request of me, in case I ever become a burden to our love, I give you the tool that could cancel this marriage. Do you accept it?"

Maryen smiled sweeter and wider at Dani-el. She eagerly took the device. However, instead of retaining it, she gave it back to Gabri-el. Immediately, she exclaimed.

"Dani-el, I reject it; I am giving it to Gabri-el to be destroyed!
Since the heaviest burden you, my beloved Dani-el, could place upon me would be as light and pleasant as the clothes that I am now wearing, I publicly renounce my right to a marriage termination. Only you, my spouse, will hold that right!"

With his best smile, Dani-el replied almost instantly.

"I equally relinquish my right!
Let it be noted today that Dani-el and Maryen shall be married until the
end of their lives!"

Raquel and Gabri-el held and squeezed hands, but the pressure between
them was tender. They had just heard a wedding vow very similar to their
own. As many years accumulated, their love for each other increased not
to become a burden but to enlarge the internal flame burning deep inside
their hearts. The closer they got to their God, the more beautiful this flame
became; correspondingly, their love grew equally more beautiful!

**Can we describe Love when it has no physical bounds and no
intellectual limitations?**

One more time, the wedding couple touched both palms of their hands
and raised them upward in joint prayer, looking to the sky, both exclaimed
together.

"Dear God, as You are our witness, this ceremony is completed!"

As Dani-el and Maryen embraced and passionately kissed, the
participants plus the audience burst into deafening cheering! From the
terraces above, hi-tech colored confetti spread over the open space,
sending light flashes as it spiraled down and reflected any available light.

Pleasant music filled the whole location, but it was hardly noticeable
due to the loud celebration. After a full minute, Micha-el raised his hand,
asking for silence.

When silence finally arrived, Raquel and Maryen began to sing a
special reciprocal duet.

To appreciate the song, one must remember that angels can sing with
upper and lower tones next to the center melody. It started like this.

(Raquel) ♪ **Our love, the light of our lives...♪**

(Maryen) ♪ **Love, as bright inside our minds... ♪**

As the song progressed, the incredible melodic duet captivated the
audience, practically making them forget anything else; the quality of their
combined voices reached a plateau never heard before. The
complementary reverberation of Maryen increased the melodic and
indisputable best voice on the planet, the one from the beautiful Raquel.

The singers converged where the words were equal or similar in their
phonetic vocal expression. They diverged, where the word's sounds did
otherwise. Three Terra's minutes later, they concluded their fantastic song.

(Raquel) ♪ **... so I can now tell you, that I love you! ♪**

(Maryen) ♪ **...I know that is beautiful. As love is to you! ♪**

The ovation turned as emotional and loud as the wedding's ending.
People cheered with both hands up. Food and music followed; the party
had just begun.

All participants rejoiced and enjoyed the celebration. Many visitors had come to this pretty city just for this occasion. They mixed with the initial participants to transform the festivity into an entire city's celebration.

Dani-el and his wife shared intense emotional interactions with the enormous number of visitors flooding the city. The visitors were anxious to be part of the event, to personally touch and talk to the married couple. Doing such an act, even for an instant, was equivalent to them being at the center of the whole festivity as one of the main celebrants. The married couple knew about this joyful drive to be at the center of the celebration as a healthy custom, and they would not have it in any other way. In this manner, many old friendships strengthened, and many new ones flourished. The binding glue of love attached many thousands of beings as its invisible threads connected their existences in ways beyond their imagination.

The party continued until ten seconds before midnight. At that moment, everybody stood still in silence. They were waiting for the flashing signal indicating that it was midnight. Like Trillium, the SA citizens stopped all activities as they sang or prayed to God, thanking Him for the benefits of the passing day and welcoming the new one.

The angels of The Core and the SA did not take God and their existence for granted; they accepted the divine gift for what it was every day!

Dani-el and Maryen held hands and kissed. Their blood carried their love across the boundaries of their skins. They had never experienced so much joy in their long lives. The closeness that they felt with each other was intoxicating. The warmth, the tingling on their skin, the merging of their souls, the sight of their loved ones, and even their smell, all became the euphoria of happiness.

They could hardly wait to sing with a hymn, the many thanks to God for His many gifts, for the best day in their lives, for Love!

A flash from all the buildings indicated midnight. It also pointed out:

$T_0 = -70:00$ (Seven days left!)

SBC, Pristeen, SA. Second sunrise since the wedding.

A white blanket of snow covered the southern base; the sun barely shined as it rose above the nearby mountain range, merely offering a reddish tint reflected as pink on the snow's surface. Since the sun leaned heavily in the northern direction, it was late in the morning: 4:20 hours.

A faint haze hung almost to a standstill, slightly drifting upwards and allowing the place to warm up slowly. Otherwise, the skies stayed clear; no clouds appeared on this balmy winter day. For this base, this was an unusual heat wave; the temperature remained above 10°C. Even the snow began to melt in the middle of the winter!

A structural complex ramified from a centered building 40 stories high. Circular structures, connected with pathways, radially projected in all directions. None of these pathways was open to the outside; all were enclosed within squashed cylindrical domes that resembled the top half of the cross-sectional area of an aircraft's cylindrical structure. Everything looked peaceful, but it was possible to identify clusters of laser and plasma cannons menacing heads sniffing the cool morning air for enemy crafts; it was a military base.

Two Overlords stood at a round overlooking platform, which crowned the center of the highest building. A Throne, leaning against the rail, faced the rising sun while submerged in a reflexive mode.

"Everything looks so peaceful," he mentally told his companion, *"It is hard to believe there is a threat beyond the horizon!"*

The other Overlord placed his right hand over his shoulder; almost melancholically, he exclaimed.

"I am truly sorry for interrupting your honeymoon so soon! Nevertheless, my brother, I am almost sure we are running out of time! The NA is activating all its military resources. Even when many think it is just a military exercise, I am convinced that Lucif-er is preparing for war.

You also know that the only way he could expect to win such a war is by disabling the 4-D Matrix defense system!"

Still staring away at the far sunrise, Dani-el responded, *"You have a point. Show me the report you got yesterday; I know it includes X-ray mapping of the NA!"*

To satisfy his companion's request, Gabri-el proceeded to send mental images. They transferred swiftly from his brain to Dani-el's. Now, as Dani-el knew precisely the same data that Gabri-el had held in his memory, he remarked.

"You are right! I have never seen such massive military preparations; all their armies are moving to locations where they could be flown for deployment. Even the defensive structures around all capitals have been mostly completed. The big question is... How will it be done?"

Gabri-el placed his hands on the rail that demarcated the upper platform. He stared at the sun, so low on the horizon that it could not stay up much longer; he knew it would be setting one hour after the noon's zenith. He looked at his friend and indicated.

"Micha-el agreed with me; he has to be an Overlord! Except for Mervyn, you know that the Matrix program is too complex to be understood by anybody other than an Overlord!"

"I can see you want to do this by an elimination process! ... If we start with Micha-el and Rapha-el, we know they are out of the list. In addition, you agree with me when I state that we can trust each other. Only four left!"

After a brief pause, Gabri-el turned sideways, facing Dani-el, and mentally pointed out.

"After Mervyn disclosed the existence of the Matrix to all the SA Overlords, what would you have done... if you were a traitor?"

Without any hesitation, Dani-el replied.

"I would have sent the information to the NA. The same night! Deployment of the Matrix had to be prevented at any cost. However, I could not send a message without exposing myself!"

"That is correct. There were only two choices: You could risk sending the message or find somebody to deliver it!"

This time, Dani-el paused for two seconds. He recalled.

"Platoon C from the NA was active at that time... Is it possible that I knew about them without them knowing about me?"

"Emphatically, yes! It was imperative that they did not know you! Next, you could contact Dagon, the platoon leader," added Gabri-el; while showing deep concentration, he continued, *"However, since this individual died trying to kill Micha-el and me, one enormous favor we both owed to our Creator, we never learned about such contact!"*

"When the rest of the platoon was killed or captured by our forces, two soldiers were missing: C-2 and C-3... We found out from the survivors' questioning that they went back to the NA!"

Looking at his companion, Dani-el insinuated a burning question, *"If they carried the message and the missing Matrix program copy, why did the NA do nothing? ... It is obvious that the NA did not receive such a message!"*

Gabri-el glanced at the faraway mountains; briskly, he announced.

"That is a big question! ... Let us go down and check all data banks and logs for the same day, plus a few more after the Matrix announcement. Dani-el, we will find <u>who</u> this Overlord is, even if it is the last thing we will ever do!"

Two kilometers underground, the heart and computer center of SBC throttled with activity. Many terminals with electronically controlled overlaying maps of land and sky activities supported such activity; about 200 technicians, engineers, and even two scientists worked in the compact underground facilities. The supporting arches and pillars designed from hard polymer materials helped this structure to be a solid place.

As the elevator stopped at the bottom, the two Overlords exiting the transporting machine faced a round room, the largest of the facilities. Many angels were walking in and out of this place, but only the ones near the Overlords greeted them; the rest continued with their jobs.

Two officers rushed to meet the Archangels. The higher ranking, a Seraph, mentally spoke to Gabri-el hastily.

"Sir! Our great leader Micha-el ordered alert status: 9!"

"Abdren, it was necessary. I must inform you that we will be using the main computer; please ensure we will be free from interruptions!"

"It will be done as requested! Sir!" exclaimed the officer.

The two officers moved ahead of the Overlords toward the computer. They signaled the angels working there to close their programs and to exit promptly. Twenty seconds later, the electronic workstation became empty.

The two Archangels sat in adjacent chairs, and in front of them, a massive terminal awaited instructions. They looked at each other; for a moment, they shared sadness. Spying on their Overlords was not a pleasant activity. How could they, when finding the traitor, rationalize in their minds an appropriate response? Together, both imagined the outcome.

"We loved you as a brother; now we despise you! We would have given our lives for you; now, your own life is worthless to us! We trusted you; now we know you are a liar and a traitor!"

These poignant statements… result from just pointing an accusing finger. How much and how fast can the perspective we use to judge our companions change instantly?

They both felt deeply saddened; at this moment, they understood much better why Micha-el opposed an investigation of the Overlords.

The large screen facing them split into two sections. Each Overlord entered their requested information, not word-by-word but page-by-page.

>**Authorization: G-P-SBC-002**
OK
>**Computer: Priority 1, scan.**
>**Search for all available data on SA Overlords location.**
Date: 205047/147/6:00
Deviation: 0/-5/6:00↑
End.

As Gabri-el sorted the data available, all the unconfirmed gaps in the information for placing an Overlord location; starting the day Mervyn disclosed the Matrix plus five days were compiled. Next, he asked the computer for the exclusion of an individual if all his time was accounted for. The result:

Samu-el

>**Authorization: D-P-SBC-002**
OK
>**Computer: Priority 1, scan.**
>**Search for all missing individuals from the village named: Hazenor**
(120 Km west of Dawnel)
Date: 205047/147
Deviation: 0/-10
END

Dani-el waited patiently as all the records for the town of Hazenor were analyzed.
Shortly afterward, the display showed the requested data.

Nereus   P-3780549
Ektor   P-3766348
NA Immigrants
Work: Transport supplies to B3 island.
Date missing: 205047/143

The two Overlords, assimilating both sections of the screen, looked at each other. Gabri-el, faintly smiling, spoke first.

"Only three choices left!"

"The commander of B-3 Island may tell us what happened?" Dani-el quickly added.

As the two Overlords continued their search, it was not long before the inexorably advancing time reached midday.

$T_0 = -55:00$

****

Someplace south of Absalom, SE Sector, NA

At past midnight, this place was neither still nor quiet. The sky, dotted with bright lights descending in a spiraling pattern that landed on a designated area only a few kilometers away, turned out to be large NA transport cylinders.

In the opposite direction, a 50-strong squadron of attack aircraft fighters zoomed overhead, rattling the location with their powerful engines. They fanned upwards and outwards, moving like spears thrown high in the sky.

Lucif-er, Magog-el, and Azami-el stood close to each other, watching the activities with great interest. The place they stood in remained poorly illuminated, but we could tell all wore jumpsuits. However, Azami-el had a military outfit practically invisible at night; only the flashing lights of the landing crafts revealed his location. Exposed by the lights showed that he was carrying weapons; his belt held a handgun, and somehow attached to his back, a high-power, long-range sniper plasma gun could be seen; a model similar to the one C-1 had in his hands when ambushing the SA Overlords. Only one difference existed: Azami-el did not wear a telemetric helmet; he did not need it.

In front of them, platoon thick rows of ten soldiers continued marching. Dressed for combat, the soldiers were hardly visible, appearing like rows of shadows. The army marching in front of the Overlords comprised thousands of soldiers, like an endless sea of angels moving wave by wave as dark undulating sheets that extended forward in a threatening manner.

Lucif-er seemed unhappy; he just barked at the open fields.

"The third army is one day late; where is Razari-el?"

Magog-el turned to Azami-el and barked at him in a similar style.

"We only have 39:21:68 hours left; he should be here!"

Azami-el seemed undisturbed by his two bosses' demands and calmly answered.

"The NE Sector has had severe flooding for the last 30 days. I am sure he is blaming the rain for this delay. He will be arriving in 22 minutes!"

After a short pause, he said something else, *"Why are we not hiding the deployment of our armies?"*

Since Lucif-er continued displaying an unfriendly mood, Magog-el responded.

"What for? The SA already suspects our intentions! By doing it in the open, we hope to reinforce their belief that this is only an 'exercise'!"

Lucif-er was restless; he started pacing the place. His wings began to glow in an eerie way. The sound of his grinding teeth could be heard above the outside noise. Magog-el stared at his superior and exclaimed.

"I understand how you feel... I can hardly wait to give the order to destroy the SA!"

Lucif-er's response came thundering and full of hate. He had never forgotten the humiliation he had suffered under the leader of the SA. He clearly expressed it by looking at his hands posed as the claws of a wild beast.

"Exactly! ... The order to kill Micha-el!
I only wish I could rip his flesh with my own hands!"

****

Approaching Dawnel, a large aircraft had almost a thousand angels inside, including a couple pressing against each other sideways; they gazed outside the wide transparent window facing them at the green mountain ranges slowly moving under the vessel's path.

Far ahead, in the center of an incoming valley, the shiny towers of Dawnel sparkled like jewels with many facets. The city reflected the bright afternoon sun, so at a distance, the sparkling from the skyscrapers cascading from their tops to the lower structures emerged as a fountain of light.

One individual from the couple, an attractive brunette with long eyelashes, pointed her index finger to the approaching city; she said with excitement.

"There! ... I can see Dawnel; it is beyond that big mountain!"

Her companion, also with brown hair and the same color as her eyes, focused on the indicated direction and acknowledged.

"Yes, I can see it!"

"Every time I come to this city, it looks more beautiful than before," she asserted.

He commented, changing his focus to her and utilizing a very soft voice.

"I used to think the same way but found something much prettier than that city!"

She looked into his eyes, adorned her face with a lovely smile, and kissed him. With their heads touching sideways, they continued watching the moving scenery. They also held hands tightly; these two angels were deeply in love.

Eugenius felt his wife's warmth, producing such a comforting feeling in him that he knew he would not be alone anymore. She cared for him so much that their lives stayed intertwined into a web of mutual love called marriage.

For a moment, while watching outside, she stared blankly. He noticed and asked.

"Claire, are you worried about moving to the big city?"

She paused for two seconds; then she replied.

"A little bit... I am so used to the quiet life I lived for so many years in Graceland that I don't think I will ever forget my hometown, Green Valley!"

He placed his second hand over the top of hers, staring at the buildings that were continuously growing as the craft approached the city. He felt somewhat hesitant; it would be a significant change.

However, something irresistible drove him to meet his benefactor, Micha-el, the Archangel, whom he credited with saving his life.

He hoped that in their free time, he would have the chance to face him and have one more opportunity to thank him and to admire his zeal and dedication to God. If he could have been half as dedicated and grateful to the Creator as compared to the way Micha-el always acted, his present life would have been so much different.

He knew God had been generous with him; Claire was the latest example. He gazed one more time into the open window of his wife's mind, her pretty eyes. Even when almost hidden by her thick eyelashes, he saw only goodness; he kissed her cheek and gently spoke to her closer ear.

"Don't worry, my love... Everything is going to be OK!"

$T_0 = -33:79$ (Only 33 hours and 79 minutes left.).

SBC, the next day's evening, just past 8:00 hours.

Gabri-el and Dani-el worked at the same large screen at the center of the base's underground facilities. They knew now that the incident caused by the scientist Tanner's research vessel set up the circumstances for the destruction of C-2/C-3 craft over B2 Island, the only incident preventing the copy of the Matrix from reaching the NA!

Piles of data continued to stack on top of each other, but no further breaks in the investigation were found. The two Overlords continued to work with a split screen, doubling their input and output capabilities. A message appeared in the upper right-hand corner of Gabri-el's section.

Mervyn-PD-002

Gabri-el acknowledged with a flick of his finger. The top left quadrant of the large screen, or half of his viewing area, was overtaken by the video display of Mervyn's face.

Since he looked a bit disturbed, and his curly hair was more tangled than usual, Gabri-el assumed this to be caused by the scientist rubbing his head in disgust; the incoming message could not be any good news. The image on the screen spoke sharply.

"My friend, I am glad that I found you!" Seeing Dani-el sitting at Gabri-el's right side, he greeted him, *"Hi, Dani-el!"*

He quickly returned his attention to Gabri-el and proceeded, *"I have been away for a few days at the Green Ridge satellite launching site in Graceland. When I came back to my lab, as I always do, I checked the Matrix supervisory program! To my horror, I found out that there had been an unauthorized entry into the main computer! ... When I sent a trace to identify it... I could not find it!"*

Gabri-el almost interrupted as he verbally replied.

"This is very serious; it could be a virus! Did you notify Micha-el?"

Mervyn took a bite of his left hand's thumbnail and, nodding affirmatively, responded.

"Yes!... He is the one who recommended contacting you immediately. Gabri-el, I am apprehensive about this incident; if the Matrix is turned off, we will be in grave danger!"

"Calm down, my friend; give me the parameters related to this entry!"

Mervyn swallowed once, cleared his throat, and, still in a disturbed state, spoke again.

"The original intrusion program must have been inserted when the SA's security was much lax. At present, this is not possible!

The entry, or program, is lock-activated. Since we can't talk to any part of it, its program access must be closed. The result of a search for unlisted program identification failed!

This means the program we seek is fragmented and attached to many other valid files. It also means that it has multiple links! Because if you check for any valid file, it detaches from the file being inspected... In this manner, you cannot isolate even a fragment! The only way to destroy this 'virus' is by erasing all memory banks. This means... turning off the Matrix! ... Most of our defensive and offensive devices are up in the sky with the Matrix; if it is disabled, we could not stop the NA from destroying us!"

Gabri-el appeased Mervyn with a hand gesture. Calmly, he asserted.

"We know. Please return to your normal work. We will continue the investigation from this site. From here, we will inform you of any significant development, and most importantly, do not let any undue anxiety take over your existence. Remember that God is always at our side. Turn your thoughts to Him, and He will comfort you and give you <u>peace of mind</u>!"

Mervyn agreed; he tried to slow down and return to normal.

"Thanks, my friend!" He spoke through the electronic machine.

He ended the communication after raising his right hand up and away, which was a greeting when the arm stayed close to the chest and saying goodbye when the arm moved away from the chest.

The screen returned to the split text format. The two Archangels stared at each other; this was terrible news. The NA's behavior and the secret enemy's actions hidden among the SA Overlords' top echelon were merging... Time... must be running out!

Dani-el advanced his statement first.

"I agree with you; there is no use rerunning the 'tracer' on the main computer in Dawnel. If Mervyn said: It cannot be found over there; it must be that way! However..."

As Gabri-el's green eyes sparkled strangely, Dani-el retorted, *"You must be right! Mervyn probably does not know that the main computer server, which handles the file transfers, is the only server in the SA that keeps a log, in <u>addition or as a duplicate</u> to the attached computer's log!"*

"Accessing the server records, relevant dates, entered," Dani-el added. The display before him showed the local computer activity churning millions of files. It compared the transferred files logged in the server against the ones stored in the capital of Pristeen, which also was Micha-el's operating computer.

Minutes passed by as the analysis reached the billions!

Then, the stream of high-speed data stopped. Only one entry remained displayed in Dani-el's working section.

IZ797

"It is an Izma-el file; I cannot believe it is him!" The Overlords, linking their thoughts, agreed.

Gabri-el rubbed his forehead like he felt pain. In a sad mental message to his companion, he indicated.

*"Ask him to report to this base... **immediately!**"*

$T_0 = -21:45$

The next day, at noontime, Gabri-el's craft landed in the main airport of SBC when the sun was at its highest point in the sky but still very low above the horizon. The good weather had remained almost motionless, with the balmy temperatures going down two degrees to 8°C, with only a mild breeze disturbing this clear and sunny day.

After landing on a designated parking space, the two armed pilots quickly positioned outside the craft, one at each side of the exit door. As Gabri-el and Dani-el stepped out of the cylinder, the first Overlord looked at his pilots with a minor sadness due to their present militaristic attire, which included weapons. He never got used to seeing Reuben and Norvel as soldiers. He liked the old times when he had time to socialize with his pilots. At chest high, he gave them a casual hand salute.

Both Cherubim smiled, and they similarly returned the salute.

The two Overlords walked to a handrail overlooking the landing complex. This area remained as the reserved parking space for the Overlords. Three top-design vessels occupied this location.

Gabri-el and Dani-el exclaimed.

"Zeri-el is here, and we did not know it!"

A distant figure, followed by four soldiers, came closer from another entrance.

"There, he is coming this way!" Gabri-el stated.

A Cherub, also an Archangel, wore a jumpsuit in his favorite color, dark red. Quickly, he approached the two standing Overlords. He looked short but muscular, and his long, skillfully styled hair was neatly kept. As he stopped close to his colleagues, using both hands simultaneously, he offered a one-hand salute to the other two. Without sound, he talked first.

"Greetings, my brothers! I can see that you are surprised to find me here!"

Gabri-el, after responding to the initial salute, stated.

"That would be an understatement! Why did you not visit us at the underground facilities? You knew that we were there!"

Zeri-el's green eyes stared directly into Gabri-el's, and the first explained.

"My brother, a very menacing storm is moving toward SBC and the rest of the mainland; it will hit here tomorrow night and then spread into Pristeen and Zarinia.
I am concerned because it will affect our defense exercises. Furthermore, I did not stop because I was in a big rush to return immediately to Zarinia to fix some unexpected emergencies. I know both of you want to talk to me; however, I need to leave now."

"It is important." Gabri-el insisted.

"I promise… I will be back tomorrow night!"

Dani-el, anticipating a question, responded.

"The investigation is going fine. We are questioning Izma-el today. We will talk to you tomorrow, and since Lari-el is also too busy now, we will meet with him in two days."

"Good! I will do __anything__ to find this no-good traitor. I only hope that it is not Izma-el because I like him; on the other hand, since he came from the North, he is the prime suspect! ... One thing I know for sure is that I am glad I am not investigating this big problem; therefore, I do not have to point an accusing finger toward him or anybody else… yet, Micha-el and Rapha-el checked him to be OK. I do not think Lucif-er has enough power to conceal such a guilty conscience from our two highest Overlords?"

"We completely agree with your statement!" Gabri-el and Dani-el responded.

Zari-el ended the conversation with a short remark.

"Until tomorrow, 9:90 hours."

As Zeri-el moved away in the direction of his craft, which was in the same direction where the four escorting soldiers were waiting and almost 10 meters away, he passed between the two other Overlords. At that moment, Gabri-el sent a message to Dani-el.

"Dani-el, after lunch with the wives, meet me at the underground facilities at 6:50 hours."

A high-tech military cylinder, like the one Gabri-el owned, came down at the special parking place where Dani-el and Gabri-el stood.

A tall, medium-built Cherub stepped out of the craft. He was an Overlord and must have ordered his military escort to remain inside the craft because no one else got out. He wore his new colors, a gray jumpsuit with a bicolor white/green belt and a silver cross forged over his chest. He saluted with both hands up, first to Gabri-el and Dani-el shortly afterward.

With a half smile, he asked, *"I know this meeting is not an invitation for lunch; tell me, what is on your minds?"*

At short range, Gabri-el stared into the eyes with a color like his. Inside, he did not see any evil; therefore, he hesitated to accuse his colleague. Izma-el read his concern and added.

*"I am coming from Dawnel, and I did hear about the computer problem with a possible 'virus' infiltration. I did not know, it was IZ797... **one of my files?**"*

Gabri-el, still looking intensely at the questioned Overlord, said.

"My friend, you must explain what happened. The tracer in the file log did not identify you in any public place; you have no alibi!"

"Even if it has my codes, it is not my file; I have never seen it before! However, regardless of what I say, it is not what you both want to hear. You demand... proof! What do you want me to do? I can only give you, my word!"

Gabri-el and Dani-el felt that the questioned Archangel was truthful, but at present, with the impending danger of the NA getting ready to strike... It was not enough!

This time, Dani-el took the word.

"It bothers us to question your integrity. Nevertheless, we have no choice! ... Yes, you are right! You must allow us to merge our minds into a single one!"

Izma-el, in a sad mental telepathic message, recollected.

"It does not matter that I have already taken such a test with our leaders, Micha-el and Rapha-el... what difference do you expect to find?"

Gabri-el placed one hand on his shoulder and looked directly into his eyes, not aggressively but compassionately and genuinely understandingly. He declared.

"My brother, my heart is entirely sure that you are an Archangel serving our Lord. It is just a formality; it will place you permanently in the clear. Also, in anticipation of such an intrusion on your personal identity, we greatly apologize!"

Izma-el looked down, stayed silent for just a moment, then nodded affirmatively. Finally, he exclaimed with a burst of energy.

"Let's do it!"

The two Overlords doing the investigation stood beside each other, facing Izma-el at arm's length. The three Overlords made a triangle by touching each other at the side of the head. Izma-el saw two sets of eyes merging into his, one green, one reddish.

The surrounding scenery began rotating and fading away as Izma-el fell into a spiraling, bottomless dark well. Visual information started to flash among the three powerful minds. As the speed of exchange continuously increased, it added to the vertigo of the down-spiraling hole, like looking at a tornado from the top, in which suddenly, the Overlords had been thrown inside its center!

Images, sounds, and formulas all added to the spinning vortex. The speed of exchange became almost impossible to follow, like looking at a computer running at its own speed. With little to focus on, everything becomes just a speeding blur.

At that point, the blur suddenly fell apart... Just three silent, bright white lights remained at the bottom of the spiral. They slowly merged into just one white and larger light!

In unison, all three announced.

"In the light, we are the servants of the Lord!"

$T_0 = -14:88$

****

CWC, CD, NA.

Two kilometers underground, the Central War Center looked extremely busy. Lucif-er, Magog-el, and Azami-el continued supervising the hectic pace of the vast angelic force inside the base; it was almost midnight.

The place operators ran to do errands. The multiple screens remained eagerly monitoring the NA activities and the SA responses simultaneously.

The three Overlords faced each other. Azami-el, still militarily dressed, only carried a handgun inserted into a holster on the left side of his belt; his high-power rifle stayed attached straight up on a nearby wall.

Lucif-er, still not in any friendly mood, exuded hate. As the moment of revenge approached execution, he became more restless and bloodthirsty. With a cynical smile carved on his face, Azami-el felt the same evil forces growing inside him, getting stronger, ready to explode and destroy.

Magog-el focused his attention on one of the larger screens displaying the tactical deployment of the NA armies. After analyzing the data, he smiled with sadistic satisfaction, ready to send a mental message to Lucif-er, but even as the leader of the NA was not looking at the large screen, he stayed ahead of Magog-el.

"Finally, the Third Army is fully deployed!" Lucif-er, briskly stated.

"Lucif-er, all seven Armies are now ready for action!" Magog-el overlapped.

"And we still have ten hours to wait!" Azami-el added.

Lucif-er pointed his claws toward the South and exclaimed.

"Yes, Micha-el, only ten hours left… only one single day! I will give many riches to the angel that brings me back, the carbonized remains of the leader of the SA… Micha-el!"

Soldiers and technicians scrambled to escape his path as he paced the busy corridors like in a trance. The blue color of his eyes remained tinted with a bloody red while his sculptural muscles stayed tensed with the flow of his ominous power. His twelve blue wings persisted scintillating with an eerie display much closer to the ultraviolet than the visible light.

He knew it was past midnight. He cynically exclaimed with impatience, with anger, and with hate.

"Citizens of the SA… Have a nice day! Tomorrow… The pleasure shall be all mine!"

A satanic laugh pervaded the place. It filled the corridors, echoing back from the dark crevices of the underground base. It also became a hair-raising experience for the non-Overlords working in this subterraneous place.

****

Same day at a nearby lake close to SBC, 6:00 hours.

Two couples sitting on a grassy hill looked northwest at the slowly setting sun's red disk. A mild and cool breeze blew Raquel's hair in an undulating way, almost sensual. Since the temperature got cooler, now only four °C, she was dressed in a better-insulating green jumpsuit this time. The cool air on her face and hands still chilled her; she was not used to these cold temperatures. Argentan, the capital of Cheruban, where she came from, always had good warm weather.

She pressed harder against Gabri-el's warm body, who, responding to the stimulus, placed his right arm across her back. She felt much cozier under his snug embrace; in gratitude, she rubbed her charming left cheek softly against her husband's.

Close to them, moved at a slight angle so the other couple partially faced them, Maryen sat next to Raquel with Dani-el being next in line but very close to his wife... no air pockets between them.

All four stared toward the red disk slowly disappearing over the faraway mountains, outlining the farther end of this pretty lake. Because of the calm water surface and the setting sun's undulating reflection, as always does to the observer when the angle of reflection is shallow and the surface is reflective, it stretches across the entire lake.

Overhead, flocks of birds flew north, their aerodynamic, colorful bodies contrasting with the sunset's darker blue skies. This sky color was only broken by a tantalizing aquamarine color located near the red disk. Gabri-el, displaying a tender smile to his wife, did notice.

"My love, the color of the sky, next to the sun, is the same color as your beautiful eyes!"

"Thank you, my dearest husband. I thought that the color of my eyes was the reflection of the ocean when it came close to a sandy beach," she responded. At the same time, she touched him like a feather brushing against his lips, but it was a kiss.

After a moment of enjoying the touch, Gabri-el stared at the birds and the gray clouds approaching from the South, somewhat sadly; he added a soft message.

"Since all the birds are moving north, this incoming storm will be a bad one. And it is going to be here tonight!"

Dani-el quickly annexed something to the statement.

"It will have winds up to 50 meters per second, and the temperature will drop to -10°C."

Both girls shivered at the thought of such a windy and cold night. Maryen, in a sweet manner, requested, *"Could Raquel and I join both of you at the underground command center? Just the thought of staying on the surface gives me the chills!"*

Both Overlords looked at each other while jokingly inferring with a mannerism that indicated, 'Chill, from what?' Without any more delays, Gabri-el, squeezing his beloved wife a bit harder, took the word.

"Of course, we would love to have you down there. However, since we have work to do with the computer and at 9:90 hours Zeri-el will be arriving at SBC, you fabulous-looking angels can stay in the recreation area until we finish our work. Afterward, we could go to the cafeteria and have a snack before retiring to our private quarters for the night."

As he talked, Gabri-el saw another large flock of birds flying above the horizon where only a tiny portion of the sun's red disk remained. For a moment, he considered the feeling of being able to fly away from an incoming storm. If he could only do the same, fly away from a much worse storm, in contrast, this one approaching from the North.

The voice inside us, our conscience, our spirit, or whatever, just spoke to Gabri-el, **"You will!"**

A chill, curious enough, also a sadness, started from the inside and radiated to his outer body; Raquel was not an Overlord, but her sharply tuned senses to the Archangel she loved were unmatched. She only thought.

"Anything wrong, my love?"

Gabri-el knew the question without even being asked. He promptly replied while trying to avoid any sadness in his words. At the same time, he ran two fingers across such a lovely face, only stopping when touching her upper lip.

"Sweetheart, would it be great if we could fly away from our worldly problems like the birds fly away from an incoming storm?"

With a gorgeous half smile, Raquel, while turning her head to watch the overhead flying birds, exclaimed with an inner knowledge that she had already experienced, *"It would be fantastic for us to be able to fly... It is such an awesome feeling!"*

As her head moved sideways and upwards, he could not resist but rub her long, silky hair. He could not think of himself without including Raquel; it was true... Love unites two beings into only one.

As Gabri-el noticed the other couple closely watching them, he asked. *"What about the newlyweds, still want to stay together... forever?"*

He got a big smile for a response. Next, the newlywed couple eagerly responded together, *"More than ever!"*

Maryen, with starry-looking eyes, added.

"We just completed seven days since our marriage... it already feels like a lifetime! I love my husband..." she interrupted by giving Dani-el a passionate and sexy kiss that lasted for five pleasurable seconds, *"...more than ever! ... I can't imagine anybody who would be in a situation to end their matrimony. Did I hear correctly that the institution of marriage is disappearing in the North?"*

Dani-el, licking his lips still tingling and warm because of his spouse's stimulus, responded.

"It is true! The NA citizens are losing the perspective of what sex should be: an integral part of Love. Individuals are looking now at the opposite sex as objects to satisfy their lust and pleasures. In this manner, sex that should be an act to reinforce our love for each other is becoming an evil tool to separate the offenders from meaningful relations and their God."

"That is very sad to hear!" Both female angels, equally sorrowful, responded.

Most of the solar disk had disappeared. A purple glow began advancing from the opposite side; since the days were so short in the middle of the winter, the night came early.

A colder breeze capriciously moved their hair. The temperature was down another two degrees; it would be below freezing very soon.

From the south direction, darker clouds started to pile up.

Both Overlords stood at the same time; they helped their spouses to do similarly.

Where the sun had just gone away, Gabri-el took a last look at the remaining not-so-bright reddish glow and softly said.

"It was an excellent idea to come after lunch to watch this pleasant and relaxing sunset. It is time to return to the base, but let's take the warmth and beauty of this joyful event with us!"

$T_0 = -3:90$

It is a burning question!

What would we be doing one day, perhaps only hours before a devastating nuclear attack on the country and the city where we live? Would we have some premonition warning us of this terrible danger? Or, on the contrary, could the last day of our lives be another monotonous or boring experience? One more of the almost never-ending string of similar days ends up in a homogeneous soup called 'monotony,' a sedating monster that eats dreams, quenches ambitions, dulls the senses, and makes our lives appear to be so short!

Perhaps we could be lucky, and it could be a day of joy. We could be getting married, buying a new house, being blessed by the birth of a new child, or maybe just taking a vacation day. How unfortunate that everybody around, including the newborn, will have only a few hours to live… Still, it would be a day of joy up to that last moment.

Perhaps it could also be a day of great sorrow. A day when we lost somebody very close and very loved… Even though, this sorrow would be greatly diminished if we could only know we would be joining our loved one only a few hours later.

We may even say, "If we only knew!" However, knowing could worsen it; anticipating a horrible end could be unbearable. Even if we could get to the streets and yell our lungs out to accept the imminent danger and avoid its consequences, how many would believe us? Will we considered to be out of our minds? ... Another crazy preaching for the end of the world?… While most of the skeptics standing around (us) believe the End will never come, or at least not in our lifetimes!

It is better not to know. We could be spared the double torture of knowing and facing the event. If today was the last day of our lives, it could also be the last day of the whole planet… the last day of the Universe!

Afterwards, we certainly would not care. At the other side of **'the end of life'** door, our vision of life, the meaning of our existence, and especially our perspective regarding Eternity… **All are <u>so</u> different.**

Back to the same subterranean section of the base two kilometers underground, Gabri-el commanded the central computer to work at its utmost capabilities. He expected Dani-el to join him in only one minute; it was 6:49 hours.

After 100 seconds passed, in answer to his requested high-speed commands, images, and data stayed feverishly flashing on the main display. His internal clock told him 6:50 had arrived, but Dani-el had not!

For the Overlords, being late was not an option. If a delay had unexpectedly occurred, he would have sent a message to notify Gabri-el of a postponement. Gabri-el became seriously concerned as he quickly pointed to some controls; the upper left quarter of the screen read.

Link>Dani-el

Slowly, three seconds passed before the screen selected quarter lit with a full display of Dani-el's face. He smiled as he asked.

"What is it, brother?"

"It is past 6:50 hours!" Gabri-el responded.

From the other side of the screen, Dani-el, with his expression becoming more serious, stated, *"Did you expect me to meet you at this hour? I did not receive a message!"*

In the next instance, Gabri-el, searching for his own memories, speculated why Dani-el had not received his personal and telepathic message. What went wrong? ... In his mind, he saw Dani-el moving behind a dark silhouette. He sent the message when the other being completely occluded Dani-el, the recipient of his telepathic message.

Only an individual whose mind had an implanted evil block so the truth could not be revealed could create an involuntary barrier that had such an effect on such a telepathic message. A mental scream filled the Overlord's mind.

"Zeri-el!"

Dawnel, Pristeen, SA

At the top of the tallest and central building in the city, Micha-el was seated facing west. Half of the circular walls in his office facing the west direction were transparent. This gave him a great view over the city skyline; he was attentively observing the sun as it was setting.

It called his attention that the sky had been absolutely clear; only in the past minutes had a band of fluffy puffs of collected moisture organized in overlaying streaks quickly moved in to express, in a glorious and spectacular way, 'good night' to the disappearing sun.

The whole western section of the sky became ablaze with bright yellows. Light rays pierced some clouds, offering a majestic perspective pointing at the sun. Micha-el felt lucky to have a clear view of this magnificent sunset.

The colors had just changed to bright gold. Farther away from the sun and higher in the sky, beautiful oranges shined like a heavenly crown.

Mesmerized by the magnificent display, Micha-el thanked God for such a treat. However, the more he looked at the rainbow's colors changing one at a time and by now shifting to the reds, the more he saw his Creator. Deep inside, he felt like He was calling him!

"In my long life, I have never seen such a beautiful sunset!" He thought, "Dear God, the spectacular beauty offered to my senses is overwhelming, but regardless of its beauty, it is only a pale display compared to Your magnificence. My soul craves for Your presence! ... **I am ready... I have always been!**"

He paused for a moment as sadness invaded his whole being. It was not for himself but for billions of souls under his care and guidance. What will happen to his loyal citizens? The burden of the thought felt heavy indeed.

When he looked at the sunset, now endowed with rich reds and fantastic maroons, he saw blood! Lots of blood!

With desperation invading his mind, his fists closed super tight. The temperature of his body, chilled by the thought, made him shiver. If possible, he would have cried.

Standing tall, he did not even remember getting up from his chair. The blood in the sky went away quickly. The rich maroons approached the disappearing solar disk as the reddish-darker browns took over the outlying regions.

Suddenly, he felt as if an immense burden had been removed from his shoulders; it was not his anymore; he knew that God had taken the burden over to Himself!

Why worry? God could take care of the faithful in a much better way than he could imagine. With a renewed outlook, he breathed calmly; the view was meant to cause not pain but pleasure. Micha-el saw the sun vanishing around the planet's curvature; only purple, gray, and darkness remained.

A 'ding' called his attention. It merely duplicated the previous flash he noticed coming on his personal screen display. This machine, located behind him, had remained unusually quiet.

As Micha-el turned around, the image of Gabri-el and Dani-el filled the screen. The former talked first in a sober manner.

*"Greetings, my brother; we have sad news: we found the traitor! He is... **Zeri-el!**"*

Micha-el frowned in disbelief and sadly exclaimed telepathically to the machine, *"He is like my brother... Is there any doubt?"*

"None! He excludes telepathic messages. He has no alibis for the most critical events. He is the one who trained Izma-el on the SA computer system. Obviously, he stole his ID and tried to frame him as the traitor."

"I know you are telling me the truth... still, I find it so hard to believe!"

"Likewise, my brother... Just yesterday, Dani-el and I saluted him as being our brother!"

After a brief pause, Micha-el continued, *"It is going to be quite a shock for the citizens of Zarinia Province to accept. Regardless, I must order his immediate arrest!"*

Gabri-el almost interrupted.

"He is supposed to report to my base at 9:90 hours. If we arrest him at the SBC airport, we may avoid an unpleasant confrontation."

Micha-el approved by nodding affirmatively while thinking of the hidden time bomb, a program that needed to be diffused. The pressure for immediate action was tremendous. However, after his last experience moments ago, he felt less anxious; the will of God will prevail, no matter what!

He stared into Gabri-el's eyes. The Cherub corresponded similarly; Dani-el also tuned in. A spark flew through their minds since they knew something big would happen. Nothing was said, but the communion among their souls was vast. To their realization, this happening could not be possible because it transpired across the electronic lines of communication!

Without any anxiety shown on his face, Micha-el requested.

"Bring him to me as soon as he is under arrest!"

$T_0 = -3:25$

Iris, Irisan, SA; 7:05 hours.

Rapha-el took a momentary stop from his vigorous walking. As he placed his left foot on top of a small rock protruding next to the center path of this street for pedestrians, he leaned forward, placing both hands over his left knee. He had reached the center of a nicely decorated garden's pathway neatly placed in the middle of a busy wide avenue, with his final destination still at a faraway point near West.

A moderate number of people walked along the elegant pathways. Four Seraphim, his armed guards, kept some distance apart, even though they fanned individually in all directions surrounding the Overlord.

One angel, struggling with his jogging, approached Rapha-el's place of relaxation. This stocky individual remained perspiring and breathing heavily, his black hair in disarray. He addressed the Overlord vocally speaking. The Archangel greeted him with a smile.

"Dear friend Rapha-el!... I have been trying... to catch up with you... for the last five kilometers!"

"I am sorry, Sergius! I was aware that you were following me, and normally, I would have waited for you, but I had this incredible urge to arrive at this place before the sun went away!"

Sergius dropped to the nearest flat surface, trying to catch his breath.

Rapha-el looked again down the long and straight avenue where the sun began approaching the end of another day. The glitter from the building's reflections, overhead pathways, and flying cylinders moving above in their fixed air channels all contributed to a shower of sparkling reflections. As the sun moved behind some far-away overpasses, it cast a shadow... **It was a cross!**

The top of the cross' shadow, drifting away from its origin, slowly moved up toward the two angels; ultimately, it directly reached Rapha-el's feet and started to climb over his whole body.

As the Overlord looked far ahead down the street into the partially occluded solar disk, he saw a dark cross. Around the distant cross, a glow of dazzling white light compelled him to stare at the sign. It became an invitation to join the sunset... to go away with the setting star!

Rapha-el felt his body filling with a unique sensation... He remembered the same feeling that overwhelmed him when he touched the flower delivered by Gabri-el... a gift from God, with a fire that did not destroy but brought new life and love!

This time, the sunset brought back to him the same immense joy that he had previously felt.

As the sun went farther down, the cross disappeared. Yellow and gold reflections tunneled to impact the observers with a million reflections!

Sergius' mouth opened as he remained mesmerized by the incredible display. He was ready to comment, but when he saw the outside edge of the Overlord's skin, clothes, and hair bathed with a sparkling golden shower, with his face like being in a trance, he relinquished and remained silent.

Only minutes later, the sun was gone, and the reflections ended.

"I have never seen anything like it... it was incredible!" Sergius exclaimed.

Touching him on the shoulder, Rapha-el remarked with a bit of sadness in his voice. Like Micha-el, he also knew the implications of the event just witnessed; soon, it would be affecting all his fellow citizens.

"It was divine! It was a small window which allowed us to see a spark of the Glory of our Lord shared with our humble existence!"

Rapha-el, looking directly at his friend, emphasized.

"Sergius... tonight at midnight, come to the upper terrace of the Arts Center Building for the new day's praying and singing," as the Overlord gently touched his companion on the shoulder, he continued, *"I apologize for cutting this conversation short; I wish I could stay and talk to you about some critical events, but I must go now. I shall see you... at midnight!"*

Rapha-el, with swift steps, walked briskly toward the next building. About 30 meters away, he turned his head back and yelled just high enough for Sergius to hear him clearly.

"Do not forget... and please, <u>do not be late!</u>"

It was 7:11 hours.

$T_0 = -2:89$

SBC, Pristeen, SA; Main Airport, 9:89:00 hours

The wind continued howling with surging energetic dashes at a well-illuminated landing site. The temperature dipped way under the freezing point. Snow ran adrift, falling lightly but speedily because of the driving winds. The tiny white, puffy, frozen water droplets rolled on the floor; some bounced off the feet of two Overlords standing at the very edge of the landing location.

Three platoons fully armed with high-power rifles drawn at a 45° angle stayed ready for action, equally spaced in a large circle encompassing the landing site. Overhead at about two kilometers high, inside a thick cloud cover that made them invisible to the ground observers, a whole squadron of military cylinders remained hovering over the entire airport, waiting for the arrival of a particular individual.

A bright dot became visible as it approached from the western direction. On the crisp, cold, heavily cloudy, and windy night, it was in and out of sight while descending to the allocated landing place.

The vessel came into full view; it was Zeri-el's flagship. It came to rest in the assigned parking area, with its engine's noise drowned by the screaming wind.

The two Overlords quickly approached the vessel's exit door. As soon as it opened, three military Seraphim stepped into the stormy outside. From this group, the leading angel, a commander by his uniform insignias, mentally spoke first, *"Greetings, Great Overlords! I am here as you requested!"*

"Zeri-el sent you instead!" exclaimed Gabri-el.

"What a snake!" Remarked Dani-el.

As the commander and his two subordinates stared at the Overlords, baffled by their statements, Gabri-el ordered.

"Commander! Since it is obvious that you have no idea where your boss is, you and all your crew, please follow us to the underground command center. Dani-el and I will explain on our way there the extremely serious charge against your province Overlord, Zeri-el!"

After a speedy return to the underground main command post, the Overlords and the crew from the Province of Zarinia were in front of the main computer. This time, Gabri-el addressed one of the nearby operators for the request he needed. As he stood behind him, placing one hand on his shoulder to prevent him from standing up for the standard salute, he asked, *"Give me all unauthorized air departures presently moving away from Zarinia!"*

The operator quickly inspected various access ports, which yielded only one answer in return.

"Sir! There is only one!" he exclaimed.

"South-west direction... and it is now approaching the South Pole," Gabri-el casually noted.

The operator accessed a map of the province, revealing a blinking red dot moving away from Zarinia. He was surprised that the Overlord knew the exact location, he retorted with some excitement.

"Exactly there! Sir!"

Returning to his companions, Gabri-el noted, *"Before he gets out of range from the last armed satellite, we still have 20 minutes to stop him!"*

$T_0 = -0:05$

****

CWC, CD, NA; 2 Km underground.

The activity at the Central War Complex resembled near chaos, while four Overlords in a single line faced the largest displays on the base. They were the top echelon of the NA, Lucif-er, Magog-el, Gorgon-el, and Azami-el. Behind them, a large screen split into three equal parts displayed the faces of the three missing Overlords. They also had a front view of this critical countdown from their distant locations.

All around, soldiers and operators feverishly worked, nobody walked, and any movement between stations was hastily done; the Overlords had all their attention directed to the large screens in front of them. The center one displayed a huge map of the whole planet with delineated borders of the provinces or sector areas. Notes were overlaid, indicating the locations of significant armies, launching sites, and others.

To the right, multiple displays showed troop movements, missile launching status, and other critical data. To the left, another large display concentrated on the Matrix Defense System. Many red dots in a 3-D display were constantly being analyzed for any change in their activity. A column next to the array had a constant pouring of information that kept upgrading the data available at a hectic pace. Below the array, a clock was ticking. It displayed the remaining time!

$T_0 = -0:00:92$

$T_0 = -0:00:91$

$T_0 = -0:00:90$

$T_0 = -0:00:89$

Lucif-er's hard-set face glanced back to Razari-el's image from the back monitor; in a predetermined sequence arrangement, the latter Overlord had just stated to Lucif-er,

"Done!"

Lucif-er, addressing the other two images with a deep stare, got a speedy response from Kroma-el and Ezek-el, who pointed their left-hand thumbs up while responding in unison.

"All systems, O.K.!"

The leader of the NA returned his attention to the countdown, even when he knew the time to the millisecond. All his hate, outpouring from the inside, existed to do its worst.

He could hardly wait seconds later to give that ominous command of mass destruction; his subordinates stayed no less involved. Each one was looking forward to the destruction of the SA, for the removal of the only obstacle still preventing them from becoming the supreme rulers of the planet.

The clock read.

$T_0 = -0:00:21$

Magog-el, making tight fists, demanded the impossible from the timepiece. With a loud growl, he impatiently ordered the time-counting device, *"Stupid clock, just show what we are waiting for!"*

Time continued its inexorable journey. Nobody, God excepted, could add or subtract one single microsecond! ... The current time:

$T_0 = -0:00:15$

As more eyes stared at the countdown and minds could no longer think of anything more critical than the incoming instant, the noise and activity in this large war room steadily decreased. It was the turning point; Evil had its claws extended, its fangs exposed, and its muscles tensed and ready for the kill!

$T_0 = -0:00:10$

The entire Seraphim Overlord team in front of the display saw blood already. Their deep blue eyes, normally attractive and seductive, became tinted with a reddish glow, reflecting the sadistic and hateful outpouring of their inner souls. The monsters striving to be gods were posed to destroy the remaining force opposing their devilish ways.

The rest of the crew, technical and military, nervously followed each second's disappearance. Heavy breathing and perspiration caused by many hearts approaching their failure points were the norm of the moment.

They watched in the same manner as anyone facing a time bomb ready to explode in a matter of seconds would. All the present continued being trapped inside a sea of anxiety, where you could do nothing to stop the count... only look!

$T_0 = -0:00:05$

The whole underground base personnel stayed hypnotized for the last few seconds. All eyes were on the clock. Even the NA military located far away had their vision on the same fateful time-keeping device.

The underground base, only seconds ago teeming with incredible activity, was now at a dead calm... Nothing could be heard; everybody held their breath to count the very last second. Perhaps, if listening carefully, the only perceptible noise in the room became the drumming of so many stressed hearts!

The last five seconds, for the anxiously waiting for its passing, stretched the time base.

Finally!

T$_0$ = 0:00:00

All eyes switched to the 4-D Matrix displayed above the ominous clock, which was almost losing its important grip on so many lives.

Next, it became the Matrix display's turn to absorb all the attention!

The many red dots representing the complex array stayed red at this moment!

The next instant: No change, they were **red**!

The next instant: The same, still **RED**!

GREEN

The dots representing the Matrix had changed to green.

The SA defense system, the 4-D Matrix, the protecting shield for billions of angels, had been turned... **OFF!**

A *"YES!"* uproar shook the war room!

All went back to their assigned tasks. Lucif-er, with arms and fingers twisted grotesquely, screamed to his subordinates a fatal command ever spoken by anyone!

"Attack! ... Kill them all! ... Specially, Micha-el!"

With an unusual praise from his tight lips, Magog-el exclaimed.

"Good job, Zeri-el!

Nevertheless, you better rush to get out of the SA... or we will fry your ass, along with all the bastards from the rotten South Alliance!"

****

Trillium, The Core.

At the top of the city's tallest and most central structure, 28 years before, this was the same place where the Overlords from all Alliances walked the circular path surrounding the attractive dome above the most massive building in this pretty metropolis. Here, while they strolled along the curved pathway, the day's most critical issues became discussed. The exact location where Nobiel, the council members, and other elite continued enthusiastically singing to God, thanking Him for the new day.

As usual, all activities and air travel were stopped entirely. The song of praise emanating so strongly from the vocal cords of so many angels reverberated among the buildings and connecting pathways.

The night sky remained as pristine as ever. The stars shined spectacularly and were accompanied by two full moons that added to the mysticism of the moment.

Nobiel stayed singing as hard as his lungs would allow him.

♪**"Under Your wings is the city of love.**

Across the sky..." ♪

He suddenly became distracted as he raised his arms and head toward the night sky. From the north, approaching at great speed, a meteor shower began climbing the dark sky; hundreds, perhaps thousands of streaking points of light, shining like the stars, moved toward the zenith. However, unlike meteors, they did not fall or stop; they continued moving south!

Many of the singers stopped as they became as alarmed as he was. Nobiel, without looking down, mentioned to one of the council members standing next to him, *"This is not a meteor shower! ... Those are orbital projectiles or satellites with a shallow trajectory! Possibly, only twenty kilometers high!"*

His companion did not respond.

Nobiel, focusing his eyesight on the moving cloud of brilliant spots, suddenly realized that a second higher mass of smaller dots flying at a higher location was also moving south!

When he focused again, this time on the smaller dots, a cold shiver rumbled through his whole body. Even higher, a third faint cloud of dots also traveled in the same direction... He froze! Something big was happening, but his mind refused to accept it!

A nearby door sliding open caught his attention. From the brighter inside, a Cherub came running out. Colliding with people standing on the pathway, he aimed for Nobiel. His face scared the peace-loving angels looking at his expression; it was a face distorted by the influence of utter panic, sheer terror! Nobiel became very concerned by this angel's action, but before he even reached him, he heard the scream being uttered from his lungs,

"The SA... The SA Matrix is down... And the NA is attacking!"

Nobiel looked at the night sky one more time... At that instant, the view became quite different; this time, he saw thousands of nuclear warheads on their way for the most unthinkable destruction! The next horrifying thought pointed out that they were on the way to slaughter his most precious friends!

He did not realize he had grabbed the 'messenger' by his tunic and started shaking him out of control. Releasing him, Nobiel raised both hands, imploring the Creator.

"Why? Why my loving God? Why did You abandon the ones that love You?"

After screaming, he went mute... He saw the monster of nuclear holocaust above him. It was not even after him or his city... **just passing by!**

Regardless, the terror it inflicted chilled the Seraph to his deepest bones. Out of immense despair, he pulled the Cherub's tunic in front of him again and begged him, *"Please... set a link with SBC; I have to communicate with Gabri-el!"*

Not too far away, standing in the middle of a beautiful terrace on top of the Arts Center Building, Rapha-el addressed a congregation of angels, which included many old friends.

Even when he anticipated the incoming dreadful event, when the message from his command center through his communicating device told him the Matrix had been turned off, he felt a deep and searing pain. His thoughts were not to himself but to his beloved friends, who, at his request, had accepted his invitation with no hesitation. He closed his eyes for a moment; he saw his province's cities and towns, but not the buildings, only the people; his heart bled for them!

He would have done the impossible to spare them from this incoming suffering; nevertheless, he would not question his Creator's choice to bring the faithful to His presence.

The howling of the warning sirens interrupted him!

The friends gathered around him immediately questioned, some vocally, others telepathically.

"What is happening? Are we under attack?"

"Rapha-el, did we lose the Matrix?"

The Overlord looked at them sadly. He quickly responded in a way that all could understand.

"My dear citizens and close friends!
Yes! It is my sad answer to your questions. We have lost our protective umbrella, and the NA is attacking us.

I want to be sincere: without our satellite defense system, we cannot stop all the incoming warheads… Only a few minutes remain before their arrival!"

Fear and panic struck the gathering around the Overlord. Incredulous eyes popped open in disbelief. A cold of fear, which numbs our senses, petrified the angels. Many of them wanted to run; the question remained… to where?

"Please, Great Overlord and friend, help us… Don't let us die!"

They screamed to the Overlord.

Rapha-el called their attention in a powerful burst of mental and verbal interaction.

"My dear friends, calm down! … Since our Lord has decided to call us to His presence, there is nothing I can do to stop the deadly rain from bearing down on us.

Be strong; I beg you to concentrate on what is essential. Let us not disappoint Him with our behavior; we must pray together to focus on His love, which will help us with the strength to discard any fear or anxiety."

Rapha-el's fearless face emphasized his words, his voice had a soothing effect, and the power of his conviction began splitting apart the grip of fear and darkness, he declared.

"Let us show Him that our hearts are fully open to accept His divine gift… and what is happening around us is NOT that important; our souls meeting with His Spirit is the final and ultimate achievement!"

From the north, several flashes comparable to lightning pierced the dark horizon! A reddish glow that appeared like an early sunrise slowly increased in intensity. More lightning strikes followed!

All the angels on the terrace looked in that direction. Even when most felt overwhelmed by the terrifying situation, the panic had vanished.

"Let us hold hands… let us show our love to each other; let us pray to our loving Lord and Creator as if we were just one!" Rapha-el continued.

Sergius, close to Rapha-el, became the first to grab his right hand. From both sides of Rapha-el, an angelic spiral grew until all the people on the top terrace of the Arts Center Building joined together. Sergius addressed the Archangel.

"My dearest friend! There was a time when I became so afraid to live that I was willing to waste my life; however, I am not afraid anymore because of your caring and kindness toward what once was my sick and confused body and mind. With God's help, you pulled me away from the dying… If I lose my life now, I know that it will be for something much better! … My faith in God is very strong because I know a fundamental fact: HE is the ETERNAL LIFE!"

Rapha-el smiled with great satisfaction, squeezing Sergius' hand tighter, and exclaimed, *"Bravo! I could not have said it any better!"*

The city's perimeter facing the north direction came alive. A barrage of laser and plasma cannons pierced the darkness, hunting for falling missiles. Many streaks of bright and pale lights continued climbing from the northern horizon. Many were hit! Small flashes and occasional little balls of fire from great distances above the ground indicated impacts on warheads.

However, there were just too many!

High in the atmosphere, at its zenith, three extremely bright flashes staggered to make it more powerful, generating a tremendous triple magnetic wave that hit the city of Iris!

It caused minor dust and vibration; it fried most electrical circuits!

Rapha-el became the only angel seriously affected by the magnetic wave; as it passed through his body, the powerful surge of energy caused him to squeeze his teeth to almost their breaking point.

Then, the city's lights went off. Partial darkness attenuated by the two moons shining in the night sky was broken by the firing cannons at many points. However, now they were less since most became lost to the magnetic surge generated by the nuclear explosions. Farther away, the bright, massive flashes of light began approaching.

Rapha-el closed his eyes... Out of his body, a blue glow made his six wings shine, as they never had before. The glow merged into both hands, then propagated to the whole angelic spiral, uniting all the minds and bodies into one entity. This conglomerate had no fear or anxiety, only a sublime and peaceful peace of mind; furthermore, they shared only one communal concern: to be ready to receive love directly from its source... from God!

Even when Rapha-el's eyes stayed closed, he saw the missile coming. As it flew very low, it had already penetrated the defense perimeter, aiming directly at the city's heart!

With all the concentration that his being allowed him, with a sublime intensity radiating outwardly, he exclaimed... Actually, since all the present followed his actions as their own, they all exclaimed in unison.

"Dear God... We love You!"

An intense flash of blinding light, escorted by searing heat, abruptly ended this testimony!

In Dawnel, Micha-el grabbed his heart; a great vacuum inside his spirit suddenly emerged. In the middle of the tumultuous wailing warning sirens, sadly and in pain, he exclaimed.

"Rapha-el... I shall not miss you; I am coming to join you!"

Micha-el was not alone. Izma-el's green eyes showed the NA leader what he also felt as he placed his right hand over Micha-el's left shoulder; he responded to the empathetic affection by placing his right hand over his companion's while Mervyn restlessly watched nearby.

All three stood at the main entrance of the Central Building, the headquarters for Micha-el's operations. The Archangel, the leader of the SA, anticipated Mervyn's anxious question, spoke mentally.

"Yes, Mervyn! If you can and still have time to reactivate the Matrix, please do it! However, my friend, do not worry unnecessarily. It is immaterial, and for the place where we are going soon, it will not make a difference!"

Izma-el, understanding the message better than the addressee and sympathetic to reducing anxiety to this great scientist, volunteered.

"Mervyn, I will be glad to help you!"

The scientist, lightly shaking, was pleased by this great offer.

"Thanks! ... Let's hurry up!" He quickly replied.

Micha-el, knowing this was the last time he would see these close friends, said with deep emotion to both.

"So long, my brothers! If you succeed, send the activation code and firing sequence to Gabri-el!"

He said goodbye by touching both open palms separated from the body, first from Izma-el and next to Mervyn. The palm contact stayed much longer than usual.

Three sets of eyes, one blue and two green, with a deep understanding of the priorities, met for one more ecstatic moment.

As the two Cherubs entered the building, one of Dawnel's commanders, followed by an armed platoon, rushed to face Micha-el.

"Great Overlord, please hurry to your vessel. We may have a chance to escape!" The commander telepathically yelled.

Micha-el, while placing both arms on his shoulders, answered.

"My dear friend, the pattern of nuclear bombing on capitals includes a set of peripheral explosions,100 kilometers from the initial ground zero, to prevent the Overlords from escaping. There is no time to get that far! Most importantly, I cannot run away. Soon, my people will arrive looking for my support; if I abandon them, they will panic and scatter in terror!

I am staying; nevertheless, if you still think you can get away, take my vessel and try it! And God be with you!"

The commander hesitated for a moment, fighting his most important duty to preserve the life of his leader; however, he also knew Micha-el. It would be useless to try to change his mind. As the Archangel had anticipated, he decided to try it. As he ran away, Micha-el heard his loud last comment.

"Thank you, Sir! ... And God be with you also!"

A huge and noisy crowd began approaching from all directions. They merged in the location where the Overlord stood tall but alone. The noise level drowned the sirens, and the uncoordinated screaming became deafening. The horror threatening their lives distorted the faces of so many, and all of them yelled.

"Great Overlord, Micha-el!
Please, save us!
Do not abandon us!
Don't let us die!"

CWC, CD, NA; same underground place.

All four Overlords were staring at the main center screen, which showed the progress of nuclear destruction. Like a wave, many dots of light showed the impacts on the SA as they advanced south. Irisan, Graceland, and the B3/B4 islands became devastated!

The leading nuclear-exploding edge continued approaching the borders of Pristeen. Moreover, the most crucial target: Dawnel, where the central command resided... and Micha-el!

The Overlords allowed the highly trained personnel of the base to direct the missile attack. Only when something did not meet their high criteria did they intervene and use a sharp and precise command directed to the officer in charge of such incidental operation.

In the middle of the noisy operation, Azami-el, when noticing that Graceland province resistance reached the edge of collapse, sent a crisp and surgical command that pierced the brains of a nearby officer.

"Reroute backup missile wings 275 and 369 to attack Pristeen from the West!"

The addressee, startled for just an instant, responded with determination.

"Sir! ... It will be done in 5 seconds!"

The screen showing the action in 3-D clearly displayed the attack's three-dimensionality. The tiny clusters of green dots moving in a southern direction inexorably advanced deeper into the SA. Other intermediate and low-flying missile groups reaching their assigned targets turned into bright and wider light spots. Still, even when represented as tiny specs on a display terminal, they announced the death of millions of angels.

The stern faces of the NA Archangels did not show any concern for the lives being consumed in the nuclear holocaust. They had one goal impatiently awaited: the end of Dawnel and his hated leader, Micha-el!

Fourteen seconds had passed since Azami-el's last command. Two groups of many small green dots floating over Graceland changed their direction. They now approached the borders of Pristeen from the west.

SBC, Pristeen, SA; also, 2 Km underground.

Gabri-el and Dani-el remained working in front of the main display. Both showed signs of pain as the provincial capital cities of Iris and New Hope became annihilated. The pain became greater since they also knew that Rapha-el and Samu-el were gone!

Their 3-D display showed the incoming warheads and corresponding explosions, a different layout than the NA, but the facts remained similar. However, one crucial difference existed; for the low-flying missiles, the location of these devices stayed very sketchy. Without satellite information, only a tiny percentage could be located appropriately. Their whereabouts were sorrowfully discovered only in the last instant when a new bright spot illuminated a new zone of destruction!

A small section on the display, at the lower left corner, read.

>**Trillium**

Nobiel → Gabri-el

As Gabri-el accepted the requested message, the same area on the screen showed the concerned face of the council leader of The Core. The image quality stayed sporadic, frequently breaking apart. Nobiel instantly cried out.

"Gabri-el... You --must leave-- -- SBC imm-ediately!
The NA --is -- att--acking!"

The magnetic interference was brutal. Every time Nobiel's voice would break apart, his image on the display would also rip in all directions.

Gabri-el calmly responded.

"My dear friend, please do not worry about me. If it is God's will to take me tonight, just accept the fact that it is not a punishment; it is a reward! With open hands, I will gratefully cross that gate to His Glory. And from there, with all the faithfully departed, we shall wait for the superb moment you will join us!"

Nobiel clinched both hands as shown by the display, sporadically and in a broken manner, his pain accentuated by the ominous interruptions, responded.

"I am--- g-oing to -- --- miss you! ... Why did our Lord- - **choose this- -- way--** *--- to recall His loyal servants?"*

Gabri-el, smiling with compassion to his friend, stated.

"My brother... How we die is not the issue!
But at the instant when we relinquish our spirit, what becomes permanently imprinted in our soul is the ONLY thing that matters!
Will it be Love? Or will it be Hate?
Goodbye, my brother! That Love stays with you, now and forever!"

The Seraph at the other end sadly raised both arms and hands, giving the Overlord the sign for 'goodbye.' Gabri-el equally responded.

The small window to The Core, uniting two friends who shared so many things for so many years... had closed. Gabri-el, showing deep sadness, looked at Dani-el, who responded to a missing question.

"I cannot contact Micha-el; the interference is too great!"

The Overlords noted the sound of two individuals running fast and approaching from the corridor. The distinctive sound of shoes, combined with the approaching sense of two deeply loved angels, alerted them. Their wives, Raquel and Maryen, had hastily arrived!

Their faces showed fear because of the impending mortal danger; however, this fear, felt as a tiny part of themselves, mainly remained directed toward the safety of their husbands.

Both Overlords stood up as their wives plunged into their arms and tightly embraced their loved ones. It was unique, like each couple desired to become one entity.

The Archangels' emphatic abilities quickly absorbed the pain and suffering of their consorts. Gabri-el warmly kissed Raquel on her forehead while sadly stating what Dani-el equally conveyed to Maryen.

"Yes, my love, what you heard is absolutely true!
The NA, with the help of Zeri-el, turned off the Matrix. You already know that we are under attack and in grave danger!"

Raquel's beautiful, slightly larger-than-normal eyes looked up to the Archangel's; she, comforted by his powers, knew they only had a few minutes left to live! When she spoke telepathically, her strong mental message said.

"My beloved husband... When God is in my soul, and you are at my side, I have <u>nothing</u> to fear!"

Dawnel, Pristeen, SA.

An intense bright light, high in the night sky, illuminated the city. When it gradually dissipated, darkness surrounded the buildings, now void of electrical energy. The moons bathed the towering structures close to the zenith with a silvery tint. Sporadic reflections from the buildings' tops heralded what appeared to be a still-distant lightning storm!

A weird purplish tint remained suspended in the sky above the city. Most of the stationary stars and the ones moving south now looked reddish. Even the moons' surfaces turned to blood.

Micha-el looked above; the colors stayed the same as in his dreams. Along with a vast crowd, he was on his way to the central plaza. Yet, unlike the dreams, the crowd did not drag him; he remained in control!

Like a good shepherd, he led his citizens to meet their earned destiny. The multitude grew exponentially; it resembled a giant magnet pulling angels from all directions, all wanting help, all in dire need of support and guidance. Their leader did not abandon them; he personally took them to the place of exaltation.

From across the street, a couple went directly to Micha-el. The Archangel recognized them; before the male angel had time to open his mouth, he greeted him.

"Eugenius, I am glad to see you again! I can also see that you married this beautiful angel named Claire!"

The two angels were practically shaking with fear from the unexpected terror. Somehow surprised that Micha-el recognized him, Eugenius exclaimed.

"Great Overlord! You still remember me?"

"Of course, my friend. However, I sense that fear has invaded both of your minds and is tormenting you. Let me help you!"

As Micha-el touched both angels on their shoulders with his hands, they felt an immense relief.

It is the same as when you are shaking on a freezing night, and somebody offers you a warm cup of coffee or blanket; the soothing and warming effect makes your day.

"Time is short, my friends," Micha-el spoke, and after a short pause, continued, *"Please, join us in our short journey to the central plaza. This time, even when I cannot save your lives, what you can expect in return is much more important. To this moment of darkness and horror, rejoice!*

The source of light and love is near... My dear friends, we are on our way to meet our CREATOR!"

Next, addressing the whole congregation, his voice powerfully rebounded on the street alleys.

"My brothers and sisters… follow me!"

In the center of the plaza, where the centered podium stood as a statement, Micha-el climbed the steps to its top surface. As he did, he looked at the three massive round pillars towering into the night sky: the central skyscrapers at the plaza's edge. A completely coalescent view of the incoming events became evident in his mind. The symbols, which in his first dream caused anxiety and concern, became part of the stairway to Heaven!

Micha-el smiled at their sight; he was even glad to see them again. Unlike those dots of light ominously moving closer to bring death and destruction, an incoming single light immensely more powerful than all the others combined brought the good angels just the opposite.

The leader of the SA turned around to face the vast crowd. His piercing blue eyes scanned the many faces hungry to hear his voice, hoping to be saved from descending oblivion by a divine miracle. Yet, he mostly sensed… FEAR!

As the uncountable many begged for help, a murmur grew into a muffled roar. Micha-el smiled since his heart extruded empathy. He raised his open hands fast and high. The crowd understood and became silent.

Micha-el proceeded to announce the good news.

"My dear citizens!
Once more, we gathered at this plaza like so many times before, where we had expressed our concerns and love for each other. Even more important, it has been an altar where we had worshiped our Lord; therefore, it is the ideal location for our last meeting!"

Micha-el gazed into the hungry eyes, looking for help. What he proposed was not what they initially expected but something much better, with innate inspiration, he said.

"I know that you are expecting me to help you, but my cherished citizens and friends, the help you are so ardently looking for is already part of you! … Look inside your hearts and minds, inside your souls, for the God you love so much… He is in you! He has not abandoned you! He has always been with you!
Since the moment you were conceived and became an Angel, you were waiting for this instant. This is not a time to be afraid of the dark or the incoming terror; this is a time to rejoice!"

A million eyes stared at Micha-el; the fear inside them began fading away. A gentle but inherently powerful breeze blew it away! The hand of God, working through Micha-el, appeased their spirits.

This dynamic Overlord never looked so impressive; he was a beacon of energy overflowing from his soul with such intensity that he could reach the unreachable!

The not-so-faint glow from both moons lit the otherwise dark plaza with an iridescent radiance, which made the Archangel visible to everybody... The flashes of light continued getting closer.

After a brief pause, he added.

"Get ready to meet your Creator. Throw away all those fears caused by the presence of the unknown. Look at this incoming door, called 'death,' in a positive way because whatever you are when you cross it is what you will be <u>forever</u>!

We are fighting a war, not between the North and the South, but between Good and Evil, and you, as individuals, are about to win it!

Detach yourselves from all your material concerns and possessions, including your own lives, because they are material and finite. We are about to start a new era where all that is material has no place for being... it has no value!

This era will become a spiritual journey through the Universe and Eternity. Most importantly, it will include seeing God as He is... Our minds cannot even imagine the sight or the meaning of this divine event!"

Using his Overlord powers, Micha-el saw the white dot above the night sky without turning to look. Like the other countless dots adorning the sky, it was there but moving. It split into a cluster of smaller dots. Most of the smaller dots moved away outwardly.

One didn't. It sat still and started to grow. He knew it was coming straight down to the plaza!

His face lightened up, his eyes gleamed in the deepest blue, and his six wings glowed to incandescence. The bulging of his muscles stretched to their maximum, outlining his extraordinary physical conditioning. This time, when his voice came out, it was overwhelming.

"Time is short; prepare your spirits to meet your Lord!"

Looking directly at the incoming nuclear warhead, his palms projecting upwards by the maximum extension of his arms, he screamed with all the power of his lungs!

"GOD OF LOVE AND LIGHT! MY BODY, MY MIND, AND MY SOUL ALL BURN WITH THE DESIRE TO MEET YOU!"

A bright light illuminated the plaza. For just an instant, a cross became visible. Then, a blinding flash of intense light turned the night brighter than the day

[100x]> It burned everything in sight!

Under the searing nuclear reaction heat, Micha-el's eyeballs and flesh vaporized instantly. At this first millisecond of the blast, despite the blinding flash, upwardly emerging out of the charring body of the Archangel was an ethereal silhouette glowing with an immaculate white; it moved up like being pulled by an invisible hand!

Equally alike on or near the plaza, a million angels displayed their pure white glowing spirits, more beautiful than their original bodies; they ascended toward the high skies and away from their now carbonized remains. Only a few milliseconds later, the 20-megaton thermonuclear shock wave reduced the angels' remains to microscopic dust!

Next, in slow motion, it could be seen when the ground and all nearby skyscrapers, already bursting in flames, were blown away into unrecognizable debris!

As the shock wave rebounded from the ground, it lifted enough dirt to create a crater several kilometers wide. With all its dust-collected additions, the shock wave promptly joined the immense fireball racing for the stratosphere! <[100x]

A slick and shiny aircraft speeding away from Dawnel continued accelerating tremendously. It was Micha-el's craft, the best in the SA.

The commander, who had just asked Micha-el to run for his life, looked out of a window toward the shrinking downtown area when the big flash engulfed the city. The transparent window of the craft must have been made from a transitional material sensitive to light, which automatically darkened the surface. It prevented the pilots and passengers from becoming blind in the event of a nuclear blast.

His heart almost stopped when his beloved city burst on fire from the searing heat escorting the intense thermonuclear flash. As the city's central area vaporized and a giant mushroom ball of fire roared upwards, it was preceded by several massive lightning strikes to the ground. The shock wave moved radially outward, destroying most of what remained of the city in its devouring path!

As the commander lowered his head in deep pain, he partially opened his mouth to let out a low and sad moan. At that same instant, another nuclear explosion released a new diabolic horror!

Ground zero was so close that it shattered the flying cylinder windows and practically melted its metal exterior! Compared to the mammoth new expanding infernal ball consuming everything standing in its way, for only a fraction of a second, the crew inside the craft lived to see their craft blown away into a much smaller fireball!

Five nuclear blasts covered the outside perimeter of the city. Joining the first blast, all six blazing giant mushrooms climbed upwards, illuminating the whole region of devastation! The interaction of their shock waves sent pieces of buildings flying aimlessly, like a giant ocean riptide destroying once... Destroying all over again!

Angels, like us humans, could release the monster of nuclear war, the intense horror, the enormous destruction, and the immense casualties. It even seemed better to die in the attack than to survive and live in new horrors due to radiation poisoning and starvation. Perhaps, even seeing the terror of the survivors being hunted, plus the oblivion of seeing your family and country… gone!

It may be the closest thing resembling Hell on our planets.

For the good angels who died in the hell of nuclear war, they only experienced it for an instant! Would the attacking angels of the North Alliance experience it for an ETERNITY?

CWC, CD, NA; 2 Km underground.

Like a giant magnet, the main screen had all eyes drawn to its display. In vivid detail, it showed the progress of the nuclear holocaust inside the SA. The real-time acquisition system revealed six bursts over Dawnel.

Even the Overlords screamed, *"YESSS!"*

The edge of destruction had overcome the capital city of the SA. For them, Micha-el's death became equivalent to the statement: **The war was already won!**

The three Overlords from the back screen noisily joined the event, congratulating each other. The base was momentarily a mad house; however, when Lucif-er extended his right hand up, the roar almost died instantly; he loudly spoke to all present.

"Finish them; then, we celebrate!"

He immediately addressed the other Overlords with a satanic smile and telepathically commented with a personal group message.

"We did it! … We killed Micha-el!"

Induced by the immense pleasure of an enemy's death, he glutted into a sadistic trance. Then, he loudly exclaimed, mainly to himself.

"Micha-el, you carbonized piece of garbage! … Did your god help you? Where was he? He would have never allowed anything to happen to you if he existed! You would be alive if you had taken my offer to join me! Or… maybe not!"

He laughed maliciously. The other three Overlords in the place joined him with similar enthusiasm. Azami-el, after analyzing the data being displayed, made an excited remark.

"Lucif-er! Look at the warhead video data!

The recording shows a large crowd in Dawnel's central plaza. Somebody is addressing them… It is an Overlord! It must be Micha-el! We dropped one nuke right on top of his head!"

"He ate it!" Gorgon-el jokingly resounded.

Again, all burst laughing!

Lucif-er placed a hand on Azami-el's shoulder. The latter was already anticipating his boss's unspoken praise. His eyes opened widely when a searing pain ripped his shoulder; Lucif-er suddenly got dead serious and almost crushed it!

All three Overlords facing the leader of the NA stared at his blue eyes; they saw them turning to fire as an uncontrollable rage burst out of the Overlord. Typically, it was impossible to read Lucif-er's mind, but this time, the intensity and fury of his thoughts emerged so loud that they overflowed his tight mental shell!

In unison, the other three Overlords inside the base turned their heads at lightning speed and stared at the frontal left screen.

The indicator light for the SA 4-D Matrix Defense System was...
RED!

A chilling silence froze all the personnel in the base... and the three participants even beyond. For the second time in their lives, the seven Overlords had a taste of fear!

The operators closer to the Archangels trembled at the rage from their leaders; even death by a nuclear explosion remained less intimidating. After all, the menacing fury next to them could mean instant death! Meagerly, even afraid to look at Lucif-er and the rest of their leaders, they went nervously back to their jobs.

The NA's leader approached the point of spitting fire. His distorted face, bursting muscles, and almost flaming 12 wings made him look like a malevolent dragon! He would have leveled the place, but he knew he needed the instrumentation and the supporting staff... He turned the heat off... he kept the hate!

Magog-el, violently shaking a pillar, asked.

"Zeri-el destroyed the Matrix program! The main computer in Dawnel is gone! ... What is going on?"

Lucif-er did not answer; he became introspective. After a second, he ordered something from the central computer. The 4-D Matrix program covering about half of the left screen became displayed as an overlay; its three-dimensionality was accurately drawn.

For six seconds, he stared at the basic program modules. His powerful mind must have been working in overdrive; nobody dared to interrupt him!

Quick like lightning, his closed fist hit the same supporting beam that Magog-el had previously shaken. A loud 'thud' shook the adjacent area. Minute pieces of debris flying rapidly fell around the same adjoining area. Squeezing his teeth, he remarked with anger.

"It makes sense... NOW!
All those extra handles for the Matrix Supervisor program were not there to support additional future programs; the program was already there! ... Rotten Mervyn! He did install a second supervisory program with an invisible hyperlink! And because it was connected to the main program, only with handles, which do not allow transfer of 'search and destroy X-nodules,' it was left untouched!"

"I said it before!" exclaimed Magog-el, *"Why did we not kill him?"*

Azami-el felt like killing somebody but could not since the boss refrained from doing it. In desperation, he pulled his hair hard with both hands. The pressure of impending death grew overwhelming; he decided to drift to the nearest exit. Suddenly, he sensed the dagger-sharp stare of Lucif-er, and he also mentally heard.

*"That is **not** a good idea! What is your problem Azami-el? Is it getting too hot for you?"* Lucif-er said cynically, and he continued almost instantly.

*"If you mention, 'We could have a better chance to survive outside!' It could be the stupidest thing that you ever said. You know there are 10 to 1 odd in favor of surviving... **if you stay here!**"*

"OK!" Admitted Azami-el while rejoining the group, but he still felt like a caged wild animal.

Gorgon-el, showing his trademark foxy look as he faked a false 'cool' attitude, pointed his right-hand menacing fist at an invisible enemy and questioned, *"The main computer was destroyed! Did Mervyn have time to transfer command to Gabri-el?"*

Lucif-er just gave him a **'What do you think?'** look.

Gorgon-el made an ugly face to himself and hit his forehead with an open hand. If the Matrix was reactivated, he must have the time. Fear started clouding his usually high intellectual abilities.

Azami-el barked an order to nearby officers and leading operators.

"Reprogram Centrum defenses! Not the city, but WE at this base have ALL priorities!"

"Yes, Sir!" They immediately responded.

The bad guys began sweating now. The monster they had unleashed on the SA was now poised to devour them... equally unmercifully! Only a moment ago, they exploded celebrating a big triumph; now, their lives, seemingly eternal to live, lingered at risk of being diminished to only a few minutes long!

Even if they could survive the nuclear attack, the NA would be devastated; not many subordinates would be left to give orders. No more cities... actually, no more NA! Their fate could be like Dawnel's citizens; their bodies could be reduced to smoldering chunks of charcoal in a few minutes!

Returning all his attention to the main screen displaying the advancing wall of fire approaching the last main center of resistance, SBC, Lucif-er, full of violent animosity, exploded with his naked vile intentions; his telepathic message conveyed his enormous hate.

"Gabri-el!... You soft-bellied politician!

Think about me, who used to be your 'brother'! Think about all the billions of lives you can kill by pushing one button! Think about the garbage that radiates from your heart, and you call it LOVE!"

While projecting all his hate outwardly, he yelled.

"Gabri-el, you bastard! Don't touch the Matrix firing button!"

SBC, Pristeen, SA; still 2 Km underground.

A bright dot illuminated the screen location of Dawnel. Both Archangels present lowered their heads and closed their eyes; the pain became real and merciless. At an angle, the tips of Gabri-el's right-hand fingers touched Dani-el's left-hand fingers. They communicated to each other the painful fact: at this moment, they became the only two surviving Overlords of the SA; not long ago, Lari-el's life was extinguished!

They turned to console their consorts. Gabri-el looked into the moist-ridden, wide-open, beautiful aquamarine eyes; he saw the ominous but small dot of light reflected from their surfaces as they stared at the electronic display showing a nuclear explosion. At the next moment, there were six dots. Gabri-el did not glance back to the screen; he knew about the nuclear cluster bombing.

"My God... Micha-el is gone!" Raquel exclaimed with deep sadness.

"Oh my Lord, I can't believe what I see!" Maryen closely followed.

Raquel embraced her husband, burying her pretty head into one of his shoulders, she lamented.

"Micha-el is gone! ... I already miss him so much! ... I should rejoice because he went to meet God, but I feel more pain than joy!"

Gabri-el, while caressing her long and silky hair, remarked.

"My love! I completely understand your feelings; they are identical to mine!"

Something happened in the upper right-hand corner of the main display. This time, both Overlords turned around and quickly returned to the computer controls. The Matrix Defense System had been reactivated! A brief message tagged along read:

"My brothers, as per Micha-el's instructions, the Matrix controls have been rerouted to SBC. Yours will be the final decision on whether to counterattack.

I have no time left. My Lord is requesting my presence, and I am ready. This is no farewell... until soon!

Izma-el."

As the message disappeared and two sets of boxes requesting the Archangels' DNA for an ID replaced the text, Gabri-el responded.

"My brother, go to the presence of God!
Dani-el and I will be joining you soon!"

Maryen, somehow excited and hopeful, quickly asked.

"The Matrix has been reactivated! ... Does this mean we will survive?"

Dani-el gently rubbed her face while looking deeply into her hopeful eyes, and he answered.

"No, my precious, 80% of our ground defenses are gone! Even with the help of the satellite network, we will now destroy many more of the

incoming missiles, but not all. Our defense space has been seriously compromised; it is too late for a fix!"

She lowered her eyes further, saddened by a hopeful wish not materializing. Raquel moved closer to her for direct physical and mental support.

Right then, Gabri-el intercepted a message directed at him, but it had not yet been mentally spoken. It was from one of the nearby operators, it would have said.

"Sir! The aircraft moving to the South Pole and away from Zarinia will be out of range in just two minutes!"

In his brain, before he had time to convey the message, he heard Gabri-el's acknowledgment, *"Thanks, I got it!"*

Both Archangels placed their right hand, palm open, facing the screen. A laser read their DNA code, and the computer responded.

Matrix connection to Automatic Nuclear Offense > READY
Maximum Security Scan   > OK
All super-lattice projections   > DONE
Target acquisition systems   > LOCKED
Firing sequence   > ACTIVE
Code: N SW [E+W] NE [NW+SE] S >C; Time: <0.1 Second

A bright red blinking switch array with the four cardinal positions plus the in-between locations and a **C** for the center and activating button became visible. All the eight switches and **C** were to be manually operated in the proper sequence and inside the time limit; only an Overlord was fast enough to do it. The power to unleash the destruction of a continent, a whole Alliance, billions of lives, all at the fingertips of an Archangel! ... All in one single switch!

Gabri-el glanced at the ominous device in front of him. If he had a temptation to use the power at his fingertips to get even with the NA's brutal attack, he remained immune to it!

He did not activate it. Instead, he sent a message to the operator tracking the cylinder flying south.

"Request an ID! Give him 10 seconds to respond!"

A medium-built and stocky Overlord, Zeri-el, concentrating on the current craft's location as displayed by a frontal screen, became excited; he was about to reach a safe distance from the SA defense artillery. While squeezing his frontal teeth, he exclaimed to himself.

"Just 200 seconds, and it is goodbye to all of you, suckers!"

He smiled because he was very pleased with himself. He thought how cunning he had been; single-handedly, he had sabotaged the SA's main defenses. Lucif-er would have no choice but to give him the best reward available in the NA, and of course, he would accept all the power available to the Northern Overlords but non-existent in the SA. This alone was worth it all!

A sound triggered by a message just received called his immediate attention.

SA SBC Main Command
Visual ID requested. You have 10 seconds to respond.

Zeri-el cursed the message on the display. He decided to stall; he was so close to being out of range. Caused by the rage at being threatened, his green eyes saw blood.

He glanced at the cylinder controls set for the aircraft's maximum attainable speed. It could not extract any extra juice from the engines without placing them in a risky and overloaded condition.

He did nothing... except wait.

The SBC operator announced without taking his eyes off his screen. *"No response, Sir!"*

Gabri-el let the message be delivered even when he knew it before being emitted; he calmly said, *"Thank you, Octavius! Please reroute control to the main screen; I will take over this operation!"*

In a snap, a new electronic window opened in front of Gabri-el; he immediately sent a new request to the speedily moving away vessel.

"This is Gabri-el.

Zeri-el, I know you are there; I am sure you will be glad to know that The Matrix has been reactivated.

You already know that we have positive satellite tracking of your craft. To respond, these are your last ten seconds!"

Zeri-el eyes opened in disbelief after reading the message.

"It is not possible! You must be bluffing, you rotten bastard!" He screamed furiously.

His breathing and heartbeat suddenly increased. He stared at the very last displayed line. A cold feeling ran down his spine; he did not like this feeling at all. This was not allowable for an Overlord, and he felt extremely disturbed.

A new line read.

SA Plasma Cannon.
Targeting Telemetry's condition on this craft: LOCKED

He paused for a few seconds to control the disturbing furor blazing inside him; he forced himself to look peaceful on his outside skin. Telepathically, he pushed the connecting video communication button.

The stern faces of Gabri-el and Dani-el appeared on the control screen; behind them were the inquisitive looks of their female companions, who had difficulty keeping pace with the fast communication rate.

He ignored the females and locked his vision with both Overlords. He stated calmly but somehow evasively.

"Greetings, my brothers! What is the meaning of this threat?"

Dani-el's index finger pointed harshly toward Zari-el's image; utterly disgusted, he burst out through an electronic transmission.

"You treacherous coward, you do not know how hard it is to stop me from erasing you from the sky.

You did something evil when sentencing billions of beings to a fiery death! ... You, who was loved and cherished as a brother!

Is there no guilt, remorse, or compassion left in your soul?

Lucky for you, I cannot hate you, but I do feel pity for you."

Gabri-el added, in a superimposed manner.

"Tell us, Zeri-el. What did Lucif-er offer you that is worth the lives of so many? Perhaps... the power of being a god?"

At his craft, the accused remained silent, but only momentarily; he finally exploded to justify himself as he sent the following message.

"Yes, he offered me much more than Micha-el ever dreamed.

You, as Overlords of the SA, live in a rigid cage constructed by your non-existing god and _that_ which you call 'love.' You have no freedom... You have no courage to win this war. Micha-el was too weak to lead the SA; therefore, you had no chance... I feel sorry for you!"

Gabri-el's soft look became a piercing emerald stare like the jewel of his eyes being enhanced by a thousand spotlights. Very serious but in a milder tone, he telepathically sent his answer to the transmitting machine first.

"Your concept of winning is all wrong! The hate inside you has clouded your mind; consequently, you have chosen one instant of glory instead of a much greater Eternity!

Zeri-el! Do not feel sorry for us; we truly do it for you. You have chosen the wrong team; you are the big loser!

Let me share a symbol on my screen with you. I am sure... you will know what it means!"

Gabri-el raised his left hand, with its flat palm facing Zeri-el's vision path. Its shape rippled for an instant; then it became a shiny mirror, like looking through a fish-eye optical lens that, in its reflection, Zeri-el could see the whole main screen, including his own image. Nevertheless, something else caught his horrified attention!

A red blinking array; the Matrix nuclear attack activation button...

It was armed!

Zeri-el froze!

He felt like standing at the edge of an abyss; if the NA were also gone, all he had done would have been for nothing!

Gabri-el's mirror undulated again; his hand became non-reflective, and he put it down. As more words came out of Gabri-el's mouth, Zeri-el appeared to be in a trance, and the words coming out of his mouth did not sound the same. Gabri-el continued.

"You can see how easily the horror being unleashed on the SA could be reproduced on the NA! ... Since we cannot hate, not even Lucif-er, we cannot hate you either. Not even the unthinkable act that you have committed against our nation could allow us to tarnish our hands with your blood, especially now when we are so close to meeting our loving Father!

We will let you go because we believe our Lord will dispense the ultimate justice!"

Back to Zeri-el's craft, the image on the screen went blank. He remained staring at the place where he had communicated with the last two Overlords of the SA. He could not believe Gabri-el's previous statement. Did he mean what he said? He remained deeply disturbed as he stared at the screen, now reading.

Craft condition: UNLOCKED
Craft now out of range.

Zeri-el had a sadistic smile on his face; he exclaimed.

"You stupid Overlords! If you had done the same to me, I would have removed all the flesh attached to your bones, one tiny piece at a time!"

The smile disappeared from his face. The concept of the NA perishing in the war chilled his bones. He quickly evaluated his options, and then, suddenly illuminated by a great decision, he retorted.

"If the NA is gone, I will fly to Trillium and tell them that I was the only survivor from the Overlords of the SA. The morons will believe in me, and I will be the only Archangel on the planet with plenty of servants! Either way, I still would possess the power I rightly deserve!"

A vicious but shaky laugh filled the front cabin of the cylinder.

Still, at the center screen, Gabri-el and Dani-el stayed seated, spearheading the last SA defense against the incoming nuclear tidal wave; alongside, all personnel in the base worked feverishly to stop the holocaust.

The Overlords' wives stood behind their husbands, precariously hanging from their powerful torsos with the tips of their fingers. They prayed in silence, hoping for a miracle!

The Archangels operated the consoles' controls at blinding speeds, pushing the instruments to their maximum capacities; they were ready to do the impossible.

To the left section of the screen, a tactical display of SBC surroundings covering a circular area of about 300 kilometers in diameter showed many warheads penetrating the perimeter. As they attacked the previous cities, they stayed layered in three levels: One high-altitude group, an intermediate cluster, and the low-altitude group hiding or hugging the ground around hills and canyons. Indeed, there were so many!

To the right, another large portion of the huge central screen now displayed the surface above the underground control of the SBC Defense system. The storm blowing with hurricane force hardly allowed the lighted nearby structures to be visible from the entrance location.

Snow was falling, but almost horizontally. Howling with furor, the wind blew any loose particles in its path to the North. It appeared this massive blizzard wanted to repel the attacking warheads and push them back to their origins!

The Overlords looked one last time at the ominous red blinking nuclear attack activating switch in the center of the screen, a button that could erase the NA from the face of the planet! For an instant, their eyes met... After exchanging a torrent of mutual emotions, an agreement was reached about something devoid of hate. Even when the murderous and vicious attack on the SA continued raging over their heads, the destruction of the NA would have solved nothing. The war was lost, and the act of retaliation to get even could not save them anyway; therefore, they decided to allow billions of citizens from the Northern Alliance to live. Even Lucif-er, the foremost cause of such evil unleashed on Terra, became spared!

After all, God is love, but He is equally just. He will dispense His divine justice in a way comprehended by Him alone!

When the Overlords returned to the controls, only a fraction of a second remained before the plasma, laser cannons from the base, and the satellite network in space started a barrage of fire. As displayed on the frontal screen, they began intercepting many incoming dots.

From space, the 4-D Matrix looked awesome; laser and plasma blasts rained toward the lowest section of the continent. They did not miss their moving targets.

Sadly, one-third of the world could be seen on fire from above. Inside the burning SA, many new lightning flashes coalesced together to resemble an ocean of iridescent blood; it illuminated the darkened side of Terra with a reddish glow.

With so many missiles destroyed, two holes appeared in the cloud of attacking devices. Unfortunately, either by targeting programs or by accidentally exploding nuclear bombs, thermonuclear explosions filled the holes just created. Each explosion generated a vast magnetic field blocking the area from electronic detection. New warheads would penetrate the same perimeter, but they would be undetected. In effect, these holes in the surveillance remained lost ground for the defense systems.

It would take precious minutes before the same area was available for proper scanning again. By then, it would be too late! The base personnel

watched with horror as the diameter of defense was reduced to 100 km...
and then to 60 km.

The screen section showed the upper outside world being besieged by
what appeared to be a terrific electrical storm. Even the density of the
naturally occurring raging storm did not impede the intensity of the bright
nuclear flashes, which pierced the darkness, making it much brighter than
daylight. The nearby illuminated buildings seemed to emulate strange
monsters ready to attack and crush the survivors.

The underground SA personnel did not wait too long for the monster
to arrive; only seen through the screen, an intense white light flashed inside
the underground complex! It was like a strobe light that froze everybody
in time, except for the two Overlords who twisted with pain!

Two kilometers above, ground zero was not far away! The blinding
light and enormous heat set the whole complex on the surface afire. It also
evaporated the adjacent snow and nearby clouds, creating a hole in the
raging blizzard from the South Pole.

Only seconds later, the shock wave raced furiously across the land. It
ripped the buildings to pieces, resembling a giant sledgehammer smashing
everything in its path.

An enormous ball of fire raced to the dark sky. It was a malevolent
mushroom of destruction, with its center stem pulling dust and debris from
the ground and projecting them at great speed through its core, aiming for
the stratosphere.

Its outer ring of fire rolled from the inside edge to the outside edge over
the top and back to the rising stem from the bottom. In this manner, the
stem continued to feed the monster of fire as it grew projected above the
clouds. Even at great heights, bright tongues of fire still rolled along with
the rubble in a donut-like circular rotation.

As the smoke and dust cleared from the ground, a few fragmented
pieces of the nearby buildings remained visible, smoke and fire gushing
from their damaged guts.

On a lonely remaining wall, on what once was a shiny and pretty
surface, a dark tree-like silhouette now adorned its smoldered and charred
remains. The shape of a twisted trunk projected upwards on the vertical
flat surface, close to the top of the silhouette, two upward branches also
twisted and convoluted, each ending in five skinny and long protuberances
pointing upwards... Was this the silhouette of a tree? Or, on the other
hand, was it perhaps the remaining shadow of an angel, the grotesque
memory of an individual who stayed alive only a few minutes ago?

A sparse but fine dust began falling from the ceiling two kilometers
below the surface. Several terminals had failed and were sparking from
electrical failures, with smoke spiraling up from their guts. The Complex

Defense lighting system decreased to about 50%, but plenty of light remained. The computer's main center screen no longer displayed the 3-D position of the attacking warheads; instead, it read in blinking red lights.

WARNING

Ground Base telemetry > Not responding.

Satellite communication > Terminated.

Some of the local instrumentation above ground must have been heavily shielded because they survived the nuclear blast. A few of the visuals on the surface stayed on but remained very grainy.

Standing, the Overlords faced their wives and held them tightly against their bodies.

The place became noisy as panic began settling upon the underground personnel. Dani-el stepped up on a nearby counter, taking Maryen up with him like she did not weigh anything. With a commanding voice so that everyone would understand, he exclaimed.

"Please! Calm down!"

As the noise quickly died out, he continued in a lower tone.

"My dear brothers! Be strong; God has not abandoned us!" While holding his bride with his left hand, he extended his right index finger, pointing high to emphasize his moral point.

"Love eliminates fear... Perfect Love eliminates ALL fears!

If you know that God loves you... You have NOTHING to fear!

Open your hearts to our Lord and let us rejoice!" Dani-el exclaimed.

The tone and emphasis in his voice must have been infused with a potion. All the angels working in the place instantly calmed down. Some looked up in ecstasy, others closed their eyes to visualize the metaphysical, and the rest just looked down in meditation and prayer; every angel in this place communed with the Creator in their own unique way!

Maryen raised her deep purple eyes to her husband. Her fluffy blond hair, covered with dust, looked grayish as if she would look like an older angel; however, she exclaimed with great zest.

"I love you Dani-el... Please, hold me tightly!"

The Archangel gently kissed her on the lips. While still holding her, he stepped down from the counter.

A close-by officer, whom Dani-el had previously addressed with the name Octavius, serenely indicated to Gabri-el in an astonishingly calm tone due to the enormous consequences of his message.

*"Sir! My local instruments detect a warhead locked in our coordinates! It will arrive soon! ... **Praise the Lord, Sir!"***

Gabri-el, already staring at the outside window provided by the now noisy and defective video monitor, lifted his eyes from the tiny shiny dot fixed over the purplish but dark sky. This dot had been increasing in brightness as it got closer. He gently locked his vision with the Seraph and promptly exclaimed.

"Thank you, Octavius! And God be with you, <u>forever!</u>"

A delicate and gentle hand caressed Gabri-el's face. The most melodious telepathic message that anyone could generate in the world filled his mind with what he loved the most on this planet, of course, with God's exception... Raquel! He heard her mental voice while her moist lips moved closer to his cheek. He knew she carried a grave concern inside her mind, but she expressed herself with incredible self-assurance while projecting the kind of outside support only possible from Archangels.

"My dear husband... I am not afraid!

I cannot possibly ask for anything more than to die in your loving arms. Take me across this door called Death to the Light and Love of our Creator. Then, bound by love, we can worship Him for Eternity... together!"

Gabri-el took a last look at that angelic face so perfectly shaped that it attained the utmost possible loveliness. It was still his to admire and deeply love for a very short instant. It seemed like a million memories poured in a second, streamed like a vast and powerful waterfall pouring into all the intricate passages in his brain and equally in his mind. It turned into an instant résumé of thousands of years, of thousands of excellent memories. God has been so good for blessing him to be her husband. It was unlikely that anyone else could have experienced a greater love than his.

A tender and caring message came out from him.

"My dearest love!" He mentally spoke while taking a deep breath, *"For a last time, kiss me; then, you should concentrate on that divine gift called Love, which unites us so tenderly. Afterward, do not think about me; think about our Lord! Then, as you rightfully stated, together, we shall present our souls to our Creator!"*

As both vocally and mentally, said.

"I will love you forever!" Their moist and warm lips sealed the promise with a feeling not equated in their lives before. It turned into the maximum that life could have offered: **one instant... worth a lifetime?**

As his soul prepared for the Almighty, Gabri-el had one last thought propagating externally. Even when it was mentally loud, it remained a respectful action focusing on his Creator.

"Life, how long should it be?
A few years, centuries, millenniums... Even a million years?

Regardless of length, it always reaches an end; it always seems to be too short. It is like the instant we are facing now, where there is no future for our earthly lives anymore. At this moment, the only thing that matters is <u>how</u> we lived such lives; without a doubt, they should have been according to the will of our Creator.

You, who are so generous to me, I could not even envision any possibility for my existence without my compliance with your great love!

Please, accept my humble soul in your presence!"

A blinding flash illuminated the screen portion, showing the upper outside section of the base, now mostly ruins. Almost instantly, it became black!

For a dreaded fraction of a second, nothing happened; nobody moved.

The underground structure was ripped into many pieces. Searing light, enormous heat, a roar, and a pulverizing blast invaded the last SA outpost.

It happened so fast that we had to see it in a much-slowed motion to obtain an idea of this last instant.

[100x]> Visually, ten milliseconds are as long as one second.

As the walls cracked with an ominous shriek, the vaporizing hot and intense light blazed its way into the underground base. The petrified motionless angels' bodies suddenly appeared to be skeletons standing up, as the immensely brilliant light made the rest of their tissues transparent!

This image lasted only briefly. An instant later, their body surfaces started to smoke and vaporize; soon, they would become charred and carbonized remains! However, as their bodies decayed and burned, their spirits became brighter and ethereally more beautiful. Dressed in iridescent white tunics, they separated from the remains of their earthly bodies. Free now, they ascended to claim their place next to the Divine Being who created them in His image!

Two couples led them. One pair stayed tightly embraced. The other, undisturbed by the inferno around them, was still tenderly kissing; their great love transcended all material disturbances since the Essence of God lived in their spirits.

Nothing was strong enough to unsettle such Presence!

A horrifying shock wave erased it from view by grinding it to dust! <[100x]

A cluster of three more nuclear warheads fell over SBC. Before they exploded, nothing remained but ruins and immense craters on the baked ground ... they did not care!

Three enormous balls of fire ripped the devastated landscape, carving new larger craters with furious and violent fire. More ashes were formed, and dust became reduced to finer dust!

Three immense mushroom-shaped fireballs raced to test which one would climb higher. They shined, roared, and evaporated the nearby clouds; eventually, they dissipated their rage into the dark domains of the night.

Gradually, the clouds and hurricane-force winds from the South Pole returned. The pyrotechnic displays had interrupted their own show, but they were back!

The skies above locked into darkness. The hot surfaces on the ground quickly cooled down. It took some time, but eventually, rain first, and snow next started to fall again. The wind howled once more as if countless souls began screaming with pain!

The storm seemed ashamed of the happening and tried to cover it up by hiding it from sight. It knew that a very short time ago, a pretty city was located on this site, and one hundred thousand angels populated its glistening buildings.

Now, a barren and lifeless land remained!

Lucif-er's underground base was silent. The large screens in front of all personnel occupying its interiors showed that SBC had been destroyed... However, nobody began celebrating! All continued staring at the Matrix's red blinking sign, still petrified.

Lucif-er broke the quietness. With a sadistic smile, the leader of the NA burst out loudly.

"You, boneless slime... You couldn't do it!"

As the roar of his powerful voice echoed through the cavities of the underground complex, everybody else screamed with euphoria. They finally realized that the nuclear warheads did not rain over their heads; now, pandemonium reigned unabashed at this location. Their fear became replaced with a much larger joyful celebration for victory.

Seconds later, Azami-el ordered one of the officers, jumping with jubilation, *"Reroute all remaining missiles to secondary targets!"*

The officer stopped his articulated celebration immediately, but with a broad smile remaining on his face, he enthusiastically responded.

"Sir! It will be done, immediately!"

With a loud thud, all four Overlords in this place connected their right-hand fists just for a second to symbolize a great victory.

The other three Overlords outside the compound, seen through the video screens, joined the festivity; Kroma-el, squeezing his short hair along his temples, announced with great satisfaction.

"The armies will be moving to attack positions!"

"Right now, I will allow our citizens to leave the shelter areas!" Ezek-el said with an almost overlapping message.

After Lucif-er sent away his three subordinates from the outside, present only electronically, he stared at Azami-el, who replaced his power rifle behind his back. The latter returned the glance and stated, *"I took command of the First Army! I will be hunting; somebody must pay for the bad time I had today!"*

After an extremely short pause for us, but a substantially long one for an Archangel, he exclaimed, *"Of course, Lucif-er! I will bring you plenty of prisoners from both sexes, unharmed!"*

As Azami-el departed, both Overlords shared a final sinister smile; as ordered, a group of officers and top-trained soldiers left with Azami-el. The NA mobilized the final death blow for the unfortunate few survivors of the devastated Southern Alliance, with mercy given to no one. However, death could be a blessing, as compared to being taken alive!

NA sector, inside a bomb shelter.
The sirens remained howling; thousands of NA citizens had nervously gathered in this massive underground facility. Nobody was talking since they didn't know if they would live or die tonight. They just listened to the outside noise while nourishing their jitters. Some even covered their ears so they would not hear the sirens. Their anxiety stayed widespread and terrifying.

Then, suddenly…Silence! … No more sirens!

Heads turned around, looking at each other inquisitively. What was happening? Could it be possible that all was over? On the other hand, could this be just wishful thinking?

A voice from a large speaker solemnly announced.

"All clear!

We inflicted a decisive defeat on the attacking forces of our enemies. We have laid their cities and their whole Alliance to smoldering ruins.

They got what they deserved; now, we are free from their menace. Let's get out of the shelters and celebrate. Let's scream joyfully because this is the biggest day in our history. The day we defeated those who hated us and plotted our destruction.

Let's have the biggest cheers for our great Alliance!"

And so, they did! As they poured into the previously empty streets, the roar from their delighted lungs disturbed the silence of the night. They ran crazily while embracing each other; they showed their jubilation by pointing angry fists toward the South. They shouted, sang, and cursed their departed enemies.

A group of angels from the choir of Virtues stood together in joyful celebration, all but one female. The group leader, a mature-looking individual, inquisitively asked her.

"What is the problem? You should be screaming with joy?"

Her glassy eyes lifted from the ground to meet his. She sadly stated.

"I was thinking about our son, Eugenius! He is probably dead by now… You are his father; don't you feel anything for him?"

He rubbed his neck almost violently. Next, he stared at the dark skies where many bright dots continued moving south. Still high in the sky, he saw the two full moons; their bloody color gave him a chill.

"It looks like the blood of my child!" He thought.

He remembered a time when he was so proud of Eugenius. What went wrong? Why did his son not listen to him? Slowly, he finally answered his wife's question.

*"I wasn't, but you reminded me that I still miss him! Why didn't he come with us? We practically begged him! If he had, he would be standing here with the rest of our family... But he chose wrongly... And he is **dead**! We chose right... And we are **alive**!"*

After an introverted thought, he closed his statement.

"What is the use of wondering about it? Let's go downtown and celebrate!"

She agreed with a sad smile; inside, a painful emptiness kept torturing her; tonight, no celebration could erase it.

A Seraph started dressing in his officer's uniform someplace in the NA. As he picked up his handgun, he reflected on the destruction of the SA.

"Maybe it is better that you are dead now. You were tormenting me with those flashbacks! What were they supposed to be, a reminder of the good old times? Here, in the NA, I found the place where I belong, where in the not-too-far future, I will eventually become an Overlord! I don't need any Gods because I will become one myself!"

After a final check for the neatness of his uniform, he walked out of the room. A completely armed platoon was waiting for him in the adjacent corridor. The platoon leader, a Seraph, stood in attention and telepathically shouted, *"Commander Arkyn! Your craft is ready!"*

At the same time on Trillium, council leader Nobiel dropped hard on his knees as he received the news that not much was left of the SA. The SBC base had been confirmed to be erased from the map. The sharp pain emanating from his knees went unnoticed; the pain inside overshadowed everything else.

He stared at the bright red full moons while his distorted face squeezed with unbearable anguish. He raised both arms above, bent his head backward, and prayed painfully.

"My dear God, why?... Why so many are gone?
*Your servants: Dani-el, Rapha-el, Micha-el... and my dearest friend, Gabri-el! They all loved You and lived only for You... **They all are dead!**"*

A council member, a Cherub, approached from behind and placed his right hand over Nobiel's right shoulder. A friend tried to console him, but he was shaking; his left hand stayed compressing his left cheek. One fingernail touching his teeth moved up and down as an involuntary nervous tick rattled his left hand.

For an instant, Nobiel almost believed that Gabri-el had touched him like he had many times in the past, and with such a touch, he could take away his anxieties and fears.

This time, they did not go away!

Anyway, he cherished his friend's effort and placed his left hand on top of his. Then, he mentally shouted.

"Why does Evil prevail? Why are the faithful being destroyed?
Why, my God? ... Why did You forsake us?"

What would happen if Evil could take control over the whole Earth? Would life be full of fears and anxieties? Is it even possible?

Unfortunately, the answer is YES!

Many millenniums ago, the people populating our planet moved away from God; they took Evil as their deity!

Only one family remained loyal to our Creator, Noah's. His family consisted of his wife, three sons, and their wives.[3]

When the floodgates of heaven opened, they were the only humans spared.

However, there is the possibly that they took with them many children from the three families, even though, there is no record of such a thing. If this happened, the recovery of humanity would have been much faster after the waters receded from the land.

This great disaster was called 'The Great Deluge.' Noah's family built a large boat named the Ark to escape the flood. The animals they took with them to the Ark were also the only survivors of their kind. The excluded birds, animals, and humans perished; many plant and animal species vanished.

A large civilization, perhaps encompassing many millions of human beings inhabiting many cities, just disappeared from the face of the planet. There is little we know about them, no names or records.

Our existence is sometimes solid, other times very flimsy. We are born and then die; these are the two most important events in our lives.

Is there anything more important?

Our Lord, by giving us a spirit created in His image, changed it all! Death is not that important anymore, but how we die and what is inside us at that instant is what matters.

At the moment of death, our souls are similar to photographs, a permanent record of the last instant of our existence. We hope that the last permanent image of any of us is pleasant to His sight!

Since God's ways are frequently not ours, He habitually reverses our worldly achievements.

---

[3] Genesis 6, 18

The big winners, people with great riches and power, become big losers
eternally.

*The God-abiding losers, the poor and defenseless, become victorious
forever.*

DECADENCE

CHAPTER 8

Half a year had passed since the destruction of the SA, and except for some NA outposts strategically placed in the Southern Hemisphere, nobody else was left alive on the devastated land. The armies that poured from the North killed almost everyone but still managed to capture about a million survivors from the obliterated Alliance, most unhurt, but some mildly injured or with minor radiation burns.

The lower continent stayed too radioactive for any immediate occupation; it would take more than a few years before any new settlements or cities could emerge from the ruins. The desolation became even worse since most of the forests had been burned or had radioactive damage. Reforestation remained a primary objective for sustaining the hordes waiting to migrate south to take possession of their newly conquered land.

The whole planet stayed covered by a thick layer of fine dust suspended in the atmosphere. This occurrence caused the planet's temperatures to plummet to freezing levels never heard before; to fight this crippling nuclear after-effect, the NA started two big projects.

The first project was a global removal of floating dust by two methods. One used alcohol dispersed as an extremely fine spray at stratospheric heights to wash down the dust particles jettisoned to those altitudes by the powerful nuclear explosions.

The other method used electrostatically charged particles that attracted and captured the dust floating in the atmosphere. When the particles became large enough, they would fall to the ground. This method worked better for particles too high in the atmosphere to be removed by the first method. The second method did not work at lower altitudes where liquid water remained present since it canceled the electrostatic effect.

The second large project used the injection of massive amounts of CO_2 into the atmosphere to increase the greenhouse effect.

Since the NA anticipated these problems, as soon as the war ended, its citizens were ready to swing into action; nevertheless, the hardly visible sun, seeing as a brownish-red disk, barely warmed the surface of the planet... and it was cold... bitterly cold.

CD, NA; Main building at Centrum.
The spacious circular dome of the central structure of the city had a great view of the town. It was another hazy day, which made the faraway rectangular buildings barely visible. The white and blue color patterns, predominant in all buildings, just merged into a pale reflection with color

differences almost impossible to discern. Lots of snow covered the top of the nearby mountains; this was not the case in the city since infrared lights constantly melted the snow, and only tiny spots remained on top of the buildings.

Looking at the not-so-attractive spectacle, Gorgon-el twisted his lips in disapproval and shook his head, whipping his curly blond hair around. Turning about face, he addressed his boss Lucif-er, who wore his favorite silvery jumpsuit.

"The temperatures are still falling; when should we start warming?" Gorgon-el mentally said.

Lucif-er watched his subordinate condescendingly. Then, he responded, *"This month... for sure."*

"My computer's projections forecasted a turnaround a week ago, but still nothing!" Gorgon-el complained.

"Listen to me! You have to wait a few more days; remember that we are in the middle of winter. Why are you so anxious anyway? If we lose an additional million citizens due to the extended projection, we are still way inside the expected casualty range!"

Looking into the hypnotic deep blue eyes, Gorgon-el decided to add more.

"I could care less about the casualties; this situation is screwing up my social life. The radioactive dust raining on us and the freezing weather ravishing the NA are causing starvation across the land. The combined effect is causing us to live indoors; I want to go outside and celebrate our great victory: The gratifying slaughter of the SA!"

The leader of the NA smiled with a sinister sneer; he was reminded of his greatest moment. However, before he continued, the front sliding door to this large room at the top of the tallest building in Centrum opened.

Two Overlords walked in. Their authoritative footsteps bounced off the shiny floors with a noticeable and sharply distinctive clatter; Azami-el and Zeri-el had just arrived.

"Glad to see you! What is the latest news?" Lucif-er, seated at the center of the place in a plush chair, faced and greeted them.

The incoming Overlords walked until they faced their leader. Zeri-el wore an attire similar to Gorgon-el's, a blue and white jumpsuit with a similar emblem on his chest. Zeri-el had achieved the same rank as Gorgon-el, third in command in the NA. This promotion was rewarded for his important role in defeating the SA and its famous Matrix Defense System. As ranking Overlord, Zeri-el took the first turn. He spoke calmly while inspecting Lucif-er's face for any indication of what he was thinking; he found none!

"The former SA continent is still too hot with radioactive fallout. We need to wait another year, until the summer, before we start constructing new cities!" After a brief pause, he added, *"I got the last report on NA*

casualties from our soldiers invading and attacking the remaining SA posts; it now stands at seven thousand. How many citizens have we lost to the nuclear winter?"

Lucif-er gave the inquisitive green eyes what they wanted to see, a smile of approval. With a profound, toned mental message, he answered.

"Two million... Two million more are projected to go before all is over."

Lucif-er, standing up, gave his subordinate a deeper glance. He startled him by touching his right arm; this was not a display of 'affection.' As his mental probe bored into his subordinate's subconscious, the NA leader said.

"I already knew what you just declared... What about the problem you are having? In addition, why are you hiding it from me?"

Zeri-el froze, nervously thinking about the cunning abilities of his new boss. How is it possible for Lucif-er to find out what he was thinking? Did he provide a symptom to tip Lucif-er about having severe nightmares, an event practically <u>impossible</u> for an Overlord to experience?

He stalled by saying, *"What?"*

Lucif-er gave him a mischievous look, then, sarcastically twisting his lips, suggested.

"Perhaps... recurrent nightmares?"

Zeri-el felt that the floor no longer supported him. The last thing he wanted was for anyone else to discover what had now become public knowledge. Even Lucif-er's platoon guarding the premises had mentally heard the leader of the NA state his secret problem!

Lucif-er read his concern because he quickly asserted.

"You are new here, and you are not quite familiar with the rules. Let me assure you that my guards are absolutely loyal to me. They will not even <u>think</u> about crossing me or any Overlord under my command!"

He chuckled with self-assurance but speedily added with deep malice.

"Or else... they will be dead!"

As Zeri-el changed his anxiety for a better self-controlled mental state, Lucif-er further assured him in the next instant.

"I understand your problem. It should not exist. Nevertheless, regardless of its source, I should be able to eliminate it. You know the 'stone,' with its help, there is no depth of the subconscious that I cannot reach. Come tomorrow to my residential building at midnight!"

From at least a dozen angels operating electronic equipment in a separate room, one Seraph approached in a hurry; before he walked close enough to communicate telepathically, Lucif-er acknowledged the incoming unspoken message and ordered.

"Transfer the signal to the main terminal!"

As the operator responded with the usual salute, the leader of the NA contacted Gorgon-el, who stood nearby at one of the large outside windows of the big room; he had been carefully observing the interchange of information among the three Overlords in the center of the room. He was focusing on Zeri-el's behavior problem when his boss contacted him.

"Gorgon-el! Kroma-el is running out of time. Kral, his capital city, is about to be run down by glaciers advancing from the North Pole.

I discussed with you how to convert a conventional nuclear bomb to a microwave-generating nuclear device. Explain it to Kroma-el and inform him that he has five days to modify 20 nuclear devices of 10 megatons each. I will be in Kral in six days, at 4:30 hours!"

Gorgon-el did not waste time walking to the main terminal, about 10 meters from his present location. His boss turned his piercing sight to lock into an almost equally sinister pair of blue eyes, Azami-el's. Lucif-er, somehow inquisitive, began communicating with Azami-el.

"Tell me about your 'peculiarity'!"

When he finally had his turn, Azami-el burst his mental message at higher-than-normal speed.

"You are right; I have no problem, only this peculiar situation. I cannot rape, maim, or torture any of the SA prisoners... because they die on me! I always thought that the SA citizens were a bunch of wimps, but this is taking all the fun out of having prisoners. At this rate, in a few months, there will be nobody left!"

"The autopsies did not disclose the reason," Lucif-er stated instead of questioning.

"Exactly! Half of the captives are in good health, with minimal traces of radiation exposure. There is no reason for them to die yet. They should have waited for me to kill them!"

The number one Archangel of the Evil Alliance smiled cynically. He remained momentarily silent, and so did the other Overlords. In the background, Gorgon-el continued transmitting instructions to Kroma-el using a communication terminal, which could faintly but clearly be heard.

"...mix 1% of inert material spaced equally at the molecular level through the plutonium core. This should lower the temperature of the nuclear reaction so the explosion would generate more microwaves than gamma rays. Use a shield alloy placed at the rear of the bomb's core, so at least 90% of the energy will be focused downwards to a selected target..."

Lucif-er, rubbing his chin with his left hand, exclaimed at Azami-el.

"Is the time-space fabric falling apart? Or, on the other hand, the radiation may have some unknown effects never seen before.

Whatever it is, it seems to be affecting even you, superior beings. However, I want to verify the situation related to the prisoners for myself. Let's go to containment area CC-23!"

CC-23: a vast, saucer-shaped indoor building.

The inside, looking more like a giant indoor stadium, stayed brightly illuminated with powerful flood lamps duplicating the outside's sunshine. The smooth ceiling, much higher at the center than the edges, remained supported by concentric rows of widely spaced columns. At about one-third of the inside radius, measured from the outside, an empty area about 30 meters wide made a perfect circle around the center portion, thus isolating it. A metallic grid followed the outside edge of this circular gap.

A single structure wrapped around the centered-supporting pillar rose to the ceiling height.

Past the one-third outside section, everything was quite different; it seemed much more luxurious. Radial channels or streets connected both sections. Three Overlords looked toward the inner section inside a structure, perhaps part of the main entrance. Lucif-er in front, Zeri-el near at his right hand, Azami-el by his left hand; both subordinates stayed positioned slightly behind. Their view was almost unimpaired; the transparent large windows allowed the best observation of the inner core.

One side door slid open. Three NA officers entered the room; the higher-ranking stayed at the front, with the two lower-ranking officers stopping at the door. Somewhere two meters from his location, the leading officer proceeded to face Lucif-er. He was a stocky Throne dressed in formal military attire and expressed his best welcome.

"Greetings, Most Eminent Overlord! I am honored to serve our victorious and eminent leader and his illustrious companions! Welcome to CC-23, a fallout shelter converted to a detention area!"

As the Overlords just stared at him, he continued with his speech.

"We have the largest prisoner population: 125,031 inmates. They wear a neck collar for identification, location, and control. Males are separated from females by using different building sectors.

All utilities and services are done through underground tunnels. We keep computer-controlled video contact with all places and for all prisoners. A metallic grill separates us from the prisoners; it is electrified to 100,000 volts!"

Lucif-er walked casually around the officer and glanced at the outside inner core as presented by the transparent windows; he did not appear to be listening. The officer paused momentarily, startled by his action; he licked his upper lip and quickly swallowed. Since the other two Overlords stayed in their places, he decided to stand at attention and continue with his speech; however, he now stared at the gap between the two remaining Archangels. He continued his telepathic discourse.

"Each prisoner has assigned tasks, so they run the maintenance of the detention area. The food allocation is..."

Lucif-er, looking outside the window, just flicked his index finger up. The officer did not see but certainly felt the following command:

"Shut up!"

Lucif-er calmly returned to his original position; from there, he moved closer. The officer tried his best to stay at attention, but such an incredibly handsome face also generated an incredible fear that could border into sheer terror... He moved one step back.

Meagerly, he looked at the face close to his. He saw Lucif-er raising three fingers, starting with the index and slowly following with the other two; they blocked his acute and disturbing eyes. To worsen his anxiety, the officer still transparently saw Lucif-er's blocked eyes.

The leader of the NA mentally commanded.

"Akron, bring me three healthy prisoners: a Seraph, a Domination, and a Principality!"[1]

Akron, obviously the officer's name, pulled all his strength to answer his ultimate superior correctly.

"I shall bring them immediately! Sir!"

The officer looked at his two subordinates standing close to the door. He snapped his thumb and middle finger so that his index finger pointed toward the exit.

They were listening to the conversation, so one took off through the door while the other got to the next available terminal; feverishly working, he requested the computer to sort the prisoners to match Lucif-er's request.

He only took five seconds to enter the request. Even faster, the computer took five microseconds to find the match. The terminal read.

MS-3578
MD-11530
MP-24767

The officer, by using electronic means, immediately requested.

> Order the three prisoners to report to their respective transfer stations.
> Notify Officer Korba of their locations.
Done

As Akron and the three Overlords watched from the outside windows, a section of the metallic grid blocking the closest access road to the center core slid open. A small vehicle hastily accelerating passed through the opening on its way to pick up the prisoners.

A few minutes went by slowly. The Overlords stood in a group, like statues, at least what they appeared to the outside spectators; they were mentally chatting at high speed but privately. The only one restless and nervous was the Throne in charge of the detention area. He could not find a location where he felt comfortable.

---

[1] One angel from the top of each Choir's Triad.

He became pleased when he saw the small craft reappearing on its way back. The same two officers returned, but this time, between them, stood the requested three captives from the SA marching in a single line.

A platoon of armed guards crossed the door and positioned along the back walls.

"Does it look like I need any protection from these prisoners?"

Lucif-er, while staring at the detention area commander, exclaimed.

Akron mumbled an incoherent statement that he did not dare communicate; he was following standard procedures. Regaining his coherence, he moved his hand, signaling to the exit door; he ordered the platoon to *"Stay outside!"*

In addition, looking directly at Lucif-er, he apologized.

"I beg your pardon, Sir!"

The soldiers cleared the location, marching out quickly. When the big boss was around, everyone moved at double speed.

The three captives stopped at the center of the room where Lucif-er approached them.

The two officers moved farther apart to give the Overlord plenty of walking space. At this point, it became noticeable that the officers carried a handheld electronic device in their right hands.

All three inmates wore gray jumpsuits. They also wore a thin metallic strip around their neck, an inmate-controlling device capable of even killing the angel captured in their vicious grip.

The original seed of Evil slowly walked around the prisoners, carefully examining them externally, internally, and mentally. The three seemed perturbed with deep anxiety, but the Seraph in the trio kept the best outside pose, apparently looking calm. He also remained in the best physical shape, with no scars or injuries.

The Domination angel had his left cheekbone bruised; a dark purple tint adorned it. The deep purple tone indicated that a blunt object had stricken his face not long ago. Lucif-er examined the depth of the damaged cheek; he noticed it was superficial, nothing serious. The Domination's brown hair almost stuck up due to the chills of being under Lucif-er's microscope-like eyes. He didn't dare to look at the face of the Overlord.

The last in the row, the Principality, persisted shaking. Lucif-er gave him his sadistic look as a welcoming smile. He shook harder.

His black hair remained unkept, even when he may not be responsible for his appearance. Looking at the floor, his black eyes moved nervously from one location to another. Lucif-er carefully stared at his bruised face. The left side, peeling off like a severe sunburn, was a radiation burn but healing properly. The left eye must have been affected since it stayed closed more than the right one.

Lucif-er agreed the captives remained in good health, with no life-threatening injuries. He pointed a finger toward the Domination; this individual looked disturbed as the two officers approached him. They grabbed him by each arm, carrying him almost off the floor, and dumped him flat on his back on a nearby table. From under the table, two wide plastic straps were pulled and tightly placed across his feet and his chest, pinning his arms flat against the table.

One of the officers moved some control devices that turned on two blue lasers directly from above the ceiling.

Akron's explanation was unnecessary since the Overlords knew much more about the subject than he could imagine, especially when it related to torture.

"This is a high-frequency, current injecting device. It produces intense muscle pain! ... Ten is the maximum accepted by a normal brain, but the individual passes out at this intensity. Therefore, we stay below that level. Let's start at level 4!"

The officer beside the controls positioned the lasers over the angel's right arm. This angel twitched with a moderate amount of pain inflicted by the needle-like lasers; being tiny spots, they penetrated his left arm muscles to a particular depth and stopped digging. One spot was at his biceps, the other close to his wrist.

With Akron staying behind them, the three Overlords approached the table for a better observation point.

The torturer set the machine for the proper current, and before pressing the red button, he took a quick view at the domination's face; the angel sweating profusely expected the worst. The officer, displaying a faint smile since he enjoyed seeing the effects of pain, pushed the button.

A faint high-frequency pitch became noticeable.

The Domination angel twisted in pain but remained in control.

"Level 5!" Akron commanded.

The twisting and shaking increased in violence.

"Level 6!" he commanded again.

The Domination started losing muscle control. His right arm shook hard, and his sweat turned plentiful as it ran from the higher locations to the table. The officer operating the controls glanced at his boss, Akron. The latter ordered again, *"Level 7!"*

The tortured angel shook violently, not only his arm but his entire body! The level of pain was not that high, but he had already reached a maximum. Then, as his head rolled to his left side, he completely stopped shaking; one instant later, he went completely limp!

Lucif-er quickly rubbed his index finger from the top of the Domination's forehead to in-between his eyes, and he explained.

"No brain activity at all; he is dead!"

"Just level 7, only across his right arm. I told you; it does not make sense!" Azami-el retorted.

Lucif-er squeezed his front teeth with inner displeasure. Turning around, his powerful steps echoed metallically as he walked directly to the Seraph prisoner. He stood directly in front of this angel. The Seraph dared to look into his piercing eyes!

Not a good idea... He felt as if his eyeballs had become incandescent! As he closed his eyes while lowering his head, Lucif-er grabbed him by the arms, lifting him off the floor. He applied his own torturing technique while his penetrating sight intruded into the Seraph's private thoughts. The captive angel, even when under the power of the most powerful Overlord in the land, kept his own identity He had no evil thoughts, just a prayer to his loving God.

With a chilling sound, the bone of his right arm broke!

Almost instantly inside his mind, no pain or anxiety remained, only a pleasant emptiness. Physically, he became innocuous to his surroundings; spiritually, he turned into a burst of energy going away.

He was also dead, and his soul had departed!

Lucif-er held the lifeless body between his hands; he could not believe what had just happened. A broken bone... and he was gone!

He became angry; the exposure of a prayer to God refreshed his hate toward the Creator. In disgust, he threw the Seraph's body to the floor, where he watched the twisted and inanimate remains.

A nervous shaking behind him caught his attention. Of course, it was that lower kind of life called a Principality. If a Seraph prisoner did not give him any satanic pleasure, this worthless being could not even be capable of wasting his time. With a violent left-arm swing, he struck the last surviving prisoner!

The unfortunate angel flew straight to the nearby transparent window, banging his head hard against the polished glass surface. A blood splash appeared radially from the site of impact. He did not survive!

The other two Overlords watched undisturbed. Azami-el ran his index finger to the edge of his mouth as if he tasted blood.

The officers felt nervous and uneasy but remained at attention. Akron indicated something to the video monitor watching the room.

"Clean up!" He stated.

The same platoon of soldiers that previously exited the room now came back running. They removed the three dead prisoners and electronically wiped the place clean. In no time, everything looked like nothing had happened.

Lucif-er addressed the commander of the place.

"From the remaining prisoners, select 666 healthy ones, 60% male and 40% female; treat them well, feed them properly. When I ask, you will deliver them to me."

"Understood, Great Overlord! Your wish shall be done!"

Lucif-er turned to Azami-el; he sent his favorite subordinate a personal message, *"When you throw a stone up, gravity is supposed to bring it down. Lately, stones are going up but not coming down... It is quite interesting!"* After a short pause, he cynically added, *"You were absolutely right... killing was no fun!"*

The sliding side door of this spacious and luxurious flying craft opened; Zeri-el stepped out of the vehicle. He wore a shiny outfit, the blue and white NA colors plus a golden circle encompassing a dark red triangular emblem across his chest, its golden margins glowing under the bright sun; his belt, as if made of diamonds, sparkled like having its own power source.

The crisp, clean air gently caressed his golden, well-groomed hair as he stared at this tropical island's fantastic view, similar to a Hawaiian spectacle.

After 100 meters of clear path, luxurious vegetation adorned the rolling hills leading to a spectacular mountain range. Crowning the steep mountains' ridges, a volcano dominated this range's elevation.

It was a peculiar mountain, not too close, approximately 50 Km away. It immediately called the attention of the Overlord since its top appeared to be uniquely shaped, like a slanted giant 'M.' Its outside edges did not look straight but at an approximately 45° angle. A dark plume of ash, towering above its top, was pushed away from the location of the Overlord by the prevailing winds.

Two gorgeous females, both Seraphim, scantily dressed in loose but silky materials that accentuated their sensual curves, dropped to a kneeling position next to each of his legs. They pressed their well-endowed breasts against his powerful thigh muscles. They looked up at him, begging for his attention by blinking their sparkling blue eyes.

He caressed their faces and mentally commanded them.

"Come to my residence in two hours!"

Their faces brightened up at the mental command, happy to be accepted for the sexual entertainment of this glorious leader. They separated, stood up, and moved backward out of his way.

Zeri-el stood when a high-ranking officer, the leader of a top-notch military platoon, rushed to stand in front of the Overlord. As soon as he reached this position, he exclaimed.

"Sir! Welcome to Central Island!"

Zeri-el nodded in approval. Regardless, he flipped his hand in an unspoken command, *"Get out of my way!"*

When his path became clear, he strode out like a king. He moved toward a cluster of buildings erected at the forest's edge. Civilians and soldiers present bowed as he passed by.

Zeri-el panned his sight around the surroundings. He smiled with a sinister intonation. He was pleased with what he saw, pleased at what he had become...

CONTIGUOUS, BUT DIFFERENT SEGMENT

Next... Zeri-el stood at the top of a ten-story building, part of a cluster of structures used for entertainment or as an observation point for the island's inhabitants; from its circular top, the view appeared fabulous. The crowd accompanying him had prepared a grand celebration in his honor; he had already anticipated what all the preparations would lead to. He became anxious for this activity to end since he would rather be at his private quarters where the two females should be waiting for him. He anticipated the threesome encounter and the screams that those females would let out when he placed his hands and his oversized masculinity on them.

He scrutinized his surroundings, which were strange yet so familiar. It felt like a repeat of something he had already seen. Even the island's colors stayed so bright, almost unreal!

He looked one more time at the smoking volcano; he felt a chill. Unhappy about the unwarranted feeling, he questioned himself.

"What could a stupid volcano mean or possess for him to shiver?"

He had just finished the angry thought when a fireball rose from the top of the distant volcano. As everyone focused on the explosion, a powerful ground shockwave hit the building!

Plastics and metals cried ominously, and window panels shattering on the upper floors rained massive amounts of debris over the ground below. The top oscillated violently, so much so that Zeri-el believed the whole building could collapse or split into two pieces.

Jumping over the outside perimeter rail, he plunged into the emptiness surrounding the building. He fell... and fell...

CONTIGUOUS, BUT DIFFERENT DREAM SEGMENT

...Next... Distorted and panic-stricken, his face did not belong to a normally fearless Overlord. Racing back to his craft, he ran for his life; however, even that short distance appeared to be so far away... Even at his top speed, the craft still looked unreachable!

The events remained so unrealistic that he furiously thought.

"This does not make any sense! If I am dreaming, why can't I end this absurd and stupid nightmare? After all, I am an Overlord, a superior being, master of billions! I should be able to control my own actions, even when they are part of the subconscious!"

The ground began shaking so violently that it made him wobble, and he almost fell... he stopped. He was copiously sweating, his heart painfully pumping blood, and his breathing so difficult that there appeared to be not enough air around him.

He thought the volcano could blow up, and he had to move farther away, or the lava would burn him. In desperation, he ran again.

Then, an awesome feeling overwhelming his whole being took over...
The black shadow of death approached him; extinction was coming his way, and he could not find a place to run or hide!

Horror invaded and devastated his superior composure. He screamed and, in panic, looked all around for the incoming devastation. He still could not see it even when he knew it was there!

From above, a searing red glow suddenly appeared; fire rained upon him! ... He assumed the volcano must have blown up!

As his entire body burned with unbearable pain, Zeri-el stuck up his hands in a futile last effort to protect his face from the searing heat. As his smoking flesh began turning to charcoal, a macabre and horrid-sounding scream pierced the surroundings.

"Nooo-o--o---o!"

END OF DREAM SEGMENTS

Zeri-el slowly opened his eyes... He was covered with sweat, but not from a cold sweat, something like acid. His skin felt on fire on the outside, like coming out of a cremation chamber!

Squeezing his teeth with utter anger, disappointment, and lingering fear, he canceled the pain. Next, he vaporized all the sweat; his clothes became as dry as if they had never been wet.

A fingernail scratched his forehead!

Very close to him, he focused his eyesight on Lucif-er's face. The leader of the NA, while staring at the small pieces of skin sticking to the tip of his fingernail, commented.

"Incredible! Your skin has been sunburned!"

Zeri-el did not answer. For a millisecond, he regrouped his last activities before falling asleep. Lucif-er used the 'stone' to erase the cause of his dreams and intruded into his subconscious to find the cause of the nightmares and eradicate them.

He was disturbed by the humming from the beautiful light-dispersing apparatus, almost giving him a headache... Lucif-er pointed to the device deactivating the modulating lasers that fed the synthetic stone. Lasers, which converted this precious-looking jewel into a diabolical instrument. Without the external source that modified its normal appearance, the 'stone' became again a spectacular diamond-looking rock with 666 cm^3.

"Well?" asked Zeri-el while intensely staring at Lucif-er.

The Lord of Darkness approached until his face became close to Zeri-el's. He communicated to his subordinate almost angrily; he was not happy either.

"You must have the worst case of guilty feelings that I have ever seen; it even includes severe psychosomatic effects affecting your whole body!"

Zeri-el got up and complained almost violently.

"What guilty feelings? I have NO guilty feelings!
I am glad the SA is gone, that Micha-el is dead, and that all are dead!
Presently, I am doing what I always wanted to do… In addition, I am an
Overlord!"

Lucif-er, unaffected by the burst of affection, retorted.

"OK! However, this problem of yours is even deeper than the
subconscious. I could not reach your dream.

It felt like it was in another dimension. The initiating mechanism of
your dream is likely located in some primal cell of your intellect,
underneath any conscious or even unconscious thought!"

After briefly pausing, he continued, *"I will not give up; I can still try*
different resonant frequencies and laser power settings. It is going to take
time, but I will prevail."

At that instant, he sent a mental message out of the room.

Magog-el, Gorgon-el, and Liliel walked into this large but exotically
complex location. Obviously, Zeri-el did not want anyone in the room
while Lucif-er probed his mind for a fix to his problem. Magog-el's
massive body placed himself first before the other two Overlords; he
immediately exclaimed, *"Obviously, it did not work!"*

"You must have a nasty case of guilty feelings!" Gorgon-el, with his
typical foxy smile, suggested while moving alongside Magog-el.

With his blood getting closer to boiling, Zeri-el stomped along the
room to face Gorgon-el. As his green eyes approached red, he stared
closely at his equally ranked co-worker, and he angrily stated.

"I have a request for you! Never mention guilty feelings again!"

He quickly turned around and walked out of the room. Gorgon-el, who
wiped the smile from his face when facing Zeri-el, returned to his grin as
soon as his colleague departed.

The big boss, watching from the corner of his eyes, smiled with
contentment. He knew about Gorgon-el's aspirations to move to a higher
commanding position, and sharing his position with Zeri-el caused the
expected friction.

In a world dominated by Evil, only the unifying totalitarian power of a
supreme leader could allow the forced but accepted pacific coexistence of
so many bloodthirsty and power-seeking Archangels. They wished
nothing else but to be the number one master of Terra. Only then could
they unleash their ultimate and dark desire: to be **a god!**

Lucif-er remained the only one with that capacity. Any other aspiring
Overlord for such a position had only to look into the depths of his leader's
eyes to instantly know that they should be content to be a sub-god!

Without Lucif-er's binding power, the other Overlords would have
engaged in what Evil is best: The total destruction of anybody or anything
that stands in the way of their ambitions.

Magog-el relayed a message.

"The Core refused again! They do not want any help to solve their radiation problem. Since they did not expect any nuclear war, they remained unprepared. They are suffering but stubborn; their answer is still no!"

As Magog-el expressed his concerns, Gorgon-el moved closer to the impressive collection of items on the walls and adjacent transparent cases. He looked with interest. He had seen most of them before, but this was the most unique gathering of collectibles on the planet.

Liliel, dressed in a low-cut, sexually insinuating jumpsuit, was displaying her best attributes; she looked astonishingly erotic. Her suit stayed tight against her buttocks, showing more curves than most males could handle. She located her insinuating shape very close to Lucif-er; after looking at his Adonic profile, she caressed the back of his lustrous hair.

Magog-el continued his chat as he was alone with Lucif-er.

"I know you want me to insist, but I am sure it is a waste of time. We should move in and take over The Core!"

"We will eventually do that, but our resources are strained at this moment, and we should wait until we recover," Lucif-er noted.

Something not displayed in an obvious manner called Gorgon-el's attention; he picked it up from a shelf. It was a small transparent cylinder perfectly sealed in a vacuum, with one strand of hair inside! He stared at the silky, gold-looking strand; it was beautiful.

There was only one female on the planet with such gorgeous hair; her name was <u>Raquel</u>; however, she was not around anymore! Gorgon-el smiled because of a morbid thought about the hair strand. At that instant, he heard a personal telepathic message from his boss, who simultaneously talked to Magog-el.

"Yes! You are absolutely right; it is from Raquel. Someday in the future, I shall clone her. Ultimately, she will be just for me; consequently, forget about having a piece from that strand of hair!"

Sensing what was happening, Liliel glanced at Gorgon-el; she saw the container. Quickly, she moved next to the Overlord; ignoring his cynical smile, she took the container from his hand and examined it.

It must be female intuition because she instantly knew to whom such a single piece of hair belonged. She also heard her lover's (Lucif-er) brain-splitting comment!

"You will be <u>extremely sorry</u> if you do what you are considering... Just put it back!"

She clenched her pretty teeth but relinquished what she intended to do; as she returned to her previous location, she began acting more seriously.

Magog-el and Gorgon-el finished their communiqué and exited the room. Now alone, he sat; she did alike but on his lap. Like a cat, she purred and rubbed against her master. While playing with his left earlobe, she asked.

"Why do you want to clone Raquel? ... I don't want to see her face again!"

Without looking at her, Lucif-er answered with a stern voice.

"Because it is my wish!"

Clenching her teeth again while containing her anger, she replied.

"The clone will look like her, but she will not be Raquel!"

"I know; she will have to do until I find somebody better."

The Overlord grabbed her face with both hands by her cheeks. She faced him like a fish with an open mouth gasping for air. She looked at him, exhaled, and remarked with a much lower tone.

"If you were not the best-looking male in the Universe, I would have traded you. But you are... and I am your slave!"

She twisted her head so one of his fingers partially entered her pretty mouth. Twisting her tongue, she wrapped it around the finger and then slid the moist and warm appendage back and forth.

Lucif-er, rubbing her long silky hair, commented, *"Liliel, there is something that you want much more than sex; it is power.*

You want to be an Overlord; I promise, you will be the first female in the ranks. You have been chosen to be the next Overlord! ... How long will it take? It depends on you; I estimate 10 to 15 years."

Her purplish eyes shined like stars while she breathed with vigor and passion. As her full lips opened, they almost dripped moisture. She violently kissed Lucif-er with sensual fury.

The Council Building in Trillium, The Core.

Nobiel sat at the head of a large oval table; he looked tired. His eyes were dim, lacking the spark characteristic of his noble position. To his right, four Seraphim representing Seraphan sat. Across the table, four Thronan delegates were also sitting; to his left, four Cherubim did likewise. He glanced sideways at a large window. Outside, the day remained gloomy. A grayish haze cutting most of the sunshine made the temperature drop exceedingly below normal. The afternoon continued to be cold and shuddery.

Outside, burned by radiation and inclement weather, the trees were dying. Nobiel sadly looked at the branches, almost bare from leaves. His beautiful city did not look the same; very few trees remained alive, and there were no flowers or fruits. The cozy patio, previously laced with exuberant and colorful vegetation, a favorite location where the council would gather in the afternoons to discuss any issue on the planet, became a thing of the past. The outside area was now barren and desolate; nobody would dare to walk its paths without the protection of the proper anti-radiation gear. Watching the few dressed in such a manner, who had no choice but to make the requested rounds along the backyard's patio, resembled watching aliens on an alien land!

He would have mourned for the trees, but a much larger pain was eating his guts; starvation, freezing temperatures, and radiation were killing millions of The Core's citizens. While food supplies became dangerously low, radiation contaminants were everywhere: in the air, in the water, and above the ground. Even using highly sophisticated devices for canceling the radiation was not enough; the load remained too big.

"Nobiel..."

The first Cherub from his left, a medium-built, round-faced individual with his blond hair arranged formally, addressed the meditating council leader; he was a close friend of Nobiel. The council leader came out of his stupor and focused on his friend.

"Sorry, Oryel, what was your last statement?" He asked him.

"The vote is unanimous; we will not accept any help from the NA, even if their leaders insist!"

"Good! I am glad that we are united on this issue. We know for a fact that if the NA armies enter our country, they will never leave!"

To the right of Nobiel, the Seraph mentally spoke to the leader.

"I am apprehensive that the NA will invade us anyway. Without the protection of the SA, there is nothing that we can do to stop them. Should we pray... harder?"

Nobiel touched him with his right hand and commented.

"Yes, praying always helps. God does answer our prayers, but the help He sends us is often not the help we expect. I used to beg God for materialistic favors; however, I hope I have grown out of such weakness... Let me share some of my personal experiences with all of you!

When my best friend Gabri-el was about to die, I communicated with him, but we talked shortly... With no fear in his heart, he emphasized one important thing to my panicking self.

'At the end of our lives, <u>no</u> material thing is important... Only the spirit!'"

After a brief pause, he continued.

"How important was this message?

I have spent countless hours reviewing its context. This is what most impressed me: in front of an imminent death, he had no fear. He was ready to join our Creator, whom he loved much more than his own life. For his love and sacrifice, I am sure our Lord is sharing His Glory with him!"

Nobiel pressed some controls, and the visual screens in front of each council member displayed a manuscript. He mentally read the page to the rest.

"This reminded me of a prophecy written countless years ago.

Listen to this paragraph from the ancient book of 'Wisdom, page 173!

'At the end of time, when great suffering falls over the land.

And when a brother fights against his own brother.

Beware, because the end of the great trial is near.
At this time, do not ask the Lord for earthly possessions.
He will not listen.
Only ask for that which concerns the spirit.
Because in His Glory, material possessions will have no value.
On the other hand, spiritual concerns will be worth everything.'"

****

The flagship of the NA, Lucif-er's aircraft, was approaching for landing at 4:25 hours. The higher atmosphere stayed more transparent than the hazy lower air masses; however, the sky above did not have a blue tone but had an ominous light purple tint. The sun, almost at noontime, remained inclined substantially below the zenith. Another mid-winter day in the northern section of Terra.

Below the highly armed but gracefully flying aerodynamic craft, a vast sheet of snow extended in all directions except straight down. Like an oasis in the middle of the desert, a city emerged clear of the fluffy and crystallized frozen water. As the craft approached the city's center and the tallest building for a sky-port landing, the ice walls moving from the North became quite apparent. Inching their way into the city's northern section, the ice walls, with the tremendous power of an advancing glacier, started destroying the buildings at the northern perimeter!

High-power infrared beams inside the city had their output energy concentrated against the advancing glacier demolishing the outskirts of the town. This action caused the melting of large amounts of water, with the resulting liquid creating small rivers along the adjacent avenues leading to such a place.

The craft hovered above the main structure in the middle of downtown. It quickly settled on the largest landing pad at the top of the building. To be noticed, all the other landing sites were empty.

After landing, nobody got out. Seconds later, the floor collapsed into the building, the same way airplanes are lowered into the inside decks of an aircraft carrier. The landing pads became empty again when the walls closed above the descending vessel.

A tall and slender Cherub, an Overlord displaying his typical crew-cut hairstyle, anxiously waited for the cylinder's passengers to exit. He was not alone; three of his top-ranking officers stood behind him. When the Overlords, Lucif-er, Magog-el, Gorgon-el, Zeri-el, and Azami-el walked across the large side aperture just slid open, he moved forward and telepathically exclaimed.

"Welcome to Kral! Everything is ready for the nuclear operation!"

Lucif-er nodded with approval and took command.

"Good, you have my authorization!" He spoke telepathically.

Lucif-er moved toward the nearest elevator, where the rest of the Overlords followed him according to their rank. The three officers waited until all the Overlords had passed by before they even moved; they tagged along as a compact single row.

The top floor of this massive building offered a great view of the capital city of the NC sector of the Northern Alliance. From here, the ice walls bearing over Kral looked ominous and menacing. Even at noontime, the cold outside was unforgiving. Without the infrared devices warming up the city, the whole place would be part of the glacier by now, one thick sheet of ice.

Lucif-er, pacing the top floor, examined the upgrades that Kroma-el had implemented. Like inspecting, he noted the changes.

"Double magnetic shielding in place.

Heavy-duty grounding microwave mesh for 9.2 Gigacycles over all openings.[2]

Dual polarized transparent panels to minimize nuclear flashes have already been installed.

You are ready; start the show!"

Kroma-el flipped a finger to the three officers. They broke their formal grouping and moved to an independent display center.

All the Overlords lined up in a single row with Lucif-er in the middle. An officer reported from another control center.

"Sir! The power grid to the rest of the city is disconnected. All other utilities are shut off!"

From behind, another officer shouted.

"Sir! All civilians have been secured in proper underground shelters! All city disaster alarms are being activated now!"

In a few seconds, the sirens outside wailing penetrated the sealed structure. It induced a high level of anxiety in all the citizens of Kral who were not Overlords. After all, nuclear blasts were not a casual everyday event. A microwave-generating thermonuclear explosion was not a picnic item, either. The population had never seen one before; all that they knew and understood was that the bombs were going to explode; close enough was sufficient to raise goose pimples and much more!

The last officer did not wait much longer to speak mentally aloud.

"Sir! The aircraft is in position, awaiting final orders!"

Kroma-el turned his face to communicate directly with this officer. In a stern statement, he abruptly retorted.

---

[2] The frequency at which water molecules best absorb microwave energy.

Note: The Angels could never use metric system nomenclature that included the names of inventors and scientists, such as 'Hertz.'

*"First explosion, at 5:00:00 hours! The rest, at 30-second intervals! I want **no** deviation from my pre-selected coordinates!"*

As Kroma-el turned away to face the outside view, the subordinate exclaimed, **"Preliminaries completed, Sir! All nuclear devices are _armed!_"**

Kroma-el turned to face Lucif-er. Since the NC Sector Overlord was taller than his leader, he first looked down, then glanced up to meet the piercing blue eyes. Only once did he make the mistake of staring down at Lucif-er; it felt like a blue laser had pierced his brain. It must have left a scar because he never did it again. The leader of the NA wasted no time establishing his superiority and domain.

"In 25 seconds!" announced Kroma-el.

Lucif-er flipped his index finger up; he had been waiting for the signal.

The seconds crawled by slowly. All the Overlords stared at the distant ice walls approaching from the North. The officers and their subordinates looked away from the windows; some hid their eyes by placing both hands over their faces as they looked concerned about being blinded by the blasts.

An intense flash of light that slowly diminished to moderate levels inundated the floor!

All electronic equipment blinked but recuperated fast.

The two Cherubim Overlords, Kroma-el and Zeri-el, covered their heads due to a painful discomfort caused by the residual magnetic flux that the shields did not altogether bypass away. The other three Seraphim Overlords squeezed their teeth while mildly squinting their eyes. Lucif-er, if he felt anything, he kept it to himself.

A strange noise increased to a peak and then decreased to a much lower decibel level. It was like pouring water over a red-hot metal plate, the same kind of searing noise!

The building made strange cracking noises.

Outside, vapor vents appeared in some locations. Some windows blew up into smoldering pieces. Some pieces of the structures popped out with small cracking explosions. Any trees barely surviving the extreme winter also blew into fragments, which split again into smaller pieces.

All the water running on the streets from the invading glacier just vaporized. A column of white vapor rose quickly, simulating immense white balloons rising into the sky.

In some places, the glacier's top surface liquefied and vaporized. Loud cracking noises indicated propagating fractures. In some areas, ice blew up violently!

Thirty seconds later, just as most events started settling down…

Flash number two brilliantly seared the surroundings again!

More noise! More explosions! Many more columns of steam climbing with furor for higher grounds! Things would be moving to less violent chaos when...

Just as brilliant! Flash number three ripped Kral and its adjacent areas!

A few minutes later, as nuclear blast number nineteen rattled the building, Kroma-el and Zeri-el held their heads in pain... this had become too much to bear!

The outside temperature of the building must have been going up because the inside became much warmer. By this time, the officers and their subordinates began hiding their heads like ostriches under stress, with moisture condensing on their foreheads.

Number twenty blasted away! The effects were similar!

Outside, minor fires had started, and many buildings had minor damages. The internal explosions inside the glacier, generated by the monstrous microwave blasts, had reduced the ice to splinters!

Massive torrents of boiling water ran unabashedly throughout all avenues of the city. The flooding went higher than the second floor of all buildings! The water did not climb higher because most of the torrents found natural drainage locations.

The entire city became covered with a thick and hot fog, occluding the towering columns of moisture reaching for the skies. Lightning was now present and abundant!

As the vapor condensed at higher altitudes, rain started to fall.

The Overlords could not see what happened outside anymore; however, the radar image on a nearby display indicated that the walls of ice pushed by a local glacier were gone!

Lucif-er smiled with sadistic satisfaction. He raised his right-hand fist with one thumb up, in a way he had not done before.

****

Half a year later, it returned to summertime in the Northern Hemisphere. Temperatures on a global scale finally began climbing up; this brought a sign of relief from both the NA and The Core.

Resources became strained, and casualties kept mounting, but finally, the sun rays became strong again, dissipating most of the haze that had hung over Terra for so many days. The frigid winter had seriously damaged the flora and fauna on the whole planet, but now, they have rebounded.

In Centrum, the weather stayed pleasant; at Lucif-er's residence, the rising reddish sun slowly illuminated a silhouette next to a window. It was from a very beautiful Throne, scantily dressed in short, silky, mauve-colored attire; however, her pretty face appeared distorted by an intense, painful grimace.

She remained holding with both hands the lowest part of her abdomen; between her bare feet, blood dripped, one drop at a time. She let go of a deep moan!

As the reddish light rays completely illuminated her face, they also dispersed the darkness in the room; not far back, a large bed could be seen, and of course, it was hexagonal. On the bed's center, leaning at an angle supported by a rather large pillow and with the lower part of his body covered by silky linen, laid Lucif-er. He observed with a faint sadistic smile the gracious contours of his mate.

Staring at the sunrise in a detached manner due to some painful experience, Liliel turned around to face the room's interior. Even when her eyelids did tremble because of pain and anger, she squeezed her teeth and complained in a mentally severe tone.

"You have gone... too far! If that thing *gets any larger... you will kill me!"*

She stopped momentarily to squeeze her tummy harder to quench a painful internal pang.

"It never crossed my mind that someday I would be stating that it could be more pleasurable to have sex with a horse than to do it with you!" She sarcastically continued.

He extended a powerful arm with his hand, calling for her; he sardonically commented, *"I may consider your concern and spare your life! ... Come, Azami-el will arrive soon. Touch my hand; I will fix you back to normal!"*

"Sure!" She sneered, *"So you can rip me apart again!"*

As she touched his hand, a flow of energy healed her up; she moaned but with pleasure!

Somehow casually, Liliel remarked.

"Painful or not... you are the best!"

Later, in the same residence but in a different room, Azami-el and Lucif-er sat comfortably in two plush chairs facing each other. Liliel, dressed in a low cut and tight jumpsuit, was seated on another chair next to Lucif-er's. The latter remarked.

"The last one of your prisoners is gone? ... It is too soon!"

"I could not help it," Azami-el explained, *"Those idiots died by just looking at them! I tried autopsies plus everything in the medical books to explain what happened... No answers!"*

While Azami-el was communicating with his boss, he glanced at the beautiful Throne seated across a piece of furniture in a sexy pose. The Overlord must have deduced what had just occurred from the excitement and temperatures in her body. He gave her a complacent evil smile indicating his approval of Lucif-er's big deed… If only **he** had been the one to ravish this foxy female!

Liliel took no time to figure out Azami-el's sneer; she didn't like it. As an offended female, she squinted and partially showed her frontal teeth.

Lucif-er, ignoring the sideshow, quickly mentioned.

"I assume that <u>my</u> 666 prisoners are still enjoying all the comforts of the NA?"

"Of course! Nobody is touching one single hair from those prisoners."

Lucif-er played with his left index finger over his upper lip, the same place where Liliel had given him a recent bite. He moved the finger forward, almost pointing it to Azami-el, and spoke telepathically.

"You have three days to set up Centrum's central plaza. I want it to be the first outdoor celebration since the war with the SA. All the Overlords, plus all my prisoners, should fit on the center platform. We shall start at noon!"

With a cynical overtone, he concluded.

"Include my kind invitation to all citizens of Centrum!"

Azami-el nodded affirmatively. Looking closer into the darkness inside the eyes before him, he insidiously asked.

"Are you planning to do what I am thinking?"

Lucif-er gave him a sinister smile and replied.

"Of course!"

Centrum; Main Plaza.

A series of large squares became concentrically smaller; each larger quadrilateral structure was higher than the one closer to the center. The smallest one, being the lowest one, was at the plaza's center. Rows of floral trees used to adorn the perimeter of each square, but the radiation and cold weather wiped them out. The dead stumps were removed, so the place looked like a barren amphitheater. The busy skyline of the towering white and blue rectangular skyscrapers surrounded this vast plaza.

A few minutes before noon, the place was completely packed with the Centrum's citizens. Since the large majority did not fit inside the plaza, all the avenues leading to the place remained entirely blocked by the largest gathering of angels in the city's history. It seemed that nobody wanted to ignore the <u>kindly</u> invitation of the master of the land!

To cater to such an enormous crowd, large screens were placed all over the plaza, even way down along the avenues; in this manner, all of Centrum's citizens could participate in this first outdoor event. The radiation finally stayed under control, and the summer temperatures approached what used to be a cool spring day.

The only unusual objects in the place were four thin towers protruding from each of the four corners of the central square, with a shiny spherical cap crowning the top of each building. Among the four caps, the monochromatic light of a red laser connected all four towers: apparently, some internal security for the center's perimeter.

A pervasive roar spread across the plaza from the angels' gathering; it gave the impression of coming from the ground, but it was from the people; the immense crowd chatting with renewed enthusiasm produced it. After all, staying indoors for most of the year turned out to be a very depressing experience. The refreshing outdoor meeting felt like a long-awaited party, exhilarating.

From high in the sky, one shiny small dot approached the plaza's center. Above it, a second dot, substantially smaller than the first, also had its sights on the center of this gathering place. As the larger dot got closer, its massive hull became apparent; it was a transport ship.

After centering its approach on the mid-quadrilateral area, this vehicle descended gracefully for a soft landing; in the process, its powerful engines rattled the plaza's congregation.

From the craft, ten platoons of heavily armed Seraphs spread out; their movements were precise and disciplined, moving at double speed. They took positions at equal intervals around the outside perimeter of the central square. One additional platoon walked outside of the massive transport's side doors to a position close to the middle of the square, where they marched to prefixed locations to form a single row at the center, everyone spaced by only a long step.

Three officers strolled out of the large vehicle, one of whom was Akron, the prison commander. They waved to someone still inside the craft to move.

Ten columns of 11 angels deep came running out of the door's gaping hole. One Seraph ran in front of them, all wearing gray jumpsuits and a metallic neck collar.

The ten soldiers standing like markers pointed to the leading prisoners where to go to assemble. In no time, all 111 prisoners had compactly converged into what looked from above a square made from angels.

The multitude, once they saw the SA prisoners, went wild; they screamed obscenities and demanded their death, *"Kill the bastards!"* became their favorite scream for blood!

After completing the first square, the ten soldiers moved to an adjacent area and repeated the task. A single Seraph prisoner, part of the first row, stood alone in front of the assembled angelic square as a group leader.

Six similar gatherings of three frontal columns, two rows deep, became lumped together. Two meters separated each square from the adjacent assemblies.

The crowd looked restless but held their position. Nobody dared cross the outside perimeter, so even when the crowd appeared rowdy, it behaved orderly.

The three officers and the platoon assembled the prisoners and moved to the outside perimeter.

The doors of the big transport closed. Its engines hummed forcefully, even silencing the noisy plaza spectators. The large cylinder moved straight upwards; its size quickly diminished until it became a stationary point in the sky. At this instant, the second dot in the sky, which had waited for the unloading of soldiers and prisoners, came down upon the same landing site. The craft was much smaller than its predecessor, but it was much more aerodynamic and graceful but menacing: Lucif-er's private vessel.

After it landed, a heavily armed platoon made of only Seraphim assembled at the side door. The soldiers were more for show than for protection. They wore fancy, shiny outfits or, if you may, the parade uniforms.

Lucif-er, dressed in a dazzling white that honored his name's meaning, stepped out of the vehicle. Instantly, a loud clamor forged with voice and telepathy shook the downtown area! Lucif-er raised his open hands, slowly turning around to accept the glorious welcome from his subjects.

The other seven Overlords planted their feet close to their leader in hierarchic order.

The roar continued unabashed. It lasted over two minutes.

The faces of the NA leaders were magnified many times and broadcast to all street monitors. Their dominant personalities dug deeper into the minds of their subjects, especially Lucif-er's face, which attracted the female side with a hypnotic magnetism that impregnated their vulnerable minds with lust and submission. The male side had its own shortcomings when facing Lucif-er, such as admiration, envy, and fear.

The wings of the Archangels, perhaps because so many admiring cheers fed them, glowed above the sunshine from the noon's sun.

Liliel, in a voluptuous pose, stood at the vessel's door. She was wearing a fancy white and blue jumpsuit, which, of course, had a low cut on the front. The two colors, interlaced with frills, made the cloth more dynamic while enhancing her feminine attributes.

Lucif-er called her to move by his side.

She avidly accepted. Soon, her face and shapely body were equally broadcast all over the city. The male population became instantly 'in love'! Little did they know that it was the female version of Lucif-er!

The group moved to a seating arrangement. One oversized chair that resembled a Throne stayed at the front by itself. Next, the rest of the Overlords sat in a '▲' shaped arrangement; Magog-el was at the center point, Gorgon-el and Zeri-el were on both sides, and so on. Lucif-er's chair, about 3 meters in front of Magog-el's, had two protruding wings or seats, one at each side and located below the level of the main seat. Did Lucif-er plan to sit two queens, one at each of his sides?

Liliel took the seat on the right side.

When all were seated, except Lucif-er, with a hand mannerism, he asked for silence.

His powerful voice could be heard across the plaza; the electronics projected it to the streets and beyond, he said.

"My beloved Centrum citizens!

Our efforts have prevailed. The residual effects from the war that the SA forced upon us, with their hate for our peaceful ways of life, are finally disappearing! Our resources are bouncing back to normal levels. Our..."

Lucif-er explained everything that exalted him and the NA; he talked for twenty minutes. The audience followed every word out of his mouth and every inflection out of his face, indicating total acceptance and submission to their leader. The audience hardly blinked; their eyes stayed glued to Lucif-er when he was in sight or to his image when the large monitors displayed his broadcast to the whole Alliance.

For the enormous crowd gathered, it was an incredible silence. This was only broken by the forceful and dominant voice of Lucif-er that appeared to permeate every crevice in the city. He paused; pointing a finger at the 666 prisoners, he continued.

"There... They are the last survivors of an Alliance that wanted your destruction! They are alive today only because I have fed and protected them!"

The Overlord paused for a short time; he surely expected a response from the audience. He was right because, almost instantly, a muffled rumor rose from the gathering. Why was their greatest leader protecting them? Lucif-er answered their indirect complaint, *"Of course, I understand your feelings... They should be dead!*

However, based on the premise that we are a generous nation, I will offer them a chance for their lives. Furthermore, if they refuse my kind proposition, the decision of their fate will be yours!"

Lucif-er majestically walked the distance, separating him from the prisoners. He planted his intimidating but incredibly handsome physique only a few steps from the central group, where a Seraph, the prisoners' group leader, stood. Lucif-er casually glanced at the prisoners and remarked.

"You heard correctly. I am offering not only your lives but also a chance to be part of this great nation. I can make you rich and powerful, and I will fulfill your desires or fantasies.

On the other hand, since I own you, I could make your lives miserable... I have the power to give life or death.

Since my desire is not to destroy you but to be magnanimous, my offer is as follows."

The Overlord, looking up to the vast crowd, continued similarly as if talking to an imaginary invisible being, *"You believe in a god who does not exist. You can pray, beg, yell, and insult him… He will never answer you! Why are you loyal to such an imaginary being that does nothing for you?*

If you need a god, I could be one for you… I will feed you, clothe you, entertain you… I shall even protect you!"

Pointing his open arms with his fingers apart, like a welcoming invitation, the leader of the NA impressed his sight onto all the prisoners' eyes. While seeding his ideas into their minds, he stated.

"Unlike your god, you can see and touch me… I am real.

Furthermore, I am offering you everything that I have!"

As the Overlord turned sideways, as a guiding gesture to entice the prisoners, his deep blue eyes locked just for an instant with another pair of almost as sinister sight as himself, Azami-el's. When the word 'everything' was mentioned, a diabolic interchange occurred between the two Overlords. Lucif-er, disengaged and facing the captive audience, spoke in a powerful but seductive way.

"What do you have to do to join the NA? It is effortless. You have to say nothing… Just step forward!

I will recognize it as a gesture to accept me and the NA."

As a dead silence fell over the plaza, Lucif-er waited six seconds. Sparks from his eyes began reflecting the internal fury building inside him. He noticed that the Seraph in front of him wanted to say something. Pointing to him, his voice saturated the place so all could understand.

"You are in charge of the whole group. Are you allowing all of them to die? What do you have to say?"

Lucif-er knew what the Seraph had on his mind but let him express his thoughts to the audience. Even when this prisoner was in an unpleasant spotlight, he replied with a firm voice.

"I know that I speak for all!

We can't accept your invitation. We have previously made a 'choice,' and our God will give us the strength to remain loyal to Him!"

Lucif-er's teeth started squeezing harder; not much patience remained. The Seraph backed up as the heat from the nearby stare burned his face. Lucif-er gave his attention to an Angel behind the talking Seraph, the lowest in the hierarchic scale, a plain Angel. Sardonically, Lucif-er remarked with a petulant tone.

"Do you want to talk too? Go ahead… It is your life! And after what you are planning to say, not much may be left of it!"

The slender Angel, with black eyes, black hair, and modestly attractive facial features, avoided the piercing eyes. Timidly but with clear and fluent words, he spoke with determination.

"Our God is not from this world, as you want to attribute yourself!

His power and divinity are on a different level, so we cannot physically perceive them. You have no power of life and death upon us, only what our Lord has allowed you to own!

If we die today, it will be because that is His wish, and we will willingly and joyfully look forward to that moment!"

Lucif-er would have killed him right there, but the angel's eloquence had perplexed him. How could a low life like a plain Angel express himself so well? He would have squashed him if he had not been on public broadcast in front of so many!

Public image… it is so important. What they see is what they believe!

Slowly, Lucif-er walked back to his throne. After taking the last step up, he did not sit. Instead, standing at the edge of the higher step, he seemed to grow. As he faced the crowd and the prisoners again, he remained in an uninterrupted silence for six additional seconds. He seemed to grow taller, to become stronger, and to be more radiant.

His hands reached out for his subjects while his eyes reached out for their souls; deep inside his mind, the darkness grew thicker and malevolent. The prisoners became the focus and the only target of his unsatisfied hate. The personification of Evil reached for a single ending goal: their death! Finally, his voice ripped the stillness.

"Citizens of Centrum. I kindly offered these SA prisoners a chance for a life with a promising future.

They not only refused, but they insulted me with their godly statements. Even when I could rightfully decide their fate, I would not do it… That decision… is only yours!"

With his eyes changing to a deeper blue emulating the darkness from his soul's depths, he hypnotically demanded.

"Do you want them… to live?"

He raised his right hand with his thumb protruding high. His face turned enigmatically distorted because he asked a question with **no** favorable outcome.

"Or do you want them… to die?"

He moved his hand partially down, the thumb facing down as if squashing an invisible bug, while his face indicated the path for a guided purpose.

Was this a prelude to the Roman Coliseum and the Christian martyrs?

The immense crowd answered him with a noisy, violent, and hateful intention. Millions of pitiless mouths opened and screamed. What came out reflected the current state of their souls.

"Kill them… Kill them, now!"

The leader of the NA smiled cynically at the 666 captives. It meant.

"You have made your choice!"

He must have mentally addressed the Seraphim platoons guarding the central square because all moved at double time from their existing positions to a compact arrangement behind the designated seating place for the Overlords. After its completion, Lucif-er raised his hand to appease the multitude. This took several seconds since the roar from the outside kept coming, even when the mouths that generated it were already shut closed.

He opened his hands in front of him like offering a concealed gift.

"My dear people, you have spoken... the prisoners are yours!"

He exclaimed jubilantly.

For a moment, the statement took the bloodthirsty crowd out of balance. When they realized they had been given full approval to be the executioners, they exploded into the centered square!

From above, it looked like watching the march of army ants converging upon defenseless adversaries. They devastated the six groups of SA captives. They punched, kicked, and strangled them. They insulted, ripped their clothes, and continued the savage beating. They did not want to stop until all the prisoners were dead!

However, even this chaotic sea of marauders who were up to no good had their priorities in sight. Many were crunched, had broken bones, and suffered severe injuries caused by the enormous pressure generated by the angelic waves moving forward. But the area where all the Overlords stood in a mixed group by no means became threatened by the crushing power of the compressing wave of people. They knew their priorities.

Liliel, standing very close to Lucif-er, was admiring the carnage; she did enjoy it. Rubbing her breasts upward against the powerful torso in front of her, she locked her pretty purple eyes with the most dominant Overlord. She kissed him on the lower jaw; over the deafening racket shaking the place, she exclaimed.

"I admire your sensitivity; you were quite generous!"

As he looked at her complacently, he extended his right arm and stopped Azami-el as he was moving toward the place of massacre. Even when looking away from his boss, this Overlord mentally saw the face of Lucif-er nodding negatively!

Azami-el wiped one side of his mouth with one hand as if he were missing a great meal! Disappointed, he turned around and faced his boss.

"Too bad!" He retorted. Then, remembering something, he commented, *"Lucif-er, I have this feeling that when you offered the prisoners, 'everything that I have!'..."* He interrupted the message with three sadistic chuckles and continued, *"I am sure that you were referring to the big one!"*

Next, leaning backward, using both hands, simulated holding a large stick in front of his pelvis. Since this was not a private message addressed to Lucif-er, all the other Overlords heard it. Simultaneously, all laughed.

They enjoyed the torture of so many because their hardened hearts remained impervious to the bloody event in front of them. They cherished their satanic ways, while only a few meters away, the blood of the innocent ran plentiful along the shiny floors of the plaza. Under the brutal attack, their lives were extinguished at an accelerated pace. Only God was aware of their unjust suffering, He made it to be very short!

His antithesis was already planning more wrongdoings when Azami-el complained, *"Now... there are no more!"*

"That is not true; somewhere South, I can see many millions still waiting!" Lucif-er promptly replied.

Azami-el's face lightened. He shared sadistic images with his leader. He knew: It's not a long wait... soon!

Lucif-er was getting closer to his goal of becoming a living god, master of the planet, and everything on its surface. The SA did not exist anymore; the only bastion still not under his control remained The Core. This country was not a military threat since it had no armies; in fact, their firm belief in being a pacifist Alliance prevented them from joining the SA.

Nevertheless, the Overlords from the dark side believed The Core to be a real threat to their security, an insane belief fueled by their expansionist desire to conquer. Also, besides the hate, there existed a masked fear of a being called **God**!

They would not stop their path of destruction until that word could only be synonymous with Lucif-er. Even the way this powerful Archangel physically expressed his inner self imitated God. Even when Lucif-er did not express it openly, he believed it to be equated to God for the following reasons.

His first six wings, awesome compared to another Archangel, equated to the First Person of the Holy Trinity: The Father.

His second and unique group of six wings, a reflection of the power of the first group, could be considered similar to the existence of the Trinity's Second Person: The Son.

Last, the intense interaction between the first group of six wings and the second group could represent the Holy Spirit equally.

Speaking materialistically, Lucif-er resembled God when he was created. The possession of such a powerful body and mind corrupted his inner self.

Envy first, next overpowering pride. They overran and erased any traces of the good that once existed inside his soul. He became worse than a barren land that produces nothing from the seeds of love and goodness because he also generated his own opposite evil seeds ready to be exported to any receptive soul to propagate hate and darkness. These seeds had their priority: the destruction of anything good. A seemingly unstoppable power overrunning everything in sight!

All affected Lucif-er in such a manner that his final conviction became. *"I am a God!"*

Humans do not have 'wings' like angels, but we are also created in His image; as a result, our souls relate us to Him.

Angel or Human, we are all God's children, and we should be aware that His love for each of us is immense. However, unhappy events in our lives sometimes cloud our vision, and we may even think that God does not love us. If we reflect on this, we will find a most essential truth.

God is like a good father; to save any of us, He would offer His Son's life to rescue us... as He has already done.

Furthermore, with no intention to confuse you... just meditate on the following statement.

The Son is also the Father![3]

****

Seven years have elapsed since the nuclear war.

As the sight of clean skies and temperatures getting closer to normal, the countermeasures implemented by the NA effectively dwarfed the nuclear winter's effect. Only at sunrise and sunset, the brighter tones of purple, mauve, and magenta tones of color were a reminder of an awesome previous event. Like Earth's major volcanic explosions, which leave similar dusty traces on the atmosphere, those color tones become more noticeable at the twilight of every day, from sunrise or sunset.

Zeri-el had just jumped out of a building and ran toward his craft. Inside his mind, desperation, terror, and fear dominated. Inside his body, sweat, trembling, a pounding heart, and heavy breathing continued tormenting his existence.

Again, as he speedily ran in the craft's direction, it appeared to move farther away. Also, he remained aware that he was dreaming.

Anger interlaced with utter fear rattled his whole body; he knew what was coming next. While his teeth clung together, he looked at the volcano; it was erupting violently!

Once more, the sky became brightly red, with the intense heat searing his body, not only on the outside but all the way to the center of his bones! In horror and enduring almost unbearable pain, he saw his flesh dissolve and vaporize; before letting go of his final scream, a flashy thought speedily crossed his mind.

"No volcanic lava can do such a thing... This stupid dream is made of impossibilities!"

Twisting with the final horror of extinction, he yelled.

"Nooo-o--o---o!"

---

[3] John 14: 9 Jesus said: "Whoever has seen me has seen the Father."

Zeri-el opened his eyes; he was awake now. The drops of sweat were burning like acid as they copiously rolled down along the outside of his seriously burned body, which vividly reminded him of the past dream. Lucif-er stood before him, the Cherub and Overlord angrily exclaimed.

"Still nothing? It did not work again?"

Lucif-er indicated with an open hand to calm down; however, Zeri-el angrily commented, *"Am I condemned to expend eternity with this idiotic nightmare?"*

His boss smiled with amusement; then, he sarcastically mentioned.

"To allow our national hero such fate? ... Never!" Then, placing his hand, which felt like a ton of iron, on Zeri-el's shoulder, he exclaimed.

"I have good news for you... I finally figured out your problem!

You know that dreams initiate in localized areas of the cerebral cortex. They pull information from other places to make a dream segment. All revolves around one theme; when the segment is finished, the dream switches to another localized cortex area, which behaves like a miniature central center, but only briefly; remember that dreams move much faster than what is our average awake speed!

This hopping continues for the duration of the whole dream. It may not be fully continuous, which accounts for the chopping action of the events and the non-related episodes that sometimes pop up; a neuron could have fired the wrong dendrite, making the wrong synapse connection to another brain cell.

The length of the dream segments has a specific duration and a related hopping frequency. Now, the problem with your dream is that the segments are not localized in the cortex but completely dispersed!"

The leader of the NA glanced at the inquiring green eyes impatiently waiting for any answer; he sadistically smiled at his pain but solemnly continued.

"We also know that such dispersion could not possibly be organized to pull information from the rest of the brain for a coordinated dream sequence or segment, but your abnormal brain is doing the impossible! ... It even believes that the dream is real!

I now have an algorithm that will handle such abnormal dispersions. Since I accurately measured the length and frequency of the dream segments, next time, I will intercept and take command of your nightmare... and make you free!"

As the incredulous Cherub would ask: *'Are you sure?'*

Lucif-er added, *"Absolutely!"*

The Lord of Darkness strolled outside the building, inspecting the vigorous growth of the newly planted trees in Centrum's downtown area. As he carefully observed a leaf gently held between two fingers, he told

Azami-el, who stood before him. Gorgon-el, also present, continued casually analyzing the trees and their new branches.

"I am satisfied that the NA resources and its military are back to normal; on account of such good news, you are free to start a border incident against The Core.

We will march against The Core and take over their land as soon as we have any excuse. I am tired of listening to their rationalizations; they are only excuses to avoid us!"

Stopping for a second, the leader of the NA raised his hand.

"You have another message!"

"Yes, Lucif-er!" responded Azami-el. He raised his right hand with his palm facing Lucif-er; he flatly touched his boss's palm. Images flew from one mind to another like a computer memory exchange. Lucif-er quickly retrieved all the relevant information and disengaged, reflectively as he visualized the images just acquired, he remarked.

"It is fascinating... The instrumental measurement of the spectral line of ionized silicon in the sun's corona shows a ten-fold increase in the strength of the magnetic fields around the corona and the photosphere. Also, it is perturbing what is happening on its surface: the asymmetric sunquakes!"

"I found these events to be very unusual!" Azami-el noted.

"Tell the Centrum lab to follow up and keep me informed."

Azami-el nodded affirmatively and departed. Next, Lucif-er faced Gorgon-el and started an inquiry.

"You could not find two better-looking females?"

The addressee twisted his foxy eyes to emphasize his reply.

"That is correct! Furthermore, I know that these two performed a threesome, and they liked it!"

"Excellent! Bring them to me."

"Any chance that Arkyn may object?"

"None!"

A small but elegant cylinder approached Centrum at high speed; it only had two occupants. In the pilot seat, a medium build Seraph was programming the frontal console; he wore the uniform of a high-ranking officer in the NA military forces. Watching him with profound attention was a very attractive female Cherub, who had predominantly large breasts and looked almost as aggressive and sensually dressed as Liliel.

The officer turned his attention to the owner of a set of two pretty green eyes. She smiled at him as she continued enjoying the great vacation they had together at BlueStar City in Eastland.

Being an idyllic place, it rekindled all the passion she felt for him. At this instant, she felt so close to him that she sensed deep warmth radiating from her inside. If he asked her to be married, she would have accepted instantly. This was unusual, considering that they lived where marriage had become outdated, and nobody wanted any new commitments.

His eyes revealed the high level of passion burning inside him; he kissed her on the cheek with some partial lips and a partial tongue. He admired her pretty face and individuality; she was independent, sexy, and intelligent. Moreover, she was quite a dish!

If he would marry anybody, she was the one. With a carefully toned-down telepathic message, he remarked, *"Deana... I can't forget the commendable time we just had together."*

She gently rubbed two fingers on his cheek. She inhaled deeply and then exhaled like you do when your mouth is packed with something hot, she said in a romantic tone.

"Arkyn, my love, I will never forget it. It was the ten best days of my life!"

With their seats facing each other, they kissed intensely and sensuously. Outside, the skirt edges of Centrum approached at high speed. Some preprogrammed control took over, as it could be deduced by the craft going into a sharp deceleration mode; from a speed of several Mach numbers, it slowed down to subsonic speeds. As the fast braking affected their kissing, they laughed. He quickly indicated, *"We will be arriving soon!"*

Next, he typed more commands into the control console.

It is to be noted that typing commands into an angel's control computer turned into a keystroke for every action. Most of the commands ran fully implemented executable programs, anticipating the response and setting up the display so it would become just a one-stroke option. This is what we call AI-assisted today.

Overlords worked differently; they used their highly developed telekinetic powers to access the computer. For Arkyn, the following task selection took only six strokes.

Landing> Sector: Downtown   Building 271
**   Site: NW 1 Floor**
 Control> Automatic

Arkyn was a high-ranking officer; even when he had assigned pilots for his craft, he preferred to do his own flying; it could be a leftover from his previous job with Micha-el. He returned his attention to his attractive companion.

As Centrum's downtown came closer, the view was spectacular. The two angels riding the craft did not care; instead, they spent that time caressing each other.

The cylinder veered into a position aiming for a conglomerate of structures second in splendor only to the central complex where the Overlords lived.

A high-pitched sound called attention to the control screen. Arkyn glanced at the display; a new message had been written.

Attention.
High Command Override
Landing Site> S1 Top Floor

Deana, after reading the message, commented.

"Was your boss waiting for you?"

"No! This must be some unscheduled meeting."

The craft moved higher until repositioning over the assigned southern landing site. There, it hovered before slowly moving down; it almost silently took one of the marked parking places.

Seconds later, the two passengers exited the craft. Arkyn looked around; sure enough, not far away, his boss was waiting for him. Two armed Seraphim, probably his two pilots, stood behind the Overlord. With Deana walking at his side, he wasted no time reporting to the Archangel.

"At your service! Sir!"

Gorgon-el half looked at him; most of his attention remained to the sexy female beside the officer. In a sharp but friendly tone, he announced.

"Congratulations, Commander Arkyn! You are the new Commander of the First Army. Report to the main Centrum base at 4:00 hours!"

Glancing at the attractive female Cherub, he also mentioned.

"Your pretty girlfriend Deana has been invited to meet Lucif-er. It is only a request; she could decline the invitation if she wishes.

Do you have any objection?"

Arkyn got a bit paler. If Lucif-er got hold of Deana, she would no longer be useful to him!

"Not at all, Sir!" he responded cautiously. *"It is up to her to decide!"*

When both sets of blue eyes converged upon her, waiting for her response, she swallowed before deciding what to answer. Inside her brain, she thought.

"No way! I will be crazy to see Lucif-er; I heard he tears females apart... He may even kill me! I am glad that I have a choice!"

As she carefully figured out a nice way to say no, her mind assembled the message's information inside her before it was sent out: "I kindly thank our Great Leader for his generous invitation, but please, I beg him to forgive me for not accepting!"

The message that came out of her mouth was so different!

The two Seraphim attentively listening for her response heard.

"This is a fantastic opportunity! Of course, I accept!"

Before the empty look on Arkyn's face could disappear, he also mentally heard.

"Excellent!" As the Overlord quickly stated. Next, Gorgon-el, waving his index finger to Arkyn, ordered, *"Go!"*

As the officer turned around, he had a chance to see Deana casually waving goodbye to him. He rubbed his face in disgust; he was absolutely sure that his girlfriend would not accept the invitation. How could he be so wrong? Just one invitation from an Overlord, and they run to them with their legs open! ... What does he care about her anyway?

He became the commander of the First Army, next only to an Overlord... his next promotion! **Is that not <u>what matters</u>?**

Deana was numb. She saw her boyfriend walking away with utter disbelief. In no time, he was gone. She felt horrified; the impression he took from her turned <u>utterly wrong</u>! She even waved goodbye against her own wishes. What is she? Just a puppet under the control of the Overlord standing next to her?

Despair filled her whole body. Seemingly, she was in control of her actions, but she could not even raise a finger to protect herself. Depressed, she meagerly walked to the craft where a cynical-looking Gorgon-el pointed for boarding. As she entered by the side door, she saw a pretty Throne seated inside; when she recognized her, Deana's eyes became wide open.

"Gail! I have not seen you for quite a while," she spontaneously exclaimed, *"What are you doing here?"*

The beautiful, purple-eyed Throne felt ecstasy; she almost screamed joyfully, *"Hi! I am so glad to see you again! ... Don't you know, we both have been invited to meet the great Lucif-er!"*

Deana sunk into a chilling fear; now, she knew what Lucif-er wanted!

Lucif-er's residence at Centrum.
Liliel walked into the large meeting room accompanied by her own typical and sensual movements. Her attire was scant the way she preferred it to be. As she aligned her direction for the door leading to the leader of the NA's bedroom, one of four Overlords, Gorgon-el, seated with the others on very modern plush chairs, stopped her.

"Liliel! We are waiting for Lucif-er; take a seat!"

As she stopped, she first glanced at Gorgon-el, who was practically using X-rays to see her naked. After giving him an 'eat your heart out' smile, with consecutive eye contact, she addressed the other Archangels. She noticed the insidious look of the second in command, Magog-el; even when she knew the Overlords could read her intimate thoughts, she said to herself. "What about that... Even the big boy is getting horny!"

Next, she quickly eye-saluted Azami-el and Zeri-el. She took her time as she allowed the spectators to follow every contour of her shapely body until she took a central seat next to Magog-el, who smiled with a satisfaction rarely allowed to permeate outside his formal self.

Liliel gave him three quick eyelash blinks, sort of a tease.

While staring at her impressive physique, the muscular Seraph broke his typically rigid behavior by commenting.

"Are you aware that you have started a new trend for female dressing?

Since they saw you on video, standing alongside Lucif-er during the execution of the last SA prisoners, most of the females are imitating the way you dress!"

Gorgon-el quickly added.

"The male population is eternally grateful to you because now they can see what they want much easier; you have no idea how many eye strains you are preventing!"

Liliel thought it was funny and laughed; from the other room, a muffled scream from a female in deep pain interrupted her laugh! It sounded like a chilling shriek encompassing pain and terror; then, a lower pitch crying, a somewhat uncontrollable moaning. Liliel, standing up, demanded an answer.

"Is Lucif-er screwing a bitch?"

Gorgon-el gave her a sinister and sarcastic answer.

"Correction! ... Two bitches!"

Since the female Throne saw the other females as a threat to her superiority, she became instantly furious and exclaimed with deep hate.

"I will kill them!"

Zeri-el ventured to say.

"Nonsense! After all, the main reason for you females to exist is for the satisfaction of our male necessities!"

Liliel did not like the remark, she speedily retorted.

"You males... You believe that by sticking a big stick into us, we will become scared and submissive. If you think that works all the time, you are wrong! ... Let me tell you something! When I become an Overlord, I will grow a clitoris so large that your penises will resemble little weenies ... Then, I will get even!"

Gorgon-el instantly replied.

"Ouch!"

"It looks like you want male power; why don't you become one?"

Zeri-el commented again.

Expecting the remark, she retorted, *"No need! ... I am going to prove that a vagina is as powerful, and even more so when it will grow teeth and eat all of you up!"*

The sliding door opened. Lucif-er emerged meagerly dressed in a light-dark red tunic, with his left hand supporting Deana, who was in intense pain but still holding her own. She breathed in deeply and frequently as she had both trembling hands together and pressed against her lower abdomen. Her clothes were partially torn with bloody spots, especially around the crotch area. She did not dare to look up since she became deeply embarrassed about her situation; she realized everyone knew what just happened to her.

Another female's whining could be heard from the currently opened room, only now it had become a bit louder.

Liliel stepped forward and slapped Deana. Even when it was a slap, Deana's head snapped to be consistent with a full fist blast. Liliel was already getting stronger and on her way to becoming an Archangel.

Deana's head bounced back to the front; her lips looked chopped and bloody. As Liliel got ready to deliver a second blow, she sharply heard.

"Enough!" Lucif-er ordered.

Even when her body was activated for more action, she refrained. She would not dare antagonize the Lord of Darkness; she knew the consequences. She knew <u>what</u> he could do… which was much more than <u>what</u> she could take!

As Liliel was prepared to ask, "Do you want to keep her?" Lucif-er briskly replied, *"Yes!"*

Moreover, before she could ask again, 'What for?' His anticipated response was, *"She is in great shape. I want to use her for a cloning experiment. Or perhaps… you may prefer such procedure is done to you?"*

Her pretty eyes, redder than purple, almost blew into flames. After giving a spiteful glance to Deana, she meagerly and slowly raised her sight to the big boss and exclaimed.

*"Cloning that whore of Raquel, in my own body? … **No way!**"*

With a cynical smile, the powerful Overlord pointed out.

"In that case, move out of the way!"

Lucif-er addressed Gorgon-el, who stayed avidly watching Liliel.

"Take Deana to the lab. It will be a year before the actual cloning can take place, but when the time comes, I want her to be completely ready. Also, transport Gail to the hospital to fix her injuries; she is all yours when she recovers."

The addressed Overlord nodded in acknowledgment and started to walk toward the opened bedroom door, already anticipating some tender and romantic interlude, Overlord style.

Liliel remained unhappy; while fuming internally, she moved toward a nearby chair; her thought kept to herself, expressed the following.

"He is not the only one that can screw around; I can do it too!"

She was shaken when Lucif-er interrupted her with a public message.

"Absolutely! You are free to choose any mate of your liking. There is only one catch; first, you must ask for my permission."

Liliel squeezed her eyes, bit her lower lip, and stared inquisitively at the leader of the NA; slowly and cautiously, she inquired.

"Did I hear you correctly? You could be teasing me?"

Lucif-er gave her the devil's smile and calmly responded.

"Yes and no!"

She was unleashed; she ran her left-hand thumbnail into the inside of her upper lip. She pulled it slowly out so her lip became sexily exposed; the curves from her shapely body moved with passion. She made a melodious and insinuating request.

"I have a choice... Could I have him, now?"

Gorgon-el, almost walking into the adjacent bedroom, stopped in his tracks; turning around, he stared with lusty hope over the sexy body undulating not far away while his blue eyes shined with intense craving.

Lucif-er responded with undisguised complacency.

"You can have Magog-el... right now!"

The chosen Overlord was incredulous; even for an Overlord, the quick change of direction took him by surprise. He became delighted, but he sent a personal telepathic message to Lucif-er.

"Are you sure?"

"Yes!"

With a sadistic smile that also showed great satisfaction, he grabbed Liliel's left hand and speedily moved toward the nearest elevator. Liliel was amused; the Overlord had kept his passion for her quiet until today. Now, she was almost dragged out of the room by the muscular Seraph, who usually remained so strict and stern that he reminded her of a stiff. She sardonically whispered in his ear.

"Hurry up! I can't wait to show you the best time of your life!"

Gorgon-el felt intense frustration; he squeezed his teeth until they made noises. However, his horny mind did not give up; he sent a personal message to the boss.

"Can I be next?"

Lucif-er looked at his subordinate in the same way as a pimp sneered at a penniless customer asking for free sex with one of his whores; he slowly moved his head in an affirmative direction. This action generated the maximum delight Gorgon-el could harbor; to his total and furious disappointment, the message that came out simply read.

"No!"

An aircraft continued flying at great speed high on a sky stamped with a clear and starry night. Like a silent meteor, it streaked way above the ground; its dark image remained barely defined by its frontal light and the lights at the tips of its wings, giving the illusion of a night bird hunting for prey.

Inside the craft, three plush chairs faced each other. Confronting the front cabin, two Overlords stayed seated contemptuously. They were Gorgon-el and Zeri-el. The chair in front of them remained empty.

One of the Overlords, a Seraph, talked to his partner, expressing his thoughts with fury and uncontrolled malice.

"You saw what Lucif-er did to me! He knows that I have a craving for nailing Liliel, so he enjoys screwing me up; I hate his guts when he does that!"

His partner, who felt a little edgy himself because of the fact it was nighttime again, the usual time for nightmares, retorted.

"He was just teasing you."

"I know; however, he should not do it when there are subordinates present. It undermines the chain of command!"

As he noticed that Zeri-el was casually staring at a butt that was partially sticking out of the pilot's cabin, he quickly changed his anger to a lusty and sodomite remark. Azami-el, who owned the body part, got an image of his behind with text attached.

"Azami-el, Zeri-el is thinking that you have a great ass!"

The Overlord with the deep blue piercing eyes was not amused. He made a gesture, which probably was a prelude to an Italian hand remark meaning: *'Up yours!'* Since both Overlords were his superiors, he refrained from any severe verbal damage. From his seat, he commented.

"Liliel surely knows how to suck your brains; both of you are still horny!"

Gorgon-el appeared to see the image of the seductive female spread across the interior ceiling of the cylinder; with a sexual overtone, he exclaimed, *"Could you imagine the kind of high level of sex that could be achieved, when she becomes an Overlord?"* He finished by sticking out his tongue and licking his own lips.

Azami-el, looking at a different ceiling's location and sharing the sensual image generated by Gorgon-el's twisted mind, coldly remarked.

"I cannot get excited by such an idea. I would not trust her with the pride of my masculinity!"

The other two Overlords laughed with their lusty and sadistic imagination running rampant.

Zeri-el, changing the direction of lewdness, asked Azami-el.

"I know you screwed some SA male prisoners. Is it possible for this homosexual act to have any advantages, as you compare it to heterosexual intercourse?"

Azami-el, rubbing his index finger up and down his chin, responded.

"It was not fun with the SA prisoners; the bastards died by only touching them! I have tried it with some NA citizens... I enjoy the full penetration, the male screams, the blood! ... Occasionally, you kill some... even better!"

Gorgon-el inserted his telepathic message, *"Lucif-er and I discussed the topic. This is the way he explained to me.*

'No male or female is 100% his own sex.

Of the males, 20% have a weak masculinity; they are prone to be homosexuals. Once they are <u>introduced</u> to this new activity, they do not wish to go back to being heterosexual.
Another 50% can be forced to develop a taste for it!
The remaining 30%, regardless of being imposed on this new activity, will still go back to being heterosexual. They are a minority!

Most important, when you own a 60 centimeters long organ, it can intimidate and terrorize both sexes! ... Males, in their presence, feel inadequate and inferior.

Forcing your way into the ass of a rebellious male makes him more submissive. It works similarly for the females you have screwed, as they become sub-dependent to your male power!

It is a new weapon to be used as another way to impose your supremacy; it is also an insidious way to increase the level of fear and submission to your enemies! ... And even to your friends!'"

As all the present chuckled with decadent wisdom, Zeri-el, rubbing his chin, indicated.

"Lucif-er has a point!
It is interesting to note that if homosexuality becomes an accepted way of life, it will change the heterosexual balance that we have maintained for many millennia... In this new scenario, we have heterosexuals, male homosexuals, and female homosexuals; six possible interactions!"

Same on Terra with the angels, as here on Earth with the humans, it is sad to notice that the original act of sex, something so noble and good due to its primary two functions, to procreate and to unify two different beings into one loving pair; because of its evil use, has become dirty and decadent. No wonder that the word 'sex' is now frequently replaced by four-letter words, which more accurately represent its new perverted meaning.

Gorgon-el asked a direct question to Azami-el.
"Is there a chance that The Core's citizens may be more fun than the SA prisoners?"

With a sadistic smile, the addressed Overlord replied.
"I hope so! I have a big stake in them! ... In two days, we will know!"

Their sordid laughs echoed through the crevices of the craft's interior. Zeri-el had to mention one more thing.

"I am going back to Centrum, Lucif-er assured me that this time he would help me to get rid of my bad dreams. I hope he is correct; I want to fully enjoy the invasion of The Core! ... I have never seen Lucif-er taking such a long time to fix a problem!"

Gorgon-el replied, *"Some gamma rays must have cooked your brain!"*
"I told you before! I was not even close to any nuclear explosion!"

The Overlords stayed deeply sunk into their decadent ways. It became a dark swamp, where the turbid waters of sin without limits completely occluded any spark of goodness. It was a loveless habitat, where nightmares were not in dreams but part of a decadent society and daily life. The real monsters remained loose and walked next to you; however, even if you became scared, it made not much difference. After all, on a smaller scale, you were one of them!

As a good soul strives for perfection as it climbs the ladder of the heavenly sky, with every step making itself better and getting closer to God and Holiness, in a similar but opposite way, the souls of the evil ones sink deeper into new and darker places where the mud is thicker and the hope of escaping non-existing.

Trillium, The Core.

Walking along the newly planted main avenue, a tall and stoic Seraph missed the beautiful flowering trees that once decorated this spectacular pathway, now dead and already removed. New plants grown inside greenhouses that protected them from the previous cold and radioactive dust started reclaiming their grounds. With their last splendor gone, only the impressive maze of green skyscrapers remained unchanged.

Nobiel, sad for the loss of such precious plants, had a much deeper pain carving a scar that produced a greater sorrow in his present life: the loss of millions of The Core citizens fallen to the nuclear winter. Equally unforgotten remained the loss of two billion SA citizens slaughtered by the merciless NA. It was hard to believe; it happened seven years ago!

Dressed in casual attire, he did not call the attention of the few other individuals, couples, or groups who finally ventured to the outdoors. Seven years ago, it was hard to walk among the cheerful crowd enjoying these locations; life was so different then.

Coming from behind him, a hurried pounding of running steps began increasing in intensity.

Nobiel stopped walking as he turned around to see the approaching runner. He was a Cherub dressed as a council member. Even at the distance needed to reach Nobiel, he appeared seriously perturbed.

After a few seconds, he finally faced the council leader. The Cherub placed a hand on Nobiel's shoulder for support, and while trying to catch up with his excited breathing, he exclaimed.

"Nobiel!" He stopped to take two deep breaths, then continued, *"You have not been notified? ... **I have... terrible news!**"*

The Core's leader asked, *"What is it? I wanted to be alone, and I disconnected my communication device!"*

"The NA is massing their armies along our borders... I am sure that this time, they will make their threats come true!"

"My dear friend Oryel, is it our turn now? Are we running out of time?"

Oryel wiped the sweat running down his round face. He asked the leader, *"Is there anything we can do to stop the NA?"*

The Seraph in charge nodded negatively. After a short pause, he indicated.

"We do not have an army. But even if we did, we could not stop the powerful military machine of the NA!"

"Should we pray for God's help?"

"Of course, all the time!

We will pray for courage! We will pray that this feeling deep inside our hearts, which allows us to stand straight and sing aloud to our Creator, will help us measure up to His last request for our loyalty.

When we talk about courage, what is courage, anyway? Is it something like faith? Something that we must believe in to act on?

People can tell you: 'You are courageous!' But only you know if that statement is true!"

Nobiel placed both hands over Oryel's shoulders as he looked squarely into his green eyes, partially clouded by anxiety. Nobiel felt a surge of courage filling his whole self with new energy, demanding to be outspoken, so he exclaimed.

"Let's go, Oryel! Let's alert the whole country!
The NA can take over our land, but they will hear our singing; they will listen that we are not afraid of the darkness!

*They will hear that we deeply love our God, and we will sing to Him louder than ever! The Evil from the NA will know that they can steal all material things we possess; however, our souls shall belong to our loving God... **now and forever!**"*

Centrum, NA; the same night at Lucif-er's mansion.

This was the same room where Lucif-er kept the 'stone' and his trophies. At this moment, the incredible artifact bathed the whole room with an unusual display of light and modulated energy, bouncing from a bed just below its position. Sleeping on it, face up, Zeri-el lay still.

The light display ran over his body with bands of colored light waves and intersecting nodules caused by resonant frequencies. The largest and primary resonant nodule was located precisely at his forehead; it distorted his facial characteristics as if his skin began moving on its own, not in one direction but simultaneously in many directions.

Lucif-er stood facing away from the bed; he talked to Gorgon-el.

"I am glad you brought the research lab report on the sun's behavior. You and I have worked many hours on our sun's thermonuclear reactions and were definitely sure that we understood all the fusion processes involved.

Starting 35 years ago, our sun behaved illogically. As time passes, its actions have become more complex and moved away from the statistic norm!"

Lucif-er stared into his subordinate colleague's eyes, making him blink twice; he ordered, *"I want you to do the following!*

Equip six satellites to be positioned in stationary orbits around the sun, equidistant from each other. They should be located barely outside the corona and at identical distances to the sun's surface.

All the satellites should work synchronously and transmit back to Terra using six multiplexing 3-D channels. Call the database: ST-6. I want long-term integrated projections!"

After a brief pause, he added, *"We may have to rewrite our thesis, 'Stars- A Nuclear Physics Treatise'!"*

Before Gorgon-el could express himself, his leader continued.

"Zeri-el will start dreaming in five seconds; you cannot stay and watch... just go."

Gorgon-el finally had the opportunity to say anything.

"I got it! Satellite launching shall be scheduled for deployment in twenty days!"

Zeri-el had landed on this tropical island again. The two beautiful females came and threw themselves at his feet. His loyal armed escort took him to the top of a nearby building. The slanted 'M' shaped volcano suddenly got violent and rattled the building.

Zeri-el escaped the crumbling structure by jumping off the top floor. Now, he began running for his life again!

The space between jumping off the building and reaching his private craft stretched in the same manner as a rubber band becomes longer as it is pulled apart.

Fear, terror, and the knowledge of what the nightmare ending became was ripping him apart. He turned his head to stare at the volcano; it continued blasting fire with an incredible display of fury!

A thunderous rumble shocked the ground; he could hear the fiery mountain speaking with a menacing roar.

"M-U-R-D-E-R-E-R!"

A chill so cold that it burned, something never experienced before, charred his mind and body! The horror stayed out of control, lashing at the most intimate locations of his mighty intellect; he yelled to himself.

"It is only a dream! ... Why can't I wake up?"

He continued his desperate running toward a place that could not be reached. Next, he was expecting the fire from above to fall on him, with the intent not just to burn but also to carbonize!

Suddenly, like a Star Trek episode, a figure materialized before him. The individual wore a radiant white tunic, and his blue-searing stare became disturbingly sharp. Zeri-el stopped flat in his tracks, exclaiming with utter unbelief.

"Lucif-er! What are you doing in my dream?"

The image extended its right arm up with his palm facing Zeri-el. The Cherub felt intense pressure on his chest, causing him to exclaim.

"I felt that... Tell me, what are you doing here?"

The questioned Overlord calmly smiled at him, and with a soft but powerful voice, he explained.

"I was checking your response to a push; since it worked, I am here to end your nightmares. Let's exit this dream segment!"

Zeri-el frowned because he was incredulous.

"There is no way out of here! How could you do it?" He questioned.

"In a very simplistic way... we just draw a door!"

As the Cherub's inquisitive eyes stared at the leader of the NA, the latter, with his index finger pointing to the emptiness of air, just drew a rectangle.

Zeri-el's incredulous eyes opened widely; a door had instantly materialized.

It appeared so unrealistic. It was like floating in the middle of nowhere... with nothing at its sides and nothing behind it!

Lucif-er flipped a finger, and the door slid open. Inside, it was dark, a solid black.

Lucif-er, with a hand mannerism, coerced Zeri-el to cross the door. The latter hesitated. Was it possible to step out of this place of horrible torture through an imaginary door?

He went for it!

As he placed one foot inside the other side, everything else in the dream fell apart. It was like a painting made with watercolors, and someone poured a bucket of water over it; the mountains, the ground, and the sky all became smeared and vanished!

Zeri-el slowly opened his eyes. The room was quiet, with no light displays. He felt unusual stress in the center of his forehead; he almost instinctively rubbed the affected skin area. As he focused on the image of Lucif-er, suddenly, he noticed.

There was no sweat, no pain, and no sunburn!

He just knew it. Finally, he was free from the nightmare. In utter satisfaction, he licked his upper lip and yelled to Lucif-er.

"I owe you... a big one!"

It had been a very long battle; smiling with the taste of success, his boss sarcastically remarked.

*"Fine! ... Just **no** kissing!"*

The Core. The main central building in Trillium.

Thirteen angels hesitantly talked to each other; they were The Core's council members. Nobiel raised both hands, begging for silence. It took a while, but eventually, the other twelve calmed down; he immediately stated.

"Yes! It is confirmed!
Three armies from the NA are invading our air space; at this instant, they are moving to take positions inside each of our states!
A detachment of the NA First Army is approaching our city directly from Centrum; it will arrive in half an hour! ... At 4:00 hours!"

A Throne council member suggested.

"Perhaps, if we don't do anything to upset the invaders, they will leave us alone! They should know; we are a peaceful nation!"

Nobiel nodded with disagreement. With sadness in his telepathic message, he remarked, *"If you breathe... You will upset them!"*

The round-faced Cherub named Oryel exclaimed.

"My dear brothers, our leader Nobiel will initiate our praying songs to our Lord; only He can give us the courage to stand straight for this intense impending trial!"

Nobiel moved away from the council table, the place where the members ran their everyday business; slightly perspiring, he considered the ominous threat to his country but remained incredibly calm. He had relinquished his effort to survive by trusting God's wisdom. When his good friend Gabri-el was still around, things happened differently; any major crisis and he would run for advice from his friend, this kindly Overlord always stayed available when help was needed. Now, he was gone. To ask for help, only God remained available!

He could not deny his concern and deep anxiety stirring his soul; however, dealing directly with the Lord filled him with a self-sufficient state of Grace.

Looking at his twelve colleagues, he planted a broad smile on his face. He knew Lucif-er's demands and the dramatic and explosive results provoked by The Core's refusal to accept them.

This was not a single individual decision but a nation's choice!

With a classy and friendly poise and using the flipping of a finger, he asked a nearby operator to connect him to the nation's broadcasting network. He addressed the present and the not visually available. Nevertheless, carried by the electronic waves, he felt equally in contact with all of them. His firm voice and stoic figure became heard and seen over the meeting room and the whole land called The Core.

"My dear brothers and sisters... citizens of The Core.
Today is the day that we have been waiting for. Today... we shall meet our loving God, our Creator, to Whom we sang for so many years.
In this way, we will praise His Glory in the manner we know best. We will sing out our gratefulness to His love, power, and splendor... for all Eternity."

The council leader paused for a moment. He looked outside a large window; the cameras could only capture his profile. Like getting introspective, without facing the cameras, he continued.

"Using this electronic link, let's synchronize our singing.

Let the Lord hear us, not as individuals, but as a whole nation. Let's start our singing with a new song that we have named: 'Love is everything, Love is God.'"[4]

The Core sang loud and passionately as never before. The song came deep from their hearts, millions and millions of voices singing in unison, making the whole land of The Core tremble with their outpouring of love towards an <u>invisible</u> God!

On the other hand... **was He invisible?**

At the top of The Temple, the magnificent building erected for the worship of the Lord with a geodesic dome having a radius of 777 meters existed a small flat area at its very summit: a shiny metallic square, 40 x 40 cm. At such an incredible height and small area, an angel stood perfectly straight!

He remained impervious to the incredible view, which appeared as deep as a canyon down to the faraway floor. The strong winds blowing at that height moved his dark red tunic as a flag tended to the wind.

There was a strange aura around his body, but he had no wings!

He paid attention to the song, enjoying what He heard, as shown by a smile; after a few minutes of appreciative listening to The Core's most loving song to God, His face brightened, and He exclaimed.

"My dearest nation! Your wish shall become a reality!

In Heaven, you will be the closest to my presence, where you shall sing to my Glory, which I will share with you.

In addition, for your love to me in the face of such great tribulation and for your beautiful singing... today, you shall be rewarded!"

Nobiel continued singing as loud as his lungs would allow it. The window caught his attention; as he casually glanced outside the tall central tower, The Temple attracted his sight. It did with such demanding force that it appeared to be the only place he could see. While he sang, he admired the beautiful lines that adorned such a spectacular building; gradually, his sight moved upwards to the top of the dome. He casually stared at the top of the distant structure.

He squeezed his eyelids while trying to focus on the highest part of the dome. A chill running down his spine caused him to stop singing abruptly.

---

[4] The Seraphim are the highest Choir of angels; except for the seven Archangels next to God, they are the closest beings in the presence of the Lord.
Isaias 6: 2-3 describes them as six-winged angels crying out the glory of God.

He could not believe it. Someone was standing at the building's top, which was impossible; only an Overlord could perform such an acrobatic feat, and none remained living in The Core.

"Who could he be?"! He thought.

He tried harder to discern the silhouette. To his astonishment, even when his body remained at the central tower, his vision moved closer and closer to the stranger. Soon, he began floating in front of this being, like Nobiel was made of spirit alone, and he could travel anywhere by just wishing it to be!

When Nobiel saw the stranger's radiant face, it did not matter that he had the shape of an angel; he knew this person could <u>not</u> be an angel!

Nobiel was filled with immense joy just by having the honor of being in His presence.

The 'Angel' in the red tunic communicated with a pure, resounding telepathic message.

"My dear son! ... I just wanted you to know that in these last moments, you and all the citizens of this land shall not walk alone, as my hand will support and guide you toward the heavens!"

Nobiel became speechless; the divine figure extended His right hand in his direction. He frantically wanted to touch it… but could he? Would this ethereal body of his allow any physical contact?

Eagerly and motivated beyond angelical means, he tried… And he did!

Like liquid fire running through every cell of his body, he felt the divine touch. His body, not even present there, shook violently with immense joy!

The next instant, his entity became exposed to this unbelievable knowledge. His incredulous but avid mind opened to this incredible richness. He saw the past, the present, and the future.

Then, he understood. The divine plan was now so clear!

For a second time, Nobiel found himself glancing out of the window.

The top of The Temple's dome became empty! The Seraph stared at the place he had just visited. He had never felt like this before; now, he felt so complete!

His wings shined like never before; even an Archangel could not surpass him. He knew why they had to depart from this planet, why God was calling them to His presence, and why he even existed.

From behind him, his close friend Oryel touched his shoulder. The Cherub retracted his hand instantly! He had felt a burning jolt of energy; confused, he asked.

"What is happening?"

Nobiel looked at him with brotherly love; then, he noticed that the rest of the council members had stopped singing and stared at him. Oryel, pointing to the hair around Nobiel's ears and temples, exclaimed with astonishment.

"Your hair is white! You have aged!"

Nobiel stayed jubilant; he knew the reason for such an unusual event. Propelled by the fire, which was diminishing but still burning along his entire body, he proclaimed.

"Nobody can stand before our Creator, touch Him, and remain the same! ... The Lord has honored us with His presence; the fire of His touch has burned me much more on the inside than on the outside!

His love and compassion did not abandon us, ever! In His generosity, He even brought us a gift!"

The council leader reflected on his previous statement. Even when all his questions were answered, he knew about the gift but did not know what exactly it was! He assumed the obvious.

"We asked for courage; God Himself has brought it to us!

I know you are anxious for me to explain; however, let all thirteen of us hold hands together, and without me pronouncing a word, you will comprehend as much as I do.

Then... we will sing!"

An aircraft cluster began approaching from the North at 4:00 hours. The peaceful and empty skies above Trillium, unusually quiet for this time of the day, became disturbed by a wave of invading military aircraft. Inside these cylinders, the NA leaders and their soldiers looked like a sinister gathering of menacing and bloodthirsty gargoyles. Even when masked on the outside by their good looks and shiny clothes, the dark forces of Evil started extending their tentacles, showing their sinister true selves to the outside. They were setting their last belligerent stance, their final plot for the destruction of the last country in Terra still glorifying God.

An ominous cloud of cylinders occluding the clear sky came into view. Leading the invasion was an elite group of high-tech aircraft. The aerodynamic shape of these machines heralded the importance of their passengers.

A wing of combat aircraft closely followed them; their mission was to have a protective umbrella for the rest. Of course, the Overlords owned all the priorities.

Finally, at the end of the procession, the large troop transports displayed their massive contours. The growing outline of the cylinders as they got closer crowded the skies; inside their hulls, fully armed soldiers were ready to slaughter the unarmed, the peace-loving, and the innocent!

A section of the combat flying devices moved upwards and dispersed over the city; at their new locations, they remained stationary.

The elite group landed on a high plateau southwest of the city. The remaining invading aircraft, after drawing a circle around the perimeter of the city with their stationary dots, landed on the ground but outside such a perimeter.

In no time, equipment and troops began disembarking.

From the flagship, Lucif-er and his seven Overlords stepped out of their stylish cylinder and stood at the edge of a plateau facing the magnificent capital of The Core. Inside their field of vision, the magnificent structural green jewel adorning the planet glittered majestically under the bright midday sun. No other city on the planet looked so majestic and spectacular.

Even with no sign of any Core's aerial activity, the city was not silent. From this distant location, the melody of an incredibly loud and synchronized singing filled the air with a song of love and worship.

Lucif-er glanced with disdain at the city he had entitled as his home for so many years and at the same place where he had become the most important and admired citizen for so many years. However, since at this site and at that time, he did not enjoy the absolute power that the founder of Evil required, he departed.

Now, he was back. His hardened soul had no mercy on sight; he also intended to level the place if his slightest request remained unfulfilled.

People of Trillium, beware! The Destroyer, the ultimate Terminator, has arrived!

The First Army commander's ship landed next to the Overlords' craft. Arkyn, followed by a fully armed platoon, took positions around the perimeter. He wasted no time reporting to Lucif-er. The Overlord made eye contact and pointed down to a nearby location; the commander acknowledged and, using his belt communicator, ordered two nearby large transports, still hovering close to the ground, to move in and touch down at the assigned location.

Arkyn also received a personal message from Lucif-er.

"Ask all council members to report to this location at 4:40 hours!"

"Sir! It will be done immediately!"

The two massive transports landing nearby caused the earth to tremble under the hum of their enormous superconducting engines. Some atmospheric eddies were generated, causing dust and small particles to fly everywhere. This disturbance did not last long, as it quickly disappeared after their engines went off. Out of their huge bowels, massive and menacing mobile cannons moved to the front line, the location where the Overlords stood.

Two batteries, each with five cannons, took position along the plateau's edge. Together, they formed a ▲ pointing to the downtown area. This was done so the Overlords standing next to the rim did not have to move. With laser-guided targeting, the cannons' menacing coils became poised for massive destruction. These huge electromechanical monsters were the most potent plasma cannons on the planet, the newest artifacts for dispensing death and destruction.

Inside the flagship, next to one of its windows, Liliel sat comfortably while looking toward Trillium. She had decided to watch from the craft because those massive cannons were noisy, and the electrostatic electricity they generated raised havoc with anybody's hairdo.

When she finishes her Overlord training in a few years, it will not matter anymore. Besides, she should be able to watch the carnage at close range using the military vehicle's telescopic sights, allowing her to observe any of her choices. There is nothing like having a front-row seat at the Coliseum!

4:38 hours. From Trillium, a small craft approached the edge of the plateau.

It hovered before the Overlords and slowly landed in front of the Archangels and their menacing cannons. The thirteen members of the council disembarked. Nobiel quickly approached the group and faced Lucif-er and Magog-el. The singing from the city remained undisturbed by the developing events.

Lucif-er immediately noticed the gray hair around Nobiel's temple and made a sarcastic remark, which amused the rest of the Overlords.

"You must be living a bad life! You are getting old!"

Nobiel did not show any concern. He was ecstatic that the fearsome terror hidden behind such a beautiful outside envelope caused no anxiety in his heart or mind. He had no fear in front of the Lord of Darkness! Before, he had dreaded such an encounter to the point of panic, but now, his worries seemed futile and unwarranted. The peace inside him stayed exalting and unshaken by anything; he even felt pity for his former leader. With a smile on his face, he responded.

"You have no idea how proud I am of these white hairs!"

Lucif-er, not amused by the response and by the attitude of the Seraph in front of him, turned on his easily provoked rage. In addition, it did not make sense that the council leader remained unafraid of him, as he had always been. Furthermore, he immediately noticed that none of the council members were either! Lucif-er, somewhat confused by such unusual behavior, lashed out with a clear message with two subtle overtones: anger and hate!

"I will be very brief... Since you already know what my demands are, you will have precisely twenty minutes to announce the acceptance of my terms!
Failure to accept will cause your city to burn! The remains, together with your dead bodies, I will make sure they become dust!"

Nobiel glanced at the fiery blue eyes before him and calmly remarked.

"We do not have an Army. Since this nation's foundation, The Core has always wanted peace. You, of all people, should know it!
You have changed so much, Lucif-er; now, you hate us. What have we done to you?"

The face of the leader of the NA got closer to the leader of The Core's council; he was baffled. How was it possible that Nobiel could be standing that close to him, unperturbed? How could he be talking to him on equal terms? He lashed with furor.

"When you hide behind a god that does not exist, who intends to banish me from the land, you have done more than enough! ... There will be no peace in this land until the god with no name is replaced by a god with a name!"

The council leader's stoic appearance, further enhanced by his encounter with God, had his personality outshine his more powerful opponent. After the last mentally spoken sentence, he sharply lashed out at the Lord of Darkness.

"Now, you have made it clear. It is not about us; you are at war with the Most High! ... You want Him to disappear because you intend to take His place; however, you are no god, a mighty angel indeed, but still an angel! ... We shall only worship what you have rightly stated: a God with no name!"

Clenching his teeth, the Lord of Darkness shouted.

"You are pushing my patience! You and all the dead people from the SA have chosen a god that is non-existent; if a god existed, he would not have allowed your destruction; he would have protected you! Take notice! Anybody that joins the NA will be protected, and he will live!"

Lucif-er, pointing a menacing finger to the forehead of the Seraph in front of him, threatened him, *"Listen, and listen well! You and the whole Core can sing to a worthless god... until noon!*

Nevertheless, just one second past the 5:00 hours with no response from you, the council, and today shall be the last day for your god... and equally, the same last day of your lives!"

With just a short pause, he yelled to the whole council.

"You spineless cowards! You do not even fight for what you believe! Go back to Trillium; count even the seconds... you have not many left!"

As the council moved toward their craft, Nobiel turned around and questioned even when he already knew the answer.

"If nobody offers any resistance... Will you... still kill us?"

Lucif-er did not answer; he just gave him a sinister grin that said it all. From behind the two Overlords, Azami-el's uncontrolled diabolic laugh broke the silence.

The seconds moved much faster at Trillium than at the location occupied by their recently camped enemies outside the city's perimeter.

Lucif-er and Magog-el stood on a plateau's edge bordering the city's southwest side. The terrain did not fall steeply but mainly like a three-degree incline that ended at the town's very fringe.

Coming from far away, the singing stayed more vital than ever, with no breaks. It was a nonstop marathon for the exaltation of a God anxious to reclaim the souls of the faithful, who were anxious to share His immense love and be awarded nothing less than the Infinite.

Can you imagine being in front of the All-Mighty God and calling Him "Father!" ... In addition, He, in return, addresses you as *"My son!"*

If you were a prince, the son of a mighty king, you could expect to share the riches of a nation, perhaps the wealth of a whole continent.

However, if God Himself calls you to share His Glory, which includes Eternity and Infinity, could you possibly imagine what kind of wealth you could expect to share?

Lucif-er grabbed his long curly hair with both hands around his temples; he pulled hard, full of indignation, he remarked.

"That stupid singing! It is giving me a headache!"

His colleague, Magog-el, quickly indicated.

"It is annoying! It is similarly affecting me. I am glad that they have only five minutes left! Yet, something else is bothering me... I still cannot figure out if the council members were in a hypnotic trance or took some drugs. The behavior of those maggots was surely odd!"

Lucif-er staring at the city with piercing hate, without turning to see Magog-el, mentioned, *"Yes! An irrational behavior! ... I believe the idiots are becoming suicidal. They may not even care anymore if they live or die! ... I care less; I am eager to fulfill their last wish!"*

Magog-el, rubbing his chin, ventured to question.

"Lucif-er! Are you sure that you want to destroy the city?
It would be extremely easy to kill all its inhabitants, and we could have such a wonderful place to ourselves! The city holds great treasures and technological developments!"

The leader of the North did not even blink. He had an empty stare at the skyscrapers that rose higher as you approached the city's center.

"Yes, I will!" He responded, *"Trillium will be an example to this world as it will show what happens to anybody who opposes me. In addition, the whole city was built to exalt god's existence; it must go!"*

After a brief pause, he continued, *"Furthermore, I have new plans for an integral city that will make all the existing ones obsolete!"*

Magog-el glanced at the emerald city, a sparkling jewel enticing his greedy eyes, *"I understand, but it is such a waste. It's the same as we are doing now, just waiting, just wasting our time! ... Those hardheaded bastards, they are not going to join us!"*

Lucif-er interrupted him; he ordered, *"Tell Arkyn to get ready to fire!"*

As they sang together, Nobiel and the rest of the council stood at the center of the central building, somewhat detached from the rest. He reflected on the power of singing. Even in the most stressful situations, singing kept his nation in focus. It bound their souls uniquely, enhancing God's love while diminishing their earthly concerns.

He looked at a timepiece across the room. Only minutes remained for Trillium to sing its last glorious instants, so he asked for a special song.

With all arms extended, everyone touched two other members, making a circle. The council leader's voice advanced his last suggestion.

"Let all in this nation express the best inside our hearts by singing our newest song to our loving God!"

The Core synchronized for an encore performance of a new song written to encompass His most important value: The power of Love.

Together, their lungs blasting to their maximum capacity, the citizens of this peaceful nation sang with passion, like they all knew that this was their last song, a melodic stepladder to the heavens where their loving Father had His hand already extended down, waiting for that final instant when the material becomes spiritual.

'Death' is not a good description of the faithful's life-ending; it only applies to sinful souls who have lost God forever. Perhaps it should be called 'Metamorphosis', a transformation: the change from a physical state to a much better form. Conceivably more fitting, we could even call it for short 'Meta,' which in Spanish means something to reach for, a goal.

The song, vocalized to its best because it came from the deepest part of their hearts, went like this.

♪ **The heavens proclaim Your glory**
The firmament affirms Your kindness
All is Love that equates to You, O Lord

You show me the path to Love
The fullness of joys in Your presence
The delights at Your right hand forever

O Lord, hear my prayer, hear my song
Listen to my pleading in Your loving faithfulness
Our hearts are open to receive You, O Lord[5] ♪

---

[5] Lines 1-2> Modified Psalms 19-2; Lines 4-6> Psalms 16-11; Lines 7-9> Modified Psalms 143-1

Arkyn, the commander of the First Army, stood next to the heavy artillery while holding a communication device in his hand. He used it to order all the plasma cannon operators around Trillium to charge up their energy banks. In this manner, they prepared to fire a massive and violent energy discharge capable of incinerating anything in its path, including the unfortunate angels living in the city!

Arkyn wore a combat telemetric helmet that matched the patterns of his shiny uniform, which was white and blue. With a firm voice, he ordered.

"To all operators of plasma cannons!
Burst frequency = 5, Plasma power = 50%, Targets: Locked.
Devices: Armed!"
After a two-second delay, he finished.
"Wait for my signal to fire!"

An ominous hum rattled the ground. Except for the Overlords, the perimeter guards and the cannons' operators felt all the hair on their bodies tingling. The massive superconducting coils generated a tremendous static and magnetic field when the extremely high voltages necessary to create the fiery plasma balls became activated. A moderate mechanical noise became momentarily noticed as the cannons moved their pointing sights to target the structures of their choice and laser-locked those final destinations.

The mouths of the cannons were not gaping holes but concave half-hemispheres that appeared smooth; in actuality, they were composed of thousands of needle endings, each independent from the others. An enormous electromagnetic wave was required to project the energetic balls of fire from the tips of the needles to the far-away targets. The tip of the targeting laser stayed at the dead center of the concave half-hemisphere.

Each large transport aircraft carried a thermonuclear reactor, which propelled the massive crafts when flying or recharging cannons on the ground. In addition, cables, telemetric instruments, massive coils, gadgets, and a crew of five maintained each cannon.

Lucif-er and the other seven Overlords moved to positions along the artillery. They positioned themselves inside the ▲ shaped cannon arrangement with only one difference: instead of being behind them, they stood between two cannons; in this manner, they would have a clear view of the city while being close to the line of fire. Inside the control cabins of the cannons, itchy fingers waited to activate the FIRE buttons. The evil ones could not wait to show their main attribute: hate!

How different does one person become when he/she allows it inside their soul?

Inside Trillium and all around the nation, impervious to the menacing dragons posed for their destruction, the citizens of The Core sang louder than ever.

♪ **Bless the Lord, for He has heard the sound of my plea**
The Lord is my strength and my shield
In Him my heart trusts, and with my song, I give Him thanks

Happy be the nation whose love is God
Happy are the people, He has chosen for His inheritance
Happy be my soul, because it has been filled with love[6] ♪

With time running out, Azami-el broke ranks and climbed to the foremost cannon's control cabin in a speedy move. The leading operator, who saw him coming, did not waste any time getting up from his chair to stand at attention from the back of the cabin.

"Stay there! I will do all the firing!" The Overlord quickly notified him.

"As you wish, Sir!" He responded.

In one second, his mind checked all the controls to his liking, and then Azami-el stopped moving. He stared at Trillium, with saliva almost dripping from his distorted lips, viciously waiting for the command to fire.

All the Overlords from the NA had developed an inherent hate for Trillium, the leading bastion of the last nation still adoring God. Azami-el behaved worse than the rest; he had an unquenchable thirst for blood!

The city projected upward to the sky as an altar to the Creator. The minds and bodies of The Core citizens had melted together in a sea of ecstasy as provided by the Most High. Their song, accepted graciously by God, had created an environment that shielded the whole nation from the Evil force bent on their destruction. Since their minds stayed properly focused on the love of God, nothing else did matter. Therefore, pleased with what He saw, the Creator was ready to dispense His final gift.

The angels of this blessed nation sang this last verse so hard that even the distant Overlords heard the words; however, in their evil brains, the song felt not pleasant but painful.

♪ **Praise the Lord in His sanctuary, praise His Everlasting Love**
Praise the Lord in all His creation; praise His generosity
And let all that has life, praise the Lord of Love! Alleluia![7] ♪

---

[6] Lines 1-3> Modified Psalms 28, 6-7… Lines 4-5> Modified Psalms 33, 12
[7] Modified lines taken from Psalms 150, (1,6)

Arkyn knew only a few seconds remained; his eyes sought and found his supreme commander. He felt apprehensive facing his hypnotic power; lucky for him, the hate emanating from the darkest blue set of eyes was not directed at him but at a defenseless city and five million inhabitants!

The singing lingered louder than ever, and even Arkyn felt affected; he sensed a rising nausea coming up to his throat. This feeling caused another kind of panic. He, the commander of the First Army, could not possibly throw up in front of his vast subordinates, all awaiting his unquestionable command! With furious determination, he concentrated on his immediate task.

Nobiel felt like he was floating on a cloud. The last verse of the new song permeated his soul, capturing the essence of what was being sung: **love!**

The song had just finished. The joint ecstasy created by so many singing simultaneously felt incredible. In their sharing, love intertwined their souls, blessing a great nation by erasing any concern for the danger pointed at them. He glanced at the clock at the back of the room and wondered:

Plenty of time existed to share God's Love, but for their lives in this material world, time had run out! ... The clock read:

5:00:00

Arkyn, still focusing on Lucif-er for the order, saw the time displayed on the upper right corner of his special helmet. This caused him to squeeze his communication device extremely hard.

It was: 5:00:01

Lucif-er's eyes, almost projecting red flames, yelled!

"Kill the singing bastards! Level their stupid city! ... Fire!"

"Fire!" Arkyn gave the same order almost instantly.

The ten massive guns sucked electrons off the ground in a way that intended to deplete the whole plateau of its negative charge. The earth trembled as each cannon shot five massive balls of fire in rapid sequence. The ominous noise sounded like a flame-thrower machine gun; however, the projected energy was much more destructive!

On its way out, it even sucked the nearby air while grasping at anything close for its immediate annihilation. Lightning sparks rose from the ground to the chassis of the artillery pieces. Even occasionally, a lightning strike would connect two of the massive cannons.

The sight of five awesome fireballs racing to their targets at supersonic speeds and converging to their doomed destinations turned hair-raising.

Only the Overlords of the North could enjoy the horrifying experience of being in the middle of ten such monstrous cannons sending wallops of mass destruction; Azami-el, in charge of one leading artillery piece, attained the fastest recharge time and caused the most destruction.

At the distance, huge mushroom-like balls of fire ignited at its final convergence. Whole sections of the largest buildings became blasted or vaporized away, sending enormous sections of debris to crash on the streets many meters below.

It turned into a horrifying demolition spectacle!

Liliel, behind a large screen, stayed manipulating some controls to get the best telescopic views of the massacre. She was so excited by the crisp images that she did not even feel her nails digging into the palms of her hands.

"Yess!" She exclaimed at the sight of half of the Central Building being blown apart from its lower section and the top plummeting one thousand meters to the ground!

It was a horrific sight of destruction; nevertheless, she even focused on the angels falling from the collapsing structure to the distant ground floor and their imminent deaths.

For five minutes, fire rained over Trillium. After this time, the city, reduced to a smoldering inferno, became filled with fire, smoke, and debris. Enormous columns of hot smoke rose, coalescing into an even bigger cloud that climbed above the entire city like a massive volcanic eruption.

Lucif-er raised his open hand above his head. The shooting around the perimeter of Trillium stopped completely. For a few seconds, loud thundering noises could still be heard from the distant blasts, even when such noises were a delayed aftereffect of destruction. Finally, the only noise remaining was the cracking noise of many fires and the thunderous falling of many structures.

Lucif-er, turning his head toward Magog-el, carved into his personal thoughts and exclaimed.

"You are absolutely right; there is something wrong about this!"

The ominous scream of a giant ball of fire hit many floors above the location where the Council's members were singing together; the explosion was horrendous!

They saw fire everywhere. A shockwave rattling even their bone cells to almost extinction ripped across the place at extremely high speed, destroying everything in sight. A loud noise that nearly ripped apart their hearing organs overloaded their brains. A searing heat, holding hand to hand with a blinding flash of enormously released energy, sautéed the surroundings!

Mayhem took over; the destructive force of the energetic plasma explosion burst most of the visible upper structure apart. It was supposed to be hundreds of floors above them, but through the holes in the ceiling, they could see the smoky fireballs rising to higher ground. The upper section of the Central Building was gone, and the top of the remaining lower section remained engulfed in smoke, dust, and fire.

Nobiel shook his head. For a moment, he had blanked out and was lying on the floor. As he stood up, he looked around, searching for his friends. He only found one. The rest had just vanished!

A Cherub's twisted body lay on the floor; he was partially hidden by the building fragments, with some of them still shooting flames and smoke in dense spiraling columns.

As Nobiel touched his shoulder, he turned around and faced him. He recognized his good friend Oryel.

The council leader was shocked; his friend became so burned and ripped apart that he must be dying amid the most horrible pain!

He fell to his knees and immediately picked up his friend's head. A friendly pair of green eyes opened and recognized Nobiel. A smile, quickly marred by a compassionate grin, adorned his battered face. Blood was dripping from his ears, nose, and mouth, but Nobiel felt disconcerted by what came out of his friend's mouth.

"My dear friend... I am fine, but you are hurt!"

As the Seraph tried to articulate a response, his friend's body gently twitched and shook. His eyes turned to an empty glare, but his eyelids, fixed in one position, did not move again.

Nobiel closed his own eyes. Pulling the lifeless head of his friend against his chest, he mourned the priceless loss. While gently caressing Oryel's hair, he thought about the previous instant.

"Oryel, my dearest brother! How could you be so insensitive to your grave wounds, and I be your only concern?"

He stopped for a moment. A massive series of nearby blasts rattled the building worse than an earthquake. The noise became intensified by explosions everywhere, except at the place where he remained hanging to his life.

Suddenly, the attack stopped!

Only the collapsing buildings and the whole city's violent firestorm still rattled the ground and the listening ears of the few survivors. Above all the noise, singing could be heard... faint, but still going!

The Seraph smiled with inner satisfaction; while doing so, he looked at himself for the first time after he had recovered from unconsciousness. At the incredible sight of severe multiple injuries, he loudly exclaimed.

"Oh my God, I am seriously injured! How can this be when I feel so good?"

At this instant, it dawned on him. Staring at the large side hole that exposed the outside inferno raging out of control, he conversed with his God. With all the love left in his earthly heart, he acknowledged with total reverence.

"Our loving God, I would have gladly died in pain for You. It would have been a small sacrifice for all that You have blessed me in my long life! But my kind and loving Lord, You have even spared us the pain and suffering of these last moments. You are so compassionate for this Nation that we shall always sing to You... Alleluia!"

Part of the flames and smoke outside dissipated. A building stood at a distance, its majestic splendor untouched: **The Temple remained intact!**

He looked for the Lord on top of that magnificent building; He was not there! He reflected, "Of course, He was not there... **He is at my side!**"

Nobiel's loving smile became a very wide expression of immense joy. The outside view of The Temple must be a miracle!

"What is going on?" barked Lucif-er. *"We are massacring millions of singing bastards, and I still hear nothing else but singing! What happened to the screaming, to the cries of terror and pain? We are boiling their guts with their own blood and still hear... **only singing?**"*

"It does not make any sense!" Shaking his head, Magog-el exclaimed.

Lucif-er, clenching his teeth until they made weird noises, stared at the remains of the smoldering city. Even after destroying the most beautiful city on the planet, he persisted in overflowing with hate. Staring at the downtown remains, blocked mainly by flames and dark smoke, he started the following statement.

"I have n..." After a brief silent pause, he exploded.

"This is impossible!"

Magog-el strained his eyesight on the pointed location, opening his mouth with incredulous acknowledgment. He also blasted away.

"I do not believe it! The Temple is still untouched!"

Azami-el, exiting the cannon's cabin, picked up the conversation. He speedily focused his piercing eyes on the same target.

"What? How could we miss it?" He angrily retorted. While showing his teeth like a rabid dog after any prey, he climbed back to the cabin and shouted.

"Anyway, I will fix it in just a second!"

From below, a powerful message froze Azami-el solid.

"Azami-el! Stop! ... Do not fire!"

The Lord of Darkness walked to the cannon with solid and angry steps. He climbed the cabin as if it were at a horizontal incline. Inside, Azami-el got away from the controls and inquired with a look. Lucif-er, with his face twisted with evil determination, explained.

"I was the chief architect who built the Temple; it is my divine duty to destroy it!"

He quickly redefined the firing sequence; soon, the terminal read.

Firing Frequency => 3

Plasma Power   => 100%

A hiss and tremor shook the cannon's cabin for three seconds as the power source loaded to a maximum plasma burst; even the outside coils glowed with an ominous blue emission. A deep frequency hum disrupted the nervous system of the regular operators inside the cabin. Nobody had ever fired this monstrous artillery piece at 100% power output!

The operators, obviously shaken by the action of their supreme leader, had a question... Would the whole thing blow up in their faces?

The display indicated the cannon status.

Target > Locked

Cannon> Armed

Without even blinking, Lucif-er mentally commanded the computer.

"Fire!"

A train of three massive fireballs raced toward The Temple's location. These three energy bursts were so massive that they generated a network of crisscross lightning strikes. The lightning flashes traversed the ground and the fireballs, as well as among the cannon, the grounds, and the plasma bursts.

Like a giant vacuum pump, the balls of fire sucked air, dust, and anything close to them. Even a longitudinal massive shock wave could be felt moving along with the enormous balls on their way to their target. The noise became menacing, but the three deep roars that started at eardrum piercing level quickly diminished as the plasma spheres sprinted away.

The blasts were moving at tremendous supersonic speed, but to the anxious onlookers, it appeared to take a long time to reach its destination. The huge spheres of fire, dwarfed by the distance, had become three small but bright dots seemingly merging into one.

Then... all three ripped through the magnificent building's exterior. Once inside, they triggered three gigantic explosions; the whole building was engulfed in fire, incinerated, and blown away!

The three explosions coalesced into the largest mushroom blast that exploded inside the city. It even looked like a small nuclear explosion. Tiny pieces of the remains of such a splendorous and sublime place rained over a large part of the city, nothing was left of The Temple built to honor and adore God; perhaps, it had finished its usefulness. As the Evil ones took over The Core and massacred its citizens, there would be nobody left to pray or sing to the Lord.

The Overlords on the ground, including Liliel inside the flying vessel, all gave Lucif-er their cheers and thumbs up as they feasted on the destruction of the altar-like structure.

Lucif-er, closely followed by Azami-el, stepped out of the cannon's cabin. The leader of the NA raised both hands in triumph. At this moment, his hair moved widely behind his face as hurricane-force winds rushed to the downtown area to feed the firestorm engulfing the remains of Trillium.

His shiny white tunic, tightly bound to his muscular body, flapped like a flag extended to the mighty winds. While his body contour, dressed in white, contrasted with the hellish background of smoke and fire, he adorned his face with a sadistic grin of satisfaction.

He yelled to the smoldering remains.

"Invisible god with no name… you have lost! All of this was yours; now, the whole planet is mine!

Your 'name' will be forgotten; only we, the Overlords of the North, will be remembered. In contrast to you, we will be like real gods. We will start a new era in which the NA no longer acknowledges the existence of any god since that belief is just a flimsy excuse for the weak and the dumb to hide from reality.

We are our own gods… we shall make our own destiny!"

Raising his open palms higher, he glanced at the sky, still engulfed with dark clouds of smoke from smoldering fires; he continued.

"Next month, as we start the construction of the first spaceship, we will begin to take our place among the stars. Then, when the spaceship is finished, we will launch the conquest of the Universe!"

Pointing a finger directly to Zeri-el, he ordered.

"You will be in charge of starting the design and construction of a spaceship capable of flying faster than 9/10 of the speed of light! … Furthermore, we are currently working on a quantum effect that could bypass the light-speed barrier; if successful, we will no longer use light speed as a reference… instead, it will become… 'Quantum Speed.'"

Zeri-el acknowledged with one thumb up. Lucif-er, turning to Arkyn, ordered.

"Command the First, Second, and Third Armies to kill all the remaining Core citizens. In six days, I want all of them dead!"

At the end of this statement, Azami-el faced Lucif-er and hesitantly inquired, *"You promised that I would have many new prisoners when we invaded The Core!"*

"I did… however, things have changed! … I do not relish the way this operation is turning out; therefore, I have concluded that The Core citizens will be worse prisoners than the SA captives. I am sure you remember well that they were NO fun! Taking any Core prisoners with their disregard for pain would be an absolute waste of time!

If you want to have any fun, do it now!"

Azami-el remained unhappy and showed it by clenching his teeth with fury. After a short mental rumble, he stepped inside the cabin, where he took a high-power rifle from the nearest soldier, almost ripping off the soldier's arm in the process of its removal. On his way out and down from the cannon, he indicated to his boss.

"I am going hunting!"

Almost superimposed on Azami-el's response, the speedily returned message stopped the Overlord.

"Just wait, we will go together!" Lucif-er requested.

Meanwhile, Arkyn, reflecting on the order, was rather shocked. With great internal anxiety, which interfered with his actions, he thought intensely.

"My very first order as the First Army Commander: To massacre five million people in Trillium!

My second order as a Commander will be: The extermination of one billion Core citizens!

Oh, Micha-el... you should be proud of me!"

His sarcastic smile vanished almost immediately. In front of him, out of the smoldering remains of the city, an ethereal wiggle took shape.

Micha-el, a life-size image of the Archangel, materialized close enough to be touched; the image, with a sad grin that wrinkled his handsome face, opened his arms and asked.

"Why Arkyn? Why do you hate me so much?"

The Seraph in charge of the First Army panicked under the vision. He backed up two steps and was ready to yell, **'Leave me alone!'** When a piercing message from Lucif-er rattled his brain!

"Anything wrong, Commander? Do you have any objections to giving the order?"

A super cold chill ran painfully by the medullae of his bones; he stared in the direction of his boss and shouted while gathering all the strength he could muster.

"None, Sir!"

Arkyn glanced at the place where the image of Micha-el had appeared; to his angry relief, nothing remained there; he speedily relayed the order to his electronic communication device. Sharply and heartlessly, he spoke with an angry overtone.

"To all Army commanders!

I order you: Attack and kill all Core citizens.

We will take no prisoners!

It is the wish of our Supreme Leader for this order to be fully implemented in six days.

Do not disappoint him!"

To his sadness, Nobiel saw The Temple reduced to ashes by a huge ball of fire. In a vision, he saw a much bigger fireball consuming all in its path; **this one was immense!**

He was glad that he would be spared such a nightmarish end; he even felt sorry for the angels of the North, who knew nothing about it. While engaged in a life of hate and destruction, they failed to see beyond their noses. Eventually, this would bring the just wrath of the Creator and their destruction.

Blessed with the wisdom and knowledge of the divine plan, he wanted to sing louder than ever. He opened his mouth to sing again... however, nothing came out.

He did not feel any pain, but looking at the floor, he saw a dark pool of liquid expanding around him; he realized that this was his own blood!

Everything around started to spin. The noise outside became fainter and fainter; as darkness approached, he knew that his 'Meta' had arrived. As his sight became like a dark tunnel, he stretched his right hand upwards while still holding Oryel's head with his left hand against his own body.

A bright light overtook the darkness of his vision; he felt a hand grasping his. He did not feel any pain before, but he surely felt this hand! This hand was warm, powerful, and immensely invigorating.

It was not the hand of Death...
It was the hand of ETERNAL LIFE!

THE IRON CONNECTION

CHAPTER 9

Once more, time continued its inexorable progression on the angels' planet. Seven years have passed since the destruction of Trillium and The Core and 14 years since the devastation of the SA.

Just outside Centrum, a tremendous hum rattled the earth like an approaching powerful earthquake!

In its entire splendor, amid massive towers holding it down, a gigantic saucer-shaped craft wanted to fly. It shook the towers violently as its mighty engines seemed angry for being restricted to the ground; however, the enormous spaceship built to travel to the stars did not move.

With a 200-meter diameter, this craft was huge; even its protruding circular edge raised 40 meters above the ground. From its silvery exterior, not many artifacts bulged to disturb the sleek appearance of this incredible machine. The shiny surface of this flying saucer was not contoured smoothly; a convex and concentric coil symmetry slightly protruded to its top, where some complex antenna crowned it.

The craft was not completely circular; since it had a front slightly streamlined by being pointed. A massive retaining wall completely blocked the spaceship at the front, preventing this vessel from going forward.

Five Overlords supervised the crew inside the ship, implementing a test run. At least a dozen Seraphim, all hi-tech engineers, operated the complex console at the bridge, the heart of this fabulous flying machine. It had no windows, but a large aggregate of sensors gave a clear display of the six planes that could be observed from all directions away from the craft. The crew was dressed in dark blue pants that appeared tight to the body but elastic enough to give full extension and freedom of movement. They wore color-coded upper jackets, a small number printed on their back and again on the right pocket above the heart, indicating their ranking position.

The jacket color code was:

    Dark red: Weapon systems.
    Dark green: Environmental control.
    Dark blue: Power control.
    Black: Security.
    Gray: Flight logistics.

This was just a test crew; the full flight support, not including the Overlord in charge and his six concubines, remained scheduled to take two thousand members to the stars. These one thousand couples would be ready to colonize any planet showing any signs of a promising environment.

As the interior shook because the bound vessel could not take flight, one angel with a dark blue top and the number 1 embossed in gold on his uniform exclaimed.

"Superconducting primary impulse power, holding at 10.01%, Sir!"

Zeri-el sternly looked at the # 1 power console operator and lashed out.

"I said 10%, exactly!"

The Seraph tried to increase his concentration by manipulating the complex set of manual and automatic controls, and in just ten seconds, he yelled back.

"Sir! Power is now: 10.0000%!"

Zeri-el did not answer; instead, he addressed Lucif-er.

"The containment towers and the forward stop cushion will take a maximum of 12% power strain; if we exceed that limit when the fusion reactor fires, the hull will become crushed!"

The leader of Terra casually looked at the consoles; he was already projecting the second stage of this test. After acknowledging Zeri-el's statement as nothing new, he requested information from Gorgon-el, who continued looking at the outside of the craft using a monitor displaying all available visual planes. More precisely, he was analyzing the shaking of the outside towers and the dust generated by the engines powered by the massive superconducting coils.

"I know that you have already implemented the changes to the fusion reactor," stated Lucif-er, *"Just give me the modification results to quadruplex the deflecting fields between the reactor and the main ship!"*

Gorgon-el glanced at his boss as Lucif-er touched his shoulder; a bluish glow, almost like a spark, transferred the complex data from his brain to Lucif-er's absorbing powerful mind. Only two seconds later, Lucif-er commented.

"It looks good! Residual radiation reaching this command bridge at 10% power, accumulated for ten years, should be 1.0% of the maximum allowed for a round trip to the nearest star. Deploy the reactor!"

Gorgon-el accessed the brain of the logistic engineer # 1 and ordered.

"Deploy the reactor!"

A Seraph with a gray jacket accepted the order and commanded his crew similarly.

A strange noise, caused by massive sliding metallic parts mixed with the rattling triggered by the holding supports as the push of the humming superconducting engines, disturbed the crew. The combination of these vibrations and noises bombarded the ears of the busy crew inside the grounded spaceship. From the rear of the ship, a large cylindrical section extending from the ship's core slowly protruded farther and farther away.

Think of it as a hydraulic shaft lifting a car. This shaft was more complex because its final outside diameter continuously became locked in place as it extended. Inside, it was like many laminated interconnecting sheets pushed to deployment by a central driving mechanism.

At the very tip of this outward-projecting device remained the original central edge portion of the spaceship's rear; this end now had the shape of a conical tip; further inside the cone, a whole circle of exhaust vents could be seen.

This was the driving power of the fusion reactor; it had 12 vents. Independently, each one was powerful enough to blast the craft into outer space. The outer shaft envelope's conical shape was designed to deflect the radioactively charged particles streaming away from the reactor. The shaft maximum extension remained at five lengths of the saucer-shaped craft; it had a very long tail: 1,000 meters long. The snapping sounds generated by the outside sheets as they locked to form the extending center shaft diminished in intensity as the process moved away.

Logistic Engineer # 1, who stayed graphically following the assembly and deployment of the shaft by following a computer layout of the event, yelled.

"Deployment completed, sir!"

Zeri-el glanced at his boss for approval. Lucif-er smiled at him, anticipating Zeri-el's deep satisfaction for the great accomplishment just instants away: A functional spacecraft capable of delivering two thousand plus angels to another solar system!

Zeri-el, glutting on the event before it happened, allowed two seconds to pass before pointing his finger at the number 1 engineer in gray uniform; even with no message, the engineer knew exactly what was required of him. On the screen's surface, the Seraph in front of the console pushed the electronic button.

Nothing happened in the first second!

Before the muffled sound, which stayed many times decoupled at the shaft, reached the control cabin, a shock wave rattled the craft forward. The roar could not be heard until 3.3 seconds later.

The spaceship did not move much; a massive containment wall shaped to match the vessel's frontal physical characteristics did not give any additional space; however, the spacecraft began pushing much harder in the horizontal direction than in the vertical one!

Ten percent of the fusion reactor power was many times the power of a superconducting engine. The vessel's internal structure squeaked and made weird noises caused by the compression of materials that could not move forward.

The space engine reactor blast looked awesome, much more powerful than any blast-off from Cape Canaveral. Since it remained horizontal, it blew fiery smoke parallel to the horizon, along with massive amounts of dust that scattered across many kilometers. As planned, the immense cloud generated by the engines' exhaust drifted away from the test site pushed by the prevailing winds, which were also blowing away from Centrum.

Magog-el and Azami-el, who were present, glanced at each other. They were somehow worried about the integrity of the supporting towers, the forward retaining wall, and the vessel itself. As both took one further glance at the leader of the NA, they were more than sure that nothing could go wrong. Lucif-er, busy assimilating data from the many displays and sensor outputs, had not even looked at any of the spaceship holding structures; he did not have to. Since the boss tracked everything and showed no concern, they did not need to worry. The test went on for exactly 100 seconds, one Terra minute.

The logistics # 1 engineer had the mental command to stop it at exactly the required time. The inertia recoiled in the opposite direction as the reactor energy output shut off; even so, the ominous roar did not stop for another 3.3 seconds.

The enormous and elongated cloud formed by the fusion reactor started to merge into a brownish mushroom cloud racing toward the upper atmosphere. Several lightning strikes bombarded the ground underneath since the dry, hot dust blown from the nearby terrain generated lots of static electricity.

At the command bridge, Lucif-er ordered the superconducting engines to be turned off.

Again, they felt the inertia as the usual starting conditions became restored; it was as if the craft had landed, even when it had never left the ground.

Lucif-er smiled while addressing Zeri-el and Gorgon-el and exclaimed.

"You both did excellent work; this spaceship is ready to go!"

Zeri-el advanced a quick comment.

"I have chosen 100 couples from the personnel assigned to this vessel to test the integrity of the bio-recycling systems for one year. The spaceship will be completely sealed, simulating the resource usage of two thousand angels. At the end of the test, it will be ready for takeoff."

In a joking mood, Lucif-er questioned.

"Which of you will volunteer to be the 'Captain'?"

The other four Overlords made the unhappy face of 'non-volunteering.' Gorgon-el spoke first; his answer reflected all their minds.

"Not me!"

The pleasures on the planet were too enticing and abundant. None of the top Overlords wanted to volunteer for a tour that would probably last, round trip, at least 20 years to the nearest star!

Lucif-er, changing his smile to a sinister grin, commented.

"Do not worry; none of the existing Overlords will take this first trip! After establishing a star colonization network and molding this planet the way I want it, I will take a tour among the stars. Now, in 20 days, Liliel

will be ready for her last boost to become an Overlord. I will provide the
last push that she needs. However, she will not go either. There are not
enough males in a spaceship to satisfy her!"

The rest of the Overlords laughed with mischievous joy. After a brief
pause to allow the slimy steam to subside, Lucif-er continued, *"In about*
one year, the training for Arkyn will be completed. He shall be the first
Overlord to go to the stars; he cannot refuse!"

Magog-el's muscular body, reflecting externally what his usual stern
internal image of himself demanded, took the initiative to send a mental
message as a reply.

"It is an excellent choice. I am glad that he will be ready, just in time."

The other three became more than happy about the conclusion; they
approved it with a unanimous evil agreement. It is hard to settle for a few
thousand slaves when you could have billions in Terra!

Lucif-er switched the conversation by pointing to Gorgon-el and
continued mentally speaking.

"I already received the information about solar activity from you. The
correlation you found with yellow stars like ours, indicating an oscillation
in solar activity and instability over a period of hundreds of millions of
years, is very interesting!

Stars, to become nova, which have similar solar masses as our sun, all
show the same increasing undulations that peak when the stars reach this
state. Your algorithm for the spectroscopic H/He ratios is very accurate
for defining the stars' age. The graph, to my satisfaction, is accurate.

I found it exciting that stars destined to become supernovas have a much
more compressed time base with a much larger peak oscillation.

Now, the big question?

Why does our sun, which is presently peaking in activity and instability,
not follow the same period as all the other stars of similar age and mass?
Why is the peak higher? Why is the period shorter?

It is too young to become a nova; it is too small to become a
supernova!"

Gorgon-el was eager to add his comment and unmasked dislike for the
data; he raised both hands and complained, *"The data from our sun does*
not make any sense. It is driving me crazy!"

Liliel, leaning against the rail of the uppermost terrace of Lucif-er's
mansion, had the lower patios in front and below her; the even lower and
circular pool adorned by a six-pointed star-shaped landscape remained the
center of attraction. It was late at night, yet the place stayed brightly
illuminated. She casually stared at the marbled type floors, where the
number '666' was dazzlingly engraved in a deep blue sapphire, the
favorite number of the master of the land.

The night felt a bit cooler, but she had become much tougher and hardly felt the temperature difference; however, she acutely knew precisely what such a difference was.

She remembered that 28 years ago, this same place looked better. Many trees, sensitive to the cold and radiation after-effects of the war against the South Alliance, had died. New ones have replaced them, but they will take a while to grow fully.

Twenty-eight years was not a long time for Liliel's lengthy life, but what a difference it made. At that time, she was weak and completely dependent on Lucif-er. Now, she felt the power running through her muscles and mind. In only 14 days, she would be ready for her lover and master to endow her with the last threshold to cross... the last step needed to rise to Overlord status!

Fourteen days of hard training and a mind melt with Lucif-er became the only steps left.

She sensed somebody moving under the dark shadow projected by a large tree. He was not alone; five more stayed close by, all strategically deployed on the terraces and the large patio. She knew exactly who they were. Incredible, she knew they were guards from Lucif-er's personal platoon; she could almost see their faces. Considering their hiding locations' distance, that was quite a feat! ... She thought.

"Being an Overlord is having such awesome power. To be so much above everybody else is a valid excuse to feel like a god... Oh yes! That is what she will become on her next step..."

She squirmed like a worm! ... A firm hand touched her shoulder, even when she did not sense anybody approaching her!

"Are you trying to seduce my guards!" A powerful mental message startled her; Lucif-er had sneaked up on her again.

She turned and looked at his dominant but irresistible face; softly, she caressed him behind his left ear with a touch as a feather moved by a gentle breeze. The terrace lighting remained moderate, so his face stayed on the hazy side, but his blue eyes did not; they glowed like a white shirt under a black light. With a seductive smile, she replied.

"Not even close; I was waiting for you!"

He faintly chuckled; then, he casually said, *"Sure."*

When she began pinching the tip of his earlobe with her thumb and index fingernails, he raised his right-hand index finger so the tip of his nail barely touched the tip of her nose. It felt like an extremely sharp object piercing against her nose, ready to split it into two pieces!

She immediately released the earlobe pinch.

"I can see that you can hardly wait for the day when you will become an Overlord," Lucif-er added casually.

"You know it! But how long will it take for me to reach Magog-el's level?"

Lucif-er smiled at his concubine's greed. With two of his index fingers, he slowly rubbed both sides of her shapely nose at the base where it rose and was close to its bottom. She must have liked it because her very faint pink wings became pinker. The Overlord stared deep into her purplish, pretty eyes; he pointed out next.

"About a thousand years... and if I help? ... 100 years!"

Liliel, gently licking her upper lip, asked what he knew where she was leading; she used her best melodic tone for this inquiry.

"And to surpass you?"

He rubbed his right hand against her left cheek in a way that suggested a very slow face slapping; meanwhile, his eyesight became more intense.

"You will never aspire to such an undertaking because you cannot afford it... It is because the price is too high... your life!
You understand, nothing personal!"

Liliel dropped her sight down. She turned around and pressed her back against his masculine front. As her neck stretched up, she gazed at the stars. She felt romantically inclined, so she commented in a soft tone.

"The stars are beautiful tonight."

Lucif-er, grabbing both of her upper and inner thighs, gently rubbed them, slowly, up and down; he stared at the bright dots of light adorning the dark sky and stated.

"Yes, indeed... However, have you noticed that they are not too far anymore!" He exclaimed.

Raising his right hand like a claw while feeding on his inner possessive power, he shouted

"I can reach you now... You will be mine!"

Halfway up the eastern sky, the sun lit a lovely balmy morning; everything stayed crystal clear, producing maximum visibility. Only in the direction of the destroyed city of Trillium, dust and puffs of smoke rose above the narrow canyon leading to Lucif-er's newest mansion.

A million workers labored at top speed to raise a new city from above the ashes of the old one. This new one will become ultramodern, with the latest technology in every beam, tile, and space.

Most of the work remained at the subterranean level; hundreds of floors underground were required to meet this new metropolis' needs, according to Lucif-er's master urban plan. He called it the city of the future, the ultimate city, a single massive structure wired for self-sufficiency. Every part, including a skyscraper, becomes one cell of a whole body interdependently aware of its location and usefulness. All to be run by a massive central computer to be wired like our brain, in a way that could sense its existence, capacity, and resources.

As we react to hunger, this enormous, metropolis-sized machine requests and takes whatever power is needed to run its countless tasks.[1]

Brazil built Brasilia, a showplace for the rest of the world to see, a town with no intersections, only beautiful avenues and modern buildings. Similarly, the NA started constructing Terra's biggest project for the planet, an undertaking so spectacular that the future observer would stand with an open mouth at the sight of such splendor.

The buildings and gardens adorning the place would be breathtaking. An incredible array of terraces and roof decor, unsurpassed on the planet, would contain the most beautiful flora collection ever assembled.

At one of the upper terraces of his new mansion, Lucif-er, sitting alone with both feet on a rail, stared in the space between his legs but in the direction of the new city; in self-reflection, he mentioned.

"You will be the gate, where I will control the whole planet... The beauty and splendor of this new city will be like a temple for me. I have chosen the proper name... You will have a royal name: **Babyl-on!**"[2]

One set of firm steps, accompanied by another set of weak ones, which sounded as if being dragged along, increased in intensity as they approached the Overlord's sitting place.

He smiled with a sinister overtone, knowing they were Gorgon-el and his new special friend, Deana. They both stopped behind him; the quick and stressed breathing of the female angel could be heard at a distance. Slowly, the planet's leader turned his seating chair to face them.

While mildly shaking, she was noticeably afraid and avoided any eye contact with Lucif-er. Gorgon-el, smiling sardonically as he watched the great concern that Deana experienced trying to avoid eye contact with the # 1 Overlord, with his index finger, lifted her face up so she had no other choice than to stare at him; Lucif-er lashed.

"I know it hurt the last time. You should not focus on the pain but on the pleasure!"

She looked at those incredibly blue eyes attached to that extremely handsome face and physique. Against her better judgment, even when she remembered the agonizing pain, she could not resist him. However, at the sight of such good-looking facial attributes, the image of a previous lover momentarily flashed by in her mind, somebody to whom she once said.

"I love you so much!"

"What was his name?" She thought. "Maybe... Arkyn?"

All appeared like a forgotten dream, a recollection of small, disconnected fragments. In fact, her previous life seemed to have been

---

[1] Lucif-er planned to build a city like the one an advanced alien civilization erected in the sci-fi movie The Forbidden Planet.

[2] The name Babylon is derived from the Akkadian bab-ilu, which means "Gate of God" (Bing.com/search.)

erased, her priorities overwritten. Whatever happened to the independent, intelligent, and dynamic Cherub named Deana?

Falling to her knees, she grabbed his leg with renewed passion; while kissing his hand, she exclaimed with a sorrowful outburst.

"Forgive me, my Master! ... I cannot forget you or live without you! My whole body is burning with passion... Please, take me!"

He ran a finger by her partially open mouth, touching her tongue as it went by her full and moist lips, he casually commented.

"I have great news for you. All those tests and preparations you have been going through are over. You have been selected as the first female to have a baby!"

She looked up; her eyes showed a deep, incredulous, blank stare.

"I... a mother?" She mumbled.

Even the word 'mother' sounded so strange. Nobody on the planet has had any offspring since the big cut-off date millennia ago. Female instincts, long-buried for necessity, surfaced with renewed excitement. Lucif-er looked at her complacently.

"Yes!" he assured her, then, anticipating an excited question, he continued, *"No such luck! You will not have my child; actually, you will be a surrogate mother. Even so, it is bound to be a prestigious honor."*

She stuck her lips out with momentary disappointment but accepted with a broad smile.

A personal message was at this time sent to Gorgon-el.

"Come back to pick her up in one hour. Then, you will take her to the hospital for the implantation!"

As Gorgon-el turned around and departed, Deana tried to stand up. The Overlord, while holding her down with one hand on her shoulder, stated.

"Since you will be going for the implant in one hour, we cannot have normal sex. Stay down! I will show you some alternate but fascinating techniques."

Her body, still shaking with desire, felt a burning sensation setting her body on fire. She wanted to have a male so badly that all her female organs stayed palpitating in unison, asking for that unique anatomic part solely capable of quenching her flaming desire.

It was bright, and the lights above half-blinded her. She did not care; both of her hands were tightly squeezed into two fists, and her deep and rhythmic breathing echoed her internal urges.

A white sheet covered her naked body, spread open as if she were ready to deliver a baby. A Throne, dressed in white, came out from between her legs; he raised his hand. An assistant deposited a narrow vial with some clear liquid inside his hand. The assistant, in a low tone, asked.

"Is she ready?"

The Throne, a doctor, nodded affirmatively while moving closer to the assistant and exclaimed.

"You cannot believe how ready she is for this cloning; she is just _perfect!"_

****

The solar disk, Star-1 for Terra residents, became displayed in its entire 3-D splendor. Backing up, we realize we are staring at a huge screen display. Numerous stationary and active numerical arrays of data began flashing around the image perimeter; at the bottom, in bold letters, it read:

DATABASE: ST-6

This display was part of an array of instrumentation dedicated to studying solar behavior. Five operators, with at least one being a scientist, stayed busy analyzing the incoming data from the stationary solar satellites. A transparent partition divided this section from another instrumentation cluster; there, Gorgon-el instructed two engineers on how to cool down a thermonuclear reactor. Complex designs and formulas flashed across the displays in front of them.

From the previous section, a red warning indicator came on. At the large screen with the solar display, a moderate but audible alarm signal became heard throughout the laboratory. Gorgon-el's medium build body sprang into action; fast like a flash, he reached the screen with the sounding alarm in just one second flat!

He saw a chilling event at the solar display in front of him. Squeezing his foxy eyes in disgust, he observed the extraordinary event in progression.

A massive ball of fire began stretching away from the sun. Due to the enormous volume of the mass shooting from the star, the event unfolded as a slow-motion phenomenon: a massive solar flare unfolded ominously. The Overlord sent a message to the computer; it acknowledged.

>Rotate: Equatorial/Planar to 90°

The image quickly rotated around its axis. The growing flare moved to the right side, now shown as an edge event. On the opposite left side of the sun, another equally massive flare was rising above the solar edge. Gorgon-el said to himself.

"Just what I thought! Two equal and opposite flares exploding along *the equatorial solar plane!"*

Quickly but without touching, he maneuvered the controls of the solar display. Many columns of data disappeared. Instead, vividly colored graphs exhibited the characteristics of the explosion in degrees Kelvin.

Most graph lines moved upwards, and the computer displayed their functions.[3]

Corona: Up 500,000 °K   To: 1,500,000 °K
Photosphere: Up 300 °K   To: 6,300 °K

Many other indicators of solar activity continued being graphed. A new warning came on.

Satellite array: 2 & 4 components in the path of a massive solar wind to be powered down.

Image deterioration: To be expected at maximum parallax compensation.

Gorgon-el turned around and activated a much smaller screen. He extended his right hand forward for DNA confirmation and commanded.

>Priority link: Gorgon-el --> Lucif-er

Three seconds later, the image of Lucif-er filled the whole area of the monitor. As soon as this occurred, Gorgon-el pointed to the screens behind him. Two seconds passed before Lucif-er had assimilated and processed all the visual data; he assessed the information.

"Another out-of-sequence event!" Lucif-er spoke through the display, *"Check for me the deviations of the carbon cycle nuclear equations, especially the last one involving C^{12} and He^4; I am concerned about the sun's core heavier elements. We have not seen another star behaving like our sun in this unprecedented manner!"*

After making a twisting grimace, the image on the screen pointed an index finger to Gorgon-el and remarked.

"This is too serious for us to leave unattended; I want you to mobilize a new task force of our best 100 technical-oriented people, including our top 20 scientists. I want the best support available. Assign commander Zoltar to supervise this group; he should report any new significant event to you!

The ▲ = 1.22 will peak at noon tomorrow![4] I want a report on global effects. Also, a solar wind moving at one million Km/hour will hit Terra tomorrow; you know what this means!"

Gorgon-el, displaying a complete set of teeth, smiled with mischievous joy when exclaiming, *"Yes! For tomorrow night, we are having a party with fireworks!"*

Centrum's Downtown.

It was almost midnight at the top terrace of one of the tallest buildings in the city, where a large gathering having a wild party began reaching its peak.

---

[3] Degrees Kelvin = Absolute Temperature.
[4] ▲ = In Terra, a mathematical handle = Δ (Black Body Radiation) x T^4

Amidst the young trees arranged in clusters or rows, the architectural design of this captivating gathering place was a sight to behold. Modern-looking cubicles, gazebo-like arrays, and a performing auditorium were intricately intertwined, creating a unique and visually stunning landscape that almost resembled a forest.

With a center location from where all the rest radiated outwardly, the whole place was intended for relaxing and having fun or for something much more decadent.

This crowded social event called attention to the anomaly of two females for each male present. An instrumental three-tone complimentary piece of music entertained the visitors; some of them paid attention to its melodic and complex rhythm, but most did not even notice. The place's lighting remained just bright enough to identify the person in front, but tonight, this was not important since the night sky became alive as it appeared to be on fire!

An incredible Aurora Borealis gave the show of a lifetime!

Not even the long-lived angels of Terra had ever seen anything like it, especially when the sky above the city of observance was so much south of the North Pole.

Ribbons of white and green colored folds speedily unwounded as they traveled across the sky like a heavenly dance magnificently orchestrated by invisible giant hands performing their routine way up into the ionosphere. Fiery rays from the horizon pierced the night sky and appeared as flaming tongues devouring the stars.

This astounding spectacle, ignited by the solar wind, battered the planet at millions of kilometers per hour. The giant solar explosions or flares caused these winds made of charged particles to interact with Terra's magnetic field. As a result, the upper layers of the atmosphere became ionized.

The intensity of the changing lights and the variety of colors provoked an eerie pattern over the faces of the party's participants. Of course, the same effect could be seen in everything in the city.

It stayed cool and windy on the high elevations at the top of this skyscraper. However, the attending crowd dressed scantly did not feel it because windbreakers and abundant heat gave everybody the sensation of a balmy summer's night.

At one of the fancier gazebos, Gorgon-el lay down with two good-looking females caressing him; not far away, commander Arkyn was equally massaged by his female companions. Suddenly, a message entered the commander's brain: *"Come closer, I have important news for you!"*

As the commander placed on standby his two companions, he got up and firmly walked to the Overlord's location. At his suggestion, he sat down in front of him.

Gorgon-el gave the commander his never-ending trademark, his foxy smile; then, he announced.

"You already know that Liliel will be elevated to Overlord status in five days. Now, I have great news for you!"

The Overlord paused for an instant to observe Arkyn's facial reaction; he was also checking his internal inquisitive mental power, which had increased substantially due to the special training the commander continued enduring as an Overlord's trainee. Internally, his boss read many mental questions from Arkyn; the Overlord allowed none to come out; next, he revealed the news.

"In less than one year... you will be the next Overlord!"

The subordinated Seraph's face stood motionless momentarily; then, he burst with newly found energy.

"Sir! ... Did you say less than one year?"

Gorgon-el nodded affirmatively; however, he quickly added.

"Yes! ... However, there is a catch. We need an Overlord to command the first mission to a nearby star; you have been chosen!"

Arkyn's open smile showed a small display of what he felt inside; he readily volunteered his existence.

"To be an Overlord in one year? I will do anything!"

"It will require some hardships; nevertheless, as an incentive, you will have the choice of six gorgeous concubines!"

Arkyn licked his upper lip sensually as the image of Deana flashed through his brain. She would have been a great choice, but now she remained out of reach.

The pretty rounded face of Deana, with dazzling green eyes, big breasts, and a shapely body. This image, decentralized by his brain neuron connections, faded away; it dispersed into the dark corners of items to be forgotten... or in oblivion.

"Sir! I will be ready!" He burst into uncontrolled jubilation.

The Overlord dismissed him with a flick of his hand.

At the center of the terrace, inside the fanciest pavilion in the entire place, Lucif-er, in the middle of a cozy corner, did not wear his usual white tunic; instead, he showed a silky red garment, which accentuated most of his superior physique. Scantily dressed, the sexy Liliel slithered next to him while kissing him on the neck with a lusty tongue and a lip workout.

He did not seem impressed. He continued glancing at the Aurora's magnificent display as it changed the surroundings to unusually colored overtones. He smiled at his lover's face as one side flashed with a deep green overtone while the other stayed illuminated by a reddish glimmer.

Perhaps she felt like a clown because she stopped what she was doing and placed her nose directly in front of him. Slowly, she rubbed the edge of his nostrils with the tip of her own nose. She was breathing heavily; at the end of a deep inhale, she exclaimed what seemed unrelated but reflected her inner being.

"Only five days left! I am going crazy waiting for the instant when I become an Overlord! ... I have some concerns... When you help me to become an Archangel, will it hurt?"

He took his time answering. With both hands, he started to caress her silky blond hair. *"Yes! It is going to be traumatic, like a butterfly coming out of a cocoon, but I know you can take it!"*

He refrained from anticipating his companion's next question as he relished seeing her sweat it out. She inquired again.

"Are you revealing my new global status during your world announcement, which is only three days away?"

"Indeed, even if you still need two more days to become an Overlord, you will be granted all the honors. I have decided to create a special niche for your situation; you will report directly to me as my assistant Overlord!"

"Yes!" She exclaimed with saliva almost dripping from her partially open mouth and sexually attractive lips. Her face, illuminated in an innovative manner by the ionic storm raging way above her head, made her appear more evil-looking.

"There is more..." Lucif-er added, *"Comet C-279, which will be in its most glorious display on the nightly sky in three days, will have the additional name of 'Liliel'!"*

With almost a grotesque manner, she twisted her tongue outside of her mouth.

"I like it!" She exclaimed but quickly added. *"Now, just lay down. I have prepared an exclusive treat for you!"*

She flicked a finger high above her head; it pointed at Lucif-er. Two female angels, standing nearby, moved closer. Liliel continued, *"I personally trained these two female Seraphim for your own pleasure!"*

Her companion retorted sarcastically.

"I know. You also screwed them... together!"

She gave him a quick sneer with no other consequences. When she was so close to her life's biggest ambition, no sarcasm could affect her; slowly and sensuously, she stated.

"We three... will give you... the rub of a lifetime!"

Lucif-er laughed with his favorite satanic connotation; challenging the females, he replied, *"You are welcome to try!"*

Before anything else could materialize inside her brain, she heard him again.

*"And since you already brought the male and female horses, choice animals for the night, let me proclaim to all: **Start the party!** Or should we call it what it is: **Start, the orgy!"**

Unknown to all, a Supreme Being watched in every detail all the transgressions the remaining inhabitants of Terra engaged in. His love was immense, but the blood of so many cried for justice; in many places, the dirt was still red, and not even the bright sun had bleached it away.

What kind of moral values remain on the planet?

Only one: all-out sinfulness. Nothing less than Sodom and Gomorrah!

Homosexuality became accepted as normal behavior; multiple sex partners were common now, and the final stain was sex with animals. When the whole planet fell into utter decadence, could the local culture still be called a 'civilization'?

The whole population did not fall into chaos only because the evilest of all, the originator of sin and the master of disobedience, Lucif-er, was in charge. No one would dare to question his commands; he, who equated himself with being a god, would have no remorse in taking one life or a million lives!

When we trade a god of Love for a god of Hate, we earn many new liberties. Our passions can be set free; no more binding commandments that restrict <u>even our thoughts</u>. The sky is the limit!

However, how sad is the deception of Evil; in trying to escape from the binding but loving arms of a Father, we find ourselves enslaved by a ruthless tyrant, who, in the end, all that he wants is described by our blood and our soul.

Embracing sin brings nothing else than what we most despise: shame, humiliation, sickness, loneliness, hopelessness, anxiety, fear, and worst of all, **hate!**

This last one, being the opposite of Love, brings the ultimate punishment from our Creator: An eternal life without seeing or sharing His Glory. This brings utter suffering, which must be faced <u>alone</u>.

God, after watching all, decided that it was enough.

At exactly midnight, He set a celestial clock for three days.

Invisible, unknown, the divine clock started the countdown. What it read became inescapable **fate!**

T_{END}= -30:00 Hours

****

Along a straight pathway adorned with bushes and trees at both sides, Arkyn continued running fast at the trail's center. Flanking him, Zeri-el and Gorgon-el kept running at the same speed. While the commander had reached his maximum, the Overlords seemed to do it effortlessly. Arkyn, feeling that he was at its top speed, complained.

"This is it... I can't go any faster!"

"Nonsense!" replied Zeri-el, who pointing his index finger to the Seraph's temple, suggested.

"It is in your brain; you must modify your metabolic rates to increase your speed. With our help, that should be easier; try harder... now!"

Some ringing invaded his head, accompanied by a mild headache. He squeezed his teeth hard and felt energy surging from places not tapped before as he shifted to overdrive.

Arkyn ran faster than ever; after one full minute of sustained running, he slowed and finally stopped. He was windless; his two companions remained breathing at the same rate as if they were seated instead of sprinting. While the commander's head stayed down, he asked the Overlords, *"How fast... did I go?"*

"20 meters/second!"[5] Gorgon-el replied to him this time.

"Wow! That is incredible! Is there... an utmost limit?"

The Overlord nodded while at the same time informing Arkyn.

"Yes! And you must find this limit by yourself; if you exceed it, you could seriously damage your body!"

Centrum's main lab.

Among the many instrumentation and screen displays, Zoltar, the previous BI Island commander, faced the chief scientist, a Seraph dressed in a tight green tunic with no unique markings; in contrast, Zoltar's uniform was shiny, almost pretentious. The golden BI markings inside the circle next to the right pectoral muscle now read CL. (Centrum Lab.)

He stretched up as being stiff-necked. He did this intentionally because, by such action, he would look down upon the scientist. This Seraph looked evasively and stated.

"Our great leader Lucif-er was correct!

The gravitational matrix constant is causing density waves that affect the thermonuclear carbon cycle. The problem arises when the unstable oxygen-15 isotope decays into a nitrogen-15 isotope! This isotope, combined with a proton, splits to a helium nucleus and the original carbon that..."

"Wait!" Zoltar interrupted, *"I am not too good with solar nuclear reactions, in layman's language; tell me what is going on!"*

The head scientist grimaced as if annoyed, but he reflected and explained again, *"The solar nucleus data indicates that our sun is denser than normal; it means that it has a larger ratio of heavier elements compared to the helium, which is normally present. For the size of our sun, this is extremely abnormal!*

I just hope we could have a computer program that would include a cross-sectional, element-extrapolating matrix with relativistic effects

---

[5] About 72 Km/Earth-hour.

compensated in exponential form. Then, we could tell where all these events are leading to."

The lab commander almost laughed at the scientist. Reaching inside his pants pocket, he extracted a small shiny cube. He retorted with a touch of superiority since all these brainy angels somewhat bugged him.

"I am almost sure; it was exactly what the soldier who delivered this unit told me. He said our Supreme Leader, Lucif-er, has already incorporated your request into this program!"

The mouth of the scientist opened with an incredulous display.

"This is fantastic! Our great leader is always ahead of us. Considering it may take several days to compute the answer, I should start the program immediately!" He exclaimed.

Zoltar, feeling better, responded with complacency.

"OK... Go ahead, Cyrek!"

Later the same day, it was almost midnight at Kral, where two Overlords were talking. Kroma-el, a Cherub with a crew haircut, stayed facing his companion, who, as far as hairdos are concerned, was the opposite. Ezek-el had lots of blond hair but not a loose strand. This Overlord also looked the opposite as physique was concerned; he remained a round-faced and stocky individual, while Kroma-el, his companion, looked taller and slender.

"Ezek-el, I received a message from Lucif-er. He said we would not attend his big upcoming speech in two days. Instead, he wants us to optimize the output of the ST-6 solar acquisition satellite network!" Kroma-el said.

The Throne Overlord, with a round face, exhibited an unhappy grimace; he retorted.

"I do not know why the boss worries so much about the sun. I am aware of the unexpected abnormalities occurring, but I am sure they are just fluctuations occurring every million years or billions of years. We will find out in the future that the variations are cyclic and <u>normal</u>!"

"I agree with your viewpoint; just do not underestimate Lucif-er. If he is worried, something must be seriously wrong! ... He also said: In two days, we should know the answer." To make a point, the speaker, pointing a finger at Ezeki-el, exclaimed, *"That is the night of the big party! Everything is ready today; I even ordered more animals... <u>sheep!</u>"*

"Kroma-el! You did read my mind; I like it! Do you know that I am developing an attraction to female sheep?"

"Yes... however, the animals have no time to show you their affection; you kill them all the time!"

Both giggle with a sinister overtone

"I have an idea to spice up the party," Kroma-el added.

Ezek-el anticipated and enthusiastically exclaimed.

"It is great! After I kill a few sheep, we can roast them over an open fire just like our ancient ancestors did, and then we can eat their flesh!"

"The thought of this makes me squeamish!"

As Kroma-el's teeth stuck out, he formed in his mind the image of the action of eating partially cooked meat, still dripping blood, as a new experience.

His partner licked his lips and remarked with sadistic gore.

"I see the image you have in mind. It is a rather... beastly behavior! I love it!"

It was precisely midnight.

T$_{END}$ = -20:00 Hours

The sun, climbing the morning sky, sparked another beautiful day on the planet named Terra. Next to the pool at Lucif-er's original mansion, three Overlords sat next to the water. The master of the place addressed the other two, Zeri-el and Gorgon-el. With a cupped hand, the latter picked up a batch of water. Both subordinates received the message.

"Zeri-el, I am sending you to fix a problem developing in the Keres Atoll. Two opposing factions are fighting; they have caused several civilian casualties. Start with the leaders; anyone unwilling to obey, terminate his existence!

Second, check the volcanic chain along the islands where two extinct volcanoes have come alive! I am sure the sun is again affecting the stability of the tectonic plates. Report anything relevant to me!"

Gorgon-el made a windy whistling noise with his puckered-up lips. At the same time, still holding the cupped water about thirty centimeters above his pants when some drops of liquid fell. The amazing thing was that they did not reach his clothes; instead, they followed 'S' shaped pathways around his legs as they fell under his chair like the drops stayed rolling along the surface of an invisible playground slide, all following the same trajectory. The Overlord commented.

"An island with a volcano? If Zeri-el refuses to go, I will do it!"

The named Archangel squeezed his teeth; he felt close to a blind fury.

"Gorgon-el! You know that has been buried in the PAST!" He angrily exclaimed.

Suddenly, the water left on Gorgon-el's hand fell and wet his pants.

While Gorgon-el passed his right hand over his pants, completely vaporizing the water and leaving his garment as dry as before, he gave his colleague an ardent look with his typical foxy glance freely included... Was hate involved?

Lucif-er barely showed any enthusiasm; after a faint smile, he continued his communiqué to Zeri-el, who now gave him most of his attention.

"Leave tomorrow afternoon; they will be waiting for you at the Atoll the next day at noon!"

Later, inside the mansion, a monitor asked for Lucif-er's attention. After acknowledging the initiation, Zoltar's face appeared on the screen; he exclaimed.

"Great Overlord! I have news for you!

Cyrek found that the black body radiation, which was supposed to return to its original level after the flares subsided, did not! Instead, it is up another 100°!"

Zoltar appeared shaken! Seeing the angry face in front of his viewing monitor became intimidating. Lucif-er looked unhappy; the furor inside him became ready to burst, but it did not. In a voice that even echoed electronically, he demanded with an unsympathetic look.

"When will my program be run to its completion?
I need that information… now!"

Zoltar swallowed first; then, he quickly but nervously responded.

*"**Sir!** I have everybody working on the project… ten hours a day! Cyrek did promise me: Tomorrow night… **For sure!**"*

At the other end of the electronic communication, Zoltar's side, the image of the fiery blue eyes pierced his vision with what Zoltar thought would be enough to melt his brain. Electronically or not, he could not discern if such a thing was feasible.

Enormous relief flooded his whole mind and body; the monitor had blinked OFF.

Another night crawled by; unknown to all, only one complete day remained. Somehow, this reminisced about the last day of the SA. Conversely, it remained dissimilar by one fact: Today will be the last day of the entire planet!

As the black veil of the night reached its darkest zenith, so the darkness inside the souls of the remaining inhabitants of Terra reached for the murky depths that only sin could provide. They engaged in the most decadent ways they could imagine; every new night, they took one more step down into an abysmal black hole.

Their immense offense to their Creator was about to reach its breaking point. A debt that had by now become greater than the material Universe had reached its collection time.

A magnificent comet stretched across the southern night sky, another unmatched spectacle for the dwellers of Terra to cherish. The largest comet ever seen in the sky was scheduled for its maximum spread tomorrow night. Was it heralding good news or bad news?

Alternatively, perhaps it came to commemorate an anniversary; tomorrow night will be exactly 14 years from the destruction of the SA!

The clock that only God could envision accurately marked the instant when the new day whispered by unnoticed.

T_{END} = -10:00 Hours

****

The brightness rising from the east began dissipating the darkness; the emerging morning colors brilliantly decorated the sky. The brightest part of the sky was the closest to the ground; when the red disk emerged above the low nearby hills, it practically dissolved the previously well-defined separation between the earth and the sky.

As a fish caught in a string is pulled out of the water, equally alike by some invisible cosmic strand, the sun seemed to be extracted from the ground; subsequently, the entire disk continued its daily journey across the sky.

A pair of intense blue eyes had imprinted on their surfaces the image of the solar disk; the owner of such eyes was Lucif-er. From a terrace of his new mansion near the site of the destroyed city of Trillium, he sat facing the sunrise. He was not alone; Liliel stayed seated next to him, observing the upward movement of the sun. She did notice his deep concentration in the event; she appeared even surprised that her partner did not anticipate her thoughts when she ventured to ask.

"What is so alluring about a sunrise that you even ignore me?"

In a reflective manner, Lucif-er rubbed two fingers on his well-formed chin. He did not answer the question immediately; in a sinister manner, he slowly retorted.

"The stupid star is too bright! ... I have serious concerns about it!"

The construction rattling from the new city of Babyl-on started to increase; it was faint because of the distance, but you could tell that many early-rising workers had just started their shift. Lucif-er continued overlooking such an enormous project from his strategically located new mansion.

Lucif-er continued with a serious overtone.

"If the sun's overall energy output increases even 10%, we will be in serious trouble!" Lucif-er, anticipating a question, continued, *"You are correct. The program Cyrek is currently running should give all the answers we need. I am angrily trying to figure out our sun's crazy behavior; at least Cyrek promised that tonight we should have the final details."*

First, Lucif-er and then Liliel became aware of the still distant platoon leader Kragen approaching to announce that the flagship assigned to Lucif-er was ready for a Centrum departure. They were already formally dressed for the occasion: He was in his blazing white outfit, and she was in a provocative, skintight red dress. The Overlord proceeded to say the final word.

"After tonight, we should know everything about our sun activity; no need to worry or guess anymore!"

T_{END} = -7:81 Hours

At the top of a snow-capped mountain, two Overlords, masters of their craft, continued their intricate work at an outdoor computer terminal. Nearby, a massive antenna array, a testament to their technological prowess, followed up every minuscule change performed on the terminal. It was freezing; to make it worse, a brisk wind blew the snowflakes around. The Overlords, seemingly unaffected by the cold, wore their summer attire, some type of lightweight jumpsuits, a testament to their resilience and adaptability.

The midday sun, judging by its inclination south, this location must have been as far north as land would allow it. A Cherub, Kroma-el, announced above the whistling noise of the crosswind.

"The array stayed out of synchronization by 1.3°.
The last magnetic solar storm must have polarized some detectors, causing the deviation. This increase in accuracy should help Cyrek meet his deadline."

"Since we are finished, let us go back to Kral. I do not want to be late for Lucif-er's speech and the big party," replied Ezek-el. *"The sheep... have they been delivered yet?"*

T_{END} = -4:78 Hours

A powerful aircraft with a top-of-the-line design took off, speeding almost violently; its leading nose remained aimed at the setting sun, the place where a colorful sunset began crowning the end of a pleasant day. As it climbed into the darkening sky, the vast work done in Babyl-on came into view. Many levels of the structures remained unfinished, with lots of work lying still ahead. When completed, the city would not just rival the stars in the sky but also the sparkling of a waterfall, the beauty of a flowering rain forest, the complexity of DNA, and the intricacy of electron orbital of heavy elements. It would become the ultimate 3-D self-supporting matrix, a living entity in its own right.

Above and most important of all, it was intended to be the capital of Evil, its gate to the Universe. Since its completion remained years to come, its real destiny became set by the last darkening curtains thrown over the land by the impending night; its future stayed well-defined... just cosmic dust; this was the ominous fate awaiting it.

Inside the speeding craft on his way to the Keres Atoll islands was Zeri-el.

T_{END} = -2:30 Hours

At the Centrum's main lab, located at the bottom of the tallest building in the city, many floors above the Overlords' meeting place, Lucif-er became ready to address its vast dominions. The planetary network was ready to transmit a very important message from its leader to all citizens of the NA.

The head scientist, Cyrek, at the lab, closely examined a large screen. Two of his top assistants, Seraphim, remained analyzing the computer data facing them. Working at almost 100% capacity, the computer showed many strings of three-dimensional data passing by at sub-nanosecond speeds. In red letters at the bottom, a message was updated in real-time.

Program completion ➔   **0:71:23 hours**
                        0:71:22
                        0:71:21

Each new entry replaced the previous one.

The scientist at the right of Cyrek had an N1 printed over his shiny outfit; he also displayed golden characters stamped over his right chest, identifying him as a nuclear physicist. The one on his left was labeled as P1, the leading programmer expert; this individual, with a bushy hairdo, advanced his opinion.

"Lucif-er's program will be completed soon, and we have enough data to start running preliminary projections. Do you want me to initialize the programming matrix, G-3V-DSC?"

Cyrek, who was squirming his buggy eyes, quickly replied.

"Yes! Start with a solar cross-sectional analysis!"

It took three seconds for the computer to display a rectangular central box using about ¼ of the whole screen. Inside, 3-D images of a cross-section of the sun started being analyzed and continually updated. All three scientists concentrated their sight on a group of information tagged next to the solar internally split view.

Sun composition: H   69%
                  He   28%
        Other elements   3%

N1 declared immediately.

"This doesn't look any good! ... Look at The Core data!"

Core   Density   254x
Temperature   21 million °C

With his blue eyes straining to absorb the multiple arrays of data, Cyrek exclaimed, *"The radiation zone and the convection zone show only minor increases in activity. The photosphere temperature is up to 6320 °K! ... **Is it increasing?**"*

The last displayed data, read.

Core   Density   255x
Temperature   21.2 million °C

P1 immediately manipulated some controls; a new smaller graph appeared and stayed next to the center. Its climbing features shook N1, who nervously asked, *"An exponential curve?"*

"No! Like T^4!" replied his superior.

Cyrek stared at his colleague. N1's hands shook momentarily; it was a nervous outpour that could not be controlled, hinting at the fear growing inside him. Tiny droplets of sweat materialized almost instantly on Cyrek's forehead! Squeezing both hands together, he swallowed with difficulty and remarked with a shaky telepathic statement.

"This cannot be right!
*This is only the first projection... however, **I am already scared!**"*
$T_{END} = -0:95:22$ **Hours**

Close to noontime.

One slick cylinder landed on a site next to an isolated building complex; the surrounding scenery was like a tropical jungle around this location. Thick forest covered the slopes of the nearby mountains. One of them, a cylindrical cone, continued emitting a dense column of smoke that drifted away from its top in a direction away from the landing site.

When the main side door of the craft opened, two armed pilots quickly stood at each side. A Cherub, Zeri-el, dressed in a shiny dark red attire, stepped out.

The medium-built but muscular Overlord stood straight, scrutinizing what lay in front of him. Only about 20 meters away, a welcoming crowd heralded his arrival. One Cherub stood before the rest; by his fancy clothes, he was obviously the Governor of the Atoll. He approached Zeri-el.

The Overlord casually gazed at the distant volcano, almost looking for the scary shape of his dreams: The dreaded 'M' shaped top... No, it just looked like any other stupid volcano!

He relaxed, letting his egocentric powers take over. He came here to hand out a swift solution to a problem, and he would make sure that they remembered his divine powers!

The governor stopped close to the Overlord, bowed, and exclaimed.

"Most illustrious Overlord! Welcome to Central Island!"

The place's name rang inside Zeri-el's brain as a bullet fired inside a metallic room with an awesome ricochet!

The Overlord's green eyes turned to an orange tone; he squeezed his teeth very hard while his appearance became fearsome. Without any comprehension of what was happening, the governor took a step backward, seriously concerned about doing something improper.

Almost instantly, Zeri-el regained his composure. He just ordered.

"Let's start examining the unruly situation!"

The crowd opened in two halves, allowing the Overlord to stroll along an ample pathway leading directly to a raised platform with one chair facing many others.

Zeri-el walked like a king; all eyes stayed on him, but only indirectly. He climbed the short stairway to the top surface and moved directly to his assigned chair, which he sat in.

The governor and the most important people of the place took seats in front of him. Many surrounded the platform, eager to see what the Overlord intended to do. Unnoticed to most, the heavily armed platoon assigned to the Overlord had taken strategic positions around the compound.

Zeri-el knew that a speaker system was set up to amplify his voice so all could hear; he talked in a mild but sinister voice. From his sitting position, he said.

"Our Great Leader is extremely unhappy about the behavior of the two fighting groups on this island. I am here to end all fighting; anyone who does not obey this command... will be terminated!"

After a planned pause given to the congregation to digest the short message, he continued with an intimidating voice, including a fatal pledge if not acknowledged.

"I want in front of me the two opposing leaders of this conflict! ... I will not wait longer than 20 seconds!"

The seconds could almost be heard as they added to the indicated amount. The two angels must have felt the pressure because at the count of '15', they broke away from the standing crowd and moved to the stipulated location.

None of the two individuals standing before Zeri-el dared to look up to him. To his left, a muscular Seraph was moving nervously at his position. At the Overlord's right, a tall Throne stayed even more nervous than his opponent. They stayed a short distance from each other; however, they momentarily forgot that they were opponents. Zeri-el commanded.

"You, as the leaders, will ensure that all your followers behave as I ordered! ... Acknowledge!"

Both, almost in unison, vocally exclaimed.

"We acknowledge, Great Overlord!"

Two seconds of silence passed. Then, suddenly, the muscular Seraph in front of Zeri-el twisted in agonizing pain. His neck snapped with the cracking sound of a broken joint; his head turned now, looking the opposite way than the front!

A grotesque body, which dropped lifelessly on the platform, horrified the congregation. The Throne, his opponent, took two steps away from the fallen corpse, afraid of being next!

The Overlord felt like spitting on that pile of garbage that just seconds before was alive; he pointed to the dead angel announcing.

*"He did not mean what he said... **I do!**"*

Only a few minutes later, the crowd seemed to have forgotten the incident. Now, all were located at the top of a wide but somewhat low structure by Terra standards, about 20 stories high. The elegant terrace at the top of this building, pleasantly adorned with flowering plants native to the atoll, became part of the festivity; the governor had this place specially prepared for the important visitors where food and entertainment were exuberantly given; even a melodic piece of music could be heard in the background of this noisy group. At opposite ends of the terrace, two large screens remained facing the congregation; even when close to noontime, the screens brightly displayed global news information.

The images of Lucif-er, Liliel, four other Overlords, and six army commanders at Centrum moved to their preassigned positions, getting ready to start the big announcement.

At Central Island, Zeri-el had the place of honor at the building's terrace, but he was not at the center; he was next to an outside edge rail so the Overlord could have an undisturbed view of the spectacular Keres Atoll.

The Governor approached the Overlord, flanked by two gorgeous, scantily dressed Seraphim females who were more tanned than the usual city dwellers. Stopping in front of Zeri-el, the governor bowed, but the Overlord rattled his brain before he could say anything.

"I will take them!"

As the governor removed himself, the archangel scanned the great female bodies with a lusty inquiry. What a coincidence, two female Seraphim, just like in the dream! This kind of coincidence, he could take any time!

The attractive females sat on each of his legs and caressed him. One raised her sight to give him an inviting glance with sexy overtones while at the same time admiring his superior appearance and power.

While ravishing her entire body, but only with his mind, Zeri-el thought.

"After I get through with your mind and body, you will not dare to look at me in this way ever again!"

Zeri-el felt immensely powerful physically, mentally, and socially. He felt so good and so much that only a god could feel this way. Both pretty Seraphim had thrown themselves at his feet. With each hand, he grabbed the hair of each female and pulled; he stopped when a cry of pain came from both angels. He glanced at them with lust and disdain.

Silence came along the whole place; Lucif-er had just started his speech. Zeri-el listened while his mind engaged in several other activities, including the simultaneous sexual fondling of his two companions.

He glanced at the outstanding view in front of him, 180 degrees from the mountainous site of the island's volcano; he could see the not-too-far shoreline. A blue ocean gap separated the Central Island from the rest of the Atoll members; dwarfed by the distance, he saw another island with another smoking mountain, another volcano. He had plenty of time; he should investigate tomorrow's volcanic activity.

Across the terrace, he saw one of his own guards listening and watching the speech. He thought.

"Stupid bastard! He should be listening, not watching! He will pay for this!"

Lucif-er's speech progressed as planned. Zeri-el knew the context throughout its length, but regardless, he elaborated on his boss's proclamation.

Suddenly, a mild earthquake shook the building!

Apart from the Overlord, all dismissed it as just another 4.0 shake. They had felt too many of those and even bigger ones to be concerned.

Zeri-el became perplexed. The direction of the wave looked very unusual: no lateral translation! Even worse, the energy direction had a **negative** value!

Something caught his attention as the Overlord searched for a solution with his brain working at warp speed. The image of Lucif-er giving the discourse had become silent; the leader of the NA now showed a reflexive stance!

This shocked Zeri-el. How could this be possible? Lucif-er was on the other side of the planet, and he felt this minor quake!

His boss, still under the camera, had interrupted his scheduled speech. In response to Gorgon-el's comment, Lucif-er, extending his open hand at his subordinate, exclaimed.

*"This was not a casual earthquake! ... **It was a gravity wave!**"*

Zeri-el dropped everything else. From the multiple tasks being performed by his powerful brain, only one took all priorities; he mentally yelled.

"That is the answer! Lucif-er, I envy you; your mind is so sharp!"

The Overlord became restless; still, a big question remained.

"From where it came?"

The island's volcano caught his attention. A larger stack of smoke began to be noticeably projected upwards. His quick perception of his surroundings made him look in the opposite direction; the volcano on the neighboring island in the Atoll had equally become more active.

A chill ran down his spine because, at an even greater distance, another island in the Atoll had now become an active volcano, and a large plume of smoke could be seen blasting its way to the stratosphere. Now, three volcanoes were active!

Zeri-el got so concerned that he quickly had a personal admonition.

"Something is seriously wrong! I cannot wait until tomorrow for this investigation to start. I hate to drop the broads, but they will have to wait... I am launching the volcanic exploration this afternoon; no way I'm getting caught with my pants down!"

Lucif-er's planetary address on the two large screens was interrupted again! Magog-el pointed his left hand's index finger to the sky; a dead silence took over Centrum.

The cameras showed the reason for this commotion. The comet, the splendorous traveler covering half of the southern sky, began disintegrating!

The event appeared on the two large screens as a shock wave rippled across the comet. First, the nucleus blew into tiny pieces. Next, a wave traveled along the splendorous tail, disturbing its peaceful display. Now, where beauty and form ruled, only chaos remained.

Zeri-el's mental stability was also collapsing, and he tightly squeezed his left hand's fist with his right hand.

"This is a bad omen!" He managed to comment.

The sun had arrived at its noon's zenith.

In Centrum, the master clock read:

0:00:00 hours

The celestial and divine clock also read:

$T_{END} = $ **0:00:00 Hours**

A chill never felt before ran deep inside the Overlord's bone marrow, the same feeling as when the first winter storm blasts the flowering annuals. The plants know that their time is up because there is nothing left to do on this planet other than to spread more seeds to preserve future generations and then die. I am sure the perishing plants go in a merry way; their lives have been splendorous through the spring, summer, and fall. Their existence was exalted by a shower of colors that attracted the eyes of so many, especially those of the pollinating bugs. Their mission had been accomplished; finally, it was time to go.

Zeri-el did not feel that way; actually, he felt just the opposite!

His sinister eyes scanned the horizon, looking for invisible monsters. By now, his breathing had become deeper but more strenuous, his heart began accelerating, and perspiration wetted his forehead. The Overlord remained horrified with the thought of his nightmare becoming a reality!

Confused by the events on the screens and at home, the two females at his legs grabbed his legs harder. Zeri-el, using both hands, threw them away from him.

His heart almost stopped when he heard the horrifying nightmare approaching; it sounded like a million freight trains converging to the point where he stood.

Like thunder hitting you on the head, a monster roared.

The seismic blast rattled the building; it felt not much different than a giant demolition ball hitting the sidewalls and causing chunks to fall off. The large screens blew in many pieces, with falling fragments injuring or killing nearby angels. Massive cracks appeared instantly on the top terrace; pieces of structure, plus branches of the landscaped trees chopped by invisible axes, rained over the congregation!

It turned into a nightmarish spectacle, which was unfortunate for the participants because this part remained a mellow beginning for what was to come.

Zeri-el moved into action; he felt the building collapsing and only one thing remaining to do... he jumped over the rail toward the faraway ground!

Like a bat with his wings extended to the wind, he fell. Around him, pieces of debris mixed with screaming angels with their eyes and mouths opened in terror fell to their crushing ends while staring at the fast-approaching floor, the surface defining life or death.

In the last instant, the Overlord broke his fall sharply; he planted both feet squarely on solid ground with a solid 'thud'! All around him, large fragments and bodies crashed into the hard surface at the base of the building.

Zeri-el turned his overdrive on. He ran at maximum speed away from the building. He had just cleared the area when the massive structure collapsed into a roaring pile of rubbish. Dust, noises, and screams mixed for a moment. Next, only dust continued expanding in all directions.

The earth remained shaking and moaning like it was in great pain. Cracks appeared everywhere, with columns of steam and smoke shooting out of the crevices. Zeri-el was the only one able to run in those conditions; everyone else stayed flat on the ground!

He sped toward his aircraft; he had to get aboard and leave the island. A red flash caught his attention, and he looked back.

A giant mushroom ball of fire and ash had erupted from the island's volcano!

As he continued running, his peripheral field of vision saw something that scared the wits out of him; the frontal center part of the volcano had collapsed.

Utterly terrorized, he closed his eyes and faced the volcano. Even with his eyes closed, he saw it: the **'M' shape of his dreams.**

A god called Zeri-el shook with fear and terror; he ran like a maniac! This was the same place where the ice-cold liquid horror had run through his veins before. He knew the fire was coming soon, so he had to reach his craft and escape this heinous atoll before it blew up!

His face, distorted by fear, had sweat pouring out of every pore on his skin; his heart started pumping lead instead of blood, and this weight began pushing him downwards. He fell to the ground.

Zeri-el rolled over and got up, but several lacerations on his face and arms started to bleed. He stopped the blood dripping. With his mouth open and running out of breath, he glanced ahead; to his astonishment, the craft stood in front of him.

Four of his crewmembers bounced from the adjacent floor, incapable of standing up. The shaking, still raging at its maximum energy, bounced the flying craft against the ground; it could become damaged!

Zeri-el, ignoring his crew, dashed into the vehicle's open door and sped like a bullet to the pilot's controls. There, he manipulated such complicated controls at incredible speed.

The rough humming of the engine was heard as the craft tried to take off. After banging one side on the rough floor, the sleek cylinder lifted off the ground; once in the air, it became like an unleashed bullet streaking away violently. The outcry of the strained engine remained short; in only a few seconds, the island's mountains looked dwarfed below.

Zeri-el had the almost uncontrollable urge to scream with utter satisfaction.

"Yes!"

He had cheated death again. The stupid atoll could blow up; now, he could care less!

In an ethereal way inside the craft, many particles came together to bring into view an image! In front of him, he saw the image of Gabri-el, equal to the one when this Overlord let him escape from the doomed SA; Zeri-el's same sardonic and evil laugh remained filling the craft's cabin.

The image of Gabri-el persisted; he did not say anything, just stared at Zeri-el. Inside the long-departed Overlord's eyes remained this disturbing sadness… The image dissolved away.

Zeri-el stopped laughing; something about seeing Gabri-el had replenished his fear and deep depression. He glanced at the islands below, where even the towering plumes of smoke and fire stayed safely below him. Why were the horror, fear, and smell of death suddenly back again?

The sun, through a window, continued hitting his body.

It felt so hot! So penetratingly… **hot!**

An immense horror shook his whole body. He went out of control, with his mind close to a nuclear meltdown, refusing to believe the inevitable; he stared at the blazing sun and screamed in a chanting way.

"This cannot be… This cannot be… This cannot be!"

Suddenly, the sky turned black!

The solar disk had, in an instant, reduced its size to a minute point.

The Archangel's mind was working at maximum speed, allowing him to see the sun blinking out and its immensely bright return. When darkness set in, he had time to scream at 50 times the normal speed.

"I am a God, I can't die! … I am immortal!"

When the searing light came back, he just had time to shout in utter terror.

"N-o-oo-...o- ...."

The incredible light and heat charred his skin like an overcooked barbecue in just an instant. His eyes did not even explode; they just vaporized into thin gases. The pain grew unbelievable; every molecule of his body was being destroyed; he became atomized! A horror never imagined before materialized; unfortunately for him, this remained just a prelude to something much worse to come. At this instant, Death was only 1/60 of a second away!

His mind, along with his body, and his whole craft dissolved into nothing!

Zeri-el was dead!

Even when he was physically gone, a grotesque and dark silhouette sank below the remains of his last material location; it became an image of Evil released by the fiery light, showing its true essence: a combination of ugliness, darkness, and hatefulness.

Below, the oceans vaporized, the mountains melted, and the atmosphere turned into fire. Amidst a blinding glow, a blast of cosmic rays and neutrinos began dissolving one side of the planet!

The sun of Terra, Star 1, became what should have been impossible!

A supernova!

****

T_{END} = -0:20:00 Hours

Twenty Terra minutes before the last event, at the Centrum downtown area, millions of angels roamed the streets avidly waiting for their leader to announce the good news. Nobody intended to miss anything from the speech and to ensure it, enough displays had been set up at strategic places for the video transmission. The talk was to be broadcast from the top of the Central Building; up there, only an elite group of angels would be present.

At such a location, a raised round platform had a higher crescent moon section assigned for the Overlords. Lucif-er sat ahead, Liliel at his side but lower, Magog-el a bit behind. Three more seats were farther behind.

Four pathways allowed easy access to the platform and its raised podium. All other seats at the top of the central skyscraper were already occupied; the seated crowd remained noisily talking to each other. The vast congregation on the town's streets caused enough uproar to be heard even at the very top; however, up there, it sounded like a hum from a distant wasp nest.

The light, more intense over the podium, stayed lower for the rest of the platform and appeared to be the least for the audience.

A 'ding' sound caused the congregation above and below the building to stop chatting and to listen. The six commanders of the NA armies, wearing their best military uniforms with attached handguns at their waistline belts, walked to the platform in a single file. At the head of the group, Arkyn led the procession. After marching to their assigned sitting places, they positioned themselves in a stand-at-attention mode.

Four Overlords, also displaying their best tunics and favorite colors, casually strolled to the center, first Magog-el with the other three behind; they also waited, standing next to their seats.

Last, the lord of the land, dressed in an iridescent white tunic, walked, displaying his sense of ownership; all eyes admired his powerful and hypnotic appearance. To his side, just a bit behind him, Liliel walked with a glow of satisfaction and earned glory. This was a big day for her; her attire showed it: an aggressive interlaced red dress with a low neckline showing most of her best assets and crisscrossed so both of her thighs occasionally became displayed.

She insidiously moved her shapely body, exuding sexuality in a wholesale manner. The jewels on the dress, a high-tech design, were so positioned that similar facets glowed simultaneously, adding to the mysticism of her walk. The NA's male citizens lusted for her; even a significant amount of the females became equally aroused.

Liliel walked to her seating location. Lucif-er did not stop at his; he continued his ceremonious stroll until he reached the center of the raised section or podium.

At this moment, Magog-el sat down; Liliel and the other three Overlords sat next. Last, the commanders took their assigned seats, with Arkyn being the first to rest on a piece of furniture.

Lucif-er stood under the light for a few seconds, his majestic personality overpowering everything else. His face glowed more than his white clothes, and his wings shined so much that their combined halo framed his body's outline. When the cameras focused on him to show his facial expressions, the enormous comet in the southern sky was displayed just above his head, like it was part of his personal belongings!

He allowed the speaker system to magnify his voice; he started with a commanding verbal message.

"My dear citizens!

*In a few minutes, we welcome a new day; this is not an ordinary day…
it is a date to remember!*

Day: 151, Year: 205,061."

T_{END} = -0:15:00 Hours

Cyrek and his two top assistants, P1 and N1, continued ferociously entering data; the rest of the crew just fed the building blocks to allow them to do so. The whole place seemed to be running on pure adrenaline.

The head scientist glanced up to check two of the sun's core parameters: density and temperature. They were still climbing up, so he checked other additional incoming data.

Sun composition: **H**   **67%**
                                     He   **27%**
                    Other elements   **6%**

"Heavier elements at the core, increasing faster!" Cyrek exclaimed.

"I don't understand what is going on!" N1 mentally yelled; he added, *"The C-N-O nuclear reaction loop is shifting to higher elements! There is* **no** *precedent for this! ... Cyrek! I am terrified!"*

The head scientist cleaned the sweat from his forehead; next, as his heart began pounding harder than usual, he rubbed his chest. Staring at P1, he requested.

"Can you program the computer to project an increasing and overlapping nuclear reaction in a simultaneous equation form? I need it soon, and I need it for the final answer!"

"I can! But it is a complex calculation; it will take several minutes!"

"Start now!"

A Seraph, wearing a fancy military uniform, walked into the large acquisition lab room. Stiff-necked, when he approached the trio, just about now, he realized that the whole place was in overdrive. Staring at the back of the three top scientists, who worked at their maximum concentration facing the largest screen connected to the computer, he noticed N1 pulling the hair that hung about his neck with an almost nervous fury. With a commanding tone, he asked.

"What is going on?"

T_{END} = -00:10:00 Hours

"...We are renaming The Core and the SA. The first will be known as the three Central Sectors. Babyl-on will be the capital of the new sectors and the capital of the whole planet!

Over the previous province boundaries, five southern Sectors will be traced!"

Lucif-er walked around so the camera view could show his explaining hand positioned just under the splendid comet display; he continued.

"Eventually, we will have new Overlords to govern each new sector. Concerning this statement, today, I am instating a new Overlord on the high command... **Lili-el!**"

At the sound of her name, she eagerly stepped up and quickly joined her boss and lover at the podium. She walked facing all cameras, so her attributes were clearly visible and appreciated. As she gracefully paced the upper platform, she could not resist, and she raised both of her fists as high as she could; Lucif-er, who supported her triumphant debut with a formal overtone, firmly stated.

"All citizens should give her the respect that her rank demands!"

At a pause from her boss, she announced with passion and triumph.

"Citizen of the NA, I will treat you according to the law of the land and with the utmost fairness! ... As my new rank requires, I look forward to many years of mutual cooperation!"

Her beautiful purplish eyes shined like stars at the audience, while her pinkish wings' halo became inviting and sensual. Above all, she felt the intoxicating ecstasy of victory. No female had ever dreamed of reaching the prestigious position of being an Overlord, an exclusive male dominion. Today, she broke that ancient rule; **she became one of them!**

As Lucif-er gave her a consenting smile, many citizens did not say it but thought of it as a roaring mental exclamation.

"Lili-el, we surely crave for the 'mutual cooperation'... Just ask, and we will be your sex slaves!"

"In honor of her new title," Lucif-er continued, *"the splendorous comet C-279... now has the additional name of Lili-el!"*

A roar of appreciation came from everywhere, but the outside cheers had to rumble their way up to the top of the building. The cheers were for the new Overlord, a beautiful female... If they could only see under her skin that a black widow spider was very tame and merciful when compared to this one!

T_{END} = -0:07:00 Hours

There were only seven minutes left, but still, nobody had figured out what was relentlessly approaching. However, inside the soul of many, oppression set much deeper than anything felt before, a subtle hint of the impending disaster. Perhaps, in this instance, it was better not to know!

Two other Overlords at Kral, Kroma-el, and Ezek-el, were already at a big party unleashed at the city's downtown area, but the noisy affair had been halted to see Lucif-er's announcement.

The local audience, including the two Archangels, was vociferous in favor of Liliel. This loud cheering remained motivated by hopeful sexual encounters with the new queen!

Inside the spacious halls of a building, many people gathered for the big orgy coinciding with Lucif-er's big announcement; it was a celebration to honor such a broadcast declaration.

In a corner, a small, fenced area separated six well-fed white sheep from the angels. In front of them were six machines, all lined up in a straight row. These machines had a supported central bar with an empty area below that showed an array of electric coils.

One female angel of the lowest choir asked a male Seraph next to her.

"I have never seen any such devices before. What are they for?"

The Seraph, a military attaché, moved his smiling face close to her and vocally exclaimed.

"They are for the sheep... We are going to cook them!"

She stared at his nose, almost touching hers, partially getting a cross-eyed vision. She wrinkled her forehead and asked again without a hint of what was going on.

"Why? ... Is it some kind of torture?"

The Seraph moved his nose back and forth, gently rubbing hers like a negative nodding. While puckering up his lips in an inviting sexual advance, he commented in a condescending manner.

"Don't you know anything? We are going to eat them!"

She opened her mouth, reflecting an incredulous mental input; two seconds later, while twisting her lips, she exclaimed, ***"Eww... gross!"***

T_{END} = -0:06:00 Hours

The Supreme Leader continued.

"...The most important aspect of this change will be the repopulation of the Central and Southern Sectors. I want the planet's population to grow until it reaches 10 billion!

Starting Day: 151, which begins in just a few minutes... I am lifting the planetary ban against having children. Any females interested in procreation are free to do so, and starting at this moment, they can make plans to start reversing their biological blocks!

The government will assist in the upbringing of the newborn. Special children's wards will be constructed to control the babies' growth and to take care of their physical and mental needs.

Parents will not be held responsible for their children's development; they will be free to pursue their ambitions and goals!"

Lucif-er could read the inner excitement in many females; Liliel was not one of them. The innate drive for a female to be a mother, even when suppressed for such a long time, remained alive. After a brief pause to let the natural excitement that the news had stirred finally subside, he opened his mouth for the following statement... **Nothing came out!**

The top of the building had shaken mildly.

Gorgon-el, springing to a standing position, commented.

"Just a mild 4.0 quake!"

His boss, still under the camera, had interrupted his scheduled speech. In response to Gorgon-el's comment, Lucif-er, extending his open hand toward his subordinate, exclaimed.

"This was not a casual earthquake! ... **It was a gravity wave!**"

T_{END} = -0:05:00 Hours

"What was that?" asked Zoltar with some hesitation.

"Just a mild earthquake!" N1 answered with a broken voice; he was sweating profusely.

The head scientist, Cyrek, raised his hand to draw attention. While holding the left side of his chest, he exclaimed, *"We have no time for that! ... P1, we have all the necessary calculations; start the program!"*

A new 3-D graph showing the activity of the sun's core started to grow. It stayed at the center of the screen, incorporating all the major factors: temperature, density, atomic elements, and time. As the graph's main line climbed due to higher densities and temperatures, its correlation to atomic numbers increased; heavier elements started coming into view.

The highest atomic number reached was 22, titanium.

The graph clearly displayed an upward discontinuity after the 18th atomic number: AR, argon element.

N1 stayed numb for an instant, but he exploded.

"It has reached Ti, and it is still climbing!"

The left hand of Cyrek remained in a slight but constant shaking; also, a minor distortion on the left side of his face became apparent; he had severe chest pain. He pointed to the discontinuity, but before he could make a statement, Zoltar, who stood behind the scientists' trio, asked.

"What does it mean?"

The head scientist ignored him; his eyes were bulging almost out of his sockets. He was wet from his own sweat, and his breathing became deeper but shortly spaced. Trying to stay in focus, he lectured.

"Oh! ... The acidic pair, 16 S and 17 Cl, have caused a discontinuity in the nuclear reactions... uh! ... when crossing over to the alkaline pair: 19 K and 20 Ca!"

About this time, the computer advanced a message; it read next to the graph.

Unable to find quake epicenter, it was not on this planet.

After a second of silence, Cyrek pointed to the message and exclaimed.

"There! ... We did not experience a quake; look at the discontinuity! It was a gravity wave! ... Uh!"

Suddenly, P1 screamed.

"Look at the graph! It is completed... It can't be!"

A chill, which can only be found at the bottom of a grave, ran through the spines of the three scientists; **it was the chill of death!**

Zoltar just stared at the end of the graph; he was too dumb to read the message.

The last atomic element displayed at the end of the graph, where all calculations had stopped and where the growth of the graph's lines had collapsed, just read in large blinking red letters!

Fe

In young stars, hydrogen (Symbol: H, atomic number: 1) is burned as fuel. In the process, a higher atomic number element is created, helium

(He, atomic number: 2). The thermonuclear energy released by this reaction prevents the star's core from collapsing under the gravitational force of its own massive weight.

As the star ages, it starts converting helium into carbon (C, atomic number: 6). For the size of our sun, it is about where it ends. However, for stars at least eight times more massive than our sun, the process continues up the atomic number ladder until the element iron (Fe, atomic number: 26) is reached.

Iron is a very stable element; therefore, it will not burn into heavier elements and supply the energy that the star requires for its existence. As a result, the star's core collapses, and the star becomes a **supernova**.

$T_{END} = -0:04:00$ Hours

Kroma-el and Ezek-el, like a synchronized dynamic duet, stood up. Kroma-el issued a command that everybody in the party's whole place could hear.

"I want everybody to shut up! Something critical is happening… I order, NO interruptions!"

Turning to his colleague, he sent him a personal message.

"Lucif-er is right! The quake had no translational displacement and a negative value; it must have been a gravitational effect!"

"Yes! But what is going on? Has a black hole entered our solar system?"

"Not likely! Let us analyze the event… The direction was from the center of Terra!"

"You are right! The sun is in complete opposition at this moment; it must be the cause. Nevertheless, whatever caused the wave could be <u>bad news</u>!"

$T_{END} = -0:03:00$ Hours

Lucif-er, very concerned about the unusual event since his scheduled speech was due in three minutes, had to check his solar program running in the lab located many floors below. The dilemma caused him to squeeze his teeth so hard that they made cracking noises. He took a deep breath and decided to continue his magnified vocal message.

"Last, it is my privilege to report that an operational spacecraft is fully equipped to travel to the stars. This vessel can speed up to 90% of the speed of light! … This could allow this great nation to colonize other solar systems!

I know you are asking the question: We have not even colonized our solar system; why are we aiming for the stars?

My answer is simple: we will colonize our solar system soon; however, since this is a short-term endeavor compared to traveling to the next star and attempting to colonize its planets, I have decided to start with the most challenging enterprise.

The spacecraft will be self-supporting. On hostile planets, it could stand alone as the first building block for transforming undesirable environments into a pleasant habitat... it is called... terraforming!

This conversion is needed to start a suitable and livable climate, which allows a planet to be inhabitable for us!"

Lucif-er pointed one finger at Arkyn. The addressee stood up and bowed.

"In a year, commander Arkyn will depart for the most encouraging nearby planetary system we can find. Our first priority will be to build an interstellar network of colonized planets... Later, we shall expand to our whole galaxy G1... Finally, G-2, and the Universe! ... Even if it takes an eternity, we shall do it!"

He stared at the viewers through the camera. Without looking, he pointed at the enormous comet stretched across the southern and pristine night sky; he spoke with a dominant and hypnotic voice.

"Look at this magnificent visitor; it is here to celebrate the new order of our glorious nation!"

Simultaneously, he sent a personal message to a medium-build Cherub, Razari-el, *"Go to the lab; my program must be run to its completion now! If necessary, contact me immediately!"*

T_{END} = -0:02:00 Hours; only two minutes left.

"We only have until midnight! ... Only two minutes!" Cyrek moaned. He felt like passing out at any moment; his face showed a bluish tone, regardless, he added.

"Dis... ouch! ... tance to the sun: 141,805,000 Km. In 4.72 minutes after the explosion, the first blast will rea... ch Terra. Shortly afterward... the... shockwave!" Cyrek struggled to explain.

Zoltar, very concerned, retorted.

"I don't believe it! It is common knowledge... It is impossible for our sun to become a supernova!"

"We have just discovered a new type of supernovae! ... Type III," responded N1, *"It is the most sickening and terrifying discovery; because... it is our own star!"*

A head bouncing from the front of the display console attracted everybody's attention. Cyrek could have gotten help, but he did not! He decided to leave earlier, avoiding the last seven minutes of the ultimate nightmare!

Zoltar checked the head scientist's neck pulse; there was none. Cyrek lay motionless in a pile of lifeless matter, and the place's supervisor exclaimed with disgust.

*"I'll be... **he is dead!**"* Then, he glanced at the graph above and immediately decided to do something. He pointed a finger at N1 and ordered.

"You! Go upstairs and report to Lucif-er what is happening... now!"

The scientist remained shaking, sweat dripping from his head, and his heart became increasingly strained by fear. Nevertheless, he stared squarely at the commander's face, showing no fear of him; the commander was nothing compared to the horrible monster, soon to be unleashed, he just replied.

"No! ... Do it yourself, I won't do it!"

The commander's face became reshaped by anger, as he was not used to insubordination. He raised his hand to strike N1's face, but the determination that he saw made him lower his fist. Very angry, he barked.

"OK! I will do it myself... but if nothing happens, I will be back to punish you! ... What do I tell Lucif-er?"

N1 sadly looked at his dead colleague and old-time friend before replying; he also glanced at P1; the top programmer had his whole face covered with both hands, sobbing because he did not want to die! Almost in a trance, N1 exclaimed.

"You won't have to say or explain anything... Lucif-er can read it directly from your brain!"

T_{END} = -0:01:00 Hours
99 Seconds

98   Lucif-er had stopped the speech, pausing to emphasize his next statement; suddenly, something caught his attention. Above him, in a not-too-distant dark corner of a structure facing the long drop to the streets, a silhouette had unexpectedly appeared.

The Overlord sensed that he was being looked at; he strained his superior powers to discern the image; his material sensors said: There is absolutely <u>nothing there</u>.

His sixth sense told him the opposite!

90   His piercing blue eyes scanned the image to make it clear. No use!

It was like us using our night vision in a dark place; we can barely see this image in front of us, but the harder we stare at it, the fainter it becomes.

Lucif-er felt mesmerized. He even took a few steps toward the above corner to see better... no help. This entity stayed out of his senses' reach!

80   While Gabri-el, Micha-el, and Nobiel did discern His image with incredible clarity, Lucif-er remained incapable of seeing anything beyond his own reflection... just darkness!

The Visitant was there.

He glanced at Lucif-er. In the same instant, He glanced at every face present on the top terrace of the Central Building!

70   He was sad. Not only did He see the exterior bodies of the present, but the ultimate depths of their souls. It was not a pleasant view to God's eyes, but a monstrous display!

Next, He turned His perception to the many below… Millions!

It was a long way to the ground floor, much farther to the end of the massive outside congregation; still, He saw every face and soul of them.

60   There were so many of them… However, not one single soul had escaped the thorny and ugly grips of sin. Inside of them, Love did not exist anymore… only Hate!

50   The sorrow caused His eyes to wet. Two tears rolled down His divine cheeks and fell to the ground below, where even Lucif-er saw them!

40   A pair of shiny pearls appeared from nowhere and gracefully followed a direct trajectory to the nearby floor next to the platform, where they displaced the surface dust in a perfectly rounded way.

30   As the Overlord stared at the sparkling site, with a puff, they vanished.

Now, Lucif-er sensed missing the Entity. Even the displaced dust, where the tears had fallen, returned to its original place.

20   No silhouette and no marks from the tears left.

The Visitant, the God of Love, had departed!

The leader of the NA shook his head in disbelief; he thought that he was seeing things.

Who was 'he' anyway? Angels do not cry!

10   Magog-el's left index finger pointed to the southern sky. Before finishing pivoting in that direction, Lucif-er saw it.

The comet's head shattered into many tiny pieces, and a ripple quickly propagated along its fabulous tail. The glorious comet was destroyed right in front of their incredulous eyes. A radiant celestial body, endowed with a beauty never seen before, was no longer in the sky; only scattered debris remained.

A dead silence took over the place as many questioning eyes stared up at the night sky, and many minds envisioned the same thought.

"This is no good… It must be a bad omen!"

All the Overlords stood up. Magog-el approached Lucif-er, who appeared to be perplexed.

0 Seconds   Terra time = 0:00:00 hours
T_{END} = 0:00:00 Hours
The end of the world had already started!
Far away from Terra, its sun, Star 1, had become a <u>supernova</u>!

Lucif-er had a cold chill running by his bone medullas; it felt like falling into a black hole. This horrid sensation had the same feeling as if his flesh had been stripped away from his soul. He blamed the invisible visitor, a relative to Death itself, who had just passed by his side!

Lucif-er nervously swallowed. He stretched his hands in front of him and looked at them; they were there! They had flesh and feelings.

Magog-el, grabbing his head like he had a severe headache, asked his visibly disturbed boss.

"What is going on?"

Lucif-er placed a finger between his teeth and bit hard; the pain did not bother him, but he hurriedly ordered his companion.

"Razari-el should be reaching the lab entrance! Call him now!"

Magog-el stopped before activating his belt communication device as both Overlords gazed to the main terrace's entrance, where a military-dressed Seraph had entered the upper building section and was running toward them at the maximum speed that his strained body could allow him; both Overlords knew that he was Zoltar.

Worst of all, at the exact moment the structure started to shake by the effect of a mild earthquake, they understood: He was bringing terrible news!

The two Overlords at Kral scrutinized the screen displays and saw the comet falling apart. Almost immediately, they felt immense depression. They both looked at each other for answers. They were confused, even scared! **They... Overlords?**

On the screen, they saw Zoltar running toward Lucif-er.

At the actual place where the video cameras continued recording the event, Zoltar finally reached his ultimate boss. Out of energy, he fell at Lucif-er's feet. The commander was shaking and out of breath; his strained heart remained pounding very hard. He opened his mouth, but he could not talk. Lucif-er picked him up by lifting his body with both hands over his head; when his sinister blue vision matched Zoltar's, he drilled the commander's eyes, scanning his brain and mind for information!

A scream of pain came from the Seraph's opened mouth as Lucif-er saw it all... **the graph! The iron connection!**

The Overlord started to shake with fury, frustration, and hate! He squeezed harder and harder; Zoltar's eyes almost popped out of their sockets. The commander let one last muffled moan, a terrified scream for help... None came... **His head had just blown apart.**

Blood and brains splattered all over Lucif-er's face and his brilliant white garments; red streaks splashed over his front attire like a painted canvas depicting a gory death. On their way toward the floor, bloody pieces began sliding along his clothes, a nightmarish view for all the citizens of Terra to see on their screens!

The death of Zoltar was gruesome, and they became shocked by the view; however, they also felt a great horror invading their souls.

Why? What was happening?

Lucif-er dropped the lifeless body to the podium's surface; he made no intent to clean himself. His distorted face was almost unrecognizable; the most handsome face on the planet had become the most distorted and ugly mask; even his wings were in incredible disarray.

Magog-el was in shock, along with Liliel and the other three Overlords present. Even the ferocious Azami-el began shaking in fear! All had read the violent extraction of Zoltar's brain information. They all knew that only a few minutes were left before the searing light would arrive.

Magog-el shook his head and cleaned himself. Next, he removed the bloodstains from Lucif-er's clothes and face. Lucif-er did not care; he felt an utter rage.

"This is not possible!" He screamed telepathically.

He raised his body temperature so much that even his clothes started to smoke. Magog-el grabbed him by one arm and mentally yelled directly at his face.

"The spaceship... The spaceship!
It is our only hope, but we must depart NOW!"

Lucif-er, in a last moment of anger, pulled his hair hard backward. His eyes were not blue anymore, just a fiery red; even Magog-el backed up at their sight. Finally, the master of the evil angels exploded in a ripping mental bark.

"You are right; there is no time to waste! Let's get out of here!"

"Razari-el?" Gorgon-el questioned.

"It will take him twenty seconds to get back here! We cannot wait!"

All the Overlords, with Liliel hanging to Lucif-er to keep pace, ran out of the camera's range at a blinding speed.

Back at Kral, the two Overlords looked stunned. They saw it all but could not hear the mental conversations; Kroma-el, highly disturbed by the events, exclaimed, *"Lucif-er just killed Zoltar! What kind of bad news could he possibly have delivered?"*

Ezek-el, introspectively searching his brain, fell in such disarray that the answers did not materialize as they usually did; it became almost a painful experience to think, anyway, he mumbled to his companion.

"He was working on Lucif-er's program... The sun's nucleus! ... Where are they going in such a big hurry?"

Kroma-el, with his hands twisted like claws, scratched his face with utter anger.

"I know, to the spaceship!

This stupid planet is doomed. We must find a way out!"

Returning to a recent previous time, an Overlord, a medium-built Cherub, energetically approached the lab entrance, moving at several times the average speed. He would have gotten here much sooner, but for some unknown reason, the gravity wave had disabled all the elevators, except one. No need to say; the elevator was on its way up when he wanted to go down! As he approached the lab's main door, his normally straight-looking hair was even straighter as the wind pushed it back; then... he almost lost his step.

He stopped. An incredible weakening wave had rattled his strong body! Mentally confused, he entered the lab; inside, he quickly planted his feet in front of the big computer screen and the three foremost scientists. He immediately knew that Cyrek was dead.

P1, still hiding his face with both hands and his forehead touching the counter where the computer's controls were located, shook out of control.

N1 turned around to see who had entered the room; by the time his head completed the 180° turn, the Overlord was already behind him; in addition, he completed a full scan of the data being displayed above.

Razari-el's face got pale!

The impossible was facing him. At the final **Fe** calculation, he closed his eyes in horror. It did not matter; it burned into his brain and became bigger with each instant. The two letters carved their place into his mind like a burning fire. Squeezing his teeth with anger, he swung his fist with ultimate hostility.

A hole in the counter was blasted into oblivion, causing tiny pieces to scatter around the place.

Razari-el, with a ferocious appearance, turned to N1. He grabbed his chin so his fierce green eyes could investigate N1's mind through the windows of his eyes. At a blazing speed, he asked.

"Did you notify Lucif-er? How long ago?"

As the scientist's brain processed the questions to answer, the Overlord already knew the response: "Zoltar did... Two minutes ago!"

The room shook and squealed like being in pain; an earthquake began rattling the place.

With a fast glance, the Overlord checked the current time.

0:00:11 hours.

"The first blast is coming at the speed of light; it will arrive in exactly 4 minutes 61 seconds!"

At tremendous speed, he additionally thought.

**"Yes! The spacecraft! There is a chance for survival!
The only asinine elevator working is at the top; it will take me twenty seconds to get back to the terrace; however, I am sure... they will wait for me!"**

As he zipped out the door, almost in a speedy blur, N1 finally exclaimed the mental message Razari-el had already accessed from his brain.

"Zoltar did... Two minutes ago!"

Lucif-er's flagship was using all its afterburners! Azami-el manipulated the engines to optimize them to their maximum without blowing out. Using a communication device, Magog-el sent an urgent computer message to the spacecraft's crew.

The Supreme Command orders an emergency takeoff; we arrive in two minutes!

I want the spaceship detached and ready for immediate departure! Move quickly!

The outside of the aircraft became hot and reddish, flying at a speed above too many Mach numbers, causing the air friction to be very high! Magog-el's massive body turned and faced his boss; he stated.

"Done! We will be arriving at the base in 2.17 minutes!"

Wiping off the sweat on his forehead, he also exclaimed.

"Lucif-er, do you know what that stupid comet reminded me of? ... The signs we saw 42 years ago in Trillium!"

Lucif-er's red eyes staring at a wall of his craft tuned in; the comment had made a connection. With glowing hate emanating from all his body, Lucif-er telepathically asserted.

"The signs were spaced 14 days apart! ... It was 14 years later for the Exodus! ... Another 14 years for the destruction of the SA!

And tonight, precisely at midnight... Another 14 years have passed!"

In disbelief, he screamed, ***"It could not be that simple! Every day for the symbols was equal to one year! ... It is so stupidly obvious that nobody saw it!"***

Azami-el, the one driving the craft, announced.

"A message for Lucif-er, from Kroma-el and Ezek-el!"

The Lord of Darkness did not care about anybody other than his own skin; without any additional disturbance to his distorted face, after glancing to watch Liliel shiver, he angrily ordered.

"Do not bother to answer... Terminate the communication!"

Kroma-el and Ezek-el became speechless. His great leader had shut the door on their faces, but only one thought, echoing in all the folds of their brain's gray matter, persisted.

"We are doomed! ... **We are doomed! ... WE ARE DOOMED!**"

Like two wild beasts let loose in the middle of a crowd, the two Overlords ran across the room. They trampled and injured many since they did not bother to run around anybody; behind their paths, they left only destruction.

It did not take long before they dashed along an empty avenue; still out of their minds, in a senseless, energetic drive, they began diving into the darkness, trying to escape the incoming light. They ran for their lives in a futile attempt to save them; unfortunately, those lives were already taken!

At midnight sharp, a blade much sharper than a bistoury will deliver an incredible event in a few minutes, during which not even the atoms will be safe. This event will not be bloody because afterward, no blood will be found, not even a tiny single drop.

With terror squeezing their bodies and minds, a tall, slender, and short-haired Cherub did not look much different from a stocky, round-faced Throne with lots of hair. Their actions, fears, and inability to recognize that they were not gods after all looked identical.

Run Overlords! … But to where?

There is NO place to go… There is NO place to hide.

Since he could not keep up with the super-fast speed of the Overlords, Arkyn became desperate as he was left behind. Lucif-er's flagship was already roaring away toward the location of the interstellar spacecraft. Arkyn's spacecraft was assigned to him, and they did not even bother to wait for him!

The other commanders also ran to the parking area, but lacking Arkyn's conditioning, they could not follow his strong stride; they were equally far behind him.

"Wait for us!" Someone yelled at him.

Among the sharp breathing bouts, he had time to sneak a sinister smile, and in a low tone, he self-commented, *"The Overlords didn't wait for me… Fat chance that I will wait for you!"*

He stressed his physical abilities well beyond his limits, a new trait he had just learned from the Overlords. When he finally touched the shiny surface of his own cylinder, it felt so cool and reassuring; his craft could deliver him to the spaceship… on time! Then, he would take the position that belonged to him: the captain, the Commander, the Overlord!

He got into the craft, skillfully setting the controls for maximum lift at takeoff, and pushed the button. The vehicle made all kinds of mechanical noises and stresses caused by the sudden liftoff. Still, among the hums and squeaks, a sudden compression and almost instant decompression followed the first event, like a gust of wind shooting across a room when allowing a window to open in the middle of a stormy night.

By the time he asked, "What was that?" the control panel had flashed a red warning.

Danger: > Side door open.

However, he had not even finished reading the message when a new one appeared in green.

No action required: ->Door closed.

As the G's deformed his face in the steep climb, he sensed someone behind him. Fighting the enormous stress flattening his back, he glanced sideways. A pair of fiery green eyes, full of hate, met his.

"Razari-el... Sir!" exclaimed Arkyn.

By now, the Gs had decreased as the craft leveled and blasted its way to the destination. Razari-el, with a flip of his hand, wiped the wet sweat off his forehead. As he took the copilot seat and adjusted the preset controls, he said with a mean overtone.

"I am glad you got this piece of garbage off the ground, but we have to travel faster!"

As more G's were activated, a severe whiplash against the cushioned back seat caused Arkyn's head to ache. The engines roared as never before; the structure's integrity began complaining loudly when a new red message appeared on the central craft's monitoring screen.

Danger: ->Engine overheating.
110%... 111%... 112%...

The message kept Razari-el unperturbed, but Arkyn could not avoid reflecting on a fact.

"If it reaches 200%, the stupid engine will blow out!"

[20x]> The Overlords entered the spacecraft's opened doors.

They moved at maximum speed. To the personnel inside the vehicle, they became shadows moving at incredible velocities. Liliel, unable to keep pace, continued to be dragged by Lucif-er.

As soon as the Overlords entered the spaceship, amid a visual and audible warning alarm, the massive main entrance doors started to close. Still running, they quickly accessed the main control cabin or the bridge, the brain of this massive craft.

Two heavily armed security guards, plus four technical operators adjusting secondary controls, stayed at this location; none were at the central controls or the guidance systems. It was probably some kind of protocol, which in case of an emergency, would help by staying out of the way of the speedy Overlords. The six non-Archangels in the room looked like frozen statues; their movements stayed so slow compared to the Overlords' accelerated pace that there appeared to be none.

As soon as the door finished closing behind the incoming group, Lucif-er dropped Liliel on the floor. She, almost out of breath due to the hectic movements to get to the spacecraft, sat on the floor's shiny surface, trying to catch up. Since she was not an Overlord yet, she lacked blinding speed, tremendous power, and ultimate control. She was close, but she had not reached the final threshold.

Lucif-er, addressing Gorgon-el, pointed at Liliel and commanded.

"Your primary mission in this takeoff is to ensure she survives! If she does not, you will be the next female!"

Gorgon-el's sweaty face wrinkled with complaints.

"Lucif-er, that is not fair! I will have a hard time just holding my own!"

"You will be holding something else if you fail!"

Lucif-er, with his bloodshot eyesight, moved to the central controls. Magog-el moved to his right, Azami-el not far to his left; Gorgon-el, lifting Liliel with one arm, moved to a better strategic location; there, he sat the beautiful but scared female Throne in a nicely padded chair. From that place, he started monitoring the nuclear reactor's control panel.

A strong quake rattled the land, pushing the spaceship into a rocking oscillation.

The approaching apocalyptic disaster made seeing each present second painful as it became part of the past. One second is not much in everyday life; it is mostly an ignored fleeting moment. However, when our lives are only seconds before extinction, a second has a new awesome and scary perspective.

Lucif-er, his mouth twisted with anger, sent a message to his subordinates and assistants.

"Superconducting primary impulse power: 100 %! ... Adjust for maximum stresses!"

At the command, Magog-el showed his teeth with concern; he commented.

"Only the Overlords can survive that crushing start; the rest of the crew will die!"

"So what? We do not need them!"

"I am glad you don't care! We have no time to waste!"

Multiple displays adorned the control screens. One of them, under Lucif-er skilled hands, displayed the incoming supernova's blast. A growing disc followed by another concentric inner circle: the initial searing blast and the following shock wave!

The first expanding blast appeared to be close, almost overtaking the planet. The horrible front, moving at the speed of light, was about to blast a planet named Terra! <[20x]

For nuclear explosions, we have grown accustomed to asking.

"How many megatons?"

In the case of a supernova, it is much better not to ask! After all, what is a 'megaton' on a cosmic scale? ... An insignificant measure of energy output!

If the supernova could be compared to the Pacific Ocean, a 'megaton' would likely be... one drop of water!

[20x]> The display, showing a decreasing time, manifested.
   -0:01:98
   With almost two minutes remaining, Terra's Supreme Leader's piercing eyes focused on Azami-el as the latter accepted a mental image from Lucif-er; shortly after, the leader announced.
   "To maximize planetary eclipsing from the sun, the optimal trajectory is already locked! All controls are: OK!"
   Gorgon-el advanced a statement.
   "An aircraft has just arrived from the city. Out of the vehicle, two individuals are approaching the spacecraft!"
   Only an instant later, he added, *"They are Razari-el and Arkyn!"*
   Lucif-er's claw-like hand just pointed to the ignition button with his merciless command!
   "Take off." <[20x]

Razari-el smiled with joy as he quickly approached the spacecraft. Falling behind, Arkyn ran to his fullest, and exhilarating excitement brightened his face. They made it; the spaceship was waiting for them!

Both waived their hands way above their heads, trying to call someone's attention; meanwhile, their avid eyes focused on the closed main access door. In any instant, the heavy opening would move up and allow them the opportunity to jump aboard. They had to be fast; the door had to be quickly closed to prevent any squandering of time, which became an incredibly expensive commodity at that moment!

The standby humming of the massive superconducting impulse engine added vibration to the strong quake rattling the ground; some dust and small rocks became blown away from the spaceship as it mildly rolled back and forth following the push of the strong seismic waves.

Arkyn just reached the same position where Razari-el stood; both angels held their breath in anticipation of the spacecraft's boarding. One second stretched its way by...

Like an explosion, a magnetic blast ripped the area around the enormous saucer.

A red glowing ring emerged from the edges of the flying machine, a fearsome donut of plasma generated by a massive magnetic pulse. A blast of dust and rocks raced away from the spaceship!

Razari-el quickly backed up while protecting his face and body with a triangular wedge that he made with the tips of his extended arms. A green glow appeared at the interface between him and the blasted material being projected all around the vessel.

Arkyn, not as powerful, was utterly blown away. While he tumbled between the ground and the sky, bouncing without control, he covered his face with both hands.

A loud hum and squeal nearly tore the eardrums of the two angels. The massive vessel lifted from the ground and accelerated with incredible velocity.

Razari-el, during the dust storm, closed one of his hands, making a fist threatening the speeding away vehicle. He yelled with all his might.

"You bastards! You cannot abandon me!"

The spaceship blasted in a vertical takeoff so fast that it sucked up part of the dust. This dust climbed like a mushroom cloud, with its center open and free of dust. From where Razari-el stood, it was similar to a rolling ring of dust moving upwards, a donut-shaped event; in its open center, the saucer-like vessel became another shiny star; however, this one glowing red.

As the noise subsided, a strong thunder rumbled overhead. The sound barrier became broken at some distance above, luckily for the ones below, the sonic energy of the massive blast was also moving away from them.

A fine rain, a mix of dust and small rocks fell over the Overlord; Razari-el, violently shaking, dropped to his knees amid a pure satanic rage!

The thought of dying overwhelmed the Overlord, while the light dust covering his face, wetted by a copious sweat, gave a thin brown layer of mud. All the enormous fear rippling through his whole body became converted into one vicious and relentless outburst of **hate**!

It became hard to recognize him; his straight but neat hair resembled a mesh of twisted bundles resembling live snakes. As his handsome face conveyed another reflection from his dark and malevolent soul, the monster inside broke loose!

From far behind, somebody came running. He stood before him, staring at the now empty sky above; only a faint dust ring was still climbing. He also glanced at the remains of the comet, now just dust in disarray; in utter frustration, Arkyn screamed to the dark sky.

"Come back! ... I am the captain! ... It is my ship!"

Full of despair, he turned around to the Overlord, looking for some empathy.

Razari-el, standing up, used his fiery eyes to scan the commander's ripped clothes and many superficial wounds on his face, hands, body, and the dust encrusted in Arkyn's skin and clothes. Some blood dripping from the commander's face made small trails of a red/brown murky mixture; amazing enough, Arkyn had survived the blast with only minor injuries!

At the same time, the Overlord yelled, *"Shut up!"* With tremendous speed and power, he hit the commander's rib cage!

A sharp cracking noise echoed by the place as the commander flew across the air to finally roll against one of the support structures used for the spacecraft's testing. He was seriously hurt; the impact was meant to be fatal! Only his superior training allowed him to survive such a massive blow.

Arkyn ached all over, especially on his right side, where several ribs felt broken. Blood began running out of his nose and mouth, but since his face remained lying on the floor, the blood dripping did not go too far before wetting a layer of dust on the ground.

Like a sandcastle when a big wave comes to its base, all his dreams crumbled into nothing!

The outside pain became huge, but it was hardly felt because the pain inside was much worse. As his soul tortured his mind, this added more pain to his battered body... Abruptly, his life had become worthless!

Razari-el went into a furious rampage. He ripped a section of the building, kicked chunks of hard construction plastics, and threw heavy pieces high into the dark night. He made his external rage equal to his internal rage.

The ground shook harder, and pieces of the nearby buildings came thundering to the ground. The planet knew it was agonizing, not to be outdone, went into its own rage!

[20x]> Inside the spacecraft now in space.

Everything ran at maximum Overlord speed. The takeoff felt like an exploding bomb in slow motion. Only the robust design of the vessel, for such a horrendous initial vertical lift, prevented it from collapsing. Nevertheless, the craft complained loudly; squeaks, rumbling noises, and metallic moans of large plates under massive stresses, the whole place became a nerve-racking source of sonic horrors.

The first angels to succumb were the six ones at the bridge. The initial trust just flattened them on the floor, but as the G's increased, their bones and skulls fragmented and soon collapsed, causing their oblivion. Blood gushing out of their wounds became flattened into growing pools that did not expand concentrically but in a tentacular way.

Lucif-er's tight jaw was the only sign of stress. Gorgon-el and Azami-el cussed as they fell to the ground; on their knees, with their hands in front of them, they stopped their fall.

Magog-el did better because his massive body took most of the strain; only when his legs wobbled, he grasped a solid nearby counter for stabilization.

Liliel was hit harder; the unbearable pressure distorted her face, molding her pretty facial skin to look like an 80-year-old woman, as wrinkles and bulges appeared everywhere. Even laid on top of a cushion, she became squashed too much.

Blood appeared from her nostrils and ran in two fine strings to her ears. More blood in smaller quantities began popping out of her ears; her eyes, flattened by the pressure, looked bloodshot!

Gorgon-el angrily noticed the serious stress affecting the queen of darkness. While making an extraordinary effort to support himself with a single hand, he painfully elevated the other to fully cover the female head. A bluish glow from his hand tried to shield her from the grinding event; amid this effort, he shouted at her.

"Don't die on me… you bitch!" <[20x]

Even the downtown area seemed to fade away as the two Overlords continued their frantic escape to nowhere. They were not alone; groups of NA citizens screaming off their heads also ran in all directions, although the Overlords moved so fast that no one else had a chance of interacting or stopping them.

The ground shook harder. A big earthquake began seriously damaging the city of Kral, causing the buildings to fall and partially blocking the streets. Screams of terror combined with screams of death filled the air, already occupied by the blasting noises of massive building chunks hitting the ground. The earth's ominous rumbling became stronger!

It must have taken the panic-stricken Overlords an eternity to consume the last two minutes of their lives, but they did. Suddenly, both Overlords stopped on the spot.

The ground felt like it was sinking, while gravity felt like it was doubling. An intense white light, making an arc from the North, appeared as a sudden blinding flash!

In the next instant, the night sky lit up like a torch.

Again, from the North, a wall of fire as high as the whole atmosphere came at a blazing speed, devouring everything in its path. It was a horrible monster, insatiable and merciless!

For an instant, Kroma-el and Ezek-el became petrified; both extended their hands to protect themselves from the flames. Unfortunately, this did not work; their hands burned to crispy charcoal microseconds before the rest of their bodies were consumed and blown away!

While coughing blood and breathing with difficulty. Arkin knew one of his lungs became punctured and bled internally. He knew the end was near; his eyes wetted to a glassy haze as he felt like crying. With only one eye above the ground, he glanced at the undulating and moaning ground… nobody else could be seen around!

He was alone; he, who almost became a god! Where were the slaves, the servants, and the gorgeous females? What would remain of him… **nothing? … Not even a hint that he had ever existed?**

A fierce loneliness stabbed his mind!

As death approaches, the self-exclusion of love from God brings this immense vacuum. It is the failure of a soul to accomplish what it was created for, its ultimate fulfillment: to see God and to share His Glory!

Only the denial of this innate force can bring such immense self-annihilation. It is impossible to feel such a depressing state of mind when living. Regardless of the misery that anyone can be immersed in, if we are alive, there is <u>Hope</u>!

As death defines our choice of Good or Evil, as we fail the trial, there is no more Hope. At that instant, a temporary loneliness in our souls becomes an eternally barren wasteland of despair. In Hell, there are enormous quantities of evil doers' souls; it does not matter; the condemned will feel utterly... <u>alone</u>!

He coughed again. The pain turned so unbearable that he almost crossed the threshold to fainting... No! He could not faint; that would be the end!

He would rather stay around to enjoy the last seconds of his life... the ultimate nightmare!

A blinding glow permeated the darkened nightly atmosphere; just a second later, he felt the ground below move like a pile of collapsing gelatin. This lasted for an instant because a sharp rebound lifted the earth's surface toward the sky!

The noise became intolerable, and the ground cracking nearby spewed fire, steam, and smoke. Nearby mountains instantly became fiery volcanoes, spewing lava and ash in immense quantities. A furious lightning mesh crisscrossed the upper atmosphere while massive electric bolts struck the ground!... a Dantean maelstrom of destruction!

A red glow approached, continuously intensifying. It appeared to come from all directions but most intensely from the North. With the dust covering his whole body, Arkyn's left eye remained the only shiny object still reflecting the awesome events unleashed on the planet.

It was hot around him but not inside his soul. Inside there, a polar chill blown by his lonely end began devastating the remains of his ego. One could say, "There was nothing left inside his mind or soul!" But that would have been incorrect...There was something very big, still untouched. It was a dark, sinister monster whose powerful claws held his spirit in bondage. Its name: hate.

It would be part of him for eternity. Hate and loneliness are a frightening pair for anyone to be bound, slaved, and tortured... <u>forever</u>!

Arkyn's moist and blue eye... blinked.

Subsequently, it remained fixed on the spectacle. For an instant, Arkyn's surroundings appeared so familiar. Could it be possible that he was <u>already there</u>? ... (At this time, the commander did not know the name of the place; we could help him: **Hell!**)

A sinister grin slowly moved his lips; then they froze in one position. The inside shine in his eye vanished, and even when light remained reflected from his opened eye, nothing alive lingered inside.

[20x]> *"I am losing her!"* Gorgon-el mentally screamed to Lucif-er.

The leader of Evil barely glanced at the graph of a climbing line reaching its apex before answering.

"We passed the maximum acceleration peak; the Gs are going down!"

After staring at the instrumentation, Lucif-er, whose forehead became wet with perspiration, addressed the subordinate Overlords: "I am very concerned about the calculations; they are *too close for comfort!"*

Pointing to a complex graph showing two events with approaching converging points, he indicated with unmasked anger.

"The first convergence! It is our immediate problem!

We have to deploy and fire the thermonuclear reactor... **before** *the planet disintegrates, and we lose its shielding effect! Later, the reactor itself should protect us from the cosmic rays and the neutrino blast emitted by the supernova! In addition, the spacecraft's exceptionally reflective outside surface should minimize the heat and radiation going through the hull!"*

For what appeared as normal speed, he must have flipped his finger faster than the speed of sound because a lower frequency cracking sound (due to the faster speed of this frame) echoed throughout the bridge. The pointed location turned out to be the second convergence point.

He followed quickly.

"We must accelerate fast enough to prevent the second blast, the shock wave, from overtaking us. Fortunately, we know the fixed speed at which it will travel; the computer accurately tracks its arrival and displays it in graphical form!

Gorgon-el, forget about Liliel; use all your abilities to maximize the reactor's power output! No time to waste! Start the reactor deployment, NOW!"

Azami-el, grinding his teeth due to the enormous pressure of the moment, stated.

"Reactor deployment: **Activated!***"*

This time, even when deployed at maximum speed, the mechanism appeared to be running so slowly for the Overlords that it looked like it took forever. The noises sounded like a record played at slow speed, with low and elongated sounds.

Since the spacecraft was moving away from the planet with its bottom surface aligned with the center of Terra but not aligned with the sun's location, the flying saucer started to add some lateral translation to match a new path. In this manner, when the fusion reactor's deployment is completed, its exhaust should be pointing to the center of Terra <u>and</u> the location of the exploding sun!

The bridge, as a rotating unit, moved in a synchronized motion that followed the vessel's rotation. In this manner, the accelerating force always remained axial to the standing operators.

All the Overlords were aware of the spatial change. With the G's down, they could move with ease; they even had an instant to glance at the slowly decreasing diameter of Terra, a black circle with an outside bluish edge. However, the incoming glow vanished, all the stars twinkling. Moon and Moony, now visible, stayed illuminated, but only as crescent moons.

On Terra's dark side, the NA appeared bright, with many cities showing their glitter. Less could be seen from the Central Sectors; in the Southern Sectors, only darkness remained.

"Half of a second for the supernova's first blast on our planet!" Lucif-er warned.

As the computer continued connecting the laminated sections of the extending shaft in a conical manner, the Overlords paused for about 'five-tenths of a second' of their accelerated speed.

Suddenly, the sky got darker. The atmospheric blue ring around the edge of Terra vanished into darkness! ... This was a brisk instant of calm before a storm of cosmic proportions unleashed its devastating fury!

A wave of intense light passed by at 300,000 Km per second.

It saturated everything around them; even the Overlords felt overwhelmed. However, since the planet blocked most of the blast, they survived. In amazement, the four Overlords saw the immense power of the explosion.

A ring of fire burned around the dark side of the planet. It appeared slow under these accelerated conditions; however, they knew that on the planet, it was moving **fast**!

Out of nowhere, red dots and fiery cracks appeared on the planet's surface; Terra was being turned inside out! A bluish glow indicated massive electric storms raging in the atmosphere. The Overlords' eyes stayed visually glued to their vanishing planet, but deep inside, they could not avoid feeling a vast depression squeezing their spines. Magog-el, sensitive to the pain, exclaimed.

"If we had stayed... We all would be dead!"

Moon became a ball of fire. Moony, alike in flames, blew up in a fiery display!

If the same happened to the planet before the shock wave arrived, they all would be dead instantly. The expectation was killing them!

Azami-el broke the suspense.

"The Quadri flex deflection shields: In place!"

A moment later, he announced what the rest already knew.

"The reactor is fully deployed!

Activating H-He^3/He^4 mixture to 80% saturation!"

As they started to watch the graph showing the progress of charging the mixture into the reactor's core, as displayed on one screen, Lucif-er, with a penetrating and dominating mental command, demanded.

"No! I want the mixture at 100% saturation!"

Even Magog-el got pale when he heard the command. He quickly checked, *"Lucif-er! Are you sure?"*

Azami-el's ferocious stand melted. The superconducting engine's jackrabbit start would appear as nothing when compared to the next acceleration crunch!

Gorgon-el moaned and squeezed his head. They all hoped to hear the boss retracting his demand; instead, the dreaded message came swiftly.

"Yes! We have no other choice! Do it, immediately!"

"Reprogramming..." like saying his own death sentence, Azami-el spoke mentally. As the Seraph quickly glanced at the monitors around him, he added.

"Cooling system, in line!

Retaining magnetic fields: activated!

Superconducting coils feeding the heating plasma, ready to start at... ten million °C.

At your command, I am ready to fire!"

Lucif-er twisted his lips in a spiteful manner, reflecting on the burning inside him. The loss of his planetary dominion was not a small deed; he extruded hate from every pore in his skin. He did not wait; his powerful but silent command activated a button labeled.

FIRE <[20x]

[20x]> The dark side of the planet was no longer black.

Only a pale red extracted from the bloodstain of so many dead. Moving away at great speed from the holocaust, the spacecraft started the ignition of its nuclear reactor.

All twelve vents at the end of the shaft projection, where the thermonuclear engine stayed, simultaneously ignited a blast of reddish/blue fire.

The action-reaction effect became so strong that the vessel took off in a similar manner that a baseball is blasted away at the contact with a powerfully swung bat. Except for Lucif-er, all the Overlords fell to the floor; heads, extremities, and butts bounced all over the place, driven by an excruciating crunch!

Unlike the superconducting engines, where the acceleration using smaller numbers could be variable, the maximum fusion reactor's acceleration worked at a constant value, but this was a scary number; the craft was barely designed to be strong enough to take this unbelievable stress since no one ever considered using the maximum range of acceleration, 0 to 100%, in one single leap!

All kinds of noises surfaced, but the most ominous screams came from the internal structure, begging for immediate relief.

Liliel, unable to see anymore, just saw flashes of light generated by her compressed and damaged retinal cells that unevenly contacted with their related and equally compressed optical nerves; above all, severe pain led the extreme suffering.

Her bones became compressed; only her superior training had kept her alive, but now, a new terrifying compactor had turned on! She did not hear the outside noises; her own internal structure collapsing began making enough noise to become an internal pandemonium; the chilling cracking and snapping noises of her bones being crunched became horrifyingly painful!

She tried breathing one more time; however, nothing came in. Her cranial bones were deformed to their utmost; her beautiful face became a flattened mess that nobody could recognize as being hers. At the last moment, her mind begged for help in a faint mental whisper.

"Lucif-er... where are you? ... Are you, letting... me die?... I hate y..."

Snap. A sharp noise interrupted; it was the last sound she heard and the last flash of light she ever saw!

When your skull is squashed open, and your brains are laid as a flat pancake on the floor, you can see, hear, and live... no more. An instant silence in a new place where you could see nothing since not even darkness existed.

All the Overlords knew she was gone, but only Magog-el had a kind thought for her.

"What a waste! I am going to miss the whore!" <[20x]

[20x]> The planet became smaller due to the increasing distance.

It caused more of the supernova's blinding glare to overflow around the edges. The crushing acceleration had not changed; it was still strong enough to pulverize bones; nevertheless, the fallen Overlords had a chance for readjustment and recovery.

First, Magog-el, channeling his powers to overcome the crunch, stretched a hand to Lucif-er, asking for help getting up. The Lord of Darkness just looked at him; he did not even show a condescending attitude. After all, he was the only important entity who had to survive since he was a living god. If he stayed alive, even if the rest died, it would still count as a victory.

If necessary, on his own, he could spawn a whole new generation of super-angels. Then, he would have all the sexual companionship that his strong masculine power required, even if that meant screwing his daughters; nothing wrong with that. After all, they would be much better-looking and tougher than Terra's top females!

Looking at his boss doing nothing for him must have inspired Magog-el; he managed to get up. Leaning against the instrumentation panel, he began turning back to the tough, mean, and vicious second-in-command Overlord. He avidly scanned the graph.

Obviously, the first conversion was successful. The 3-D graph now showed the shock wave reaching Terra, with its front moving toward them at the incredible speed of 40,000 Km/sec. To be able to escape… it would be a close call!

Azami-el pushed his face away from the floor; he had broken teeth and cut lips; he was trying very hard to stop the bleeding. With an internal ferocious outburst, his deep anger prevailed; the blood vessels became sealed! He glanced at his two superiors, but his eyes locked with Lucif-er's.

He knew his leader better than he knew anyone else. If he could not get himself up from the floor, he was no better than a wounded beast in a similar situation when belonging to a pride of lions. Together with other ferocious lions, they will help each other hunt down the prey; however, if you were on the ground, incapable of standing on your own, you could not expect anybody to raise a paw to help you. At that instant, consider yourself dead!

The pain felt excruciating, but after two failed attempts, Azami-el also stood up.

All three stared at Gorgon-el, who breathed with difficulty due to blood running out of his nostrils. A glazed stare from his eyes told the story; the Overlord was hurt. He probably hit the floor too hard; if he could not keep control of his inner powers, he could also be a goner soon!

The foxy smile was gone from his lips; only a twisted grimace squashed by the tremendous outside pressure, viciously trying to squeeze the life out of him, remained.

He became a wounded beast. He knew it, and he was horrified; this could not be the end, but when he tried to move, only spasmodic vibrations rippled through his extremities!

In a cold but excited tone, Lucif-er told Azami-el.

"We do not need him. At least he did finish optimizing the nuclear core!"

Azami-el, hanging for his life on the countertop, asked.

"Are we... going to make it?"

Before Lucif-er had time to answer, all available eyes stared at the display screen monitoring the rearview; since this graph monitor continued showing the shock wave as it overtook the planet, all saw a horrifying spectacle!

The planet had blown up into tiny pieces!

A massive ball of fire had destroyed it. The remaining debris immediately became part of the advancing edge of devastation, which induced enormous fear and anxiety into the minds of the three standing Overlords because the diameter of that immense ball of fire continued increasing at a tremendous velocity!

Inside the craft, two alarms went off.

Warning: $R_C + R_G$ ➤ ⇈⇋10%$\Delta\Sigma$

Radiation levels are increasing to dangerous levels.

$T_o + T_I$ ➤ ◈✚◈<100°/sec>□<1°/sec

Vessel temperature is becoming critical <[20x]

A horrendous ball of fire, now larger than the orbit of Terra, was devouring a planetary system. The supernova explosion was ten times brighter than Type I or Type II supernovae, a billion times brighter than a typical star's absolute brilliance!

Type III leaves no Black Holes, no Neutron Stars, and no White Dwarfs. As the star of this type of explosion is much richer in Hydrogen and Helium than the other two types, it burns everything, even the core. The only thing left is an immense volume of space in utter devastation!

Watching it come at you at a fraction of the speed of light must be the most terrifying sight in the Universe. Everybody agreed; this was not a good place to be!

The three Overlords may not have shown it on the outside, but their insides must have been churning into ground meat. When you are like a god, and your godly existence can be terminated in a blazing instant, even an evil Overlord has no choice but to shiver at the sight of a monster much bigger than him!

Even the most powerful, the Lord of Darkness, stayed profusely perspiring; his tight jaw indicated his profound concentration on avoiding his own extinction.

The Overlords moved at incredible speeds while operating the bridge's controls, but what could an ordinary angel see if they were observing the same bridge activity?

With the Overlords in high overdrive, an angel saw only blurs and streaks, shadows too fast to focus on. Some body parts became visual as legs, heads, or torsos, as they remained stationary by only fractions of a second!

To an observer, Lucif-er fixed the two new problems before the computer message could be read. The computer then announced what appeared to be an instant second message.

Warning terminated:
>**Quadruplex negative shields:**
Exclusive adjustment -> Shield Bridge
>**Temperature control: Global parameter**
Maximum cooling --> To outside shield
Bridge enclosure   --> 75<80>200°C

These computer messages were primarily for the layman, as 3-D complex data streams and graphic displays continued speedily being shown over the main screen. Only the expert could follow the data; the graphic displays remained self-explanatory.

Magog-el must have stared at the rearview panel for a while because his image became visible. He said this in a manner that would have been impossible for the average angel to listen to.

[20x]> *"The temperature of the outside surface is above 2,000 °C!*

I am glad that we are using the best thermally insulating alloy, and that this material extrudes non-heat conductive gases, which creates a shielding heat gradient! Otherwise, by now, we would be toast!"

The outside image showed that the rear half of the spaceship was glowing red. A trail of vapor was left behind; however, the relentless cosmic and gamma rays bombardment interacted with the vapor trail in a unique way. Molecules being vaporized from the outside surface became demolished by the super-intense cosmic ray activity. This did not happen as a uniform effect but as a wave or quantum effect!

Azami-el, very strained and tired, looked for a momentary distraction. Breathing heavily, he checked Gorgon-el's body; with a sinister half smile, he self-commented.

"Foxy is playing his last moments right... That is exactly what I would have done! ... A triangular maximum deflection effort to protect the chest and brains, and yes, a hibernation with an overdrive muscular link, slow your vital signs, but use whatever you have for that next heart pump cycle... You bastard! Soon, you may be gone anyway!"

As the minutes passed, it felt like an eternity at this speed. This became a never-ending torture, with a growing ball of fire getting closer and closer, slowly incinerating the tough alloys that comprised the outside hall of the spaceship.

How long could this go on before collapsing? The drill digging into their brains asked exactly this.

How long before the computer finishes the second convergence point? Why is it taking forever?

Some of the parameters must have been changing, affecting the final answer. Even so, the machine must have listened to their telepathic inquiries because it displayed the following bulletin.

Spaceship speed: 10,000 Km/sec

The so-long-awaited convergence point was finally displayed on the graph: The spaceship's climbing acceleration projection racing against time versus the steady speed of the shock wave.

A note next to the point of convergence explained:

Second Convergence: Spaceship----> @ 20.58 minutes
Shock Wave -> @ 20.78 minutes.

Three Overlords saw the most glorious display of their lives. It ignited an instant outburst of joy. A great jubilation for a great victory, a big celebration for life itself!

Even Lucif-er demonstrated outward emotion as he stepped closer to Magog-el and banged their closed right-hand fists. Quickly, Lucif-er advanced in front of Azami-el, with most of the fire gone from his eyes; he locked his penetrating stare with the sight of his most understanding subordinate; he even placed a hand on his shoulder!

In a mind lock, all three exclaimed in unison.

"Yes... we did it! We survived!"

Lucif-er felt so jubilant that he took time to inspect Gorgon-el's condition; smiling widely, he exclaimed with a sarcastic overtone.

"You lucky bastard! With my help, you still have a chance to reach the convergence point!"

The six winds of the subordinate Overlord remained barely visible, indicating that Gorgon-el had little left. His breathing

remained widely spaced and weak. While lying flat on his back
with his arms locked over his chest, he had his hands over his face
like he was in a praying position. Lucif-er stood at his side; he
mildly kicked him on the head.

Energy transfer became visible at the point of contact as a faint
blue flash. Almost immediately, Gorgon-el took a deeper gasp for
air. He still did not move, but Lucif-ed received a faint mental
message.

"Tha... thanks..."

The now ex-leader of the NA did not answer. He just glanced
at the collapsed and the flattened corpse of his girlfriend, a
pancaked pile of crushed bones with grounded muscles still
extruding blood! He made a disgusted grimace with his lips; the
only image of what Liliel used to look like was now solely
imprinted in his brain.

He went back to Azami-el and the controls in front of him.
Academically, he ordered, *"At precisely the time the spaceship
reaches the convergence point, reduce the acceleration constant
by changing the H-He^3/He^4 mixture to <u>80% saturation</u>!*

*This will allow us to perform our duties in a more acceptable
environment; meanwhile, we will be gaining distance with respect
to the shock wave. Gorgon-el will appreciate it since he can
survive at such reduced Gs-acceleration crunching!"*

Making sure Azami-el remained aware of a string of complex
data, he continued, *"The second parameter indicates that this
supernova is ten times more powerful than any other type...
Consequently, it will not last long; only seven days!"*

Lucif-er rubbed his hair and, with renewed hate and anger,
quickly retorted.

*"A day, a night! ... Now, just meaningless measures of time!
From now on, 10 hours are meant to be One Tac. A primary time
unit of angelic cyclic physiology!"*

His piercing eyes stared into the black circle that demarcated
the transparent cornea at the center of Azami-el's eyes, where his
blue iris adorned and controlled the amount of light getting in. In
this case, by instinct, the opening got smaller. His boss continued.

*"In 70 hours, the coherent leading shell of the shock wave will
start to dissipate.*

*Chaotic forces will take the upper hand; by then, the shell will
break apart, with some masses beginning to lump together.*

*At this moment, there will be almost no more cosmic rays, and
the gamma radiation will be drastically reduced. When this
happens, reduce the mixture to 50% ... Together, we will work on*

a destination course based on the stellar data already loaded into the computer.

Also, it is imperative to restart or repair the bio-systems as soon as possible!"

The leader of the small crew pointed a finger at Azami-el's nose and indicated.

"I know... by that time, we will have serious DNA damage! Still, I assure all of you that we should be able to cope with the radiation damage and reverse the effects!"

Almost superimposed, first Azami-el, next Magog-el; both exclaimed.

"I am relieved; I was afraid my flesh would start falling apart!"

"This was a big concern of mine! ... I am glad that you believe it can be done!" <[20x]

Like a speeding bullet fired repeatedly, the saucer-shaped craft, propelled by its massive rear-extended nuclear reactor, moved faster with each passing instant. The convergence graph still showed the shock wave closing in, moving at a higher speed than the vessel; however, it became evident that the spaceship would reach the cross point first. Afterward, the spacecraft would move faster than the shock wave and be permanently free from its massive claws!

Since the intense acceleration remained constant, the horrible squeaks and noises had mainly disappeared. The two main engines generated two mild hums: superconducting and fusion. Their frequencies were different, the first engine having a much higher tone.

Looking at the rearview screen, we could see a horrible large ball of incandescent white fire gradually growing; its thermonuclear fangs continued to open with only one sinister intention: total destruction. The most appalling fact of this extraordinary event was not its deafening growl or intimidating roar... it was **its absolute silence!**

... A new, hardly noticeable shake... had just started.

[20x] A new vibration... Lucif-er listened for an instant... **he froze!**

His eyes opened widely, his face became white, and his breath did stop. Like unleashing a raging dragon, his eyes turned to fire, and his breath became deep and furious; the next breath turned more profound and more violent; the third one, a horrid snort that caused the adjacent instrumentation to vibrate!

His hair, this incredible blond aggregate that enhanced his fantastically handsome face, became like tongues of fire twisting as tormented snakes!

When the noise started, his three subordinates had a question mark written on their faces, and their expressions suddenly changed to fear when they saw the dragon. Then, on their own, they noticed that the increasing new noise came from the harmonic frequency of the superconducting engine hum... Now, they knew why Lucif-er became so infuriated!

Their fear increased to a place of ultimate horror!

The vibration, gradually climbing, now mildly rattled the spaceship.

A vibrant and noisy attention-calling alarm went off!

The computer's display showed an ominous red blinking message!

Warning!
The molecular structure of superconducting coils is damaged by cosmic radiation.
▶▶IMMINENT ENGINE FAILURE◀◀

Azami-el squeezed his teeth so hard that the just-sealed wound cracked open and spilled new blood down from his lower lip! Pulling his hair like a crazy individual, he screamed at the electronic display.

"Stop it! ... Fix it!"

A sharp cracking noise, like a shrieking scream, rattled the bridge. The superconducting engine had gone from its 'superconducting state' to its 'normal state'! In other words, it did not work anymore!

Next, the falling domino effect. The power supply generating millions of volts ran out of juice. As the magnetic field collapsed inside the thermonuclear reactor engine, the nuclear reaction stopped...

All twelve exhaust vents instantly became dormant!

As the nuclear engine shut down inside the spacecraft, inertial negative stresses were instantly generated... it hit like a **'bang'**! [25x] Lucif-er alone moved to a higher performance level.

The Overlords' maximum performance peaked at 20 times the average speed. He could reach a pinnacle where his twelve wings, the only Archangel with so many, allowed him to do better than the maximum performance of any other Archangel!

In other words, what could we do in a millisecond? Nothing!

It takes 1/10 of a second for our brain to process a single visual image; it is our limitation. The average Archangel could do ten times better than that. Lucif-er alone, twice as much! Of course, there were limitations when related to movement because there exists a finite speed for joints and muscles to execute movement without falling apart; therefore, fingers and hands could move faster, but moving their whole bodies would be restricted to much lower speeds, surely not 20x, perhaps 10 times maximum.

Both Magog-el and Azami-el appeared at this fast speed, like moving in slow motion. Lucif-er just flinched as the negative G's hit the bridge, and the other two slowly floated off the floor. By grabbing the counter's edge, both managed to hang upside down, thus avoiding being tossed against the walls.

Gorgon-el had no such luck. He moved slowly at this speed but violently fast in normal conditions; along with him, all the dead angels that became squashed on the floor moved sideways. Also, some instrumentation pieces violently ripped off their sites amid smoke and sparking electrical disrupted connections, equally moved toward the rigid bridge's walls!

At this moment, the power feeding the illumination blinked off, but the emergency backup came on almost instantly.

All the bodies and debris, even when seen in slow motion, crushed violently against the side edges. The debris became ground to smaller pieces; the dead did not care; only the one living saw his last moment arriving... A fast-moving wall with insufficient energy left to block the crushing collision!

As seen by Lucif-er in slowed motion, Gorgon-el only had time and effort to raise one hand to protect himself from the massive impact, which was unfortunately generated by his own weight!

In the middle of a horrified scream, Gorgon-el's hand bones crushed into many pieces as they hit the hard surface. Next, his arm, piece by piece, shattered violently on contact. Last, against all the power he had left, his head hit the hard material! ... As he became squashed into a mesh of bones and brains, his last mental scream was heard.

A scream of pure terror... **"Aaah! ... ah..."**

All that moved and crashed on the walls bounced back in all directions. What was left on its surface, scratches, smoke damage, and horrid bloodstains resulted from paintbrushes making a bizarre mural. Instantly painted, it became a grotesque reminder of the sordid event.

The future did not appear to be so kind. As the two Overlords hanging sideways came down to their steady feet, they remained free from the enormous inertial pressure. They were eager for action; however, what could the three Archangels do?

They remained inside a vessel going nowhere, destined for destruction; they might as well be imprisoned inside a death cell, where the executioner had already pushed the life-extinguishing button!

Inside the bridge, smoke propagated in undulating sheets, and electrical shorts generated strange balls of fire moving in slow trajectories. These left behind interesting trails of smoke with unusual patterns before they also turned into smooth, expanding waves.

What a contrast, from a massive crunching acceleration to a sudden no gravity at all. As all the loose objects started to float or bounce around, the computer announced.

0 Gravity: Magnetic floors activated.

The boots worn by the spaceship's crew were magnetic. They 'clunk' as their shoes' soles made contact and held to the floor's surface. Even though the crew was no longer alive, their shoes stuck the flattened remains of their feet vertically to the ground; 90% of the debris hit the floor and stayed there.

A hazy bridge remained; some instruments went out of commission, some stayed sparkling, and others only smoked. The computer displayed another message, this one with an ominous death sentence. Alarms sounded, and red blinking signs appeared; meanwhile, all hope disappeared!

Warning:
   Spaceship speed = 30,000 Km/sec
   Shockwave speed = 40,000 Km/sec
   >>>TOTAL DESTRUCTION<<<
         @ 5:00 Minutes
4:99
4:98
4:97

The protruding eyes of three Overlords stared at the computer display; it showed a horrifying nightmare, but they knew they were awake. While his subordinates, terror-stricken, slowly turned to Lucif-er for a hopeful suggestion, he screamed with utter anger.

"You idiots! There is __nothing__ that I can do!"

His own words echoed with a sadistic overtone through the dark corners of his evil mind. Was he admitting defeat, the living god named Lucif-er?

His powerful mind could not take it since the hate inside him became too much to keep inside; he focused on the being that he knew was responsible; he vocalized with extreme loudness.

"You... You, out there!
I know you exist! ... Talk to me, you coward!"

As his blasting words rattled a sonic boom inside the bridge, his fiery eyes focused on the incoming supernova's shock wave; he continued with renewed hate.

"You said: We have the freedom to serve you, or __not__ to serve! You liar! Why can't you accept my choice? Why didn't you leave me alone?"

Lucif-er took a break to rearrange his offensive outburst. A sinister spark illuminated his eyes; he jumped to a sudden conclusion.

"I can see it now… It was you sneaking on us at Centrum; you were that shadow I sensed floating close to where I was giving the speech to welcome Lili-el as an Overlord! … You are no different than we are; you were there to see our blood run, our bodies mangled, and our brains splattered! … Sure, you are god… a bloodthirsty one!"

Azami-el, normally a fearsome Overlord, looked terrorized. In the face of imminent death, he became yellow; his last remaining drive to escape became a running event. As seen by Lucif-er, he slowly turned around; next, in slow motion, he dashed for the exit door.

Lucif-er raised a finger to stop him, to warn him about the horrendous heat outside the bridge; instead, he said to himself.

"Screw him!" <[25x]

[20x]> The corridor felt like a blazing oven.

Azami-el had just stepped in when his blond hair immediately caught fire. As he ran to nowhere, his clothes lit up like a torch!

All his skin began to be charred like pork rinds on an open fire. He ran further, fanning the flames encircling him. The corridor stayed partially covered with smoke, and several fires burned at different locations, with new ones spontaneously flaring up from nowhere!

He must have had pain so great that he felt nothing; only his blue eyes remained spared from the super-heated air, which was ideal for quickly cooking a well-done broiled steak. Unconsciously, the Seraph had diverted his powers to shield his eyes completely.

He reached an intersection. While he decided which way to go, a highly polished surface called his attention; there, in a mirror, he saw a horrifying monster… **himself!**

His hair had become a pile of ashes, his ragged clothes were on fire, and his skin looked like rough charcoal, but he still had a pair of malignant blue eyes! … At the sight, his heart almost stopped!

He took two steps backward, shocked and frightened by his own image!

Now, the pain arrived with a vengeance, a terrifying pain that not even his superior powers could diminish. The pain overcame him, and he fell to the floor. There, he wiggled like a worm on a hot plate. By now, his eyesight had vanished!

Struggling, his heart missed a beat... pumped... missed two beats... pumped...missed again... and from there on, it was forever silent. <[20x]

[25x]> Even the bridge was getting too hot.

Magog-el was dripping with sweat, some because of the heat, some because of his internal terror. Lucif-er also remained perspiring, but at this moment, he stayed silent while staring fearfully at the screen displaying the rear of the spaceship.

The edge of the shock wave appeared so close that the entire field of vision beyond the spacecraft became an ominous firewall!

The extreme heat started destroying the computer, one by one, its functions stopped; visual displays went blank, with only three remaining active... Was it an extreme oddity that one of the few remaining turned out to be the screen monitoring the incoming supernova's shock wave?

By this unusual condition, the two Overlords still alive could see the grasping hand of death mercilessly reaching for their lives, a horrifying visual event being delivered up to the last instant!

A red/silvery edge touched the tail where the reactor remained inactive; almost instantly, the whole section where the fusion engine was located blew up into tiny pieces! In a flash, all the debris, pushed by enormous forces, became part of the fast-moving front.

The dreaded shock wave had arrived!

Lucif-er's mind continued working at its utmost speed. Even though the disintegrating front ripped the extension to the tail at incredible speed, the blast moved so quickly that the vessel had no time to shake, twist, or even rattle! And, of course, all this massive and total destruction happened in dead silence!

As the blazing inferno reached the spaceship's central section, Magog-el turned around and screamed with a last desperate plea directed to Lucif-er, to whom the former second in command of the NA had grown dependent on solving the impossible!

"PLEASE! ... H...E...L...P... M...E."

As he screamed to his boss, the awesome power of the supernova blast vaporized the section where Magog-el was standing. This took place just after he yelled past the second letter of 'HELP'… then, he was gone! The rest of the phrase was spoken by a ghostly and horrible monster, the evil spirit of another malevolent entity, the last words of another fallen god!

As the sound waves found a medium to propagate, the noise generated was unique and immensely loud. It encompassed the disintegrating blast blowing apart everything, even molecules! The cracks, the squeaks, the explosions, and the screams of the former living all melted together. Even included was the never heard before… the ominous roar of a supernova's shock wave! This incredible noise must have reached **1,000** dbs.[6]

As Lucif-er saw his colleague dissolving into the blazing fire, he just had time to extend his arm forward with his palm facing the blast's fast-moving interface in a futile attempt to stop its devastating progress. The edge touched his hand slightly, becoming concave around its perimeter! An intense blue glow emanating from his hand mixed with the red/silvery front of the shock wave interface! … The intensity of the blast increased!

The blazing front went past his resistance.

Lucif-er saw the flesh of his hand dissolve into incandescent gases. In just a fleeting instant, the bones followed!

At the next instant, when he felt a tingling sensation from his face and from the front of his body, he knew:

This was the end; he was being… **vaporized!**

With the last energy left in him, he angrily cursed God.

"I HATE YOU"   <[25x]

(His departing spirit added)
"I WILL HATE YOU… FOREVER"

At that instant, when the supernova blast disintegrated the spaceship and the last Overlord survivor, the faint image emerging from the atomized remains became the most horrifying ever!

Lucif-er, the most handsome, intelligent, and powerful Archangel to ever walk the planet Terra, became transformed into a monstrous dragon, a nightmarish dark image more terrifying than anything seen before.

It became the antithesis of Love and Beauty, the exclusion of Goodness. What remained… it was just too ugly to contemplate.

Lucif-er was dead… Satan had just been born!

Nothing remained of the planet of Angels, not a small piece that could be found by an alien race, not a single piece that could have symbolized the prominent achievements of a unique and great civilization. In fact, no

---

[6] One hundred and thirty decibels of sound is considered painful.

physical evidence remained that they ever existed; however, their story was not over since the last chapter of their existence remained essential and had not yet been written.

A remarkable event destined to occur in a place that nobody had ever heard of before, at a location where the angels' spirits awaited their rewards and their punishments to be administered!

A cataclysmic event so awesome that, in comparison, a supernova explosion looked like a harmless firecracker, a minute flash of light hardly noticeable over the whole cosmic Universe, where its overall effect remained so negligible that it almost made no difference! Nevertheless, to the angels, it made all the difference!

Now, the next event unfolds; unlike a supernova, its aftermath shall last for an ETERNITY!

HEAVEN AND HELL

CHAPTER 10

The Universe, an impressive word challenging the limits of our understanding, embodies all we can perceive, even if such perception is only an infinitesimal part of its wholeness.

Nonetheless, is our comprehension of such a place a valid speculation? Is it possible that we are looking through a window located on one floor of a complex multi-story building, where our narrow perception allows us to see only the floor where we are standing? How many floors or dimensions could possibly exist in the whole Universe?

What about God? Does He exist in all dimensions?

For the last question, since many humans believe that He is the Creator, it is accordingly evident that He must exist in all dimensions; however, as obvious as it sounds, it is beyond our capabilities to prove it. There is one unmistakable statement related to verification: We know very little about any other dimensions; furthermore, most of what we know is only speculation and hypothesis.

Visualizing such localities and recognizing any connections to our dimension is tough. In the true sense, we are barely learning how to understand the structural and complex dynamic interactions of our own Universe or dimension; not many years have passed since our vision of the Cosmos was all wrong or nonexistent.

It is worth noting how changing size affects our cosmic perspective; each individual size exclusively determines a unique perception of the Universe on our planet. It may help us to visualize a new perspective if we imagine being as small as an ant. How drastically different the world where we live becomes?

Everything surrounding us is gigantic; the world becomes much more dangerous and scarier. Our well-known landscapes, including our home's backyard, could turn into a savage jungle where staying alive for a single day could become a task to cherish.

In this strange habitat, the value of life does not carry the same weight, with its length and value to be considered short and precarious; there are so many ways to die because it is so easy to be killed or eaten.

Just picture yourself being one small ant working your butt off, day and night, minding your own business. One morning, as you quickly walk across this large flat and arid gray expanse, a wasteland that looks unnatural when compared to everything else, you hear this incoming rumble. It could be from one of the many unknown moving giants that come and go at tremendous speed. When they come, you have very little warning. By the time you feel the ground shaking like a quake, it is too late; you have been flattened to the ground!

Most of the time, you can consider this to be an unfortunate accident. Occasionally, your last visual observation could have told you that this giant monster went out of his way to squash you on purpose! Forget about Godzilla; for your small size, these two-legged monsters are worse!

Now imagine being the size of bacteria... What a drastically dissimilar environment.

The place on sight is an alien landscape that could almost instantly change from a friendly environment to a hostile place, from cold to hot, from dry to flooded, and from organized to complete chaos. A frightening environment where survival is not geared to the individual but to the species; when conditions are in your favor, you reproduce to generate thousands, even millions of offspring, many generations all done in hours to assure that when adversity comes again, the survival of a few is almost guaranteed.

And could it even occur to you that the red rivers, mountains of pulsating living cells, endless fibrous connections, and much more, all as large as a whole planet, could be <u>one single living entity</u>?

At that level, one human being could be planet Earth; the planet, the entire unreachable Universe.

Finally, imagine being at the atomic level... This would be the strangest of all places.

In its relation of mass to empty space, it is like our solar system, except, in this place, the events develop at incredible velocities, up to the speed of light. Electromagnetic waves, photons, electrons, and even massive nuclei interact frenetically.

I cannot visualize life being able to exist at such a level, but God is there. In addition, how can we reconcile the fact that at the molecular level, life seems impossible, and yet those same molecules could be part of a living organism? Furthermore, as those same molecules and elements are the remains of supernovas and our bodies became made from such molecules, how can we all be created from stardust?

For Him to be accordingly present, from what dimension must He be? I assume He must be at some level higher than a three dimension.

Unfortunately, we are incapable of visualizing such a locality. The closest we can get to explain God's position with our references is to assume that we live in a two-dimensional world and God is in a three-dimensional one. That perspective could give us the insight that it is impossible for us to see God, even when He is in front of us!

Our dimension limitations would not allow us to visualize a three-dimensional person or object; however, we could readily theorize that a three-dimensional world could exist. In contrast to our limited perception, God can see everything we do and where we are going. This is easily predicted at His level since our narrowness of vision and mind prevents us from seeing our future's obvious outcomes.

You could draw your own perspective about how the Universe should be; by now, you could also figure out that I am trying to add my grain of sand to the immense pool of knowledge. When I do so, it may become apparent that I do not know much of anything.

When you go from one linear dimension to two dimensions, a planar, the latter is immensely larger than the first one.

When you do the same from two dimensions, a planar, to three dimensions, a volume, the latter is equally immensely larger than the previous.

Now, from three dimensions to four dimensions, the same relation should hold. Therefore, as far as we are concerned, God is immensely larger than we are. Our whole visible Universe is just like a flat piece of paper in front of him; however, it could be more than just one flat piece of paper in His presence; there could be many!

So, invisible to us, alternate spaces exist, probably even universes. Or what we call, perhaps improperly, other dimensions.

Next, we continue with our angels' story in a not yet specified after-death dimension.

From the surface of a planet-looking extraterrestrial singularity, the sky displayed the most incredible cosmic whirlpool ever seen. Even at the center of this strange land, the astonishing event could only be seen partially.

At the closest layer to the ground, starlight small blue dots slowly passed by; then, as the layers got farther away, the dots belonging to those layers moved faster. The last faint ones, extremely distant, were the fastest in motion. Purple flashes of lightning, silently jumping from the faraway levels to the closest ones, moved downward in random fashion. Once the lightning reached the lowest level, the flashes diverged away like branches from a tree's main trunk; the lightning also behaved like a profuse cloud-to-cloud lightning burst. Finally, after flashing at the lowest level, they dissipated away; however, a bolt of lightning would occasionally strike the ground of this strange place.

As an ominous background to all, a very dark and deep violet sky stared at the ground.

The terrain, flat for a vast distance, finally became jarred at the faraway horizon; it was an immense valley surrounded by towering mountain ranges. The enormously large mountains of this range were like crystal growths, with their shiny and jarred faces simulating lances stabbing the sky at incredible heights; at that distance, they resembled massive jewels with ruby, amethyst, and tanzanite colors. One immediately observed difference revealed that they did not reflect light; they generated it. The color of the immense valley, a polished and extremely flat surface, had a uniform mesmerizing dark maroon.

Something odd in this strange place became apparent. A shiny, straight, and thin white line ran along the middle of the valley; it also projected upward an extremely thin, faint, and white wall. This wall propagated from the ground line to as far above as it could be seen; actually, it split the flat valley into two equal sections.

From the upper depths of the sky, a purple flash dropped to the closest layer of blue light dots. A bright multi-branched lightning spread at the nearest orbit above the ground; a single powerful bolt hit the ground before dissipating.

Now, a dark figure stood at the stricken place, which had stayed empty before. It was Lucif-er!

His eyes remained full of hate. His face did not look as handsome as it used to be, with protruding parts distorting what used to be flawless skin. His black wings matched the dark tunic covering his body.

He looked as if he had come out of a nightmare because his distorted facial features showed intense emotion and fear. His spiritual shape continued twisting like it had just been removed from an oven!

Instantly later, amid great confusion, he somehow calmed down and glanced around at his strange surroundings. Nobody could be seen in front of him, yet closely behind; his seven subordinated Overlords stood in a single row. They looked mean and ugly, but he immediately noticed that all the Overlords' wings had become black. A strange emotion permeated from their beings; they felt intense internal fear and confusion, precisely as he did!

Not far behind his colleagues, a vast crowd extended as far as he could see; they were billions of his followers. In front of this immense multitude stood Liliel, Arkyn, Zoltar, Dagon, Kragen, and the rest of the top NA-ranked soldiers and close servants. His favorite female had lost her stunning sensual figure; less than an ugly shadow remained of her previous self.

In an inquisitive style, the spirit of ultimate Evil looked again at his surroundings. As he moved around, he kicked some of the maroon dirt. The particles, small, perfectly shaped spheres, flew on multiple circular orbits to the ground. After bouncing two or three times above the top surface, they pushed their weight into the floor lattice. The ground repaired itself along the void caused by the kick, filling everything back to its original shape... a perfectly flat floor.

The thin white line stretching beyond sight in both directions above the ground, with its faint and thin wall propagating as high as the 'stars' called his attention... As he looked down, he became startled!

On the other side of this thin wall, Micha-el and the rest of the SA Overlords also stood in front of another vast crowd... billions again!

"How could so many be nearby, and he did not sense even a single individual?" He thought.

His eyes fired at Micha-el with hate; soon afterward, Lucif-er moved toward the separating wall of light. As he moved in the direction of the leader of the SA and got closer to the mostly transparent wall, he felt an awesome rejection, like trying to push together two powerful magnets, one pole against the same other equally magnetized pole; the closer they get, the stronger the repulsion becomes.

The same happened to Lucif-er; he never touched the light wall when he projected his hand intending to cross the barrier. It felt like an impregnable wall of solid steel, an absolute obstacle that grew immensely stronger as his hand got closer to this light's interface!

Lucif-er looked with disbelief at his crushed hand, a painful incident.

On the other side, Micha-el saw the event and walked beside the wall. He faced Lucif-er, but the sight of the leader of the NA made his heart ache with compassion. Lucif-er did not sense Micha-el's feelings but deduced them by his actions. The Lord of Darkness exploded.

"Keep your stupid pity to yourself!"

The fire of anger burning inside him was not enough to prevent him from questioning Micha-el, *"You, who have been here for a while, explain! Where are we?"*

Micha-el's face, including his whole body, wings, and garments, glowed with a dazzling white. He showed no offense by the remark and responded.

"I have been here... only for an instant before your arrival!"

As Lucif-er stared at one of the angels behind Micha-el, the ex-leader of the SA anticipated another question. He continued with a soft and friendly voice, *"Yes! He is one of our early ancestors. However, he has been here an instant longer than I have...*

Let me explain our location: To start, this place is an intermediate dimension! Look above... you can see Time passing by. One instant here is equal to a million years above!

We are at the center of the whole creation. The upper sphere passing by represents all the time allotted to the Universe: the beginning and the end. From the initial Big Bang to the final collapse of matter into an anti-Big Bang, all that our Lord deposited for the creation of the Universe shall be back to Him!"

After a brief pause, Micha-el, staring at the above fantastic display, continued, *"At the place where we stand, all Time that was previously created is at equal distances to any event, Past, Present, or Future. Time is a commodity that affects the living and all the material things.*

God is timeless... God's existence has no beginning and end; He is everything!"

Lucif-er squeezed his forehead while questioning a situation that disgusted him.

"How do you know all these things, and I don't?"

The answer became painful for Micha-el to convey since it resulted from a 'choice' now permanently embedded in their souls. He stated the facts.

"Knowledge... it is like a thirst.

God is like an ocean of knowledge. When you want to know, you drink from His vast pool; then, you are not thirsty anymore because you know. You do not know because you have refused to acknowledge His existence and have disobeyed His commands! Your actions have denied any possible access to such divine knowledge!"

As Micha-el extended his hand to emphasize his statement, his fingers passed across the dividing barrier... analogous to passing a finger across a beam of white light, with no effort required.

Lucif-er, in his inner self, turned furious about the entire God's praising by Micha-el, but he did immediately notice the fingers crossing the barrier's phenomenon. He angrily asked again.

"Your hand goes across the barrier, but I cannot even touch it?"

"For the same reason that you do not know. In God's grace, we have no constraints; in contrast, everybody on your side does! You are enclosed... like in a prison."

Not too far down the divider, a male Virtue stood close to a female Domination, Eugenius, and Claire. Both full of God's grace, when they looked at each other, their eyesight reflected their new inner state: a pure and perfect love filling their souls. They patiently waited for the final judgment, which they knew would happen soon.

It was odd to note that even when sound did not propagate in this dimension, the angels in their spiritual form could communicate by voice or telepathy.

From the opposite side, Eugenius saw a group of Virtues getting closer to the barrier. He felt a deep sadness at the sight of five individuals staring at him from across the barrier: his parents, two brothers, and a sister; his whole family!

Even when the sadness remained deep, he felt no remorse. The Holy Spirit must have blessed his soul with a deep understanding of God's justice. In the past, if he had listened to his family's pleas, he would have ended up on Evil's side; that did not lessen his compassion.

His mother, not looking the way he remembered, stretched her hands toward him; she cried.

"My dear son! ... I beg you! Please, help us!"

The rest of his family also screamed in desperation.

"Eugenius! You can help us; pull us to the other side. You can do it!"

With saddened eyes, he responded.

"I am sorry, mother; I am sorry for all of you, but pulling you to this side is one of the few things I cannot do. Please, do not ask me any more; it is impossible! ... And you already know it!"

His father looked at him with anger and remarked.

"I despise you, son! You didn't do anything to stop us from moving to the NA; if you were so sure that we were doing the wrong thing, you should have stopped us!"

Eugenius looked at his father with undisturbed compassion and replied.

"You all made a choice... If I had forced you to stay, it would not have affected this outcome!"

His father twisted his already deformed face and exclaimed.

"You bastard, I wish that I had never had you! Let's get out of his sight!"

As the family group moved away from the divider, his mother turned her face for a last look. It was a sad glance, full of fear and hopelessness. Torn by the sight, Eugenius sadly waved goodbye to his mother and the rest of his family, whom he had loved so much in Terra. Even after losing them to the dark and evil side, he would always love them!

The glowing hand of Claire, sensitive to the sorrowful event, consoled him. She remarked with sweetness in her voice.

"Far away into the left side's crowd, I know I have a brother screaming in loneliness for my help! I am glad he did not come to my presence to personally demand what your family did; I would be as sad as you are for rejecting him... We thank you, Lord, for giving us the strength to say goodbye to our loved ones.

We all have a friend or relative we sadly lost to Evil; however, who has lost the most? And so many? ... but You, our loving Father!"

The blue points of light, alike stars, oddly resonated. The intensity increased from the outer layers to the nearest one; it was like a collapsing wave finally being focused on this strange land's nucleus. The ground followed suit by reproducing small undulating ripples along its smooth surface. The sharp jewel-like peaks, the ridges in the distance, were hit by massive bolts of purple lightning. The billions of spectators could feel the electricity extraordinarily propagating through space but in silence. Down from the mountains' peaks, lightning bolts propagated along the valley's floor like glowing red/purplish expanding waves, like the waves created by throwing rocks into a calm water pond. All the present watched the colorful ripples interacting under their feet and as the disturbance vanished. The only undisturbed feature in the whole place was the white dividing line and the wall it projected upward; it remained a solid barrier.

Azami-el walked closer to Lucif-er; suddenly, he stopped; for some reason, he could not access the same row where his leader stood. He was feeling lonely and miserable but also perplexed by the situation. When he tried to question Lucif-er, he glanced to the other side and saw behind the good Archangels a beautiful female moving to the front of the crowd. He sadistically smiled when he recognized Raquel; immediately, Azami-el communicated with his boss.

"Lucif-er! Look who is at the front of the other side's horde!"

The number one Evil Overlord glanced toward the indicated location. A lusty and sardonic smile further deformed his damaged appearance. Under her white glowing tunic, he could admire her perfect shape; she looked even better than he remembered.

He moved his sight to catch Gabri-el approaching in his direction. The Archangel stopped next to Micha-el, just at the edge of the white light barrier; as he did, he locked his green eyes with Lucif-er's, making the latter feel uncomfortable. The stare was friendly, so Lucif-er looked back; scornfully, he lashed at the radiant Cherub.

"Hi 'brother'! I hope you have no hard feelings about nuking you! ... We miss you... Care to join us?"

Gabri-el nodded with disapproval; he had no hard feelings at all. Instead, he felt sorry for Lucif-er; he was given so much in the other life and wasted such talents by doing so much evil to others. With an altruistic intention, he responded to Lucif-er's sarcastic remark.

"It is a pity you still cannot comprehend the full extent of your predicament; by the Grace of the Lord, I can see it coming ahead!

You were like a brother, the one reason why I ache about your incoming fate, but by our own choices, we stand on opposite sides. Concurrent with such a choice, my reward will be immense, but your punishment will be equally extensive... I do not wish you this fate; however, the Lord's divine justice gives me no choice!"

For an instant, as Gabri-el extended his hand beyond the barrier, the evil Lucif-er stared at its location; then, he went for it. He tried to pull Gabri-el to his side!

Grabbing the extremity with both powerful hands, he pulled with all his mighty power. To his disbelief, he could not even move one finger from Gabri-el's hand. The good Overlord slowly and gently flipped his hand inside his territory; the frustrated Lord of Darkness remained incapable of preventing it. He stood in rage, staring with hate at the two Overlords that were so close to him but, at the same time, so far away. Gabri-el, without any change in his attitude, remarked.

"Lucif-er! We are not on the same basis anymore. You do not have any power against us, as you do not have any power against God. However, we do share His power against you!"

Lucif-er, partially opening his mouth to release some internal heat from the burning furnace of hate, took two steps backward. Frustrated, he shifted his anger by refocusing on Raquel's gracious shape; with utter lust, he sized her up and down. At that time, he made a mistake...

Remembering how he had mentally terrorized this female, his piercing eyes now blacker than any blue, locked into the prettiest eyes that existed in their previous life. All the mental energy emanating from the Overlord remained like a still wind, incapable of moving one strand of her glorious hair... But her sight, more potent than a high-power laser beam, scared him!

He shook as he tried to stare her down. The longer he tried, the worse he got; finally, amidst violent convulsions, he could not take it anymore. The leader of the dark side broke down the stare and sheepishly glanced at the floor. The humiliation was intense; Lucif-er could not even stand a stare from a <u>female</u>!

His teeth rumbled; his nails dug deep into his palms as his fists closed so hard; his eyesight was on fire while smoke came out from his nostrils. He did not scare anybody on the good side; only his colleagues became nervous; the closest crowd's bystanders, his followers, became afraid of him.

Lucif-er did not look at the good side; instead, he blazed his full-of-hate stare toward his seven subordinated Overlords. None of them dared to return the stare at him!

He felt somehow relieved; after all, he still did have his full power over them. Furious because of the humiliation, he projected his scouring hate toward his subordinates.

Micha-el and Gabri-el returned to their original front row; however, Gabri-el did not stop there; he continued moving until reaching the love of his past life.

Gently, their hands met; their eyes filled with perfect love looked at each other. As dazzling as they were before, now they looked even better; inside their minds, they had no mixed feelings, anxieties, or questions. A shared mutual understanding that something much better than they had ever experienced before was coming their way. As both lips met in a silky and tender touch, their eyes did not close; they left open the windows to their souls. What was inside was truly precious but not completely fulfilled. One more critical step remained: to see God... as He really is!

Slowly, their lips separated. In a short time, their hands followed the same course. When Gabri-el turned around and rejoined the other six Archangels, Raquel returned to her previous location; even when both stayed separated, their intimate touch continued to be part of them.

Timeless love dwelled inside them, forever present!

The seven bad Overlords in a restless row, plus Lucif-er, remained exuding fear as they sunk into deep anxiety. They did know that something frightening was on the way, but what? Was this the ultimate punishment predicted by the ancient books? And where was this God who had summoned them here?

They had not seen Him yet, but all the spirits on the evil side did intrinsically know about His existence. You could not deny it in this place like His name was carved in every little sphere on the ground and every bright blue dot in the sky. It became impossible to disclaim it; after all, He was the only reason for them being there.

The violent end to their lives, still present, had two main ingredients remaining active: Fear and hate! ... Now, something new was added: total confusion.

Their hostility toward all, including God and themselves, remained the glue that bonded them. As Love stayed embedded deep into the good angels, Hate persisted in being equally carved with indelible ink among the evil angels.

The North Alliance Overlords did not talk much; their presence in this place reminded them of their failure in their now-past lives; the result caused their colleagues to be like strangers standing in front of each other. Every time they stared at any of the others, cold chills ran down along where their spines used to be. The now spiritual beings had similar body structures as compared to their past living counterparts, but their bodies, without any matter, just lacked any material functionality.

To their sight, their colleagues had become the ugliest beings they had ever seen. What a horrifying thought when they knew that they were not different! They even thought of this being their final transfiguration. The angels on the other side felt saddened by the intuitive realization that this state was only a metamorphic cocoon leading to something utterly bizarre and horrifying, still yet to come.

Not far behind, Arkyn stared hatefully at the Overlords; he could not forgive them for leaving him behind to die. His spirit boiled internally at the thought and horror of his last moments in Terra as he continued to go over and over past events. Another feeling, one of utter loneliness, had surfaced with a vengeance... He could have been with Micha-el on the other side, celebrating. Instead, he harbored this horrible fear, which continued devouring his inner being. The void of loneliness went deep indeed, but abundant hate overfilled the cracks; he concentrated on the latter. He detested all of them, especially Micha-el.

It is much easier to hate the one who did not do enough to save your soul, regardless of how hard he tried, because he was now far and distant than to hate the one that most hurt you because he was now closer to you than ever, and he scared you!

Again, on the good right side and somewhere in the middle of a vast crowd, an angel of the choir of Principalities had all his being full of the Love and the Grace of God. All the angels around him, equally blessed with the same gift, continued sharing the incredible joy of the Lord's gifts.

Most of them had violently died amidst a nuclear fire; however, unlike the other side, where the dwellers hated and trembled at the way their life ended, the angels in this location remembered their death as a glorious event: A sacrifice with the utmost reward, a step to a higher existence.

A glowing face revealed an angel named Sergius. The image of his benefactor, a great friend named Rapha-el, crossed his mind. With incredible speed, even when he stood in the same place, he saw himself instantly projected to a position next to the Overlord's row.

Rapha-el perceived his arrival because he turned around and greeted him, *"My dear friend, it is an honor to see you again!"*

Sergius, who did not communicate telepathically before, did now; in fact, it felt as natural as an inborn characteristic. Joyfully, he replied.

"Rapha-el, the honor is all mine! I shall be eternally grateful to you for all the patience and help you offered me in the other life... and to you, Gabri-el, I am equally indebted!"

This named Archangel had also moved around and joined the meeting, Gabri-el exclaimed.

"Nonsense! As servants of God, it was our duty."

"I know, but I will always love you for the personal effort that both of you placed on my person!"

Sergius, full of happiness, had the thought of a lost friend momentarily breaking the enchantment. Just thinking about Marcus, who remained his closest friend for so long, he saw him across the barrier. The sight was painful; his friend's face and body, covered by a dark tunic, were ugly. Amid many more fallen angels, he used a low, raspy voice, screaming for mercy, for help, <u>for Sergius</u>!

"I didn't want to join Lucif-er! ... It was a mistake! Help me out of here! ... Sergius, you abandoned me! I blame you for what happened to me... I hate you!"

Sergius said to himself, *"The day you chose the NA over my complaints, you broke my heart! ... I will always cherish all the good times we had together; if only you could feel the same way. Evil, with its merciless grasp on you, will use the sharp talons of hate to drag you away into a darkness and horror never seen before.*

There, amidst an eternal fiery torment, our friendship will vanish. Any thought regarding our life in Terra will increase the already unbearable torture.

Why did you reject our loving God? He is the essence of all beauty and joy. Without Him, what is left is what you can perceive now!"

With sadness, Sergius detached from the image. His companions shared his concerns by supporting him. Micha-el, Nobiel, and Raquel also joined the growing chat. An increasing circle, in which all the participants conversed very unusually; without leaving their locations, they joined a gathering of souls by projecting themselves to a different location where thoughts and actions were exchanged.

As Nobiel approached Gabri-el, the latter greeted him with a two-hand salute at chest level.

"My brother! I am proud of how you faced the onslaught of Evil," the Archangel exclaimed. *"Even our Lord blessed you with His presence!"*

"Gabri-el, you showed me the way with your dignified example!" Nobiel responded.

"Blessed is God, Who enlightened us to find the proper direction!" Gabri-el said enthusiastically.

Joyfully, Micha-el, Izma-el, Dani-el, Samu-el, Lari-el, and Maryen increased the circle of exchange. Here, freely and instantly, all accomplished a communal gathering. Even in a very large group, all talked in harmony, without interruptions, without overlapping, and without any confrontation... furthermore, all shared the wisdom of perfect Love and its corresponding understanding.

After a while... Could we say, 'minutes later,' in a timeless place?

Micha-el raised both hands.

At the same instant, everyone involved in the chat instantly returned to their original place.

Micha-el's face, bursting with excitement, proclaimed with immense and unrestrained joy.

"The Lord, our loving God... is coming!"

The fastest moving objects in the sky, also the farthest away, as represented by the small blue points of light embedded in the deep violet sky providing a background to all the fireworks above, suddenly, this upper layer came to an abrupt stop!

An all 'star' to 'star' purple flashing connected the upper layer.

As part of a contagious event, the lower layers began slowing to a standstill; it looked like a simultaneously collapsing sheet of lightning converging toward the strange land below, the solid nucleus of this unusual dimension. Billions of good angels raised both hands up, welcoming the Creator. Billions of disobedient angels moved backward, like running away from the crushing impact of a collapsing wall of purple lightning!

When the final blow arrived, the sky, the mountains, the valley, and everybody present became blinded by a purple glow, a saturating hue that overpowered everything in this dimension.

Next, exactly at the center of the white light dividing wall, at a point in front of both sides where all the angels stood, at a spot facing everybody and where nobody stood behind, a bright white point of light emerged!

It looked like a dazzling explosion in reverse. The white point grew in size as it siphoned the purple glow from the sky, valley, and the ground below!

It was the sight of a collapsing sphere of cosmic size. From the outer reaches of space, it quickly reduced its boundaries to the mountain ranges; an instant later, it collapsed into a two-meter-diameter blinding white sphere. At this moment, no more purple glow remained.

All eyes looked intently at the front, unblinking, mesmerized. Many showed intense joy, while others became torn by intense fear. While some widely opened their eyes to welcome the divine visitor, others covered them to protect themselves from the burning light.

Slowly, the shimmering glow decreased. Like the unfolding facets of a giant diamond sparkling into a shape, the image of the Creator materialized!

He stood facing all the angels. His left foot remained firmly planted on the left side of the white dividing wall, while his right foot remained equally steady on the right side. His glowing body and white tunic emanated light with unmatched radiance.

Micha-el took two steps forward and kneeled in front of the Lord. The remaining six Archangels immediately followed their leader's spontaneous response. Bowing to the divine presence, Micha-el, full of the Holy Spirit, proclaimed with ardent love.

"My Lord! My spirit has long waited for this moment!
From this loyal servant, please accept my humble adoration!"

The Lord touched his head, a gentle touch like a father caressing the curly hair of a preferred child. When He talked, His voice propagated clearly and concisely to everyone present!

"Micha-el, my son, your love and loyalty are unsurpassed by anyone else; therefore, I will reward you accordingly by appointing you as the commander-in-chief of the faithful!"

Micha-el recognized the voice; he had heard it some time ago when he was alive on Terra; he raised his eyes to see what he already knew. The Lord, holding his hand, raised him up.

"You will be in charge of all my children!" He continued, and addressing all the loyal Archangels, announced, *"All seven of you shall always be at my side!"*

Micha-el's face, ignited by the fire of perfect love, grew brighter with God's proximity, and so did the spirits of the other six Archangels; together, all praised the Lord!

God's face became evident to the seven closest angels in his presence. Standing in a dimension where time existed as an intrinsic circle, time now stood still. Nothing in the firmament moved. Time was placed on hold!

The divine visitor and judge was easily identified. They recognized Him as: **The Visitant.**

The new inherent knowledge, now part of the good angels, gave them the answer to all their questions. They knew that the image of God, now in the presence of all, was not the full vision of the Lord. To see Him as He really is, the individual must be exalted to a much higher level. This level may rightfully be called the primary dimension, a location where it is possible to envision the magnificence of a Being in His timeless immensity!

Only a divine gift of unbelievable proportions could allow anybody this immense capability. Just think for a moment for the clue to achieve this endeavor… In His own words, the Creator asked us to call Him, Father!

What a joy it must be to be at the right hand of God at His last judgment; on the other hand, finding yourself at his left side must be the most horrifying living or after-death nightmare possible. Even before God's judgment, you will know one instant after your death that you have failed!

The permanent loss of God brings the most dreadful loneliness. It is a dark and frigid cage; inside, a soul sinks into this abysmal and depressing isolation. No place in the material Universe could induce such a devastating blow to your identity. Your relatives and friends, even if facing you, would be like strangers wearing dark masks in front of you; they also would be equally demolished.

Anybody outside you is a dark and faceless shadow waiting in fear for something worse, something that you could only imagine; however, when it comes, you should find out that your imagination was not even close.

To visualize the impact of this harrowing predicament, imagine yourself as a tall building condemned for demolition. One instant, you are a solid structure facing the sky; even when harboring multiple defects, you rise to the clouds. It only takes seconds amid thunderous, well-placed detonations, and you and your ego collapse into a pile of rubbish, the center of a dark and dusty expanding cloud. This is a poor analogy; the collapse of your soul's individuality is much worse! … You could blame yourself, your relatives and friends, Lucif-er, and even God; it shall not make a difference; the imprint in your soul is permanent!

God will be looking during the judgment of our deeds for mercy, sacrifice, and Love. For the ones to be condemned, He will not find any of the above… only selfishness and hate! These two, and many similar bad attributes, will be the company of the damned during their eternal torment.

The finger of God pointed toward His right side.

The servants of the Lord stood there. Communion among the Spirit of Love and billions of blessed followers remained a totally harmonious event since the Grace of God endured inside their souls; very little needed to be explained or added to the utmost joy filling their spirits. They anxiously waited for their final reward, to see the Creator as He is: three persons, but one single God. For us, this is another great mystery beyond our comprehension!

It is impossible to visualize God as one single entity. Why should we even try for His three different and inherent personalities?

I know that some of us may want to try anyway.

This is the starting point. Begin by tracing a straight but vast line connecting the infinitesimally small with the immensely large. The subatomic particles are not the smallest particles that exist, but we could start there. Also, the known Universe is not the whole Universe, but we could end there.

Now we include time, so our view is not fixed but dynamic, a Universe in motion. Note that as we move along the sampling line toward the smallest, the measuring units of time to see any movement also become smaller, microseconds, nanoseconds, etc. If we move to the cosmic perspective, our units of time to see any movement again are in the millions or even billions of years.

Could we visualize our sampling line, which includes the smallest and the largest, to expand in 3-dimensional space to include the whole Universe? Furthermore, could we still visualize it if we added billions of years so the whole thing moves in an immense circle where the beginning and the end are in the same place? … Up to here, it has already become a mind-boggling event!

Myself, I cannot even visualize two different places along the sampling line at the same time. I can only visualize one region at a time, sort of a sequential probe; if I try two, it becomes chaotic, and I lose control of my imagination. It is like how our eyes are built; we can only focus at one distance. If we try for two different depths, we strain our eyes and end up flipping back and forth between any two points.

By now, we have a good perception of our visual Cosmos. Unfortunately, this is not enough to guess how God may look. He is multidimensional!

After we figure out how all of this works together, we have the final task of solving the Holy Trinity of God, the creator of all these places.

Just think about it. The understanding of God's existence is so much beyond our comprehension that only by his divine wish may we one day be blessed to see Him and fully understand it all.

The good angels had arrived at the door of this incredible gift. The anticipation of their reward must have overwhelmed their spirits. By tapping into the well of divine knowledge, they knew the basics to see and experience the Glory of our Lord as the ultimate experience. The Visitant communicated individually and communally with all; each one of the billions of the servants of the Lord talked to Him, personally and simultaneously!

God pointed his left-hand finger toward the evil angels.

In anticipation, grinding teeth, moans, and crying came out of the large crowd; they could not find a place to run away. Fear of God became real and present. They could not move; they were in bondage, anchored to their assigned locations.

Lucif-er alone faced the Visitant's initial wrath.

So much piled against Lucif-er, the seed of Evil himself! The weight of his sins remained enormous. Pride had been his downfall. He, who was giving the most, abused his powers and disobeyed. Nevertheless, the worst was that he had deceived billions of angels to follow his thwarted and evil path!

Lucif-er wanted to scream, to blaspheme; however, he was not allowed at this instant. As his tongue painfully twisted out of control, only ineligible groans came out of his mouth.

The sight of the Visitant with its divine glow burned the surface of Lucif-er's skin. His black and ragged tunic did not smoke, but all his skin did. In utter pain, he fell to the ground, twisting like a snake.

Lucif-er could not stare at the Creator's laser-like eyes; he tried desperately to protect his face from the divine Entity before him. The presence of the Lord became a fearful and painful sight for the sinful.

The seven Archangels in the next row were next. One by one, the Lord exposed their sins. Zeri-el became last since God was especially stringent on condemning him. So many souls asked for justice; they had died because of his cruel and merciless treason, although his punishment had started even before he died. In his dreams, he suffered many painful and horrifying deaths, much before the real one came about.

Billions more followed to be personally and simultaneously condemned. An ocean of disobedient angels flexed under divine justice. Like a lashing stroke, their condemnation surfaced the worst fears and horrors. They already knew that they were no good, but hearing God sending them to eternal punishment developed into an agonizing moment. The cries of so many sounded like the ominous noise hurricane winds make as they lash the land, a howling that chills the bones, a sinister warning that sends people looking for cover; however, there was none in this place!

The Visitant moved His left foot and whole body inside the right-side area next to the thin light wall.

God made a request to the land below and to the firmament above; **it was a divine order!**

At the white line separating both sides...

From above, it seemed as if the sky became sucked into the thin white glowing plane separating the good from the bad. Similarly, as a black hole sucks matter from its surroundings to never give it back, so God's request to split left from right did. However, instead of matter, it sucked energy. Every 'star,' or whatever the bright blue bodies adorning the sky gave part of their intrinsic energy. Like a cosmic-sized Aurora Borealis, strings of light were extracted from every one of the countless 'stars.' All these energies cascaded into the dividing plane toward the ground. Its colors were primarily purple and blue; next, red and green with less intensity; last, a shade of orange and yellow.

At the separating interface, all this immense energy became concentrated. If this was not enough, from the maroon soil, streaks of orange, red, and purple all began being sucked from the vast dimensional core and into the ground below the surface of the dividing white line. An increasing underground reddish glow grew delineating the subterraneous white line.

The good angels did not move. The bad ones stepped away from this ominous wall as an increasing level of terror invaded their souls; the scream of billions propagated outward in a horrifying manner. Suddenly, the evil angels were not bound to a specific place; as a result, the vast crowd spread aimlessly but away from the restricting and impassable wall.

The floor at the white line interface became glowing white-red!

The trembling ground moved, moaned, and hissed like a tortured snake over hot asphalt. Something awe-inspiring approached, so vast that it deeply affected all the present.

Then... An **EXPLOSION!**

An incredibly powerful blast rattled the whole dimension!

So vast was the energy spent that a supernova, in comparison, looked like a harmless firecracker. If this dimensional core became analogous to an enormous black hole, what kind of energy would be needed to split such a massive black hole into two separate parts?

The energy coming into the plane moved faster than the speed of light! However, if a particle is accelerated to the speed of light, its mass becomes infinitely large. What could it cause if it passed this known barrier for our known Universe?

Many neutrino particles at the ground location of the barrier became accelerated beyond the light's speed, thus negating the formula of $E = mc^2$

The sky and the ground rippled beyond reality as the fundamental laws of Physics no longer applied! No sound propagated in this strange place, but the electromagnetic ripples blasted the present with an immense cry from matter stressed beyond the limits established at their long-ago creation. The shriek spiked so powerfully that it caused the evil spirits present to question their eternal existence!

Along the thin separating plane, the ground split!

But this was beyond the usual crack; the whole fabric of this dimension had split in two. Not since the Big Bang primordial explosion had that much energy been spent!

Looking in the same direction to the dividing white thin wall, the attending saw God, whose right was their left; incredible hot tongues of fire emanated from the interface and propagated **only** across the right side. It appeared as if the right side of the land had become heavier while the left side was lighter. As one sank, the other floated upwards!

As still seen from our point of view, an unnerving scream of pain and horror filled the right side of the barrier as the wailing and grinding of teeth overpowered the loud noise, which happened to be something else than sound. Billions of condemned angels felt the charring pain of a fire that did not consume; it only burned. Additionally, it shall continue its merciless scorching for an eternity!

Their dark robes burned away as the shapes below began turning into horrible creatures.

Lucif-er's spirit, as hinted when he died, turned into the most grotesque and harrowing creature. The closest description of his new appearance could be described as a horrifying dragon. Even the Archangels that had followed him shook in fear at his sight; although they did not look as bad as their leader, they became scary creatures themselves!

The good angels began glowing with an iridescent shine, an increasingly brighter glow of pure white light that made their shapes harder and harder to discern.

Seven bright shapes stayed close to the Creator, now emanating a blinding but beautiful radiance. The Seraphim assembled next, closest to God; after them, the Cherubim did similarly; closely behind them, the Thrones followed. The top triad was completed; immediately, they started to sing together, praising God and His Glory. Gradually, all the good angels became integrated into such Glory.

The charming melody was a performance fitted to satisfy their divine Creator, a truly angelical performance. Their final wish had become a reality!

Lucif-er, amidst fire and acrid sulfuric smoke, furiously and in pain, thrust his angry and twisted index finger upward. The projected message was raspy and ugly sounding; it overpowered the horrible noise and screaming, saturating the collapsing side. He angrily shouted.

"Micha-el, I detest you! But before you go, I want you to hear me! This is not over yet… You and I will fight again!"

From above, one of the seven bright spots next to God, a voice became projected so Lucif-er could hear; it was from Micha-el. Not even the ominous noise around affected its clarity or context.

"Lucif-er, you are correct.

We will fight again… not between you and me, because you cannot cause me any harm, but for the eternal souls of an alien race.

Since Good and Evil have been defined, this war will be more vicious, like a second and more complex level of confrontation. We, the good angels, will help them, while you, the fallen ones, will seek their damnation. However, their choice will be the same, just as ours; they will decide to serve God or to serve you.

In addition, since they would not be able to recognize Lucif-er for what he once was because now you have become the master of that horrible place where you are, they will know you by your new name… Satan!

That alien race will call themselves… humans!"

During the violent upheaval, the whole left section rose high in the sky. Only a single bright, sparkling white light from the ascending section could be seen.

Equally as fast, the sinking right section fell into an ominous dark abyss. Fire and smoke remained the main elements of that tortured place.

Suppose it could be possible to stand right at the center of the dividing plane as a spectator opposing the place where God did stand, in the same direction as all the angels faced. What would you sense if we allowed the white line interface to split your whole body into two equal parts?

Since the left side of your body would be placed on the good angels' side and the other right half on the evil angels' side, the contrast given by your sensory organs would be overpowering!

While your left eye would see the most pleasant and lovable light emanating from God, your right eye would see a Dantean nightmare of fire and torture.

Your left nostril would catch the smell of perfumes and flowers as if you were taking a stroll in a floral landscape on a pristine early morning in the middle of the spring season. Searing heat and sulfuric stench would pierce your right nostril, just like walking along a moving lava flow, with the heat and smell unbearable.

One side of your mouth will sense sweetness, the other utter bitterness. One side of your body experiences the ultimate pleasurable sensation, while the other side experiences the ultimate pain. I cannot possibly picture anything else depicting such two extremes!

The good angels ascended higher and higher; the bad ones fell deeper and deeper into a dark, bottomless abyss. We think about a black hole as being the ultimate abyss; however, even a black hole, which some also know by the name of 'singularity,' has the distinctive possibility of being recycled by an anti-Big Bang event or destroyed by simple evaporation as described by Stephen Hawkins. Therefore, when compared to the place where the evil angels became bound, it was not even close; this heinous new location was the ultimate abyss!

There is no way out! You are there, FOREVER, eternally DAMNED.

It is easy for me to imagine being in the place where the good angels went, even considering that I have but a faint idea of precisely what that place is supposed to be. Conversely, I refuse to believe or to imagine dwelling on the opposite side of the heavenly place, the other horrible location… for eternity!

I think there is a reason why so many people are not afraid of this place. It is so horrible that they have blocked it from their minds, 'If it doesn't exist, why should I worry about it?'

Regardless of any rationalization… it is there!

In a corkscrew effect, each side of the dividing plane ripped apart the time-space fabric of this strange dimension, causing unimaginable chaos in its basic structure. Both judgment areas, one ascending and one descending, vanished!

When peace finally came to the battered land, the first thing to be noticed was that the original enormous valley had returned, and it looked like a desolate place with no angels in sight! The dividing plane, the white line separating the vast valley of the maroon-colored ground into two distinct sections, was gone!

Once more, we faced an extensive valley with sparkling red flashes connecting whole sections like electric needles sewing the deterioration; quickly, the cracks and the damage to its surface were repaired. The gigantic faraway mountain ranges, mostly destroyed by the upheaval, entirely re-crystallized to their original shape.

The sky became crystal clear again, except something was not the same. The 'stars' above looked not blue anymore. Now, all shined with a sparkling yellow. Far away, the deep violet background had changed to a deep purple.

The cosmic clock, represented by the stars, resumed its trajectory. Again, millennia passed away far above while only a single instant was spent below. It appeared that this whole dimension became ready for another judgment. I wonder who it would be?

From our glancing eyes into the starting intermediate dimension, two new dimensions had been created, and they were now invisible to us.

One was where God had placed his loyal angels: A place of light, joy, and ultimate love.

The other was where Satan became the master: A place of darkness, suffering, and brutal hate.

Most of us have heard about these two completely opposite destinations.

We casually call them…

HEAVEN

AND

HELL

EPILOGUE

**Two and a half million years later.
The light from one specific Andromeda's supernova arrives
at the Milky Way.**

For a second time, we levitate in deep space, facing the same spectacular view of the beautiful galaxy of Andromeda. We can see its fiery orange center, with its large gravitational pull, is the dynamo that spins around the massive spiral arms. However, as we compare our present view to our previous sighting, we notice that its spiraling arms barely move around its huge, bright center. When you know that one full rotation, a galactic year, is longer than 200 million years, the reason is apparent. Accordingly, we still admire the remarkable spectacle majestically presented to us briefly before, a mere 2.5 million years ago.

We continue viewing what is a whirlpool of immense proportions compared to ourselves. A vision that could demean our human vanity, humbling us further. This galaxy is just another minute dot lost amid the universal cosmos.

Still mesmerized by the view, we move away at a mere one light-year/second!

Could you visualize this speed? Reaching the nearest star would take only four seconds from our solar system at this speed. Even with the swiftness of light, it would take four years to travel the same distance; at the speed we are talking about, count from one to four, and you are already there. However, traveling from Andromeda to our Milky Way would take 176 hours at this same blazing speed!

Traveling from one star to another is an immense undertaking; traveling from one galaxy to its next-door neighbor defies the imagination. If we could ever send humans from our galaxy to Andromeda, a trip lasting 2.53 million years, the beings reaching their destination would be total aliens by our race standards! Except, of course, if the travelers remain frozen for the length of the trip; in that case, humans existing in that far future would be alien when compared to them!

As our speed increases, Andromeda's size starts to shrink. As its bright color diminishes as we move away, its spiral nature becomes more predominant; by now, the galaxy gives us the visual effect of sinking into the pure black background of the abysmal void of space.

Moving along an enormous arc spanning 3 million light-years, we float from our previous close view of Andromeda to a closer view of its nearby sister galaxy. Since our last view of the Milky Way stayed at a 12-degree tilt concerning its galactic plane[1], we swiftly moved around to attain a similar full view of our galaxy as we had of Andromeda.

As we accelerate to a blazing 100,000 light-years/sec, it takes only 25 seconds for us to reach our new lookout point: a spectacular panoramic outlook of a similar spiral galaxy, in this case, our Milky Way. About 25% smaller in diameter, its features are very similar to its sister galaxy, now much smaller and fainter because we have moved away a great distance.

The most striking feature of our quick trip was the vast emptiness of space. However, the duration of the journey is by far the most impressive accomplishment of our minds; nothing travels faster than our imagination!

I reiterate that even assuming we can travel near the speed of light, it will take years to reach the nearby stars. Commuting between galaxies boggles the mind... millions of years... only one way!

Could we wish for 'warp speed' to exist? Or, perhaps, for wormholes allowing travel through 'singularities' to be a reality? Unfortunately, I think that both of the above may be nothing else than wishful thinking! Maybe quantum mechanics could open a door!

Using physics and mathematical calculations, we can predict that some of these incredible hypotheses may be feasible. A good example is traveling through black holes to other places in the Universe, which some claim is possible due to the duality of matter (matter and anti-matter). In this case, they are absolutely right about the duality; if you travel through a black hole, you will definitely go to either of two places: Heaven or Hell!

Just think about it: we cannot even get close to a black hole without our body's atoms being ripped into elementary particles. Are we really dreaming when planning to go through a black hole and survive? Only our imagination can do such feats!

Some of these predictions are accepted in the scientific world due to the fundamental abstractions of mathematics. At the basic level, there are positive and negative numbers, real and imaginary numbers. We use these two basic mathematical concepts to solve problems, and the solutions we attain are valid; however, some may not always be true in real life.

Let's take one of the most basic of mathematical calculations.

$4-6 = -2$

In real life, taking away what I do not have is impossible. Let's use something not as arbitrary as money but as physically tangible as oranges. The solution to that equality is:

$4-6 = 0$! Same as $4-4 = 0$

I know, you can say that I owe you two oranges... Well, that is just another arbitrary setup related to time since, in reality, you will be waiting for me to gain +2 of whatever you are taking away to remove it from my possession, which is always a positive quantity.

---

[1] Similar to an edge view of the galaxy.

If you carry all these abstractions into complex math calculations, you will find yourself flying through a black hole and reappearing somewhere else, at the same time, or a different one. This scenario creates a virtual universe, like what a computer creates; virtual images are so real that we may even forget they are not!

Since we were talking about black holes, let's also talk about the future of the Universe. There are three possible scenarios related to the Universe and the Big Bang.

The first one: the Universe will continue to expand forever.

The second one: the Universe will collapse into an anti-Big Bang and disappear.

The final one: the Universe will continue oscillating between Big Bangs and anti-Big Bangs.[2]

I do not know which one is your favorite, but mine is the second scenario. The reasoning I use for such a statement is that If the Universe expanded forever, all energy would be spent someday. The cosmic debris would be nothing else than dark chunks of matter frozen to almost absolute zero temperatures and drifting farther apart from each other for all eternity; this is a meaningless end to God's creation. One way or another, I am sure all the created Universe will be back to Him.

Everything will someday, for an instant, have infinite density, pressure, and temperature; that is what God is all about. He gave us a spark of Himself at the Creation of the Universe; He will take it all back in a final anti-creation event!

That will be the end of matter, energy, and time!

Time… an invisible mesh holding everything together in an immense circle. It started with the Big Bang; its gigantic loop will finally close with the anti-Big Bang, which will also mark the end of Time.

Time can never be moved forward or be reversed on its tracks; in fact, it cannot even be stopped. Using relativistic approaches, it can be slowed down or sped up; nevertheless, that is only the case because a local point of reference is used. Regardless, Time is always moving forward.

If Time could be allowed a shortcut access by jumping into the Future or going back into the Past, we would have ended up with infinite Universes. All would be multiplying and diverging in all directions, a chaotic situation I am sure God would have never allowed.

After the last instant, when the Universe ceases to exist, the spirit of God will continue to move through the ether, which is a massless and timeless void. However, He will no longer be alone; countless billions of creatures in His presence will sing to His Glory. In contrast, in another

---

[2] Currently, it is believed that the Universe will expand into oblivion and all matter, including black holes, will evaporate eventually.

dimension, countless other billions will not sing but scream as they burn in the eternal fire.

A question should arise. Will He do it all over again?

He may not, but if He does, I am sure our Lord will try something completely different: A new Universe with new looks, rules, and absolute values. It should be a new challenge for the Supreme Being!

We are still admiring the Milky Way's beauty as we slowly get closer. In our approach, we are not moving toward the center but aiming toward one arm of this spiral mass of billions of stars. We focus on someplace 33,000 light-years from the center, at a single yellow star.

This star shines alone, with similar companions just a few light-years away. It is almost unnoticeable due to the galaxy's enlarged arm, which is rich with detail. Large nebulae, clusters of new bluish stars, and older aggregates fight for attention, a distracting spectacle that makes it almost impossible to focus on such an average-sized star. Nothing seems to be critical about it, but from such a faraway distance, how could you tell that such a minute speck of light is of the utmost importance? ... Why?

Because of humanity, billions of souls exist, most with undecided outcomes. Because God created man in His own image, each person's soul is considered invaluable. To follow up on this issue, let's analyze the value of our innermost possessions.

If you could be offered to be the master of the planet Earth for a thousand years, with the condition that you would lose your soul to the devil, you should have <u>no</u> choice but to turn the offer down! ... It is a lousy deal!

A thousand years, when compared to Eternity, is equal to **zero**.

All the planet's riches, when compared to Infinity, are equal to **zero**.

The choice seems to be obvious... Why do we surrender such a priceless gift for practically nothing? Mainly because we are in the middle of an incredible war between Good and Evil, and most of the time, we do not even realize its immense implications.

We need to wake up and understand that if we reject the love of God, we could lose the Infinite, and we could lose it for an Eternity! Even worse, we could lose the most valuable gift of all: to share the Glory of God. An incredible richness that outshines any other absolute; it is the ultimate reason for our existence, even if we do not know it.

Evil has **no** mercy on us. It is determined to drag each one of us to the same horrible place where it dwells. Unfortunately, it has a big advantage over us, mainly because it has been around for a long time! If only for that reason, Evil knows how our own minds work better than we do.

Let's review some basic Psychology concepts to emphasize our weaknesses. Freud's description of our minds was accurate enough; he divided the mind into three main parts, named as follows:

The *id*. Our primordial instincts, needs, and passions.

The *ego*. The continuously changing perception of ourselves.

The *superego*. The conscience oversees our actions and decisions.

Evil, of course, can induce temptations from our most basic instincts or *id*. If lust does not work, anger expressed as violence could do, or greed, vanity, gluttony, etc. Even for the individual who methodically follows God's commandments, pride could be their downfall; in this case, placing their values above the sinful could corrupt even the *superego,* causing this person to become self-righteous.

Another way to understand the vicious grip of Evil on our souls is by comparing it to a drug addiction; the latter works in a very similar manner. If we take a drug just once, we probably could discontinue its use with easiness. If we do it several times, it will be hard to quit. If we do it many times, we may have to fight the addiction for the rest of our already shortened lives!

Evil is a similar whirlpool; as we approach its deeper, centered vortex, we find ourselves trapped and incapable of escaping.

As with any addiction, we know when our minds tell us that such a thing is not cool or fun anymore because it is destroying our bodies and could eventually even kill us. However, since the drug has also destroyed our will to fight, we must retake it on the account that we need it <u>so much</u>… Equally similar to drug abuse, the sinner has the same deception to reality.

For example, we may drink alcohol until we pass out, or we may smoke and be unable to quit, but to a direct question concerning our habits, we may answer, "I am NOT a drug addict!"

In this case, we are already inside the whirlpool, inside a place where it would be much easier to move to a deeper section. Pot, cocaine, and other similar uppers and downers could further provide a downward repositioning. Even there, there is other 'stuff' that could move us closer to the center, to that place where there is no spiraling water anymore, only a black ominous hole!

Evil, in a likewise manner, wants you to be <u>bad</u>. Once there, it wants you to do <u>worse</u>!

Without the help of God and His good angels, we do not have a chance to win. In reality, the avoidance of such help is the cause of so many of our downfalls from God's grace. We accept the deception of Evil, thinking that we can defeat it by our own strength and cunningness!

All the horrors we have seen from our wars, inequalities, and crimes are only a background. The real battle, which is still raging, is much more vicious and ruthless; its spoils become the ultimate of choices.

This battlefield is more complex than the one the angels fought; this should not discourage us since we should focus on what is essential. We are in the middle of this battlefield only because we are imperfect; we must remember that we have a choice only because of such a precondition.

To win is to strive for perfection, which we gain as we approach God. Evil will work very hard to derail our destination by preying on every one of our weaknesses. By channeling our strengths, God and His good angels will guide us to a sublime outcome. In addition, if we fall, they will help us to get up. If we are standing up, we will be pushed to move forward!

Just think how precious we are that God in human form came down to Earth to die for us, to save us from the dark whirlpool of sin demanding our souls as payment. Jesus paid that debt and gave us another chance for eternal life. Nevertheless, it is still up to us to accept this gift by making one single choice!

Why did Jesus, to redeem us, die on the cross? If you stand up, pull your feet together, and extend both arms horizontally, you become a cross! **We** are the reason Jesus came to Earth and spilled His blood on **us, the cross,** to rescue our souls from the grip of evil!

As a last thought to be shared, what will happen after the passing of humanity? I wonder what is beyond; would our human conflict be the last war between Good and Evil?

Could Armageddon, the last battle between Good and Evil, be fought away from our planet? In a faraway place... in a distant future... by another alien race?

Returning to our present time, you will eventually find that this story is no longer about the angels because it was not written for the angels' sake but for humanity, specifically for someone you care the most... **yourself.**

We continue looking at one yellow star hung by invisible strings inside one of the spectacular arms of the Milky Way galaxy. As we glance above the galaxy's plane from far away into the infinite horizon, we see an extremely bright dot approaching; its cosmic disturbance is beyond our imagination!

Again! Time... space... dimension; there are no boundaries for the approaching shockwave. This incoming event is traveling at billions of light-years/seconds! In no time, it is here!

It spawned a screeching white line, which separated our field of vision into two planes: a left side and a right side.

After its cataclysmic arrival, small bright dots appear on both sides along the line. They are free to move across the plane, with some choosing to stay on one side all the time. Eventually, after moving for a short time, the dots become rigid, fixed inside one of the sides. They have made their final choices!

Immediately after their fixation, if they stayed on the left side, they started radiating a pure white glow. Unfortunately, if the dots chose the right side, they began to emit a reddish glow mixed with sinister blackness.

As many dots become stationary, many new ones are emerging. In no time, they are multiplying in great numbers; the mobile dots are in the millions! Instantly later, in the billions!

From this location, Heaven and Hell seem so distant; yet, the white line, our **choice** between Good and Evil, is an ominous reminder of what is coming next. Beyond the perception of our senses, a horrifying crevice is about to open again; it shall separate God's loyal servants from the Devil's followers!

The abyss between them will be the same as when it separated the good angels from the fallen ones. This is a scary and breathtaking reality because this bottomless pit is…

Immense!
Impassable!
ETERNAL!

The Last Judgment

*When the Son of Man comes in
his glory, escorted by all the angels
of heaven, he will sit upon his royal
throne, and all the nations will be
assembled before him. Then he will
separate them into two groups, as a
shepherd separates sheep from
goats. The sheep he will place on
his right hand, the goats on his left.
The king will say to those in his right:
'Come. You have my Father's blessing!
Inherit the kingdom prepared for you
from the creation of the world.'*
Mt 25, 31-34
*Then he will say to those on his left:
'Out of my sight, you condemned, into
that everlasting fire prepared for the
devil and his angels!'*
Mt 25, 41

Acknowledgments

First, I thank my Bible for the passages that made this book possible. In addition, I thank whoever dictated those great ideas for the book into my mind, which I was not good enough to record as they came. Was 'he' my guardian angel?

I am grateful to my daughter Leticia, who helped with the book editing and the drawings, including the book's cover. And years later to proofread it again.

Equally to my son, Adrian, who helped with the website and selling of the book.

In addition, I thank all the people who gave their time to edit the book and gave me valuable advice. I am not giving names, but you know who you are.

Finally, I also want to thank Robert L. Holt, the author of "How to Publish, Promote, and Sell Your Book." Even though the book I bought was somehow outdated (© 1987), it did save me from making a serious mistake.

I am Jose E. Vazquez, born February 12, 1938. I saw my first light in Merida, Yucatan, Mexico. I am primarily of Spanish origin, with a bit of Portuguese from my mother's side (Peniche) and another bit of Mayan ancestry from both parents.

I came to the USA when I was 22 years old, so I missed picking up the 'good' English that you get in high school. You may have noticed some slang caused by my lack of childhood experiences in this country. In other words, I am an ESL writer.

I worked most of my life at IBM, first in manufacturing and then as a test technician. Later, I worked as a lab specialist and an engineer at the Almaden Research Center in San Jose, California. At the age of 55, I was pushed into early retirement by company downsizing. I was not ready to retire then, but maybe it turned out for the better; otherwise, this book would have never been written.

ANG publishing
Website

www.angpublishing.com

Please visit us on our website for ordering books, e-mail comments, and specific facts about the angels. Also, for the sequel of this book, where we humans must make a similar moral choice.

An Apocalyptic narrative

A H A
ANGELS/HUMANS/ANGELS

eBooks available on Amazon for only $9.99